Dynamics of Islam in the Modern World

Social, Economic and Political Studies of the Middle East and Asia

FOUNDING EDITOR: C.A.O. VAN NIEUWENHUIJZE

Editor

Dale F. Eickelman (*Dartmouth College*)

Advisory Board

Bettina Gräf (*Ludwig-Maximilians-University München*)
Robert W. Hefner (*Boston University*)
Ruth Mandel (*University College London*)

VOLUME 130

The titles published in this series are listed at *brill.com/seps*

Jamal Malik, Bonn, 2020. Photo by Shabi Hussain

Dynamics of Islam in the Modern World

Essays in Honor of Jamal Malik

Edited by

Saeed Zarrabi-Zadeh, Armina Omerika,
Thomas K. Gugler and Michael E. Asbury

BRILL

LEIDEN | BOSTON

Cover illustration: Nasir al-Mulk Mosque or "Pink Mosque," Shiraz, Iran. This nineteenth-century mosque utilizes unconventional, pink-colored tiles and stained glass and incorporates depictions of European architecture. Photo by Amin Abedini.

Library of Congress Cataloging-in-Publication Data

Names: Zarrabi-Zadeh, Saeed, editor. | Omerika, Armina, editor. | Gugler, Thomas K., editor. | Asbury, Michael E., editor. | Malik, Jamal, honouree.
Title: Dynamics of Islam in the modern world : essays in honor of Jamal Malik / edited by Saeed Zarrabi-Zadeh, Armina Omerika, Thomas K. Gugler and Michael E. Asbury.
Description: Leiden ; Boston : Brill, 2022. | Series: Social, economic and political studies of the Middle East and Asia, 1385-3376 ; vol. 130 | Includes index.
Identifiers: LCCN 2022006631 | ISBN 9789004512399 (hardback) | ISBN 9789004512535 (ebook)
Subjects: LCSH: Islam–21st century. | Islam–Social aspects–21st century.
Classification: LCC BP161.3.D96 2022 | DDC 297.209/05–dc23/eng/20220222
LC record available at https://lccn.loc.gov/2022006631

Typeface for the Latin, Greek, and Cyrillic scripts: "Brill". See and download: brill.com/brill-typeface.

ISSN 1385-3376
ISBN 978-90-04-51239-9 (hardback)
ISBN 978-90-04-51253-5 (e-book)

Copyright 2022 by Koninklijke Brill NV, Leiden, The Netherlands.
Koninklijke Brill NV incorporates the imprints Brill, Brill Nijhoff, Brill Hotei, Brill Schöningh, Brill Fink, Brill mentis, Vandenhoeck & Ruprecht, Böhlau and V&R unipress.
All rights reserved. No part of this publication may be reproduced, translated, stored in a retrieval system, or transmitted in any form or by any means, electronic, mechanical, photocopying, recording or otherwise, without prior written permission from the publisher. Requests for re-use and/or translations must be addressed to Koninklijke Brill NV via brill.com or copyright.com.

This book is printed on acid-free paper and produced in a sustainable manner.

Contents

Acknowledgements XI
Notes on Transliteration XII
List of Figures and Tables XIII
Notes on Contributors XIV

Introduction
Dynamics of Islam in the Modern World 1
   Ali Altaf Mian

PART 1
Islam, Modernity and Science

1   Islam and the Global History of Secularity   17
    Reinhard Schulze

2   Negotiating Modernity through Constructions of History in Modern Muslim Religious Thought   38
    Armina Omerika

3   Between Science and Mysticism
    Sabir Multani and the Reform of Humoral Medicine in Pakistan   63
    Stefan Reichmuth

PART 2
Islamic Activism and Radicalism

4   Peaceful and Militant Interpretations of Jihad
    A Comparative Study of Contemporary South Asian Exegetes   93
    Tariq Rahman

5   The Word of God for the Indian Muslim of Today
    Abul Kalam Azad's Tarjuman al-Qur'an   121
    Jan-Peter Hartung

6   Post-Migrant Dynamics of Islam
    Muslim Youth and Salafism in Germany   141
        David Yuzva Clement

PART 3
Islamic Normativity and Shariʿa

7   Islam and Human Rights
    Breaks and Continuity in a Complex Debate   177
        Mouez Khalfaoui

8   Islamic Law
    The Struggle against Time   205
        Reik Kirchhof

9   Negotiating Everyday Lived Islam
    A Case Study of Pakistani Diaspora in Canada   236
        Syed FurrukhZad

PART 4
Islamic Mysticism and Globalization

10 Prophetic Descent in the Early Modern *Tariqa Muhammadiyya Khalisa*   267
        Soraya Khodamoradi

11 Dynamics of Mystical Islam in the American Space
    Ahmed Abdur Rashid's "Applied Sufism"   292
        Michael E. Asbury and Saeed Zarrabi-Zadeh

12 "Transplanted" Sufism
    Complications of a Category   323
        Marcia Hermansen

PART 5
Islamic Pluralism and Dialogue

13   Discourses of Tolerance and Dialogue in Contemporary Islam   347
       Itzchak Weismann

14   Religious Pluralism and Religious Plurality in Pakistan   371
       Hasnain Bokhari

   Afterword
   Dynamics of Islam in Context   398
       Pnina Werbner

Honoring Jamal Malik

   Tabula Gratulatoria   409

   Jamal Malik's Publication List   411

   Index   433

Acknowledgements

The editors would like to thank the Academy for Islam in Research and Society (AIWG) at the Goethe University Frankfurt and the University of Erfurt for their financial support of this volume. Thanks also go to Brill's editing staff in Leiden, especially Nicolette van der Hoek, Nienke Brienen-Moolenaar, and Pieter te Velde, who have been an invaluable source of encouragement and advice while preparing this volume for publication. Furthermore, Yousra Ibrahim did an excellent job in preparing the manuscript. Finally, we are indebted to the contributors for shedding light on different facets of the dynamics of Islam in the modern world and to the signers of the Tabula Gratulatoria, all of whom accompany us in honoring Prof. Jamal Malik for his lifelong and precious scholarship in the field of Islamic Studies.

Saeed Zarrabi-Zadeh
Armina Omerika
Thomas K. Gugler
Michael E. Asbury

Notes on Transliteration

Transliteration of words in Arabic and other Islamic languages that use non-Latin scripts follows the system of the *International Journal of Middle East Studies* (IJMES). For the ease of the English reader, we have avoided diacritical marks throughout the book and wherever applicable opted for the common English usage of foreign terms and standard names. Full transliteration has been kept in quotations as well as in the titles of references already published in European languages.

Figures and Tables

Figures

3.1 Flow of activities between vital organs 71
3.2 Circulation of blood and humors between the main life organs 80
3.3 Position of man in the universe (poster) 85
14.1 Representatives of all five *wafaq*s at Hafez-Goethe monument in Weimar 380

Tables

3.1 Simple Organ Theory (*Qanun-i Mufrad A'za'*), as taught by Sabir Multani and his school 72
4.1 Hafiz Muhammad Sa'id's commentary 101
4.2 Mas'ud Azhar's commentary 107
4.3 Wahiduddin Khan's commentary 109
4.4 Jawed Ahmad Ghamidi's commentary 114
14.1 List of madrasa boards (*wafaqs*) in Pakistan 379
14.2 Madrasa degrees/certificates in Pakistan 381
14.3 List of participating madrasas in *Towards an Ethics of Peace* project 393

Notes on Contributors

Michael E. Asbury
completed his PhD at the Chair of Muslim Cultural and Religious History at the University of Erfurt in Germany in 2021. His dissertation, entitled "Seeing with the Heart: The Mysticism of an Islamic Sufi Lineage from India in the West," studies the arrival and development, from the perspective of mystical doctrines and practices, of one multiple-*tariqa* line that expanded, beginning in the late 1970s, from India to the Euro-American sphere and beyond. His research interests include mysticism, comparative religion, Islam and Sufism in South Asia and in Europe and North America, the Naqshbandiyya, New Religious Movements and Western Esotericism.

Hasnain Bokhari
works as a Research Fellow for Internationalisation and Digitalisation of Education at the Willy Brandt School of Public Policy, University of Erfurt. He worked as an Assistant Professor (Wissenschaftlicher Mitarbeiter) at the Chair of Muslim Cultural and Religious History at that university, where he developed projects on the topics of cyber culture (funded by the DAAD) and peace education (funded by the German Federal Foreign Office, GFO). In addition, he has served as an independent consultant for a KFW/GFO-funded project. He is also associated with the Centre for Digital Development, University of Manchester, UK. He holds an MA and PhD from the University of Erfurt.

David Yuzva Clement
is a lecturer at Carleton University's School of Social Work. He received his doctorate in Religious Studies from the University of Erfurt and his Diploma of Social Work from the Catholic University of Applied Sciences in Cologne, Germany. He is affiliated with the Canadian network for research on Terrorism, Security and Society (TSAS). He has held a variety of positions in social work and has recently published *Offene Kinder- und Jugendarbeit im Kontext des Salafismus: Soziale Arbeit und Radikalisierungsprävention* (2020).

Syed FurrukhZad
is a lead researcher working in Diversity, Equity and Inclusion (DEI) field with various research organizations in Canada. He received his PhD from the University of Erfurt, studying cultural politics of islamophobia in Western Europe, and MPhil in International Relations from Quaid-i-Azam University

Pakistan. He taught at National Defence University, Quaid-i-Azam University and National University of Modern Languages in Pakistan. In addition, he is a peace practitioner and academic consultant with different organizations in Canada and Pakistan. His many research interests, reflected in his writings, focus on issues of diaspora, genocide, islamophobia and peace studies.

Thomas K. Gugler
is a member of the Frankfurt Research Center on Global Islam at Goethe University. He graduated in South Asian Studies, Religious Studies and Psychology from LMU Munich and received his PhD with distinction at the University of Erfurt with a dissertation on Islamic missionary movements. He has been a research fellow at the Leibniz-Zentrum Moderner Orient Berlin and a member of the Clusters of Excellence "Normative Orders" at Goethe University in Frankfurt/Main and "Religion and Politics" at WWU Münster. His monographs include *Mission Medina: Daʿwat-e Islāmī und Tablīġī Ǧamāʿat* (Würzburg, 2011) and *Ozeanisches Gefühl der Unsterblichkeit* (Berlin, 2009).

Jan-Peter Hartung
is Senior Research Fellow at the Erlangen Centre for Islam and Law in Europe at the University of Erlangen-Nuremberg. His previous positions include a Readership in the Study of Islam at SOAS, University of London. He received his PhD in the Study of Religion from the Max Weber Center for Advanced Cultural and Social Studies at the University of Erfurt, and his Senior Doctorate (*Habilitation*) in the Study of Islam from the University of Bonn. His many research interests, reflected in his publications, include prominently the history of ideas in Islamicate South Asia and the wider Indo-Afghan world with an emphasis on political ideologies, the history of concepts and Indo-Muslim philosophy since the early modern period.

Marcia Hermansen
is Director of the Islamic World Studies program and Professor in the Theology Department at Loyola University Chicago where she teaches courses in Islamic Studies and the academic study of religion. She received her PhD in Arabic and Islamic Studies from the University of Chicago. Her numerous authored and co-edited books include *Varieties of American Sufism* (2020), *Islam, Religions, and Pluralism in Europe* (2016), *Muslima Theology* (2013), *Shah Wali Allah's Treatises on Islamic Law* (2011) and *The Conclusive Argument from God* (1996). She writes on Islamic thought, Sufism, Islam and Muslims in South Asia, Muslims in America, and Women and Gender in Islam.

Mouez Khalfaoui
is a senior Professor of Islamic Jurisprudence and Islamic Thought at the University of Tübingen. He started his academic career at the University of Tunis and earned a PhD in Islamic Studies from the University of Erfurt. He was Lecturer for Islamic Studies and Arabic at several Western universities and in the Islamic world. His main research fields are Islamic law and ethics, minority law, human rights and Islamic education. He is a member of several publishing, advising, social and political boards in Europe and worldwide.

Soraya Khodamoradi
is a contract lecturer at the University of Erfurt. She is a specialist in the field of Islamic Studies and the intellectual history of Islamicate India with a focus on Sufism. She has been active in different international research projects such as "Perso-Indica, An Analytical Survey of Persian Works on Indian Tradition," and "Prophet Muhammad in the Mirror of His Community in Early Modern and Modern Islam." Among her publications are *Sufi Reform in Eighteenth Century India: Khwaja Mir Dard of Delhi (1721–1785)* (Berlin: EB Verlag, 2019) and a joint article with Carl W. Ernst entitled "Risāla-yi Shaṭṭāriyya" (in *Perso-Indica*, 2018).

Reik Kirchhof
graduated with a Master in Near and Middle Eastern Studies from the School of Oriental and African Studies in London and was awarded a PhD in Islamic Studies by the University of Erfurt. His research is mainly devoted to foundational research on theories of normative orders and law with a focus on Islam. He is currently working on a theoretical framework for the study of social integration. Most recently, he authored the book *Grundlegung einer Soziologie der Scharia* (2019). He furthermore graduated in law and is practicing as a barrister-at-law in Berlin.

Ali Altaf Mian
is Assistant Professor of Religion and Izzat Hasan Sheikh Fellow in Islamic Studies at the University of Florida. His research has been published in *Islamic Law and Society, History of Religions, Der Islam, Journal of Urdu Studies, Qui Parle* and *ReOrient*. He is currently working on two book projects: *Muslims in South Asia* (for Edinburgh University Press) and *Surviving Modernity: Ashraf ʿAli Thanvi (1863–1943) and Genres of World-Making in Modern South Asian Islam*. He is also the editor of *The Bruce B. Lawrence Reader: Islam beyond Borders* (Duke University Press, 2021).

Armina Omerika
is Professor of the Intellectual History of Islam at the Goethe University Frankfurt am Main. She obtained her PhD in Islamic Studies (2009) at the University Bochum with a thesis on the history of Islam in Bosnia and Herzegovina in the twentieth century. Since 2005, she has conducted teaching and research activities in the History of Islam and Islamic Studies at universities in Germany, the US and Switzerland and had visiting professorships in Islamic Studies at the Universities of Hamburg (2014) and Zurich (2017). She has published on the intellectual history of Islam in Southeastern Europe in the modern period, as well as on current developments in transnational Islamic religious thought.

Tariq Rahman
is Dean of the School of Social Sciences at the Beaconhouse National University, Lahore, and a Distinguished National Professor. He has a PhD (1985) and DLitt (2014) from the University of Sheffield and was the first Pakistani to be given the Humboldt Research Award in 2012. He was a Salzburg Seminar fellow and a member of the Common Room at Wolfson College at the University of Oxford. He has been the incumbent of the Pakistan Chair at the University of California, Berkeley and has taught briefly at the University of Aarhus, Denmark and the Peace University in Spain.

Stefan Reichmuth
is former Professor of Arabic and Islamic Studies, at present Senior Researcher, at Ruhr University Bochum (Germany). His research has focused on the history of Arabic and Islamic education and learning in a transregional perspective, on Arabic language and literature in Africa, and, more recently, on the Prophet in the mirror of Muslim society, culture and politics since the early modern period. He was chief editor of the journal *Die Welt des Islams* (2002–2016), member of the scientific council no. 106 of the DFG (2008–2016), and chairman of the Islamological section of the German Oriental Society (DMG, 2011–2019).

Reinhard Schulze
is Director of the transdisciplinary Forum Islam and the Middle East, University of Bern, Switzerland. After studying Islamic Studies, Semitic Studies and Linguistics at the University of Bonn, he earned his doctorate in 1981 and then held positions at the universities of Hamburg, Essen and Bonn. After his postdoctoral research (*Habilitation*), he was appointed as a professor

at Ruhr-University Bochum, University of Bamberg and the University of Bern. His recent publications include *Der Koran und die Genealogie des Islam* (Basel: Schwabe, 2015) and *Geschichte der islamischen Welt: Von 1900 bis in die Gegenwart* (Munich: Beck, 2016).

Itzchak Weismann
is Professor of Islamic Studies and former Director of the Jewish-Arab Center at the University of Haifa. His research interests focus on modern Islamic movements and ideologies. He published widely on the Muslim Brotherhood, Salafism, Sufism and jihadi organizations in the Middle East (especially Syria, Egypt and Saudi Arabia), in South Asia and worldwide. His latest monograph is *Abd al-Rahman al-Kawakibi: Islamic Reform and Arab Nationalism* (Oneworld, 2015). He is also scientific editor of the Sahar (Crescent) series of translations into Hebrew of major modern Islamic texts.

Pnina Werbner
is Professor Emerita of Social Anthropology, Keele University. She is author of "The Manchester Migration Trilogy," including *The Migration Process* (1990/2002), *Imagined Diasporas* (2002) and *Pilgrims of Love* (2003), on South Asians in Britain and Pakistan. She has edited several theoretical collections on Sufism, hybridity, cosmopolitanism, multiculturalism, migration and citizenship, including *Anthropology and the New Cosmopolitanism* (2008) and *The Political Aesthetics of Global Protest* (2014). Her most recent books are *The Making of an African Working Class* (2014) and *African Customary Justice: Living Law, Legal Pluralism, and Public Ethics* (2022).

Saeed Zarrabi-Zadeh
is a habilitated lecturer in Islamic Studies at the University of Erfurt. His research is mainly devoted to the study of Sufism (in both medieval and modern times), comparative mysticism and Persian literature. His recent publications include *Practical Mysticism in Islam and Christianity* (Routledge, 2016) and *Sufism East and West: Mystical Islam and Cross-Cultural Exchange in the Modern World* (Brill, 2019, co-edited with Jamal Malik). He is co-editing, along with Marcia Hermansen, *Sufism in Western Contexts* (Brill, forthcoming), is the guest editor of *Sufism in the Modern World* (special issue of *Religions*), and is an associate editor of the *Mawlana Rumi Review*.

Introduction

Dynamics of Islam in the Modern World

Ali Altaf Mian

How have Muslims in the modern world interacted with its seismic epistemological shifts, political challenges and cultural transformations? This question can be addressed adequately with a combination of methodologies and insights from both the social sciences and the humanities.[1] Yet throughout much of the twentieth century, the study of Islam in Germany has rarely adopted this interdisciplinary approach. Rather, the strengths of German-language scholarship on Islam have been source criticism, philology and historical reconstruction, especially in relation to subjects such as the Quran, Islamic law and Sufism.[2] Modern-day Islam and Muslim societies only became objects of scholarly study after World War II. Orientalist scholarship on the textual traditions of Islam, on the one hand, and the social-scientific study of Muslim societies, on the other, were largely pursued as two autonomous academic enterprises. This situation changed, however, in the 1990s and 2000s, with the work of scholars such as Reinhard Schulze, Gudrun Krämer, Jamal Malik and others.[3] Islam was no longer to be approached as an antiquated object of philological and historical analysis; rather, Islam and Muslims in the modern world illuminated broader realities such as colonialism, anti-colonial insurgency, post-colonial nation-building and globalization. This new approach encouraged scholars to situate beliefs, experiences and texts in their social, economic and cultural contexts and to examine the interplay among global movements, trans-regional

---

1 To some extent, this combinatory approach informed the late nineteenth-century disciplinary formation of *Religionswissenschaft* ("the science of religion"). This academic discipline, in Germany but also in Europe more broadly, sought to illuminate "the enormous impact of religion on political, social, and cultural life." Arie L. Molendijk, "Tiele on Religion," *Numen* 46, no. 3 (1999): 242.
2 On Islamic Studies in Germany, see Annemarie Schimmel, "Islamic Studies in Germany: A Historical Overview," *Islamic Studies* 49, no. 3 (2010); Dietrich Jung, *Orientalists, Islamists and the Global Public Sphere: A Genealogy of the Modern Essentialist Image of Islam* (Sheffield: Equinox, 2011).
3 See Florian Zemmin, Johannes Stephan, and Monica Corrado, eds., *Islam in der Moderne, Moderne im Islam: Eine Festschrift für Reinhard Schulze zum 65. Geburtstag* (Leiden: Brill, 2018); and Bettina Gräf, Birgit Krawietz and Schirin Amir-Moazami, eds., *Ways of Knowing Muslim Cultures and Societies: Studies in Honour of Gudrun Krämer* (Leiden: Brill, 2018).

networks and local traditions. The volume in your hands, or on your screens, brings together experts of the Islamic textual traditions and Muslim societies who have shaped or been shaped by this academic transformation.

The contributors to this volume posit Muslims not as docile and autonomous but as relational and interactive agents of change as well as continuity. They depict Muslims as interacting with Islamic(ate) sources of self and society but also with resources from other traditions of thought and practice. This volume understands intra- and intercultural relations as fluid and metamorphic, not as static and isomorphic. While attuned to the local, the following chapters also direct their gaze to the global. The contributors highlight the "dynamics of Islam in the modern world" – namely, the diachronic dialectical components of Islamic thought and culture as well as the diverse ways Muslims interact with broader frames of reference as they navigate the challenges and opportunities of the modern world. These include, to name only some of the prominent themes examined here, secularization, colonialism, religious insurgency, human rights, the nation-state, globalization, migration and pluralism.

This volume makes a rich contribution to Islamic Studies and its contributors represent multiple disciplinary approaches. They are historians, anthropologists, sociologists, political scientists, lawyers and theologians. Collectively they seek to document and analyze a staggering set of Muslim voices, practices and institutions in three geographical settings: South Asia, the Middle East and Euro-America. The temporal framework is that of "the modern world," which is a contested category with a bewildering set of competing, and sometimes conflicting, definitions. In order to produce some analytical clarity about this term, we may turn to the world historian Marshall Hodgson (d. 1968), whose prescient insights about modernity and global Islam are relevant even today.[4]

Hodgson locates the emergence of the modern world between 1600 and 1800, a period of crucial cultural changes in Europe that paved the way for large-scale shifts in inter-state relations and established "European world hegemony." Hodgson calls these cultural changes "the Great Western Transmutation" (GWT). The decisive historical process undergirding this transmutation is "technicalization," which he defines as "a condition of calculative (and hence innovative) technical specialization, in which the several specialties are interdependent on a large enough scale to determine patterns of expectation in the key sectors of a society."[5] Industrialist production, colonialism and revolutions

---

4 On Hodgson, see especially Edmund Burke III and Robert J. Mankin, *Islam and World History: The Ventures of Marshall Hodgson* (Chicago: The University of Chicago Press, 2018).
5 Marshall Hodgson, *The Venture of Islam: Conscience and History in a World Civilization*, vol. 3 (Chicago: University of Chicago Press, 1974), 186.

have been some of the most noticeable consequences of the GWT. Yet Hodgson also emphasizes the paradoxical nature of the change in human subjectivity inaugurated by the GWT, that is, a dehumanization of interpersonal connections but also the positing of a "distinctive ideal human image."[6] The modern world thus harbors conflicting forces: capitalist exploitation, colonial domination, technological alienation and secularist authoritarianism, on the one hand, and the discourse of freedom, dignity, rights, and a certain "gentling of manners" and openness to religious and cultural differences, on the other hand. The essays collected in this volume, which focus especially on the period beginning with the eighteenth century onwards, situate several facets of Islam within this paradoxical context of "the Great Western Transmutation." In doing so, they avoid Eurocentric interpretations of modernity and, instead, invest Muslims with agency in the pluralistic and global scenes of alternative and multiple modernities.[7]

To be more precise, Part 1 looks at definitions of modernity and the legacy of the Enlightenment *vis-à-vis* Islam, concentrating particularly on secularism, history and science. Muslims' interactions with this legacy are diverse and dynamic, including civic action, political activism and insurgent uprising. Yet each of these modes of engagement can be further complexified in terms of historical context, types of sources and research questions, as well as the social locations and analytical objectives of those conducting research. Part 2, "Islamic Activism and Radicalism," sheds light on the idea and practice of violence, the need for pluralism in multi-religious settings, and new experiences of citizenship as Muslims grapple with what it means to live as a cultural and religious minority in Europe.

The consequences of the GWT and the legacy of Enlightenment norms are today debated in an uneven global public arena, both on- and off-line. Muslims interact with broader questions of social norms and cultural values from a range of differing perspectives. The complex issues of human rights, the nature of normativity in the Islamic legal tradition, and everyday ethical negotiations are examined in Part 3. The Islamic legal tradition has seen a complicated trajectory in the aftermath of the GWT – from legal Orientalism to the weakening of the traditional law schools to Islamization. This particular trajectory severs the legal tradition from other genres and experiential modes. Be that as it may, Islamic legal and mystical traditions continue to overlap and reinforce each other in the modern period. Contrary to the depoliticized image

---

6 Ibid., 190.
7 Dilip Parameshwar Gaonkar, ed., *Alternative Modernities* (Durham, NC: Duke University Press, 2001); Shmuel N. Eisenstadt, "Multiple Modernities," *Daedalus* 129, no. 1 (2000).

of "Islamic mysticism," which is prevalent in the modern West, Sufi actors in Muslim-majority societies as well as "Sufi transplants" in the diaspora have fortified Islamic law and ethics. Part 4 examines three interactions between the legal tradition and "Islamic mysticism" in the modern world, concentrating on the use of the prophetic ideal to renew Muslim society in eighteenth-century India, the dynamic translation of past teachings in modern-day forms of "Applied Sufism" and Sufi transplants in America. The final part of the volume examines the question of pluralism and the challenges but also opportunities afforded by dialogue.

The division of the following contributions into five sections neither exhausts the subject matters of "Islam in the modern world" nor reflects, at least not in any systematic way, Malik's academic trajectory (which I cover in more detail below). Rather, these five sections highlight some of the most salient categories that allow researchers and readers to observe and analyze the dynamics of Islam in the modern world. That none of the following chapters deal extensively with gender and sexuality should not be taken to imply the insignificance of these important subjects for either Malik or his interlocutors. On the contrary, Malik's revised, enlarged and updated second edition of his classic work, *Islam in South Asia*, for example, makes a concerted effort to afford greater attention to these issues. Furthermore, it is hoped that these neglected topics of inquiry will be included in future edited volumes on Islam in the modern world. Let us now turn to each part to discuss some of the salient issues highlighted therein.

1   Islam, Modernity and Science

Is the division between the religious and the secular entirely a product of Western political history? Do Muslim-majority societies have their own genealogies of this division? In the first chapter of this volume, Reinhard Schulze contributes to a global history of secularity by offering a retrospective genealogy of the secular in Muslim-majority societies. For him, the articulation of Islam in political terms is both a response to colonial and postcolonial political realities as well as a continuation of certain indigenous mechanisms for dividing consciousness and social life. Thus, conceptual mechanisms to divide life are not exclusive to the West; the origin of this dividing epistemological impulse is almost impossible to delineate. In Islamic history, the *din* and *dunya* binary stands out as a salient candidate for this proto-conceptualization of secularity. Schulze argues that the globalization of the particular Western genealogy of secularity has also intensified the authority of the subject and the individual. If secularity reinforces religious institutions and actors, does it do so by exacerbating the authoritarian tendencies of the individual? This seems to be the case since secularization sanctions the personalization of truth and the formation of a "clear identity." Schulze's contribution enables us to appreciate the salience of tracing retrospective genealogies of different conceptual and political dynamics of Islam in broader historical and conceptual frameworks.

In the next chapter, Armina Omerika explores the centrality of history for understanding the multiple connotations of modernity in Muslim thought over the last one and a half centuries. "History," she writes, "has become the major framework of reference in Muslim identity negotiations." This parallels the rise of history as a source of legitimacy in modern nationalist and ethnocentric projects across the globe. In Muslim reformist thought, history, and more specifically civilizational discourse, becomes a vehicle for social change and critical interpretation. Omerika then considers a second trend in modern Muslim thought – namely, the close reading of the Quran to distill a theology of history. This scripturalist project, while affirming God as the ultimate shaper of human destiny, emphasizes a dynamic view of history, one in which human activism shapes society. A third view of history – that is, the historical construction (or historicity) of human experience – has largely been neglected in modern Muslim political thought and movement. Throughout, Omerika emphasizes that each view of history is connected to broader questions of epistemology and culture.

The discourses of modernity and historical change intersect with those of science and medicine. Stefan Reichmuth illuminates the tradition of Humoral Medicine in Pakistan by contextualizing the practice of "Greek Medicine" (or *Yunani Tibb*) in South Asia and by briefly outlining the theories of the famed physician Sabir Multani (d. 1972). The latter's legacy continues to influence the practice of several "traditional healers" in Pakistan and elsewhere, including Germany. Reichmuth explains the key reason behind Multani's success: he creatively reformed *Yunani Tibb* by engaging with other healthcare traditions, such as modern biomedicine and Ayurveda. Multani was able to retain the basic outlines of Humoral Medicine while also making it a means to reactivate the public and social relevance of Sufi teaching and practice. This is captured by the pithy saying of one of his followers: "A *Tabib* ["physician"] who wants to be a *Hakim* ["sage"] has to be a Sufi." Reichmuth also discusses how Multani related his Sufi-based medical discourse and practice to sectarian religious orientations in Pakistan.

2 Islamic Activism and Radicalism

The examination of how some contemporary South Asian exegetes interpret Quranic verses on jihad is the aim of Tariq Rahman's chapter. He focuses on scripture since it is this source of authority that is most often mobilized by modernists, traditionalists and radical Islamists alike. The various deployments of jihad in the history of South Asian Islam mirror its broader historical trajectory. Rahman surveys four postcolonial interpreters, giving us a sense of the starkly different approaches of modernists and radical Islamists in India and Pakistan. Modernists tend to practice the interpretive strategy of restriction – they contextualize the text, restricting the applicability of an injunction to its historical circumstances – while the militant interpreters generalize scripture, often ignoring questions of historical context and traditional exegeses. In the end, the results are not surprising: the militants advocate for both offensive and defensive jihad, encouraging perpetual armed conflict between Muslims and non-Muslims. The modernists, however, endorse peaceful co-existence and permit only defensive jihad. All four exegetes endeavor to portray their interpretations as representing "true Islam."

Jan-Peter Hartung also addresses the primacy of scripture in modern Islam in his essay on the Indian Muslim theologian, political activist, educator and literary figure Abul Kalam Azad (d. 1958). The latter's Quran commentary contains a strong political message in the form of a "pronounced intra-faith coherency" between Islam and Hinduism but not between the latter two and Christianity. It is ironic, as Hartung points out, that in making this anti-colonial argument, Azad relies on a colonial construction, namely, the notion of a unified "Hinduism." Hartung deftly summarizes the four key elements of Azad's intra-faith coherency: "first, humankind has been created as one; second, humankind has fallen apart due to artificial dissent; third, God has sent messengers in every era and to every community with one and the same message, warning them of the consequences of dissent; and, finally, because of that, no one can claim to have had no knowledge of God's message and will therefore be similarly accountable to God without exception."

In his chapter on the post-migrant dynamics of Islam, David Yuzva Clement sheds light on the diverse forms of Salafism among Muslim youth in Germany. Islam and Muslims have been racialized over the last fifty years and it is in this context that Muslim youth construct their identities. Clement is attentive to the many different elements of identity construction, from interpersonal relationships to psychological factors to socio-economic conditions. He offers several correctives to the existing literature on the securitization and radicalization of Muslim youth in Germany. Clement critiques the "misleading assumption that greater Islamic religiosity automatically carries a higher potential for extremism and thus presents a higher risk for national or social security," while also deconstructing the "essentialist dualism between 'German' and 'Muslim.'" Finally, he problematizes the exaggerated attention to religion we see in many extant analyses, as if the complex identities of Muslim youth are only shaped by a single factor.

3   Islamic Normativity and Shariʿa

The discourse of human rights has increasingly posed a challenge both to ordinary Muslims' religious understanding and practice as well as to Muslim-majority states. In his chapter, Mouez Khalfaoui critiques the unexamined citation and application of classical-era shariʿa norms in some contemporary Muslim-majority states, arguing that these premodern norms are "incompatible with modern human rights norms." Yet he also suggests that "international human rights, including the rights of women and children, can theoretically be deduced from Islamic doctrine." He therefore calls on Muslim jurists and ethicists to creatively think within the framework of international human rights to articulate and embody their own "norms of freedom, gender equality and other values of human rights." According to Khalfaoui, if Muslims were to attend to this interpretive and practical task, they would not only be improving their own globalized image, but would also make a valuable contribution to democratizing and pluralizing the regime of international human rights. Otherwise, Khalfaoui argues, Muslims, particularly those living in Europe and North America, risk isolationism.

In his analysis of Islamic normativity, Reik Kirchhof encourages us to take seriously the material (read: practical and contingent) basis of any normative order. In the context of studying "Islamic law," this means that we ought to consider those conditions in which human beings make everyday decisions, share mutual expectations and relate to each other in social institutions. The material conditions that shape today's competing normative orders differ greatly from those in which the divine norms or shariʿa were first articulated and embodied. Modern normative orders elaborate distinct modes of human socialization, cross-cultural communication, global trade and political power. This is why many Muslims themselves experience something out of joint in the normative order of classical shariʿa. According to Kirchhof, in order to resolve the "felt" and "perceived" incongruency between shariʿa and several different orders of norms and values in the modern world, Muslims adopt different programs involving an imagined global but united Muslim community (*umma*), including conservation of tradition, critical traditionalism, modernist reform and Islamist state-making.

In his examination of the negotiations of everyday lived Islam in a majority-non-Muslim setting, Syed FurrukhZad shares with us five case studies of Pakistani Muslim migrants to Canada. He fleshes out lived Islam by analyzing his interlocutors' perspectives on and practices of creedal matters and ritual as well as the daily choices they make in navigating their Pakistani ethnic and linguistic, Islamic and Canadian frameworks of identity. He draws on theorists of ordinary life, space and lived religion to contextualize how his interlocutors cultivate and preserve their identities as diasporic subjects. FurrukhZad documents and analyzes how "multiple expressions of religiosity are constantly being (re)invented, (re)produced and (re)formed by migrants amid constructions of religious space through implicit and explicit negotiations with society at large." He argues that his interlocutors' everyday lives demonstrate "inventiveness, plurality and flexibility." He thus effectively shows how individuals deploy micro-strategies to produce coherence in dominant structures of power that render minority traditions incoherent.

4   Islamic Mysticism and Globalization

Currents of continuity and historical change in the Sufi tradition are discussed in Soraya Khodamoradi's study of the eighteenth-century Sufi-poet Mir Dard (d. 1785). She demonstrates how Mir Dard renovates the image of the Prophet Muhammad. While keeping intact his spiritual stature and the Sufi focus on interiority, annihilation in God and ascent, the thrust of Mir Dard's prophetology remakes Muhammad as an exemplary social and political ideal, shifting his image in order to underscore normative behavior, subsistence with God and societal engagement. Khodamoradi examines this shift in the context of what Mir Dard says about the viceregency of God, patience and gratitude, clear and hidden announcement, and the idea of "pure Muhammadness" (*Muhammadiyya khalisa*). The case is then made that this image of the Prophet better served the social and political needs of Muslims living in contexts where the Islamic imperium was experiencing decline and decay, such as eighteenth-century Delhi.

In order to offer a dynamic understanding of the themes of change and continuity in the broader Sufi tradition, Michael E. Asbury and Saeed Zarrabi-Zadeh analyze the category of "Applied Sufism," as articulated by the American practitioner of institutional Sufism, Ahmed Abdur Rashid (b. 1942). This American Sufi oversees a Sufi community in Virginia where he directs disciples and delivers lectures on a weekly basis. He also stays in close contact with disciples in other parts of the world. Asbury and Zarrabi-Zadeh analyze how he carries forth but also tweaks the teachings of his Indian Sufi master, Azad Rasool (d. 2006). In so doing, Abdur Rashid creatively draws from the broader history of Sufism while adapting this tradition to the American context. Thus, his renewed emphasis on societal engagement and pluralism at once appears to be both continuity and transformation. It is here that the authors contribute to the theoretical discourse on historical Sufism by insisting that the binary of change and continuity is inadequate and that we should instead see Abdur Rashid's "change-in-continuity" through the metaphor of dynamics.

Marcia Hermansen draws on her foundational contributions to the study of Sufism in America to complicate the category of "transplanted Sufis." This category belongs to a three-part typology previously elaborated by Hermansen herself, the other two groups being "hybrid Sufis" and "perennial Sufis." All three terms extend the garden metaphor for understanding Sufi communities and sociality. Sufi transplants are "smaller groups of co-ethnics who follow a Sufi teacher and/or Sufi order in much the same way as they might have done in their original cultural settings." They are "most likely local and ephemeral" and their small communities in US megacities such as Chicago reinforce immigrant religiosity and spirituality along ethnic lines. However, according to Hermansen, in order to survive in the American Muslim landscape, it seems that Sufi transplants "must hybridize." In other words, the growing influence of multiple homogenizing religious figures – from "New Age" Sufis to madrasa-trained traditionalists to Salafi-influenced imams – often make it hard for Sufi transplants to sustain their institutions. They thus gather at certain mosques or homes and in transient ways host events at banquet halls and in graveyards.

5 Islamic Pluralism and Dialogue

Itzchak Weismann's chapter examines discursive formations of "tolerance and dialogue" in contemporary Islam by discussing four principal religious players from the Middle East. First, he examines the writings of the Qatar-based theologian Yusuf al-Qaradawi (b. 1926) and detects a shift from the latter's 1970s invocation of "the protected people" (*ahl al-dhimma*) to his 1990s use of the language of "minority rights" and "citizenship." Weismann then turns his focus to the Turkish Gülen Movement, which seeks to displace the concept of armed struggle with tolerance and dialogue. The third case study is the Iranian philosopher and reformer Abdolkarim Soroush (b. 1945), who emphasizes the "universal vocabulary of democracy and human rights, freedom of thought and public accountability." Finally, Weismann considers national and international attempts on the part of the Saudi state to contribute to inter-religious dialogue, which have mostly reproduced the regime's exclusivist image of universal salvation through Islam. For Weismann, however, al-Qaradawi, Gülen, Soroush and the Saudi State have largely failed to promote the broader aims and objectives of pluralist dialogue and cosmopolitan tolerance. Their efforts are thus questioned by Western critics, Muslim autocrats and radical Islamists alike.

Hasnain Bokhari examines the concrete efforts of Jamal Malik to interact with Pakistani madrasa cultures in his two-year project, "Religious Pluralism and Religious Plurality: Towards an Ethics of Peace" (2016–2018). The project consisted of workshops on historiography, critical religious studies and religious pluralism. Madrasa teachers and students from Pakistan's five key religious orientations – namely, Barelvi, Deobandi, Shiʿa, Ahl-i Hadith and Jamaʿat-i Islami – attended these workshops in Erfurt, Germany. While the alleged role of Muslim religious schools in encouraging hate speech and extremism has been highlighted in global and geopolitical debates, especially after 9/11, the participants in these workshops discussed values like justice, pluralism and religious diversity, while trying to situate them within Islamic tradition. Bokhari's chapter not only discusses the fruits of Malik's efforts, but it also sheds light on the history of madrasa cultures and their attendant sectarian dynamics in Pakistan.

The volume concludes with an insightful "Afterword" by the distinguished social anthropologist Pnina Werbner. She highlights how Jamal Malik brings his "contextualizing insights and interpretive perspicacity" to the study of Islam and Muslims in the modern world, especially in South Asia and the South Asian diaspora in Europe. She also underscores how his work, sometimes in subtle ways, draws attention to the "dynamic interaction between Islamic mysticism and politics." Finally, Werbner comments on how the recent takeover of Afghanistan by the Taliban serves as an illustration of "the imbrication of religious movements in politics and economics."

6   Conclusion

The above overview has highlighted how the various contributors to this volume touch on the dynamics of Islam in the modern world from different angles. Jamal Malik is a distinguished scholar who has enriched academic discussions on such dynamics over the last several decades through his monographs, edited volumes, articles and book chapters which straddle the themes, regions and time periods covered by the essays in this volume (see "Jamal

Malik's Publication List"). His scholarship sheds ample light on how Islam and Muslims have been transformed by interacting with what Hodgson calls the Great Western Transmutation. In so doing, Malik bridges the gap between philological and sociological approaches in Islamic Studies, in Germany and internationally, which can be easily observed by looking at the trajectory of his scholarship.

At the beginning of his career, Malik drew on his training in political science and wide-ranging familiarity with modern South Asian history to analyze the Khaksar Movement of the mid-twentieth century. His doctoral research examined the persistence of colonialism in Pakistani nation-building projects and how various elected governments and military regimes have used Islam to modernize – and thus make governable – traditional agrarian and urban sectors.[8] His postdoctoral thesis offered a descriptive-historical examination of North Indian scholarly culture and paved the way for a generation of younger scholars to conduct research into the intellectual, social and cultural dynamics of the Islamic discursive tradition in colonial and postcolonial South Asia.[9] This postdoctoral research also enabled Malik to sharpen his grasp of urban studies, modern Urdu literature and South Asian Sufism. In short, by the mid-1990s, Malik had made a strong case for pursuing Islamic Studies in the disciplinary frameworks of the social and cultural sciences.[10]

In February 1999, Malik was appointed as the Chair of Muslim Cultural and Religious History in the Department of Religious Studies at the University of Erfurt. His inaugural lecture was titled, "Europäische Muslime oder muslimische Europäer?" ("European Muslims or Muslim Europeans?"). This prestigious position has allowed Malik to assume a stronger role in researching Islam in Europe, which he has often pursued in a comparative framework, for example, through the project "Religious Pluralism in South Asia and Europe."[11] The post-9/11 context also demanded a critical return to Muslim institutions in South Asia, resulting in the volume *Madrasas in South Asia: Teaching Terror?*[12] Malik's research on Sufism also deepened with the edited volume, *Sufism in*

---

8   Jamal Malik, *Colonialization of Islam: Dissolution of Traditional Institutions in Pakistan* (New Delhi: Manohar; Lahore: Vanguard, 1996).
9   Jamal Malik, *Islamische Gelehrtenkultur in Nordindien* (Leiden: Brill, 1997).
10   Jamal Malik, ed., *Perspectives of Mutual Encounters in South Asian History, 1760–1860* (Leiden: Brill, 2000).
11   Jamal Malik, ed., *Muslims in Europe: From the Margin to the Centre* (Münster: LIT, 2004); Jamal Malik and Helmut Reifeld, eds., *Religious Pluralism in South Asia and Europe* (New Delhi: Oxford University Press, 2004).
12   Jamal Malik, ed., *Madrasas in South Asia: Teaching Terror?* (London and New York: Routledge, 2008).

the West.¹³ Since then, his research projects have continued to deal with an increasing variety and range of topics: dialogue and Muslim belonging in Europe and North America, Islamic *daʿwa* (preaching and proselytism) in the modern world, religious pluralism and social media.¹⁴ He also honored the work of the late Annemarie Schimmel by organizing an international conference on Sufism, the proceedings of which were recently published as an edited volume.¹⁵

No account of Malik's accomplishments as a scholar would be complete without mentioning his magisterial *Islam in South Asia*, which remains the most comprehensive Anglophone survey of the subject matter.¹⁶ In this volume, Malik ventured beyond Pakistan and subjected the entire primary and secondary historiographical corpus of Muslim South Asia to the rigors of historicist denaturalization. What resulted was nothing short of a deconstruction of the dominant analytical categories available to social scientists and humanities scholars for understanding the diversity of Islam in South Asia from the seventh century of the common era up to the present.

Malik's scholarly output has transcended South Asia insofar as he has documented and analyzed the integrationist predicaments of Muslims in Europe and North America in the context of challenges such as neocolonialism, racism and xenophobia but also opportunities such as dialogue and pluralism. At the broadest level, Malik's work has explored patterns of cross-cultural dialogue as well as the potentials but also limitations of religiosity in modern democratic societies. The chapters collected in this *Festschrift* contain ample evidence of the analytical dividends of interacting with Malik's dynamic scholarship.

Bibliography

Burke, Edmund and Robert Mankin, eds. *Islam and World History: The Ventures of Marshall Hodgson*. Chicago: University of Chicago Press, 2018.

Eisenstadt, Shmuel N. "Multiple Modernities." *Daedalus* 129, no. 1 (2000): 1–29.

---

13   Jamal Malik and John R. Hinnells, eds., *Sufism in the West* (London and New York: Routledge, 2006).

14   Jamal Malik and Itzchak Weismann, eds., *Culture of Daʿwah: Islamic Preaching in the Modern World* (Salt Lake City: The University of Utah Press, 2020).

15   Jamal Malik and Saeed Zarrabi-Zadeh, eds., *Sufism East and West: Mystical Islam and Cross-Cultural Exchange in the Modern World* (Leiden: Brill, 2019).

16   Jamal Malik, *Islam in South Asia: A Short History* (Leiden: Brill, 2008); Jamal Malik, *Islam in South Asia: Revised, Enlarged and Updated Second Edition* (Leiden: Brill, 2020).

Gaonkar, Dilip Parameshwar, ed. *Alternative Modernities*. Durham, NC: Duke University Press, 2001.

Gräf, Bettina, Birgit Krawietz and Schirin Amir-Moazami, eds. *Ways of Knowing Muslim Cultures and Societies: Studies in Honour of Gudrun Krämer*. Leiden: Brill, 2018.

Hodgson, Marshall G.S. *The Venture of Islam: Conscience and History in a World Civilization*, 3 vols. Chicago: University of Chicago Press, 1974.

Jung, Dietrich. *Orientalists, Islamists and the Global Public Sphere: A Genealogy of the Modern Essentialist Image of Islam*. Sheffield: Equinox, 2011.

Malik, Jamal. *Colonialization of Islam: Dissolution of Traditional Institutions in Pakistan*. New Delhi: Manohar; Lahore: Vanguard, 1996.

Malik, Jamal. *Islamische Gelehrtenkultur in Nordindien*. Leiden: Brill, 1997.

Malik, Jamal. *Islam in South Asia: A Short History*. Leiden: Brill, 2008.

Malik, Jamal. *Islam in South Asia: Revised, Enlarged and Updated Second Edition*. Leiden: Brill, 2020.

Malik, Jamal, ed. *Madrasas in South Asia: Teaching Terror?*. London and New York: Routledge, 2008.

Malik, Jamal, ed. *Muslims in Europe: From the Margin to the Centre*. Münster: LIT, 2004.

Malik, Jamal, ed. *Perspectives of Mutual Encounters in South Asian History, 1760–1860*. Leiden: Brill, 2000.

Malik, Jamal and Helmut Reifeld, eds. *Religious Pluralism in South Asia and Europe*. New Delhi: Oxford University Press, 2004.

Malik, Jamal and Itzchak Weismann, eds. *Culture of Daʿwah: Islamic Preaching in the Modern World*. Salt Lake City: The University of Utah Press, 2020.

Malik, Jamal and John R. Hinnells, eds. *Sufism in the West*. London and New York: Routledge, 2006.

Malik, Jamal and Saeed Zarrabi-Zadeh, eds. *Sufism East and West: Mystical Islam and Cross-Cultural Exchange in the Modern World*. Leiden: Brill, 2019.

Molendijk, Arie L. "Tiele on Religion." *Numen* 46, no. 3 (1999): 237–68.

Schimmel, Annemarie. "Islamic Studies in Germany: A Historical Overview." *Islamic Studies* 49, no. 3 (2010): 401–10.

Zemmin, Florian, Johannes Stephan and Monica Corrado, eds. *Islam in der Moderne, Moderne im Islam: Eine Festschrift für Reinhard Schulze zum 65. Geburtstag*. Leiden: Brill, 2018.

PART 1

Islam, Modernity and Science

CHAPTER 1

Islam and the Global History of Secularity

Reinhard Schulze

In my contribution, I will argue why it makes sense to speak of Islamic modalities of secularity. I will first briefly discuss the concept of the secularization of the social order and show that it was not only in the Euro-American sphere that the secularization paradigm determined the normative order of the social field, but also in the Islamic world up to the 1950s and 1960s. A special feature, however, characterizes this development in the Islamic world. Between the 1960s and 1990s, Islamic communities and parties succeeded in attaining hegemony in the political public sphere, making decisive contributions to the regulation of social processes and orders. But this also meant a transformation of the Islamic tradition towards a secular order. We can also put it this way: unlike in the West, in the Muslim-majority world, the secularized social order has in fact been symbolically represented by Islam since the 1960s. While Western viewers saw this as a confirmation of the religious character of the Islamic order, many Muslim commentators insisted that Islam was not at its core a religion, but rather a worldly order.

But it would be wrong to conclude from such difference in the symbolic representation of secularization that there are essential differences in the social history of Western and Islamic modernity. Since the 1990s, there has also been a process in the public spheres of many Muslim countries towards a new post-secular condition. Yet this should not be understood as a process of de-secularization. Rather, it must be assumed that the religious communities (as well as the churches) have lost their normative regulatory power, and not only over the social field, but even over the religious field as well. This process also particularly affects the Islamic tradition. On the one hand, this involves a growing willingness of religious actors to justify the secularization process in religious terms, while on the other hand, the post-secular situation causes a disintegration of the religious field in which institutions of the religious communities have largely lost their regulatory sovereignty. In fact, according to the thesis of the present chapter, this process amounts to a disintegration of Islam as a religious tradition.

1   Secularization as a Guiding Concept in Political Debates

Secularization and secularism still are highly contested concepts in discussions of the place of religion within the social order. Though the conceptual difference between both concepts is often ignored in favor of a general statement on the social divide between religion and society, we should stress the importance of a clear distinction. The term "secularization" stands for a social and institutional process which creates the divide between religion and society as two normative orders. In contrast, "secularism" designates an intellectual, political or even ideological affirmation and justification of such a divide that established what Talcott Parsons called the modern normative order. A less frequently used term, "secularity," refers to a social or political entity which has undergone a process of secularization and has thus acquired the quality of having been "secularized." Yet this formal distinction does not help to establish a common meaning of the basic notion of what it means to be "secular," as it is perhaps best analyzed as a "thick concept" (Hilary Putnam, Bernard Williams).[1] It simultaneously has a descriptive meaning ("having been freed from the rules of religious institutions") and evaluates that meaning, for example as "good," "bad" or "necessary." In addition, the Latinist foundational term "secular," which nowadays functions as the prototype of any semantic and lexical representation of "secularity," contains a kind of prescription for how to address "secularity." The historically established connotations of the term refer to spatial separation, to temporal order and to a process of transition from a religious to a worldly order. Thus the term to be used should first, stem from a religious background (though no longer be subject to the rules of a religion), second, have a conceptual opposite ("world") and third, be transferable into an affirmative self-concept of a non-religious social agent. In many languages, this semantic convergence has relied on lexical entries that reciprocally translate the idea of "world,"[2] while some languages use terms that reflect the idea of "dissolving"[3] and still others simply integrate "secular" as a new item into their own lexicon.[4] The multi-religious background of the Arabic language offered

---

[1] For our purposes, see Hilary Putnam, *The Collapse of the Fact/Value Dichotomy and Other Essays* (Cambridge, MA: Harvard University Press, 2002), 34.

[2] For example, Arabic دنيوي (*dunyawi*); Dutch *wereldlijk;* Russian мирской (*mirskoy*); Greek κοσμικός (*kosmikós*); Armenian աշխարհիկ (*ashkharhik*); Chinese 世俗的 (*shisúde*).

[3] For instance, Modern Hebrew חִלּוֹנִי (*ḥillōnī*), properly: to bore, i.e., (by implication) to wound, to dissolve; figuratively: to profane (a person, place or thing).

[4] For instance, Japanese 世俗的な (*sezoku-tekina*); Malay, and most European languages: *secular*.

both a Christian term (*ʿalmani*, derived from the Syrian-Aramaic term *ʿalman*, meaning a monk not subjected to monastic rules of the *regulares*) and a Muslim term (*dunyawi*). The possible Jewish reading using a lexical derivation of the root ḥ-l-l ("to dissolve") was never realized, as nineteenth-century Jewish authors in the Middle East seldom published texts in Arabic during the time when discussions on "secularity" became important. I will come back to that.

This said, we may take as a starting point the fact that West European narratives of the divide between religion and world as "secularization" has become the dominant paradigm of interpreting the modern normative social order. Since the 1990s, the master narrative which had claimed for secular society a growing hegemony over any other social form, including religions and confessions, has gradually lost its explanatory force. One of the reasons for this has been the shift in how immigrant identity is perceived and categorized. Up to the mid-twentieth century, Muslim immigrants have typically been classified in terms of their supposed ethnic origin, but since then, it has become more common to categorize them based on religious affiliation. At the same time, the tendency among Muslim immigrants to also choose Islam as a reference for their public identity has intensified. The entry of Islam into the public sphere, which resulted from this two-sided cross-cultural endeavor to establish identity in many Western European countries, was and still is highly controversial. The debates alternate between two poles: on one side, it has been argued that the secular, even laical identity of European societies and states should be strengthened in view of the validity claims of Muslim communities. At the opposite pole, others have asserted that in view of this situation, Europe must become aware of its own roots and values, which are said to have been decisively shaped by Christianity and Judaism. European identity was likewise classified along religious patterns. This of course did not mean that European politicians and public players collectively decided to start attending Sunday services. Religion itself has been placed into the "secular frame," and thus radically secularized. For many secularists, religion has come to be understood as culture.[5] But regardless of the political debates, it has been argued that the secular order which had finally won recognition in most Western European

---

5   In this regard, Niklas Luhmann was very explicit. He underlined that culture is foremost a secularist interpretation of religion. This corresponds to the religious interpretation of society as "secular." For a more detailed discussion with references to Luhmann, see Reinhard Schulze, "On Relating Religion to Society and Society to Religion," in *Debating Islam: Negotiating Religion, Europe, and the Self*, ed. Samuel M. Behloul, Susanne Leuenberger and Andreas Tunger-Zanetti (Bielefeld: Transcript, 2013), https://doi.org/10.14361/transcript.9783839422 496.333.

countries in the 1950s and 1960s at the latest,[6] and which had replaced the denominationalism that had prevailed up to then must be discussed anew, and even re-established. The transition from a secular to a "post-secular" society was already anticipated in the 1980s and 1990s, and the presumed emergence of a "post-secular religion" became a central theme from the 2000s onwards, clearly enhanced by Jürgen Habermas' rather spontaneous use of the term "post-secular" in 2001.

2 Religion in Post-Secular Times

In his Frankfurt speech held on October 14, 2001, only a month after the 9/11 terrorist attacks, Jürgen Habermas called for European societies to become aware of the dialectic of their secular orders and suggested that the attribute "post-secular," at its core, meant that people ideally no longer exclude each other on the basis of either a religious or a non-religious attitude. Post-secularism[7] refers to how state and society deal with the effects of secularization, which is no longer thought of as a process of privatizing religion, but as a normative order in which religion and society could coexist harmoniously and without a renewed *Kulturkampf*.[8] Thus, as Italian sociologist Massimo Rosati put it, in a post-secular situation, societies are concerned with the establishment of a balance between religion and society.[9] But as Niklas Luhmann underscored, in order to make this coexistence possible, both "systems" would have to learn. Thus secular society, i.e., a society that is not subject to any rules of a religion, must recognize that today the idea of religion is no longer represented by a single denomination, but by a plurality of religious traditions. For the sake of social peace, society would also have to recognize religious validity claims for the justification of a system of values and for participation in public space. On

---

6 In Switzerland, "non-denominationals" have only been included in censuses since 1960. At that time, only about 27,000 people stated that they were non-denominational; but by 2016, there were over 1.6 million.
7 A very useful summary of the debates on post-secularism is Matthias Lutz-Bachmann, ed., *Postsäkularismus: Zur Diskussion eines umstrittenen Begriffs* (Frankfurt am Main: Campus Verlag, 2015); furthermore, see Adam Possamai, *The i-zation of Society, Religion, and Neoliberal Post-Secularism* (Basingstoke: Palgrave Macmillan, 2018); Francesco Molteni, *A Need for Religion: Insecurity and Religiosity in the Contemporary World* (Leiden: Brill, 2021).
8 Jürgen Habermas, *Glauben und Wissen: Rede zum Friedenspreis des Deutschen Buchhandels 2001, Laudatio: Jan Philipp Reemtsma* (Frankfurt am Main: Suhrkamp, 2001).
9 Massimo Rosati, *The Making of a Postsecular Society: A Durkheimian Approach to Memory, Pluralism and Religion in Turkey* (Farnham: Ashgate, 2015).

the other hand, religion would have to learn to finally renounce any claim to formulating rules for social coexistence, or even to enforcing such rules. The struggle is therefore about the new balance between religion and society, or – staying with the terminology of Emile Durkheim – about the balance between the norms that constitute a society and the plurality of value orders that justify and define these norms as values. Thus, it also becomes clear that any value fundamentalism claiming that only one tradition can and may establish existing norms as values seriously disturbs this balance.

It is controversial whether this post-secular order presents itself as a real order of interpersonal coexistence, i.e., as a modern social fact to some extent, or whether it merely represents a social imagination of certain groups in a society. If one considers the weak institutional position of religious communities and the increase of non-denominationals, the impression is reinforced that such a post-secular order does not exist as a social reality. On the contrary, as people increasingly turn their backs on the churches, other, new religious communities in Europe, above all Muslim communities, must also acknowledge that society refuses to follow their institutionalized religions or denominations. Societies are increasingly justifying their norms through their own, non-religious, civil values.

De-confessionalization[10] – i.e., the fading out of the normativity of denominations within lifeworlds and political orders – therefore means neither de-secularization[11] nor the loss of significance of the religious sphere. Yet since secularization was linked to the confessionalization[12] of religions, at least in

---

10   The German term "Entkonfessionalisierung" was first used at the fourth Reichsbekenntnissynode in Bad Oeynhausen, 18–22. February 1936, see: Wilhelm Niemöller, *Die vierte Bekenntnissynode der Deutschen Evangelischen Kirche zu Bad Oeynhausen* (Göttingen: Vandenhoeck & Ruprecht, 1960), 158. In the late 1950s, the term was increasingly used in the German press.

11   Peter L. Berger, ed., *The Desecularization of the World: Resurgent Religion and World Politics* (Washington, DC: Ethics and Public Policy Center, 1999). On the German use of this term in the early nineteenth century, see Hermann Zabel, "Zum Wortgebrauch von 'Verweltlichen/ Säkularisieren' bei Paul Yorck von Wartenburg und Richard Rothe," *Archiv für Begriffsgeschichte* 14 (1970).

12   I use this term to translate the German expression "Konfessionalisierung" into English. The concept of "confessionalization" and its historical emergence have been discussed recently by Wolfgang Reinhard for Catholicism, and then by Heinz Schilling for the Reformed Church in the Old Reich, based on research by Ernst Walter Zeeden. The term was first used around 1890. By confessionalization, I understand the formation of a normativity of religious communities with regard to social practice in lifeworld and political orders. Normativity is enforced by structural violence without direct involvement of the state executive. This means that almost all biographies, life stories and life decisions are framed by the normative order of a particular religious denomination.

many Western European countries, and since this made it possible for the state to delegate its sovereign tasks to ecclesiastical institutions, the confessionalization of religion demands a redefinition of the secular order. Being "secular" does not equal behaving indifferently toward religions; in such an order, the state declines to regulate the religious field, to subject the religious to state control or to push it completely into the private world. Such secular solutions are not based on any contractual partnership with the religious denominations.

To summarize the picture thus far, secularization essentially refers to the differentiation of a social order through the categorical separation of religion and society. This separation provided for an autonomy of religion, which in turn allowed it to control ever-larger areas of the social field, above all social ties, education, health care and everyday rituals. This process is called "confessionalization." A "confession" is more than simply a community based on a common confession, they are religiously defined social orders. In German-speaking countries, secularization has promoted the dominance of denominations as a social order; in the *Kulturkampf* of the late nineteenth century, the hegemonic reach of denominations has been horizontally limited, yet at the same time vertically deepened. The history of confessionalization is closely interwoven with the history of nation states, where it has significantly shaped the specific faces of secularization. Deconfessionalization, on the other hand, was not limited to certain nation states, but unfolded in what we call in a political sense, "the West." For this reason, it makes sense to understand secularization as a problem of global history.[13]

3   Islam and the Global History of Secularity

Let me begin my reflections on how to write a global history of secularity with a short remark on Talal Asad's concept of secularism. I share some of the views and ideas that he developed regarding secularization and its affirmation as political secularism.[14] This includes, among other things, the observation that

---

13   Michael Rectenwald, Rochelle Almeida and George Levine, eds., *Global Secularisms in a Post-Secular Age* (Berlin: de Gruyter, 2015). Although the title of this book promises a discussion of the term "global secularisms," neither the term nor its implications are dealt with in the single chapters. More profitable is the important study by Todd H. Weir, "Germany and the New Global History of Secularism: Questioning the Postcolonial Genealogy," *Germanic Review* 90, no. 1 (2015), https://doi.org/10.1080/00168890.2014.986431.

14   Talal Asad, *Genealogies of Religion: Discipline and Reasons of Power in Christianity and Islam* (Baltimore and London: John Hopkins University Press, 1993); Talal Asad,

historically, secularization has been closely linked to the post-Reformation period in terms of concept and content. Likewise, and at the same time, a new meaning of the word "religion" emerged as the social order that the public has called "secular" since the nineteenth century. Thus, Asad's genealogy of "religion" is simultaneously reflected in a genealogy of "secularity." He of course understands his genealogy critically: since religion and secularity have only one shared history (that is both became hegemonic in the context of colonial expansion and finally also conceptually nestled in the languages of the colonized elites), it is fundamentally important to criticize these two hegemonic orders from a post-colonial perspective, so that local, communal counter-drafts of the subalterns become possible. Hadi Enayat rightly stated in his 2017 essay that Asad's critique of the secular rests on three pillars: (a) formalizing Nietzsche's concept of genealogy as a method, including references to Heidegger and Foucault, (b) an anti-humanist reading of Edward Said's *Orientalism* as a fundamental critique of a universal modernity and (c) the communitarian rediscovery of tradition and community.[15] Taking up Stephen Holmes' criticism of anti-liberalism,[16] Enayat understands this Asadian tradition as anti-liberal.

But what is the problem? There is no doubt about the actual secularity of a multitude of lifeworlds on a global scale. Asad maintains that secularity and secularism are concepts that bring together "certain behaviors, knowledges, and sensitivities in modern life."[17] As proposed by Monika Wohlrab-Sahr and Christoph Kleine, we may understand secularity as "institutionally as well as symbolically embedded forms and arrangements of differentiation between religious and other social spheres, practices, interpretive frameworks, institutions and discourses," or simply as "modalities of making distinctions."[18] Yet such an analytical definition underestimates the above-mentioned quality of "secularity" as a "thick concept." Used in public and even academic discourses, the term denotes a selective view of reality along with a moral and even normative evaluation of what has been perceived. In fact, "secularity" works as a public hermeneutical concept, and it is extremely difficult to transfer its

---

    Formations of the Secular: Christianity, Islam, Modernity (Stanford: Stanford University Press, 2003), 1–20.
15 Hadi Enayat, *Islam and Secularism in Post-Colonial Thought: A Cartography of Asadian Genealogies* (London: Palgrave Macmillan, 2017).
16 Stephen Holmes, *The Anatomy of Antiliberalism* (Cambridge, MA: Harvard University Press, 1993).
17 Asad, *Genealogies*, 25.
18 Christoph Kleine and Monika Wohlrab-Sahr, *Research Programme of the HCAS 'Multiple Secularities – Beyond the West, Beyond Modernities'* (Leipzig: Leipzig University, 2016), 8, https://doi.org/10.36730/2020.1.msbwbm.1.

public meaning into scientific language without retaining its evaluative connotation. Moreover, though the expression "modality of making distinction" sounds neutral, it still connotes that the very modality of making distinctions has gained worldwide hegemony, and what Charles Taylor has called "Western Secularity."[19] Thus, secularity defines a relational property between two social orders, or better two normative social orders. In short, secularity itself has become a normative order of typicality, one which today serves as a global standard for successful secularization.

A look into the Arabic conceptual history of "secularization" gives us clear indications of how this process of standardization worked out and how the "Western modality of distinction" gained hegemony. Early lexical attempts of the nineteenth century to reduce modern life to a single concept still made use of either the attribute *dunyawi* ("worldly," if affirmative) or more rarely *dahr* ("materialist," if negative[20]), but their Arabic history obviously prevented these words from becoming real equivalents to the word "secular." Maronite authors in Lebanon, on the other hand, employed their Arabic church language to denounce Protestant religious and educational policies, in the same way that their European Catholic partners did. For this they borrowed the Syrian term *'almani,* a lexical equivalent to the Latin adjective *secularis,* which, as already stated, designated those church people who were not subject to the rules of a monastery. The latter were regarded as *regulares,* which Christian Arabs translated as *shar'i.* The anti-Protestant polemics of the Maronites had already used the expression *'almani* since the 1870s, and Arab Muslim journalists very hesitantly took up the notion shortly before the First World War.

At first, the term was not very successful. This was certainly due to the fact that in the nineteenth century in the European modality, the term *secularization* still referred to the history of Christian church law. In 1882, the German *Brockhaus' Conversations-Lexikon* did not even mention the term *secular.* A theory of secularization beyond church history did not yet exist. Germans understood *säkular* either as "centennial" or as not *regular.* In the nineteenth century, secularization was primarily related to concepts such as politics, proselytism, education and church goods. It was not until the 1920s that the

---

19   Charles Taylor, *A Secular Age* (Cambridge, MA: The Belknap Press of Harvard University Press, 2007), 41.

20   In Urdu, the expression *la dini* ("not religious") is also used to indicate something not concerned with or devoted to religion. This use does not correspond with the meaning of the Arabic term *la dini,* which rather denotes deism, atheism or agnosticism. It first came into use in the Ottoman public in the 1880s and was then Arabized by the Maronite scholar Louis Cheikho at the beginning of the twentieth century.

secularization of society was mentioned,[21] and the Germans did not perceive a secular society before the 1950s.[22] The term *secularism,* coined by George Jacob Holyoake in the late 1840s for his ideas on the criticism of religion, only became gradually meaningful beyond its ideological frame during the 1920s. If one examines the term *secular* in European languages, it becomes clear that the lexicalization of the redefinition of relations between religion on one side and the state, law and society on the other began only in the 1920s. It will also become apparent that secularization did not actually refer to the structure of the social order until the 1960s. This took place – certainly not coincidentally – at the same time that social scientists and historians rediscovered Max Weber's work and reduced his theories to labels such as "secularization thesis" or "secularization theory."

It was only now that *secularization* was also addressed in the sense of a process in the Arab public sphere. *'Almana,* the Arab term for secularization, was used for the first time in the context of Lebanese domestic political debates, where it was set in contrast to "sectarianism" (*ta'ifiyya*) and filled the need to create a discourse on a Lebanese problem. Hence, Lebanese *secularization* sought to deprive religious communities of sovereignty over social worlds and social relations. Such a discourse called for the communitization or

---

21 For a conceptual history, see Ian Hunter, "Secularization: The Birth of a Modern Combat Concept," *Modern Intellectual History* 12, no. 1 (April 2015), https://doi.org/10.1017/S1479244314000158. Hunter states: "I shall propose, then, that if prior to the early 1800s nobody spoke about secularization as an epochal transition from religious belief to autonomous rationality that is in part because the language in which to do so had not been invented and in part because no such transition had taken place." See also Todd H. Weir, *Secularism and Religion in Nineteenth-Century Germany: The Rise of the Fourth Confession* (New York: Cambridge University Press, 2014). Weir argues that secularism arose as a belief system. He reconstructs three stages of its evolution, starting with the initial development phase of the secular as a worldview of "free religion" from 1844 to 1847; followed by a stage of both repression and internal consolidation in the 1850s, also characterized by a flourishing of communities and their participation in political activities in the 1860s; and ending with a third stage marked by taking up positions in the "culture war" (*Kulturkampf*) of the 1870s. The latter was finally resolved in the 1880s by a repositioning under the banner of socialist laws on the one hand and anti-Semitism on the other hand.

22 Prominent authors who used this expression were Paul Tillich, Alfred Weber, Ernst Bloch, Gustav Eduard Kafka and Franz Altheim. In German, the expression appeared at the same time as the term "*Entkonfessionalisierung*." In the English tradition, the expression "secular society" (homonymous with the name of Charles Badlaugh's famous National Secular Society of 1866 with its slogan, "challenging religious privilege"); referring to a societal sphere *in toto,* as distinguished from the church; was already used in the 1880s, see for example Ágost Pulszky, *The Theory of Law and Civil Society* (London: T. Fisher Unwin, 1888), 400.

socialization of the Lebanese population into a unified "nation," one in which confessions would no longer determine membership and social privilege.

Thus, the possible implications of the term *secularization* became clear in Muslim environments as well. It was far more than a matter of redefining the relationship between religious institutions and the state. To address this dynamic, Europeans had a second lexical concept at their disposal by resorting to the ecclesiastical expression *layman*. European languages profited from a double terminology, which had a Greek and a Latin background. The Greek word λαϊκός (*laikós*, "layman," literally meaning "member of the people") has been used in the church language as the opposite of κλῆρος (*klíros*, "clergy") since about the third century.[23] The derivations of *laïque* (*laïcité, laïcisme*, etc.), first used in French in the early 1870s, denote the idea that the people had gained sovereignty over the institutions of religion. This, of course, did not imply that the people (λαός, *laós*, Ar.: *sha'b*) as a whole should exercise control over religious institutions, rather, the expression referred to the state authorities as a *totum pro parte*. That is why religious actors perceived laicism as a nationalization (*etatization*) of religious institutions.

While secularizing a social order did not successfully dissolve the hegemony of denominations (confessions) prior to the second half of the twentieth century, relations between the state and religious institutions have been repeatedly renegotiated for centuries. The negotiation processes had once again reached a climax in the *Kulturkampf* of the nineteenth century, and since then, the relationship between state and religion has been stabilized in most Western and Central European countries. An analogous process took place in Middle Eastern countries between 1880 and 1930, with the religious laws of the young Turkish Republic being a culmination that attracted worldwide attention.

The global history of secularization and secularity is thus particularly tangible for the period after the Second World War, and even more specifically, since the 1950s and 1960s. The matter of fact way in which religions had intervened in the social order was lost, thus in order to preserve supremacy, religions had to reinvent themselves. This was especially true for modern Islamic history. Now, the self-secularizing society radically claimed its autonomy, and at the same time, religious traditions also radicalized their claim. This global history resulted in a worldwide accepted standard framing for the concepts of secularity and religiosity. In the West, the last *Kulturkampf*, this time between religion and society, lasted till the 1970s. The winners were the secularists: not only did they push social autonomy through, they also succeeded in creating a positive

---

23   In Arabic, this is often *rijal al-din* ("men of religion").

identity for the *secular*. Within Muslim societies, this *Kulturkampf* is still going on, but looking at the current situation, we may predict a victory of the secularists there as well, albeit vested with a religious legitimation (called religious secularism).[24] Not surprisingly, most religious actors have rated secularity negatively, and even for advocates of a secular order, the attribute "secular" does not always imply a positive judgement – as the example of the controversial and highly ambiguous term "secular religion" clearly demonstrates.[25]

But back to the global history of secularity. If it is undisputed that (a) for large parts of a society, secularity represents a normative order in the sense of Talcot Parsons, and (b) the functional differentiation[26] between society and religion thus reflected the divergence of values (religion) and norms (society, state), then contemporary Islam must also be interpreted in the light of this order. However, as Florian Zemmin has recently shown,[27] the interpretation of Islamic discourses is complicated by the fact that the modern term "Islam" means, on the one hand, "religion," but on the other, "society" as well. In principle, there is also a similar peculiarity in the modern Jewish tradition, but here the secular and socialist idea of Judaism was given a different name, Zionism. Gershom Scholem therefore viewed Zionism as secularized,

---

24   Naser Ghobadzadeh, *Religious Secularity: A Theological Challenge to the Islamic State* (New York: Oxford University Press, 2015).

25   "Secular religion" was understood as either a religionization of political ideologies or secular worlds of knowledge (Eric Voegelin), or a religious order that refrains from normative interventions in civil society while still participating in it. The conceptual vagueness increases even further when, as Voegelin did, one equates the secular with the political. For a critical stance and rejection of Voegelin, see Hans Kelsen, *Secular Religion: A Polemic Against the Misinterpretation of Modern Social Philosophy, Science, and Politics as "New Religions"* (Vienna and New York: Springer, 2012). Kelsen worked on his criticism of Voegelin and of his view that modern philosophies are merely "failed" religions between 1952 and 1964, but did not publish the final manuscript himself.

26   A recent discussion of theories of differentiation has been provided by Detlef Pollack, "Die Genese der westlichen Moderne: Religiöse Bedingungen der Emergenz funktionaler Differenzierung im Mittelalter," in *Postsäkularismus: Zur Diskussion eines umstrittenen Begriffs*, ed. Matthias Lutz-Bachmann (Frankfurt am Main: Campus, 2015). See also a stimulating study of the transcendentality of the concept "secular": José Casanova, "Exploring the Postsecular: Three Meanings of 'The Secular' and Their Possible Transcendence," in *Habermas and Religion*, ed. Craig Calhoun, Eduardo Mendieta and Jonathan VanAntwerpen (New York: Wiley, 2016), 27–48. See also Casanova's famous contribution, "The Secular, Secularizations, Secularisms," in *Rethinking Secularism*, ed. Craig Calhoun, Mark Juergensmeyer and Jonathan VanAntwerpen (New York: Oxford University Press, 2011).

27   Florian Zemmin, *Modernity in Islamic Tradition: The Concept of 'Society' in the Journal al-Manar (Cairo, 1898–1940)* (Berlin: de Gruyter, 2018).

socialized Judaism,[28] and Max Nordau was of the same opinion, albeit in a positive, apologetic sense. But there is no analogous naming of Islamic secularity, so that Islam of today must equally and simultaneously represent both social imaginaries. This conceptual peculiarity and semantic ambiguity led to the fact that the de facto distinction between a "religious Islam" and a "secular Islam" was not understood by the Western publics, which then accused Islam of failing to separate religion and society (state, politics, etc.). Upon closer examination, however, it becomes clear that those Muslim actors who want to assign Islam a societal order, i.e., Muslims who are generally typologized as Islamists, are in fact true advocates of secularism.[29] They shift Islam's area of validity from religion to the world and claim that Islam must be realized as a worldly order. It is not, therefore, a matter of aligning legal norms with religious values, which is called for by many conservative communities, but of making Islam a worldly order. Islamization can also be understood as secularization, and even the fashion of wearing a headscarf that emerged in the 1970s would – at least in Scholem's eyes – be part of a secularization process. But this is a different story.[30]

The fact that this actual secularization of social worlds was accompanied by rapid social change and that it intensified at the beginning of the 1970s, when the new globalization began to intervene in the social order, is important for a global history of secularity. This process shaped secularity into a fairly uniform order, even if it was expressed through a variety of traditions. Therefore, it only makes sense to pluralize the concept of secularity if at the same time a generic concept of secularity is recognized, analogous, for instance, to the expression "capitalisms," which Wolfgang Schluchter used to describe Max

---

28 Christoph Miething, ed., *Politik und Religion im Judentum* (Tübingen: Niemeyer, 1999).

29 Jamal Malik, "From Salafism to Secularism: The Dialectic of Political Islam and Secular Nationalism in the Case of Azad's Thought," *Journal of South Asian and Middle Eastern Studies* 37 (2014): 32–45, is a telling analysis of a possible convergence of "Islamism" and secularism. Jamal Malik has been able to demonstrate the close epistemological and social interconnection of Islamization and secularization of the religious order in Pakistan. Jamal Malik, *Colonialization of Islam: Dissolution of Traditional Institutions in Pakistan* (New Delhi: Manohar Publications; Lahore: Vanguard, 1996).

30 As a consequence, classical Islamism of the 1960s and 1970s could be interpreted as a "political religion" in the sense of Voegelin, which would have paved the way for the deconfessionalization of society. Here an analogy to fascism would arise: fascism as "political religion," as was repeatedly argued by church institutions in particular, had destroyed the confessional social-moral milieus and thus facilitated the later secularization of society.

Weber's analysis of capitalism in terms of a typology.[31] We would then, however, have to dispense with the term "secularity," otherwise hegemony would continue to exist in one particular interpretation of this process, namely that of the Western Protestant tradition from which the term emerged. We therefore need a theory that provides information about what the term "secularity" in effect construes and signifies. Yet in order to trace this generic term, it is not only the normative orders assembled by the Protestant term "secularity" that we should take as a starting point. Rather, a suitable theory must meet such a complexity that it can also integrate other experiences into the processes of interpretation. However, I do not want to use the metaphor of a "common denominator" here, but I instead propose deriving a theory in the form of a retrospective genealogy.[32]

Naturally, the global history of secularity also investigates the question of why one of these secularities, namely the tradition that we are acquainted with in the *gestalt* of Western Protestant interpretation, became hegemonic and why it was able to assert itself in such a way that particular, conceptually independent interpretations of "secularity" disappeared. While Talal Asad would agree with the first part of the question, he would certainly frown on the second part. It implies that today's secularity has a multitude of ancestors that are "similar" to one another, with the degree of such similarity increasing as they come closer to the present time. This second part of the question thus also implies a process of convergence that increased this "family resemblance" and supplemented processes of differentiation. Consequently, it also means that the further we look back into the past, the more dissimilar the uses of tradition become, specifically those uses which potentially serve as ancestors of contemporary *modalities* of secularity.

Logically, however, a family resemblance disclosed in a retrograding genealogy is restricted to a certain lineage. As within a specific lineage, "resemblance" is of a purely formal nature (lexical, conventional meaning), so the metaphor of "family resemblance" should only be used to denote the result of conceptual convergence. The further we advance toward the present, the more similar the heterogeneous traditions of interpretation become. Family resemblance may thus be understood as the property of similarity, which emerged out of a gradual process of convergence.

---

31 Wolfgang Schluchter, *Die Entzauberung der Welt: Sechs Studien zu Max Weber* (Tübingen: Mohr Siebeck, 2009), 69.
32 A closer look at this method can be found in my book, *Der Koran und die Genealogie des Islam* (Basel: Schwabe, 2015).

Therefore, the history of a retrospective genealogy of secularity cannot be interpreted as a "development." Hence, a formulation such as "the development of secularism in Turkey" (Niyazi Berkes) contradicts this model. Instead, the modelling of a retrospective genealogy as a cluster definition starts from reconstructing the modalities of addressing secularity and assigns a plurality of lineages to this reconstruction. It is thus simply impossible to identify an origin of secularity.[33]

Secularity is always part of a social imaginary, to take up a term first coined by Cornelius Castoriadis in 1975, further elaborated by the sociologists Ulf Himmelstrand and Michael Rustin and finally elegantly systematized by Charles Taylor in 2007.[34] The traceability of the genealogies of secularity applies to the way a given public addressed the order that came to be standardly referred to with the term "secularity." I will very shortly consider some uses within the Middle Eastern context. So, what term replaced the Arabic concept ʿalmani, which had gradually become a synonym for secularity since the 1920s? Evidently, ʿalmani has modernized two very traditional attributes, namely dunyawi and dahri. These two Arabic terms, however, had represented different conventionalized, lexicalized meanings: both attributes observed and evaluated an orientation towards the world, or better a worldliness, though dunyawi in a positive way, and dahri in a negative one. Of course, this is connected to the history of their lexical meanings. The dunya ("world"), to which the attribute dunyawi refers, meant basically "living within a social world," so the term was often used to translate the Greek βίος (νίος, "life"). Rather anachronistically, we can translate dunya as "lifeworld." The meaning of (al-hayat ["life"] al-)dunya becomes explicit when we take into account the complementary term din (today "religion"). The tradition of separating life into two distinct spheres goes back to early Islamic times, as found in the distinction between an existence that serves the cult (din) and an existence that serves the social environment (dunya). The two spheres were clearly distinguished from

---

33   Azzam Tamimi, "The Origins of Arab Secularism," in *Islam and Secularism in the Middle East*, ed., John L. Esposito and Azzam Tamimi (New York: New York University Press, 2000), 17. Tamimi simplifies the story by stating that in the mid-nineteenth century, secularism "came to the Muslim world in the company of other related terms such as modernity, Westernization and modernization within the context of colonialism" (ibid., 13).

34   Michael Rustin, "Place and Time in Socialist Theory," *Radical Philosophy* 47 (1987); Ulf Himmelstrand, ed., *Sociology: From Crisis to Science?*, vol. 2, *The Social Reproduction of Organization and Culture* (London: SAGE Publications, 1986). Today, "social imaginary" is simply defined as a "set of values, institutions, laws, and symbols common to a particular social group and the corresponding society through which people imagine their social whole."

one another, while Islamic law defined and monitored the demarcation line. It was just as impossible to transfer sovereignty over something that had hitherto been under the control of the cult world to the social world – i.e., secularization in the true sense of the word – as it was vice versa.[35] *Din* and *dunya* signified two earthly forms of human existence, or as we would say today, two well differentiated social roles. Since *islam* was only the name of the cult (*din*) and the social situation in which the cult was practiced, there was a fundamental separation of Islam and the lifeworld.[36]

Secularizing the concept of time (*seculum*) was decisive in Church Latin, as it also was in Christian Syrian Aramaic and even in the Rabbinic tradition. Actually, the concept *seculum* meant, analogously to the Greek αἰών (*aión*), a worldly time that was regarded as permanent. Through exegetic reasoning, the Church Fathers modified this concept of time: first, they lifted it up into heaven as timeless eternity, thus transcending mundane time, and second, in quite the opposite direction, they anchored it within creation by using it to denote the "temporally limited physical world" or "cosmos." This differentiation created an ambiguity in the meaning of *seculum*, which also marked the use of the parallel Syrian-Aramaic term *'alam*. The Quranic reading of *'alam*, on the other hand, only referred to its immanent meaning as cosmos. The Arabic term *dahr* passed on the old meaning of the world's lasting temporality and was still used in Arabic translations of many texts from the classical Greek canon to reproduce αἰών. Theologically, *dahri* became the simple signifier of a denier of God. In the nineteenth century, when "secular" was still mostly perceived as an ecclesiastical term, *dahri* was used to signify the then dominant metaphysical naturalism, especially materialism.

That way there were sufficient terms in Arabic (and thus also in the languages that incorporated Arabic terminology) to discuss how to address the hidden meaning of the secular. But what was this hidden meaning of the secular? Obviously, the term served as a metaphor for a process of differentiation which took place within the epistemic order. This order framed the assumption and recognition of a real, transcendental truth which interpreted the cosmos, and hence reality, as a comprehensive correspondence of its property called "truth." This truth, which had hitherto been realized in the cosmos, then

---

35 This only became possible in postmodern times.
36 For details, see Schulze, *Der Koran*, 529–49. Whereas *dunya* signified the world as life, the term *'alam* referred to a geographical, physical world as cosmos. Arabic translators occasionally understood the word βίος (*víos*, "life") as *'alam*. Technically, the term referred primarily to the environment of Neoplatonist and "Monistic" traditions (*Ikhwan al-Safa'*, Ibn 'Arabi).

evolved into two autonomous, self-organized systems. What was crucial was the fact that divinity, i.e., transcendental truth, no longer had to prove itself in the reality of the world. In short, the world was freed from heteronomous governance and was granted autonomy. At the same time, truth, previously understood as transcendence, also attained absolute autonomy and thus came to be called "belief." This, however, demanded a change in the epistemic procedures with which truth and the world were grasped and understood. I can only refer here to a few diverging pairs: The transcendental truth was subordinated to certainty (*certitudo*), to which man could refer by "faith" (*credere*), the testimony of which was an inner-psychic act, which subordinated "believers" to their own "conscience." Cult practice now served to bear witness to this very piety. Obedience was replaced by "insight into necessity." This new order was defined as "*religio*." Thus, the arrangement defined as a religion was freed from the task of having to prove itself in the world. It became literally autonomous. At the same time, the self-sufficient religion unintentionally abolished the heteronomy of the world, which as an autonomous order became "worldly" in the true sense of the word. This had far-reaching consequences for human existence in the world. A believer, being subject to his or her conscience and the grace of God only, could develop a form of self-reference and subjectivity, which imparted to him/her a new perspective onto the world, or better said, which partially secularized him/her. This empowered the believer to view him or herself as a "self" and a "subject" (in the Cartesian sense), thus disposing of a clear identity. These terms signify the *leitmotif* which marks the model of an "epistemic break."[37]

In fact, this process, which coincides historically with early modernity, has been studied very thoroughly, albeit controversially, by a variety of historians, philosophers and theologians, but only in the Western world. Nonetheless, there are many indications that this modern break of the epistemic order also took place in the Middle Eastern world. I would just like to point out that while many theological and legal texts of the sixteenth and seventeenth centuries very precisely documented the reinterpretation of Islam as religion, we still know rather little about the parallel "discovery of the world" as autonomous order. It is due to historical reasons that we are only unilaterally informed about (a) the increase in significance of the term Islam as *religion* and the reformulation of the concept *iman* as "faith," which previously had the lexical meaning of "fidelity" or "allegiance," (b) apprehending Islamic truth norms as

---

37   I discuss the emergence of the concept of "identity" in detail in "The Ambiguity of the Religious Self in Pre- and Post-National Social Worlds: Examples from 17th-Century Morocco and 20th-Century Germany," *Numen* (forthcoming).

certainty and (c) the formation of an internalized conceptualization of conscience. In short, we are well informed about how a Muslim "religious self" emerged in early modernity, but we know very little about the way natural philosophers explored the world and its autonomy independently from the norms of Islamic truth. Yet there is a great deal of evidence which proves that the modern division of the metaphysical structure into a dichotomy of transcendent religion and mundane world was in fact part of the new order of Muslim empires. The introduction of the printing press to the Middle East during the eighteenth century may serve as a helpful example, as it unveiled an existing consensus on distinguishing between secular and religious knowledge. The emerging public positively identified this division by using the conventional terms *din* and *dunya*.

All in all, the differentiation process went rather smoothly. In contrast to the Western world, there were hardly any great hegemonic conflicts, either in the field of sciences or in the social organization of knowledge. This is probably due to the fact that such a new distinction between religion and the world could fall back on much older social resources, namely those which rested on a meticulously upheld demarcation between a cult practice (*din*) and a social lifeworld (*dunya*). The cultic performance of fidelity to God and his truth and the associated expectation of salvation were strictly limited to this cult world. Of course, some Muslim theologians, and in particular actors in the broader social field of lived piety, argued for a justification of fidelity through works (*Werkgerechtigkeit*, legalism). They maintained that God's favor could be achieved by good deeds, but this was by no means formalized and ritualized to the extent it had been in Christianity. Interestingly enough, Islamic puritans of the seventeenth century radically criticized existing convictions of the possibility of "buy[ing] a place in God's mercy" by good deeds.[38]

4 Same Spectacle Everywhere, Only Performed by Different People (Marc Aurel)

Retrospective genealogy allows us to relate the factual secularity experienced by people in the contemporary Middle Eastern worlds to an historical process of differentiation in the epistemic order which we call *pars pro toto* and, due to the hegemony of the Western interpretation of this process, "secularization."

---

38 For details, see Reinhard Schulze, "Arbeit als Problem der arabischen Sozialgeschichte," in *Semantiken von Arbeit: Diachrone und vergleichende Perspektiven*, ed. Jörn Leonhard and Willibald Steinmetz (Cologne: Böhlau, 2016).

Thus, in our times, "secularization" is the family name conventionally used to define one predominant lineage. But there is undoubtedly a multiplicity of lineages, so that we could theoretically use a different family name, for example *tadniya*.[39] However, hardly anyone in the Western world would understand the meaning of *tadniya*, since early Islamic expressions of distinguishing between religion and society are not in use there. We may therefore accept globalizing social theories of secularization as they represent the de facto family resemblance, but we should avoid generalizing Western strategies and models of historical justification of secularization. In order to conceptualize a global history of secularization, we would have to work out a theory that considers the plurality of corresponding experiences. This theory could be useful for exploring the existing secularity through a variety of narratives and liberating it from the hegemony of the interpretations of Western and Central European experiences. A narrative would be an inversion of a retrospective genealogy. Such a theory would therefore necessarily be historical and would help to recognize that the modern social imaginary we conventionally call secularization has a multiplicity of lineages.

A global history of secularity should therefore not only take into consideration the multiplicity of secularities, but the multiplicity of genealogies or lineages of secularity which have converged over the last decades and even centuries. The global common thread in these genealogies is that they are all related to a thorough transformation within the epistemic order. As scholars, we may reconstruct a variety of Middle Eastern genealogies, but of course, it would be up to engaged Muslim scholars to transform the retrospective genealogy into a Muslim narrative of secularization. As we have seen, there are compelling arguments for composing a plausible narrative, and I am sure that all of the evidence we have at our disposal would provide for a Muslim narrative of secularity which is at least as equally convincing as those of Charles Taylor or of Ernst Troeltsch.[40]

---

39   This lexical expression does not exist in Arabic. The word *tadniya* means "minimization" and is derived from the adjective *dani* ("low and close").

40   Ernst Troeltsch, *Die Bedeutung des Protestantismus für die Entstehung der modernen Welt* (Munich: Oldenbourg, 1928 [1911]); see also Georg Pfleiderer, "'Säkularisierung': Systematisch-theologische Überlegungen zur Aktualität eines überholten Begriffs," *Praktische Theologie* 37 (2002).

Bibliography

Asad, Talal. *Formations of the Secular: Christianity, Islam, Modernity*. Stanford: Stanford University Press, 2003.

Asad, Talal. *Genealogies of Religion: Discipline and Reasons of Power in Christianity and Islam*. Baltimore and London: John Hopkins University Press, 1993.

Berger, Peter L., ed. *The Desecularization of the World: Resurgent Religion and World Politics*. Washington, DC: Ethics and Public Policy Center, 1999.

Casanova, José. "Exploring the Postsecular: Three Meanings of 'The Secular' and Their Possible Transcendence." In *Habermas and Religion*, edited by Craig Calhoun, Eduardo Mendieta and Jonathan VanAntwerpen, 27–48. New York: Wiley, 2016.

Casanova, José. "The Secular, Secularizations, Secularisms." In *Rethinking Secularism*, edited by Craig Calhoun, Mark Juergensmeyer and Jonathan VanAntwerpen, 54–74. New York: Oxford University Press, 2011.

Enayat, Hadi. *Islam and Secularism in Post-Colonial Thought: A Cartography of Asadian Genealogies*. London: Palgrave Macmillan, 2017.

Ghobadzadeh, Naser. *Religious Secularity: A Theological Challenge to the Islamic State*. New York: Oxford University Press, 2015.

Habermas, Jürgen. *Glauben und Wissen: Rede zum Friedenspreis des Deutschen Buchhandels 2001, Laudatio: Jan Philipp Reemtsma*. Frankfurt am Main: Suhrkamp, 2001.

Himmelstrand, Ulf, ed. *Sociology: From Crisis to Science?*, vol. 2, *The Social Reproduction of Organization and Culture*. London: SAGE Publications, 1986.

Holmes, Stephen. *The Anatomy of Antiliberalism*. Cambridge, MA: Harvard University Press, 1993.

Hunter, Ian. "Secularization: The Birth of a Modern Combat Concept." *Modern Intellectual History* 12, no. 1 (April 2015): 1–32, https://doi.org/10.1017/S1479244314000158.

Kelsen, Hans. *Secular Religion: A Polemic Against the Misinterpretation of Modern Social Philosophy, Science, and Politics as "New Religions."* Vienna and New York: Springer, 2012.

Kleine, Christoph and Monika Wohlrab-Sahr. *Research Programme of the HCAS 'Multiple Secularities – Beyond the West, Beyond Modernities'*. Leipzig: Leipzig University, 2016, https://doi.org/10.36730/2020.1.msbwbm.1.

Lutz-Bachmann, Matthias, ed. *Postsäkularismus: Zur Diskussion eines umstrittenen Begriffs*. Frankfurt am Main: Campus Verlag, 2015.

Malik, Jamal. *Colonialization of Islam: Dissolution of Traditional Institutions in Pakistan*. New Delhi: Manohar Publications; Lahore: Vanguard, 1996.

Malik, Jamal. "From Salafism to Secularism: The Dialectic of Political Islam and Secular Nationalism in the Case of Azad's Thought." *Journal of South Asian and Middle Eastern Studies* 37 (2014): 32–45.

Miething, Christoph, ed. *Politik und Religion im Judentum*. Tübingen: Niemeyer, 1999.

Molteni, Francesco. *A Need for Religion: Insecurity and Religiosity in the Contemporary World*. Leiden: Brill, 2021.

Niemöller, Wilhelm. *Die vierte Bekenntnissynode der Deutschen Evangelischen Kirche zu Bad Oeynhausen*. Göttingen: Vandenhoeck & Ruprecht, 1960.

Pfleiderer, Georg. "'Säkularisierung': Systematisch-theologische Überlegungen zur Aktualität eines überholten Begriffs." *Praktische Theologie* 37 (2002): 130–53.

Pollack, Detlef. "Die Genese der westlichen Moderne: Religiöse Bedingungen der Emergenz funktionaler Differenzierung im Mittelalter." In *Postsäkularismus: Zur Diskussion eines umstrittenen Begriffs*, edited by Matthias Lutz-Bachmann, 289–333. Frankfurt am Main: Campus Verlag, 2015.

Possamai, Adam. *The i-zation of Society, Religion, and Neoliberal Post-Secularism*. Basingstoke: Palgrave Macmillan, 2018.

Pulszky, Ágost. *The Theory of Law and Civil Society*. London: T. Fisher Unwin, 1888.

Putnam, Hilary. *The Collapse of the Fact/Value Dichotomy and Other Essays*. Cambridge, MA: Harvard University Press, 2002.

Rectenwald, Michael, Rochelle Almeida and George Levine, eds. *Global Secularisms in a Post-Secular Age*. Berlin: de Gruyter, 2015.

Rosati, Massimo. *The Making of a Postsecular Society: A Durkheimian Approach to Memory, Pluralism and Religion in Turkey*. Farnham: Ashgate, 2015.

Rustin, Michael. "Place and Time in Socialist Theory." *Radical Philosophy* 47 (1987): 30–36.

Schluchter, Wolfgang. *Die Entzauberung der Welt: Sechs Studien zu Max Weber*. Tübingen: Mohr Siebeck, 2009.

Schulze, Reinhard. "Arbeit als Problem der arabischen Sozialgeschichte." In *Semantiken von Arbeit: Diachrone und vergleichende Perspektiven*, edited by Jörn Leonhard and Willibald Steinmetz, 191–208. Cologne: Böhlau, 2016.

Schulze, Reinhard. *Der Koran und die Genealogie des Islam*. Basel: Schwabe, 2015.

Schulze, Reinhard. "On Relating Religion to Society and Society to Religion." In *Debating Islam: Negotiating Religion, Europe, and the Self*, edited by Samuel M. Behloul, Susanne Leuenberger and Andreas Tunger-Zanetti, 333–56. Bielefeld: Transcript, 2013, https://doi.org/10.14361/transcript.9783839422496.333.

Schulze, Reinhard. "The Ambiguity of the Religious Self in Pre- and Post-National Social Worlds: Examples from 17th-Century Morocco and 20th-Century Germany," *Numen* (forthcoming).

Tamimi, Azzam. "The Origins of Arab Secularism." In *Islam and Secularism in the Middle East*, edited by John L. Esposito and Azzam Tamimi, 13–28. New York: New York University Press, 2000.

Taylor, Charles. *A Secular Age*. Cambridge, MA: The Belknap Press of Harvard University Press, 2007.

Troeltsch, Ernst. *Die Bedeutung des Protestantismus für die Entstehung der modernen Welt*. Munich: Oldenbourg, 1928 [1911].

Weir, Todd H. "Germany and the New Global History of Secularism: Questioning the Postcolonial Genealogy." *Germanic Review* 90, no. 1 (2015): 6–20, https://doi.org/10.1080/00168890.2014.986431.

Weir, Todd H. *Secularism and Religion in Nineteenth-Century Germany: The Rise of the Fourth Confession*. New York: Cambridge University Press, 2014.

Zabel, Hermann. "Zum Wortgebrauch von 'Verweltlichen/Säkularisieren' bei Paul Yorck von Wartenburg und Richard Rothe." *Archiv für Begriffsgeschichte* 14 (1970): 69–85.

Zemmin, Florian. *Modernity in Islamic Tradition: The Concept of 'Society' in the Journal al-Manar (Cairo, 1898–1940)*. Berlin: de Gruyter, 2018.

CHAPTER 2

Negotiating Modernity through Constructions of History in Modern Muslim Religious Thought

Armina Omerika

1   Introduction: The Discovery of History During the "Saddle Time"

The political, social and discursive entanglements of the modern period,[1] which in the Muslim world had especially intensified since the beginning of the "colonial situation"[2] from the mid-nineteenth century onwards, have provided a foundation for a dynamic of Muslim identity discourses that has remained vital until the present day. The complexities of Muslim-European cultural encounters since the mid-eighteenth century and their consequences for dynamical identity-building processes in South Asia have been examined in Jamal Malik's publications as well.[3] The perceived or experienced military, technological and scientific superiority of the great European powers during the colonial era strongly influenced Muslim negotiations of modernity. This put references to – real or imagined – Europe or the West at the core of all modern debates on collective identity and alterity in the Middle East, whereby a wide range of positions could be found, ranging from acceptance and adaptation to opposition and distancing.[4] These identity negotiation processes take place in the broader context of societal debates on the meaning and handling of the historical, scientific and cultural heritage of Islam in their own

---

1   On these entanglements, see Shmuel N. Eisenstadt's *Die Vielfalt der Moderne* (Weilerswist: Velbrück Verlag, 2000) and *Comparative Civilizations and Multiple Modernities* (Leiden: Brill, 2000). For an approach towards the history of Muslim modernity which combines several theoretical frameworks in a complementary way, see Dietrich Jung, "Multiple, Entangled, and Successive Modernities: Putting Modernity in the Plural," in *Muslim History and Social Theory,* ed. Dietrich Jung (London: Palgrave Macmillan, 2017).
2   Reinhard Schulze, "Die islamische Welt in der Neuzeit (16.–19. Jahrhundert)," in *Der islamische Orient: Grundzüge seiner Geschichte,* ed. Albrecht Noth and Jürgen Paul (Würzburg: Ergon, 1998).
3   See, for example, Jamal Malik, ed., *Perspectives of Mutual Encounters in South Asian History 1760–1860* (Leiden: Brill, 2000).
4   Bekim Agai, "Freiheit neu entdeckt? Vergessene gemeinsame Erfahrungen des Nahen Ostens und Europas," in *Arabische Zeitenwende: Aufstand und Revolution in der arabischen Welt,* ed. Asiye Öztürk and Zerrin Karta (Bonn: Bundeszentrale für politische Bildung, 2012), 19.

particular contexts. In the Arab world, they are inevitably linked to the manifold discussions on "cultural heritage" (*turath*). However, identity debates are also a central part of the discussions on how to deal with modernity (impregnated by the West or perceived as such) in its various dimensions and aftermath, which since the nineteenth century have been an integral part of the debates on how to shape Muslim societies. Similar patterns of discussion can be observed among Muslims outside the Arabic-speaking world: For those Muslims of the Russian Empire, for instance, who embarked upon projects of social and intellectual modernization and educational reform of their communities, the debates on Muslim identity were strongly informed by references to the Russian Empire – not surprisingly considered as part of "Europe" in these contexts.[5] Even for communities of Muslims in Bosnia and Herzegovina, who came to be regarded as "European" Muslims, the debates on Muslim identities over the twentieth century, up until today, featured a strong, albeit highly ambivalent emphasis on their relations to "Europe."[6]

The development of modern Muslim religious thought has unfolded as much against the background of these identity negotiations as in the context of entanglements that were triggered by direct European presence in the Muslim world – and vice versa.[7] Recent scholarship, such as the works of Dietrich Jung,[8] has increasingly pointed out that modern Muslim conceptualizations and constructions of Islamicity are the results of adaptations of older Islamic epistemological and normative traditions to modern European thought, a product of a joint endeavor of Western scholars of Islamic Studies and influential *'ulama'* and Muslim intellectuals. Among the latter, it is particularly proponents of the so-called Muslim reformism who, starting from the

---

5 Edward J. Lazzerini, "Ismail Bey Gasprinskii and Muslim Modernism in Russia, 1878–1914" (PhD diss., University of Washington, 1973); Adeeb Khalid, *The Politics of Muslim Cultural Reform: Jadidism in Central Asia* (Berkeley: University of California Press, 1998).

6 Armina Omerika, *Islam in Bosnien-Herzegowina und die Netzwerke der Jungmuslime (1918–1983)* (Wiesbaden: Harrasowitz, 2014), 22–30, 122–25; Kerim Kudo, *Europäisierung und Islam in Bosnien-Herzegowina: Netzwerke und Identitätsdiskurse* (Baden-Baden: Nomos, 2016); Xavier Bougarel, "Bosnian Islam as 'European Islam': Limits and Shifts of a Concept," in *Islam in Europe: Diversity, Identity and Influence*, ed. Aziz Al-Azmeh and Effie Fokas (Cambridge and New York: Cambridge University Press, 2007).

7 See, for example, the studies on the reports of travelers from the Orient to Europe in Bekim Agai and Stephan Conermann, eds., *'Wenn einer eine Reise tut, hat er was zu erzählen': Präfiguration – Konfiguration – Refiguration in muslimischen Reiseberichten* (Berlin: EB-Verlag, 2013); and Bekim Agai, Umar Ryad and Mehdi Sajid, eds., *Muslims in Interwar Europe: A Transcultural Historical Perspective* (Leiden: Brill, 2015).

8 Dietrich Jung, *Orientalists, Islamists and the Global Public Sphere: A Genealogy of the Modern Essentialist Image of Islam* (Sheffield and Oakville, CT: Equinox, 2011).

mid-nineteenth century, have had a significant share in this process. Muslim reformist intellectuals were part of overlapping intellectual milieus of the Ottoman Empire, Egypt, South Asia and the European West, and they participated in shared discourses in transnational public spaces, something that Jung has labeled *the emerging public sphere*.[9]

This perspective inevitably places the focus on the fact that Europe and the Muslim world have a shared history of modernity, in addition to a number of other shared histories.[10] Due to differing social, political and economic conditions, the answers to the challenges of this commonly experienced modernity were diverse. But these differences have not impeded the permeability of certain concepts, ideas and epistemes which had their theoretical origins in Europe, but which since the nineteenth century became universalized and reproduced globally, including in the Muslim world.[11] This included ideas related to societal order such as "sovereignty" and "society,"[12] but also and very importantly, categories of collective identity such as "nation" or "people," which came to be imagined as historically constituted and conditioned, and hence justified in historical terms, both within and outside the confines of the scholarly discipline of historical studies.

Reinhard Koselleck has described the period of European history from the mid-eighteenth to mid-nineteenth century as "saddle time" (*Sattelzeit*) – a time in which certain political and social concepts developed and became imbued with the meanings they still carry today.[13] Recently, the term "saddle time" has also been cautiously used for the societies of the Middle East since the nineteenth century, since it was from this period that modern terms and concepts pertaining to social and political life first came into use, and these continue

---

9   Ibid.
10 See, e.g., Sanjay Subrahmanyam, "Connected Histories: Notes Towards a Reconfiguration of Early Modern Eurasia," *Modern Asian Studies* 31, no. 3 (1997); Sebastian Conrad and Shalini Randeria, "Geteilte Geschichten: Europa in einer postkolonialen Welt," in *Jenseits des Eurozentrismus: Postkoloniale Perspektiven in den Geschichts- und Kulturwissenschaften*, ed. Sebastian Conrad and Shalini Randeria (Frankfurt am Main: Campus Verlag, 2002).
11 Jürgen Osterhammel, *The Transformation of the World. A Global History of the Nineteenth Century* (Princeton: Princeton University Press, 2014); and Dietrich Jung and Kirstine Sinclair, "Multiple Modernities, Modern Subjectivities and Social Order: Unity and Difference in the Rise of Islamic Modernities," *Thesis Eleven* 130, no. 1 (2015).
12 For the conceptual history of "society" in the journal *al-Manar*, see Florian Zemmin, *Modernity in Islamic Tradition: The Concept of 'Society' in the Journal al-Manar (Cairo, 1898–1940)* (Berlin and Boston: de Gruyter, 2018), https://doi.org/10.1515/9783110545845.
13 Reinhart Koselleck, "Einleitung," in *Geschichtliche Grundbegriffe: Historisches Lexikon zur politisch-sozialen Sprache in Deutschland*, vol. 1, ed. Otto Brunner, Werner Conze and Reinhart Koselleck (Stuttgart: Klett-Cotta, 1972), xv.

to inform the political imageries and public debates up to the present.[14] We should, of course, keep in mind that the asymmetrical power relations of colonialism as the framework within which Muslim experiences of modernity took place have made this transfer of ideas a quite one-sided issue: Muslims could at best reactively determine how the modern world of globally reproduced ideas should be shaped and in which direction it was to develop.

A central element of the European "saddle time" was the "discovery" of history, or rather something which the German Catholic theologian Peter Hünermann has termed "the breakthrough of historical thought,"[15] namely "a new way of being-in-the-world,"[16] the most important feature of which was probably "the historical constitution of reality on the whole."[17] Koselleck speaks of the "temporalization" (*Verzeitlichung*) of the categories for interpreting the world:

> The relation of the acting and suffering human to historical time has changed ever more thoroughly both in theory and in practice. "History itself" is discovered in a way it never had been experienced before.[18]

Like in post-Enlightenment Europe, an increased interest in history can be also observed in the Muslim world since the nineteenth century. History began to assume an identity-generating role. What Geert Hendrich has stated for modernity in general applies to Muslim societies as well: History is an issue, and historical discourses are identity discourses which accompany the processes of societal change and transformation.[19] One manifestation of this new role of

---

14 Agai, "Freiheit neu entdeckt?," 20–21. For a more detailed discussion of the applicability of the "Saddle Time" approach to the conceptual history of Arabic terms, see Zemmin, *Modernity in Islamic Tradition*, 39–44.
15 Peter Hünermann, *Der Durchbruch geschichtlichen Denkens im 19. Jahrhundert* (Freiburg: Herder, 1967). Translations of German texts are mine.
16 Ibid., 14.
17 Ibid., 14.
18 Reinhart Koselleck, *Begriffsgeschichten: Studien zur Semantik und Pragmatik der politischen und sozialen Sprache* (Frankfurt am Main: Suhrkamp Verlag, 2006), 77.
19 Geert Hendrich, "Identitätskonstruktion und Geschichtsbilder im arabo-islamischen Modernediskurs," in *Geschichte und Erinnerung im Islam*, ed. Angelika Hartmann (Göttingen: Vandenhoeck & Ruprecht, 2004), 31. On Muslim contexts in India, see Jamal Malik, "Constructions of the Past in and about India: From Jahiliyya to the Cradle of Civilization. Pre-colonial Perceptions of India," in *Globalized Antiquity: Uses and Perceptions of the Past in South Asia, Mesoamerica, and Europe*, ed. Ute Schüren, Daniel Segesser and Thomas Späth (Berlin: Reimer, 2015), and idem, "Andaman Islands in Muslim Cultural Memory and Fadl-e Haqq Khairabadi," in *Manifestations of History: Time, Space,*

history was the emergence of national historiographies in various regions of the Muslim world. These historiographies were of course shaped by a myriad of different factors and consequently cannot be assessed nor even subsumed under one category.[20] Later on, the twentieth century saw further diversification of historiography in the Muslim world due to the emergence – and competition – of ideologically driven approaches, such as Marxist or feminist historiographies.[21] Regardless of the ideological divides, however, history – in the sense of "the condition for the possibility of all individual histories"[22] – has become the major framework of reference in Muslim identity negotiations, similar to the developments that Yvonne Haddad has described with regard to the Arabo-Islamic world:

> Utilized in the last century as a rallying cry against the erosion of confidence in Islam as a viable way of life in the modern world, the concept of history has served as a basis for political unity for nationalists and supranationalists alike, as a focus of pride in the heritage of the elders and as a common memory of a great achievement that endows the individual with pride and dignity.[23]

The centrality of historical references can also be observed in the decidedly religious debates from the nineteenth century and throughout the twentieth century. Representations of the past have been crucial to many modern discourses on cultural authenticity since the nineteenth century, including, for instance, both traditionalist and feminist Muslim perspectives on gender and gender relations. As Aysha Geissinger critically points out, it is particularly the (female) figures from early Islam who have provided a number of modern actors, male as well as female, with justifications for their current stance on gender issues.[24] In fact, several major intellectual "scandals" in the Muslim

---

      and Community in the Andaman Islands, ed. Frank Heidemann and Philipp Zehmisch (Delhi: Primus Books, 2016).

20   Ludwig Amman, "Geschichtsdenken und Geschichtsschreibung von Muslimen im Mittelalter," in *Die Vielfalt der Kulturen: Erinnerung, Geschichte, Identität*, ed. Jörn Rüsen et al. (Frankfurt am Main: Suhrkamp Verlag, 1998), 215; idem, "Kommentiertes Literaturverzeichnis zu Zeitvorstellungen und geschichtlichem Denken in der islamischen Welt," *Die Welt des Islams* 37, no. 1 (March 1997).

21   For the Arabic-Islamic world, see Yvonne Yazbeck Haddad, *Contemporary Islam and the Challenge of History* (Albany, NY: SUNY Press, 1982), 24–70.

22   Koselleck, *Begriffsgeschichten*, 80.

23   Haddad, *Contemporary Islam*, XVI.

24   Aisha Geissinger, "Feminist Muslim (Re)Interpretations of Early Islam," in *Routledge Handbook of Early Islam*, ed. Herbert Berg (London: Routledge, 2017).

world during the twentieth century, with significant echoes in public debates, revolved around the question of the interpretation of religious texts and were strongly tied to the issue of historicity and the historicization of the Quran and/or hadith with methods of modern historical scholarship.[25] This chapter deals with modern Muslim constructions of history and, more specifically, with the consequences these constructs have had on some formulations of Muslim religious thought throughout the twentieth century.[26]

2 The Decline Model of the *Islah* Intellectuals

The roots of modern Muslim religious imageries of history were to a large extent laid down by Muslim reformist intellectuals of the nineteenth century; among whom the pan-Islamic activist Jamal al-Din al-Afghani[27] (1838–1897) and the religious scholar, and in the period from 1899 to 1905 acting Mufti of Egypt, Muhammad 'Abduh[28] (1849–1905) are probably the best known and most influential protagonists. They met in Cairo in 1871, and the latter can be

---

[25] This was the case with Taha Husayn's (1898–1973) *Fi al-Shi'r al-Jahili* ("On Pre-Islamic Poetry," 1926), in which he expressed doubts about the historical factuality of Abraham's Arabic descent, as it is traditionally derived from the Quranic narrative. Similarly, Muhammad Ahmad Khalafallah (1916–1997), who in his dissertation *Al-Fann al-Qasasi fi al-Qur'an al-Karim* ("The Narrative Art of the Holy Quran," 1947) questioned the historiographical value of Quranic prophetic stories, was heavily criticized for allegedly putting even the value of "conventional books of history" over the Quran. The literary scholar Nasr Hamid Abu Zaid (1943–2010) was exiled and declared a non-Muslim by an Egyptian court for arguing that the Quran is a cultural and historical product, with the revelation having adapted itself to the linguistic and intellectual horizon of its first audiences. Fazlur Rahman's (1919–1988) critical stance on the historical authenticity of the written prophetic tradition (hadith) also resulted in public criticism and hostile campaigns, which ultimately forced him to leave Pakistan and go into exile.

[26] While different approaches to the history of the Islamic world and to Islamic religious history as advocated by Western scholars of Islam, such as W.C. Smith, have undoubtedly had an impact on the modern historical imageries of Muslims as well. The exact trajectories of these interactions and transfers of ideas are still in need of further research.

[27] For al-Afghani's life and work, see Nikki R. Keddie, *Sayyid Jamāl ad-Dīn 'al-Afghānī': A Political Biography* (Berkeley: University of California Press, 1972), idem, "Sayyid Jamal al-Din 'al-Afghani'," in *Pioneers of Islamic Revival*, 2nd edition, ed. Ali Rahnema (London: Zed Books, 2005); Thomas Hildebrandt, "Waren Ğamāl ad-Dīn al-Afġānī und Muḥammad 'Abduh Neo-Muʿtaziliten?," *Die Welt des Islams* 42, no. 2 (2002).

[28] For 'Abduh's life and work, see Anke von Kügelgen, "'Abduh, Muḥammad," in *Encyclopaedia of Islam*, 3rd edition, ed. Kate Fleet et al. (Leiden: Brill, 2008), http://dx.doi.org/10.1163/1573-3912_ei3_COM_0103; Hildebrandt, "Waren Ğamāl ad-Dīn al-Afġānī"; Mark Sedgwick, *Muhammad Abduh* (London: OneWorld, 2010).

described as a student of the former. Both thinkers had networks of students (and later religious scholars and intellectuals) and their work enjoyed broad resonance throughout the Muslim world. Both had travelled extensively and were in close contact with contemporary scholars, philosophers and intellectuals from the Muslim world as well as Europe – through correspondence, personal visits, acquaintanceships and not the least, through public polemics.[29]

Al-Afghani and ʿAbduh provided a foundation for an understanding of history that integrated traditional Islamic concepts with elements from the philosophy of history of the Enlightenment along with European national-romanticist historiography and historicism of the nineteenth century. These conceptions of history admittedly differed in some important details and were later critically referred to by the philosopher Muhammad Arkoun as the "*islahi* mode."[30] Yet they subsequently became formative for the meaning of and references to the past in modern religious thought, despite the variations they were to experience later in the elaborations of their disciples and other Muslim scholars.

For al-Afghani,[31] history is acted out by collective historical units (nations, peoples),[32] although he changed his definitions of what constitutes and justifies a nation several times.[33] He regarded these historical subjects as organisms, analogous to a body, with individuals being the organs that functioned as closed units within. The organism derives its strength from the strength of its individual components or members. Accordingly, history is an oscillation between, on the one hand, an original essence consisting of integrity and unity, and on the other, the decline thereof. The coherence and unity of the essence exists as long as the factors that stimulate and ensure it are present, otherwise a decline occurs.[34] For al-Afghani, the transfer of these considerations to Islam resulted precisely in the construction of a historical model of decline – the collective entity known as "Islam" appears as a historical subject, as a bearer of history, a subject that had once existed as a vital, coherent organism, but has fallen away from its essence and landed in a state of subjugation.

---

29   Jung, *Orientalists, Islamists and the Global Public Sphere*, 230–31.
30   Mohammed Arkoun, "Rethinking Islam Today," *Islam: Enduring Myths and Changing Realities, The Annals of the American Academy of Political and Social Science* 588, no. 1 (July 2003): 22, https://doi.org/10.1177/0002716203588001003.
31   Jamal al-Din al-Afghani, *Al-Aʿmal al-Kamila*, ed. Muhammad ʿImara (Cairo: Dar al-Kitab al-ʿArabi li al-Tibaʿa wa al-Nashr, 1968).
32   Ibid., 153.
33   Keddie, *Sayyid Jamāl ad-Dīn ʿal-Afghānī*.
34   Al-Afghani, *Al-Aʿmal al-Kamila*, 430–31.

Echoes of this idea can be found in 'Abduh's work. According to several scholars, 'Abduh was one of the first modern Islamic scholars to approach the Islamic textual sources in a decidedly historical perspective,[35] and he is said to have had a particular interest in history.[36] 'Abduh also advocates a historical model of decay, albeit with different accents. For 'Abduh, history takes place in an evolutionary process, which unfolds according to certain recurring laws (the "sunnah of God," *sunnat Allah*) and according to principles of causality.[37] This evolution is at the same time a maturing process, in which humanity goes through various stages, and it corresponds to a permanent development of rationality. For 'Abduh, however, and unlike the French writer Voltaire (d. 1778), whose views are echoed here and with whose philosophy of history he was most likely well acquainted;[38] this process was at the same time the history of religions, which appear here as actors of history, with Islam being the peak of the historical evolution of rationality. More precisely, this evolution had reached its zenith among the first Muslims with their rational interpretation of the Quran; hence, this historical period, the era of the "pious ancestors" (*al-salaf al-salih*) is in fact the very past that needs to be restored. Everything after that period is a history of decline, which 'Abduh sees as a decline of rationality expressed in the loss of independent interpretation of the sources, although he does attest to the exemplary character of some major scholars of the later, classical period of Islam.[39] Accordingly, 'Abduh saw the renewal of Islam in the revival of rationality. For him, one of the means to achieve this was comprehensive educational reforms.

The thought of al-Afghani and 'Abduh developed within the context of the increased direct imperial presence of the major European powers in the Muslim world since the second half of the nineteenth century. In fact, al-Afghani had even dedicated his entire life to activism against European imperialism. Both men's ideas about history based on a model of deterioration, as well as their appeals for the renewal of Islam, were part of a comprehensive narrative about decline (*inhitat*), within which the Middle Eastern intellectuals of the time, but also Muslims in other contexts, generally formulated their

---

35 Ömer Özsoy, "Pioniere der historischen Koranhermeneutik: Amīn al-Ḫūlī, Fazlur Rahman und Nasr Hamid Abu Zaid," in *Historizität und Transzendenz im Islam: Offenbarung, Geschichte und Recht*, ed. Jameleddine Ben Abdeljelil (Berlin: EB-Verlag, 2017), 24–26.

36 Rotraud Wielandt, *Offenbarung und Geschichte im Denken moderner Muslime* (Wiesbaden: Franz Steiner Verlag GmbH, 1971), 49.

37 Ibid., 56–72.

38 Ibid., 63–64.

39 Ibid., 71.

demands for social and cultural reform.[40] The notion of the corrosive progress of time and history was by no means new at that time and was rooted in earlier Muslim thought. Thus they also docked onto the older theological idea that the restoration of right faith and religious practice had to take place through a permanent "renewal" – expressed for example in the well-known semantic repertoire of terms for renewal or revival, namely *islah, tajdid* or *ihya'*. These ideas are in turn connected to the topos of the "corruption of time" (*fasad al-zaman*), which is also strongly represented in pre-modern Islamic religious literature.[41] In his *Muqaddima*, the Muslim historian Ibn Khaldun (d. 1382) had already represented the model of the cyclical rise and fall of civilizations; indeed, 'Abduh himself gave a series of lectures on the *Muqaddima* in Cairo in 1879.[42]

The new element in the thought of reformers like al-Afghani and 'Abduh, however, was the transfer and systematization of these ideas of decay and corruption of times and of the renewal repertoire into a universal, evolutionary view of history combined with the construction of the historical entity of "Islam," in the sense of a closed, delimitable and above all essentially determinable historical unit. It is probably no coincidence that these elaborations of Islamic reformers took place in close interaction – polemics, but also other exchanges – with scholars of Islamic and Oriental Studies from the West. It is also significant that this transpired at a time when the idea of a spatially and culturally delimitable entity called "Islam" began to emerge, and that it became consolidated in Muslim thought around the same time that "Islam" as a civilizational unit became the object of scholarly inquiry in Western Islamic Studies.[43] Nevertheless, thorough investigations into exactly how and through which channels the transfer of ideas took place, and how it influenced the

---

40 Manfred Sing, "The Decline of Islam and the Rise of *Inḥiṭāṭ*: The Discrete Charm of Language Games About Decadence in the 19th and 20th Centuries," in *Inḥiṭāṭ – The Decline Paradigm: Its Influence and Persistence in the Writing of Arab Cultural History*, ed. Syrinx von Hees (Würzburg: Ergon, 2017); for an example (1912) of the same paradigm among Tatar Muslims, see Musa Jarullah Bigi, "Why Did the Muslim World Decline While the Civilized World Advanced?," in *Modernist Islam 1840–1940: A Sourcebook*, ed. Charles Kurzman (New York: Oxford University Press, 2002); for numerous examples of the decline paradigm among Bosnian Muslim intellectuals of the twentieth century, see Omerika, *Islam in Bosnien-Herzegowina*, 22–30, 108–41, 221–51, 322–26.

41 Geert Jan van Gelder, "Good Times, Bad Times: Opinions on *Fasād az-Zamān*, 'the Corruption of Time'," in *Inḥiṭāṭ – The Decline Paradigm*, ed. von Hees.

42 Wielandt, *Offenbarung und Geschichte*, 50.

43 Jung, *Orientalists, Islamists and the Global Public Sphere*, 157–214; see also Alexander Haridi, *Das Paradigma der 'islamischen Zivilisation' – oder die Begründung der deutschen Islamwissenschaft durch Carl Heinrich Becker (1878–1933): Eine wissenschaftsgeschichtliche Untersuchung* (Würzburg: Ergon, 2005).

conceptual history of the term "Islam" in modern Muslim contexts, remain to be done.

Despite references to the early history of Islam and assertions of continuous historical decline, which was now to find its way into Islamic thought as an essential model for the interpretation of the passage of time, al-Afghani and ʿAbduh were not advocating a historical re-enactment of an ideal Islamic community from the past. Rather, they were concerned with the adoption of what they viewed as rational methods in the independent interpretation of the Islamic sources, which they identified with the period of the early history of Islam and its actors. They regarded these methods as means to master the technological and scientific developments of modernity in a supposedly "authentic" way. So in their view, rather than a reconstruction of early Islam, rationality as its characteristic feature was to lead to novel interpretative solutions in new and changing historical situations.

This body of thought among nineteenth-century Islamic reformers was developed in different directions, just as the historical model on which it was based was related to social practices in various ways. These developments did not, however, significantly change the diagnosis of the present crisis and historical decline, even if these were argued in different ways. Thus, in the wake of al-Afghani and ʿAbduh, we find decidedly modernist, even secular thinkers such as Taha Husayn (1889–1973) or Mustafa ʿAbd al-Raziq (1885–1947), as well as some later modernists of the twentieth century across the Muslim world. Some feminist readings of Islam, for example, argue within the same paradigm of historical decline when they assume the existence of an originally egalitarian Islam which has turned patriarchal over the course of time. Thus, in order for the originally egalitarian core message of Islam to be revived and made fruitful for contemporary contexts, the patriarchal "overload" of history (usually framed as the historically grown male interpretations of the classical texts) has to be eliminated.[44]

At the same time, along the trajectory of al-Afghani and ʿAbduh, we find conservative interpretations of political Islam; as expressed early on, for example, by ʿAbduh's student Rashid Rida (1865–1935) and later by thinkers like Sayyid Qutb (1906–1966) and a number of other authors and activists from the twentieth century.

---

44   For two highly influential feminist interpretations along these lines, see Asma Barlas, *Believing Women in Islam: Unreading Patriarchal Interpretations of the Qurʾan* (Austin, TX: University of Texas Press, 2002) and Fatima Mernissi, *The Veil and the Male Elite: A Feminist Interpretation of Women's Rights in Islam* (New York: Basic Books, 1991).

3 The Past as a Model for Activism

The political upheavals of the twentieth century, which in one form or another affected the entire Muslim world – such as decolonization, the establishment of new forms of statehood, the search for political unity, secularization and, not the least, the minority situations of Muslims in newly emerging states, such as those in Eastern and Southeastern Europe – consolidated the field of history as an arena for the justification of new world views. Religious thinkers and scholars saw themselves confronted even more strongly with new forms of historiography that did not argue within an Islamic framework of legitimation, as well as with materialistic world interpretations in general. At the same time, the challenges posed by Western Islamic Studies, which were increasingly defining themselves in terms of cultural history, as well as by new theoretical assumptions and methods in text-related scholarly disciplines, such as literary studies, were also more present and tangible. One response to these challenges by Islamic authors – scholars, but also laymen from the activist spectrum – especially in the second half of the twentieth century, was an active production of works on history. Some of these were theologies of history that relied on some popular historical paradigms originating from European contexts, but that were basically always founded on the claim of situating "Islam" in relation to history and working out "authentically Islamic" models of history.

An important characteristic of the theologies of history that we encounter with many authors of the second half of the twentieth century is the effort to extrapolate a philosophy of history from the Quran.[45] The Quran as a framework for interpreting history was considered to provide examples of objective history through which God's wisdom and laws (*sunan*) are perceived; laws which, in turn, control the dynamics of the historical process.[46] In this understanding, the past has a didactic and exemplary function, for it provides information about the best realization of God's will for the present. These considerations sometimes bore resemblances to classical Islamic theological discourses – for instance to the concept of habit (*'ada*), known from the classical

---

45 Numerous examples of this line of thought can be found in Haddad, *Contemporary Islam*, 145–204; for a similar approach, see also Mazheruddin Siddiqi, *The Qur'ānic Concept of History* (Islamabad: Islamic Research Institute, 1965). For a critical view of the attempts to develop a philosophy of history from the Quran, see Abdoljavad Falaturi, "Zeit- und Geschichtserfahrung im Islam," in *Glauben an den einen Gott: Menschliche Gotteserfahrung im Christentum und im Islam*, ed. Abdoljavad Falaturi and Walter Strolz (Freiburg: Herder, 1975).

46 See the writings of Muhammad Kamal Ibrahim Ja'far, Rashid al-Barrawi and 'Imad al-Din Khalil, in Haddad, *Contemporary Islam*, 174–204.

kalam discussions and according to which God acts uniformly so that man can rely on God's "habitus" to orient himself in the world.⁴⁷ In spite of such similarities with the past, the theologies of history outlined here can be regarded as syntheses of these pre-modern ideas with elements of modern universal historical paradigms. Often in direct connection to Western cultural theorists of the twentieth century, such as Oswald Spengler or Arnold Toynbee, they identify major collective categories – nations, religions or civilizations – as actors and carriers of the historical process.⁴⁸ Thus, "correct" historical action in this perspective means orientation towards the Quranic narratives of the rise and fall of peoples, which in these theologies came to be exemplified by the rise and fall of great civilizations like the Roman Empire.⁴⁹ In accordance with these classifications, "Islam" also appears as a separate historical entity, or rather, a civilization.

What is striking about these views of history, however, is the implicit rejection of the absolute predetermination of history: Historical laws and regularities are determined by God, but the Quranic concept of history is at the same time regarded as dynamic. History is admittedly bound to a specific purpose, but it also offers space for human action, and within this framework, human beings are granted the possibility of dealing with the present in a creative way. As part of the historical process, man is even called upon to play an active role in shaping events in a way that best reflects the divine plan and intention for humanity.⁵⁰

In relation to Islam, this action-oriented aspect did not mean the departure from historical models of decline. Yet the present, which in comparison with an idealized past was perceived as being in a deep crisis, was now more at stake. It is therefore hardly surprising that we find emphasis on the active human role in history strongly advocated among activists of political Islam in the 1960s and 1970s,⁵¹ although not exclusively in these milieus. In their works, authors such as Sayyid Qutb, Mahmud al-Sharkawi and Anwar al-Jundi

---

47 For a prominent view on this issue within al-Ghazali's cosmology, see Dominik Perler and Ulrich Rudolph, *Occasionalismus: Theorien der Kausalität im arabisch-islamischen und im europäischen Denken* (Göttingen: Vandenhoeck & Ruprecht, 2000), 88 ff.
48 Haddad, *Contemporary Islam*, 81–82.
49 Ibid., 123.
50 Ibid., 102 f.; for similar positions from the South Asian context, see Siddiqi, *The Qur'ānic Concept of History*, 195–226; Jawdat Sa'id, *Hatta Yughayyiru ma bi Anfusihim: Bahth fi Sunan Taghyir al-Nafs wa al-Mujtama'* (Damascus: n.p, 1972).
51 See Sayyid Qutb, *Fi al-Tarikh: Fikra wa Minhaj* (Beirut and Cairo: Dar al-Shuruq, 1974) and Anwar al-Jundi, *Al-Islam wa Harakat al-Tarikh: Ru'iya Jadida fi Falsafat Tarikh al-Islam* (Cairo: Matba'at al-Risala, 1968).

(1917–2002) in Egypt as well as ʿAli Shariʿati (1933–1977)[52] in Iran assume an active human role in historical events and in historical change. In the thought of these authors, however, this human capacity to act is linked to demands to restore an ideal condition of the past. This ideal past is construed in various ways, with different references and periodizations. For Shariʿati, for instance, the exemplary role model for current political actions is to be found in the early Shiʿa,[53] while the frames of periodization suggested by other activist writers vary from being restricted to only the Medinan community to including all the way up to the time in which the major schools of law were being systematized. Yet the entity "Islam," constructed by the earlier reformers, is here understood as a totality or a "system," which in its ideal form produces answers to all dimensions of human existence, including social and political life. The answers are already present in this system, one only needs to retrieve them correctly. The restoration of the ideal is guaranteed by the establishment of an "authentically Islamic" socio-political order, tied to the construct "shariʿa,"[54] which became the central political instrument of mobilization for political Islamic activists.

In their appeals for change and renewal, the theologies of history, as elaborated by authors across the spectrum of political Islam, are evocative of the urgent calls for change issued by preceding generations of *islah*-reformers, which had also originated from a diagnosis of general social and religious decline. One important difference, however, seems to be of an epistemic nature: The reformers at the turn of the century sought ways to establish Islam, which they also understood to be a separate civilizational unit, as a co-actor of global developments of modernity through adaptations and apologetics. In contrast, "authentic Islam" in the thought of the Islamists of the 1960s and 1970s (notwithstanding the irony that their own epistemes and categories were also founded in modernity) is constructed as something that is permanently exposed to threats through the adoption of "foreign" ideas, concepts and methods. Accordingly, Qutb stated that Islam was the best social order for humanity and not in need of "foreign imports."[55]

---

52   ʿAli Shariʿati, *Islam-Shinasi* (Mashhad: Tus, 1968).
53   Katajun Amirpur, " 'Jeder Tag ist *ʿĀšūrāʾ*, jeder Ort ist Karbalāʾ": Zur schiitischen Sicht der frühislamischen Geschichte," *Frankfurter Zeitschrift für islamisch-theologische Studien* 4 (2018): 108.
54   Dietrich Jung, "Dschihad: Zur Transformation eines ambivalenten Begriffs," *Zeitschrift für Missionswissenschaft und Religionswissenschaft* 96, no. 3–4 (2012): 219.
55   Haddad, *Contemporary Islam*, 95.

The activist view of history of the 1960s and 1970s, which was admittedly not limited to actors of political Islam,[56] is concerned with people as opposed to time or an objectively conceived historical reality. Humans can intervene in the course of events and are even called upon to shape them in order to realize divine intentions, according to the "lessons" and examples of the past. But this process, in turn, has no repercussions for man; the essential human condition remains unchanged in this connection between past and present. In this still popular understanding of history in Muslim religious thought, history is externalized; its transformations do not include humans. Neither man's own temporality nor the contingency of human knowledge and cognition are considered. In other words, the manifold preoccupation with history as an arena for negotiation processes and the concessions to the possible change of "historical circumstances" did not necessarily result in an engagement with the historical nature of human experience itself.

4   Theological Inquiries into the Historicity of Human Knowledge

Muslim criticism of these images of history that portrayed an ideal Islamic past and solidified models of salvation history, came from different sides and was formulated on various bases. Already at the turn of the twentieth century, secularly oriented Arab intellectuals such as Farah Antun (d. 1922) criticized the idealization of the Islamic past by Muslim reformers as a means to overcome the crisis of the present.[57] Accusations of ahistoricity came in the course of the twentieth century from Arabic-speaking authors who argued on secular historiographical grounds, such as Malek Bennabi[58] (d. 1973) or, some decades later, ʿAbdallah al-ʿArwi (Abdallah Laroui, b. 1933).[59] This critique is also strongly pronounced by Aziz al-Azmeh (b. 1947), who explains the strong focus on the past in modern Muslim historical thought by pointing to, among other things, the influences of European Romanticist philosophy and its organic understanding of history, but at the same time also examining older concepts of nativeness in

---

56   Neither Siddiqi's *The Qurʾānic Concept* nor Saʿid's *Hatta Yughayyiru* belong to the spectrum of political Islam.
57   Angelika Hartmann, "Einleitung," in *Geschichte und Erinnerung im Islam*, ed. Angelika Hartmann (Göttingen: Vandenhoeck & Ruprecht, 2004), 16.
58   Ibid.
59   ʿAbdallah al-ʿArwi, *Al-ʿArab wa al-Fikr al-Tarikhi* (Beirut: Dar al-Haqiqa, 1973); see also Abdallah Laroui, *La crise des intellectuels arabes: traditionalisme ou historicisme?* (Paris: François Maspero, 1974).

Islamic thought.[60] With regard to religious reasoning specifically, the Pakistani scholar Fazlur Rahman (1919–1988) formulated a harsh criticism of the ahistorical premises and methods used in the traditional handling of the hadith. In doing so, he relied strongly on the state of the art of Western Islamic Studies and methods of modern historical source criticism.[61]

Another form of criticism came from theologians who posed the question of the historical contingency of human experience and categories of knowledge in general, something that, as noted, had been ignored by popular Islamic discourses on history. It was above all in connection with modern hermeneutical and literary approaches to the Quran that the relations between human subjects and history came to the fore in a new form, evolving around the question of the historicity of the Quran itself. The hermeneutical key to these debates was provided by twentieth-century protagonists of literary Quranic exegesis who considered the Quran as a literary text, such as Amin al-Khuli (1895–1966), Muhammad Khalafallah (1916–1991) and Nasr Hamid Abu Zaid (1943–2010) in Egypt, or the already mentioned Fazlur Rahman in Pakistan. The Quran as God's transcendent and universal message, it was assumed, could only be uncovered if one knew and comprehended the historical, cultural and linguistic worlds and conditions of understanding of its first audiences.[62] Aysha 'Abd al-Rahman (1913–1998), one of the first modern female scholars of Quranic exegesis and a pioneer of literary *tafsir*, applied the historical approach in her works on gender issues and women's rights. In general, literary Quranic exegesis, which has been further developed and expounded upon in varying degrees of refinement by a number of religious scholars, also draws on the central role of history elaborated by the reformers of the late nineteenth and early twentieth centuries,[63] but continues it in a way that differs from that of the authors of political Islam.

We find a consistent demand for a historicization of the Quran, and at the same time new accents in the religious discourses on Islam and history,

---

60 Aziz Al-Azmeh, *The Times of History: Universal Topics in Islamic Historiography* (Budapest and New York: CEU Press, 2007), 9–31. For similar Arabic-speaking approaches who assume an influence of European philosophies of history on modern Arab historical thought, see Hartmann, "Einleitung," 17–18.

61 Fazlur Rahman, *Islamic Methodology in History* (Karachi: Central Institute of Islamic Research, 1965), 27–84.

62 Johanna Pink, "Striving for the New Exegesis of the Qur'ān," in *The Oxford Handbook of Islamic Theology*, ed. Sabine Schmidtke (New York: Oxford University Press, 2016), 780, https://doi.org/10.1093/oxfordhb/9780199696703.013.013.

63 For a placement of historical hermeneutics of the Quran within a line of continuity from al-Afghani and 'Abduh, see Özsoy, "Pioniere."

being strongly advocated by some Turkish theologians of the late twentieth century. They referred to the historicist idea of the uniqueness and singularity of each individual historical epoch, while also including modern hermeneutical approaches to historicity – for instance with Wilhelm Dilthey, Hans-Georg Gadamer and E.D. Hirsch. These Quran hermeneuts, with their evolutionary model of history, also presented an unsparing criticism of those images of history proffered by their Muslim contemporaries who, on the one hand, refused the present and fled into a transfigured and romanticized past, but on the other, neglected the historical constitution of the human self.

So in 2000, the Ankara theologian Mehmet Paçacı wrote: "Basically, the Muslims see modern history as a pseudo-history that should not have happened."[64] According to Paçacı, prevailing Muslim thought does not recognize as legitimate historical situations that have developed differently from the alleged ideal state – as embodied in the time of revelation and the period immediately following it – and it accordingly denies those changed historical situations the right to have an impact on the shaping of religious thought. Those who advocate such an understanding will never find a historical period in which they can get involved in history; rather, they prefer to wait for the "true history" to happen. Our present times are, according to Paçacı's clearly historicist position, historically unique and singular. His contemporary and at that time fellow exegete from the University of Ankara, Ömer Özsoy, also criticized traditional Muslim views for not accepting the time after the "Age of Bliss" ('asr al-sa'ada), namely after the period of the Prophetic revelation, as an adequate framework in which changes in the normative system of Islam can be made.[65] These two exegetes locate the reason for the dominant understanding of history of their contemporaries in a certain attitude towards the Quran: Muslims see the Quran as the final point of the development of mankind towards perfection. Consequently, post-Quranic changes of the social reality that have created new historical and social facts are rejected. Instead of considering the present times as a new historical framework, Muslims try to squeeze their historical reality back into the structures of the Quran.[66]

---

64   Mehmet Paçacı, "Der Koran und ich: wie geschichtlich sind wir?," in *Alter Text – neuer Kontext: Koranhermeneutik in der Türkei heute,* trans. and ed. Felix Körner (Freiburg: Herder, 2006), 55.
65   However, Özsoy is equally critical of the glorification of the modern period by Islamic modernists. See Ömer Özsoy, "Erneuerungsprobleme zeitgenössischer Muslime und der Koran," in *Alter Text – neuer Kontext,* trans. and ed. Körner, 20–21.
66   Ibid., 20.

In this context, Özsoy in particular points to another decisive moment that motivates the longing for the past and underlies the historical models of decline, and thus also a negative attitude towards modernity: "But they [Muslims] are more like a retired bus driver who does not want to ride a bus that someone else is driving."[67] This is a clear allusion to the confrontation with European-influenced modernity and the experience of European superiority, which had made the loss of the political, military, cultural and other strengths of medieval Muslim Empires visible. What is now perceived as historical decline is basically the inability to overcome this loss of strength – meanwhile someone else is steering the bus. In our view, Özsoy's pictorial statement also implicitly contains a further diagnosis of the problem with the historical decline model; namely, the tendency to admit only those religious terms and concepts as authentic that have been established in the context of Muslim strength or in a position of Muslim superiority.

It was in the context of their Quranic hermeneutics, which were developed along the lines of the above-mentioned "pioneers" of the historical hermeneutics of the twentieth century, that the Ankara theologians very centrally emphasized the dimension of the historicity of human understanding. Every attempt at a historical understanding of the Quran is at the same time shaped and informed by existing preconceptions and by the preconditions of understanding inherent to the reader. Religious interpretations that are to be scholarly tenable and relevant for the present times can only be obtained through a simultaneous awareness of the historicity of the texts on the one hand, and of one's own historicity on the other.

The aftermath of this approach in Turkey can still be felt today. The ongoing theological debate between the so-called "universalists" and "historicists," that was spurred by the writing of Ankara theologians since the mid-1990s, is primarily a struggle about the definition of history and its meaning for theological thought, as well as about the implications of historicity for the present development of religious normativity and the corresponding hermeneutics.[68]

Among other Muslim academic authors of the second half of the twentieth century who have critically examined the historical imagery of Islamic religious thought within the framework of their respective research fields,[69] the Moroccan-French philosopher and professor of the intellectual history of

---

67 Ibid., 27.
68 Mustafa Öztürk, "Geschichtlichkeit und Übergeschichtlichkeit im koranischen Kontext," trans. Ertugrul Sahin, *Frankfurter Zeitschrift für islamisch-theologische Studien* 3 (2016).
69 For some influential voices, see 'Abd al-Majid al-Sharfi, *Al-Islam bayna al-Risala wa al-Tarikh* (Beirut: Dar al-Tali'a, 2001); idem, *Al-Islam wa al-Hadatha* (Tunis: Al-Dar

Islam at the Sorbonne, Muhammad Arkoun (1928–2010), stands out as probably the best-known voice advocating radical historicization. Arkoun applied this demand not only to religious texts, but also to Islamic thought in general, and thus to theological epistemology at large. In several of his writings, Arkoun, clearly influenced by the French academic context he was working in, uses discourse analysis and deconstructivist approaches to those positions that, not least due to constellations of political power, have been established as religious orthodoxies. The decisive factor in his deconstruction of the epistemes of the Islamic tradition was his understanding of religious ideas as historically determined human categories, and not as essences external to man. This way, according to Arkoun, scholarly work is to reveal the historically marginalized positions in Islamic discourses, i.e., all that which has been deemed "unspeakable" or even "unthinkable" in the processes of the monopolization of interpretation by the manifold Islamic orthodoxies. At the same time, Arkoun criticizes two dominant epistemological paradigms that he identifies in contemporary Islamic thought. He rejects the position of modern reformers that a "correct" procedure of norm derivation existed in the past which was now to serve as an example for present-day Muslims; and he criticizes the adherence to concepts, procedures and categories that were established in pre-modern Islamic scholasticism. According to Arkoun, pre-modern concepts do not contain any self-reflexive reference to either the historicity or the developmental character of our own positions:

> All semiotic productions of a human being in the process of his social and cultural emergence are subject to historical change which I call historicity. As a semiotic articulation of meaning for social and cultural uses, the Qur'ān is subject to historicity. This means that *there is no access to the absolute* outside the phenomenal world of our terrestrial, historical existence. The various expressions given to the ontology, the first being the truth and the transcendence by theological and metaphysical reason, have neglected historicity as a dimension of the truth. Changing tools, concepts, definitions, and postulates are used to shape the truth.[70]

The contingency of cognitive processes, expressed in the diversity of changing concepts, definitions and assumptions, is something that was both

---

al-Tunusiyya li al-Nashr, 1991); Mohammed Aziz Lahbabi, *Le personnalisme musulman* (Paris: Presses Universitaires de France, 1964); see also Wielandt, *Offenbarung und Geschichte*, 160–67.

70   Arkoun, "Rethinking Islam," 24.

"unthinkable" and "unthought" in pre-modern Islamic thinking. If one believes Arkoun, the present-day situation he was referring to at the beginning of the twenty-first century did not look much better either: "Historicity is the unthinkable and unthought in the medieval thought. It will be the conquest – not yet everywhere complete – of intellectual modernity."[71]

Arkoun is in line, although much more explicit, with the above-mentioned Ankara theologians when it comes to criticizing the way modern Islamic thought deals with modern concepts and epistemes. Islamic thought is seen as being still rooted in categories, themes and procedures that were established in the scholastic period (seventh-eighth century A.H.), while at the same time neglecting the pluralism of ideas of the so-called classical period of Islamic history.[72] It is not only these categories, but also the metaphysical reasoning underlying scholasticism and the Aristotelian definitions of logic and abstract categories that need to be subjected to a revision in order to turn to semiotic theories of the genesis of meaning as well as the historical contingency of reason itself.[73] In a certain sense, Arkoun also seems to suggest a certain decline in the history of ideas, which he does not, however, locate in conceptions of salvation history, but rather in the victory of the scholastic dogmatism of the post-classical period over the pluralism of the classical period of Islamic intellectual history. At the same time, Arkoun is critical of the modern paradigms established by Muslim reformers, which, by the way, he does not deem very modern at all:

> I do not need to emphasize the well-known trend of *salafi* reformist thought initiated by Jamāl al-Dīn al-Afghānī and Muḥammad ʿAbduh. It is what I call the *iṣlāḥī* way of thinking which has characterized Islamic thought since the death of the Prophet. The principle common to all Muslim thinkers, the *ʿulamāʾ mujtahidūn*, as well as to historians who adopted the theological framework imposed by the division of time into two parts – before/after the Hijra (like before/after Christ) – is that all the transcendent divine Truth has been delivered to mankind by the Revelation and concretely realized by the Prophet through historical initiatives in Medina. There is, then, a definite model of perfect historical action for mankind, not only for Muslims. All groups at any time and in any social and cultural environment are bound to *go back* to this model in order to achieve the spirit and the perfection shown by the Prophet,

---

71 Ibid., 26.
72 Ibid., 27.
73 Ibid., 24–26.

his companions, and the first generation of Muslims called the pious ancestors (*al-salaf al-ṣāliḥ*). [...] This is at the same time a methodology, an epistemology, and a theory of history. It is certainly an operative intellectual framework used and perpetuated by generations of Muslims since the debate on authority and power started inside the community according to patterns of thinking and representing the world specific to the *islahi* [sic!] movement.[74]

According to Arkoun, to overcome these forms of thinking requires, among other things, the already mentioned acknowledgement of the historicity of every form of knowledge, but also the questioning, and in the end, abandoning of those parts of traditional religious systematic sciences whose epistemologies are no longer relevant today.[75]

5   Conclusion

This radical proposition by Arkoun at the beginning of the twenty-first century may best illustrate the scope in which paradigmatic shifts and developments of modern Muslim religious thought have taken place. Certain transformations of the period from the mid-nineteenth through twentieth centuries have been regarded by some researchers as characterizing the "saddle time" of modern Islamic conceptual history. This involved the adaptation of modern, albeit varying and changing, notions of history as constitutive elements of collective identities. These were not only expressed in the rise of secular ideologies like nationalism in the Muslim world, but these notions have also been incorporated and adapted in the field of religious thought and theology. They led to specific configurations of "Islam" as a historical and civilizational unit, but they have also had consequences for religious reasoning and epistemology. In many ways, these developments were the results of the engagement and participation of Muslim thinkers within transnational discursive spaces. Furthermore, they form a part of larger discussions on the manner of dealing with modernity and its after-effects, which since the nineteenth century have been an integral part of the debates on how to shape societies in the Muslim world. The shift concerned both religious deliberations on history and, in turn, the degree to which historical change was considered to have a (justified) impact on religious thought.

---

74 Ibid., 22.
75 Ibid., 25.

The foundation for the "historic" paradigm in the field of religious thought, incorporating elements from contemporary European philosophies of history as well as traditionally established Islamic epistemology, was laid out by reform intellectuals at the turn of the twentieth century, only to be developed further in different and not always mutually compatible directions. The trajectory of "historicizing" ideas could result in calls to activism to overcome the perceived "decline of Islam" and to reconstruct an idealized Islamic past, usually imagined by the actors of political Islam as the embodiment of some form of shariʿa-centric order. On the other hand, certain academic, theological and philosophical reflections on history, and especially on the notion of historicity, led to the questioning of the adequacy and validity of some well-established epistemes of religious thought. Thus, integrating methods of modern hermeneutics as well as historical and literary studies into religious thought has important epistemological implications. The way one's own historicity, and thus the significance of the historical change for one's own processes of cognition and understanding, is reflected upon determines how new stocks of knowledge, categories of understanding and methodological procedures are dealt with as well as whether they are regarded as legitimate enough to be accepted as (still) authentically Islamic.

Bibliography

Al-Afghani, Jamal al-Din. *Al-Aʿmal al-Kamila*, edited by Muhammad ʿImara. Cairo: Dar al-Kitab al-ʿArabi li al-Tibaʿa wa al-Nashr, 1968.

Agai, Bekim. "Freiheit neu entdeckt? Vergessene gemeinsame Erfahrungen des Nahen Ostens und Europas." In *Arabische Zeitenwende: Aufstand und Revolution in der arabischen Welt,* edited by Asiye Öztürk and Zerrin Karta, 18–31. Bonn: Bundeszentrale für politische Bildung, 2012.

Agai, Bekim and Stephan Conermann, eds. *'Wenn einer eine Reise tut, hat er was zu erzählen': Präfiguration – Konfiguration – Refiguration in muslimischen Reiseberichten*. Berlin: EB-Verlag, 2013.

Agai, Bekim, Umar Ryad and Mehdi Sajid, eds. *Muslims in Interwar Europe: A Transcultural Historical Perspective*. Leiden: Brill, 2015.

Amirpur, Katajun. " 'Jeder Tag ist ʿĀšūrāʾ, jeder Ort ist Karbalāʾ": Zur schiitischen Sicht der frühislamischen Geschichte." *Frankfurter Zeitschrift für islamisch-theologische Studien* 4 (2018): 99–124.

Amman, Ludwig. "Geschichtsdenken und Geschichtsschreibung von Muslimen im Mittelalter." In *Die Vielfalt der Kulturen: Erinnerung, Geschichte, Identität,* edited by Jörn Rüsen, Michael Gottlob and Achim Mittag, 191–216. Frankfurt am Main: Suhrkamp Verlag, 1998.

Amman, Ludwig. "Kommentiertes Literaturverzeichnis zu Zeitvorstellungen und geschichtlichem Denken in der islamischen Welt." *Die Welt des Islams* 37, no. 1 (March 1997): 28–87.

Arkoun, Mohammed. "Rethinking Islam Today." *Islam: Enduring Myths and Changing Realities, The Annals of the American Academy of Political and Social Science* 588, no. 1 (July 2003): 18–39, https://doi.org/10.1177/0002716203588001003.

Al-'Arwi, 'Abdallah. *Al-'Arab wa al-Fikr al-Tarikhi*. Beirut: Dar al-Haqiqa, 1973.

Al-Azmeh, Aziz. *The Times of History: Universal Topics in Islamic Historiography*. Budapest and New York: CEU Press, 2007.

Barlas, Asma. *Believing Women in Islam: Unreading Patriarchal Interpretations of the Qur'an*. Austin, TX: University of Texas Press, 2002.

Bigi, Musa Jarullah. "Why Did the Muslim World Decline While the Civilized World Advanced?." In *Modernist Islam 1840–1940: A Sourcebook*, edited by Charles Kurzman, 254–56. New York: Oxford University Press, 2002.

Bougarel, Xavier. "Bosnian Islam as 'European Islam': Limits and Shifts of a Concept." In *Islam in Europe: Diversity, Identity and Influence*, edited by Aziz Al-Azmeh and Effie Fokas, 96–124. Cambridge and New York: Cambridge University Press, 2007.

Conrad, Sebastian and Shalini Randeria. "Geteilte Geschichten: Europa in einer postkolonialen Welt." In *Jenseits des Eurozentrismus: Postkoloniale Perspektiven in den Geschichts- und Kulturwissenschaften*, edited by Sebastian Conrad and Shalini Randeria, 9–49. Frankfurt am Main: Campus Verlag, 2002.

Eisenstadt, Shmuel N. *Comparative Civilizations and Multiple Modernities*, 2 vols. Leiden: Brill, 2000.

Eisenstadt, Shmuel N. *Die Vielfalt der Moderne*. Weilerswist: Velbrück Verlag, 2000.

Falaturi, Abdoljavad. "Zeit- und Geschichtserfahrung im Islam." In *Glauben an den einen Gott: Menschliche Gotteserfahrung im Christentum und im Islam*, edited by Abdoljavad Falaturi and Walter Strolz, 85–101. Freiburg: Herder, 1975.

Geissinger, Aisha. "Feminist Muslim (Re)Interpretations of Early Islam." In *Routledge Handbook of Early Islam*, edited by Herbert Berg, 296–308. London: Routledge, 2017.

Haddad, Yvonne Yazbeck. *Contemporary Islam and the Challenge of History*. Albany, NY: SUNY Press, 1982.

Haridi, Alexander. *Das Paradigma der 'islamischen Zivilisation' – oder die Begründung der deutschen Islamwissenschaft durch Carl Heinrich Becker (1878–1933): Eine wissenschaftsgeschichtliche Untersuchung*. Würzburg: Ergon, 2005.

Hartmann, Angelika. "Einleitung." In *Geschichte und Erinnerung im Islam*, edited by Angelika Hartmann, 9–30. Göttingen: Vandenhoeck & Ruprecht, 2004.

Hendrich, Geert. "Identitätskonstruktion und Geschichtsbilder im arabo-islamischen Modernediskurs." In *Geschichte und Erinnerung im Islam*, edited by Angelika Hartmann, 31–49. Göttingen: Vandenhoeck & Ruprecht, 2004.

Hildebrandt, Thomas. "Waren Ğamāl ad-Dīn al-Afġānī und Muḥammad ʿAbduh Neo-Muʿtaziliten?." *Die Welt des Islams* 42, no. 2 (2002): 207–62.

Hünermann, Peter. *Der Durchbruch geschichtlichen Denkens im 19. Jahrhundert*. Freiburg: Herder, 1967.

Al-Jundi, Anwar. *Al-Islam wa-Harakat al-Tarikh: Ru'iya Jadida fi Falsafat Tarikh al-Islam*. Cairo: Matbaʿat al-Risala, 1968.

Jung, Dietrich. "Dschihad: Zur Transformation eines ambivalenten Begriffs." *Zeitschrift für Missionswissenschaft und Religionswissenschaft* 96, no. 3–4 (2012): 211–25.

Jung, Dietrich."Multiple, Entangled, and Successive Modernities: Putting Modernity in the Plural." In *Muslim History and Social Theory*, edited by Dietrich Jung, 13–32. London: Palgrave Macmillan, 2017.

Jung, Dietrich. *Orientalists, Islamists and the Global Public Sphere: A Genealogy of the Modern Essentialist Image of Islam*. Sheffield and Oakville, CT: Equinox, 2011.

Jung, Dietrich and Kirstine Sinclair. "Multiple Modernities, Modern Subjectivities and Social Order: Unity and Difference in the Rise of Islamic Modernities." *Thesis Eleven* 130, no. 1 (2015): 22–42.

Keddie, Nikki R. *Sayyid Jamāl ad-Dīn 'al-Afġānī': A Political Biography*. Berkeley: University of California Press, 1972.

Keddie, Nikki R. "Sayyid Jamal al-Din 'al-Afghani'." In *Pioneers of Islamic Revival*, 2nd ed., edited by Ali Rahnema, 11–29. London: Zed Books, 2005.

Khalid, Adeeb. *The Politics of Muslim Cultural Reform: Jadidism in Central Asia*. Berkeley: University of California Press, 1998.

Koselleck, Reinhart. *Begriffsgeschichten: Studien zur Semantik und Pragmatik der politischen und sozialen Sprache*. Frankfurt am Main: Suhrkamp Verlag, 2006.

Koselleck, Reinhart. "Einleitung." In *Geschichtliche Grundbegriffe: Historisches Lexikon zur politisch-sozialen Sprache in Deutschland*, vol. 1, edited by Otto Brunner, Werner Conze and Reinhart Koselleck, XIII–XXVII. Stuttgart: Klett-Cotta, 1972.

Kudo, Kerim. *Europäisierung und Islam in Bosnien-Herzegowina: Netzwerke und Identitätsdiskurse*. Baden-Baden: Nomos, 2016.

Lahbabi, Mohammed Aziz. *Le personnalisme musulman*. Paris: Presses Universitaires de France, 1964.

Laroui, Abdallah. *La crise des intellectuels arabes: traditionalisme ou historicisme?.* Paris: François Maspero, 1974.

Lazzerini, Edward J. "Ismail Bey Gasprinskii and Muslim Modernism in Russia, 1878–1914." PhD diss., University of Washington, 1973.

Malik, Jamal. "Andaman Islands in Muslim Cultural Memory and Fadl-e Haqq Khairabadi." In *Manifestations of History: Time, Space, and Community in the*

Andaman Islands, edited by Frank Heidemann and Philipp Zehmisch, 18–36. Delhi: Primus Books, 2016.

Malik, Jamal. "Constructions of the Past in and about India: From Jahiliyya to the Cradle of Civilization. Pre-colonial Perceptions of India." In *Globalized Antiquity: Uses and Perceptions of the Past in South Asia, Mesoamerica, and Europe*, edited by Ute Schüren, Daniel Segesser and Thomas Späth, 51–72. Berlin: Reimer, 2015.

Malik, Jamal, ed. *Perspectives of Mutual Encounters in South Asian History 1760–1860*. Leiden: Brill, 2000.

Mernissi, Fatima. *The Veil and the Male Elite: A Feminist Interpretation of Women's Rights in Islam*. New York: Basic Books, 1991.

Omerika, Armina. *Islam in Bosnien-Herzegowina und die Netzwerke der Jungmuslime (1918–1983)*. Wiesbaden: Harrasowitz, 2014.

Osterhammel, Jürgen. *The Transformation of the World: A Global History of the Nineteenth Century*. Princeton: Princeton University Press, 2014.

Özsoy, Ömer. "Erneuerungsprobleme zeitgenössischer Muslime und der Koran." In *Alter Text – neuer Kontext: Koranhermeneutik in der Türkei heute*. Translated and edited by Felix Körner, 16–28. Freiburg: Herder, 2006.

Özsoy, Ömer. "Pioniere der historischen Koranhermeneutik: Amīn al-Ḫūlī, Fazlur Rahman und Nasr Hamid Abu Zaid." In *Historizität und Transzendenz im Islam: Offenbarung, Geschichte und Recht*, edited by Jameleddine Ben Abdeljelil, 23–45. Berlin: EB-Verlag, 2017.

Öztürk, Mustafa. "Geschichtlichkeit und Übergeschichtlichkeit im koranischen Kontext." Translated by Ertugrul Sahin. *Frankfurter Zeitschrift für islamisch-theologische Studien* 3 (2016): 37–64.

Paçacı, Mehmet. "Der Koran und ich: wie geschichtlich sind wir?." In *Alter Text – neuer Kontext: Koranhermeneutik in der Türkei heute*. Translated and edited by Felix Körner, 32–69. Freiburg: Herder, 2006.

Perler, Dominik and Ulrich Rudolph. *Occasionalismus: Theorien der Kausalität im arabisch-islamischen und im europäischen Denken*. Göttingen: Vandenhoeck & Ruprecht, 2000.

Pink, Johanna. "Striving for the New Exegesis of the Qur'ān." In *The Oxford Handbook of Islamic Theology*, edited by Sabine Schmidtke, 765–92. New York: Oxford University Press, 2016, https://doi.org/10.1093/oxfordhb/9780199696703.013.013.

Qutb, Sayyid. *Fi al-Tarikh: Fikra wa Minhaj*. Beirut and Cairo: Dar al-Shuruq, 1974.

Rahman, Fazlur. *Islamic Methodology in History*. Karachi: Central Institute of Islamic Research, 1965.

Saʿid, Jawdat. *Hatta Yughayyiru ma bi Anfusihim: Bahth fi Sunan Taghyir al-Nafs wa al-Mujtamaʿ*. Damascus: n.p, 1972.

Subrahmanyam, Sanjay. "Connected Histories: Notes Towards a Reconfiguration of Early Modern Eurasia." *Modern Asian Studies* 31, no. 3 (1997): 735–62.

Al-Sharfi, ʿAbd al-Majid. *Al-Islam bayna al-Risala wa al-Tarikh*. Beirut: Dar al-Taliʿa, 2001.
Al-Sharfi, ʿAbd al-Majid. *Al-Islam wa al-Hadatha*. Tunis: Al-Dar al-Tunusiyya li al-Nashr, 1991.
Shariʿati, ʿAli. *Islam-Shinasi*. Mashhad: Tus, 1968.
Schulze, Reinhard. "Die islamische Welt in der Neuzeit (16.–19. Jahrhundert)." In *Der islamische Orient: Grundzüge seiner Geschichte*, edited by Albrecht Noth and Jürgen Paul, 333–403. Würzburg: Ergon, 1998.
Sedgwick, Mark. *Muhammad Abduh*. London: OneWorld, 2010.
Siddiqi, Mazheruddin. *The Qurʾānic Concept of History*. Islamabad: Islamic Research Institute, 1965.
Sing, Manfred. "The Decline of Islam and the Rise of *Inḥiṭāṭ*: The Discrete Charm of Language Games About Decadence in the 19th and 20th Centuries." In *Inḥiṭāṭ – The Decline Paradigm: Its Influence and Persistence in the Writing of Arab Cultural History*, edited by Syrinx von Hees, 11–70. Würzburg: Ergon, 2017.
Van Gelder, Geert Jan. "Good Times, Bad Times: Opinions on *Fasād az-Zamān*, 'the Corruption of Time'." In *Inḥiṭāṭ – The Decline Paradigm: Its Influence and Persistence in the Writing of Arab Cultural History*, edited by Syrinx von Hees, 111–30. Würzburg: Ergon, 2017.
Von Kügelgen, Anke. "'Abduh, Muḥammad." In *Encyclopaedia of Islam*, 3rd ed., edited by Kate Fleet, Gudrun Krämer, Denis Matringe, John Nawas and Everett Rowson. Leiden: Brill, 2008, http://dx.doi.org/10.1163/1573-3912_ei3_COM_0103.
Wielandt, Rotraud. *Offenbarung und Geschichte im Denken moderner Muslime*. Wiesbaden: Franz Steiner Verlag GmbH, 1971.
Zemmin, Florian. *Modernity in Islamic Tradition: The Concept of 'Society' in the Journal al-Manar (Cairo, 1898–1940)*. Berlin and Boston: de Gruyter, 2018, https://doi.org/10.1515/9783110545845.

CHAPTER 3

Between Science and Mysticism

Sabir Multani and the Reform of Humoral Medicine in Pakistan

Stefan Reichmuth

Alongside other forms of traditional medicine as well as modern biomedicine, *Yunani Tibb* (literally, "Greek Medicine"), nowadays widely known as Humoral Medicine or Unani Medicine, continues to enjoy wide popularity and much public recognition in the countries of the Indian Subcontinent.[1] Its presence is equally attested to among the Indo-Pakistani communities in the Middle East, South Africa and East Asia, and increasingly also in Europe, America and Australia. With several public and private higher institutions of medical training and pharmacological production being devoted to *Yunani Tibb*, not to mention it being practiced by a large number of active physicians (*hakim*, pl. *hukamāʾ*)[2] with their clinics and pharmacies in different parts of India and Pakistan, Unani Medicine has maintained itself in a plural medical setting, facing the challenges of hegemonic biomedical institutions, of Ayurveda and Siddha medicine in India, and of homeopathy across the whole Subcontinent.[3]

---

1 The author expresses his profound gratitude to Saskia Hohenberger, B.A. (Bochum), for her German translation of some of the Urdu writings of Sabir Multani, and to Hakim Saim Jamil (Okara, Punjab, then also a PhD student at Hamdard University, Karachi). Together with his father, Hakim Jamil Ahmad, and his uncle, Munir Ahmad, he provided crucial information on Sabir Multani's medical theory and practice. Saim Jamil also undertook a survey of Unani therapeutic and teaching institutions in Pakistan (still unpublished) for the research project on Unani Medicine funded by the DFG and directed at Ruhr University Bochum (2008–2015). He also collected the information and source material for the Sufi center in Sargodha and provided an English translation of the poster text which is described in the last part of this article.

2 This older Arabic and Persian term denoting wise men, philosophers and physicians is still used for the scholars and practitioners of Unani Medicine in South Asia.

3 For the history and present state of Graeco-Islamic Medicine in the Indian Subcontinent, see the following selection of studies: Guy Attewell, *Refiguring Unani Tibb: Plural Healing in Late Colonial India* (Hyderabad: Orient BlackSwan, 2007); Altaf Ahmad Azmi, *History of Unani Medicine in India* (New Delhi: Centre for History of Medicine and Science, Jamia Hamdard, 2004); Maarten Bode, *Taking Traditional Knowledge to the Market: The Modern Image of the Ayurvedic and Unani Industry 1980–2000* (Hyderabad: Orient BlackSwan, 2008); Kristy Bright, "The Travelling Tonic: Tradition, Commodity, and the Body in Unani (Graeco-Arab) Medicine in India" (PhD diss., University of California, 1998); Waltraud Ernst, ed., *Plural Medicine,*

This article deals with a reformed school of Unani Medicine which was founded in Lahore by the Hakim and pharmacist Sabir Multani (1906–1972) and which can be seen as a response to the challenges of Western medicine and of medical pluralism in Pakistan. It has gained many adherents, and a large number of the Pakistani Hakims of today are followers of his theories and therapeutic approaches. His medical theory is based on a revision of the basic concepts of Humoral Medicine, bringing them into a triadic system of corresponding elements of the human body, including tissues and humors along with psychic and emotional qualities, and relating them to an equally triadic concept of nature and the cosmos. Although building their system at a pronounced distance from Western medicine, Multani and his followers have integrated a wide range of biomedical concepts as well as diagnostic and therapeutic devices into their theory and practice. Their system also includes a strong religious dimension, culminating in a triad of mystical *haqiqa* in partnership with *tariqa* and shari'a. This apparently novel attempt at a synthesis of medical science and mystical religiosity can be seen as a revival of the Sufi dimension of the Indo-Persian and Islamic medical tradition in the Subcontinent,[4] which is pursued with remarkable success in the context of

---

Tradition and Modernity, 1800–2000 (London and New York: Routledge, 2002); Rahbar Faruqi, *Islami Tibb Shahana Sar-Parastiyun Men* (Hyderabad: A'zam Esteem Press, 1937); Om Prakash Jaggi, *History of Science and Technology in India*, vol. 8, *Medicine in Medieval India* (Delhi: Atma Ram & Sons, 1977); Usmanghani Khan, Aftab Saeed and Muhammad Tanweer Alam, *Indusyunic Medicine: Traditional Medicine of Herbal, Animal and Mineral Origin in Pakistan* (Karachi: University of Karachi, 1997); Claudia Liebeskind, "Arguing Science: Unani Tibb, Hakims and Biomedicine in India, 1900–1950," in *Plural Medicine, Tradition and Modernity, 1800–2000*, ed. Waltraud Ernst (London and New York: Routledge, 2002); Claudia Preckel, "Healing the People and the Princes: Hospitals, Ḥakīms and Doctors in Bhopal," in *Hospitals in Iran and India, 1500–1950s*, ed. Fabrizio Speziale (Leiden: Brill, 2012); Stefan Reichmuth, "Wissen, Praxis und pluraler kultureller Kontext der graeco-islamischen Medizin (*yūnānī ṭibb*/Unani Medicine) in Nordindien," in *Muslim Bodies: Body, Sexuality and Medicine in Muslim Societies*, ed. Susanne Kurz, Claudia Preckel and Stefan Reichmuth (Berlin and Münster: LIT Verlag, 2016); Kira Schmidt Stiedenroth, *Unani Medicine in the Making: Practices and Representations in 21st-Century India* (Amsterdam: Amsterdam University Press, 2020); Fabrizio Speziale, ed., *Hospitals in Iran and India, 1500–1950s* (Leiden: Brill, 2012); idem, "'Muslim or Greek?' Past and Present of Muslim Traditional Medicine in the Deccan Sultanates," in *Global Medical Geography: Essays in Honour of Prof. Yola Verhasselt*, ed. Rais Akhtar and Nilofar Izhar (Jaipur: Rawat Publications, 2010); idem, *Soufisme, religion et médecine en Islam indien* (Paris: Karthala, 2010); Sayyid Zillur Rahman, "Indian Hakims: Their Role in the Medical Care of India," in *History of Science, Philosophy and Culture in Indian Civilization*, vol. 4.2, *Medicine and Life Sciences in India*, ed. B.V. Subbarayappa (New Delhi: Centre for Studies in Civilizations, 2001). The following account is largely based on these texts, often without specific reference.

4 Speziale, *Soufisme, religion et médecine*.

contemporary Pakistan. This will be documented through the case of a Sufi medical center in the Punjab (Astan-e Fazal, in the city of Sargodha) and its own presentation of its Sufi-cum-medical view of the human being.

1 Unani Medicine in India and Pakistan

The name *Yunani Tibb*/Unani Medicine, which has prevailed in India and increasingly also in Pakistan over the more general terms *tibb* or *hikmat*, has been an established term in South Asia since the eighteenth century at the latest.[5] It refers to the Hellenistic origins of a therapeutic school based on the concept of the four elements (Ar. *arkan*, sing. *rukn*) of fire, air, water and earth, alongside the four bodily fluids composed of them (the "humors," Ar. *akhlat*, sing. *khilt*), namely blood, phlegm, yellow bile and black bile. Like the elements, each of these bodily fluids is given a specific combination of the properties of hot/cold and humid/dry, which as "temperament" (literally "mixture," Ar. *mizaj*, pl. *amzija*) also determines the human constitution. The life processes are based on physical and mental forces (Ar. *quwan*, sing. *quwwa*). They take place with the help of the "spirits of life" (Ar. *arwah*, sing. *ruh*), which are produced in the liver and heart, are effective in the whole body and drive the activities of the various organs. A healthy life consists of achieving a balance of the respective temperament of the humors and organs and can be achieved by controlling the "six necessary causes" (*al-asbab al-sitta al-daruriyya*), i.e., the factors of air, nutrition, movement/rest, sleeping/waking, voiding/continence and psychological/mental effects and activities. Diseases are interpreted as one-sided disturbances of the constitutional temperament, which are to be treated by counteracting therapeutic measures and drugs (*contraria contrariis*), for instance heat against excessive cold, or dryness against excessive humidity. The categories of therapeutic measures are "treatment by cure" (*'ilaj bi al-tadbir*), including bloodletting, cupping, leech treatment, drainage, purge, vomiting and sweating, as well as baths, massages and gymnastics; "treatment by diet" (*'ilaj bi al-ghidha'*), "treatment with remedies" (*'ilaj bi al-dawa'*) and surgical, "manual treatment" (*'ilaj bi al-yad*), which is, however, hardly practiced in today's Unani Medicine.

This doctrine, which was decisively influenced by Greek physicians such as Hippocrates (d. ca. 370 BC) and Galen (d. ca. 210 AD) and further developed

---

5 The following historical overview is largely based on Reichmuth, "Wissen, Praxis und pluraler kultureller Kontext."

within the Islamic world, was, as is well known, also held in high esteem in Europe until the eighteenth century. Its transfer to South Asia took place in connection with the foundation of Muslim states in Northern India from the late twelfth century onwards. The rulers of the Sultanate of Delhi (1206–1526), of various states in South India and especially of the Mughal Empire (1526–1530, 1555–1858) all promoted and patronized Graeco-Islamic medicine at their courts and in their territories. Between the thirteenth and eighteenth centuries, a large number of physicians from Iran and Central Asia moved to India, which also led to a flourishing of Persian medical literature. Likewise, many of the Sufi centers of the Mughal Empire cultivated not only Sufi therapy but also Graeco-Islamic medicine, and many important physicians belonged to the Sufi brotherhoods. Since the fourteenth century, an intense engagement with the Ayurvedic medical tradition resulted in many translations and adaptations of Sanskrit medical writings into Persian, and also in extensive interaction and cooperation between representatives of the Graeco-Islamic and Ayurvedic medical traditions.[6]

The important position Graeco-Islamic medicine had assumed in the Mughal Empire, which was characterized by close cooperation of the authorities with local scholars and physicians, was initially retained in the early phase of British rule in the eighteenth and early nineteenth centuries. With the tightening of colonial rule after the Mutiny (1857–1858), however, European biomedicine came to dominate in the health administration of British India. The representatives of older medical schools found themselves in an ambiguous situation, retaining many of their local customers but generally losing state recognition and support. An exception was the Oriental College in Lahore, where state-subsidized courses for Unani doctors were established in 1872 and which came to be widely attended by local scholars. Moreover, the rulers of the Muslim princely states, like Hyderabad and Bhopal, continued with their promotion and patronage of Graeco-Islamic Medicine.

Since the end of the nineteenth century, some leading representatives of this medical school engaged on practical as well as theoretical grounds with European biomedicine and its scientific hegemony. Their efforts for self-assertion and medical reform led to the founding of various schools which, in order to obtain public recognition, fused basic elements of biomedicine with the Unani tradition. The later development of Unani Medicine before and after

6 For this in particular, see the *Perso-Indica* research and publishing project that is producing a comprehensive analytical survey of Persian works on Indian learned traditions, based at the CNRS in Paris and accessible online at: www.perso-indica.net/index.faces; Fabrizio Speziale, *Culture persane et médecine ayurvédique en Asie du Sud* (Leiden: Brill, 2018).

independence and the partition of India in 1947 is characterized by the emergence of larger pharmaceutical companies, like Hamdard, and the foundation of hospitals and educational institutions, even up to the university level, which are all devoted to this traditional form of medical care.[7] The interaction of these reformist attempts with the various institutions of Muslim educational reform in British India, like the *Dar al-'Ulum* in Deoband, Aligarh Muslim University, and *Nadwat al-'Ulama'* founded in Lucknow, remains to be further studied.[8] The general impression until now remains that of a rather autonomous field of medical currents and initiatives based on quite specific family traditions and institutional dynamics.

After the foundation of India and Pakistan, Unani Medicine was officially recognized in both states and put under the supervision of state health authorities. This development was still based on recommendations of the joint conference of the Ministers of Health of the provincial governments in 1946, which explicitly recommended research and education in Ayurveda and Unani Medicine. With the 1965 *Unani, Ayurvedic and Homeopathic Practitioners Act*, Pakistan also created a legal and administrative framework for these older medical schools alongside homeopathy. About thirty mainly private *tibbiyya* colleges have come to offer diploma courses, but it has only been in the last few years that a Bachelor of Eastern Medicine and Surgery (BEMS) was introduced at two universities (Hamdard University in Karachi and Government Islamia University in Bahawalpur), after the legal basis for this was created in 2003.

The growing integration of Unani Medicine into the public health care systems of India, Pakistan and other countries of South Asia follows the increased national and international interest in "traditional" forms of medicine, which are often described with terms such as "traditional medicine" and "complementary and alternative medicine" (CAM), and seen as a welcome and

---

7 For the case of Hamdard, see Bode, *Taking Traditional Knowledge*; Anna Vanzan, "Hamdard, How to Share Pain in a Muslim Way," in *Hospitals in Iran and India, 1500–1950s*, ed. Fabrizio Speziale (Leiden: Brill, 2012); Reichmuth, "Wissen, Praxis und pluraler kultureller Kontext," 360–61, 365ff., 386, 391.

8 For Deoband, see Barbara Daly Metcalf, *Islamic Revival in British India: Deoband, 1860–1900* (Princeton: Princeton University Press, 1982); for Aligarh University, where a Unani college and hospital were established in 1929, see David Lelyveld, *Aligarh's First Generation: Muslim Solidarity in British India* (Princeton: Princeton University Press, 1978), and Stefan Reichmuth, "Wissen, Praxis und pluraler kultureller Kontext," 375–88; for the *Nadwat al-'Ulama'*, founded in Lucknow in the late nineteenth century, see Jamal Malik, *Islamische Gelehrtenkultur in Nordindien: Entwicklungsgeschichte und Tendenzen am Beispiel von Lucknow* (Leiden: Brill, 1997); and for general overviews, see Jamal Malik, *Islam in South Asia: A Short History* (Leiden: Brill, 2008), 291–345 and his *Islam in South Asia: Revised, Enlarged and Updated Second Edition* (Leiden: Brill, 2020), 396–480.

inexpensive addition to general health care. According to the WHO Medical Atlas of 2005, there were 43,330 registered Unani doctors for India and 39,584 for Pakistan. On top of this, the number of unregistered practitioners trained within their families or by other Hakims might be in the same range. The role of family and organizational connections remains important for the individual practitioner's reputation and success. Like Ayurveda, Unani Medicine has a considerable number of customers, especially among the middle classes of the Subcontinent, who regard these "traditional medicines" as part of their national identity. It must be stated, however, that the old cooperation and exchange between Ayurvedic and Unani practitioners has given way to a strict distinction between them as different "medical systems," and to their increasing competition on the national and international fields. In this competition, Unani Medicine, although having an increasing intake of Muslim customers outside South Asia, falls far behind the global successes of Ayurveda in Asia, Europe and the Americas.

2   Sabir Multani – Glimpses on His Life, Background and Writings

The scarce biographical material available for Sabir Multani[9] already provides some insight into the interaction between the different medical traditions and institutions that existed during the colonial period in British India. Born in Multan in the Punjab in 1906 as Dost Mohammad, he would later replace his birth name with the *nom de plume* Sabir Multani. He completed his early education at a technical cantonment school in his hometown with excellent marks. He also took examinations in Urdu and Arabic and received degrees for these languages from the University of the Punjab in Lahore. After that, he studied Unani Medicine at the private *tibbiyya* college founded in 1926 by the Islamic organization Anjuman Himayat al-Islam in Lahore, where he also, with great success, passed the exams to become *Hakim-i Hadhiq* ("Skillful Physician"), *Zubdat al-Hukama'* ("Cream of the Physicians") and finally *Mumtaz al-Atibba'* ("Most Excellent Physician"), diploma titles that had been recognized by the colonial educational authorities. These studies also included courses in biomedical disciplines, where he is also said to have excelled, as part of the

---

9   See "Mukhtasar Sawanih-i 'Umri-yi Hakim-i Inqilab," in Sabir Multani, *Kulliyyat-i Tahqiqat-i Sabir Multani,* ed. Hakim 'Urwa Wahid Sulaymani, vol. 1 (Lahore: Idara-i Matbu'at-i Sulaymani, 2012), 21–31, with additional oral information collected in Pakistan in March 2013, especially in Okara (4–11 March) from Saim Jamil, his father, Hakim Jamil Ahmad, and his uncle, Hakim Munir Ahmad.

medical training for Unani doctors. He furthermore gained some familiarity with Ayurvedic Medicine.

For a time, Sabir Multani worked as a medical practitioner in private healthcare institutions, at first with a strong inclination towards biomedical treatments, but later on developing his own medical approach. This came to be based on Unani principles and therapies blended with concepts and methods derived from Western science and medicine ("allopathy"), but also from Ayurveda and homeopathy, which at that time had already gained popularity in British India. He is additionally reported to have worked as a pharmacist, and to have developed a strong Sufi orientation. His own medical system, which grew out of his synthesizing efforts over several decades, informed by his practical experience as well as critical exchange with other prominent Unani Hakims, was laid out in a series of publications from the 1950s onward. With these efforts, he claimed to have created a medical theory that was independent from western allopathy, which he had come to regard as unscientific and as basically wrong.[10] His writings were compiled into two large volumes, which were published in Lahore in 2012.[11] Until his death in 1972, he had gathered a considerable number of students and followers, who continued to write about his medical concepts, summarizing and further elaborating upon them.[12] Today, his school and his medical theory, known as the "Simple Organ Theory" (*Nazariyyat-i Mufrad A'za'*, or also as *Qanun-i Mufrad A'za'*), have become dominant among Unani practitioners in Pakistan. His followers refer to Sabir Multani as the "Hakim of the Revolution" (*Hakim-i Inqilab*) and as the "Renewer of Medicine" (*Mujaddid-i Tibb*).[13] A former disciple of Sabir Multani, Arshad Mirza (d. 2009), even established a dietary consulting practice in

---

10 Sabir Multani, "Farangi Tibb Ghayr 'Ilmi awr Ghalat he," in Multani, *Kulliyyat-i Tahqiqat-i Sabir Multani*, vol. 1, 181–285.
11 Multani, *Kulliyyat*.
12 See, for example, Hakim Muhammad Yasin, *Ta'aruf: Qanun-i Mufrad A'za'* (Dunyapur and Lahore: Yasin Dawakhana wa-Tibbi Kutubkhana, n.d.), accessed April 17, 2020, https://archive.org/details/TarufQanoonMufradAzaTibbBook/mode/2up; Hakim Muhammad Siddiq Shahin, *Mukhtasar Qanun-i Mufrad A'za'* (Lahore: Maktabah Danyal, n.d. [1974]); and the list at the end of Multani, *Kulliyyat*, vol. 1, 952.
13 For instance, see Jaffar Ali, "Qanoon E Mufrad Aza: A Revolution to Health Science, What is Qanoon E Mufrad Aza: Also known as Simple Organ Theory," blog, accessed April 17, 2020, https://qanoonemufradaza.blogspot.com/2016/03/what-is-qanoon-e-mufrid-aza-qanoon.html; Hakeem Mohammad Khalid Mehmood, "Simple Organ Theory: A Revolution in the Medical Science," accessed April 17, 2020, https://hakeemkhalid.com/sot.html.

Dortmund, Germany in 1979, which is now continued by his daughter.[14] A pediatrician of Iranian origin in Witten, Germany, Dr. Amir Bahrinipour, himself also a student of Arshad Mirza, offers therapeutic consulting along the lines of the methods of Sabir Multani.[15]

The following overview of Sabir Multani's medical theory makes use of some of his writings,[16] but it is based on information gained from interviews with Hakim Arshad Mirza (Dortmund) that took place in Bochum in 2008, as well as with Hakim Saim Jamil (Okara, Pakistan), at that time a PhD student at Hamdard University in Karachi, and his father Hakim Jamil Ahmad and uncle Hakim Munir Ahmad, during a stay at their home in Okara in March of 2013.[17]

3 Sabir Multani's "Simple Organ Theory" and Its Triadic Structure

The following diagram, which can be found in an online presentation of Sabir Multani's theory, summarizes its basic underlying structural elements. The three controlling and directing organs of the body (brain, heart, liver) are connected by directional arrows in three colors, blue (brain), red (heart) and yellow (liver), which originate from these organs, suggesting a directed flow of bodily activities that is controlled and managed by these organs and their respective realms in the body.

Starting out with reference to Avicenna on the above-mentioned basic concept of the four elements of the cosmos and the four humors of the human body, Sabir Multani soon moves towards a structure of correspondences that appears to be thoroughly triadic, including physiological, psychological and religious qualities.

This far-reaching triadic structure with multiple correspondences is based on the genetic distinction between the three germ layers from which the different tissues and organs of the human body are formed.[18] Muscle tissues originate from the mesoderm; glands and gland-related organs such as the liver,

---

14   Anna Fatima Ahmed and Mansoor Ahmed, "Ernährungsberatung Mirza & Ahmed nach Avicenna," accessed April 14, 2020, www.ernaehrungsberatung-avicenna.de/mirza-ahmed.
15   Amir Bahrinipour, "Grundgesetze der Medizin: Von Saber Multani, veröffentlicht 1.02.1958," accessed April 17, 2020, www.bahrinipour.de/upload/file/Grundlagen.pdf.
16   Translations of selected writings of Sabir Multani provided by Saskia Hohenberger; see also Bahrinipour, "Grundgesetze."
17   Already mentioned above in footnote 1.
18   See, for example, Scott F. Gilbert, *Developmental Biology*, 7th ed. (Sunderland, MA: Sinauer Associates, 2003).

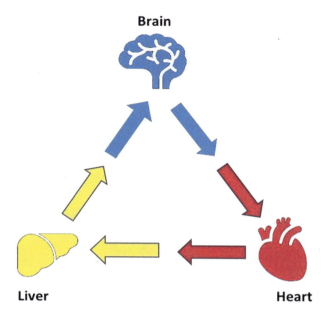

FIGURE 3.1   Flow of activities between vital organs.
STEFAN REICHMUTH, FREE ADAPTATION FROM: JAFFAR ALI, "WHAT IS QANOON E MUFRAD AZA, ALSO KNOWN AS SIMPLE ORGAN THEORY (SOT)," QANUN E MUFRAD AZA: A REVOLUTION TO HEALTH SCIENCE (BLOG), POSTED MARCH 31, 2016.

lungs and others from the endoderm; and the brain and nerves, eyes and also the skin from the ectoderm. Multani describes these tissues as "simple organs" (line 2 in the table below) in the sense that each part represents the whole and assumes a mutual influence between all bodily parts consisting of one of these tissues. The main organs (a'za' ra'isiyya, line 1) formed out of each tissue are also called "vital organs" (hayati a'za'). These are the heart (muscular, 'azalati), the liver (related to the glands, ghuddi) and the brain (related to the nerves, a'sabi). They are at the center of all bodily activities and are the major representatives of the three "simple organs." Sabir Multani puts these old Avicennan notions[19] to a novel use along the lines of modern genetic physiology.

---

19   For the "simple organs" (a'da' mufrada), see Abu 'Ali al-Hussain ibn 'Ali ibn Sina, Al-Qanun fi al-Tibb, vol. 1, ed. Muhammad Amin al-Dannawi (Beirut: Dar al-Kutub al-'Ilmiyya, 1999), 36–37; translation by Oskar Cameron Gruner as, A Treatise on the Canon of Medicine of Avicenna (New York: AMS Press, 1973 [1930]), 94–95; Abu 'Ali al-Hussain ibn 'Ali ibn Sina,

TABLE 3.1 Simple Organ Theory (*Qanun-i Mufrad A'za'*), as taught by Sabir Multani and his school

1	Main organs (*a'za' ra'isiyya*)	Heart	Liver	Brain
2	Simple organs* (*mufrad a'za'*) (body tissues)	Mesoderm muscles, bones *'adulat*	Endoderm glands *ghudda*	Ectoderm nerves, brain *a'sab*
3	Celestial bodies	Earth	Sun	Moon
4	Sources of medicine (*mawalid*)	Minerals (*jamadat*)	Animals (*hayawanat*)	Plants (*nabatat*)
5	Colors	Red	Yellow	Blue
6	Humors	Black bile *sawda'*	Yellow bile *safra'*	Phlegm *balgham*
7	Sources of energy	Gas, air *hawa'*	Heat, fire *hararat*	Humidity, water *rutubat*
8	Energy, forces	Mechanical	Chemical	Gravitation
9	Atomic structure, electricity	Proton, positive (produces "dynamo electricity" through movement of muscles)	Neutron, neutral (produces chemical electricity)	Electron, negative (produces electricity by gravity attraction)
10	Chemical elements	Carbon (C)	Oxygen (O_2)	Hydrogen (H_2)
11	Organic forces	Immunity	Vital	Gravitational attraction
12	Taste	Sour	Salty	Tasteless

Al-Qānūn fi'l-Ṭibb: English Translation of the Critical Arabic Text, Book I, trans. anon. (New Delhi: Department of Islamic Studies, Jamia Hamdard, 1993), 30–31; for "main organs" (*a'da' ra'isiyya*) see Ibn Sina, *Al-Qanun* 1–38, translated as "vital organs" by Gruner, and in Ibn Sina, *Al-Qānūn: English Translation*, 38.

TABLE 3.1   Simple Organ Theory (*Qanun-i Mufrad A'za'*) (*cont.*)

13	"Spirits of blood" (*arwah*, gases)	Animal (*ruh hayawani*), *quwwa mudabbira*, controls and coordinates chemical processes in the body	"medical" spirit (*ruh tibbi*), organizes chemical processes	Psychic/mental spirit (*ruh nafsani*), organizes inner and outer perception
14	Psychological quality	Positive, outward-going	Neutral	Negative, inward-oriented
15	Senses, forms of perception	Analogy, *qiyas*, intuition, *kashf* (also supernatural), "understanding"	Inner senses, thought (*idrak*, *wijdan*), "awareness"	Sensual perception, outer senses (*ihsas*), knowledge and memory, "knowing"
16	Emotions *inbisat* > secretion *inqibad* > stops secretion	Joy > secretion Sorrow > stops secretion	Shame > secretion Rage > stops secretion	Pleasure > secretion Fear > stops secretion
17	Human activities and professions	Craftsmen, drivers, drunkards, robbers, police, army. In religion: passion, spirituality, eroticism, geniality; but also: arrogance and stubbornness	Business, science, art, bureaucracy	Philosophy, education, teaching

TABLE 3.1 Simple Organ Theory (*Qanun-i Mufrad A'za'*) (*cont.*)

18	Religious soul qualities	Inciting soul (*nafs ammara*)	Self-accusing soul (*nafs lawwama*)	Soul at peace (*nafs mutma'inna*)
19	Religious types	Spirituality (*haqiqat* > *ma'rifat*), Pakistan: Sufi-Hanafi, Barelwi	Physical-spiritual (*tariqat*); Pakistan: Deobandi Sunni (also using force)	Solely Quran and sunna (*shari'a*); Pakistan: Ahl-i Hadith

* In some presentations, "connective tissues" are set apart as a fourth tissue, with earth as its correlated element and cold quality; see e.g. Mehmood, "Simple Organ Theory." This seems to reflect the traditional four elements structure, but this is normally not developed in any greater depth and its place in the system has yet to be further clarified. It should be noted that this online presentation includes a good number of additional triads drawn from diagnostic observation, chemical examination, food, etc.

The triadic classification also pertains to celestial bodies (3), to the natural kingdom, which is also a source of medicine (4), atomic structures (9), chemical elements (10), sources of energy (7) and colors (5). Earth is placed in correspondence with the heart, the Sun with the liver, and the Moon with the brain. In terms of the elementary particles of the atomic structure, protons are placed in relation to the heart, as underlying the movement of the muscles and thus producing "dynamo electricity," the neutrons are related to the liver as resources of chemical electricity, and the electrons as producers of electricity by gravitation. Among the chemical elements, carbon (C) relates to the Earth and the heart, Oxygen (O_2) to the Sun and the liver, and hydrogen (H_2) to the Moon and the brain. As sources of energy, gas and air (*hawa'*) correspond to the muscles, heat and fire (*hararat*) to the glands and the liver, and humidity and water (*rutubat*) to the nerves and the brain. This arrangement clearly differs from the traditional one, where coldness and dryness are presented in correlation with heat and humidity, a scheme which is replaced here with an energetic perspective. The colors red (heart), yellow (liver) and blue (brain, nerves) are equally shown as belonging to the basic qualities of the respective tissues and their products, and they are of important diagnostic value. References to physical and chemical terms are thus combined with older concepts and qualities derived from traditional Humoral Medicine and cosmology.

The arrangement of the humors themselves (6) differs from the traditional one. Blood is left out and regarded as a carrier of other humors, as opposed to being seen as a humor in its own right. It is treated by Multani as an admixture of heat, humidity and gases ("winds"), carrying nourishment for the tissues.[20] Black bile (*sawda'*) is related to the heart and the muscles, yellow bile (*safra'*) to the liver, and phlegm (*balgham*) to the brain. Another category relates to "organic forces" (11), which include "immunity" as a defensive quality, vitality as a pure force of living, as well as gravitational attraction and general receptivity. The first is attributed to the heart, the second to the liver and the third to the brain and nerves. Qualities of taste (12), which were always of high diagnostic importance, are equally connected with the humors and their main organs. Black bile is sour, yellow bile salty and *balgham* remains tasteless. Blood itself, i.e., the general carrier of the humors, is said to be of a sweet quality.

The old category of "vital spirits" (*arwah*) evinces an important reformulation of its functions (13). The "animal spirit" (*ruh hayawani*), endowed with a "controlling force" (*quwwa mudabbira*), controls and coordinates chemical processes in the body. It is related to the heart. The "medical spirit" (*ruh tibbi*), located in the liver, organizes these chemical processes. Inner and outer perception are organized by the psychic or mental spirit (*ruh nafsani*) of the brain. The different modes of perception and thought (15) also have relations to the main organs. Reflection by analogy (*qiyas*), intuition as well as natural and supernatural "understanding" are rooted in the heart. The inner senses (*idrak*) and the "awareness" derived from them belong to the sphere of the liver.

Psychological qualities (14) are distinguished in terms of their positive and outward-going or their negative, inward-looking direction. The positive and outward-going quality belongs to the heart, the neutral stage to the liver, and the negative and inward-looking habitus to the brain. The force/energy derived from physical gravity (8) corresponds to mental perceptivity (15) and psychological receptiveness (14). The connection with the main organs and with the humors is related to the emotions (16). For each organ, two types of emotions are distinguished, which refer to their function of either triggering or stopping inner secretion. As for the heart and black bile, joy is the trigger of secretion, while sorrow stops it. Regarding the liver, shame and rage are mentioned for each of these respective functions, and for the brain, pleasure and fear (for more on the emotions, see further below).

---

20   Multani, *Kulliyyat*, vol. 1, 541.

Types of human character, activities and professions (17) are likewise grouped in relation to the elementary and main organs. As for the heart group, craftsmen, drivers, policemen and soldiers are mentioned together with more violent characters and activities, such as those of drunkards and robbers. Passionate characters and eroticists, artistic geniuses and religious spiritualists are classified as heart-dominated, but also as arrogant and stubborn people. The dominance of the liver could be felt with people active in business, science, art and bureaucracy, and the brain-oriented character is associated with philosophers and teachers. This was extended by the informants to religious qualities of the soul (18), i.e., the inciting, self-accusing and peaceful souls (*nafs ammara, nafs lawwama, nafs mutma'inna*) and even to different religious types in Pakistan (19). The people shaped by the heart would be found among those striving for spirituality, mystical truth (*haqiqa*) and gnosis (*ma'rifa*), with Hanafi Sufis and Barelwis being mentioned as examples (the group to which my hosts themselves belonged). The combination of physical and spiritual efforts, rooted in the liver, was said to dominate among the people of the other organized Sufi groups (*tariqat*) and the Deobandi Sunnis, who were seen as sometimes being prone to using coercion or force. As for the influence of the brain on religious life, it was held to result in a strong focus on the Quran, sunna and shari'a in Pakistan, represented by the Ahl-i Hadith. It was thus not only a person's character, but also his or her religious inclination which was understood to be in close relation to the basic humoral categories of the Simple Organ Theory. It was furthermore stated that among political and religious leaders, negative qualities like arrogant obstinacy, imperiousness and megalomania can be related to the effect of excessive black bile.

The arrangement of the three humors – with blood relegated to being a carrier fluid for all of them – shows striking similarities to the concept of the three *dosha*s (*tridosha*) in Ayurveda, which function as basic elements and forces shaping the human body with their respective properties. Sabir Multani explicitly identifies *balgham* with the Ayurvedic *kapha*, yellow bile with *pitta*, and black bile with *vata* ("wind").[21] The *vata* concept appears to underlie the role attributed to "gas, air" (*hawa'*) in the triad of the "sources of energy" (6). In Ayurveda, as in this version of Unani Medicine, the function of blood is regarded as distinct from the humors, despite being related to them.[22]

---

21 Ibid., 527, 531.
22 For blood (*rakta*) in Ayurveda, see G. Jan Meulenbeld, "The Constraints of Theory in the Evolution of Nosological Classification: A Study on the Position of Blood in Indian Medicine (Āyurveda)," in *Medical Literature from India, Sri Lanka, and Tibet*, vol. 3, ed. G. Jan Meulenbeld (Leiden: Brill, 1991); for the synthetic attempts of Persian medical authors, see Speziale, *Culture persane*, 81–82, 92–96.

The engagement of Muslim scholars of the Graeco-Islamic medical tradition with the Ayurvedic *doshas* dates back to the fourteenth and fifteenth centuries, when similar efforts to reconcile the humoral and *dosha* categories are documented in Persian medical writings on the Subcontinent.[23] Yet this new attempt by Sabir Multani does not seem to derive from the Persian writings of earlier authors. Rather, it represents a personal effort of his own, which testifies to the ongoing interaction of Unani scholars with Ayurveda in South Asia.

Sabir Multani's amalgamation of the Unani conceptual framework with notions and categories derived from the natural sciences appears particularly striking. Resources from chemistry and physiology are tapped for this synthetic attempt, and he shows considerable interest in these sciences, despite his far-reaching critique of allopathic medicine. At the same time, remarkable Unani continuities persist in the psychological and perceptional fields, testifying to their roots in Sufi psychology. A system is thus created which promises to provide links between the cosmos and the human body as well as with the internal world of human perception, emotion and religiosity.

4 Dynamic Processes

Sabir Multani's theory also conceives of the dynamic processes within the human body and within the simple organs along a tripartite cyclical sequence of "stimulation" (*tahrik*), "calming" (*taskin*) and "dissolution" (*tahlil*). In these processes, all three organs are interrelated and participate with their own cyclical sequences, with different peaks and troughs. He describes this process as follows:[24]

> The individual organs are also interrelated. Through this relationship, excitations in the human body move from one organ to another. If, for example, there is excitation in the glands, then we must know that there is a connection between this excitation and the muscles [...]. Also, as far as the temperaments are concerned, an elementary quality can never be singular. For example, it must be connected with another quality. Heat and

---

23 Fabrizio Speziale, "The Persian Translation of the *Tridoṣa*: Lexical Analogies and Conceptual Incongruities," *Asiatische Studien* 68, no. 3 (2014); idem, *Culture persane*, 55, 75–76, 80–101, 169–73, 190ff., 214, 222–23; Puyan Mahmudian and Stefan Reichmuth, "Qāsim ibn Quṭb ibn Yaʿqūb, Ḥikmat-i Sulaymān-Šāhī," Perso-Indica, accessed April 17, 2020, www.perso-indica.net/work/medicine/hikmat-i_sulayman-sahi.

24 Multani, *Kulliyyat*, vol. 1, 541–42.

cold are never found alone, but are always found in the form of heat and humidity or heat and dryness, or cold and humidity or cold and dryness. The same applies to the organs; that is, a stimulation will be *glandular-muscular* (warm-dry) or *glandular-neuronal* (warm-moist), etc.

You should keep in mind that the name of the organ that is mentioned first in the stimulation is called the "mechanical component" and the name of the organ that comes after it is called the "humoral" or "chemical component." The stimulation of the simple organs in the second place therefore means that their influence is present in the blood in a qualitative, humoral and chemical way. In order to create a balance, the regulating nature of the body has intensified the activity of another organ, and has further increased the activity of the organ that is mechanically active, in order to bring the elementary qualities of the humors and the chemical conditions back into balance. If, for example, a *glandular-muscular* stimulation is taking place, there will be excessive heat, dryness, yellow bile or sulphur in the blood, in terms of general, humoral and chemical ways. Similarly, when *glandular-neuronal* stimulation occurs, there will be excessive heat, moisture, dryness, yellow bile or sulphur in the blood, and in qualitative, humoral and chemical terms, there will be much heat, moisture, redness and high salinity, etc. This sequence of stimulation continues in all simple organs and their interrelationships remain intact.

The first term mentioned in each bundle thus indicates the organ affected by a mechanical stimulation, whereas the second term refers to qualitative, humoral and chemical impulses that maintain the balance within the process against the first, mechanical one. With the decrease and calming of the stimulation of one organ, that of the neighboring organ increases, and so on. The cyclical processes originating from this movement, which might be caused by internal or external factors, are described in six stages:[25]

1. neuronal – muscular (*aʿsabi – ʿazalati*)
2. muscular – neuronal (*ʿazalati – aʿsabi*)
3. muscular – glandular (*ʿazalati – ghuddi*)
4. glandular – muscular (*ghuddi – ʿazalati*)
5. glandular – neuronal (*ghuddi – aʿsabi*)
6. neuronal – glandular (*aʿsabi – ghuddi*)

The mechanical stimulation of one of the three organs may affect the whole range of organs belonging to the same type of tissue, which allows for assessing

---

25 Ibid., 542, 546. The order follows the second quotation.

symptoms over different parts of the body. But this stimulation also implies the calming or weakening of the others, which then gain in strength again when the effect of the stimulation of the first one declines. The second name relates to the status of the related humor and its influence.

As the six stages reflect the circulation of blood and the ensuing stimulation of the different organs, Sabir Multani and his school relate them to different parts of the body. The left and right hemispheres of the body differ in their qualities, even for organs and other parts that come in pairs. They are listed from top right to bottom left as follows:[26]

1. neuronal – muscular: right hemisphere of the head, right eye, right ear, right part of nose and mouth, gums, teeth, tongue and neck.
2. muscular – neuronal: right hemisphere of chest and abdomen, right shoulder, lung, arm, right part of the stomach.
3. muscular – glandular: liver, right part of intestines and urinary bladder, right testicle, right part of the anus, right leg down to the toes.
4. glandular – muscular: left hemisphere of the head, left eye, left ear, left part of nose and mouth, gums, teeth, tongue and neck.
5. glandular – neuronal: left hemisphere of chest and abdomen, left shoulder, lung, arm, left part of the stomach.
6. neuronal – glandular: spleen, left part of intestines and urinary bladder, left testicle, left part of the anus, left leg down to the toes.

It should be noted that the heart itself is not given a location in any of these six areas, presumably because of its specific function as the "motor" for circulating blood; with its components of heat and humors, gases and wind; throughout the body. This circulation is presented as leading from heart to liver (that is, from the main organ of muscular tissue to the primary glandular one), from liver to brain (main organ of nerve tissue) and from there back to the heart. This direction has already been indicated in the above diagram, where the arrows of different colors depict the dominance of one of the major life organs (and its corresponding humor) within its own vicinity, which then decreases and recedes the closer circulation comes to the next one, giving way to another set of correspondences. The following diagram, taken from an internet presentation of the Simple Organ Theory, further illustrates this.

As in the first diagram, the domain of each of the three main organs is marked by the color related to it. The gradual transitions between the three primary colors indicate the blood's changing saturation of humors from phlegm and the brain (blue) to black bile (here indicated as red, as the basic humor

---

26   Ibid., 546–47, 566–90.

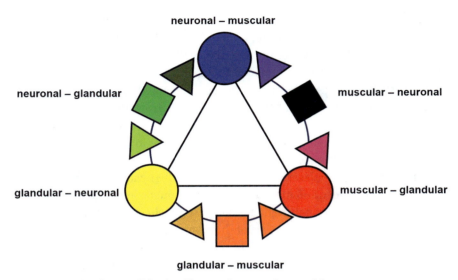

FIGURE 3.2 Circulation of blood and humors between the main life organs.
I AM GRATEFUL TO SAEED ZARRABI-ZADEH, WHO TRANSLATED AND ADAPTED THE DIAGRAM FROM "FREE TIBBI CAMP," FACEBOOK GROUP, POSTED SEPTEMBER 14, 2013.

related to the heart, see above) and to yellow bile in the vicinity of the liver, from where it gradually comes under the influence of phlegm and the brain again. The triangles of different colors, and the black, orange and green squares indicate the intermediary stages of this circulation, which Multani describes at length with its healthy and unhealthy aspects as well as signs and symptoms thereof.[27]

According to this theory, the changing stages of the circulation of blood, humors and energies in the body provide many indicators for healthy and unhealthy developments, and for the balance or imbalance of the organs and their humoral state. Unani physicians maintain that all diseases originate from a disbalancing of one of the simple organs. They argue that infection by microbes can only affect a weakened body, so those are consequently seen as only the secondary causes of a disease. The basic circular model is used as a basis for both diagnostics and therapy. The diagnostics used to be based on a combination of pulse and urine analysis. These have been increasingly complemented with laboratory tests, which are nowadays used without hesitation

---

27   Ibid., 567–90.

by Unani physicians of all schools. Although laboratory tests are regarded as based purely on science, Unani physicians do not view them as being restricted to use in biomedicine. On the contrary, they are eager to collect laboratory results for the documentation of their own therapeutic successes. This is common among Unani physicians in India as well as in Pakistan, who readily show the documentation of their successful treatments to visitors.[28] As already mentioned above, the *hawa'* ("wind") component of the blood evokes the role of *vata* ("wind") as a source of movement for the human body in Ayurveda and seems to further strengthen the dynamic character of Sabir Multani's model.

Unani physicians belonging to Sabir Multani's schools are well-known for their continuing attachment to the practice of urine and pulse diagnostics, something that has earned them the respect of other Unani physicians, who have by now often abandoned these traditional forms of diagnostics. The differences in color and viscosity of the urine are interpreted according to the scheme described above.[29] In terms of therapy, the school has become known for its preference for simple drugs and dietary applications, which are used to restore the stability and harmony of a disbalanced system of organs. This distinguishes them from other Unani physicians, who largely depend on compound drugs and the widespread *qarabadin* ("pharmacopoeia") literature that has dealt with them in South Asia for centuries. In this respect, as in so many others, the school of Sabir Multani clearly differs from the Graeco-Islamic medical tradition on the Subcontinent.

The tendency among adherents of the Simple Organ Theory to extend their triadic and hexadic schemes to diverse aspects of the bodily system – and possibly beyond – and to establish their mutual correspondences is articulated with remarkable clarity, including in their classification of human emotions and related physiological secretions (no. 16 in table 3.1):

1. neuronal – muscular: fear (*khawf*) – immediate inward-direction (*inqibad*) of the soul (*nafs*), stopping secretion.
2. muscular – neuronal: lust (*ladhdhat*) – slow direction inward and outward.
3. muscular – glandular: joy (*masarrat*) – slow outward direction (*inbisat*) of the soul, slowly stimulating secretion.

---

28 Kira Schmidt Stiedenroth, "Beyond Evidence: Eminence and Therapeutic Success in Unani (Greco-Islamic) Medicine," *Asian Medicine* 14, no. 2 (2019), https://doi.org/10.1163/15734218-12341450.
29 See the translation from Multani made by Bahrinipour, "Grundgesetze," 45–48.

4. glandular – muscular: grief (*ghamm*) – slow inward direction (*inqibad*) of the soul, slowly stopping secretion.
5. glandular – neuronal: shame (*sharmindagi*) – immediate inward and outward direction of the soul.
6. neuronal – glandular: rage (*ghussa*) – immediate outward direction (*inbisat*) of the soul.

This scheme also presupposes therapeutic value in the stimulation, calming or dissolution of emotions. Hakim Muhammad Siddiq Shahin, a prominent disciple of Sabir Multani who is the author of several books on the Simple Organ Theory and a very famous therapist, is said to have not hesitated to insult even prominent patients when trying to stimulate their liver in order to activate the secretion of yellow bile. He obviously considered the ensuing rage healthy. Imbalances of the humors and of the stages in which they are involved during their circulation are also regarded as the initial cause for emotional disorders like melancholy.

5   Simple Organ Theory and Sufi Theosophy in a Sufi Center in the Punjab

The religious dimension of Sabir Multani's Simple Organ Theory has already been touched upon. It can be seen mainly in the final triad (19) of table 3.1, whose intense connection with the religious landscape of Pakistan is certainly striking. Multani's strong Sufi background certainly played a role in his effort to base his therapeutic approach to the human body and psyche on a merger of medical, scientific and religious categories. The importance of the Sufi aspects of his doctrine is further attested to in the outlook of a Sufi medical center in Sargodha, Pakistan, which runs its own hospital. The Al-Khair Free Tibbi Hospital was founded as a simple therapeutic unit in 1964 by the Qadiri Sufi Hakim Akbar Ali Naseem. Administratively overseen by his NGO, the Anjuman Astan-e Fazal (Sargodha),[30] the hospital was upgraded in 1984 with indoor and outdoor departments. The treatments given to patients there follow the Simple Organ Theory, a topic about which the hospital's founder published several books of his own.[31] One of these is a monograph on laboratory tests and their

---

30 See their page "Astan-e Fazal," Facebook page, accessed April 17, 2020, www.facebook.com/Astan-e-Fazal-243403589156652.
31 Akbar 'Ali Nasim, *Tibb ke na'i Ufuq* (Sargodha: Anjuman Astan-i Fazal, 2008); idem, *Tibb awr Lebaratri Test* (Sargodha: Anjuman Astan-i Fazal, 2009); idem, *Fayzan-i Tibb* (Sargodha: Anjuman Astan-i Fazal, 2010).

application, which testifies to the above-noted great importance given to this diagnostic tool among contemporary Unani physicians. Apart from the hospital, although in close proximity to it, the Anjuman Astan-e Fazal maintains a Sufi congregational center (*mahfil-khana*) and also another building which is crowned by a large earth globe that turns along with the changing time of the day and is described as "World Wonder Moving Globe" on their posters and in their publications.[32] As can be gleaned from the website, this center continues its activities, even though the founder was killed some years ago, apparently by an anti-Sufi assailant.

The Anjuman Astan-e Fazal also publishes didactic posters of medical-cum-religious content. One of them (figure 3.3) shows the position of man in the universe, as God's "masterpiece" (*shahkar*) and most dignified creature, along with the relations of the parts of the human body with the different forces and elements of the created world. The cosmology laid out in its upper part is shaped entirely by Sufi theosophy, with the world originating in God, the "necessary being" (*wajib al-wujud*), and in the three "immutable entities" (*aʿyan thabita*), which are levels of His unity (*ahadiyyat, wahdat, wahidiyyat*). The created world begins with the "external entities" (*aʿyan kharija*) of the spheres of spirit (*ruh*), image (*mithal*) and body (*jism*). Following these six spheres, man originates in the seventh stage of creation. This scheme shows a strong influence from the cosmology of the Andalusian Sufi Ibn ʿArabi (d. 1240), and it also celebrates the unique position of man as God's vicegerent on Earth, who has been endowed by his loving creator with an unlimited wealth of qualities. Despite being only like a dot in the vast universe, he finds himself at its center wherever he looks, passing from the helplessness of his childhood on to adulthood and then in his old age becoming a traveler on his way to God.

The circular image at the center of the poster shows the position of man and his body within the natural world. The human figure in the middle and its bodily parts are related through a series of fourteen circles to the twelve segments of the zodiac and then to the planets and days. Further astrological information is given for professions and areas of study and for the preferable ascendant of the marital partner. Other correlations include metals, precious stones, colors, birthday numbers and the first letter of one's name, followed by illnesses, blood groups (!), humors and temperaments, as well as useful food and pharmaceuticals. The fact that only three humors are mentioned and blood is lacking and replaced by a reference to blood groups shows the clear influence of the Simple Organ Theory, as followed by the founder of the center.

---

32 Picture on the cover of their Facebook website.

The outermost circle includes correlations with the divine names, thus providing a bridge towards the transcendental spheres described in the poster's upper portion.

Apart from the influence of the Simple Organ Theory, it can be noted that the correlation of the human body and its parts with the zodiacal signs follows a model found in late medieval Europe, the so-called "zodiac man," or "man of signs" (*homo signorum*) in Latin. This model was used to indicate periods when operations and bloodletting from specific parts and organs were to be avoided, due to the influence of the respective zodiac sign. The transmission of this image of a "zodiac man" within Middle Eastern and South Asian Muslim culture remains to be further documented,[33] and possible models for this complex circular diagram are yet to be traced. At any rate, it may serve here as a striking example of the attempted synthesis of older medical traditions with modern scientific categories, something that is so characteristic of Sabir Multani and his school. The theosophical cosmology depicted in the poster illustrates the strong connection of Graeco-Islamic Medicine with Sufism in Indian Islam, which has already been studied in depth by Fabrizio Speziale[34] and which seems to have survived among a good number of Unani practitioners in Pakistan. Sufism and medicine are merged in a cosmic optimism which sees man as God's masterpiece in the created world. As a younger Hakim in Pakistan put it during my visit in 2013: "A *Tabib* who wants to be a *Hakim* has to be a *Sufi*."

This does not mean that, in the Pakistani context, Sabir Multani's school is only represented among the Sufi-oriented circles in the country. One of its prominent Hakims whose clinic we visited in Lahore was Muhammad Rafiq Shahin (brother of Hakim Muhammad Siddiq Shahin and editor of his writings), who belonged to the *Ahl-i Hadith*. But the Sufi dimension of Multani's school remains significant and it strongly differs in this respect from the general outlook of the institutions of Unani Medicine in present-day India. A sense of equal footing and even superiority *vis-à-vis* "Western" medicine and

---

33 On the roots of the "Zodiac man" in antiquity, see Charles West Clark, "The Zodiac Man in Medieval Medical Astrology" (PhD diss., University of Colorado, 1979). A sample from fifteenth-century Germany can be found in Ad Stijnman, Stefanie Gehrke and Berram Lesser, "Medizin unter dem Einfluss der Sterne: Der Tierkreiszeichenmann," in *Die Sterne lügen nicht: Astrologie und Astronomie im Mittelalter und in der Frühen Neuzeit*, Exhibition catalogue, ed. Christian Heitzmann (Wolfenbüttel: Herzog August Bibliothek, 2008). For an example from nineteenth-century Iran, see a manuscript at the Wellcome Library, "The Zodiac Man: Watercolor Painting by a Persian Artist," Wellcome Collection, accessed April 17, 2020, https://wellcomecollection.org/works/rmeas6b2.

34 Speziale, *Soufisme, religion et médecine*.

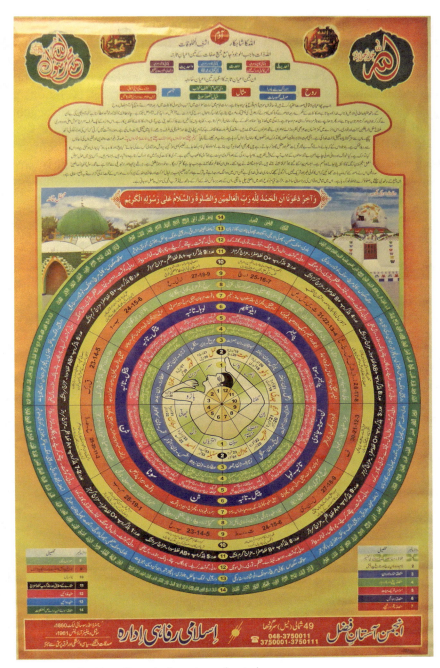

FIGURE 3.3 Position of man in the universe (poster).
ANJUMAN ASTAN-E FAZAL, SARGODHA (PUNJAB); COLLECTED BY SAIM JAMIL (OKARA), MAY 13, 2013.
IMAGE: STEFAN REICHMUTH.

other Indian medical traditions is shared by many Unani practitioners in both India and Pakistan, even if the institutional struggle for full public recognition of their own medical school still persists.[35]

Only a very preliminary and in many ways superficial description of Sabir Multani's reworking of the Unani medical tradition, regarded as revolutionary by his adherents, could be given here, and also the development of his school would certainly deserve further in-depth research. If anything, his medical theories and their impact illustrate the dynamics of cultural change within the Muslim societies of South Asia, the description and analysis of which have been among Jamal Malik's major contributions to the field of Islamic Studies.

Bibliography

Ahmed, Anna Fatima and Mansoor Ahmed. "Ernährungsberatung Mirza & Ahmed nach Avicenna." Accessed April 14, 2020, www.ernaehrungsberatung-avicenna.de/mirza-ahmed.

Ali, Jaffar. "Qanoon E Mufrad Aza: A Revolution to Health Science, What is Qanoon E Mufrad Aza: Also known as Simple Organ Theory." Blog. Accessed April 17, 2020, https://qanoonemufradaza.blogspot.com/2016/08/basicprinciples-of-qanoon-e-mufrad-azaa.html.

Anjuman Astan-e Fazal. "Astan-e Fazal." Facebook page. Accessed April 17, 2020, www.facebook.com/Astan-e-Fazal-243403589156652.

Attewell, Guy. *Refiguring Unani Tibb: Plural Healing in Late Colonial India*. Hyderabad: Orient BlackSwan, 2007.

Azmi, Altaf Ahmad. *History of Unani Medicine in India*. New Delhi: Centre for History of Medicine and Science, Jamia Hamdard, 2004.

Bahrinipour, Amir. "Grundgesetze der Medizin: Von Saber Multani, veröffentlicht 1.02.1958." Accessed April 17, 2020, www.bahrinipour.de/upload/file/Grundlagen.pdf.

Bode, Maarten. *Taking Traditional Knowledge to the Market: The Modern Image of the Ayurvedic and Unani Industry 1980–2000*. Hyderabad: Orient BlackSwan, 2008.

Bright, Kristy. "The Travelling Tonic: Tradition, Commodity, and the Body in Unani (Graeco-Arab) Medicine in India." PhD diss., University of California, 1998.

Clark, Charles West. "The Zodiac Man in Medieval Medical Astrology." PhD diss., University of Colorado, 1979.

---

35   See especially the recent studies by Schmidt Stiedenroth, "Beyond Evidence," and *Unani Medicine in the Making*, especially Chapter 5, 193–226.

Ernst, Waltraud, ed. *Plural Medicine: Tradition and Modernity, 1800–2000*. London and New York: Routledge, 2002.

Faruqi, Rahbar. *Islami Tibb Shahana Sar-Parastiyun Men*. Hyderabad: Aʿzam Esteem Press, 1937.

"Free Tibbi Camp." Facebook group. Accessed April 14, 2020, www.facebook.com/tibbicamp/posts/only-qanoon-mufrad-aza-hukuma-mareez-ko-elaj-tajwiz-kejiye/239884546162015.

Gilbert, Scott F. *Developmental Biology*. 7th ed. Sunderland, MA: Sinauer Associates, 2003.

Ibn Sina, Abu ʿAli al-Hussain ibn ʿAli. *Al-Qanun fi al-Tibb*, vol. 1, edited by Muhammad Amin al-Dannawi. Beirut: Dar al-Kutub al-ʿIlmiyya, 1999.

Ibn Sina, Abu ʿAli al-Hussain ibn ʿAli. *Al-Qānūn fiʾl-Ṭibb: English Translation of the Critical Arabic Text, Book I*. Trans. anon. New Delhi: Department of Islamic Studies, Jamia Hamdard, 1993.

Ibn Sina, Abu ʿAli al-Hussain ibn ʿAli. *A Treatise on the Canon of Medicine of Avicenna*. Translated by Oskar Cameron Gruner. New York: AMS Press, 1973 [1930].

Jaggi, Om Prakash. *History of Science and Technology in India*, vol. 8, *Medicine in Medieval India*. Delhi: Atma Ram & Sons, 1977.

Khan, Usmanghani, Aftab Saeed and Muhammad Tanweer Alam. *Indusyunic Medicine: Traditional Medicine of Herbal, Animal and Mineral Origin in Pakistan*. Karachi: University of Karachi, 1997.

Lelyveld, David. *Aligarh's First Generation: Muslim Solidarity in British India*. Princeton: Princeton University Press, 1978.

Liebeskind, Claudia. "Arguing Science: Unani Tibb, Hakims and Biomedicine in India, 1900–1950." In *Plural Medicine: Tradition and Modernity, 1800–2000*, edited by Waltraud Ernst, 58–75. London and New York: Routledge, 2002.

Mahmudian, Puyan and Stefan Reichmuth. "Qāsim ibn Quṭb ibn Yaʿqūb, Ḥikmat-i Sulaymān-Šāhī." Perso-Indica. Accessed 17, April 2020, www.perso-indica.net/work/medicine/hikmat-i_sulayman-sahi.

Malik, Jamal. *Islamische Gelehrtenkultur in Nordindien: Entwicklungsgeschichte und Tendenzen am Beispiel von Lucknow*. Leiden: Brill, 1997.

Malik, Jamal. *Islam in South Asia: A Short History*. Leiden: Brill, 2008.

Malik, Jamal. *Islam in South Asia: Revised, Enlarged and Updated Second Edition*. Leiden: Brill, 2020.

Mehmood, Hakeem Mohammad Khalid. "Simple Organ Theory: A Revolution in the Medical Science." Accessed April 17, 2020, https://hakeemkhalid.com/sot.html.

Metcalf, Barbara Daly. *Islamic Revival in British India: Deoband, 1860–1900*. Princeton: Princeton University Press, 1982.

Meulenbeld, G. Jan. "The Constraints of Theory in the Evolution of Nosological Classification: A Study on the Position of Blood in Indian Medicine (Āyurveda)."

In *Medical Literature from India, Sri Lanka, and Tibet*, vol. 3, edited by G. Jan Meulenbeld, 91–106. Leiden: Brill, 1991.

Multani, Sabir. "Firangi Tibb Ghayr 'Ilmi awr Ghalat he." In *Multani, Kulliyyat-i Tahqiqat-i Sabir Multani*, edited by Hakim 'Urwa Wahid Sulaymani, vol. 1, 181–285. Lahore: Idara-i Matbu'at-i Sulaymani, 2012.

Multani, Sabir. *Kulliyyat-i Tahqiqat-i Sabir Multani*, 2 vols., edited by Hakim 'Urwa Wahid Sulaymani. Lahore: Idara-i Matbu'at-i Sulaymani, 2012.

Nasim, Akbar 'Ali. *Fayzan-i Tibb*. Sargodha: Anjuman Astan-i Fazal, 2010.

Nasim, Akbar 'Ali. *Tibb awr Lebaratri Test*. Sargodha: Anjuman Astan-i Fazal, 2009.

Nasim, Akbar 'Ali. *Tibb ke na'i Ufuq*. Sargodha: Anjuman Astan-i Fazal, 2008.

Preckel, Claudia. "Healing the People and the Princes: Hospitals, Ḥakīms and Doctors in Bhopal." In *Hospitals in Iran and India, 1500–1950s*, edited by Fabrizio Speziale, 191–214. Leiden: Brill, 2012.

Reichmuth, Stefan. "Wissen, Praxis und pluraler kultureller Kontext der graeco-islamischen Medizin (*yūnānī ṭibb*/Unani Medicine) in Nordindien." In *Muslim Bodies: Body, Sexuality and Medicine in Muslim Societies*, edited by Susanne Kurz, Claudia Preckel and Stefan Reichmuth, 357–406. Berlin and Münster: LIT Verlag, 2016.

Schmidt Stiedenroth, Kira. "Beyond Evidence: Eminence and Therapeutic Success in Unani (Greco-Islamic) Medicine." *Asian Medicine* 14, no. 2 (2019): 209–32, https://doi.org/10.1163/15734218-12341450.

Schmidt Stiedenroth, Kira. *Unani Medicine in the Making: Practices and Representations in 21st-Century India*. Amsterdam: Amsterdam University Press, 2020.

Shahin, Hakim Muhammad Siddiq. *Mukhtasar Qanun-i Mufrad A'za'*. Lahore: Maktabah Danyal, n.d. [1974].

Speziale, Fabrizio. *Culture persane et médecine ayurvédique en Asie du Sud*. Leiden: Brill, 2018.

Speziale, Fabrizio. "'Muslim or Greek?' Past and Present of Muslim Traditional Medicine in the Deccan Sultanates." In *Global Medical Geography: Essays in Honour of Prof. Yola Verhasselt*, edited by Rais Akhtar and Nilofar Izhar, 305–34. Jaipur: Rawat Publications, 2010.

Speziale, Fabrizio. *Soufisme, religion et médecine en Islam indien*. Paris: Karthala, 2010.

Speziale, Fabrizio. "The Persian Translation of the *Tridoṣa*: Lexical Analogies and Conceptual Incongruities." *Asiatische Studien* 68, no. 3 (2014), 783–96.

Speziale, Fabrizio, ed. *Hospitals in Iran and India, 1500–1950s*. Leiden: Brill, 2012.

Stijnman, Ad, Stefani Gehrke and Berram Lesser. "Medizin unter dem Einfluss der Sterne: Der Tierkreiszeichenmann." In *Die Sterne lügen nicht: Astrologie und Astronomie im Mittelalter und in der Frühen Neuzeit*, Exhibition catalogue, edited by Christian Heitzmann, 39–47. Wolfenbüttel: Herzog August Bibliothek, 2008.

Vanzan, Anna. "Hamdard, How to Share Pain in a Muslim Way." In *Hospitals in Iran and India, 1500–1950s*, edited by Fabrizio Speziale, 215–29. Leiden: Brill, 2012.

Wellcome Library. "The Zodiac Man: Watercolour Painting by a Persian Artist." Wellcome Collection. Accessed April 17, 2020, https://wellcomecollection.org/works/rmeas6b2.

Yasin, Hakim Muhammad. *Ta'aruf: Qanun-i Mufrad A'za'*. Dunyapur and Lahore: Yasin Dawakhana wa-Tibbi Kutubkhana. Accessed April 17, 2020, https://archive.org/details/TarufQanoonMufradAzaTibbBook/mode/2up.

Zillur Rahman, Sayyid. "Indian Hakims: Their Role in the Medical Care of India." In *History of Science, Philosophy and Culture in Indian Civilization*, vol. 4. 2. *Medicine and life Sciences in India*, edited by B.V. Subbarayappa, 292–325. New Delhi: Centre for Studies in Civilizations, 2001.

PART 2

Islamic Activism and Radicalism

∵

CHAPTER 4

Peaceful and Militant Interpretations of Jihad
A Comparative Study of Contemporary South Asian Exegetes

Tariq Rahman

1   Introduction

In May of 2005, Professor Jamal Malik invited me to a conference on Islamic seminaries at the University of Erfurt. The proceedings of that conference were published as *Madrasas in South Asia: Teaching Terror?*. It was the question in the sub-title which was the crux of the matter in our post-9/11 world. Malik left the answers about specific regions of South Asia to others, but he gave a theoretical formulation which puts Islamist radicalism in perspective. He suggested that global modernization assumes a universalizing code and is state-led. So, it "is met with counter-globalization(s) which at the same time takes recourse to the imagined concept of *umma* and also indigenizes global Islamic knowledge."[1] The terms "political Islam," "Islamism," "Islamist radicalism" and even the pejorative "Islamic terrorism" and "Islamic militancy" (in the context of the "War on Terror") were discussed. The concept of "jihad," and the fact that it is often used interchangeably with all the terms mentioned above in journalistic writings, was also addressed, though in passing. Later, I decided to find out how this concept has been interpreted, especially by the authors of Urdu commentaries on the Quran in South Asia. The present chapter is based upon this endeavor.

The term jihad, often understood as "holy war" enjoined upon Muslims by their religion, is a part of the everyday vocabulary of international affairs. Most Muslims insist that jihad refers to fighting in self-defense as well as to the quest for moral improvement. Yet some —Islamists, radicals, militants and the like – assert vociferously that it is the duty of all Muslims to fight against the "West" and/or the rulers of their own countries, and that this must go on continuously until these foes are either eradicated or subdued under Islamic rule. Indeed,

---

[1] Jamal Malik, "Introduction," in *Madrasas in South Asia: Teaching Terror?*, ed. Jamal Malik (London and New York: Routledge, 2008), 11.

there is much debate about what Islam *really* says about jihad. This chapter[2] focuses on how peaceful and militant interpretations of jihad are arrived at by some South Asian exegetes using hermeneutic – the term is used interchangeably with "interpretive" – devices for understanding the foundational texts of Islam, namely the Quran and the hadith.

There are many studies on jihad, both by Western and non-Western scholars (Muslims among them), and it would take too much space to discuss these at any length. However, the ones which are relevant for this essay, are mentioned here. One such study is the American academic Asma Afsaruddin's book, *Striving in the Path of God*. Her conclusion is that the Quran "advocates only limited, defensive fighting when peaceful overtures and stoic, non-violent resistance have failed and the adversary attacks first. The religious affiliation of the adversary in itself is irrelevant."[3] Ayesha Jalal, a famous historian of Pakistan, also considers jihad as defensive. She asserts that "the Qur'an does not lend itself well to the notion of jihad as holy war, and far less to the idea of continuous warfare against infidels, how did this discrepancy between the text and the later, legally based interpretations of the concept arise?"[4] Still, Afsaruddin refers to the Quran, its exegeses in Arabic and the hadith for argumentation, whereas Jalal does not analyze the concept of jihad with reference to the Quran in her book. She assumes, on the basis of a hadith which does not occur in any of the six collections of hadiths considered authentic by Sunni Muslims,[5] that jihad means the quest for moral improvement.

This study follows Afsaruddin's methodology by focusing upon Quranic exegeses, though those she examined are in Arabic, while the ones used in this study are in Urdu. Focus here is laid on exegeses of the Quran by two modernists and two Islamist militants. The modernists are Jawed Ahmad Ghamidi (b. 1951) of Pakistan and Maulana Wahiduddin Khan (b. 1925) of India.[6] The

---

2   This piece is based on my recent book *Interpretations of Jihad in South Asia: An Intellectual History* (Berlin: de Gruyter, 2018; Karachi: Oxford University Press, 2019; New Delhi: Orient BlackSwan, 2020).
3   Asma Afsaruddin, *Striving in the Path of God: Jihād and Martyrdom in Islamic Thought* (New York: Oxford University Press, 2013), 297.
4   Ayesha Jalal, *Partisans of Allah: Jihad in South Asia* (Cambridge, MA: Harvard University Press, 2008), 7.
5   See Annexure below, no. 5. There is, however, a hadith which says "the struggler is one who struggles against his self" (*al-mujahid man jahad nafsahu*). This hadith has been used by Shibli Nu'mani and Sulaiman Nadwi, *Sirat al-Nabi*, vol. 5 (Lahore: Al-Faisal, 1991), 224. Ayesha Jalal, in common with many who use the weak (*da'if*) hadith mentioned above, do not use this, though it is considered more authentic by scholars.
6   For brief notes on both, see Jamal Malik, *Islam in South Asia: Revised, Enlarged and Updated Second Edition* (Leiden: Brill, 2020). In particular, see Ghamidi's Annexure 14, 579–82 and Wahiduddin Khan's Annexure 15, 615–18.

militants are Hafiz Mohammad Sa'id (b. 1948) and Maulana Mas'ud Azhar (b. 1968), both from Pakistan. I have taken two verses from the ninth chapter of the Quran (*Surat al-Tawba*) and compared the different ways they have been explained by the above writers. Both verses are explained with reference to certain interpretive devices which are explained succinctly below. These verses are:

> Q 9:5:[7] Then, when the sacred months have passed, slay the idolaters wherever ye find them, and take them (captive), and besiege them, and prepare for them each ambush. But if they repent and establish worship and pay the poor due, then leave their way free. Lo! Allah is Forgiving, Merciful.

> Q 9:29: Fight against such of those who have been given the Scripture as believe not in Allah nor the Last Day, and forbid not that which Allah has forbidden by His messenger, and follow not the Religion of Truth, until they pay the tribute readily, being brought low.[8]

2 Definitions of Terms

The expression "radical Islamist" is used here for people or groups who believe it is justified to use violence to create an Islamic state or fight "Western" powers which, in their perception, exploit Muslims or prevent Islam from gaining political ascendancy over the world. Other studies, generally by political scientists, often use the term "Islamism" for the expression given above. Islamism is defined by Volpi in his introduction to *Political Islam* as "the political dynamics generated by the activities of those people who believe that Islam as a body of faith has something crucial to say about how society should be organized, and who seek to implement this idea as a matter of priority."[9] However, it is true to say that "actual Islamist groups do not necessarily fall neatly into either of these ideal-type categories." Moreover, "movements frequently change their

---

7 The abbreviation Q is used for the Quran, which is followed by the chapter (*sura*) and verse number.
8 Translation is from Marmaduke Pickthall, *The Holy Qur'an: Arabic Texts with Transliteration in Roman and English Translation* (Karachi: Iqbal Book Depot, 1989).
9 Frédéric Volpi, "Introduction: Critically Studying Political Islam," in *Political Islam: A Critical Reader*, ed. Frédéric Volpi (Abingdon: Routledge, 2011).

identity over time, becoming more radicalized or more 'mainstream'."[10] But our interest is in the ideas of those who believe in initiating wars, attacks and armed insurrections with reference to "Islamic referents – terms, symbols and events taken from the Islamic tradition."[11]

The term "modernist" is used for interpreters of Islam who seek to "rethink or adapt Muslim institutions, norms, and discourses in the light both of what they take to be 'true' Islam, as opposed to how the Islamic tradition evolved in history, and of how they see the challenges and opportunities of modernity."[12] The term "progressive" is reserved for contemporary Muslim interpreters who basically share the same concerns, though they operate in a post-colonial situation rather than a colonial one. There are, despite some continuities, differences between the two situations which warrant the use of disparate terms for both.[13]

Let us now look at the interpretive devices which are mentioned in this study. One of these is to argue about meaning as constructed by words (*lugha*) and the entire range of meanings implicit in these words, including denotations and connotations (*ma'na*). Since words can have several alternative meanings and even more connotations, exegetes resort to what may be called semantic expansion in order to produce interpretations that they prefer. For instance, the word "*fitna*" – literally meaning to heat, to melt but metaphorically expanded to include some great trial or trouble – in the verses Q 2:193 and Q 8:39, both of which order the Muslims to fight till there is no more *fitna*, hinges on the meaning of this term. If *fitna* refers to the persecution the early Muslim community faced, then there is no need to fight once this comes to an end. However, if it means unbelief, then the fighting will never come to an end.

Another device used very often by classical exegetes is abrogation (*naskh*). Among the classical writings on it are Abu 'Abd Allah ibn Idris al-Shafi'i's (d. 810) *Risala* and 'Ubayd al-Qasim ibn Sallam's (d. 839) *Al-Nasikh wa al-Mansukh fi al-Qur'an*. The understanding of the concept of *naskh* is that it refers to "abrogation or annulment of a divine ruling by a later divine ruling."[14] Another

---

10 Guilain Denoeux, "The Forgotten Swamp: Navigating Political Islam," in *Political Islam*, ed. Frédéric Volpi, 70.
11 Ibid., 60.
12 Muhammad Qasim Zaman, *Modern Islamic Thought in a Radical Age: Religious Authority and Internal Criticism* (Cambridge: Cambridge University Press, 2012), 2.
13 For a more detailed discussion, see Rahman, *Interpretations of Jihad*, 1–2.
14 David S. Powers, "The Exegetical Genre *Nāsikh al-Qur'ān wa Mansūkhuhu*," in *Approaches to the History of the Interpretation of the Qur'ān*, ed. Andrew Rippin (Oxford: Clarendon Press, 1988); John Burton, *The Sources of Islamic Law: Islamic Theories of Abrogation* (Edinburgh: Edinburgh University Press, 1990); Abu 'Ubayd al-Qasim ibn Sallam,

interpretive device is using the occasion for the revelation of a Quranic verse, the *asbab al-nuzul* ("reasons for revelation"), to determine its significance. The main person mentioned in connection with this kind of exegesis is Abu al-Hasan 'Ali ibn Ahmad al-Wahidi al-Nisaburi (d. 1075). His book, *Kitab Asbab Nuzul al-Qur'an,* became a model for later exegetes and is widely available even now.[15] The method of appealing to the circumstances of a given revelation may make verses "specific for a certain time and place" (*takhsis al-zaman wa al-makan*). Thus peaceful interpretations of jihad can be created by restricting aggressive warfare to only apply to use against Arab polytheists (as in Q 9:5) on the basis of the causes of the revelation of that verse.

While the above interpretive devices have traditionally been used by exegetes of the Quran, there are others which are used more by modernists. One of these is privileging principles over particulars. A major protagonist of this approach is the Pakistani scholar Fazlur Rahman, who calls it "double movement":

> First, one must move from the concrete case treatments of the Qur'ān – taking the necessary and relevant social conditions of that time into account – to the general principles upon which the entire teaching converges. Second, from this general level there must be a movement back to specific legislation, taking into account the necessary and relevant social conditions now obtaining.[16]

The idea is that one should not be preoccupied with the literal meaning of words in the foundational texts of Islam, but instead focus on the spirit which lies behind them. Thus, if a certain practice was made more humane in seventh-century Arabia, then it should become even more humane in the modern age.

It seems, however, that a major interpretive device people use, sometimes knowingly and sometimes not, is ideological imperative (or ideological assumptions). People come to a text with certain ideas about it based on their overall worldview or ideology. These ideological assumptions color their

---

Al-Nâsikh wa'l-Mansûkh fî'l-Qur'ân/ The Abrogating and Abrogated in the Koran, ed. Fuat Sezgin (Frankfurt am Main: Institut für Geschichte der Arabisch-Islamischen Wissenschaften,1985); Louay Fatoohi, *Abrogation in the Qur'an and Islamic Law: A Critical Study of the Concept of "Naskh" and Its Impact* (New York and Oxfordshire: Routledge, 2013).

15 Andrew Rippin, *The Qur'an and Its Interpretative Tradition* (Aldershot: Ashgate, 2001), 1–15. Also see, Muhammad bin Idris al-Shafi'i, *Ash-Shafi'i's Risalah: Basic Ideas,* trans. Khalil I. Semaan (Lahore: Sheikh Muhammad Ashraf, 1961).

16 Fazlur Rahman, *Islam and Modernity: Transformation of an Intellectual Tradition* (Chicago: University of Chicago Press, 1982), 20.

understanding of the meanings of the text. Other related interpretive devices include bias in selection, emphasis or deemphasis of texts which agree or do not agree with one's ideological imperative. For instance, an exegete who favors peace, might emphasize the hadiths about peace, while one who favors war will ignore them, call them weak (*da'if*) or try to restrict them (*takhsis*) to a certain place or people. With these definitions of terms, we can scrutinize how jihad is understood in modern South Asia by radical Islamist militants and modernist interpreters.

3   Militant Islamist Interpretations

While Syed Abul A'la Mawdudi's (1903–2003) significant work on jihad, *Al-Jihad fi al- Islam*, was not given the centrality it deserves in tracing out his journey towards a radical theoretical framing of the concept of jihad until Jamal Malik drew attention towards it,[17] recent work has attempted to suggest that he was the pioneer of political Islam in South Asia.[18] Because of a paucity of space, however, we shall have to direct the reader to other sources for Mawdudi's thought while focusing here on the Islamist radicals from Pakistan mentioned earlier. Let us begin with the interpretations of jihad by Hafiz Muhammad Sa'id. He is said to have liked verses about jihad even in childhood when he memorized the Quran – hence the title *hafiz* (one who remembers the Quran by heart). Most of his family members, like himself, are involved in Islamic organizations, such as his brother-in-law, 'Abd al-Rahman Makki (b. 1948), who is his "close partner and holds a powerful position in his *Markaz* at Muridke."[19] Sa'id was influenced by 'Abdullah 'Azzam (d. 1989) and Shaikh 'Abd al-'Aziz bin Baz (d. 1999), the Grand Mufti of Saudi Arabia, and his organization was supported at some level by Osama bin Laden.[20] Thus, he imbibed radical Islamist ideas from these Arab militant sources in addition to developing some of his own.

Sa'id's ideas have been disseminated in the form of sermons, pamphlets and on the website of Lashkar-e-Tayyaba (LT). They have also been discussed

---

17   Jamal Malik, "Maudūdī's *al-Jihād fī'l-Islām*: A Neglected Document," *Zeitschrift für Religionswissenschaft* 17 (2009).
18   Among others, see Rahman, *Interpretations of Jihad*, 167–92.
19   Amir Mir, *The Fluttering Flag of Jehad* (Lahore: Mashal Books, 2008), 162.
20   Samina Yasmeen, *Jihad and Dawah: Evolving Narratives of Lashkar-e-Taiba and Jamat ud Dawah* (London: Hurst & Co., 2017), 58.

in great detail by Yasmeen, Fair and Wilson.[21] The gist of studies about the narratives offered by Saʿid himself as well as by other members of his organization is that jihad is a duty for every Muslim in the absence of the Islamic State. Moreover, Saʿid negates the ideas that: (a) jihad needs to be ordered by the state; (b) it is not incumbent upon Pakistani Muslims since they have not been attacked; (c) international treaties would have to be renounced before any attack; and (d) Pakistan is too militarily and economically weak to win a war, and thus it should not initiate one. He maintains, like ʿAbdullah ʿAzzam and Osama bin Laden, that if there is no Muslim ruler ready to order jihad openly, the Muslim community can choose one for that purpose and, as he himself is the head (*amir*) of his organization, it is implied that he is the one who has been *de facto* chosen. He claims, again like the two Arab militant leaders mentioned above, that Muslims have indeed been attacked. In this context, he presents the case of Kashmir, which he says has been occupied by India illegally and is being subjected to human rights abuses. Given this situation, he argues that India has already broken international peace agreements, so he is merely responding defensively on behalf of Pakistan. As for the last point, he refers to the small size of the Muslim army at the Battle of Badr *vis-à-vis* the Quraysh, arguing that it is courage and faith which are needed and not military superiority. Indeed, when his fighters as well as regular Pakistani soldiers had to withdraw from the Kargil peaks, which they had occupied in 1999, he quoted seven verses of the *Surat al-Maʾida* (Q 5), to argue that Prime Minister Nawaz Sharif (b. 1949) had "gone against Quranic injunctions that prohibit Muslims from befriending Jews and Christians."[22] The relevant parts of those verses can be summarized as follows:

> Q 5:51: Do not take Jews and Christians for friends.
> Q 5:52: Spiritually diseased people run towards them (Jews and Christians) fearing a change of fortune, whereas God can give them victory.
> Q 5:53: The believers will question whether they are the same People of the Book who swore oaths that they were with them (the Muslims) but who have failed them.
> Q 5:54: If Muslims become renegades from their religion, God will bring others to replace them who will strive (*yujahiduna*) in His way.
> Q 5:55: Only God and his Messenger can be your true friends.
> Q 5:56: Those who take God and His Messenger as friends achieve victory.

---

21 Ibid.; C. Christine Fair, *In Their Own Words: Understanding Lashkar-e-Tayyaba* (London: Hurst & Co., 2018); John Wilson, *The Caliphate's Soldiers: The Lashkar-e-Tayyeba's Long War* (New Delhi: Amaryllis Manjul, 2011).

22 Yasmeen, *Jihad and Dawah*, 96.

> Q 5:57: Do not choose as friends the People of the Book and those who disbelieve and make fun of your religion.

The fact that Sa'id interpreted these verses differently from more standard readings and that other verses, such as Q 60:8, which have been interpreted by others to allow friendship with non-belligerent non-Muslims, were not privileged sheds light on his ideological imperative: to fight all non-Muslims, especially Hindus.

Although Sa'id and the members of his organization have disseminated their ideas through a number of sources, the most relevant for our purposes is his exegesis of *Surat al-Tawba* (Q 9). Samina Yasmeen gives a historical account of this work, placing it both in the context of the political situation after the September 11 attacks and the development of Sa'id's thought. It is comprised of lectures to students being trained for jihad at his center in Muridke during the summer of 2004. In the era of America's "War on Terror," Sa'id's aim is to inspire Pakistani Muslims not to give up their struggle against India and to legitimize it with the text of the Quran itself.

Sa'id begins by saying that the infidels who most resemble the Arabs of the seventh century are the Hindus, since they worship many deities. Then he goes on to classify the Jews as those who associate other powers with God (*mushrikun*) on the grounds that they called Ezra ('Uzayr) the son of God. He also alleges that Christians fall in the same category because they worship the trinity. This classification serves the purpose of making the present situation analogous to that of the time when Q 9 was revealed.[23] He lays down rules for declaring Muslims heretics (*takfir*) by arguing that if people call themselves Muslims but neither pray nor give the alms tax, then they are not to be taken at their word. However, their confession of Islam should be taken at face value until this aspect of their behavior becomes evident.[24] Sa'id's main thrust is that it is because Muslims have abandoned jihad that they are oppressed and powerless in the world. His ideas as expressed in his exegesis of Q 9, with reference to other verses dealing with jihad, are summarized below.

In addition to the Quran, Sa'id also uses hadith to support his ideological assumptions that jihad is necessary to enable Muslims to gain glory and power in the world and that it must go on continuously until non-Muslim powers are either eradicated or subdued under Islamic rule. To support the latter view, he uses the hadith that the Prophet was sent to keep fighting till everyone has recited the Muslim creed. This is one of those traditions which is invariably

---

[23] Hafiz Muhammad Sa'id, *Tafsir-e Surat al-Tawba* (Lahore: Darul Andlus, 2006).
[24] Ibid., 609.

TABLE 4.1 Hafiz Muhammad Sa'id's commentary

Verse	Commentary	Interpretive device
Q 9:5	The verse orders fighting unbelievers. It is also applicable nowadays, e.g., in Kashmir, Palestine, Afghanistan and Iraq (p. 40). A local commander for jihad can be appointed just as Abu Bakr was appointed the *amir* of *hajj* and 'Ali was given the responsibility of announcing this verse to the polytheists (p. 39).	generalization; ideological assumption
Q 9:29	Open war with the People of the Book is ordered as their beliefs are wrong till they give *jizya* and live in humiliation (pp. 127–28).	generalization

SOURCE: HAFIZ MUHAMMAD SA'ID, *TAFSIR-E SURAT AL-TAWBA* (LAHORE: DARUL ANDLUS, 2006).

quoted by radical Islamists (see Annexure below). Yet the word "human beings" or "people" (*nas*) used in this account has also been interpreted as meaning the polytheists of that period (seventh-century Arabia); not all people of all times.[25] Sa'id, however, takes the tradition as applying to all people all of the time. He goes on to refute the idea that one should enter into peaceful negotiations with infidels without fighting them because of the Prophet's having done so with the Treaty of Hudaybiyya. He says that this was only to build up military strength to ensure victory. Thus, instead of making peaceful negotiations, one's objective or real aim should be fighting to achieve victory.

While Kashmir is Sa'id's special concern, he praises all Muslims fighting against invasions by non-Muslims, such as the Palestinians. But as for Kashmir, he does not even conceal the fact that he sent armed militants into the

---

25 As mentioned by several scholars, notably Yusuf al-Qaradawi in his *Fiqh al-Jihad: Dirasa Muqarana li-Ahkamihi wa Falsafatihi fi Daw' al-Quran wa al-Sunna* (Cairo: Wahba Press, 2009). Source used in this chapter, Sheikh Rachid al-Ghannouchi, "What is New about al-Qaradawi's Jihad?," in *Twenty-First Century Jihad: Law, Society and Military Action*, ed. Elisabeth Kendall and Ewan Stein (London: I.B. Tauris, 2015). Also see Muhammad Afifi al-Akiti, *Defending the Transgressed by Censuring the Reckless Against the Killing of Civilians: Mudāfi' al-Mazlūm bi Radd al-Muhāmil 'alā Qitāl Man Lā Yuqātil* (Hellenthal: Warda Publications; Birmingham: Aqsa Press, 2005), 31.

Indian-administered part of the former state because, in his opinion, Kashmir is Muslim territory forcibly occupied by India. Indeed, those who have been killed while fighting for Kashmir are remembered in inspirational hagiographies. C. Christine Fair collected 918 such hagiographies of these fighters and points out that they celebrate rather than conceal their being recruited for jihad.[26] In the *tafsir* itself, he mentions how one of his devoted fighters carried out a spectacular attack (*fidayi ma'raka*). The fighter found himself in a military camp in Indian-administered Kashmir. He had dozed off during the night and when he woke up, it was morning and people were up and about. He took aim in the sunlight, killed many soldiers and then walked out peacefully from the camp.[27] Another such case, that of an American called Abu Adam Jibril al-Amriki (d. c. 1997), who attacked Indian army posts in Kashmir, is given in sources proudly owned by the Lashkar.[28]

Sa'id and his associates were temporarily held in custody in the aftermath of the attacks in Mumbai on November 26, 2008. To this adversity, he responded characteristically by using the Quran. He wrote a commentary on Q 12 entitled *Tafsir-e Surat-e Yusuf.* This chapter of the Quran narrates the story of the Prophet Yusuf (Joseph in the Bible's Book of Genesis), who is betrayed by his brothers by being sold into slavery in Egypt. In the story as given in the Quran, he resists the advances of the ruler's wife, and finally ascends to a position of responsibility in the country. In the end, his brothers are humbled and he achieves success. The virtue Sa'id emphasizes in this exegesis is patience in the face of adversity. In his opinion, his own situation is comparable to that of Joseph, since he too is oppressed by the state, his followers are incarcerated and he has to remain steadfast to the cause. He also emphasizes public service in order to claim a high moral ground in the eyes of the public and to ensure survival. Jihad must go on, he says, but at times it is necessary to conceal it.[29]

In this matter, Sa'id's view is different from that of the Arab radicals mentioned earlier in that they justify fighting their own rulers. While vehemently supporting militancy against India, the US and Israel, Sa'id rules out any hostility towards the rulers of Pakistan. Indeed, he specifically claims that he does not allow any attacks to be conducted within Pakistan.[30]

The second militant figure to be discussed here is Mawlana Mas'ud Azhar, whose Jaish-e-Mohammad is alleged to have attacked India several times

---

26   Fair, *In Their Own Words*, 185.
27   Sa'id, *Tafsir-e Surat al-Tawba*, 66.
28   David Cook, *Martyrdom in Islam* (Cambridge: Cambridge University Press, 2007), 183.
29   Hafiz Muhammad Sa'id, *Tafsir-e Surat-e Yusuf* (Lahore: Darul Andlus, 2009), 273–74.
30   Ibid., 319.

and who preaches the necessity of jihad through his lectures, pamphlets and books. At the age of twenty, he went to Afghanistan in order to undertake a course on handling weapons and basic tactics. He apparently got a chance to fight against the Soviets, though the jihad in Afghanistan was winding down. In 1989, still enthusiastic for jihad, he returned to Pakistan and joined the Harakat al-Mujahidin, which was training young men for jihad in Kashmir. Mas'ud was now entrusted with a mission that took him to Srinagar, where he was arrested in February 1994. For several years, he remained incarcerated in jail, but was quite unexpectedly rescued when religious activists hijacked an airplane from Kathmandu and landed it in Kabul, which was then ruled by the Taliban. Back in Pakistan, Mas'ud was welcomed and, it is rumored, facilitated by the Pakistani intelligence services in setting up his own militia called the Jaish-e-Mohammad.

Mas'ud tells us about his career as an author in the preface of his book *Fada'il-e Jihad* ("The Blessings of Jihad"), which is also the name of the genre of writing on jihad, the first work of which was by 'Abd Allah bin al-Mubarak (d. 797). Mubarak's book has 262 hadiths about the rewards for martyrs.[31] Out of these, thirteen discuss beautiful women with large and black eyes in paradise (*hur al-'ayn*) who are married to the martyr and whose charms are superior to those of his earthly wife.[32] This kind of literature was probably written to inspire youths to jihad. In Mas'ud's case too, the purpose was to recruit youths to the project of jihad against India. The book began as a pamphlet in 1994. The author initially put in some Quranic verses and forty Prophetic traditions from *Bukhari* to explain the high religious significance of jihad. One of his major arguments is that jihad was aggressive during the time of the expansion of Islam and those who portray it as being merely defensive are simply misleading the world and causing damage to Muslims, since such misrepresentations dilute their spirit of conquest and resistance. He implores Muslims not to abandon jihad. And this is only possible if, to begin with, Muslims do not concern themselves with theoretical considerations like the "lesser" and the "greater" jihad.[33]

Although the book was reprinted several times, the author always regarded it as an incomplete work.[34] He got a chance to complete it by offering a

---

31   Maher Jarrar, "The Martyrdom of Passionate Lovers: Holy War as a Sacred Wedding," in *Ḥadīth: Origins and Developments*, ed. Harald Motzki (Aldershot: Ashgate, 2004). For some traditions about the blessings of jihad and the high rank of the martyr, see Annexure below.
32   Ibid., 334.
33   Muhammad Mas'ud Azhar, *Fada'il-e Jihad* (Karachi: Maktaba-yi Hasan, 1999), 118.
34   Ibid., 3.

summary and commentary on a book on jihad by Ibn al-Nihas Abu Zakariyya (d. 1411) which belongs to the *fada'il al-jihad* sub-genre of Islamic writing. This particular book captured the attention of Mas'ud, who translated it into Urdu with additions and explanations and published it in 1999. It gave the author an opportunity to disseminate his own views about the ongoing jihad, which he says is already taking place. He narrates that a copy of the book was brought to him in the Tahar Jail in India, where he had no books of reference nor did he have any peace of mind.[35] He then constructs his anti-Western narrative in which he sees the English language and even Western medicine as part of the conspiracy to subdue Muslims. There is, however, a way to overcome Europe and eventually "enslave" it – and that is jihad.[36]

The book itself has chapters on aspects of jihad: the high spiritual position of those who fight, the great rewards of fighters (among them, beautiful women in paradise) and so on. Each chapter begins with verses from the Quran followed by a number of hadiths and quotations from scholars supportive of jihad. At the end of every chapter, Mas'ud gives his own ideas, applying them to the conditions of Pakistan and Afghanistan in particular and the whole world in general. He distinguishes between jihad as a duty discharged by a few people who fight or are professional soldiers (*fard al-kifaya*) and that which is incumbent upon all Muslims (*fard al-'ayn*). The first necessitates attacks or raids on territories held by the infidels at least once a year. This, he says, is not being carried out. Instead, infidel forces are in Muslim lands, which makes jihad a *fard al-'ayn*. Thus, it is not necessary for anyone to acquire permission from authorities, be they familial or governmental.[37] While discussing the duty of guarding the borders of Muslim lands (*ribat*), he asserts that Spain, Eastern Europe and India were all once ruled by Muslims so they too must be considered as within the borders of the Islamic territory. It is only because they were not guarded that they slipped out from Muslim control.[38]

In common with all radical militants, Mas'ud takes pains to refute the traditionally held ideas about jihad among South Asian Muslims. This he does throughout the book and, for further emphasis, he also sums up his views in an annexure. First, he says that if one wants to fight either a single unbeliever or a group of them, no permission from a ruler (*amir*) is required. Likewise, if the ruler has abandoned jihad, then here too no permission is required. If there is no ruler or it is probable that he will not permit jihad, then once

---

35   Ibid., 9–10.
36   Ibid., 11–14.
37   Ibid., 34–36.
38   Ibid., 260–61.

again, no permission is required. And finally, a leader can be appointed by consensus instead of relying on rulers who do not govern according to shariʿa.[39] He also dispenses with the condition that the opponent should be invited to accept Islam before declaring war. This is only necessary if the opponent has never been invited to Islam, but not otherwise. Moreover, if the Muslims have already been attacked, such invitation is out of the question. In the same way, he argues that using fire or cannons and attacking at night are all permissible, even if women and children are present.[40]

In addition to this work, Masʿud also provides an exegesis of those verses of the Quran which directly or indirectly deal with jihad in a four-volume book entitled *Fath al-Jawwad: Fi Maʿarif Ayat al-Jihad* ("The Victory of the Generous One: In the Exposition of the Verses about Jihad").[41] Masʿud uses several interpretative devices to propound the militant understanding of jihad. One of these is interpolation, sometimes parenthetically, while elucidating the meaning of verses. This is generally done in his explanation of the verse and it leads the reader to his preferred meaning. His translation of Q 2:114, which condemns people who forbid others to worship in mosques, deviates from the literal meaning of the text. He claims that mosques should be made secure through jihad. Those who make the mosques desolate will be punished through jihad and their power will be taken away.[42] In Q 2:195, which deals with spending money in the way of God and not putting oneself in destruction, he adds that such expenditure should be on jihad and defines self-destruction as abandoning jihad.[43] While explaining a verse in Q 3, which asks Muslims rhetorically whether they would turn away from Islam if the Prophet were to die, he substitutes jihad for the faith so that the question becomes: "would you people turn away from jihad or Islam [if the Prophet dies]?" (Q 3:144).[44] While explaining the concept of *taghut* – in this case, in a verse in Q 4 which exhorts people to fight for God and not the devil (Q 4:76) – he uses semantic expansion to define *taghut* as not just idol, devil, magician and evil as traditional Arabic dictionaries do. For him, it is any individual, power or philosophy which opposes Islam. Among the examples he gives of such powers are colonial rulers and, at present, the US. Moreover, modern ideologies such as nationalism, capitalism, etc.,

---

39 Ibid., 629–30.
40 Ibid., 630–33.
41 Muhammad Masʿud Azhar, *Fath al-Jawwad fi Maʿarif Ayat al-Jihad*, 4 vols. (Lahore: Maktaba Irfan, 2007).
42 Ibid., vol. 1, 14.
43 Ibid., 45.
44 Ibid., 245.

are also included in the scope of *taghut*. In short, his expanded meaning of the term makes the Quranic command relevant for the targets he has in mind for his mission of jihad.⁴⁵

One of Mas'ud's favorite interpretive devices is semantic expansion. The term "*fitna*" is explained with reference to other exegetes, especially those who think it refers to unbelief.⁴⁶ Yet exegetes who have equated it with the sin of attacking Muslims or persecuting them are passed over in silence.⁴⁷ In a different place, while giving another definition of *fitna* as sin, he calls it the sin of creating differences among Muslims to weaken their military prowess, innovation and tardiness in fighting (*jihad me susti*).⁴⁸ These meanings have implications for interpreting the verses relating to fighting. For instance, the injunctions in Q 2:193 and Q 8:39 – about fighting till *fitna* ends – become orders to wage an eternal war even in contemporary times if the term refers to unbelief. If, however, other meanings are preferred, they can be interpreted differently. Mas'ud says that some classical exegetes take both as general orders while others use the hermeneutic device of specification, applying them to the Arab polytheists of that period. He is of the view that, whether these verses are general or restricted, they refer to *fitna* in the sense of "that power which can threaten Muslims." Hence, they command warfare to break the power of the unbelievers, which actually implies that jihad is an ongoing, valid duty, even in contemporary times.⁴⁹ Below are Mas'ud's explanations of the relevant verses.

Mas'ud makes efforts to explain away verses which advocate living in peace either by citing exegetes who regard them as having been abrogated (*mansukh*) or by giving alternative explanations (*ta'wil*). His ideological assumptions, like those of Hafiz Sa'id, are: jihad is aggressive, the downfall of Muslims is because they have abandoned it, and the current leaders of Muslims are either cowards, apostates or Western stooges who have given up jihad. Hence, verses for peace are also rendered ineffective through his interpretations. For instance, the offer of peace in Q 2:192 – "but if they desist; you do the same" – is interpreted as "desist from unbelief," not "desist from fighting," hence non-aggression is changed to conversion.⁵⁰ Another verse (Q 4:90) – "if they do not fight you, or join people with whom you have a treaty of peace, then do not fight them" – which allows Muslims to live in peace with non-belligerent non-Muslims, has

---

45   Ibid., 385–89.
46   Ibid., 40–41.
47   Ibid., 41.
48   Ibid., vol. 2, 147.
49   Ibid., vol. 2, 388–89.
50   Ibid., vol. 1, 37.

TABLE 4.2   Mas'ud Azhar's commentary

Verse	Commentary	Interpretive device
Q 9:5	Unbelievers may be fought with wherever found. Mas'ud quotes a hadith on four swords: Arab polytheists (Q 9:5); People of the Book (Q 9:29); hypocrites (Q 9:73); and Muslim rebels who fight other Muslims (Q 49:9). It is general and still valid, and it abrogates verses of peace (vol 2: 380–81).	abrogation; generalization
Q 9:29	Fight the People of the Book and other unbelievers for their wrong beliefs till they accept the political dominance of Islam, pay *jizya* and are humiliated (vol 2: 473–81). Mas'ud also explains it with reference to *dhimmi* rules (vol 2: 479).	generalization

SOURCE: MUHAMMAD MAS'UD AZHAR, *FATH AL-JAWWAD* (LAHORE: MAKTABA IRFAN, 2007).

also been explained in such a way that it does not lead to any tenable version of peaceful co-existence.[51]

Mas'ud's commentary on Q 9 gives him a chance to expand upon his philosophy of aggressive jihad and make it relevant to the present context. He explicitly tells contemporary Muslims to obey the order in the verse, suggesting that it has abrogated all the verses allowing peace treaties. While explaining Q 9:8, which is about non-believers not caring for friendship with Muslims when they are powerful, he asserts that non-believers intrinsically hate believers. Here he explicitly mentions the United Nations and human rights organizations which, he claims, are meant to make Muslims lose their spirit for combativeness and give up jihad.[52] He also uses his explanation of Q 9:5 to justify *takfir* (declaring Muslims as unbelievers), which is a practice of radical Islamists. According to him, the verse says that those who say their prayers and give alms will not be killed, which means that these are the only visible signs of being a believing Muslim. By the same logic, those who do not adhere to these two norms of outward behavior may be killed by an Islamic state.[53]

---

51   Ibid., vol. 1, 423.
52   Ibid., vol. 2, 388–89.
53   Ibid., vol. 2, 379.

It will be observed that Mas'ud Azhar uses two discourses to justify jihad. The first is derived from his use of the commentaries of classical jurists and his own interpretations of the verses of the Quran. Using the interpretive devices of semantic expansion, favoring exegetes who consider the pro-peace verses abrogated and giving alternative explanations of such verses, he promotes the discourse of aggressive jihad on theological grounds. The second, however, combines the Muslim grievance of being under attack from non-Muslim powers. This strand of the narrative refers to Palestine, Bosnia, Kashmir and Chechnya, etc. He also justifies suicide attacks on the grounds that in the classical era of Islam, there were examples of single champions attacking an armed host for the greater glory of Islam. If such missions of devotion (*fidayi hamla*) are to intimidate the enemy or to benefit Muslims in war, then they are justified.[54]

4   Modernist Interpretations

Modernist interpretations of Islam in India were a response by Indian intellectuals to the critiques of the Orientalist scholars of the colonial era. Among them, Chiragh 'Ali (1844–1895), a contemporary of Sir Sayyid Ahmed Khan, very spiritedly defended the view of jihad as defensive warfare and especially argued that women cannot be enslaved or taken into concubinage as part of such conflict. His argument is based on *Sura al-Muhammad* (Q 47) – which says that prisoners of war should either be exchanged for money or released as a favor (Q 47:4). This being so, he insists, there is no third alternative for taking prisoners.[55] Later, another world-shaking event, 9/11, provoked South Asian thinkers, including some ulama, to distance themselves from the narratives adduced by radical Islamists to justify violence and the enslavement of women. In India, Mawlana Wahiduddin Khan, who was the President of the Islamic Centre in New Delhi, took the lead in refuting radical Islam. He wrote a number of works, and of these, we first consider his exegesis of the Quran originally written in Urdu and later translated into English. The main points of his exegesis are outlined in the chart below.

As we can see, Wahiduddin Khan's special theory, or ideological imperative, is that if a group of people do not accept guidance from a prophet, especially one sent to reform them, then God himself destroys them (*sunna ilahiyya*).

---

54 Azhar, *Fada'il-e Jihad*, 351–54.
55 Chiragh 'Ali, *Tahdhib al-Kalam fi Haqiqat al-Islam* (Hyderabad, Deccan: Kitab Khana Asifiya, 1918), 219–21.

TABLE 4.3   Wahiduddin Khan's commentary

Verse	Commentary	Interpretive device
Q 9:5	Orders to kill the polytheists and give them no quarter were God's way (*sunna ilahiyya*), and such orders are addressed to prophets only. These orders are specifically meant for the Arab polytheists. Thus, Muslims are not to fight anyone except in defense (vol 1: 463–64).	ideological imperative; specification
Q 9:29	The Jews had been hostile to Islam and its prophet. That is why they had to be fought against until they were defeated, accepted Muslim rule and paid *jizya*. Except for the Arab polytheists of that period, other groups could remain unmolested by paying this tax (vol 1: 473–74).	ideological imperative; specification

SOURCE: WAHIDUDDIN KHAN, *TAZKIR AL-QUR'AN* (NEW DELHI: GOODWORD BOOKS, 1985).

In his exegesis, he explains his ideas about jihad with reference to the *asbab al-nuzul* of the verses. This allows him to use the hermeneutic device of specification so that, except for a specific historical group of Arab polytheists, no other group is to be fought with. Otherwise, jihad is only defensive and in proportion to the aggression. The norm should be peaceful co-existence with non-Muslim nations, though preparation for war to deter aggression is always necessary. The same hermeneutic device – restricting jihad to a particular age and people with reference to the reasons of the verse's revelation – is also used while explaining Q 2:217, which says that in the sacred months, killing is bad, but expelling people from their homes and preventing them from rightful worship and disbelief is even worse. This, he argues, applied only for the initial period of Islam "but in the contemporary world this is not necessary."[56] As for Q 9:29, the verse about fighting the People of the Book, he effectively glosses over and deemphasizes it. Indeed, he merely confines himself to the statement that the defeated People of the Book should give *jizya* with their hands. Like Shibli and others, he translates *saghirun* as *chote* ("small"), i.e., "they should

---

56   Wahiduddin Khan, *Tazkir al-Quran*, vol. 1 (New Delhi: Goodword Books, 1985), 92.

live like subordinates" (*chote ban ke rahe*).⁵⁷ On the whole, he makes it clear that he interprets Islam as recommending peaceful relationships of mutual amity between nation states.

Khan also expressed his ideas about jihad in other accessible publications in both English and Urdu, such as *The True Jihad* and *Din aur Shari'at*. For the commands in the Quran urging Muslims to "kill them wherever you find them" (Q 2:191; Q 9:5), he specifies that "such verses relate in a restricted sense, to those who have unilaterally attacked the Muslims" but are not permanent, general commands. He points out that the *Bhagavad Gita*, a sacred book of the Hindus, urges Arjuna to fight his kinsmen, since at that time it was a duty. In the same way, Christ said "do not think that I came to bring peace on earth. I did not come to bring peace, but a sword" (Matthew 10:34). For him, such statements are contextual and do not make Hinduism or Christianity religions of war.⁵⁸ The implication is that Islam should not be judged on the basis of contextual statements of an aggressive kind. What is permanent is that the Prophet "has been termed a 'mercy for all mankind' " in the Quran (Q 21) and that God has sent him as a "mercy for the worlds" (Q 21:107).⁵⁹ Khan also explains Q 2:193, the verse which commands fighting till *fitna* comes to an end, using both semantic expansion as well as the argument of change according to circumstances (*tataghayyar al-ahkam bitaghayyur al-zaman wa al-makan*). He defines the term *fitna* as a "coercive system which had reached the extremes of religious persecution."⁶⁰ He argues that, since people can now preach Islam peacefully, the duty of ending *fitna* by force of arms has also ceased to exist. As for the dominance of Islam and open practice of the faith (*izhar al-din*), this has been prognosticated and promised in the Quran – "the unbelievers want God's radiance to be extinguished but God will not allow it" (9:32); "God has sent his Messenger to make his religion dominant" (Q 9:33) – but it refers to peaceful propagation of the faith which will lead to a moral revolution.⁶¹ Since the fall of Communism, there is an intellectual vacuum and "the place is vacant for an ideological superpower, and that, potentially belongs to Islam."⁶² So the only jihad left for Muslims is to establish peace through non-violent means.

---

57 Ibid., 473.
58 Wahiduddin Khan, *The True Jihad: The Concepts of Peace, Tolerance and Non-Violence in Islam* (New Delhi: Goodword Books, 2002), 41–42.
59 Ibid., 43.
60 Ibid., 61.
61 Ibid., 71–75.
62 Ibid., 83.

In short, by using semantic expansion, specification, abrogation and change of rules according to circumstances for the Quranic verses about *qital* ("fighting"), along with questioning the authenticity of certain hadiths, Khan abolishes aggressive wars in the name of jihad, insurrections against rulers, suicide attacks and indeed all that radical, militant Islamists stand for. He concludes that "violence has been practically abandoned" and that it was "an abrogated command in the language of the *shariah*."[63] In his interpretation of jihad, non-combatants cannot be harmed and non-violence is the norm, only to be deviated from when actually attacked by an enemy. Here he gives the specific example of the September 11 attacks and suicide attacks, making it clear that neither are allowed in Islamic law.[64]

Wahiduddin Khan's interpretations were sharply refuted by critics who pointed out that his abolishing of jihad was very much like that of Mirza Ghulam Ahmad (d. 1908), the pioneer of the Ahmadi (Mirzai, Quadiani) sect, which is considered as heretical by both Sunnis and Shi'a in Pakistan. One such critic was Muhammad Rashid, a Pakistani scholar of Islam, who wrote a trenchant critique of an article by Khan called *"Jihad ka Tasawwur Islam me"* ("The Idea of Jihad in Islam"). Khan's article was published as a chapter in his above-mentioned book *Din aur Shari'at* and it summarizes his views about jihad as found throughout his writings. Rashid vehemently objects to the distinction Khan makes in this article between peaceful struggle (*pur amn jad o jahad*) and violent struggle (*pur tashaddud jad o jahad*). In Rashid's view, such a distinction cannot be made, since jihad was a combination of both. This is testified to by the battles that were called jihad in the classical period of Islam, and these remain models of behavior for Muslims forever. He also objects to Khan's use of the hermeneutic device of "change in laws as a consequence of change of circumstances," mentioned above to justify the abolition of aggressive jihad.[65] While Khan asserts that the world has become much more peaceful than it was among the Arab tribes of the seventh century, Rashid argues that it has not. He (Rashid) points to Western colonialism, the world wars, Israel, Vietnam, Afghanistan, Bosnia, Chechnya, Kashmir and Iraq to argue that *fasad* ("mischief") still exists. Moreover, Khan delegitimizes the struggle of Muslims against their oppressors, since it comes under his definition of *fasad*.[66]

---

63   Ibid., 22.
64   Ibid., 36–37.
65   Muhammad Rashid, "Pur Aman Tariqa-i kar ba Muqabalah 'pur Tashaddud Tariqa-i kar'," *Al-Shari'a* 23, no. 3 (March 2012).
66   Ibid., 357.

Perhaps the most powerful voice against radical Islamist interpretations is that of Jawed Ahmad Ghamidi (b. 1948), a liberal Islamic scholar who has been forced to leave Pakistan because of multiple threats to his life. Ghamidi's organization, Al-Mawrid, carries out research on Islam and publishes a journal entitled *Renaissance*, which is administered by his son. Al-Mawrid has branches in the UK, US and Australia, and its main function is to keep the issue of the interpretation of Islam alive in accordance with the broad principles laid down by its pioneer.

Ghamidi's interpretive approach is based on an emphasis on language and the literary appreciation of the Quran. Asif Iftikhar, a Pakistani academic, places it in the hermeneutic tradition of Hamiduddin Farahi (d. 1930) and Amin Ahsan Islahi (d. 1997).[67] Farahi was Islahi's teacher in India and the latter wrote his own exegesis of the Quran in Pakistan using some of his ideas. He points out the differences in the interpretations of Mawdudi and Islahi, arguing that they use discrepant hermeneutic criteria. According to Iftikhar, "contrary to the general assumption of the classical/medieval exegetes Ghamidi believes that the Qur'an primarily addresses the Ishmaelites, Israelites, and the Nazarites of Arabia in the Prophet's times."[68] This makes it possible to consider its verses, especially those relating to aggressive war, as being specific rather than universal in their application.

Ghamidi presents his theories through his essays, lectures and talks as well as in his book entitled *Mizan*.[69] This book covers all aspects of Islamic thought and behavior, but the chapter on jihad is especially relevant for us.[70] He starts by dividing jihad into two kinds. The first is defensive and is only permitted to resist *fitna*, which is defined as cruel persecution of Muslims and efforts to alienate them from their religion. Subsumed under this is cruelty, exploitation and antagonism. Muslims facing these conditions are permitted to fight by the orders in *Surat al-Hajj*— "those against whom war is going on and they are being oppressed are allowed to fight" (Q 22:39); "these are those who have been expelled from their homes, and if God does not confront such people through others, then mosques, churches and other places of worship would have become desolate" (Q 22:40). More detailed injunctions for this kind of

---

67   Asif Iftikhar, "Jihād and the Establishment of Islamic Global Order: A Comparative Study of the Worldviews and Interpretative Approaches of Abū al-Aʿlā Mawdūdī and Jāved Aḥmad Ghāmidī," (Master's thesis, McGill University, 2004).
68   Ibid., 62.
69   Javed Ahmad Ghamidi, *Mizan* (Lahore: Al-Mawrid, 1990). English translation by Shehzad Saleem, *Islam: A Comprehensive Introduction* (Lahore: Al-Mawrid, 2010).
70   Ibid., 577–607.

defensive war are given in Q 2:190–93, which have been quoted repeatedly in the present chapter. As noted earlier, the operational issue is the elimination of *fitna*. However, two conditions should apply: first, this is an order for the whole Muslim community, not individuals or groups acting on their own.[71] Second, armed resistance should be undertaken only when one's military power has reached a certain level.[72]

The second type of jihad Ghamidi addresses is aggressive, and can be found in Q 9:5 and Q 9:29. He begins here by determining the addressees of the Quran, which are the Ishmaelite polytheists, Israelites and Nazarites of Arabia in the seventh century. Thus, many of the actions consequent upon these people's rejection of the Prophetic message are particular to them and not relevant for later peoples. While this is the familiar use of the hermeneutic device of specification, Ghamidi brings in the theory of God's own tradition (*sunan ilahiyya*) in support of it. According to him, God has an unalterable law which is His own prerogative. When he sends a prophet (*rasul*) to guide a group of people and they do not obey, God punishes them, as in the case of the people of Lot and others.[73] The verse Q 9:5, about giving no quarter to the non-believers after four months, is divine punishment that is only reserved for the Arab polytheists and not to be inflicted upon any other people. Similarly, the Jews and Christians who were to be subjugated after aggressive warfare and made to pay the poll tax by the commands in Q 9:29 were those who had rejected the Prophet's message and this was, again, divine punishment. These orders are not valid anymore and therefore Muslims cannot fight aggressive wars, nor force people to pay *jizya*. The only jihad they can undertake now is defensive.[74]

The gist of these arguments is that Ghamidi uses two major interpretive devices, namely theories about divine punishment (ideological assumption) and the restriction of aggressive war to a particular people and period (specification). This application results in his final pronouncement that aggressive warfare in the name of jihad is completely banned. Moreover, he also refutes the arguments of radical Islamists for fighting on their own initiative despite a disparity of military power compared to the enemy. Additionally, he emphasizes that non-combatants should not be killed, nor anyone burnt to death. For both, he cites hadiths (see Annexure below). It was probably because of

---

71 Ibid., 579.
72 Ibid., 584.
73 Ibid., 597–99.
74 Ibid., 599; Asif Iftikhar, "Jihād and the Establishment of Islamic Global Order," 78–79; Muhammad 'Ammar Khan Nasir, "Jihad: Ek-Mutala'a," *Al-Shari'a* 23, no. 3 (March 2012).

TABLE 4.4 Jawed Ahmad Ghamidi's commentary

Verse	Commentary	Interpretive device
Q 9:5	This war of extermination is only for the Arab polytheists. This was a punishment reserved only for them by God (*sunan al-ilahiyya*). Such kind of war is no longer permissible (pp. 597–99).	ideological assumption; specification
Q 9:29	This applies only to those Jews and Christians who had specifically rejected the Prophet's message. Thus, this kind of war is no longer permissible (p. 599).	ideological assumption; specification

SOURCE: JAVED AHMAD GHAMIDI, *MIZAN* (LAHORE: AL-MAWRID, 1990).

such clear refutation of the ideas of the radical Islamists that they have seen Ghamidi as a threat.

5   Conclusion

To understand militancy in the name of Islam, one could proceed from the theories of the impact of modernity and globalization upon traditional Muslim societies, as Jamal Malik suggests in his *Colonialization of Islam*. Simply put, the state extends its power to areas hitherto left in the private domain and supervised by the ulama. This process of homogenization, a reflection of US-led globalization, has "led to an increasing radicalization" among the "isolationist" ulama and madrasa graduates who see it as "their only possible and legitimate way of self-defence and self-preservation." Such has been labelled variously as political Islam, Islamism or Islamist radicalism. In such cases, they follow the methods of interpretation of the foundational texts of Islam, as indicated in this chapter.[75] One could also go on to other tangents, exploring the psychological, economic or social dimensions of jihad. This study, however, is limited to the interpretations of this concept offered by certain South Asian

---

75 Jamal Malik, *Colonialization of Islam: Dissolution of Traditional Institutions in Pakistan* (New Delhi: Manohar; Lahore: Vanguard, 1996), 306.

exegetes, though without delving into the interpretations offered by the theorists of the recent Taliban takeover in Afghanistan or groups such as *Daʿish* which are active there. This may be a task for future researchers.

From the data presented in this study, it appears that the modernists allow only defensive military engagements while the militants believe in an ongoing war against "Western" powers, India, Israel and those Muslim rulers who oppose them or do not rule according to Islamic law. Moreover, the militants also add certain other imperatives not found in classical works. For instance, they allow jihad without a Muslim ruler (*amir*) ordering it, attacks upon non-combatants, suicide attacks and violation of international treaties.[76] In short, they allow terrorist attacks in the name of jihad to be carried out by non-state actors across the globe.

One factor common to all groups of interpreters is that they construct a belief-system which they call "true" Islam. In so far as this deviates from traditional, conservative and historical understandings of the faith, it constitutes a discontinuity with past authority. And, as Michael Cook has observed, the dominant trend in the modern Muslim world is to equate the injunction to "command right and forbid wrong" as "a praxis for spreading Islamic, not liberal, values."[77] In the case of the interpretations of jihad, this means, at least in the hands of self-educated Muslims getting their information from the internet and their peer group, imbibing the idea that war, rather than peace, is the norm of international relations in Islam.

The diversity of interpretations we have noted above has been called the "fragmentation of authority."[78] The manifold interpreters all employ the concept of objectification, defined as "the process by which basic questions come to the fore in the consciousness of large numbers of believers."[79] One consequence of this engagement with Islam as a definer of identity is that it causes an increasing number of Muslims to "take it upon themselves to interpret the textual sources, classical and modern, of Islam." Thus, there is a fragmentation of authority and the issue of who represents Islam "becomes central to Muslim politics."[80] This being the case, the modernist/progressive and Islamist

---

76 For their views as expressed in books and exegeses of the Quran on Jihad, see Rahman, *Interpretations of Jihad*, 76–88.
77 Michael Cook, *Commanding Right and Forbidding Wrong in Islamic Thought* (Cambridge: Cambridge University Press, 2001), 515.
78 Dale F. Eickelman and James Piscatori, *Muslim Politics* (Princeton: Princeton University Press, 1996), 38.
79 Ibid., 43.
80 Ibid., 43.

radical interpretations compete against each other for the minds of Muslims. Which understanding will win out depends on the politics and economics of Muslim countries along with the way Muslims perceive they are treated by Western powers, Israel and India, rather than on the scholarly merits of the various interpretations or the degree of their deviation from the foundational texts of Islam.

Annexure

The prophetic traditions on jihad mentioned in this chapter fall into the following categories according to subject.

1. Extolling the virtues of jihad and the high merit of those who sacrifice their lives. For instance, they are awarded a place in the highest level of paradise:

Yahya bin Saleh etc. narrates on the authority of Abu Hurayra that the Prophet said: [...] Paradise has hundreds of levels and those are created by Allah for those who do jihad for His sake. Any two levels are as distant from each other as the heavens and the earth. So if you pray, then pray for Firdaus which is the highest level of paradise. I think he also added that only God's throne is above it and the streams of paradise flow from here.[81]

2. That jihad will go on forever or till everyone accepts Islam:

[list of names] [...] narrate on the authority of Hadrat Abu Hurayra that the Prophet said I have been ordered that I do jihad with the people till they say "there is no deity except God." Then whoso says "there is no deity except God" his life and wealth will be protected in exchange for the Truth. His salvation is then with God. This has also been reported by Hadrat 'Umar and ibn 'Umar.[82]

---

81 Abu 'Abdullah Muhammad ibn Isma'il al-Bukhari, *Bukhari Sharif*, vol. 2, trans. [into Urdu] Amjad al-'Ali, Subhan Mahmud, Abul Fath Hammad, and Qari Ahmad (Karachi: Idara-i Islamiyat, 2003), item 58, "Kitab al-Jihad wa al-Siyar"; Imam Abu 'Abdullah Muhammad bin Yazid ibn Maja al-Quzwini, *Sunan Ibn Maja*, vol. 2, trans. [into Urdu] Sa'id Mujtaba Sa'idi (Lahore: Maktaba Islamia, 2015), item 2753, "Abwab al-Jihad."

82 Al-Bukhari, *Bukhari Sharif*, item 204; Imam Hafiz Sulayman ibn Ash'ath Abu Dawud, *Sunan Abu Dawud*, vol. 4, trans. Nasiruddin al-Khattab (Riyadh: Darussalam, 2008), item 2484 "Kitab al-Jihad," says it will go on till the war with the Dajjal, an Islamic eschatological figure somewhat analogous to the Christian Antichrist.

3. That non-combatants such as women, children, old men, hermits and those who cannot fight will not be killed:

> Ishaq bin Ibrahim, Abu 'Usama, 'Ubaidullah, Nafe' narrate on the authority of Hadrat ibn 'Umar that the Prophet saw a woman killed in a jihad and forbade the killing of women and children.[83]

4. The militant Islamists quote another tradition to counter the above hadith (no.3):

> [List of names] [...] narrate on the authority of Sa'b bin Jithama that in the place called Abwa' or Wadwan the Prophet passed by and was asked about the polytheists who were hostile. The question was that when they were raided at night their [the polytheists'] women and children are also killed, so he replied "they are of them also."[84]

5. The hadith often quoted by those who consider jihad primarily as moral improvement is:

> When returning from a war the Prophet said: "we are returning from the smaller jihad (*al-jihad al-asghar*) and going towards the greater one (*al-jihad al-akbar*)." The Companions asked: "which is the greater Jihad?" He replied "the jihad of the heart" (*jihad al-qalb*).[85]

Bibliography

Abu Dawud, Imam Hafiz Sulayman ibn Ash'ath. *Sunan Abu Dawud*. Translated by Nasiruddin al-Khattab. Riyadh: Darussalam, 2008.

---

83 Al-Bukhari, *Bukhari Sharif*, item 267, also item 266; Ibn Maja, *Sunan Ibn Maja*, items 2841 and 2842; Abu al-Husayn 'Asakir al-Din Muslim, *Sahih Muslim*, vol. 5, trans. [into Urdu] Waheed uz Zaman (Lahore: Maktaba Islamia, 2014), item 4047, "Kitab al-Jihad wa al-Siyar"; Imam Hafiz Abu 'Isa Muhammad ibn 'Isa Al-Tirmidhi, *Jāmiʻ al-Tirmidhī*, vol. 3, trans. Abu Khaliyl (Riyadh: Darussalam, 2007), item 1569, "Abwab al-Siyar."

84 Al-Bukhari, *Bukhari Sharif*, item 265; Ibn Maja, *Sunan Ibn Maja*, item 2839; Muslim, *Sahih Muslim*, item 4049 adds that it should be in a nocturnal raid and not deliberate; Al-Tirmidhi, *Jāmiʻ al-Tirmidhī*, item 1570.

85 This is *considered* a weak hadith (*daʻif*) and is not in the books considered authentic by the Sunni ulama (*Sihah Sitta*).

Afsaruddin, Asma. *Striving in the Path of God: Jihād and Martyrdom in Islamic Thought.* New York: Oxford University Press, 2013.

Al-Akiti, Muhammad Afifi. *Defending the Transgressed by Censuring the Reckless Against the Killing of Civilians: Mudāfiʿ al-Maẓlūm bi Radd al-Muhāmil ʿalā Qitāl Man Lā Yuqātil.* Hellenthal: Warda Publications; Birmingham: Aqsa Press, 2005.

ʿAli, Chiragh. *Tahdhib al-Kalam fi Haqiqat al-Islam* [Urdu], Published from the manuscripts of the author by Maulvi ʿAbdullah Khan. Hyderabad, Deccan: Kutab Khana Asifiya, 1918.

Azhar, Muhammad Masʿud. *Fadaʾil-i Jihad.* Karachi: Maktaba-yi Hasan, 1999.

Azhar, Muhammad Masʿud. *Fath al-Jawwad fi Maʿarif Ayat al-Jihad,* 4 vols. Lahore: Maktaba Irfan, 2007.

Al-Bukhari, Abu ʿAbdullah Muhammad ibn Ismaʿil. *Bukhari Sharif.* Translated into Urdu by Amjad al-ʿAli, Subhan Mahmud, Abul Fath Hammad and Qari Ahmad. Karachi: Idara-i Islamiyat, 2003.

Burton, John. *The Sources of Islamic Law: Islamic Theories of Abrogation.* Edinburgh: Edinburgh University Press, 1990.

Cook, David. *Martyrdom in Islam.* Cambridge: Cambridge University Press, 2007.

Cook, Michael. *Commanding Right and Forbidding Wrong in Islamic Thought.* Cambridge: Cambridge University Press, 2001.

Denoeux, Guilain. "The Forgotten Swamp: Navigating Political Islam." In *Political Islam: A Critical Reader,* edited by Frédéric Volpi, 55–80. Abingdon: Routledge, 2011.

Eickelman, Dale F. and James Piscatori. *Muslim Politics.* Princeton: Princeton University Press, 1996.

Fair, C. Christine. *In Their Own Words: Understanding Lashkar-e-Tayyaba.* London: Hurst & Co., 2018.

Fatoohi, Louay. *Abrogation in the Qurʾan and Islamic Law: A Critical Study of the Concept of "Naskh" and its Impact.* New York and Oxfordshire: Routledge, 2013.

Ghamidi, Jawed Ahmad. *Islam: A Comprehensive Introduction.* Translated by Shehzad Saleem. Lahore: Al-Mawrid, 2010.

Ghamidi, Jawed Ahmad. *Mizan.* Lahore: Al-Mawrid, 1990.

Al-Ghannouchi, Sheikh Rachid. "What is New about al-Qaradawi's Jihad?" In *Twenty-first Century Jihad: Law, Society and Military Action,* edited by Elisabeth Kendall and Ewan Stein, 334–50. London: I.B. Tauris, 2015.

Ibn Maja, Imam Abu ʿAbdullah Muhammad bin Yazid al-Quzwini. *Sunan Ibn Maja.* Translated into Urdu by Saʿid Mujtaba Saʿidi. Lahore: Maktaba Islamia, 2015.

Iftikhar, Asif. "Jihād and the Establishment of Islamic Global Order: A Comparative Study of the Worldviews and Interpretative Approaches of Abū al-Aʿlā Mawdūdī and Jāved Aḥmad Ghāmidī." Master's thesis, McGill University, 2004.

Jalal, Ayesha. *Partisans of Allah: Jihad in South Asia.* Cambridge, MA: Harvard University Press, 2008.

Jarrar, Maher. "The Martyrdom of Passionate Lovers: Holy War as a Sacred Wedding." In *Ḥadīth: Origins and Developments*, edited by Harald Motzki, 317–38. Aldershot: Ashgate, 2004.

Khan, Wahiduddin. *Tazkir al-Qur'an*, 2 vols. New Delhi: Goodword Books, 1985.

Khan, Wahiduddin. *The True Jihad: The Concepts of Peace, Tolerance and Non-Violence in Islam.* New Delhi: Goodword Books, 2002.

Malik, Jamal. *Colonialization of Islam: Dissolution of Traditional Institutions in Pakistan.* New Delhi: Manohar; Lahore: Vanguard, 1996.

Malik, Jamal. "Introduction." In *Madrasas in South Asia: Teaching Terror?*, edited by Jamal Malik, 1–22. London and New York: Routledge, 2008.

Malik, Jamal. *Islam in South Asia: Revised, Enlarged and Updated Second Edition.* Leiden: Brill, 2020.

Malik, Jamal. "Maudūdī's *al-Jihād fī'l-Islām*: A Neglected Document." *Zeitschrift für Religionswissenschaft* 17 (2009): 61–70.

Malik, Jamal, ed. *Madrasas in South Asia: Teaching Terror?.* London: Routledge, 2008.

Mir, Amir. *The Fluttering Flag of Jehad.* Lahore: Mashal Books, 2008.

Muslim, Abu al-Husayn 'Asakir al-Din. *Sahih Muslim.* Translated into Urdu by Waheed uz Zaman. Lahore: Maktaba Islamia, 2014.

Nasir, Muhammad 'Ammar Khan. "Jihad: Ek-Mutala'a." *Al-Shari'a* 23, no. 3 (March 2012): 109–340.

Nu'mani, Shibli and Sulaiman Nadwi. *Sirat al-Nabi*, vol. 5. Lahore: Al-Faisal, 1991.

Pickthall, Marmaduke. *The Holy Qur'ān: Arabic Texts with Transliteration in Roman and English Translation.* Karachi: Iqbal Book Depot, 1989.

Powers, David S. "The Exegetical Genre *Nāsikh al-Qur'ān wa Mansūkhuhu*." In *Approaches to the History of the Interpretation of the Qur'ān*, edited by Andrew Rippin, 117–38. Oxford: Clarendon Press, 1988.

Al-Qaradawi, Yusuf. *Fiqh al-Jihad: Dirasa Muqarana li Ahkamihi wa Falsafatihi fi Daw'i al-Qur'an wa al-Sunna.* Cairo. Wahba Press, 2009.

Rahman, Fazlur. *Islam and Modernity: Transformation of an Intellectual Tradition.* Chicago: University of Chicago Press, 1982.

Rahman, Tariq. *Interpretations of Jihad in South Asia: An Intellectual History.* Berlin: de Gruyter, 2018; Karachi: Oxford University Press, 2019; New Delhi: Orient BlackSwan, 2020.

Rashid, Muhammad. "Pur Aman Tariqa-i kar ba Muqabalah 'pur Tashaddud Tariqa-i kar'." *Al-Shari'a* 23, no. 3 (March 2012): 341–59.

Rippin, Andrew. *The Qur'an and its Interpretative Tradition,* Aldershot: Ashgate, 2001.

Sa'id, Hafiz Muhammad. *Tafsir-e Surat al-Tawba.* Lahore: Darul Andlus, 2006.

Sa'id, Hafiz Muhammad. *Tafsir-e Surat-e Yusuf.* Lahore: Darul Andlus, 2009.

Sallam, Abu 'Ubayd al-Qasim ibn. *Al-Nâsikh wa'l-Mansûkh fî'l-Qur'ân/ The Abrogating and Abrogated in the Koran*, edited by Fuat Sezgin. Frankfurt am Main: Institut für Geschichte der Arabisch-Islamischen Wissenschaften, 1985.

Al-Shafi'i, Muhammad bin Idris. *Ash-Shafi'i's Risalah: Basic Ideas.* Translated by Khalil I. Semaan. Lahore: Sheikh Muhammad Ashraf, 1961.

Al-Tirmidhi, Imam Hafiz Abu 'Isa Muhammad ibn 'Isa, *Jāmi' al-Tirmidhī.* Translated by Abu Khaliyl. Riyadh: Darussalam, 2007.

Volpi, Frédéric. "Introduction: Critically Studying Political Islam." In *Political Islam: A Critical Reader*, edited by Frédéric Volpi, 1–7. Abingdon: Routledge, 2011.

Wilson, John. *The Caliphate's Soldiers: The Lashkar-e-Tayyeba's Long War.* New Delhi: Amaryllis Manjul, 2011.

Yasmeen, Samina. *Jihad and Dawah: Evolving Narratives of Lashkar-e-Taiba and Jamat ud Dawah.* London: Hurst & Co., 2017.

Zaman, Muhammad Qasim. *Modern Islamic Thought in a Radical Age: Religious Authority and Internal Criticism.* Cambridge: Cambridge University Press, 2012.

CHAPTER 5

The Word of God for the Indian Muslim of Today
Abul Kalam Azad's Tarjuman al-Qur'an

Jan-Peter Hartung

Other than post-Ottoman Turkey, where the principle of *laïcité* was – by proxy of the Swiss Civil Code of 1907 – copied from the French post-revolutionary political paradigm, early twentieth-century British India turned out a stage almost as paradigmatic as British-occupied Egypt for countless Indian intellectuals to frame their political predicament and possible solutions through the prism of their respective religious or spiritual persuasions. These ranged from ultra-communalist Hindus like "Vir" Vinayak Damodar Savarkar (d. 1966) and his political ideology of "Hindutva," via Master Tara Singh (d. 1967) and Dr. Vir Singh Bhatti and the ideology of "Khalistan," that is a sovereign Sikh state in greater Punjab,[1] to a plethora of Islamically-grounded outlines for the political future of the British crown colony. The most prominent of the latter are certainly the more radical communalist ones, first and foremost the consequential so-called "Two-Nation-Theory," which evolved from Muhammad Iqbal's (d. 1938) Allahabad address to a large Muslim League (ML) gathering in December 1930 and was subsequently embraced by the ML as its core-tenet, but also the Islamist ideology of Sayyid Abul A'la Mawdudi (d. 1979) and the Jama'at-i Islami (JiI) or the Fascism and National Socialism-inspired ideas of 'Inayatullah Khan "al-Mashriqi" (d. 1963) and his militant Khaksar Movement.[2] Other,

---

1 See Jan-Peter Hartung, *Viele Wege und ein Ziel: Leben und Wirken von Sayyid Abū l-Ḥasan ʿAlī al-Ḥasanī Nadwī (1914–1999)* (Würzburg: Ergon, 2004), 142–54. This work, in fact, has emerged with only a few revisions from my doctoral dissertation at the Max-Weber Centre for Social and Cultural Studies of the University of Erfurt (2003), supervised by Jamal Malik.
2 There is insufficient space here to list all the relevant works on the "Two-Nation Theory," the ML led by Muhammad 'Ali Jinnah, and its material consequences in the Islamic Republic of Pakistan. A classic representative is Ayesha Jalal, *The Sole Spokesman: Jinnah, the Muslim League and the Demand for Pakistan* (Cambridge: Cambridge University Press, 1985). On Mawdudi and the JiI, see Seyyed Vali Reza Nasr, *The Vanguard of the Islamic Revolution: The Jamaʿat-i Islami of Pakistan* (Berkeley: University of California Press, 1994); idem, *Mawdudi and the Making of Islamic Revivalism* (New York: Oxford University Press, 1996); Jan-Peter Hartung, *A System of Life: Mawdūdī and the Ideologization of Islam* (London: Hurst; New York: Oxford University Press, 2013). On 'Inayatullah "al-Mashriqi," see S. Jamal Malik, "Al-Mashriqi

in retrospect less successful, visions, which stressed the possibility of the co-existence of all religious communities in an undivided India after the end of direct British colonial rule, have received comparatively less academic attention, possibly because they were oftentimes seen as mere appendices to the more secularist ideological framework of the Indian National Congress (INC), spearheaded by Mohan Das "Mahatma" Gandhi (assassinated 1948) and even more so by Jawaharlal Nehru (d. 1964).[3]

With Barbara Metcalf's analysis of Husayn Ahmad Madani's (d. 1957) important *Muttahida Qawmiyyat awr Islam* (1938),[4] a first foray has been made into looking more closely at lines of argument firmly grounded in Islamic theological and legal arguments which run against the dominant separatist/communalist frameworks that eventually succeeded. In a similar non-separatist vein, though highly independent from the pull of the Deobandi universe, one of Madani's contemporaries was Abul Kalam Makki, better known by his pen name "Azad." He served as the first Minister of Education for the independent Indian Republic and has primarily been studied as a political actor in the orbit of Gandhi and the INC, yet his own genuinely religious reasoning for "composite nationalism" has so far received little attention. Once again, historical research appears to flow with the winners, in the process knitting a narrative that marginalizes those visions which may well provide for alternative narratives to be entertained, especially by contemporary historians of ideas.[5] The ways in which such – historically unsuccessful – visions fade into oblivion seems to sometimes be echoed in the lives of their originators: Azad, for one, was increasingly disappointed by the political developments in the

---

    und die Khaksars: Eine religiöse Sozialbewegung indischer Muslime im 20. Jahrhundert" (Magister thesis, University of Bonn, 1982); Markus Daechsel, "Scienticism and its Discontent: The Indo-Muslim 'Fascism' of Inayatullah Khan al-Mashriqi," *Modern Intellectual History* 3, no. 3 (2006), https://doi.org/10.1017/S1479244306000874.

3 A case in point here is Mukhtar Ahmad Ansari (d. 1936), who appears to have been more of a political activist and educationist alongside Gandhi, but has argued little outside the INC conceptual framework. See Mushirul Hasan, *A Nationalist Conscience: M.A. Ansari, the Congress and the Raj* (New Delhi: Manohar, 1987); idem, *M.A. Ansari: Gandhi's Infallible Guide* (New Delhi: Manohar, 2010).

4 Barbara Daly Metcalf, "Observant Muslims, Secular Indians: The Political Vision of Maulana Husain Ahmad Madani, 1938–57," in *From the Colonial to the Postcolonial: India and Pakistan in Transition*, ed. Dipesh Chakrabarty, Rochona Majumdar and Andrew Sartori (Oxford: Oxford University Press, 2007).

5 For supportive arguments, see the seminal essay of Hayden White, "The Question of Narrative in Contemporary Historical Theory," *History and Theory* 23, no. 1 (1984), https://doi.org/10.2307/2504969.

Subcontinent, such that he gradually retreated from the arena of daily politics and sought solace more and more in heavy drinking.[6]

The focus on Azad, therefore, gives credit to another rather unsuccessful Islamically sustained political vision for a de-colonized India. It dramatically highlights the vast variety of Islamic articulations within the Indian Independence Movement that have, inter alia, informed Jamal Malik's diverse academic contributions as well as shaped those of his students and fellow researchers, and thus exploring this topic seems an apt way of honoring him.

1 Situating Azad

Despite the honorific "Mawlana," usually only bestowed after the successful completion of the *'alimiyyat* stage in traditional *madrasa* education,[7] Azad was renowned for his quite liberal interpretation of the authoritative textual foundation of Islam. It is conceivable, however, that this was a result of his education at the hands of his father Abu l-Khayr (d. 1908) and one Mawlavi Muhammad Ya'qub, both from among the Indian expatriate community in the Hijaz, which calls upon us to take a brief detour to this formative period in Azad's life. While Azad himself claimed to have studied the legendary *dars-i nizami*[8] – a proclamation that scholars like Ian Douglas were all too willing

---

[6] Mawlana Abul Kalam Azad, *India Wins Freedom: The Complete Version* (New Delhi: Orient Longman, 1988), 224–48; even more obviously in Humayun Kabir's very personal preface to the 1959 edition of this account (see pp. xi-xiv); Ian Henderson Douglas, *Abul Kalam Azad: An Intellectual and Religious Biography*, ed. Gail Minault and Christian W. Troll (Delhi: Oxford University Press, 1988), 251–52, and references in n. 142. Azad's later drinking habit was also corroborated by an eyewitness report to Robert S. Anderson (Burnaby, BC), retold at the conference "Cultural Institutions and Knowledge Arenas Post-1947: Revisiting the Role of Maulana Azad," held at Nehru Memorial Museum and Library, New Delhi, on March 22, 2013. The present chapter evolved from my own presentation at this conference.

[7] If Azad himself is to be believed, then he took his traditional education only as far as the *faziliyyat* stage, which is the level below the *'alimiyyat*. Mawlana Abul Kalam Azad, *Khud-nivisht* (Delhi: Educational Publishing House, 2002), 140. This work is apparently identical with *Azad ki Kahani Khud Azad ki Zabani*, dictated by Azad to his faithful disciple 'Abd al-Razzaq Malihabadi (d. 1959).

[8] Next to Francis Robinson, it was once more Jamal Malik who devoted much attention to the successive institutionalization of the subject matters of formal religious instruction, epitomized in the term "*dars-i nizami*." See his *Islamisierung in Pakistan 1977–84: Untersuchungen zur Auflösung autochthoner Strukturen* (Wiesbaden: Franz Steiner, 1989) and *Islamische Gelehrtenkultur in Nordindien: Entwicklungsgeschichte und Tendenzen am Beispiel von Lucknow* (Leiden: Brill, 1997). For a critical appraisal of *dars-i nizami* in the light of prevalent scholarship on it, see Jan-Peter Hartung, "Abused Rationality?: On the Role of *Ma'qūlī* Scholars in the Events of 1857/1858," in *Mutiny at the Margins: New*

to take at face value⁹ – some greater caution may be displayed here, pending a much closer look into the works he studied and especially the manners in which he did so.

After all, while the works that Azad named would indeed suggest a quite comprehensive religious education, the fact that he stresses how his father would teach them in a rather general and less detailed manner certainly puts the initial impression somewhat into perspective. In fact, what Azad depicted as the virtue of "not restrict[ing] himself to elaborating on a specific issue or on the commentaries and glosses [of a work],"¹⁰ but instead focusing on what he considered to be its general essence, would very soon also be reflected in Azad's own approach to the textual tradition. The conviction that there is an essence of meaning in the texts that one could extract and then apply to temporally and spatially variant conditions appears obvious in most of Azad's religious writings, from the articles in his journals *al-Hilal* and *al-Balagh*, to his later *Tarjuman al-Qur'an*, a massive and yet rudimentary interpretation of only about one fifth of the Quran. Azad's interpretations are strongly informed by his political proclivities; therefore, the social, political and cultural landscapes of late-colonial India constituted the backdrop against which Azad read, interpreted and finally propagated the Islamic textual tradition.

Therefore, we may discern some political consideration behind almost all of Azad's interpretations of religious concepts and core narratives in the authoritative texts. At the heart of the political, social and wider cultural issues that Azad was concerned with were deliberations about a de-colonized future of India. Such a future, however, could have hardly been built anymore on the political dominance of a single religious minority, divinely declared to be the "best community that I [i.e., God] have brought forth among humankind; you enjoin the commendable and prevent the reprehensible."¹¹ A re-establishment of the predominance that Muslims had enjoyed in the Subcontinent almost uninterruptedly for about eight centuries had been effectively rendered impossible by the less than a century of British colonial administration. Their dominance had not been based upon claims of their supremacy as a faith community, but on unprecedented new social, cultural and political values,

---

Perspectives on the Indian Uprising of 1857, vol. v: *Muslim, Dalit and Subaltern Narratives*, ed. Crispin Bates (New Delhi: Sage, 2014), 136–39. These critical comments have substantially evolved from my work in the DFG-funded research project 1786/8-2 "The School of Khayrabad" (2005–2007), which was directed by Jamal Malik.

9   See ibid.; compare Douglas, *Abul Kalam Azad*, 40–41.
10 Azad, *Khud-nivisht*, 146.
11 Q 3:110.

which the British almost irreversibly introduced to India and imposed upon their colonial subjects; values to which any eventual heir to British colonial rule would inevitably have to relate.

The question was thus whether these competing values, some of which lay claim to supreme force because they have been established by extra-human agency, could be harmonized or were inherently antagonistic and irreconcilable. Therefore, many politically inclined thinkers in early twentieth-century India, be they Muslims, Hindus or members of other religious communities, almost inevitably engaged with this question and proposed a vast array of responses to it. The reactions of Muslim thinkers, who answered it with reference to the authoritative texts of Islam, ranged from a categorical rejection of the possibility of any overlapping values to strong arguments for their general commensurability.

On the uncompromising end of the spectrum, we see, for example, Abul A'la Mawdudi, whose purportedly comprehensive concept of a polity based solely on Islamic precepts developed at around the same time that Azad was also engaged with such questions, but did not even allow for full citizenship of members of other religious communities.[12] Of course, given that Mawdudi's vision was never properly realized, one could well argue that it is actually Muhammad Iqbal with whom Azad should be contrasted.[13] However, Iqbal's notion of the Indian Muslims as an absolutely distinct and incommensurable "nation" (*qawm*), which would therefore require – very much in line with nineteenth-century European ideas of nationhood[14] – a separate and autonomous national territory, was first and foremost based on philosophical speculation, as opposed to being an attempt to derive this notion, or at least get corroboration for it, from the authoritative texts, over and above the Quran.[15]

---

12   Hartung, *A System of Life*.
13   See, for example, Farzana Shaikh, "Azad and Iqbal: The Quest for the Islamic 'Good,'" in *Islam and Indian Nationalism: Reflections on Abul Kalam Azad*, ed. Mushirul Hasan (New Delhi: Manohar, 1992).
14   Jan Penrose, "Nations, States and Homelands: Territory and Territoriality in Nationalist Thought," *Nations and Nationalism* 8, no. 3 (2002): esp. 286–91, https://doi.org/10.1111/1469-8219.00051.
15   See the most consequential "Presidential Address of Dr. Muhammad Iqbal, All India Muslim League, Twenty-First Session, Allahabad, 29–30 December 1930," in Fateh Mohammad Malik, *Iqbal's Reconstruction of Political Thought in Islam* (New Delhi: Media House, 2004), 46–69.

In contrast, both Mawdudi and Azad did at least claim to derive their understanding of the political needs of the hour from a close scrutiny of the Quran.[16] This does not necessarily come as a surprise, as the above-mentioned Husayn Ahmad Madani, principal of the Dar al-ʿUlum at Deoband between 1933 and his death in December 1957 and president of the INC-affiliated Jamʿiyyat al-ʿUlamaʾ-i Hind (JUH) for about the same term, also based his argument for "composite nationality" (*muttahida qawmiyyat*) on Quranic precepts and Prophetic precedent. For him, nationality was based on commonly inhabited territory (*vatan*), not affiliation to a trans-territorial identity such as a religious community. This was the exact reverse of Iqbal's idea of the Indo-Muslim communities as one single nation (*qawm*), which therefore entitled them to a distinct national territory. The aging and ailing Iqbal composed a sharp-tongued couplet in Farsi that later made its way into his posthumously compiled anthology *Armaghan-i Hijaz* and in which Madani's perspective is clearly mocked:

> Obviously, the non-Arabs do not yet know the subtle points of [our] *din* [*rumuz-i din*],
> or else, Husain Ahmad of Deoband: what is this jugglery supposed to be?
> A song from down the pulpit that a nation [*millat*] [defined] by a homeland [*vatan*] is!
> From the position of Muhammad, the Arabian, how clueless is he!
> Merge your self with Mustafa, as his *din* is complete!
> If you do not arrive at him, a complete Abu Lahab you are![17]

In his response, Madani obviously had to prove himself as a true Muslim, faithful to the Prophetic precedent (*sunna Muhammadiyya*), and he did so with ample references to Quranic passages, widely accepted Prophetic hadith and

---

16   Indeed, political relevance became one of the prominent features of Quranic exegesis since the late nineteenth century. See Johanna Pink, *Sunnitischer Tafsīr in der modernen islamischen Welt* (Leiden: Brill, 2010), 34–36.

17   Muhammad Iqbal, *Armaghan-i Hijaz* (Lahore: Shaykh Mubarak ʿAli, 1938), 278. By the comparison with the Prophet's uncle and early arch-enemy "Abu Lahab" ʿAbd al-ʿUzza ibn ʿAbd al-Muttalib (d. 624 CE), explicitly mentioned in Q 111:1 f, the trained jurist Iqbal implicitly and quite knowingly accused Madani of unbelief (*kufr*), and thus cast him out of the Muslim community at the expense of any legal protection. Remarkably, this and a few other polemical couplets are not included in current Pakistani editions of the *Kulliyat-i Iqbal*, either in Farsi or Urdu. Perhaps this was a political decision in recognition of the enormous significance of Deobandiyyat in Pakistan and the inseparably linked deep respect for Husayn Ahmad Madani.

sira. After having disentangled the Quranic semantics of *qawm*, *milla* and *umma*, Madani's core argument pivoted on the socio-political practice of the co-habitation of different religious communities in one territory during the Prophet's time, the communal confines of the validity of any religious legislation and the subsequent need for a trans-confessional legal framework to administer the territorially defined polity.[18] While the controversy between Iqbal and Madani, perhaps because of the public status of both men, received a lot of attention at the time. Each presented their respective arguments in the form of poetry, semi-personal correspondence and pamphlets,[19] thus utilizing the contemporaneous literary genres for political debate. Mawdudi and Azad, however, instead dared to employ the supreme discipline of Muslim religious discourse: *tafsir*. This, I argue, helped to give their political arguments a deliberately traditional and formal framework, which added substantial weight to their views, *vis-à-vis* the more contemporaneous and less regimented approaches.

It needs to be acknowledged that by that time, at least outside the institutions of higher Islamic learning (such as the Dar al-'Ulum at Deoband in India or the Jami'at al-Azhar in Cairo), the genre of *tafsir* and its various subdivisions was not necessarily followed according to the principles established by legions of classical exegetes, or *mufassirin*.[20] Perhaps the most prominent work in this regard, which had already broken with the classical *usul al-tafsir*, is the *Tafsir al-Manar*. This exegesis is attributed to Muhammad 'Abduh (d. 1905) and was compiled by his protege Muhammad Rashid Rida (d. 1935), with whom Azad appears to have had some rather early interaction.[21] This is indicated by the serialized publication of an Arabic translation of Azad's *Mas'ala-yi Khilafat va Jazira-yi 'Arab* from 1920 in Rida's journal *al-Manar* only two years later. It may well be that Azad drew some inspiration from the rather thematic order of the discourses in *Tafsir al-Manar*.[22]

---

18   Husayn Ahmad Madani, *Muttahida Qawmiyyat awr Islam* (Lahore: Maktaba-yi Muhammadiyya, 1939), 38–49 and 61–67.
19   See the edited correspondence between Madani and Iqbal on the issue in ibid., 3–24.
20   The benchmark for the principles of Quranic hermeneutics in the Deobandi tradition of religious learning remains Shah Waliullah Dihlawi, *al-Fawz al-Kabir fi Usul al-Tafsir*, 2 vols. (Delhi: Matba'-i Ahmadi, 1834), with the strong emphasis on the traditionist approach (*bi-al-ma'thur*).
21   Pink, *Sunnitischer Tafsīr*, 44–45.
22   Compare Mawlana Abul Kalam Azad, *Mas'ala-yi Khilafat va Jazira-yi 'Arab* (Lahore: Nami Press, 1963) and idem, "al-Khilafa al-Islamiyya," *al-Manar* 23, nos. 1–10 (1922): 45–56, 102–6,

Both Azad and Mawdudi did not merely render the Arabic text into Urdu, as the common idiom of the Muslims in North India and beyond, but they went much further by translating its meaning into the here and now. It is therefore no accident that the names each of these thinkers gave their respective pursuits appear quite closely related: what for Azad was the "Translation of the Quran," was the "Understanding of the Quran" for Mawdudi.[23] The fact that in 1932, the latter named the journal for the main propagation of his ideas *Tarjuman al-Qurʾan* seems to corroborate this assumption.[24] While not being primarily concerned with Mawdudi here, reference to him needs nonetheless be made every now and then, as this contrast may help to better appreciate Azad's endeavor, as well as to highlight their differently expressed underlying assumptions. Moreover, and this is a fundamental difference from Madani's reflections on "composite nationalism," the arguments of neither Azad nor Mawdudi pivoted on the discussion of Quranically sustainable concepts of social community formation, but rather on the more idealist conception of *din* as an all-comprehensive worldview.

2   The Abrahamic Triad

Two features are usually emphasized in relation to Azad's *Tarjuman al-Qurʾan*. The first is his assertion that the opening chapter of the Quran (*al-Fatiha*) contains the essence (*khulasa*) of the entire Quranic message,[25] which caused him to adopt the not uncommon label *umm al-Qurʾan* for this chapter,[26] a label

---

193–201, 282–89, 361–72, 466–71, 509–12, 691–95 and 753–57. Also, see Jan-Peter Hartung, "Who Speaks of What Caliphate?: The Indian Khilafat Movement and its Aftermath," in *Demystifying the Caliphate*, ed. Madawi al-Rasheed, Carool Kersten and Marat Shterin (London: Hurst; New York: Columbia University Press, 2013), 87–90.

23   Mawlana Abul al Kalam Azad, *Tarjuman al-Qurʾan*, 4 vols., 7th ed. (New Delhi: Sahitya Akadimi, 2010); Sayyid Abul Aʿla Mawdudi, *Tafhim al-Qurʾan*, 4 vols. (Lahore: Idara-yi Tarjuman al-Qurʾan, 1972). On the latter, see Feras Hamza and Sajjad Rizvi, with Farhana Mayer, eds., *An Anthology of Qurʾanic Commentaries* vol. 1 (New York: Oxford University Press, 2008), passim; Hartung, *A System of Life*, 83–90 et passim.

24   In its programmatic headline, the journal claims to be the "source for understanding the message of Noble Quran [sic] in the contemporary era [*tarjuman-i Qurʾan dawr-i hazir men Quran-i majid ki payghām ko samajhne ka zariʿa he*]." Mahnama-yi ʿAlami Tarjuman al-Qurʾan, "Taʿaruf," accessed March 11, 2013, http://tarjumanulquran.org/about-us.

25   Azad, *Tarjuman*, vol. 1, 3–6.

26   Ibid., 4. The permissibility of employing this very label has prominently been suggested by the medieval polymath Abu Hamid al-Ghazali (d. 1111) in his expositions about the Quran written from the perspective of an Ashʿarite theologian. See Abu Hamid al-Ghazali,

that close resembles *umm al-kitab*, the celestial matrix of all divine revelation to humankind.[27] This appraisal of the opening chapter is most certainly the reason why this chapter received a substantially more expansive discussion in *Tarjuman al-Qurʾan* than any other chapter of the Quran. The second feature, and inseparably related to the first, is the development of perhaps his central metaphysical notion, the "oneness of *din*" (*vahdat-i din*), which would eventually have to support Azad's socio-political vision of a de-colonized India that is not divided along denominational lines.

The particular notion of *vahdat-i din*, consistently developed in Azad's expansive deliberations at the beginning of his *Tarjuman al-Qurʾan*, has in the past – perhaps rather prematurely – been occasionally associated with the popular panentheistic concept of *wahdat al-wujud*.[28] The validity of such an association is, of course, very much dependent on the semantics of "*din*." It was perhaps the late Reverend Douglas's own religious proclivities that led him to see no issue in translating this term as "religion" (whatever this is supposed to mean), thus proposing the notion of *vahdat-i din* as Azad's manifesto for, in a nutshell, a peacefully coexisting multi-religious society. We need to bear in mind that such a translation carries a heavy Christian bias, a bias, moreover, that is not discernible in early Latin translations of the Quran,[29] but seems to be rather of much more recent origin.[30] Traditionally, and quite consistent with the views held by classical Muslim exegetes, "*din*" in the Quran appears in three different meanings, the first two of which mirror their meaning in Akkadian and Pahlavi:[31] it can refer to (a) the accountability of each part of

---

    Jawahir al-Qurʾan, 3rd ed., ed. al-Shaykh Muhammad Rashid Rida al-Qabbani (Beirut: Dar Ihyaʾ al-ʿUlum, 1990), 64–72. Also, see William A. Graham, *s.v.* "Fātiḥa," in *Encyclopaedia of the Qurʾān*, vol. II, ed. Jane Dammen McAuliffe (Leiden: Brill, 2002).

27 On the *umm al-kitab*, see idem, *s.v.* "Scripture and the Qurʾān," in *Encyclopaedia of the Qurʾān*, vol. IV, ed. Jane Dammen McAuliffe (Leiden: Brill, 2004).

28 See, for example, Aijaz Ahmad, "Azad's Career: Roads Taken and not Taken," in *Islam and Indian Nationalism: Reflections on Abul Kalam Azad*, ed. Mushiral Hasan (Delhi: Manohar, 1992), 134 and 138.

29 In early sixteenth-century Latin translations of the Quran, for example, "*din*" still appears rendered as "lex [Machumetis]." See Théodore Bibliander, *Le Coran en Latin*, ed. Tristan Vigliano and Henri Lamarque (Lyon: Les Mondes humanistes et classiques, Université lumière Lyon II, 2010), 38. For a long-overdue historical analysis, see Reinhold Glei and Stefan Reichmuth, "Religion between Last Judgement, Law and Faith: Koranic *Dīn* and its Rendering in Latin Translations of the Koran," *Religion* 42, no. 2 (2012), https://doi.org/10.1080/0048721X.2012.642575.

30 See, for example, the survey in Wilfred Cantwell Smith, *The Meaning and End of Religion* (New York: Macmillan, 1962), 25–51 et passim.

31 For the Akkadian, see Jeremy Black, Andrew George and Nicolas Postgate et al., *A Concise Dictionary of Akkadian*, 2nd ed. (Wiesbaden: Harrassowitz, 2000), 60 (lemma: *dinu[m]*);

creation for a future Day of Judgement (*yawm al-din*); (b) the ritual customs and code of social conduct that God had laid out for all human beings at all times (*sirat al-mustaqim*); or (c) exclusively the "folk of Abraham" (*millat Ibrahim*),[32] a concept that would gain exceptional prominence for the justification of an exclusive claim for Muslim leadership in contemporary times that, if necessary, is to even be enforced with violent means.[33]

While a shift towards a multitude of *din* (pl. *adyan*), can be detected between the first Meccan and Medinan periods in the history of the Quranic revelation,[34] from the perspective of Islam, the one God would bring forth only one "*din*," as the single benchmark for the evaluation of everyone's deeds and beliefs. What appears to be a multiplicity of *adyan* is nothing but a mere illusion; in reality, these appearances are only variant degrees of adherence to, and deviation from the "straight path," the *sirat al-mustaqim*. This is indeed the view adopted by Azad in his elucidation of Q 3:67, where Abraham is explicitly styled as "not a Jew, or a Christian, but [rather] a Hanif, a Muslim, and not one of the *mushrikin*."[35] As a proto-believer, Abraham's creed is the same as that of the Jews that would follow, then the Christians and ultimately, the Muslims.[36] Consequently, for Azad, being of the "folk of Abraham" necessarily included all three creeds. Moreover, in his reflections on the crucial Q 2:135; which exhorts to following neither Jewish nor Christian guidance, but only "the folk of Abraham, a Hanif, who did not belong to the *mushrikin* [*bal-millata Ibrahima hanifan wa ma kana min al-mushrikin*]"; Azad stressed that this passage needs

---

for the Pahlavi, see D.N. MacKenzie, *A Concise Pahlavi Dictionary*, rev. ed. (London and New York: Oxford University Press, 1986), 26 (lemma: *dēn*). Also, see Arthur Jeffery, *The Foreign Vocabulary of the Qurʾān* (Baroda: Oriental Institute, 1938), 131–33.

32   See, for example, Muhammad ibn Jarir al-Tabari, *Tafsir al-Tabari: Jamiʿ al-Bayan ʿan Taʾwil Ayat al-Qurʾan*, ed. ʿAbd Allah ibn ʿAbd al-Muhsin al-Turki (Cairo: Dar Hajr, 2001), vol. I: 149–59 [Q 1:4] and 170–99 [Q 1:6f], vol. X: 44–45 [Q 6:161]. While the term is mostly rendered as "*religion* of Abraham," I wish to stress here the aspect of a collective agent in the term "*milla*," that is, a group whose members all necessarily share the same beliefs, rather than a passive abstract "religion."

33   A prominent contemporary example where this is advocated is Abu Muhammad ʿAsim al-Maqdisi, *Millat Ibrahim wa Daʿwat al-Anbiyaʾ wa al-Mursalin wa Asalib al-Tughat fi Tamyiʿiha wa Sarf al-Duʿat ʿanha* (n.p.: Minbar al-Tawhid wa al-Jihad, 2010 [1984]).

34   Gerhard Böwering, *s.v.* "Chronology and the Qurʾān," in *Encyclopaedia of the Qurʾān*, vol. I, ed. Jane Dammen McAuliffe (Leiden: Brill, 2001), esp. 326–31.

35   Translations of the Quranic passages here and elsewhere in this chapter largely follow Arthur J. Arberry, *The Koran Interpreted* (London: Allen & Unwin, 1955). Arberry's translation of "*hanifan musliman*" is widely shared, yet it is contested by some who consider both signifiers as non-homologous, with "*hanif*" being a special form of Muslim, thus making Abraham a "*hanif* Muslim." See, for example, M. Arkoun. *s.v.* "Islam," in *Encyclopaedia of the Qurʾān*, vol. II, ed. Jane Dammen McAuliffe (Leiden: Brill, 2002), 569.

36   Azad, *Tarjuman*, vol. II, 315.

to be read together with the statement in the following verse that calls upon believers to "make no difference between one and another of them [i.e., the prophets]," and also, to consider in this context Q 6:161. This verse once again refers to the "folk of Abraham," who possess a right religion (*dinan qayyiman*) and follow God's guidance on a straight path (*ila siratin mustaqimin*), and Azad summarized its core statement as "My universal path is the path of affirmation [*meri rah-i 'alamgir tasdiq ki rah he*]."[37] In his elaboration on this statement, Azad stressed the pivotal position of "affirmation by faith" (*tasdiq*): as long as this is given, all three monotheistic Abrahamic traditions are equally valid and none of them is superior to the others.

For Mawdudi, in contrast, while acknowledging the polysemy of *"din,"* his emphasis was on the possibility of the parallel existence of different *adyan*, as Q 109:6 suggests: "For you is your *din*, and for me is my *din* [*lakum dinukum wa liya dini*]."[38] Among those various *adyan*, only one could be equivalent to the *sirat al-mustaqim*, namely the *"din* of Truth," which the Quran stipulates in Q 9:29:

> Fight those who believe not in God and the Last Day and do not forbid what God and His Messenger have forbidden – such men as practice not the religion of truth [*din al-haqq*], being of those who have been given the Book – until they pay the tribute [*jizya*] out of hand and have been humbled.[39]

How then did Azad position himself in relation to these Quranic verses that carry a rather disturbingly blunt notion of *din*, a notion that, after all, formed the backbone of Mawdudi's understanding of the concept as one of the four axiomatic pillars on which his entire systematic outline was to rest?

Two points need to be stressed here. First, the *Tarjuman al-Qur'an* breaks off after the twenty-forth chapter of the Quran, conveniently circumventing any engagement with verses like the aforementioned Q 109:6. Second, with those verses that still appear in the work, Azad either attempts a rather favorable translation that avoided the constitution of an exclusive community, or he simply explains their temporally and spatially invariant importance away by applying them exclusively to a very concrete historical context. The former strategy was employed in his translation of Q 6:161, where the *"millat Ibrahim"*

---

37 Ibid., vol. II, 98.
38 Sayyid Abul A'la Mawdudi, *Quran ki Char Bunyadi Istilahen*, 7th ed. (Delhi: Markazi Maktaba-yi Islami, 1996), 101–8.
39 Cited in ibid., 109.

was rendered as "path of Abraham" (*Ibrahim ka tariqa*),[40] and the latter in his annotations to his translation of the above-mentioned verse Q 9:29.[41] For the development of his particular notion of *vahdat-i din*, however, Azad seems to have needed little more than the opening chapter of the Quran; which is at least suggested by the fact that this is the context in which he discussed this notion.

In order to prove that this is a central notion of the whole Quranic message, only concentrated in the opening chapter, Azad quoted verses from across the entire Quran, deliberately leaving aside the chronology of their revelation, as well as, inseparably linked, the respective circumstances of the revelation of these verses (*asbab al-nuzul*), something that no traditional Quranic exegesis would have dared to disregard.[42] The reason for Azad's approach, however, seems obvious: by ignoring significant shifts that occurred between the early revelations to Muhammad in Mecca and the establishment of a Muslim polity in Medina, Azad was able to claim that even under changing circumstances, the essentials remained unchanged. In doing so, four distinct assertions can be identified from the twenty Quranic quotations that he draws on:[43] first, humankind has been created as one;[44] second, humankind has fallen apart due to artificial dissent;[45] third, God has sent messengers in every era and to every community with one and the same message, warning them of the consequences of dissent;[46] and, finally, because of that, no one can claim to have had no knowledge of God's message and will therefore be similarly accountable to God without exception.[47] The quintessence of Azad's exposition relies heavily on the Islamic emphasis on oneness (*tawhid*): the one God creates one single humankind, whose members are related to each other by the fact that their origins are one and the same (hence, the notion of

---

40 Azad, *Tarjuman*, vol. II, 813.
41 See ibid., vol. III, 261. Here, Azad explained this verse as a reflection of the early Islamic warfare against not only the polytheists among the Arab tribals, but also against the Arab Jews as well as the Syrian Christians, resulting in the Quranic enshrinement of the poll-tax (*jizya*) for the "People of the Book" (*ahl al-kitab*). There is, however, no discussion of the problematic notion "*din al-haqq*," translated as "*sachcha din*," which suggests, at least in terms of formal logic, the existence of other *adyan*.
42 Andrew Rippin, s.v. "Occasions of Revelation," in *Encyclopaedia of the Qurʾān*, vol. III, ed. Jane Dammen McAuliffe (Leiden: Brill, 2003).
43 Azad, *Tarjuman*, vol. I, 351–65.
44 Q 10:19; Q 23:52.
45 Q 2:213.
46 Q 3:3f.; Q 5:46; Q 10:47; Q 13:7; Q 21:25; Q 35:24; Q 40:78; Q 42:13; Q 43:6; Q 46:4.
47 Q 14:9; Q 16:36; Q 17:15; Q 21:24f.; Q 28:59.

umma wahida, which Azad rendered as "one single group of human beings" [*insanon ka ek hi groh*]).[48] While in time and space, this *umma wahida* consists of numerous communities (*aqwam*), they are still required to relate to one and the same source of origin. Therefore, every message (*risala*) sent out from this source of origin, which outlines their purpose and objective in the one created world, cannot but also be essentially one and the same. This ever repeated message, finally contains what may be subsumed under the label "*din*," although its variance in time and space causes the emergence of different legal and cultic frameworks (*shar'*).[49] It is then merely the difference in the temporally and spatially variable framework that causes the emergence of what Azad would see as empirically manifest religious traditions, the *mazahib*.[50]

Without toying around with the philosophical categories of essence and accident, or universals and particulars, which could have well been employed instead for the much crisper depiction of the relationship between *umma* and *qawm*, as well as of *din* and *mazhab*, this is what appears to be the gist of Azad's explication. It is this rather clever differentiation that allowed for a pronounced intra-faith coherency, wherein all existing systems of belief and cultic practices would be united by a common principle. Quite the opposite, Mawdudi's emphasis on the multiplicity of coexisting *adyan* required clear criteria for the justification of the one "true" *din*, while at the same time allowing for humankind to choose between adherence to it, or to any other *din* instead. Obviously, Mawdudi was deeply engaged in a struggle with competing ideologies, first and foremost with varieties of Communism and Fascism, all of which he regarded as *adyan*,[51] while Azad tried to take the wind out of any possible competition between various *adyan*, be they "religions," in the colloquial understanding of the term, or prevalent political ideologies. In contrast to Mawdudi's self-proclaimed deductive approach,[52] Azad's had been inductive, being informed in the first place by the empirical situation that he encountered in British India, and by his quest for a political future, following the eventual de-colonization.

---

48 Azad, *Tarjuman*, vol. 1, 353.
49 Ibid., vol. 1, 366–78.
50 Ibid., vol. 1, 373–78.
51 Hartung, *A System of Life*, 44–59 and 96–99.
52 Sayyid Abul A'la Mawdudi, *Islam ka Nazariyya-yi Siyasi* (Delhi: Markazi Maktaba-yi Islami, 1972), 5.

3 A Covenant for the Republic

This empirical situation suggested the existence of numerous coexisting systems of belief and cultic practices (*mazahib*) in the Subcontinent, which needed to be evaluated with regard to their respective degree of emulation of the *din*, as laid out in the Quranic revelation. It is at this point that Azad's anti-colonialist sentiments came into play when he dismissed Christianity, after all the dominant religion of the British colonial establishment, as a *mazhab* that ostensibly rejected the fundamentals of the *din* as derived from the Quran.[53] At the same time, however, Azad portrayed Hindu beliefs and practices as perfectly in line with the Quranic concept of *din*. To be able to do so, and to argue for a political unity between Indian Muslims and Hindus that would result from this understanding, he needed to handle the Quran in a very innovative manner, which in turn produced a rather questionable result. In fact, it may be this very idealized and somewhat distorted image of Hindu beliefs and practices that would clash with realities and eventually result in the collapse of Azad's societal vision.

In portraying Hindu beliefs and practices as corresponding fully with the Quranic concept of *din*, Azad first differentiated between temporally and spatially variant cultic practices (*'amali mazahib*) and an underlying "monistic philosophy" (*tawhidi falsafa*). It is this very fundament that Azad aligned with the Islamic ontological monism epitomized in the above-mentioned popular concept of *wahdat al-wujud*, a concept that, as Azad stressed, could be perfectly derived from the text of the Quran.[54] This "monistic philosophy," which Azad claimed to have found in Hindu beliefs and practices, was entirely and explicitly derived from the *Ṛgveda*, a text that had little if any relevance for

---

53 Azad, *Tarjuman*, vol. 1: 283–85. Tellingly, Azad also dismissed the Judaic religion as a *mazhab* that does not endorse the notion of the essential equality and oneness of humankind in correspondence with the oneness of God (*tawhid*), and instead stresses its claim of the divine choiceness of the Jews. See ibid., vol. 1, 281–83.

54 Ibid., vol. 1, 263–73 and 332–33. In the latter passage, Azad quoted Q 2:115; Q 50:16; Q 55:29 and Q 57:3 for corroboration, and he also stated that Shah Waliullah Dihlawi (d. 1762) had assured the possibility of deriving affirmation for the idea of *wahdat al-wujud* from the Quran and the Prophetic hadith. Azad himself provided no reference for his quote from Shah Waliullah in Urdu; it seems, however, that this passage has been translated from the *Risala fi Tahqiq Wahdat al-Wujud*, or *al-Maktub al-Madani*, a response to a letter from an Isma'il ibn 'Abd Allah al-Madani on the matter. In any case, the concept of ontological monism seems to have kept his mind employed for quite some time, as his poetic letter from the Ahmadnagar jail, dated October 18, 1942, provides evidence for. See Mawlana Abul Kalam Azad, *Ghubar-i Khatir*, 11th ed., ed. Malik Ram (New Delhi: Sahitya Akadimi, 2012), 119–20.

the beliefs and practices of the Hindus in Azad's time.[55] The resulting view appeared completely detached from all empirical reality, a fact that may have eventually contributed to Azad's later disappointment in the developments in and around 1947.

In his idealization of the unitive metaphysical basis of Hindu beliefs and cultic practices, Azad somehow followed the historical precedent of a philosophically underpinned justification of an imperial ideology based on peaceful coexistence of the various religious communities in Mughal times. Indeed, Azad's notion of *vahdat-i din* seems to emulate the earlier idea of the *din-i ilahi*, or rather the *silsila-yi irada*,[56] believed to have been the religious foundation of Mughal *padishah* Akbar's (d. 1605) domestic policy, viz., the notion of *sulh-i kull*, or "peace with all."[57] However, while there are certainly parallels to Sufi thought, restraint ought to be exercised against hastily pushing Azad's religious conception into this very corner. Moreover, whilst Azad had certainly appreciated the socio-religious policies of Akbar and Jahangir in the late sixteenth and early seventeenth centuries, especially towards their breaking the monopoly on defining the ulama, the quarrels among whom Azad argued were over minor issues and encouraged dissent, he certainly never endorsed the normative basis upon which these policies lay.[58] In Azad's view, for a policy to be sustainable, it must not, as happened here, be derived from a divination of imperial authority, but only by recourse to the normative foundations of the religiously inclusive concept of *din*, that is, the Quran. Only extra-human agency can provide for such authority that transcends man-made social, political and cultural boundaries.

Yet Azad's derivation of the notion of *vahdat-i din* from his understanding of the quintessence of the Quran, as allegedly contained in its opening chapter,

---

55   Idem, *Tarjuman*, vol. 1, 263.
56   The notion of *din-i ilahi*, or *tawhid-i ilahi*, appears prominently in the chronicle of Bada'uni, which is known for its bias towards the *padishah* and the inner circle of courtiers. See 'Abd al-Qadir Bada'uni, *Muntakhab al-Tavarikh*, ed. Mawlavi Ahmad 'Ali Sahib, vol. II (Tehran: Anjuman-i Asar va Mufakhir-i Farhangi, 2001), 134–90 et passim. A more favorable discussion by Akbar's confidant Abul Fazl 'Allami (d. 1602), suggests that Bada'uni's portrayal actually referred to a kind of exclusive Sufi fraternity at the court, the *silsila-yi iradat* or *iradat-i gazinan*, which revolved around the *padishah* as its spiritual head, and could therefore perhaps even be regarded as an "imperial cult." See Shaykh Abul Fazl 'Allami, *A'in-i Akbari*, ed. H. Blochmann, vol. I (Calcutta: Baptist Mission Press, 1872), 160.
57   Athar Ali, "Sulh-i Kul [sic] and the Religious Ideas of Akbar," *Studies in History* 4, no. 1 (1982).
58   Mawlana Abul Kalam Azad, *Tazkira*, 9th ed., ed. Malik Ram (New Delhi: Sahitya Akadimi, 2010), 40–43 and 263–65.

was apparently not best suited to providing a compelling argument for unity and mutuality (*ittihad*) between Indian Muslims and Hindus. This makes one wonder why he ultimately chose to follow this highly normative path, given that, while he was already working on the *Tarjuman al-Qur'an*, he had provided a much more practicable argument, which he could have in fact equally bolstered with Quranic references. In August 1921, he derived the possibility, even necessity of amicable relations between Indian Muslims and Hindus as a result of a social contract (*'ahd-i ittifaq*), modelled explicitly after the so-called "Constitution of Medina" (*Sahifat al-Madina*), allegedly drafted by the Prophet Muhammad.[59] This document stipulated that those of the Jewish tribes of Medina "who follow us"[60] were to all be included in the original *umma*: "Neither shall they face injustice nor shall their enemies be aided."[61] Conveniently leaving out the further history of the relationship between the Muslims and Jews in Medina, Azad concluded that making a covenant with whosoever would join in against an overpowering force of evil, in his case referring to a partnership with the Hindus against the British, would be "a religious act [*mazhabi 'amal*] for Muslims."[62]

This earlier model had a significant advantage over the idea of *vahdat-i din*, in that it allows for the dissolution of unity in the very moment that the stipulations made in the contract are no longer recognized by one or both of the contractual parties. It is perhaps the tragedy of Azad that, overall, he obviously felt the considerably less flexible argument, based on his rather libertine exegesis of the Quran, to be more compelling. But cruel political realities had already long taken over, proving once more the insurmountable discrepancy between high normative expectation and empirical reality. Azad appeared deeply hurt by those whom he held solely responsible for ripping apart what he considered to be a single nation, whose "cultural life is and will remain one."[63] His acquiescent personal account of the last decade of the Indian struggle for independence, penned a mere six months before his death in February 1958, clearly reflects his bitter disappointment in humanity when it repeatedly

---

59 See his presidential address to the *All-India Khilafat Conference* on August 25, 1921 at Agra in idem, *Khutbat-i Azad*, 6th ed., ed. Malik Ram (New Delhi: Sahitya Akadimi, 2012), 48–51. The text of the *sahifa*, however, is only found in Ibn Hisham's redaction of Ibn Ishaq's *Sira Nabawiyya* and can therefore hardly claim extraordinary normative force.
60 'Abd al-Malik ibn Hisham, *al-Sira al-Nabawiyya*, vol. II, 2nd ed., ed. Mustafa al-Saqqa et al. (Cairo: Mustafa al-Babi al-Halabi, 1955), 503.
61 Ibid.
62 Azad, *Khutbat*, 54.
63 Idem, *India Wins Freedom*, 214.

displays its inability to live up to the ethical benchmark established by God in His repeated revelations to humankind.

Yet, to the best of my knowledge, Azad never attempted to solve this dilemma, which may well be defined more precisely, and in a theological manner, as the "theodicy problem." Perhaps his deep involvement in everyday political affairs did not leave him with enough space for such systematic reflection. It may, however, also be that Azad did not see the point in engaging in a theological explanation of what had happened in and around 1947. After all, India now was divided, "the new State of Pakistan is a fact,"[64] and in the eyes of Azad, there was precious little that could be done about it.

Hence, Azad appeared resigned to this fate, concluding that "history" alone – here seemingly envisioned as a metaphysical principle close to, if not identical with God – "will decide whether we had acted wisely and correctly."[65] It thus seems that he, quite consistently with his elaborations on the opening chapter of the Quran in his *Tarjuman al-Qur'an*, was referring the ultimate judgement at the *yawm al-din*, when God will decide over the degree of adherence of each individual to His *sirat al-mustaqim*.

Bibliography

Ahmad, Aijaz. "Azad's Career: Roads Taken and Not Taken." In *Islam and Indian Nationalism: Reflections on Abul Kalam Azad*, edited by Mushirul Hasan, 122–75. New Delhi: Manohar, 1992.

Ali, Athar. "Sulh-i Kul [sic] and the Religious Ideas of Akbar." *Studies in History* 4, no. 1 (1982): 24–39.

'Allami, Shaykh Abul Fazl. *A'in-i Akbari*, 2 vols., edited by H. Blochmann. Calcutta: Baptist Mission Press, 1872–77.

Arberry, Arthur J. *The Koran Interpreted*. London: Allen & Unwin, 1955.

Arkoun, M. s.v. "Islam." In *Encyclopaedia of the Qur'ān*, vol. II, edited by Jane Dammen McAuliffe, 565–71. Leiden: Brill, 2002.

Azad, Mawlana Abul Kalam. "al-Khilafa al-Islamiyya." *al-Manar* 23, nos. 1–10 (1922): 45–56, 102–6, 193–201, 282–89, 361–72, 466–71, 509–12, 691–95 and 753–57.

Azad, Mawlana Abul Kalam. *Ghubar-i Khatir*, 11th ed., edited by Malik Ram. New Delhi: Sahitya Akadimi, 2012.

64　Ibid., 248.
65　Ibid.

Azad, Mawlana Abul Kalam. *India Wins Freedom: The Complete Version*. New Delhi: Orient Longman, 1988.

Azad, Mawlana Abul Kalam. *Khud-nivisht*. Delhi: Educational Publishing House, 2002.

Azad, Mawlana Abul Kalam. *Khutbat-i Azad*, 6th ed., edited by Malik Ram. New Delhi: Sahitya Akadimi, 2012.

Azad, Mawlana Abul Kalam. *Mas'ala-yi Khilafat va Jazira-yi 'Arab*. Lahore: Nami Press, 1963.

Azad, Mawlana Abul Kalam. *Tarjuman al-Qur'an*, 4 vols., 7th ed. New Delhi: Sahitya Akadimi, 2010.

Azad, Mawlana Abul Kalam. *Tazkira*, 9th ed., edited by Malik Ram. New Delhi: Sahitya Akadimi, 2010.

Bada'uni, 'Abd al-Qadir. *Muntakhab al-Tavarikh*, 3 vols., edited by Mawlavi Ahmad 'Ali Sahib. Tehran: Anjuman-i Asar va Mufakhir-i Farhangi, 2001.

Bibliander, Théodore. *Le Coran en Latin*, edited by Tristan Vigliano and Henri Lamarque. Lyon: Les Mondes humanistes et classiques, Université lumière Lyon II, 2010.

Black, Jeremy, Andrew George and Nicolas Postgate et al. *A Concise Dictionary of Akkadian*, 2nd ed. Wiesbaden: Harrassowitz, 2000.

Böwering, Gerhard. s.v. "Chronology and the Qur'ān." In *Encyclopaedia of the Qur'ān*, vol. I, edited by Jane Dammen McAuliffe, 316–35. Leiden: Brill, 2001.

Daechsel, Markus. "Scienticism and its Discontent: The Indo-Muslim 'Fascism' of Inayatullah Khan al-Mashriqi." *Modern Intellectual History* 3, no. 3 (2006): 443–72, https://doi.org/10.1017/S1479244306000874.

Dihlawi, Shah Waliullah. *al-Fawz al-Kabir fi Usul al-Tafsir*, 2 vols. Delhi: Matba'-i Ahmadi, 1834.

Douglas, Ian Henderson. *Abul Kalam Azad: An Intellectual and Religious Biography*, edited by Gail Minault and Christian W. Troll. Delhi: Oxford University Press, 1988.

Feras, Hamza and Sajjad Rizvi, with Farhana Mayer, eds. *An Anthology of Qur'anic Commentaries*, vol. I. New York: Oxford University Press, 2008.

al-Ghazali, Abu Hamid. *Jawahir al-Our'an*, edited by al-Shaykh Muhammad Rashid Rida al-Qabbani, 3rd ed. Beirut: Dar Ihya' al-'Ulum, 1990.

Glei, Reinhold and Stefan Reichmuth, "Religion between Last Judgement, Law and Faith: Koranic *Dīn* and its Rendering in Latin Translations of the Koran." *Religion* 42, no. 2 (2012): 247–71, https://doi.org/10.1080/0048721X.2012.642575.

Graham, William A. s.v. "Fātiḥa." In *Encyclopaedia of the Qur'ān*, vol. II, edited by Jane Dammen McAuliffe, 188–92. Leiden: Brill, 2002.

Graham, William A. s.v. "Scripture and the Qur'ān." In *Encyclopaedia of the Qur'ān*, vol. IV, edited by Jane Dammen McAuliffe, 558–69. Leiden: Brill, 2004.

Hartung, Jan-Peter. *Viele Wege und ein Ziel: Leben und Wirken von Sayyid Abū l-Ḥasan 'Alī al-Ḥasanī Nadwī (1914–1999)*. Würzburg: Ergon, 2004.

Hartung, Jan-Peter. "Abused Rationality?: On the Role of *Ma'qūlī* Scholars in the Events of 1857/1858." In *Mutiny at the Margins: New Perspectives on the Indian Uprising of 1857,* vol. V: *Muslim, Dalit and Subaltern Narratives,* edited by Crispin Bates, 135–55. New Delhi: Sage, 2014.

Hartung, Jan-Peter. *A System of Life: Mawdūdī and the Ideologization of Islam.* London: Hurst; New York: Oxford University Press, 2013.

Hartung, Jan-Peter. "Who Speaks of What Caliphate?: The Indian Khilafat Movement and its Aftermath." In *Demystifying the Caliphate,* edited by Madawi al-Rasheed, Carool Kersten and Marat Shterin, 81–94. London: Hurst; New York: Columbia University Press, 2013.

Hasan, Mushirul. *A Nationalist Conscience: M.A. Ansari, the Congress and the Raj.* New Delhi: Manohar, 1987.

Hasan, Mushirul. *M.A. Ansari: Gandhi's Infallible Guide.* New Delhi: Manohar, 2010.

Ibn Hisham, 'Abd al-Malik. *al-Sira al-Nabawiyya,* 2 vols., 2nd ed., edited by Mustafa al-Saqqa et al. Cairo: Mustafa al-Babi al-Halabi, 1955.

Iqbal, Muhammad. *Armaghan-i Hijaz.* Lahore: Shaykh Mubarak 'Ali, 1938.

Jalal, Ayesha. *The Sole Spokesman: Jinnah, the Muslim League and the Demand for Pakistan.* Cambridge: Cambridge University Press, 1985.

Jeffery, Arthur. *The Foreign Vocabulary of the Qur'ān.* Baroda: Oriental Institute, 1938.

MacKenzie, D.N. *A Concise Pahlavi Dictionary,* rev. ed. London and New York: Oxford University Press, 1986.

Madani, Husayn Ahmad. *Muttahida Qawmiyyat awr Islam.* Lahore: Maktaba-yi Muhammadiyya, 1939.

Mahnama-yi 'Alami Tarjuman al-Qur'an. "Ta'aruf." Accessed March 11, 2013. http://tarjumanulquran.org/about-us.

Malik, Fateh Mohammed. *Iqbal's Reconstruction of Political Thought in Islam.* New Delhi: Media House, 2004.

Malik, Jamal. *Islamische Gelehrtenkultur in Nordindien: Entwicklungsgeschichte und Tendenzen am Beispiel von Lucknow.* Leiden: Brill, 1997.

Malik, S. Jamal. "Al-Mashriqi und die Khaksars: Eine religiöse Sozialbewegung indischer Muslime im 20. Jahrhundert." Magister thesis, University of Bonn, 1982.

Malik, S. Jamal. *Islamisierung in Pakistan 1977–84: Untersuchungen zur Auflösung autochthoner Strukturen.* Wiesbaden: Steiner, 1989.

al-Maqdisi, Abu Muhammad 'Asim. *Millat Ibrahim wa Da'wat al-Anbiya' wa al-Mursalin wa Asalib al-Tughat fi Tamyi'iha wa Sarf al-Du'at 'anha.* N.p.: Minbar al-Tawhid wa al-Jihad, 2010 [1984].

Mawdudi, Sayyid Abul A'la. *Islam ka Nazariyya-yi Siyasi.* Delhi: Markazi Maktaba-yi Islami, 1972.

Mawdudi, Sayyid Abul A'la. *Quran ki Char Bunyadi Istilahen,* 7th ed. Delhi: Markazi Maktaba-yi Islami, 1996.

Mawdudi, Sayyid Abul A'la. *Tafhim al-Qur'an*, 4 vols. Lahore: Idara-yi Tarjuman al-Qur'an, 1972.

Metcalf, Barbara Daly. "Observant Muslims, Secular Indians: The Political Vision of Maulana Husain Ahmad Madani, 1938–57." In *From the Colonial to the Postcolonial: India and Pakistan in Transition*, edited by Dipesh Chakrabarty, Rochona Majumdar and Andrew Sartori, 96–118. Oxford: Oxford University Press, 2007.

Nasr, Seyyed Vali Reza. *Mawdudi and the Making of Islamic Revivalism*. New York: Oxford University Press, 1996.

Nasr, Seyyed Vali Reza. *The Vanguard of the Islamic Revolution: The Jama'at-i Islami of Pakistan*. Berkeley: University of California Press, 1994.

Penrose, Jan. "Nations, States and Homelands: Territory and Territoriality in Nationalist Thought." *Nations and Nationalism* 8, no. 3 (2002): 277–97, https://doi.org/10.1111/1469-8219.00051.

Pink, Johanna. *Sunnitischer Tafsīr in der modernen islamischen Welt*. Leiden: Brill, 2010.

Rippin, Andrew. s.v. "Occasions of Revelation." In *Encyclopaedia of the Qur'ān*, vol. III, edited by Jane Dammen McAuliffe, 569–73. Leiden: Brill, 2003.

Shaikh, Farzana. "Azad and Iqbal: The Quest for the Islamic 'Good'." In *Islam and Indian Nationalism: Reflections on Abul Kalam Azad*, edited by Mushirul Hasan, 59–76. New Delhi: Manohar, 1992.

Smith, Wilfred Cantwell. *The Meaning and End of Religion*. New York: Macmillan, 1962.

al-Tabari, Muhammad ibn Jarir. *Tafsir al-Tabari: Jami' al-Bayan 'an Ta'wil Ayat al-Qur'an*, 26 vols., edited by 'Abd Allah ibn 'Abd al-Muhsin al-Turki. Cairo: Dar Hajr, 2001.

White, Hayden. "The Question of Narrative in Contemporary Historical Theory." *History and Theory* 23, no. 1 (1984): 1–33, https://doi.org/10.2307/2504969.

CHAPTER 6

Post-Migrant Dynamics of Islam
Muslim Youth and Salafism in Germany

David Yuzva Clement

1   Introduction

By no means whatsoever do young Muslims in Germany represent a single homogeneous group. On the contrary, recent research has demonstrated a high degree of diversity among German Muslim youth and their milieus. Yet this has not always been the case, as can especially be seen from pre- as well as post-9/11 studies, which were overwhelmingly concerned with the intersection between Islam, integration and violence. More recently, research has suggested understanding Muslim youth in Germany through the lens of hybrid identity. This rather active identity process includes the navigation and negotiation of what it means to be German *and* Muslim within the context of personal interests, gender norms and youth cultures, with their languages and aesthetics. Thus, there are pluralistic concepts of identity, and in an individualized society, it requires effort to piece together one's own identity. However, multiple factors can influence this process, such as the adolescence-related withdrawal from parental authority and the turning to peer groups. Adolescence is especially characterized by the quest for identity, which implies the questioning of societally accepted norms.

The purpose of this chapter is twofold: first, it explores how Islam has evolved in Germany. Thereby, it aims to deconstruct monolithic perceptions of Islam that are dominant within the public sphere. Second, it discusses different milieus of German Muslim adolescents and cases of Islamic activism and engagement, including the question of the appeal of "Salafism" for some youth in Germany. Both parts are connected by a critical discussion of policies of securitization and practices of othering.

Although at first sight it may seem very similar to other cases of civic engagement, young people who take part in Salafist groups; for example those who participate in so-called "street-*daʿwa*," a Quran distribution campaign which operated in various European cities, including Germany; in fact retreat from the wider social context and undergo a process which can be understood as a "socialization in extremism"[1] – or what is usually referred to as a radicalization process – which can be potentially harmful. By drawing on Talal Asad's understanding of Islam as a discursive tradition and Naika Foroutan's understanding of Germany as a post-migrant society, this chapter attempts to contextualize persons turning towards "Salafism" as being influenced by contemporary structural, social and individual issues and contexts. It additionally seeks to show how their choice was also shaped by religious attitudes and practices that have been addressed by historical and contemporary individuals and groups or circles alike. Further still, this chapter explores ways in which pedagogy, particularly in social work but also in other fields, can respond to radicalization. Although this chapter focuses on Germany, instances from other countries will also be discussed for comparison.

2   A Short History of Islam in Germany

In the collective memory, Islam in Germany is associated with post-war labor migration in the 1960s and 1970s and bilateral recruitment agreements between West Germany and several countries, including Turkey (1961), Morocco (1963) and Tunisia (1965). Although this narrative may at first glance seem correct, a deeper dive into history provides a quite different picture. The earliest documented instances of Muslims arriving in Germany speak of prisoners of war. Around 1701, there were open diplomatic negotiations between the Prussian King Friedrich I and Sultan Mustafa II. In 1731, it was ordered that Muslim prisoners of war be given a prayer room.[2] Yet another important milestone of the Prussian-Ottoman relationship was the opening of the Islamic cemetery for deputies and soldiers of the Ottoman Empire in Berlin in 1866. The history of Islam in Germany was also influenced by the Enlightenment, as can be seen with Gotthold Ephraim Lessing (1729–1781), one of the most important poets of this epoch. His famous "Ring Parable" leaves open the question of whether Christianity, Judaism or Islam possesses the only truth.[3] In the context of the

---

1   Fabian Srowig and Andreas Zick, "Persönlichkeit oder Gruppe: Wo liegen die Wurzeln extremistischer Radikalisierung?," in *Radikalisierung und De-Radikalisierung in Deutschland: Eine gesamtgesellschaftliche Herausforderung*, ed. Magdalena von Drachenfels, Philipp Offermann and Carman Wunderlich (Berlin: Epubli, 2018).
2   Ursula Spuler-Stegemann, "Der Elefant des Kalifen: Wie der Islam nach Deutschland kam," *Der Spiegel*, accessed January 5, 2020, www.spiegel.de/spiegel/spiegelspecial/d-56323062.html.
3   Monika Fick, "Lessings *Nathan der Weise* und das Bild vom Orient und Islam in Theatertexten aus der zweiten Hälfte des 18. Jahrhunderts: Überarbeitete und erweiterte Fassung des

First World War and Germany's geostrategic interests, the first mosque in Germany was established in a detention camp for predominately Muslim prisoners in 1915.[4]

The interwar period in Berlin witnessed the arrival of various Ahmadiyya missionary groups and their transnational networks, such as "the Lahore branch who actually managed to build a mosque in 1924,"[5] one which still exists today. Over the course of the Second World War, Nazi Germany established alliances with some majority Muslim countries and their leadership: "The reasons for Germany's efforts to promote an alliance with the Muslim world were closely connected to the course of the war, which reached Muslim territories in 1941–1942 [...]. Islam was, in this context, seen as a political force that could be employed against the Allies."[6] Efforts to instrumentalize Islam included the establishment of Muslim intermediaries and units, the presence of Muslim leaders, such as Amin al-Husayni in Berlin, and acknowledging pan-Islamic and Islamic anti-imperialistic views and movements.

Moving into the post-war period, with the "guest workers" and subsequent family immigration from countries with significant Muslim populations, the presence of "Islam" was magnified in Germany. The German government, however, had envisioned that their working in (West) Germany would only be a temporary arrangement, which meant that there were very few actively implemented integration policies.[7] Nevertheless, the foundation of major Islamic umbrella organizations offering social, cultural and religious services during the second half of the twentieth century demonstrated the willingness and capacity of immigrant families and communities to make Germany their new home. The foundation of Muslim youth organizations, which will be discussed in detail below, points in the same direction.

In addition to those hailing from Turkey, Morocco and Tunisia, the current Islamic landscape in Germany further includes the aforementioned

---

Vortrags am 10. Mai 2016 im Rahmen des Lessing Festivals in der Herzog August Bibliothek, Wolfenbuettel," accessed January 5, 2020, Goethezeitportal.de, www.goethezeitportal.de/db/wiss/lessing/fick_orient.pdf.

4 Gerhard Höpp, "Die Wünsdorfer Moschee: Eine Episode islamischen Lebens in Deutschland, 1915–1930," *Die Welt des Islams* 36, no. 2 (January 1996): 204, https://doi.org/10.1163/1570060962597490.

5 Gerdien Jonker, *The Ahmadiyya Quest for Religious Progress: Missionizing Europe 1900–1965* (Leiden: Brill, 2015), 64.

6 David Motadel, *Islam and Nazi Germany's War* (Cambridge: The Belknap Press of Harvard University Press, 2014), 315.

7 Klaus J. Bade and Jochen Oltmer, *Normalfall Migration* (Bonn: Bundeszentrale für politische Bildung, 2004), 71–85.

Ahmadiyya, Muslims of Arab, African and Bosnian origin, Sufi groups, Alevis and various Shi'a communities. There are also various initiatives, such as the "House of One"[8] in Berlin, an inter-religious house of worship built by Jewish, Christian and Islamic communities, or the Ibn Rushd–Goethe Mosque,[9] inaugurated in 2017, located in Berlin and self-declared promoter of a liberal and progressive version of Islam, to which we will return at a later point.

3   Risking Social Cohesion: Othering, Violence and Securitization

With the fall of the Iron Curtain in the late 1980s and the war in Yugoslavia in the early 1990s, the number of asylum seekers rose sharply, reaching 438,000 in 1992 according to federal asylum statistics.[10] This was followed by a polarized debate regarding asylum, which led to the adoption of the new article 16a of the German constitution in 1993. It was accompanied by violent and deadly attacks on centers for asylum seekers and housing for immigrants, such as the arson attacks in Rostock-Lichtenhagen, Mölln and Solingen.[11] As a consequence of these and other right-wing extremist riots and violent attacks, the federal government of reunified Germany reacted with a new program for the prevention of violence and right-wing extremism. This program, implemented in 1992, was criticized for its sole focus on the East German provinces and its aimless activism. It was also during this time that the right-wing terrorist organization National Socialist Underground (NSU) was formed.

Since September 11, 2001, researchers have witnessed and described a global paradigm shift when it comes to discourses of belonging, defining this change as a "religious turn."[12] As the fear of terrorism increased, so did "the public scrutiny of individuals sharing the same religion as the perpetrators."[13] Within the Western context, it is arguably not religion per se which functions as a

---

8   Stiftung House of One – Bet – und Lehrhaus Berlin, "The Concept," House-of-One.org, accessed July 9, 2020, https://house-of-one.org/en/concept.
9   Ibn Rushd-Goethe Moschee, "Die Moschee," accessed September 6, 2021, https://ibn-rushd-goethe-moschee.de/die-moschee/.
10 Bade and Oltmer, *Normalfall Migration*, 87, 106.
11 Ibid., 113.
12 Willy Klawe, "Die Lebenswelt junger Muslime und die Faszination des Islam: Von der Fremdenfeindlichkeit zur Islamophobie – Der 'religious turn' im Fremdheitsdiskurs," *Deutsche Jugend: Zeitschrift für die Jugendarbeit* 64, no. 9 (September 2016).
13 Carolin Goerzig and Khaled al-Hashimi, *Radicalization in Western Europe: Integration, Public Discourse, and Loss of Identity among Muslim Communities* (Oxon and New York: Routledge, 2015), 48.

demarcation line between belonging and non-belonging. The macro-level *religious turn* that Willy Klawe points to might be better understood as an essentialization of Islam as a prime factor and overarching identity, intertwined with anti-immigrant racism. In the context of integration politics and media representations of Muslim communities in Germany, Jamal Malik described this essentialism as the "confessionalization of the integration discourse," fueled by a reduction of Muslims to *homo religiosus*.[14] This Islamization of "the other" becomes the social mirror against which "the other" is being positioned, fixated and evaluated. Such essentialism is clearly not without consequences at the micro-level for the people being labeled and othered. A few repercussions come to mind: it cuts out any other identity factors for understanding a person and their lived experience. Correspondingly, children and adolescents are automatically identified with the religion of their parents or the dominant faith of their family's country of origin, which in the case of Islam is often simultaneously used for the attribution of a so-called "Islamic identity."[15] Instead of diversity, essentialism demands "homogenisation and disciplination."[16]

Furthermore, the essentialist attribution "Muslim" is not a neutral social categorization. A recent study on the socialization of adolescents in Germany concluded that Muslim adolescents are more frequently exposed to discrimination and disadvantage compared to non-Muslim youth.[17] Similarly, another study from the University of Leipzig shows that asylum seekers, Muslims as well as Sinti and Roma, are being racialized to a much higher degree than other groups.[18] In addition, discussions of othering are framed by two powerful discourses, which are also apparent in the "headscarf-debate": the securitization of integration and immigration legislation on the one hand, and the secular-modernist idea of a decline as well as privatization of religion on the other. Both frameworks are guided by the misleading assumption that greater Islamic religiosity automatically carries a higher potential for extremism and thus presents a higher risk for national or social security. Consequently, binary oppositions and logics of equivalences are constructed, such as the divide

---

14   Jamal Malik, "Medien reduzieren Muslime auf ihre Religion," *Tages-Anzeiger* (December 8, 2007).
15   Klawe, "Die Lebenswelt junger Muslime," 376.
16   Jamal Malik, "Integration of Muslim Migrants and the Politics of Dialogue: The Case of Modern Germany," *Journal of Muslim Minority Affairs* 33, no. 4 (2013): 499, https://doi.org/10.1080/13602004.2013.866350.
17   Jürgen Mansel and Viktoria Spaiser, *Ausgrenzungsdynamiken: In welchen Lebenslagen Jugendliche Fremdgruppen abwerten* (Weinheim and Basel: Beltz Juventa, 2013).
18   Oliver Decker, Johannes Kiess and Elmar Brähler, *Die stabilisierte Mitte: Rechtsextreme Einstellung in Deutschland 2014* (Leipzig: University of Leipzig, 2014).

between "Europe" and "Islam"; the latter of which "is related to signifiers such as fundamentalism, intolerance, and backwardness [...] in opposition to [...] moderate, tolerant, and progressive, [forcing] Muslims in Europe into an either-or decision."[19] Attempts to establish a "Euro-Islam" are subject to the same dichotomy. Bassam Tibi, one of the main protagonists of such a concept, recently declared that, as he writes, "headscarf Islam" has triumphed over "Euro-Islam,"[20] ignoring the various ways of hybrid or lived religious practice, which will be discussed below.[21]

In the context of contemporary European identity politics against immigrants and refugees, discriminatory immigration policies first and foremost constructed, or rather, as Malik elaborated,[22] confessionalized refugees in a pejorative way as "Muslims," which co-constructs the "myth of a 'Judaeo-Christian' tradition in Europe"[23] and revokes the neo-racist race-religion constellation, which also constitutes the so-called "*Leitkultur*" debate in Germany. Such essentialization had tangible real-life consequences. Poland, Slovakia, the Czech Republic and Hungary were particularly united by their rejection of a majority decision on the distribution of refugees by the Council of EU Interior Ministers in 2015.[24] "One justification for this stance is the assertion that those seeking asylum from predominantly Muslim countries pose a security threat from which citizens must be protected."[25] In such situations, elected government representatives refer to the "great replacement," a right-wing extremist conspiracy narrative which argues "that white European populations are being deliberately replaced at an ethnic and cultural level through migration and the growth of minority communities. [...] Certain ethnic and religious groups – primarily Muslims – are typically singled out as being culturally incompatible with the lives of majority groups in Western countries and thus a particular threat."[26]

---

19 Goerzig and al-Hashimi, *Radicalization in Western Europe*, 35–36.
20 Bassam Tibi, "Warum ich kapituliere," *Cicero* (June 2016).
21 Meredith B. McGuire, *Lived Religion: Faith and Practice in Everyday Life* (New York: Oxford University Press, 2008).
22 Malik, "Medien reduzieren Muslime auf ihre Religion."
23 Anya Topolski, "The Dangerous Discourse of the 'Judaeo-Christian' Myth: Masking the Race-Religion Constellation in Europe," *Patterns of Prejudice* 54, no. 1–2 (2020), https://doi.org/10.1080/0031322X.2019.1696049.
24 Alexander Beribes, Leo Mausbach and Johannes Jungeblut, "Is Islam Part of Eastern Europe?: Thoughts on History, Religion, and National Identity in the Eastern EU Countries," *International Reports by the Konrad-Adenauer-Stiftung*, no. 2 (2018): 69.
25 Ibid.
26 Jacob Davey and Julia Ebner, *"The Great Replacement": The Violent Consequences of Mainstreamed Extremism* (London: Institute for Strategic Dialogue, 2019), 7.

Comparably, the travel ban enacted by former US President Donald Trump in 2017 against several countries with majority Muslim populations, including Iran, Syria and Iraq, points in a similar direction. It had discriminatory consequences, such as suspending admissions of Syrian refugees.[27] Whereas the first executive order, issued in January 2017, focused on religious identification, a second order, issued in March 2017, focused on the nationality of individuals from those countries.[28] The first travel ban, which makes reference to the 9/11 terrorist attacks, reinforces the idea that Islam and Muslims pose an overwhelming security threat to the United States. This may lead to the phenomenon of "acting Muslim," defined by Khaled A. Beydoun as "a process by which Muslim Americans strategically negotiate and publicly perform a religious identity stigmatized by counterterror policy."[29] Similarly, the UK Government's "Prevent-Strategy," introduced in 2007 and remodeled in 2011, is another example demonstrating how "counterterrorism policies in general and the new Prevent Strategy 2011 could lead to Muslim communities being viewed as a 'suspect' community."[30]

Furthermore, similar discourses or variants of such have, to some degree, leaked into academic research and pedagogical practice across the globe. Take for instance the assumption that terrorism is largely associated with Islamist groups, which led to a recent publication with the rather neutral title of *Canadian Terrorists by the Numbers*.[31] In a problematic approach, the study focuses solely on Salafist-jihadist terrorism. However, it is noted in the summary that research concerning other types of terrorism is lacking in the Canadian context, although research on the phenomenon of right-wing extremism and terrorism has recently begun to expand in scope. In the field of education, Iman Attia states that information events on Islam for teachers are currently immensely popular[32] – leading to pedagogical practices which

---

27 Amaney A. Jamal, "Trump(ing) on Muslim Women: The Gendered Side of Islamophobia," *Journal of Middle East Women's Studies* 13, no. 3 (2017), https://doi.org/10.1215/15525864-4179144.

28 Khaled A. Beydoun, "On Islamophobia, Immigration, and the 'Muslims Bans'," *Ohio Northern University Law Review* 43, no. 3 (2017): 454–55.

29 Ibid., 455.

30 Imran Awan, "'I Am a Muslim Not an Extremist': How the Prevent Strategy Has Constructed a 'Suspect' Community," *Politics and Policy* 40, no. 6 (December 2012): 1167, https://doi.org/10.1111/j.1747-1346.2012.00397.x.

31 Alex Wilner and Irfan Yar, *Canadian Terrorists by the Numbers: An Assessment of Canadians Joining and Supporting Terrorist Groups* (Ottawa: Macdonald-Laurier Institute, 2019).

32 Iman Attia, "Zur Bedeutung des Islamdiskurses für die Jugendarbeit," *Deutsche Jugend: Zeitschrift für die Jugendarbeit* 57, no. 2 (2009).

can add to institutionalized processes of othering. Children and youth, who are consistently being perceived through this powerful Islamic-ethnic lens, are at risk of only being listened to because of such essentialism. Attia shows that, by having to work their way through such perceptions, the cultural habitus of children and youths is being formed as well: as a culture of migrants or minorities, of diaspora or resistance, as defiant or self-confident Muslims or as vehement Islam critics.

Attia reflects an understanding of Islam in the West which is similar to Jamal Malik's contextualization of Islam through the lens of postcolonial theory, wherein he asserts that "[t]he attempt to understand contemporary Islam without the colonial experience seems to be a grave and unfortunate misstep."[33] Historically, and by referring to developments in the late nineteenth and early twentieth century, the reformist currents of Islam tried to reconcile and integrate the Islamic religion with European ideas by referring to the central concept of reason. Yet as Malik notes, "these discourses of compatibility and recognition were first and foremost based on self-interest, namely to achieve colonial acknowledgement for their own group as they were integrating in the urban colonial sector."[34] As a consequence, what he refers to as "strategic essentialism"[35] continuously standardizes the cultures of Islam until today, to an extent in which both non-Muslims and "reform Muslims" themselves disown the pluralism of Islamic life worlds and scholarships, a process which is described by Thomas Bauer as the "intolerance of ambiguity."[36] Instead of acknowledging multiple modernities, such processes add to the postcolonial marginalization and narrowing of Islamic thought.[37] Pointing towards contemporary groups, such as Salafist Muslims and their appeal towards some youths, which will be discussed in more detail below, Malik observes that a "hardened, clearly defined and self-contained Islam is the result."[38]

---

33   Malik, "Integration of Muslim Migrants," 496–97.
34   Ibid., 497.
35   Ibid.
36   Thomas Bauer, *Die Kultur der Ambiguität: Eine andere Geschichte des Islams* (Berlin: Verlag der Weltreligionen, 2011).
37   Malik, "Medien reduzieren Muslime auf ihre Religion."
38   Malik, "Integration of Muslim Migrants," 497.

4 Muslim Youth Organizations in Germany

Adolescence can be understood as a sociological process of peer-group formation and a creative way of dealing with societal and culturally predominant elements, including processes of giving meaning to and reinterpreting cultural artifacts, communication and practices in the everyday lives of young people. Moreover, in a post-migrant context, adolescence possesses the resources for social innovation, resilience against othering and systemic racism as discussed above, as well as civic engagement.

Largely ignored by German mainstream society, in recent years, young Muslims have been involved in several civic education projects, and have founded their own youth organizations, such as the Federal Association of Muslim Pathfinders in Germany (BMPPD)[39] or the Muslim Youth in Germany (MJD).[40] Like most youth organizations in Germany, these promote democracy education and leisure activities, interconnect like-minded individuals, and aim at societal participation and empowerment. The MJD was established in 1994 against the backdrop of heated debates surrounding such binary constructs as the compatibility of Islam and democracy. Following the assertion that they were affiliated with the Muslim Brotherhood, the MJD was classified as "Islamist" in various reports from German intelligence agencies in the early 2000s. Surveillance on them, partly directed by court orders, has now been suspended. The MJD focuses on the promotion of a German-Islamic identity, integration, representation of young Muslims in Germany, civic engagement and inter-religious dialogue.[41] Following a neo-conservative youth cultural pattern, most of MJD's own activities, such as weekly youth group meetings, are separated according to gender. This should not be confused with a non-emancipatory approach, but rather one can observe a hybridization of Islamic religiosity, civic engagement and modernity, including gender empowerment, though it currently ignores intersectionalities of Muslim youth who identify as LGBTQ+. The MJD is part of a movement which has been described as "pop Islam"; conservative Islamic values are self-confidently combined with stylistic elements and modern, education-oriented values and norms of "Western" society.

---

[39] Bund Moslemischer Pfadfinder und Pfadfinderinnen Deutschlands (BMPPD), "Wer wir sind," accessed January 5, 2020, www.moslemische-pfadfinder.de/verband/wer-wir-sind/.

[40] Muslimische Jugend in Deutschland, "Über uns," MuslimischeJugend.de, accessed January 5, 2020, https://muslimischejugend.de/about.html.

[41] Muslimische Jugend in Deutschland, "Junge Muslime als Partner: Für Dialog und Kooperation und gegen Diskriminierung," MuslimischeJugend.de, accessed January 5, 2020, https://muslimischejugend.de/module/projekte1/jungemuslime.html.

The BMPPD was established in 2010 with the focus of introducing scouting and outdoor activities to Muslim children and youth in Germany. As described on its website, "it finds its ethical basis in the teachings of the honorable Quran and in the Sunna of the Prophet Muhammad."[42] With many local chapters across Germany, the BMPPD's educational approach follows gender-integrated pedagogy, leadership and skill training, as well as the introduction of young people to scouting and holistic experiences of nature. The MJD and BMPPD are two contemporary examples of civic engagement of Muslim youths in Germany which suggest that comprehensive models for understanding youth identity and societal participation should include maximizing youth potential by building on strengths, diversity and capacity. These two organizations not only serve as contemporary examples of post-migrant civic engagement by German Muslim youths in public and educational affairs, but they also demonstrate the ability of such youths to engage in citizenship initiatives and to challenge polarizing ways of thinking, while promoting a strong sense of belonging, resilience and cultural creativity despite the continuous processes of othering and discrimination.

A topic that has received more public attention is the introduction of Islamic religious education in schools and, correspondingly, university degrees in Islamic theology and pedagogy. In recent years, different federal states in Germany have developed various cooperation models and curricula. Future research would reveal the extent to which the differentiation processes of Muslim communities in Germany and various milieu orientations can be incorporated into Islamic religious education and how this may lead to didactical and theological diversity.

Part of the Islamic mosaic are initiatives that empower queer Muslims living in Germany. Although not solely focused on youth, the LGBT*IQ Competence Centre of the recently founded Ibn Rushd–Goethe Mosque in Berlin aims to provide safe, inclusive and spiritual spaces for queer Muslims. "We regard every human being as God's creation, so we will not nor [sic] accept that people are excluded from religious worship because of their sexual orientation, which is contrary to human dignity."[43] Furthermore, the campaign "Love is Halal" seeks to educate mainstream society, including Muslim communities, on the

---

42 Bund Moslemischer Pfadfinder und Pfadfinderinnen Deutschlands (BMPPD), "Aktivitäten," accessed September 5, 2021, www.moslemische-pfadfinder.de/aktivitaten/.

43 Ibn Rushd-Goethe Moschee, "LGBT*IQ Competence Centre," accessed September 6, 2021, https://ibn-rushd-goethe-moschee.de/lgbtiq-kompetenzzentrum/.

intersectionality of gender diversity, sexual freedom and self-determination with Islamic religiosity.[44]

5   Scholarly Investigations: From Fundamentalism to Post-Migrant Diversity

Of Germany's approximately 82 million inhabitants, between four and five million adhere to the Islamic faith.[45] Overall, Muslims only make up about five percent of the country's population, thus discussions of "Islamic replacement" seem rather unreasonable, though this anti-Islamic rhetoric is constantly echoed in traditional and social media by right-wing extremist actors like the German political party AfD (Alternative für Deutschland) or social movements such as PEGIDA (Patriotic Europeans Against the Islamization of the Occident). A 2018 empirical study on migrant milieus in Germany confirms previous research results about only a very small milieu, the so-called religiously rooted, as being overwhelmingly guided and determined by religiosity in daily life. Compared to a precursory study from 2008, the findings on the high level of diversity amongst immigrants in Germany remains unchanged.[46] Recent attempts to construct Muslim youths in Germany as "Generation Allah"[47] fall short – even if this terminology is solely applied to those who are radicalized into religiously inspired extremism – since it leaves out of sight various other orientations among young Muslims.

It is worth looking at ways in which German academia has tried to reconstruct Muslim youth cultural participation and identity formation. Far from being exhaustive, there are three examples which will be discussed here: The first is the study by Heitmeyer et al. (1997) titled *Verlockender Fundamentalismus*[48]

---

44   Ibn Rushd-Goethe Moschee, "Liebe ist halal," accessed September 6, 2021, https://liebe-ist-halal.de/#die-kampagne.

45   Anja Stichs, "Wie viele Muslime leben in Deutschland?: Eine Hochrechnung über die Anzahl der Muslime in Deutschland zum Stand 31. Dezember 2015," *Working Paper* 71 (Nürnberg: des Forschungszentrums des Bundesamt für Migration und Flüchtlinge, 2016).

46   Bernd Hallenberg, Rainer Dettmar and Jürgen Aring, *Migranten, Meinungen, Milieus: vhw-Migrantenmilieu-Survey 2018* (Berlin: Bundesverband für Wohnen und Stadtentwicklung e.V., 2018).

47   Ahmad Mansour, *Generation Allah: Warum wir im Kampf gegen religiösen Extremismus umdenken müssen* (Frankfurt am Main: S. Fischer Verlag, 2015).

48   Wilhelm Heitmeyer, Helmut Schröder and Joachim Müller, *Verlockender Fundamentalismus: Türkische Jugendliche in Deutschland* (Frankfurt am Main: Suhrkamp, 1997).

("Tempting Fundamentalism"), which focused on Muslim youth with Turkish heritage in Germany and concluded that they overwhelmingly shared a high degree of religiously inspired tendency towards violence. However, this study was heavily criticized for its Eurocentric research design and was perceived to reproduce the heated public debates concerning integration, violence and masculinity among young Muslims in Germany.[49] At the same time, another representative study similarly focusing on German youth with Turkish heritage came to contrary findings, concluding that this demographic does not have a greater tendency towards violence when compared to non-Turkish youth in Germany.[50]

The second example is the study by von Wensierski (2007),[51] who concludes that the growing material prosperity in immigrant milieus as well as the increased cultural self-confidence of the second and third generation has meanwhile led to the development of a youth leisure and industry of culture with its own ethnic characteristics. According to the author, the Muslim habitus becomes reconstructable with regard to *two* milieus: The first of these is the so-called "Neo-Muslima," a phenomenon which can be understood as a gendered subjectivization of Islamic religiosity. On the private level, there is an individual religious orthodox practice (e.g., with regard to prayer, food choices and values), whereas at the level of public space (e.g., clothing, education and profession) there are quite different logics of action, such as emancipation, public engagement and aspirations for higher education and equality.[52] The second appearance of a specific Islamic youth scene, according to von Wensierski, consists of Islamist groups or Islamism in general. He states that Islamist groupings are somewhat comparable to autonomous left-wing extremist or right-wing extremist groups among the autochthonous populations.[53] His study, however, overlooks the hybrid and less tangible identity

---

[49] Rauf Ceylan and Michael Kiefer, *Salafismus: Fundamentalistische Strömungen und Radikalisierungsprävention* (Wiesbaden: Springer vs, 2013), 73.

[50] Ibid.

[51] Hans-Jürgen von Wensierski, "Die islamisch-selektive Modernisierung: Zur Struktur der Jugendphase junger Muslime in Deutschland," in *Junge Muslime in Deutschland: Lebenslagen, Aufwachsprozesse und Jugendkulturen*, ed. Hans-Jürgen von Wensierski and Claudia Lübcke (Opladen and Farmington Hills: Verlag Barbara Budrich, 2007).

[52] Sigrid Nökel, "'Neo-Muslimas' – Alltags- und Geschlechterpolitiken junger muslimischer Frauen zwischen Religion, Tradition und Moderne," in *Junge Muslime in Deutschland: Lebenslagen, Aufwachsprozesse und Jugendkulturen*, ed. Hans-Jürgen von Wensierski and Claudia Lübcke (Opladen and Farmington Hills: Verlag Barbara Budrich, 2007).

[53] Von Wensierski, "Die islamisch-selektive Modernisierung," 74.

formations among Muslim youths in Germany, ones in which being "Muslim" might be more flexible than in the two groups he describes, as highlighted by the two examples of the MJD and the BMPPD discussed above.

The third example is the research undertaken by Naika Foroutan (2014).[54] She provides a much more holistic picture when referring to Muslim identity concepts and youth culture, which she refers to as a "postmodern turn" in adolescent religiosity, encompassing a wide variety of orientations and references to Islam, including a decided non-orientation. Without being able to elaborate in-depth, the following milieus emerge in her analysis: Origin Muslims; Cool-/Pop-/Street Muslims; Neo-Muslims, Reform Muslims, Euro-Muslims; Orthodox Muslims; Jihadist Muslims; Cultural/Secular Muslims; Discourse/Media Muslims; Habitual Muslims; Salafists; and Anti-Muslims. Here, emphasis is given to heterogeneity instead of homogeneity, to simultaneity instead of linearity, and to histories instead of history. Foroutan, who also coined the term "post-migrant society," emphasizes how new and creative identities emerge because of the intersectionality of religion, hence rejecting linearity or the entitlement of a single social identity. The term post-migrant is not intended to describe a period of time after migration, since migration continues today. The post-migrant society is based on an epistemological turn, a radical break with the basic premise of the traditional discourse on migration and its categorical separation between migrant and non-migrant. Foroutan incorporates the two milieus mentioned in von Wensierski's study into her assessment without over-emphasizing one or the other.

In short, research on Muslim youth identities, cultures and milieus in Germany has shifted over the last two and half decades from a narrow perception focusing almost exclusively on issues of violence, security and integration – the latter being often misunderstood as a simplistic cultural assimilation – as the main points of public and scholarly investigation, to a milieu-oriented research approach which deconstructs the previously established essentialist dualism between "German" and "Muslim," which were perceived as culturally or religiously homogeneous categories. The following section will look closely at the issue of what has been referred to as "Salafism" – in Foroutan's analysis conceptualized as Salafi and Jihadi Muslims – and its attractiveness towards some youth in Western contexts.

---

54   Naika Foroutan, "Identität, Engagement und Partizipation junger Muslime in Deutschland," Akademie-RS.de, accessed January 6, 2020, www.akademie-rs.de/file admin/user_upload/download_archive/interreligioeser-dialog/20140924_foroutan_iden titaet.pdf.

6 The Contested Concept of Salafism within the Discursive Tradition of Islam

In his *Idea of an Anthropology of Islam*, Talal Asad argues that "if the anthropologist seeks to understand religion by placing it conceptually in its social context, then the way in which that social context is described must affect the understanding of religion."[55] Reconstructing Islam in such a way implies an understanding of the diversity within Islam in space and time as well as of the intersectionality within social and political contexts, which Asad refers to as a "discursive tradition," that is "a tradition of Muslim discourse that addresses itself to conceptions of the Islamic past and future, with reference to a particular Islamic practice in the present."[56] Notions of excluding Islamism or Salafist groups from that discourse, or even simply stating that Islamist actors misuse religion, contradict his discursive tradition thesis. It is more correct to state that Islamism does not, as claimed by its actors, advocate for and represent Islam.

From a critical perspective, Attia considers the very reference to "Islamism" or "Islamist" terrorism as problematic on the grounds that it already focuses centrally on "Islam" through its linguistic focus and thereby – consciously or unconsciously – links it with anti-Muslim racism.[57] She further criticizes how (Neo-)Salafism, Jihadism, (Neo-)Fundamentalism, Islamism, the "Islamic State" and other extremist or terrorist groups are neither discussed in public debates with regard to their respective specifics, nor are they related to non-Muslim religious, fundamentalist or violent movements.[58] Recent scholars of Islamic Studies have added to this confusion by stating that the term "Salafism" has replaced the use of "Islamism."[59]

Yet Attia's criticism does not take into account that governments and federal programs have begun to distinguish between different terminologies and to acknowledge the meanings of the terms in question. Furthermore, with recourse to the understanding of Islam as discursive tradition, both Islamism and Salafism can be understood as part of the tradition of Muslim discourse that addresses past and present issues; yet the task of Islamic Studies is to look

---

55   Talal Asad, *The Idea of an Anthropology of Islam* (Washington, DC: Center for Contemporary Arab Studies, Georgetown University, 1986), 16.
56   Ibid., 20.
57   Iman Attia, *Die fremdgemachte Gewalt: Zum Verhältnis von antimuslimischem Rassismus, dem Bedrohungszenario des 'islamistischen Terrorismus' und Extremismusprävention* (Berlin: Türkische Gemeinde in Deutschland e.V., 2018).
58   Ibid.
59   Susanne Schröter, *Salafismus und Jihadismus: Eine Einführung* (Frankfurt am Main: Frankfurter Forschungszentrum Globaler Islam, 2015), 1.

at how these issues are being addressed, by whom and under which circumstances. Violent extremism is never solely motivated by just one factor, thus the conflation of "Islamist" extremism or terrorism, mentioned by Attia, does not do justice to the complexity of this issue.

Henri Lauzière argues that the term "Salafi" appears occasionally and initially in medieval Islamic literature in the form of theology and as a teaching authority oriented towards the ancestors (*al-salaf al-salih*). He elucidates how "[w]ritten sources make it clear that medieval scholars used the notion *madhhab al-salaf* primarily in theological contexts, where it served as an authoritative and prestigious synonym for the Hanbali creed (*'aqida*)."[60] He criticizes the "tendency in the scholarship to suggest that premodern Muslims recognized a distinct Salafi school of thought that informed not only theology but also law. However, this view of an all-encompassing Salafi Islam may reflect modern conceptualizations more than it does medieval typologies."[61] Also, by looking at the modern era, Lauzière in fact demonstrates how "[t]he commodification of the adjective salafiyya and its use as a marketing tool, which began in 1909 with the foundation of the Salafiyya Bookstore, played a key role in popularizing the label, thus contributing to its mutation into a major concept in the West and in the Muslim world."[62] He therefore argues that Afghani and 'Abduh should not be regarded as founders of the Salafiyya. Instead, he declares that it was Louis Massignon, a French scholar of the early twentieth century, who – by reading and analyzing a journal published by the Salafiyya Bookstore – constructed the narrative of a Salafiyya movement supposedly spearheaded by Afghani, 'Abduh and Rida, a notion which still persists until today.

Frank Griffel disagrees with Lauzière's analysis. The circumstance, as presented by Lauzière, in which none of the movements that were committed to the pattern of Salafism in the major cities of the Muslim world during the late nineteenth century openly claimed to be "*al-salafiyya*," can be understood, according to Griffel, with regard to the Arabic language, "where -isms (or rather -*iyya*s) were introduced much later than the ideologies they describe."[63]

---

60 Henri Lauzière, "The Construction of Salafiyya: Reconsidering Salafism from the Perspective of Conceptual History," *International Journal of Middle East Studies* 42, no. 3 (August 2010): 372, https://doi.org/10.1017/S0020743810000401.
61 Ibid.
62 Ibid., 384.
63 Frank Griffel, "What Do We Mean By 'Salafi'? Connecting Muḥammad 'Abduh with Egypt's Nūr Party in Islam's Contemporary Intellectual History," *Die Welt des Islams* 55, no. 2 (2015): 215–16, https://doi.org/10.1163/15700607-00552p02.

Islamic modernist reformers were concerned with revival that must come "from another kind of Islam that represents an earlier stage of Islamic history, a stage when the balance of power between European and Muslim countries was reverse or at least not tipped to the disadvantage of the latter."[64] Griffel regards the revival of earlier expressions of Islam as "Salafism." He concludes that the "three reform movements of al-Afghānī and ʿAbduh as well as that of Wahhābism and the *lā madhhabiyya* initiated by al-Shawkānī express the pattern just described."[65] However, who exactly those *salaf* were was contested. For instance, for ʿAbduh they encompassed "the major theologians of Islam up to al-Ghazālī and Ibn Taymiyya," whereas for Ibn Taymiyya, "*salaf* meant the collectors and early interpreters of *ḥadīth* up to the generation of Aḥmad b. Ḥanbal."[66]

Regarding theology, also being discussed is to what extent Ahmad b. Hanbal (d. 855) can be read as the originator of a Salafist doctrine. Famhy, who favors this view, argues that this is evident from the beginnings of the conflict between Islamic rationalism and traditionalism, and Hanbal's role in it.[67] The development of a Salafi doctrine may be further established through the work of Ibn Taymiyya and Muhammad b. ʿAbd al-Wahhab.[68] Nedza, who disagrees with this perspective, argues that research should not suggest such a historical continuity. She maintains, with regard to contemporary movements, that scholarship should distance itself from the assumption that the beginnings of Salafism can already be located in the Middle Ages.[69] Similarly, Gharaibeh argues that contemporary Salafist movements try to construct a supposedly unbroken linkage to the time of the Prophet Muhammad and to modify theological views in the context of specific contemporary religious milieus.[70]

---

64 Ibid., 215.
65 Ibid.
66 Ibid.
67 Karim Famhy, "Salafismus: Definition, Ideologie und Islamismusbezug," in *Salafismus in Deutschland: Entstehung – Dynamik – Relevanz*, ed. Arbeitskreis der bei den Polizeien der Länder und beim Bundeskriminalamt eingesetzten Islamwissenschaftlerinnen und Islamwissenschaftler (Berlin: AKIPP, 2011), 16.
68 Ibid.
69 Justyna Nedza, "'Salafismus': Überlegungen zur Schärfung einer Analysekategorie," in *Salafismus: Auf der Suche nach dem wahren Islam*, ed. Behnam T. Said and Hazim Fouad (Bonn: Bundeszentrale für politische Bildung, 2014), 101.
70 Mohammad Gharaibeh, "Zur Glaubenslehre des Salafismus," in *Salafismus*, ed. Said and Fouad, 108.

According to Wiedl, "Salafism is characterized by posing clear dichotomies between *tawḥīd* (the oneness of God) and *širk* (associating others with God)."[71] Regarding Salafi-Jihadism, the central pillar of Islam is emphasized as *tawhid al-uluhiyya* ("unity of divinity"), which unfolds into the idea that in order to reach salvation, faith must be coupled with action and worship.[72] Jihadists, who believe in the absolute priority of militant *jihad*, namely to defend and disseminate Islam, have cultivated *tawhid* into a militaristic doctrine, legitimatizing violence against "infidels" and "apostates" alike.

With regard to current movements and groups, Quintan Wiktorowicz categorized Salafism into three types: "purists," "politicos" and "jihadists." His typology,[73] which continues to be very influential among scholars and policymakers, is built on the assumption that Salafists share the same creed (*'aqida*) but differ on its implementation (*manhaj*). In the recent past, attempts have been made to reformulate and criticize his understanding of Salafism. For example, Nedza argues that in order to define Salafism, one should focus on different concepts and understandings of *'aqida,* and how creed is propagated by different groups and individuals.[74] The concept of *al-wala' wa al-bara'* offers a great example of dispute within the Salafist movement.[75]

Wiedl points out that Wiktorowicz' threefold classification is based on analyses of Salafist movements in Saudi Arabia and Jordan and therefore cannot be transferred without modification to the German context.[76] She differentiates between four main tendencies of "German Salafism" which have gained momentum since 2005. A small group of "purist or quietist Salafists" are followers of Rabi' al-Madkhali (b. 1931) who spread their teachings predominantly via the Internet. Second, the group of "mainstream Salafists" follows largely purist doctrines, such as those of Muhammad Nasir al-Din al-Albani (1914–1999) and focuses on politicized *da'wa*. A third group of preachers, which Wiedl calls "radical Salafists," split off from this circle, since they theoretically legitimize revolutionary jihad against the rulers of Muslim countries through the

---

71   Nina Wiedl, *The Making of a German Salafiyya: The Emergence, Development and Missionary Work of Salafi Movements in Germany* (Aarhus: Centre for Studies in Islamism and Radicalisation, 2012), 11.
72   Shiraz Maher, *Salafi-Jihadism: The History of an Idea* (New York: Oxford University Press, 2016), 147.
73   Quintan Wiktorowicz, "Anatomy of the Salafi Movement," *Studies in Conflict & Terrorism* 29, no 3. (2006), https://doi.org/10.1080/10576100500497004.
74   Nedza, "'Salafismus'."
75   Joas Wagemakers, "Salafistische Strömungen und ihre Sicht auf *al-wala*'/*wa-l-bara*' (Loyalität und Lossagung)," in *Salafismus*, ed. Said and Fouad.
76   Wiedl, *The Making of a German Salafiyya*.

proclamation of *takfir*, but they do not directly call for the use of violence. The fourth group, "Jihad Salafists," openly call for armed combat against its targets. They are influenced, among other ideas, by the writings of Abu Muhammad al-Maqdisi (b. 1959) and Sayyid Qutb (1906–1966).

Utilizing Wiktorowicz' not undisputed definition, the concept of Salafism appeared in a 2011 report by the German intelligence service which estimated that approximately 3,800 persons could be considered as part of the political and jihadist spectrum. In 2018, this figure was placed at 11,500 persons.[77] Although the intelligence service has asserted an increase in numbers, it is unclear how they arrived at these findings. The same 2018 intelligence service report also mentions that "[d]espite the decline and fall of the ISIL 'caliphate', a scene of its sympathisers and followers in Germany and other Western countries continues to exist. For the time being, there is no way of telling what course it will adopt regarding topics, fields of action, or theaters of jihad."[78] Figures on how many youth can be linked to this movement are currently unavailable; but an analysis by the Federal Criminal Police found that in 2016, a total of 56 minors were known to have traveled to join terrorist organizations overseas.[79] These developments show that the question of radicalization is to be taken seriously.

7 Radicalization

A central debate with regard to the theoretical underpinnings of radicalization continues to play out between Gilles Kepel and Olivier Roy.[80] Whereas Kepel advocates the idea of a "radicalization of Islam," Roy posits an "Islamization of radicality." Kepel's understanding is that radical interpretations of Islam, such as Salafism, are largely responsible for promoting radicalization processes in

---

77 Federal Ministry of the Interior, Building and Community, *Brief Summary: 2018 Report on the Protection of the Constitution, Facts and Trends* (Berlin: Bundesamt für Verfassungsschutz, 2019), 26.

78 Ibid., 29.

79 Bundeskriminalamt, Bundesamt für Verfassungsschutz and Hessisches Informations- und Kompetenzzentrum gegen Extremismus, *Analyse der Radikalisierungshintergründe und verläufe der Personen, die aus islamistischer Motivation aus Deutschland in Richtung Syrien oder Irak ausgereist sind, Fortschreibung 2016* (Wiesbaden: BKA, BFV and HKE, 2016), 49.

80 Jana Kärgel, "Introduction," in *"They Have No Plan B": Radicalization, Departure, Return – Between Prevention and Intervention*, ed. Jana Kärgel (Bonn: Bundeszentrale für politische Bildung, 2018), 15.

young people's lives. This argument can intensify the problem of othering in the context of Islam, since a religion is used to apprehend (individual) actions and attitudes. In contrast, Roy does not place such a heavy weight on the religious factor as the main driving force for radicalization. In his view, radicalization is to be understood as a youth cultural phenomenon involving a radical break with society in which religion is an intersecting context: "Islam and its fundamentalist interpretations are merely a backdrop against which this radical break takes place. It could just as easily be an extreme right-wing ideology against which this radical break takes place."[81] Although the body of research is much larger when it comes to juvenile right-wing extremism, Michaela Glaser shows that there are commonalities regarding the role of ideology, experience of social disintegration and crisis, as well as the specifics of adolescence and group dynamics.[82] The change of personality and the gradual adoption of group ideology have recently been referred to as "socialization in extremism."[83]

Processes of radicalization often occur among adolescents and young adults during a phase in which a fundamental reorientation of primary social relationships takes place, frameworks of action expand, and questions of identity, inducing political identity, increase in importance.[84] During these times of storm and stress, those youth who turn towards right-wing extremism are usually younger, thirteen to fourteen years of age, than their peers who turn to Salafist extremism, these typically being aged from fifteen to nineteen.[85] Glaser contends that "[r]ight-wing extremism and Islamist ideologies provide comparable answers by offering the individual unambiguous 'explanations', clear distinctions between good and evil, and an allegedly higher objective for his or her existence and activities."[86]

However, at "the core of all analyses of the process of radicalization, whether conceptual or through case studies, is the problem of specificity [...]. Put simply, whenever we encounter an explanation of why some person or group has engaged in terrorism, we need to ask if the casual factors identified are sufficiently specific to explain why that person or group engaged in violence, since, more often than not, the factors apply equally well to a wider

---

81 Ibid.
82 Michaela Glaser, "Right-Wing and Islamist Extremism among Young People: Commonalities and Specifics in Pedagogical Responses," in *"They Have No Plan B,"* ed. Kärgel, 188.
83 Srowig and Zick, "Persönlichkeit oder Gruppe," 51–60.
84 Glaser, "Right-Wing," 190.
85 Ibid., 191.
86 Ibid.

set of individuals who did not become violent."[87] It is common, for instance, to add anti-Muslim racism to grievances held by persons who radicalize to violence in a Salafist context. Although such protest may play an important role in cases of individuals radicalized to violence, this grievance is to some extent shared by thousands of others who identify as Muslims in Western contexts. Clearly, in seeking to understand radicalization processes, it has become apparent that multiple interdependent factors can potentially have an important impact on an individual's decision to engage in (violent) extremism. To name a few, these factors include group dynamics, such as interpersonal relationships, peer-groups, and charismatic leaders agitating a specific extremist narrative; individual and personal motivations, such as risk-seeking; the quest for new (i.e., gendered) identity, feelings of emptiness or the attempt to cope with discrimination, frustration and victimization; psychological dispositions, such as narcissist or dissocial traits; as well as macro-societal factors like socio-economic marginalization or perceived or experienced political grievances.[88] The loss of social identity, frustration, individual crisis of worldview, belonging and purpose, produces a "cognitive opening," a willingness to review one's own thought patterns and to experiment with new ideas and value concepts – a process which Koehler refers to as "the de-pluralization of political concepts and values," thus focusing on the individual internalization of the notion that no other alternative interpretations of concepts and values exist.[89] Emile Durkheim and Robert Merton described this state as "anomie," the complete disassociation from the existing system and its principles and rules.

To conceptualize radicalization as a process, scholarship has both developed and criticized several models, such as pathways, pyramids, conveyor belts or staircases.[90] Radicalization can be seen as neither deterministic nor uniform; the importance of group has been stressed by research as well as the issue of so-called lone-inspired radicalization processes. The search for (religious) meaning in a state of social loneliness, during which positive interpersonal

---

87 Lorne Dawson, "Clarifying the Explanatory Context for Developing Theories of Radicalization: Five Basic Considerations," *Journal for Deradicalization*, no. 18 (Spring 2019): 149.
88 Thomas Maurer, "Die Pluralität der Radikalisierung: Eine systematische Analyse der Theorieansätze zur Radikalisierungsforschung," *Journal for Deradicalization*, no. 13 (Winter 2017).
89 Daniel Koehler, *Understanding Deradicalization: Methods, Tools and Programs for Countering Violent Extremism* (Oxon and New York: Routledge, 2017), 74.
90 Michael King and Donald M. Taylor, "The Radicalization of Homegrown Jihadists: A Review of Theoretical Models and Social Psychological Evidence," *Terrorism and Political Violence* 23, no. 4 (2011), https://doi.org/10.1080/09546553.2011.587064.

relationships are crucial, is similar to new religious movements.[91] These models are challenged by the diversity of biographies of persons who have radicalized to violence. As Dawson notes, "[m]ost glaringly, while some Western male recruits to jihadism, for example, have come from quite troubled backgrounds, with family issues, limited education, drug-abuse issues and criminality [...], others appear to have been model citizens, with happy family lives, university degrees, good jobs, spouses, and even children."[92]

By contextualizing religion within the methodological necessity to understand radicalization processes, religion should not be addressed as a fixed entity within a timeless nature, but rather as part of the multidimensionality and complexity of radicalization and violence.

In 2014, the United Nations published a report by the Special Rapporteur on Freedom of Religion or Belief on the issue of violence committed in the name of religion.[93] It was noticed that violence in the name of religion "disproportionately targets religious dissidents, members of religious minorities or converts. [...] However [it] also affects followers of the very same religion."[94] In order to understand religion as a factor in conflict, the report mentions that "[m]ultidimensional violent conflicts are often described along religious lines. Although such descriptions may capture some relevant elements of the phenomena, they fail to understand the complexity of the issue."[95] The report underscores two interlinked problems. First is the essentialism of isolating "religion" as a factor in understanding conflict; and second is the inadequacy of the instrumentalization thesis, which denies that "from the outset [...] religious motives can play a genuine role in incidents of violence."[96] It is acknowledged in the report that whatever the ultimate origins of a religious belief are thought to be, "human beings bear in any case responsibility for the practical consequences that they draw from the interpretation of their faith."[97] Dawson explains that "[t]he group believes that it has unique access to the sacred, and usually through its prophetic leader, knowledge of a divine plan for this world. At the core of this plan is the conviction that the world is fundamentally

---

91   Lorne Dawson, "The Study of New Religious Movements and the Radicalization of Home-Grown Terrorists: Opening a Dialogue," *Terrorism and Political Violence* 22, no. 1 (2009), https://doi.org/10.1080/09546550903409163.
92   Dawson, "Clarifying the Explanatory Context," 159.
93   United Nations General Assembly, *Report of the Special Rapporteur on Freedom of Religion or Belief, Heiner Bielefeldt, A/HRC/28/66* (Geneva: Human Rights Council, 2015).
94   Ibid., 4.
95   Ibid., 5.
96   Ibid., 6.
97   Ibid., 7.

corrupt and unredeemable, and that the group has a divine mandate to participate in its cleansing destruction."98

8 Salafism as Youth Culture?

Salafism in Germany has been described for quite some time as a type of youth culture in Western contexts.99 Although observations from social work, preliminary research findings as well as reconstructions of digital media support this thesis, there is a continuing lack of verifiable and methodologically transparent research. Although it is being referenced here as such, "Salafism as youth culture" is still an academic void and should be regarded as a hypothesis. According to Claudia Dantschke, Salafism appeals to young people of all social classes and religious, national and cultural backgrounds.100 Again, as discussed above, Salafism as a youth culture appears to be one contemporary milieu amongst many; it is not an all-encompassing context.

The turn towards political Salafist groups or movements is understood as a radicalization process, as discussed above. However, as Glaser argues, "an initial adolescent interest in these trends must not necessarily be synonymous with a radicalization that extends attitudes or behaviour."101 In order to deconstruct the contested term "radicalization," Glaser instead uses the notion of orientation to underscore the dynamics of creating meaning during adolescence.102 Others have argued that *radicality*, the questioning of social norms or the status quo and experimenting with different norms and ideas, is coherent with adolescence, from which processes of *radicalization* should be distinguished.103

Charismatic Salafist leaders, such as Pierre Vogel and Sven Lau, both German converts to radical Salafist Islam, address the juvenile thirst for knowledge regarding questions of identity, meaning and belonging. Their offer is

---

98 Dawson, "The Study of New Religious Movements," 13.
99 Ahmet Toprak and Gerrit Weitzel, eds., *Salafismus in Deutschland: Jugendkulturelle Aspekte, pädagogische Perspektiven* (Wiesbaden: Springer VS, 2017).
100 Claudia Dantschke, "Attraktivität, Anziehungskraft und Akteure des politischen und militanten Salafismus in Deutschland," in *Salafismus in Deutschland: Jugendkulturelle Aspekte, pädagogische Perspektiven*, ed. Ahmet Toprak and Gerrit Weitzel (Wiesbaden: Springer VS, 2017), 64.
101 Michaela Glaser, "Right-Wing," 188.
102 Ibid.
103 Bundesarbeitsgemeinschaft Landesjugendämter, *Radikalisierungstendenzen bei Kindern und Jugendlichen im Arbeitsbereich der Jugendarbeit* (Mainz: BAGLJÄ, 2018).

attractive, especially since the Islamic identity of young people – which is the focal point of the Salafist narrative – is often presented negatively in the public arena. The Salafist narrative provides both an earthly and a spiritual purpose, a utopian future with a revolutionary promise to challenge anti-Muslim racism and to rebel against society in general, which can be particularly important for youth. It does so by constructing a strict *halal-haram* dichotomy and a rigorous and univocal understanding of what is the "right" form of Islam by refusing Islamic diversity of thought and declaring a broad range of individuals and groups – including Muslims – as non-believers (*kuffar*). Salafism can be understood as something that youths can consume, a worldview that does not require any independent or autonomous thought effort; social, individual, working, political and religious life is strictly regulated and organized.

Salafist preachers address young people in a specific way, by using youth-centric language. Also, the use of German distinguishes this movement from other, more ethnically oriented Islamic organizations that were established in Germany in the second half of the twentieth century, following post-WWII labor immigration. Furthermore, emphasis is placed on the internet, with numerous websites and social media activities featuring Salafist ideas, and thus contributing to a virtual *umma* with new and competing leadership and voices within the Islamic market. In addition, street-*daʿwa*, as witnessed in many German and European cities, has been another major means for spreading their message, one in which young people vulnerable to radicalization are addressed with alternative engagement opportunities.

Salafism as youth culture offers access to the resources of both an inclusive and exclusive community. In the community of "brotherhood" and "sisterhood," which overcomes ethnic and national borders and is therefore also especially attractive for converts, prayer, fasting, studying, missionary work, etc., are all carried out collectively, yet roles, spaces and responsibilities are constructed within strict gender boundaries.[104] Marriage initiations and weddings are legitimized, and both are arranged and specifically utilized within this movement, which constitutes another factor for the recruitment of youth.

In the context of a pluralistic and democratic society, Salafism demands conformity and submission, aspects which translate into practice. Hence, Salafism can be understood as *doing Salafism*. The "unleashed fun society," with its syncretism, is juxtaposed with a counter-utopia in which everything that may

---

104   Harald Weilnböck, "Rehabilitating Perpetrators of Violent Extremism and Hate Crime: The Importance of Gender-Based Approaches and the Limits of Online Interventions," OpenDemocracy.net, accessed January 6, 2020, www.opendemocracy.net/en/can-europe-make-it/rehabilitating-perpetrators-of-violent-extremism-and-hate-crime-.

be considered "typical" for young people; like consumption, fashion, sexuality or exuberant celebration, but also engaging in social and political spaces; is rejected or comprehensively regulated, in most cases, on a voluntary basis. The rejection of "fun" within this narrative is associated with personal effort, esteem and self-control. The few "chosen ones," with their over-emphasis on identity as *homo religiosus*,[105] represent a divine order, they endure ridicule and hostility in the certainty that in the end, victory will be theirs because God is on their side. The absolute word of the sacred text, as wielded by the charismatic leader, does not tolerate contradiction or debate; its words demand obedience. This feeling of religious self-determination and emotional unity is all the greater when individuals experience powerlessness and discrimination. In this context, when joined by rebellion against one's own parents, something that is particularly apparent in cases of third-generation immigrant families, Salafism as a youth culture can also carry elements of intergenerational conflict. In comparison with other post-migrant worldviews, it is apparent that Salafism as youth culture inserts itself into relations of social domination, hate and potentially violence, reproducing rather than dissolving them.

For a long time, the so-called "Quran distribution campaigns," also referred to as street-*daʿwa* or internally as "Read!" and spearheaded by Ibrahim Abou-Nagie and Pierre Vogel, were a popular form of action within the political-missionary Salafist scene, in which many youth participated. This campaign was banned in November 2016, together with the organization behind it (*Die Wahre Religion*, "The True Religion").[106] Authorities associated participation in this campaign and other framing activities with the potential danger of violent extremism.[107] One example is the bomb attack against a Sikh temple by a group of three adolescents that was carried out in April 2016 in Essen, Germany. Two of the youths who perpetrated the terrorist attack against the Sikh temple were part of the Salafist scene in North Rhine-Westphalia. They sympathized with the terrorist organization self-styled as the "Islamic State" and participated in the Quran distribution campaign "Read!"[108] However, not all who participated in this or related activities committed, planned or even condoned violent extremist attacks.

---

105   Malik, "Medien reduzieren Muslime auf ihre Religion."
106   Diana Schubert, "Local Networking: A Practical Example from Augsburg," in *"They Have No Plan B,"* ed. Kärgel, 280.
107   Ministerium des Inneren NRW, *Lagebild Salafismus NRW* (Düsseldorf: Ministerium des Inneren NRW, 2018), 16.
108   Ibid., 84.

9 Preventing and Countering Radicalization to Violence

From a public policy perspective, it is important to distinguish between cognitive radicalization and behavioral radicalization to violence. The former can be understood as a process "by which an individual or a group gradually adopts extreme positions or ideologies that are opposed to the status quo and challenge mainstream ideas."[109] Having and expressing radical thoughts is not illegal or criminal in itself, and in most cases it is protected under freedom of thought, belief and expression. In contrast, however, behavioral radicalization to violence, which can be understood as a processual adoption of "an ideology and/or belief system that justifies the use of violence in order to advance their cause,"[110] is considered a threat to society and potentially national security. Nevertheless, non-violent positions can also have harmful impacts on individuals and groups. According to Peter Neumann, the endpoint of a radicalization process is extremism, understood as the beliefs and/or actions of people supporting violence to achieve ideologically motivated goals which deny basic human rights. The problem is that the term is "context-dependent, which means that its definition can easily be challenged and manipulated."[111] Since the guiding terminology (radicalization and extremism) is ambiguous, context-dependent and normative in terms of what and who defines the status quo, the term prevention is also too vague, since it is oftentimes unclear which situation or development must be prevented.

Governments and civil society organizations usually adopt the public health model, which is being applied in various prevention contexts across the globe. For example, the Canadian government utilizes this approach and differentiates between three forms of prevention: early prevention aims, for instance, to increase media literacy in the general population; at-risk prevention is directed towards individuals or groups in the initial stages of radicalization to violence; and third, disengagement focuses on individuals who have become involved in violent extremism.[112] Disengagement, understood as a process through which an individual abandons his or her (violent) extremist behavior, differs

---

[109] Canada Centre for Community Engagement and Prevention of Violence, *National Strategy on Countering Radicalization to Violence* (Ottawa: Government of Canada, 2018), 7.
[110] Ibid.
[111] Peter R. Neumann, *Countering Violent Extremism and Radicalisation that Lead to Terrorism: Ideas, Recommendations, and Good Practices from the OSCE Region* (London: International Centre for the Study of Radicalisation, 2017), 16.
[112] Canada Centre for Community Engagement and Prevention of Violence, *National Strategy*.

from deradicalization, which takes extremist ideology, views, beliefs and behavioral commitment as its main point of reference. The Advice Center on Radicalization, run by the German Federal Office for Migration and Refugees, refers to deradicalization as a process comprised of emotional, pragmatic and ideological dimensions. Instead of focusing primarily on behavior, emphasis is given here to cognitive aspects of deradicalization as well.[113] Some scholars argue that both concepts are interdependent, maintaining that if a disengaged person still holds on to extremist ideology, the chances of re-radicalization to violence are still present.[114] Lastly, the notion of violence within this continuum is often unclear, as are the questions of whether it only encompasses physical or also psychological forms of violence and harm, and of how "offline violence" differs from "online violence."

It is worth noting that some approaches to preventing radicalization to violence go back to the 1980s and 1990s and are still of significance today. For example, the well-known EXIT-programs provide – in short – a wide (e.g., economic, legal, social) range of support to those individuals who decide to exit violent extremist movements or groups. The Violence Prevention Network, a Germany-based organization working in the field of countering radicalization to violence (CRV), emphasizes that its programs are also reaching out to those "who have not yet, or not conclusively, decided to distance themselves from extremist thinking – or are still rooted in it."[115]

Generally speaking, the evidence base about what works in CRV is weak, with a dearth of externally conducted systematic program evaluations.[116] There are few verified benchmarks by which to gauge success, and determining appropriate outcome measures remains a work in progress.[117] For example, intervening in correctional facilities targeting "inmates who have been convicted of terrorism-related offenses, or have been identified as at risk of

---

113 Milena Uhlmann, *Evaluation of the Advice Centre on Radicalization: Final Report, Research Report 31* (Nürnberg: Bundesamt für Migration und Flüchtlinge, 2017), 19.
114 Daniel Koehler and Verena Fiebig, "Knowing What to Do: Academic and Practitioner Understanding of How to Counter Violent Radicalization," *Perspectives on Terrorism* 13, no. 3 (June 2019): 46.
115 Thomas Mücke, "Pedagogical Approaches to Deradicalization in the Area of Religious Extremism," in *"They Have No Plan B,"* ed. Kärgel, 320.
116 David Yuzva Clement, "Jugendarbeit und Salafismus: Eine rekonstruktive Studie zu professionellen Beobachtungs- und Handlungsweisen von pädagogischen Fachkräften" (PhD diss., University of Erfurt, 2018).
117 Friedrich Lösel et al., "Protective Factors Against Extremism and Violent Radicalization: A Systematic Review of Research," *International Journal of Developmental Science* 12, no. 1–2 (2018), https://doi.org/10.3233/DEV-170241.

radicalization due to demonstrating extremist views and/or associations,"[118] differs from youth work with at-risk adolescents vulnerable to radicalization to violence.[119] Prevention work by frontline practitioners and with family members of radicalized persons follows different pedagogical logics.[120] Additionally, the role of law enforcement in prevention efforts has been criticized.[121] A step toward desecuritizing prevention and intervention programs would be for law enforcement to withdraw from this field of action and leave it to civil society organizations, including social work and mental health agencies, and to only become involved when individuals have crossed the threshold of criminal activity. Moreover, interventions in the online space, such as counter or alternative narratives, the involvement of social media companies and the question of content moderation are all promising fields which require further research and program evaluation. Because radicalization processes are typically determined by an interplay of factors, "multimodal approaches to prevention" are required.[122]

10   Conclusion

Despite the currently quite popular tendencies to limit the question of juvenile Islamic activism to Salafist groups, this chapter explored different fields of activism, and correspondingly, different milieus and biographical diversity among Muslim youth in Germany. While the Federal Association of Muslim Pathfinders in Germany (BMPPD) and the Muslim Youth in Germany (MJD) association both promote democracy education and empowerment of young people, Salafist groups favor anti-democratic values which can fuel persons and groups into radicalization processes.

The concept of Salafism is multifaceted and controversially discussed in scholarship. There are two dominant positions regarding this subject within historiographical and contemporary contexts, the first being the debate

---

118   Adrian Cherney and Emma Belton, "Evaluating Case-Managed Approaches to Counter Radicalization and Violent Extremism: An Example of the Proactive Integrated Support Model (PRISM) Intervention," *Studies in Conflict & Terrorism* (March 2019), https://doi.org/10.1080/1057610X.2019.1577016.
119   Franz Josef Krafeld, ed., *Akzeptierende Jugendarbeit mit rechten Jugendcliquen* (Bremen: Landeszentrale für politische Bildung, 1992).
120   Claudia Dantschke, "The Role of the Family in Preventing Radicalization," in *"They Have No Plan B,"* ed. Kärgel, 202.
121   Imran Awan, " 'I Am a Muslim Not an Extremist'," 1167.
122   Lösel et al., "Protective Factors," 99.

between Henri Lauzière and Frank Griffel concerning the question of an all-encompassing Salafi-Islam, while the second is the disagreement between Gilles Kepel and Olivier Roy regarding the question of the radicalization of Islam vs. the Islamization of radicality. This chapter, however, argues that the issue of Salafism can be contextualized by referring to Talal Asad's understanding of Islam as a discursive tradition.

Furthermore, academic research has significantly contributed to the othering of Muslims in Germany. Thus, milieu-oriented research, which occurred more recently, can deconstruct academic as well as pedagogical biases when it comes to understanding and engaging with Muslim youths, hence the attribution "Muslim" becomes the starting point of debate rather than a prefix of identity.

Another finding of this chapter is the importance of the discussion about "what" Islam is and "how" it is being understood and practiced in public spheres such as schools, youth centers, universities and communities. It is important to acknowledge and address the diversity and ambiguity of post-migrant Islamic life worlds in order to confront and challenge what Jamal Malik has referred to as strategic essentialism, i.e., an essentialism which can manifest itself in religious exclusivism as well as in the idea of homogenous societies. Islamic Studies, social work, social sciences and other disciplines in the humanities should stimulate one another and address the issues of Islamic activism, diversity regarding gender and sexual orientations and other dynamics of Islam in the modern world through interdisciplinary studies. It is the role of Islamic Studies to problematize religious or cultural essentialism, including the entanglement of Islam and policies of integration and securitization, as well as, rather than treating religion as if it exists in a vacuum, analyzing it in the social and other discursive contexts in which it occurs.

Bibliography

Asad, Talal. *The Idea of an Anthropology of Islam*. Washington, DC: Center for Contemporary Arab Studies, Georgetown University, 1986.

Attia, Iman. *Die fremdgemachte Gewalt: Zum Verhältnis von antimuslimischem Rassismus, dem Bedrohungszenario des 'islamistischen Terrorismus' und Extremismusprävention*. Berlin: Türkische Gemeinde in Deutschland e.V., 2018.

Attia, Iman. "Zur Bedeutung des Islamdiskurses für die Jugendarbeit." *Deutsche Jugend: Zeitschrift für die Jugendarbeit* 57, no. 2 (2009): 74–81.

Awan, Imran. "'I Am a Muslim Not an Extremist': How the Prevent Strategy Has Constructed a 'Suspect' Community." *Politics and Policy* 40, no. 6 (December 2012): 1158–85, https://doi.org/10.1111/j.1747-1346.2012.00397.x.

Bade, Klaus J. and Jochen Oltmer. *Normalfall Migration*. Bonn: Bundeszentrale für politische Bildung, 2004.

Bauer, Thomas. *Die Kultur der Ambiguität: Eine andere Geschichte des Islams*. Berlin: Verlag der Weltreligionen, 2011.

Beribes, Alexander, Leo Mausbach and Johannes Jungeblut. "Is Islam Part of Eastern Europe?: Thoughts on History, Religion, and National Identity in the Eastern EU Countries." *International Reports by the Konrad-Adenauer-Stiftung*, no. 2 (2018): 68–81.

Beydoun, Khaled A. "On Islamophobia, Immigration, and the 'Muslims Bans'." *Ohio Northern University Law Review* 43, no. 3 (2017): 443–58.

Bund Moslemischer Pfadfinder und Pfadfinderinnen Deutschlands (BMPPD). "Aktivitäten." Accessed September 5, 2021, www.moslemische-pfadfinder.de/aktivitaten.

Bund Moslemischer Pfadfinder und Pfadfinderinnen Deutschlands (BMPPD). "Wer wir sind." Accessed January 5, 2020, www.moslemische-pfadfinder.de/verband/wer-wir-sind.

Bundesarbeitsgemeinschaft Landesjugendämter. *Radikalisierungstendenzen bei Kindern und Jugendlichen im Arbeitsbereich der Jugendarbeit*. Mainz: BAGLÄ, 2018.

Bundeskriminalamt, Bundesamt für Verfassungsschutz and Hessisches Informations- und Kompetenzzentrum gegen Extremismus. *Analyse der Radikalisierungshintergründe und verläufe der Personen, die aus islamistischer Motivation aus Deutschland in Richtung Syrien oder Irak ausgereist sind, Fortschreibung 2016*. Wiesbaden: BKA, BFV and HKE, 2016.

Canada Centre for Community Engagement and Prevention of Violence. *National Strategy on Countering Radicalization to Violence*. Ottawa: Government of Canada, 2018.

Ceylan, Rauf and Michael Kiefer. *Salafismus: Fundamentalistische Strömungen und Radikalisierungsprävention*. Wiesbaden: Springer VS, 2013.

Cherney, Adrian and Emma Belton. "Evaluating Case-Managed Approaches to Counter Radicalization and Violent Extremism: An Example of the Proactive Integrated Support Model (PRISM) Intervention." *Studies in Conflict & Terrorism* (March 2019), https://doi.org/10.1080/1057610X.2019.1577016.

Dantschke, Claudia. "Attraktivität, Anziehungskraft und Akteure des politischen und militanten Salafismus in Deutschand." In *Salafismus in Deutschland: Jugendkulturelle Aspekte, pädagogische Perspektiven*, edited by Ahmet Toprak and Gerrit Weitzel, 61–76. Wiesbaden: Springer VS, 2017.

Dantschke, Claudia. "The Role of the Family in Preventing Radicalization." In *"They Have No Plan B": Radicalization, Departure, Return – Between Prevention and Intervention*, edited by Jana Kärgel, 201–10. Bonn: Bundeszentrale für politische Bildung, 2018.

Davey, Jacob and Julia Ebner. *"The Great Replacement": The Violent Consequences of Mainstreamed Extremism*. London: Institute for Strategic Dialogue, 2019.

Dawson, Lorne. "Clarifying the Explanatory Context for Developing Theories of Radicalization: Five Basic Considerations." *Journal for Deradicalization*, no. 18 (Spring 2019): 146–84.

Dawson, Lorne. "The Study of New Religious Movements and the Radicalization of Home-Grown Terrorists: Opening a Dialogue." *Terrorism and Political Violence* 22, no. 1 (2009): 1–21, https://doi.org/10.1080/09546550903409163.

Decker, Oliver, Johannes Kiess and Elmar Brähler. *Die stabilisierte Mitte: Rechtsextreme Einstellung in Deutschland 2014*. Leipzig: University of Leipzig, 2014.

Famhy, Karim. "Salafismus: Definition, Ideologie und Islamismusbezug." In *Salafismus in Deutschland: Entstehung – Dynamik – Relevanz*, edited by Arbeitskreis der bei den Polizeien der Länder und beim Bundeskriminalamt eingesetzten Islamwissenschaftlerinnen und Islamwissenschaftler, 8–42. Berlin: AKIPP, 2011.

Federal Ministry of the Interior, Building and Community. *Brief Summary: 2018 Report on the Protection of the Constitution, Facts and Trends*. Berlin: Bundesamt für Verfassungsschutz, 2019.

Fick, Monika. "Lessings *Nathan der Weise* und das Bild vom Orient und Islam in Theatertexten aus der zweiten Hälfte des 18. Jahrhunderts: Überarbeitete und erweiterte Fassung des Vortrags am 10. Mai 2016 im Rahmen des Lessing Festivals in der Herzog August Bibliothek, Wolfenbuettel." Goethezeitportal.de. Accessed January 5, 2020, www.goethezeitportal.de/db/wiss/lessing/fick_orient.pdf.

Foroutan, Naika. "Identität, Engagement und Partizipation junger Muslime in Deutschland." Akademie-RS.de. Accessed January 6, 2020, www.akademie-rs.de/fileadmin/user_upload/download_archive/interreligioeser-dialog/20140924_foroutan_identitaet.pdf.

Gharaibeh, Mohammad. "Zur Glaubenslehre des Salafismus." In *Salafismus: Auf der Suche nach dem wahren Islam*, edited by Behnam T. Said and Hazim Fouad, 106–31. Bonn: Bundeszentrale für politische Bildung, 2014.

Glaser, Michaela. "Right-Wing and Islamist Extremism among Young People: Commonalities and Specifics in Pedagogical Responses." In *"They Have No Plan B": Radicalization, Departure, Return – Between Prevention and Intervention*, edited by Jana Kärgel, 187–200. Bonn: Bundeszentrale für politische Bildung, 2018.

Goerzig, Carolin and Khaled al-Hashimi. *Radicalization in Western Europe: Integration, Public Discourse, and Loss of Identity among Muslim Communities*. Oxon and New York: Routledge, 2015.

Griffel, Frank. "What Do We Mean By 'Salafi'? Connecting Muḥammad 'Abduh with Egypt's Nūr Party in Islam's Contemporary Intellectual History." *Die Welt des Islams* 55, no. 2 (2015): 186–220, https://doi.org/10.1163/15700607-00552p02.

Hallenberg, Bernd, Rainer Dettmar and Jürgen Aring. *Migranten, Meinungen, Milieus: vhw-Migrantenmilieu-Survey 2018*. Berlin: Bundesverband für Wohnen und Stadtentwicklung e.V., 2018.

Heitmeyer, Wilhelm, Helmut Schröder and Joachim Müller. *Verlockender Fundamentalismus: Türkische Jugendliche in Deutschland.* Frankfurt am Main: Suhrkamp, 1997.

Höpp, Gerhard. "Die Wünsdorfer Moschee: Eine Episode islamischen Lebens in Deutschland, 1915–1930." *Die Welt des Islams* 36, no. 2 (January 1996): 204–18, https://doi.org/10.1163/1570060962597490.

Ibn Rushd-Goethe Moschee. "Die Moschee." Accessed September 6, 2021, https://ibn-rushd-goethe-moschee.de/die-moschee/.

Ibn Rushd-Goethe Moschee. "LGBT*IQ Competence Centre." Accessed September 6, 2021, https://ibn-rushd-goethe-moschee.de/lgbtiq-kompetenzzentrum/.

Ibn Rushd-Goethe Moschee. "Liebe ist halal." Accessed September 6, 2021, https://liebe-ist-halal.de/#die-kampagne.

Jamal, Amaney A. "Trump(ing) on Muslim Women: The Gendered Side of Islamophobia." *Journal of Middle East Women's Studies* 13, no. 3 (2017): 472–75, https://doi.org/10.1215/15525864-4179144.

Jonker, Gerdien. *The Ahmadiyya Quest for Religious Progress: Missionizing Europe 1900–1965.* Leiden: Brill, 2015.

Kärgel, Jana. "Introduction." In *"They Have No Plan B": Radicalization, Departure, Return – Between Prevention and Intervention,* edited by Jana Kärgel, 13–23. Bonn: Bundeszentrale für politische Bildung, 2018.

King, Michael and Donald M. Taylor. "The Radicalization of Homegrown Jihadists: A Review of Theoretical Models and Social Psychological Evidence." *Terrorism and Political Violence* 23, no. 4 (2011): 602–22, https://doi.org/10.1080/09546553.2011.587064.

Klawe, Willy. "Die Lebenswelt junger Muslime und die Faszination des Islam: Von der Fremdenfeindlichkeit zur Islamophobie – Der 'religious turn' im Fremdheitsdiskurs." *Deutsche Jugend: Zeitschrift für die Jugendarbeit* 64, no. 9 (September 2016): 376–86.

Koehler, Daniel. *Understanding Deradicalization: Methods, Tools and Programs for Countering Violent Extremism.* Oxon and New York: Routledge, 2017.

Koehler, Daniel and Verena Fiebig. "Knowing What to Do: Academic and Practitioner Understanding of How to Counter Violent Radicalization." *Perspectives on Terrorism* 13, no. 3 (2019): 44–62.

Krafeld, Franz Josef, ed. *Akzeptierende Jugendarbeit mit rechten Jugendcliquen.* Bremen: Landeszentrale für politische Bildung, 1992.

Lauzière, Henri. "The Construction of Salafiyya: Reconsidering Salafism from the Perspective of Conceptual History." *International Journal of Middle East Studies* 42, no. 3 (August 2010): 369–89, https://doi.org/10.1017/S0020743810000401.

Lösel, Friedrich, Sonja King, Doris Bender and Irina Jugl. "Protective Factors Against Extremism and Violent Radicalization: A Systematic Review of Research."

International Journal of Developmental Science 12, no. 1–2 (2018): 89–102, https://doi.org/10.3233/DEV-170241.

Maher, Shiraz. *Salafi-Jihadism: The History of an Idea*. New York: Oxford University Press, 2016.

Malik, Jamal. "Integration of Muslim Migrants and the Politics of Dialogue: The Case of Modern Germany." *Journal of Muslim Minority Affairs* 33, no. 4 (2013): 495–506, https://doi.org/10.1080/13602004.2013.866350.

Malik, Jamal. "Medien reduzieren Muslime auf ihre Religion." *Tages-Anzeiger* (December 8, 2007).

Mansel, Jürgen, and Viktoria Spaiser. *Ausgrenzungsdynamiken: In welchen Lebenslagen Jugendliche Fremdgruppen abwerten*. Weinheim and Basel: Beltz Juventa, 2013.

Mansour, Ahmad. *Generation Allah: Warum wir im Kampf gegen religiösen Extremismus umdenken müssen*. Frankfurt am Main: S. Fischer Verlag, 2015.

Maurer, Thomas. "Die Pluralität der Radikalisierung: Eine systematische Analyse der Theorieansätze zur Radikalisierungsforschung." *Journal for Deradicalization*, no. 13 (Winter 2017): 49–100.

McGuire, Meredith B. *Lived Religion: Faith and Practice in Everyday Life*. New York: Oxford University Press, 2008.

Ministerium des Inneren NRW. *Lagebild Salafismus NRW*. Düsseldorf: Ministerium des Inneren NRW, 2018.

Motadel, David. *Islam and Nazi Germany's War*. Cambridge: The Belknap Press of Harvard University Press, 2014.

Muslimische Jugend in Deutschland. "Junge Muslime als Partner: Für Dialog und Kooperation und gegen Diskriminierung." MuslimischeJugend.de. Accessed January 5, 2020, https://muslimischejugend.de/module/projekte1/jungemuslime.html.

Muslimische Jugend in Deutschland. "Über uns." MuslimischeJugend.de. Accessed January 5, 2020, https://muslimischejugend.de/about.html.

Mücke, Thomas. "Pedagogical Approaches to Deradicalization in the Area of Religious Extremism." In *"They Have No Plan B": Radicalization, Departure, Return – Between Prevention and Intervention*, edited by Jana Kärgel, 317–27. Bonn: Bundeszentrale für politische Bildung, 2018.

Nedza, Justyna. " 'Salafismus': Überlegungen zur Schärfung einer Analysekategorie." In *Salafismus: Auf der Suche nach dem wahren Islam*, edited by Behnam T. Said and Hazim Fouad, 80–105. Bonn: Bundeszentrale für politische Bildung, 2014.

Neumann, Peter R. *Countering Violent Extremism and Radicalisation that Lead to Terrorism: Ideas, Recommendations, and Good Practices from the OSCE Region*. London: International Centre for the Study of Radicalisation, 2017.

Nökel, Sigrid. " 'Neo-Muslimas' – Alltags – und Geschlechterpolitiken junger muslimischer Frauen zwischen Religion, Tradition und Moderne." In *Junge Muslime in Deutschland: Lebenslagen, Aufwachsprozesse und Jugendkulturen*, edited by

Hans-Jürgen von Wensierski and Claudia Lübcke, 135–54. Opladen and Farmington Hills: Verlag Barbara Budrich, 2007.

Schröter, Susanne. *Salafismus und Jihadismus: Eine Einführung*. Frankfurt am Main: Frankfurter Forschungszentrum Globaler Islam, 2015.

Schubert, Diana. "Local Networking: A Practical Example from Augsburg." In *"They Have No Plan B": Radicalization, Departure, Return – Between Prevention and Intervention*, edited by Jana Kärgel, 280–89. Bonn: Bundeszentrale für politische Bildung, 2018.

Spuler-Stegeman, Ursula. "Der Elefant des Kalifen: Wie der Islam nach Deutschland kam." *Der Spiegel*. Accessed January 5, 2020, www.spiegel.de/spiegel/spiegelspecial/d-56323062.html.

Srowig, Fabian and Andreas Zick. "Persönlichkeit oder Gruppe: Wo liegen die Wurzeln extremistischer Radikalisierung?" In *Radikalisierung und De-Radikalisierung in Deutschland: Eine gesamtgesellschaftliche Herausforderung*, edited by Magdalena von Drachenfels, Philipp Offermann and Carmen Wunderlich, 51–58. Berlin: Epubli, 2018.

Stichs, Anja. "Wie viele Muslime leben in Deutschland?: Eine Hochrechnung über die Anzahl der Muslime in Deutschland zum Stand 31. Dezember 2015." *Working Paper 71*. Nürnberg: des Forschungszentrums des Bundesamt für Migration und Flüchtlinge, 2016.

Stiftung House of One – Bet- und Lehrhaus Berlin. "The Concept." House-of-One.org. Accessed July 9, 2020, https://house-of-one.org/en/concept.

Tibi, Bassam. "Warum ich kapituliere." *Cicero* (June 2016): 115–19.

Topolski, Anya. "The Dangerous Discourse of the 'Judaeo-Christian' Myth: Masking the Race-Religion Constellation in Europe." *Patterns of Prejudice* 54, no. 1–2 (April 2020): 71–90, https://doi.org/10.1080/0031322X.2019.1696049.

Toprak, Ahmet, and Gerrit Weitzel, eds. *Salafismus in Deutschland: Jugendkulturelle Aspekte, pädagogische Perspektiven*. Wiesbaden: Springer VS, 2017.

Uhlmann, Milena. *Evaluation of the Advice Centre on Radicalization: Final Report, Research Report 31*. Nürnberg: Bundesamt für Migration und Flüchtlinge, 2017.

United Nations General Assembly. *Report of the Special Rapporteur on Freedom of Religion or Belief, Heiner Bielefeldt, A/HRC/28/66*. Geneva: Human Rights Council, 2015.

Von Wensierski, Hans-Jürgen. "Die islamisch-selektive Modernisierung: Zur Struktur der Jugendphase junger Muslime in Deutschland." In *Junge Muslime in Deutschland: Lebenslagen, Aufwachsprozesse und Jugendkulturen*, edited by Hans-Jürgen von Wensierski and Claudia Lübcke, 55–82. Opladen and Farmington Hills: Verlag Barbara Budrich, 2007.

Wagemakers, Joas. "Salafistische Strömungen und ihre Sicht auf *al-wala' wa-l-bara'* (Loyalität und Lossagung)." In *Salafismus: Auf der Suche nach dem wahren Islam*, edited by Behnam T. Said and Hazim Fouad, 55–79. Bonn: Bundeszentrale für politische Bildung, 2014.

Weilnböck, Harald. "Rehabilitating Perpetrators of Violent Extremism and Hate Crime: The Importance of Gender-Based Approaches and the Limits of Online Interventions." OpenDemocracy.net. Accessed January 6, 2020, www.opendemocracy.net/en/can-europe-make-it/rehabilitating-perpetrators-of-violent-extremism-and-hate-crime-.

Wiedl, Nina. *The Making of a German Salafiyya: The Emergence, Development and Missionary Work of Salafi Movements in Germany.* Aarhus: Centre for Studies in Islamism and Radicalisation, 2012.

Wiktorowicz, Quintan. "Anatomy of the Salafi Movement." *Studies in Conflict & Terrorism* 29, no 3. (2006): 207–39, https://doi.org/10.1080/10576100500497004.

Wilner, Alex and Irfan Yar. *Canadian Terrorists by the Numbers: An Assessment of Canadians Joining and Supporting Terrorist Groups.* Ottawa: Macdonald-Laurier Institute, 2019.

Yuzva Clement, David. "Jugendarbeit und Salafismus: Eine rekonstruktive Studie zu professionellen Beobachtungs- und Handlungsweisen von pädagogischen Fachkräften." PhD diss., University of Erfurt, 2018.

PART 3

Islamic Normativity and Shariʿa

⁝

CHAPTER 7

Islam and Human Rights

Breaks and Continuity in a Complex Debate

Mouez Khalfaoui

> Instead of fostering primordial identity constructions and essentialisms—as Muslims themselves often do when they claim that Islamic practice and confession are not subject to historical change—Islam, like other religions, can be grasped as a repertory of references that enables Muslims to interpret—and hence make meaningful—their complex lifeworlds.[1]

⁂

1 Introduction

Over the past decades, an increasing number of publications have addressed the relationship between Islam and human rights. While some studies have examined the involvement of Muslim states in the development of the Declaration of Human Rights in 1948,[2] others have focused primarily on the human rights situation in the Islamic world, studying the impact of international human rights on national laws, among other things.[3] As this indicates,

---

1   Jamal Malik, "Introduction," in *Muslims in Europe: From the Margin to the Centre*, ed. Jamal Malik (Münster: LIT, 2004), 2.
2   Charles Malik, a Lebanese academic and diplomat, was a key figure involved in preparing the UDHR. In many ways, his involvement represented the Arab or rather the Islamic world. Tony Nasrallah, "Charles Malik und die Universalität der Menschenrechte," in *Kultur, Identität und Menschenrechte: Transkulturelle Perspektiven*, ed. Sarhan Dhouib (Göttingen: Velbrück, 2012). For more information, see Susan Waltz, "Universal Human Rights: The Contribution of Muslim States," *Human Rights Quarterly* 26, no. 4 (November 2004), https://doi.org/10.1353/hrq.2004.0059.
3   A main reference is Ann Elizabeth Mayer, "Universal Versus Islamic Human Rights: A Clash of Cultures or a Clash with a Construct?," *Michigan Journal of International Law* 15, no. 2 (1994).

public, political, and academic interest in the relationship between Islam and human rights is ongoing. In the context of growing Muslim minorities in Europe and elsewhere, attention has recently moved toward the role of Islamic law (shariʿa) in secular legal systems.[4] Social and cultural specialists and stakeholders have been asking whether Muslims in Europe are interested in integrating Islamic norms into their day-to-day lives as well as whether Islamic and secular laws are compatible.[5] These and other questions have shifted the geographical focus of ongoing human rights debates away from Muslim states and towards secular political systems in Europe and elsewhere.

The ambiguity that surrounds the concepts of "human rights" and "Islamic doctrine" frequently complicates discussions. To clarify, in most cases, "Islamic doctrine" is used to describe the classical premodern doctrine of Islamic law, whereas the term "human rights" is used to denote modern human rights norms. Opinions regarding the compatibility between these two notions diverge, something which in Muslim states is related to the varying roles of shariʿa in legal systems and society at large. On the one hand, Islamic doctrine is taken to embody human rights, allegedly not requiring any additional "Western concepts."[6] In these instances, lengthy debates about "Islam and human rights" are replaced by the succinct declaration: "Islam *is* human rights."[7] The latter position is frequently built around the argument that Islam improved the rights of women and slaves 1,400 years ago. Similarly, it is also asserted that the Quran continues to emphasize equality between people worldwide.[8] Others, who oppose the equating of Islamic doctrine with human rights, point to the doctrine's deficits with respect to women's rights, the status of non-Muslims in Muslim states, as well as the freedoms of thought and religion. They view

---

4 Heiner Bielefeldt, "Political Secularism and European Islam: A Challenge to Muslims and Non-Muslims," in *Muslims in Europe*, ed. Jamal Malik, 1–18.
5 Mouez Khalfaoui, "Das islamische Recht und das staatliche Recht aus muslimischer Perspektive," in *Handbuch Christentum und Islam in Deutschland: Grundlagen, Erfahrungen und Perspektiven des Zusammenlebens*, ed. Mathias Rohe et al. (Freiburg: Herder-Verlag, 2014).
6 Heiner Bielefeldt, "Muslim Voices in the Human Rights Debate," *Human Rights Quarterly* 17, no. 4 (November 1995).
7 Atique Tahir, "A True Vision of Human Rights in Islam," *Al-Adwa* 28, no. 40 (2013). Tahir finds that "when Muslims speak about human rights in Islam, they mean rights which are bestowed by Allah in the Holy Quran; rights which are divine, eternal, universal and absolute; rights which are guaranteed and protected through the Shariʿah. The rights which are not subject to any alterations or modifications, and there is no scope for any change or abrogation."
8 Bielefeldt, "Muslim Voices," 595.

human rights as an indispensable component of social progress and plead for their integration in Muslim legal systems.[9]

A close analysis of different Muslim positions about the relationship between Islam and human rights reveals two overarching questions concerning the compatibility of Islamic doctrine with (a) human rights and (b) secular national laws. The first question plays a central role in Muslim states, where the shari'a commonly constitutes a normative starting point in discussions about human rights, not least because it constitutes a primary pillar of national legislation in Muslim-majority nations.[10] The second question, which has recently gained importance in Western states, places human rights at the heart of ongoing debates, which frequently produce headlines referring to "shari'a and secular law" or "Islamic law in Europe."[11]

In this chapter, I argue that several of the classic premodern norms of Islamic law, as they are currently practiced in Muslim states, are incompatible with modern human rights norms. Yet, I also claim that international human rights, including the rights of women and children,[12] can theoretically be deduced from Islamic doctrine. However, for that to happen, the latter must be interpreted anew, taking into consideration the latest societal developments and the modern *Zeitgeist*.[13] In my opinion, Muslims could, or rather should, use international human rights as a framework for reflecting and further developing their own values so as to match modern norms of freedom, gender equality and other values of human rights. At the same time, I suggest that the development of genuine Islamic values, within a pluralistic and democratic context, would allow for a substantial Muslim contribution to the international understanding of human rights. In contrast, blindly defending premodern shari'a norms puts Muslims at risk of isolation and increases rather than solves existing problems, especially for Muslim minorities living in Western democratic societies.

---

9   Muslim positions with regard to human rights are not limited to Muslim states; they also refer to Muslim citizens and residents in Western countries. See, for example, Murad Wilfried Hofmann, "Der Islam und die Menschenrechte," *Qantara*, accessed November 29, 2019, https://de.qantara.de/inhalt/murad-wilfried-hofmann-der-islam-und-die-menschenrechte.
10 Muhammad Zafrullah Khan, *Islam and Human Rights* (Islamabad: Islam International Publications Ltd., 1967).
11 Bielefeldt, "Political Secularism."
12 Children's rights are primarily anchored in the UN Convention on the Rights of the Child (1989). Wolfgang Benedek, ed., *Understanding Human Rights: Manual on Human Rights Education* (Vienna: NWV, 2012), 233–49.
13 Niaz A. Shah, "Women's Human Rights in the Koran: An Interpretive Approach," *Human Rights Quarterly* 28, no. 4 (November 2006).

2 Human Rights

The modern concept of human rights is primarily based on the Universal Declaration of Human Rights (UDHR), first published in 1948.[14] The declaration was originally developed to secure basic rights worldwide and to thwart all forms of discrimination. Thus, it was particularly important to relatively "weak" societal groups, who frequently suffered from discrimination and had to fight for equality and respect. These groups included women, children, slaves and refugees, as well as ethnic and religious minorities. Thanks to the efforts of human rights activists and international human rights conventions, slavery is now widely deemed an illegitimate and punishable practice and has largely been abolished. The rights of women and children, by contrast, remain the subject of ongoing debate and still need further improvements. This is particularly true for societies in which the legal status of individuals is regulated by inheritable religious and cultural norms. In these cases, particularly pressing questions relate to the human rights approach adopted by religious individuals and institutions. In the Islamic world, the term "religious" is frequently equated with "Muslim," ignoring the fact that not all Muslims are religious and that their behavior might not always be religiously motivated.

Much of the continuing controversy surrounding women's and children's rights in Muslim contexts concerns the content and mutability of Islamic doctrine and shariʿa norms, not their application by individual Muslims. The norms of classical shariʿa, which were developed in premodern times, are widely treated as the opposite of human rights, including the rights of women, children and non-Muslims.[15] Thus, the desire to combine Islamic doctrine with international human rights is usually accompanied by ongoing calls for the reform of Islamic law, for instance, with respect to those issues concerning the matter of gender equality and freedom of faith as well as the rights of minorities. The above-mentioned claim that Islam improved the freedom of people in the past, thereby helping women, children and slaves,[16] the classical Islamic approach to gender roles and slaves, among other things, does not match modern conceptions of human rights. Thus, the notion of human rights is of modern origin and premodern societies had different norms regulating

---

14 For the English version of the universal declaration (1948), see Benedek, *Understanding Human Rights*, 394–97.

15 The constitutions of some Muslim states, for instance those designated as an "Islamic Republic," describe shariʿa or religious law as the main reference for state law.

16 Bernard Lewis, *Race and Slavery in the Middle East: An Historical Enquiry* (New York: Oxford University Press, 1990).

human behavior and relations. Nonetheless, it is legitimate to argue that classical shari'a law has failed to achieve legal equality between men and women, free people and slaves, as well as Muslims and non-Muslims. Likewise, classical shari'a law has failed to fully account for the rights of children – a fact that is reflected in the current practice of child marriage and the forced marriage of young girls.[17] While several Muslim commentators have tried to justify these practices with reference to the historical context of the revelation, their argumentation fails to explain the alleged usefulness of classical shari'a norms today. What was progressive and helpful in the past, is not automatically useful and appropriate in the present.

Islamic family law serves as an example here. It contains gender roles that are widely deemed unacceptably unequal today: while a man, according to the classical Islamic conception of marriage, is allowed to marry up to four women and divorce them at his free will, women cannot have more than one husband and may only file for divorce if they have cogent cause.[18] Moreover, women are accorded a legally inferior status to men, for instance, being entitled to merely half of the inheritance that men are to receive.[19] Generally, the shari'a portrays men as the legal guardians of women, granting them permission to take "disciplinary" action if necessary.[20] Besides gender roles, another central challenge is related to the legal status of non-Muslims in Muslim territories, specifically the issues of their freedom of religion, apostasy and conversion.[21]

Apart from a small group of ultra-conservative Muslims who support the literal implementation of the doctrines of classical shari'a,[22] "mainstream

---

17   Carolyn Baugh, *Minor Marriage in Early Islamic Law* (Leiden: Brill, 2017), 1–5.
18   The classical Islamic conceptions of marriage, divorce and family law can be found in compendiums of Islamic law, such as Abdul Rahman al-Jaziri, *Al-Fiqh 'ala al-Madhahib al-Arba'a*, vol. 4 (Beirut: Dar al-Kutub al-'Ilmiyya, 2002): 7–241. See also Kecia Ali, "Marriage in Classical Islamic Jurisprudence: A Survey of Doctrines," in *The Islamic Marriage Contract: Case Studies in Islamic Family Law*, ed. Asifa Quraishi and Frank E. Vogel (Cambridge, MA: Harvard Law School-Harvard University Press, 2008).
19   For more information on the current debate about this subject, see Mouez Khalfaoui, "Das islamische Erbrecht in Tunesien," *Electronic Journal of Islamic and Middle Eastern Law* 1 (2013); Shah, "Women's Human Rights."
20   The debate about the Quranic verse 4:34 is well-known. For more information, see Shaheen Sardar Ali, *Modern Challenges to Islamic Law* (Cambridge: Cambridge University Press, 2016), 32–38.
21   Claude Cahen, "Dhimma," in *Encyclopaedia of Islam*, vol. II, 2nd ed., ed. P. Bearman et al. (Leiden: Brill, 1965).
22   Adis Duderija explores ultra-conservative Muslims and their approaches to gender and civil liberties in his "Neo-Traditional Salafi Qur'an-Sunna Hermeneutics and Its Interpretational Implications," *Religion Compass* 5, no. 7 (July 2011), https://doi.org/10.1111/j.1749-8171.2011.00285.x.

Muslims" lean more toward international human rights norms in their approaches to women, children and people of different nationalities and faiths. This majority situation has resulted in the implementation of legal reforms in most Muslim states, aiding disadvantaged social groups there. For instance, ongoing reforms in the field of marriage and family law have led to a considerable improvement of the legal and social status of women in several Muslim states.[23] Even in religiously conservative Muslim states, such as Saudi Arabia and Iran, reforms have been implemented in recent years.[24] Progressive actors have described these changes – which include women's right to marry without the consent of their legal guardian, or to travel alone without a male relative as a chaperone – as insufficient. In contrast, conservative forces typically consider those small reforms to be illegitimate and extreme, at times even calling for their revision, if not reversal.[25]

An analysis of contemporary policies of Muslim governments regarding the issues of human rights suggests that the relationship between shariʿa doctrines and the above-mentioned 1948 declaration of human rights has become an important subject of political debate. The latter involves not only politicians but also civil society activists as well as members of various political parties and civil society actors. Thus, the topic of human rights is no longer limited to lofty discussions within elitist university settings. Instead, the relationship between Islamic doctrine and human rights has become an integral part of public debate. This development reflects the rising desire for freedom and human rights in Muslim populations.[26] Over the past few years, Muslim politicians have found themselves under increasing domestic pressure to push through decisions based on international agreements and universal human rights. In other instances, voices on the global stage have demanded reforms and visible commitment to human rights. Muslim governments that wish to be included and continuously recognized as equal members in the international community are frequently required to meet

---

23 Jan Michiel Otto discusses legal reforms in Muslim states in his *Sharia Incorporated: A Comparative Overview of the Legal Systems of Twelve Muslim Countries in Past and Present* (Leiden: Leiden University Press, 2010).

24 For an illustrative example, see Dawood Adesola Hamzah, "Impact of International Law on the Application of Islamic Law in Saudi Arabia" (PhD diss. SOAS, University of London, 2015), 83–135; and Ann Elizabeth Mayer, "Islamic Rights or Human Rights: An Iranian Dilemma," *Iranian Studies* 29, no. 3/4 (1996).

25 Ibid.

26 Mouez Khalfaoui, "Public Theology and Democracy: A Muslim Perspective," in *Religion and Democracy: Studies in Public Theology*, ed. Torsten Meireis and Rolf Schieder (Baden-Baden: Nomos, 2017).

certain legal requirements pertaining to human rights. Usually, these conditions have a positive impact on the national legislation on women, children and minorities. The fact that legal developments in Muslim states are, at least in part, induced by international agreements shows that human rights are indivisible and that progress in the implementation of human rights is possible.[27] Nevertheless, international pressure and influence on the human rights situation in Muslim states remains highly contested, often posing a political challenge for Muslim politicians.[28]

3 Human Rights are Indivisible

While the UDHR was initially met with considerable critique and skepticism, it has prevailed and continues to serve as a widely acknowledged reference, or rather framework, for national constitutional laws and legislation as well as for individual rights and duties. By and large, it reflects the concerns and desires of the world population.[29] Its publication in 1948 must therefore be considered a milestone in human history, specifically with regard to liberation against the arbitrary and ruthless enactment of power by religious and civil authorities.[30] From this perspective, it seems contradictory to describe human rights as an expression of Western hegemony.[31]

In the second half of the twentieth century, the human rights debate was shaped considerably by Western actors. This may explain why critical questions have primarily been directed toward non-Western states, including Muslim ones.[32] It was questioned whether and to what extent human rights were being applied and respected in Muslim countries, and through what measures the human rights situation could be improved there. Such

---

27 Abdul Aziz Said, "Precept and Practice of Human Rights in Islam," *Universal Human Rights* 1, no. 1 (January-March 1979), https://doi.org/10.2307/761831.
28 Shaheen Sardar Ali sees the CEDAW convention as a main challenge to the practice of Islamic law in contemporary societies, *Modern Challenges*, 32.
29 Bielefeldt, "Muslim Voices," 587–617.
30 Bielefeldt emphasizes that the UDHR undermined the hegemony of religious institutions such as the church. Ibid., 588–89.
31 Muslim critics of international human rights law, as well as other commentators, frequently consider human rights to be inherently Western. Huntington, for instance, views human rights as a Western concept, while several Muslim voices criticize what they view as human rights imperialism. See Jack Donnelly, "Human Rights and Human Dignity: An Analytic Critique of Non-Western Conceptions of Human Rights," *The American Political Science Review* 76, no. 2 (June 1982), https://doi.org/10.2307/1961111, 314.
32 Ibid., 306–9.

skepticism, and accompanying cases of interference, were perceived as human rights imperialism or straightforward colonialism by many Muslim actors. Against this background, it is understandable that human rights were initially approached defensively in the Islamic world. It was unclear to Muslim stakeholders whether human rights could at least be accepted in part, and if yes, on what grounds. At the same time, some discussions revolved around the (partial) rejection of human rights and possible justifications. In many cases, the dismissal of human rights stood at the forefront of public debate. Notably, both sides of the debate referred to Islamic doctrine, which was either used to support the (partial) acceptance of international human rights or to reject it.

With the beginning of the twenty-first century, the global human rights debate took on a new dimension: an increasing number of questions led to discussions about the applicability of shariʿa norms in Western states. The preceding discussion about Islam and human rights was thereby turned on its head. Rather than arguing over the implementation of human rights in Muslim states, debates began to focus on the role of shariʿa law in Western contexts. It almost seems as if the "Western offensive" that has arguably shaped international human rights discourse in the twentieth century, and was criticized as human rights imperialism, has now been replaced by a "shariʿa offensive" in Western states. This development resembles a paradigm shift: the theme of "Islam and human rights" now constitutes a topic whose geographic focus stretches from Muslim to Western states. This shift was notably promoted by the UDHR. In fact, questions concerning the applicability of shariʿa norms in Western democratic states are only thinkable, and publicly discussable, in a context marked by religious freedom, the freedom of belief and the freedom of expression.[33] All of these rights are contained in the UDHR and the national constitutional laws of democratic states. They ensure that people of different religious backgrounds are relatively unhindered in practicing their faiths. What remains to be clarified, however, is the extent to which some shariʿa norms, whose application in Western contexts is protected by the freedom of belief, are compatible with other human rights. Since human rights norms form a part of Western democratic legislation, this question is often examined with a focus on the relationship between shariʿa norms and local laws.

---

33 Article 18 and other articles of the UDHR (1948) guarantee these rights. Benedek, *Understanding Human Rights*, 193–210 and 297–316.

4 Shari'a and Human Rights in Western Democratic States

On the part of non-Muslim Europeans, questions about the compatibility of shari'a norms and Western legislation are mostly not related to the desire to learn more, or generally benefit, from the shari'a.[34] On the contrary, shari'a usually carries negative connotations in Western societies, being viewed by many as incompatible with modern views on civil rights and duties. Empirically speaking, debates surrounding the role of shari'a in Western states have frequently been tied to the presence of Muslim minorities there, especially their attempts to continue and protect controversial religious practices. While certain Islamic criminal laws, such as related to corporal punishment and the death penalty, are categorically rejected, the legal status of other practices, such as the wearing of a headscarf or the circumcision of boys, form subjects of debate. Generally speaking, shari'a norms that can be assigned to the field of rituals stand at the forefront of discussions surrounding the relationship between Islam and human rights in Western countries.

Except for Islamic criminal law, Muslim citizens who live in Western democratic states are relatively free to enact religious rituals that are based on shari'a norms. This freedom is only limited when specific practices collide with secular laws. In recent years, Western societies have experienced several of these collisions, some of which have triggered a vivid legal-political debate and have reached the highest juridical levels. Some heated topics in this regard include prohibitions against the circumcision of Muslim boys, the wearing of headscarves at public institutions and the construction of minarets in some European states. Notably, these conflicts did not concern only Muslims, but instead they formed part of a broader controversy regarding the role of religion in public space.[35] Such discussion notably involved secular jurists as well as Muslim scholars of different national origins, social statuses, ages and religious orientations. The agreements and reforms that have been reached in Western societies thus far constitute transitional solutions; they do not reflect the broad consent of stakeholders. Notwithstanding the continuance of problems, some of which have been discussed above, Muslim rituals that are anchored in the shari'a do not constitute a real challenge for modern secular societies. After

---

34   Increased interest in Islamic banking, a practice rooted in the shar'ia, might be considered an exception to the rule. Abdelaali El-Maghraoui, *Geld im Islamischen Recht: Die Grundzüge einer Geldtheorie nach der Rechtslogik ausgewählter Klassisch-Muslimischer Gelehrter* (Baden-Baden: Nomos, 2019), 17.

35   Rafael Domingo, *God and the Secular Legal System* (New York: Cambridge University Press, 2016), 8.

all, they are assured by the norms of religious freedom in secular European constitutions.[36]

In contrast to cultural issues, questions regarding interpersonal relations (*mu'amalat*), which fall within the area of civil law, spark considerable controversy. Among other issues, conflict revolves around questions of marriage and divorce, inheritance law, as well as gender roles. Since these problems are often very specific in nature, their analysis helps identify the different positions, or rather theological interpretations, adopted by Muslim actors regarding human rights. Within the area of civil law, different approaches toward marriage and divorce present a particularly interesting case study. Secular European states exhibit differences in their approaches to Islamic legal traditions in these two matters. In the UK, for instance, Muslim marriage contracts are legally recognized, provided they meet several clearly specified conditions. In other European countries, Muslim marriage contracts are not deemed legally valid, as they frequently collide with both national laws and international human rights. Among other things, Muslim marriage contracts violate the notions of equal rights and gender equality. Notwithstanding the rejection of "mosque marriages," Muslim marriage contracts that were concluded abroad may be recognized under private international law – provided that they do not collide with local laws. In other legal areas, such as trade and financial law, shari'a norms and practices like "Islamic banking" are widely accepted. That is to say, the prescriptions of classical shari'a are legally rejected in some fields like criminal law but may be applied in other legal areas. While the principles of international human rights facilitate and are frequently referred to in legitimizing the exercise of certain shari'a norms, they are also used in rejecting some other practices of Islamic legal doctrine.

5   What Do We Actually Mean by "Shari'a"?

Shari'a contains two main areas: religious norms and legal norms.[37] Religious norms pertain to rituals, such as praying, fasting and pilgrimage, whereas legal

---

36   Mouez Khalfaoui, "God's Law and Civil Law: Religious Norms in the Public Sphere," in *International Handbook of Practical Theology: A Transcultural and Transreligious Approach*, ed. Birgit Weyel et al. (Berlin: de Gruyter, forthcoming).

37   Contemporary understandings of shari'a law in Western academia distinguish between two main branches of shari'a norms, namely religious and legal norms. The classical Muslim distinction, which exists in almost all works of *fiqh*, between rituals (*'ibadat*), transactions (*mu'amalat*) and punishments (*hudud*) is rather a pedagogical/didactic distinction. Legal literature always starts with the part on rituals, then on transaction

norms contain criminal law and the area of interpersonal relations (*muʿamalat*), including issues such as marriage, divorce and economics, to name but a few examples. The conceptual division of shariʿa into these two parts facilitates the analysis of its complex relation with international human rights. Before delving into specific questions to this effect, it should be pointed out that the secular legal systems of Western democratic states serve as the only reference to national juridical questions due to the "territorial principle," engrained in the secular law of European nation states. This principle outlines opportunities for applying shariʿa law within the limits set by the secular legal frameworks of single nation states. Thus, secular laws provide clear rules regarding the implementation of the shariʿa, for instance, classical Islamic criminal law is denied any applicability. This rejection is in part based on the direct contradiction between current international human rights norms and the corporal punishments contained in classical Islamic penal law. At the same time, regardless of efforts by Salafi movements to implement the injunctions of classical shariʿa, it appears that Muslim minorities in Western states have little to no interest in implementing the criminal legal codes contained in the shariʿa.[38] Taken together, these two factors explain why a large part of the shariʿa is entirely excluded from debates about the relationship between Islamic doctrine and human rights. Likewise, classical Islamic criminal law has been removed from the official legal systems of most Muslim states.[39] The pleas of some religiously conservative groups to re-introduce Islamic criminal codes as state law is often considered to be unfounded and meets considerable opposition. The use of draconic corporal punishments by the unpopular and widely feared extremist group "Islamic State of Iraq and Syria" (ISIS) was strongly condemned by Muslims around the world. In short, criminal codes that are based on premodern Islamic doctrine are categorically rejected in Western and most Muslim states and do not therefore constitute a topic of juridical controversy.

Contrary to Islamic criminal law, religious and cultural rituals have enjoyed considerable freedom in Western states, which can in large part be ascribed to the religious freedom guaranteed by their respective constitutional laws. However, some rituals are strongly criticized, especially those that are seen as colliding with national laws and social norms. For instance, Islamic

---

and finally on punishments. See, for instance, Mathias Rohe's translation of the *Kitab al Mabsut* by the famous scholar al-Sarakhsi in *Das islamische Recht: Geschichte und Gegenwart* (Munich: C.H. Beck, 2009), 409–22.

38 Khalfaoui, "God's Law."
39 The classical shariʿa punishments are still implemented in some states such as Saudi Arabia, Iran, Sudan or Yemen.

prescriptions for dress, ritual slaughter and the circumcision of boys continue to produce tension between secular and Islamic law.[40] While practices such as wearing a headscarf or ritual slaughter are frequently defended with reference to human rights, paradoxically, human rights are also drawn on by those who oppose these very same rituals. In the latter case, the limited role and visibility of religion in secular public space constitutes a particularly relevant and oft-cited point.[41]

Besides religious and cultural rituals, a few areas of civil law are fiercely disputed, for example, Islamic marriage and family law. Although the application of classical shari'a norms is mostly denied in these cases, existing exceptions spark controversy. These contain the recognition of Islamic marriage contracts under international private law, cases of divorce, as well as inheritance laws. Western juridical authorities face an increasing number of cases that involve shari'a law – which often forms a part of their national legislation. While the current debate about Islam and human rights concerns, first and foremost, Muslim minorities and the compatibility between shari'a and secular laws, religious scholars in Muslim states and elsewhere have developed relevant opinions on these issues, which are briefly discussed in the next section.

6   Muslim Thinkers (in the West) and Human Rights: Three Different Paradigms

Undoubtedly, the compatibility of certain religious norms and the framework of human rights still constitute a challenge for many Muslims living in European states. To examine the complex question regarding the compatibility of shari'a and human rights, the following pages are devoted to arguments made by three groups of Western Muslim thinkers whose respective positions can be classified as defensive, reconciliatory or rejectionist. The first consists of the opinions of those thinkers who have a defensive attitude *vis-à-vis* modern human rights. This paradigm consists of defending classical Muslim positions against an alleged assault by Western values. The arguments of the German lawyer Murad Hofmann will be interpreted from this perspective. The second position is reconciliatory, consisting of paradigms that seek to bring Muslim

---

40   Mathias Rohe, *Der Islam in Deutschland: Eine Bestandsaufnahme* (Munich: C.H. Beck, 2018), 201–15.

41   For more information about the debate on religion and public space, see Jürgen Habermas, "Religion in the Public Sphere," *European Journal of Philosophy* 14, no. 1 (2006), https://doi.org/10.1111/j.1468-0378.2006.00241.x.

values together with modern human rights, and that also make suggestions for how to achieve this in practice. As a representative of this type of argumentation, I will deal with Abdullahi Ahmed An-Naʿim. The third position is rejectionist, being comprised of arguments against all forms of classical religious positions. This position will be discussed through reference to a group of thinkers.

6.1 The Defensive Paradigm: Murad Hofmann and the Challenge of Western Human Rights

The article "Islam and Human Rights" by former German diplomat and Muslim scholar Wilfried Murad Hofmann (d. 2020)[42] will be used to exemplify the approach adopted by some Muslim thinkers and commentators who strive to defend the positions of classical Islam on human rights by way of modern arguments.

In addressing the contradictory positions of modern conceptions of human rights and classical Islamic law, Wilfried Murad Hofmann considers questions of human rights as a sort of test whose outcome will determine the future existence of Islam in Europe. The author regards Muslim approaches toward human rights as primarily defensive against what he understands as a Western conception, a situation he aims to change by providing Muslims with a more open-minded voice. His goal is to carve out a position that Muslims can adopt with self-confidence. Among all the topics touched upon in current debates about Islam and human rights, Hofmann focuses exclusively on the examples of women rights and democracy. In the introduction to his article, Hofmann outlines the alleged differences between Muslim and Western positions, writing that "the Western and the Islamic worlds – if such things exist – seem to maintain a confrontational relationship."[43] He then attempts to develop an "Islamic response" to the international human rights debate, i.e., a response that is based on Islamic legal sources. In doing so, he finds that Muslims' initial denial of the universality of human rights is unhelpful:

> This view may be appropriate with regards to fashionable "human rights" such as the "right to fear," the "right to intoxication," or the "right to homosexual marriage" – demands that are typically made by the political left. However, this view is not appropriate when it comes to the classical core of human rights, including the right to life […], freedom of opinion and

---

42 Murad Hofmann was a prominent German lawyer who converted to Islam and wrote on different legal and religious aspects of Islamic thought.
43 Hofmann, "Der Islam"; translations into English by Mouez Khalfaoui.

conscience, freedom of religion and liberality. Muslims harm themselves if they let themselves be enticed to deny the universality of human rights.[44]

Instead of rejecting human rights as "Eurocentric," Hofmann suggests "approach[ing] the human rights phenomenon from within the Islamic framework, i.e., the framework provided by the Quran and Sunna."[45] He calls for an inter-Muslim debate about human rights that engages with Islamic religious scripts, and in doing so, he divides human rights into two main parts. He considers the first part, which contains the right to life, such as ensuring protection from murder and the death penalty, to be undisputed. He points out that the protection of life can be deduced from multiple Quranic verses (e.g., 4:92). By contrast, he considers other human rights to be highly controversial and problematic, including "(i) apostasy, (ii) slavery, (iii) the rights of non-Muslims in Muslim states, (iv) women's rights and (v) corporal punishments."[46] Yet the author maintains that the differences between Western and Muslim positions regarding the above-mentioned topics are not extreme. In outlining the Muslim position regarding human rights, he refers to contemporary Muslim thinkers:

> It emerges from contemporary *ijtihad* that the perspectives of both sides [...] are not as divergent as it seems. Reasons for this were, or rather are, Muslim scholars such as Fazlur Rahman, Muhammad Asad, Fathi Osman, Alija Izetbegovic, Hassan and Maher Hathout, Rashid al-Ghannuschi, Yusuf al-Qaradawi, Jeffrey Lang, Mohamed Talbi and Hassan al-Turabi.[47]

In his engagement with the above-mentioned topics, Hofmann pursues a strategy of trivialization aimed at de-escalating the situation. Instead of covering all aspects of the debate, Hofmann focuses exclusively on presenting selected verses of the Quran and providing his own interpretation thereof. By doing so, he ignores Muslim history as well as Muslim legal literature. Although he concludes that apostasy in the Quran is not explicitly punishable, he is sympathetic toward the legal persecution of apostasy when combined with treason. The author does not seem very concerned about the fact that apostasy, according

---

44 Ibid.
45 Ibid.
46 Ibid.
47 Ibid.

to the norms of Islamic family law, leads to disinheritance. Moreover, he views one's adherence to Islam as the equivalent of one's nationality:

> With regard to apostasy, all conflict vanishes once Muslims recognize that according to the Quran and the *sunna*, there is no punishment for the rejection of the Islamic faith (apostasy) in this world. The Quran even describes several cases of apostasy, without linking them to any timely punishments. Importantly, *la ikraha fi al-din* ["there is no compulsion in religion"] applies to Muslims as well. Originally, ex-Muslims were only persecuted criminally, and for good reason, if they committed treason (*al-ridda*), thereby actively fighting Islam (5:33) and causing trouble on earth. The punishment of treason, possibly by death (especially during war), is a worldwide practice and does not violate human rights.[48]

In the case of women's rights, Hofmann suggests a different methodological approach. Since the topic is closely tied to the notion of equality, he suggests solving gender-related questions by applying a "norm of logic," meaning that unequal things are non-comparable.[49] He argues that men and women are regarded as unequal in the Quran, therefore rejecting any comparison between both genders.

> With regards to women's rights, it must first of all be established that the principle of equality merely demands treating equal facts equally. Unequal facts must, as a matter of principle, be treated unequally. Whether it is fashionable or not, Muslim men and women assume that men and women are physiologically and thereby also psychologically non-identical, as Allah (t.) put it so deliciously in al-Imran: 36: "[...] a boy is simply not like a girl [...]."[50]

According to Hofmann, different regulations for men and women are justified from an Islamic perspective on the grounds that biological differences exist between genders.[51] By insisting on biological differences and treating them as a justification for unequal legal treatment, Hofmann quickly resolves all problems and questions surrounding matters of equality in inheritance law and other gender-related topics.

---

48   Ibid.
49   Ibid.
50   Ibid.
51   Ibid.

Both Hofmann's methodological approach and the content of his argument reflect the problematic treatment of human rights by several other Muslims thinkers. Through his article, Hofmann aims to strengthen the position of Muslims on human rights and to trivialize serious problems. However, his argument seems to achieve the opposite: Hofmann's comments are indicative of a Muslim-essentialist approach, which focuses exclusively on the "Muslim position" while ignoring contextual considerations, including the legal framework of discussion. The argument he puts forth is only supported by his own interpretations of the 1990 Cairo Declaration of Human Rights in Islam and the "Roundtable Conference" (1994).[52] He views both documents as a first step in the development of a clear Muslim position within global human rights debates, saying: "Thanks to this preparatory work, it is relatively easy now to portray the few differences which seemingly exist between Western and Islamic human rights catalogues."[53] Hofmann's critique of Muslim scholars who accept the marriage of Muslim women with non-Muslim men is particularly problematic. He considers such acceptance as a threat to the shariʿa:

> The fact that a Muslima – in contrast to a Muslim – may not enter into an inter-religious marriage with a Jew or a Christian – according to al-Maʾida: 5 – is closely related to the above-mentioned understanding of the male role in marriage; if he carries out the role of the boss, his Muslim wife cannot expect that he sensitively honors her convictions.[54]

The just discussed article by Wilfried Murad Hofmann also exemplifies other scholars' attempts to hold on to and justify classical Islamic norms with new arguments. This approach is misleading for several reasons. First, the author purposefully ignores existing core problems in his attempts to narrow the chasm between classical shariʿa norms and modern human rights. For instance, he disregards the fact that many substantial differences between Islamic and human rights law are of a historic nature. The norms of classical shariʿa emerged in a premodern context, whereas the declaration of human rights is relatively young. Hence, it can be said that classical conceptions in Islamic law, despite their improvements in premodern times, need new interpretations to meet modern norms of human rights.

---

52   The roundtable on the universality of Human Rights took place from December 10–12, 1994 in Amman, Jordan.
53   Ibid.
54   Ibid.

Another problematic aspect in Hofmann's work is his attempt to carve out a specifically "Muslim" position rather than treating human rights as universally applicable. It is widely known that several Muslim actors participated in developing the UDHR.[55] Notwithstanding scattered reservation on the part of Muslims and Muslim state governments concerning *some* human rights, the latter are, by and large, acknowledged by Muslims. In fact, the rebellions and human rights activities that have taken place in the Islamic world within just the last decade suggest that human rights are rather popular.[56]

6.2   The Reconciliatory Approach to Human Rights: Abdullahi An-Na'im
In his book *Toward an Islamic Reformation* (1990), Abdullahi An-Na'im discusses the possibility of reconciling Islam and human rights by reforming shari'a norms. He argues that the aim of his book is "[t]o enable Muslims to exercise their right to self-determination without violating the rights of others to the same." His proposed method for attaining this consists of: "identify[ing] areas of conflict between Shari'a and universal standards of human rights and seek[ing] reconciliation and a positive relationship between the two systems."[57] An-Na'im bases his argument on the "evolutionary principle," which was originally developed by the Sudanese scholar Mahmoud Mohammed Taha.[58]

> The best solution to the current Muslim dilemma of legitimizing peaceful coexistence and basic human rights from within Islam is based on the work of the late Sudanese Muslim reformer Ustadh Mahmoud Mohamed Taha. According to Taha, public Shari'a did not reflect the whole of Islam. Early jurists were working primarily with the model of the Medina state, speculating on the basis of their knowledge and understanding of the Qur'an and Sunna. Both the Medina model and the jurists' understanding of the sources were bound to their historical context. One may find the modern model of an Islamic state in the broad principles of justice

---

55   Waltz, "Universal Human Rights," 799–844.
56   Mouez Khalfaoui, "The Shift of Paradigms from Obligation to Right in Muslim Culture: Work Ethics as a Case Study," *Journal of Islamic Ethics*, forthcoming.
57   Abdullahi Ahmed An-Na'im, *Toward an Islamic Reformation: Civil Liberties, Human Rights, and International Law* (New York: Syracuse University Press, 1990), 161. For a clear and short presentation of An-Na'im's reconciling approach, see idem, "Islamic Law, International Relations, and Human Rights: Challenge and Response," *Cornell International Law Journal* 20, no. 2 (1987).
58   The "evolutionary principle" claims that laws constantly change in accordance with the developments in their broader context and due to the evolution of human civilization.

and equality contained in the Qur'an and Sunna of the earlier stage of Mecca, which preceded the migration to Medina.⁵⁹

An-Na'im also explains the discrimination against non-Muslims found in the shari'a. According to him, the Quranic verses highlighting inter-Muslim solidarity were revealed during the Medinan period of Islam. They were supposed to provide psychological support to the Muslim community at a time of heavy conflict with non-Muslims. In contrast, the fundamental and eternal message of Islam, which was revealed during the Meccan period, preaches solidarity among all humans. According to An-Na'im, Muslims should emphasize the eternal message of universal solidarity as proclaimed in the Meccan era, rather than holding on to the exclusively Muslim solidarity of the Medinan times. An-Na'im argues further that exclusive intra-Muslim solidarity would provoke non-Muslims and lead to a worldwide emergence of antagonistic "solidarity communities." This, in turn, would undermine the maintenance of peaceful global co-existence and cooperation, which is closely tied to the protection of human rights. About women's rights in Islam, An-Na'im argues that:

> The male guardianship over women, which is deduced from verse 4:34, was rationalised in response to women's dependence on men, both in their economic and physical security. Since these dependencies are not necessarily valid anymore, [...] the male guardianship over women should be abolished. Men and women must be given the same freedoms and responsibilities before the law; thereby the security and economic opportunities of all members of the community can be guaranteed.⁶⁰

The evolutionary principle rejects the marriage ban between Muslim women and non-Muslim men. The above prohibition is argued to be based on the historically specific assumption that a woman is more receptive to the influence of her husband than the other way around. In other words, it is assumed that a non-Muslim husband could push his wife into the abandonment of Islam. This reasoning is of course part of a broader sociological phenomenon, namely the lack of trust in the integrity and judgment of women.⁶¹

The reconciliatory paradigm of Abdullahi An-Na'im was published around 20 years ago. Since then, the legal status of women in several Muslim states has barely changed. Even worse, the situation of minorities in the Muslim world

---

59 Idem, *Toward an Islamic Reformation*, 180. See also Idem, "Islamic Law."
60 Idem, *Toward an Islamic Reformation*, 180–81.
61 Ibid.

has deteriorated, save for some minor exceptions. In a region that has long been marked by brutal conflict, civil wars, rebellions and protests, it is especially women, children and minorities who are at risk. Even where relatively progressive legislation on women rights can be found, for instance in Tunisia, these remain contested. Tunisian women who take part in the labor force are publicly blamed for the unemployment of men, among other things. Overall, the current situation in Muslim countries does not indicate any extensive or in-depth reform in the near future. This is especially true for reforms that emerge from within, not those that respond to external pressure.

6.3 The Rejectionist Paradigm

What I have called the "rejectionist" paradigm is advocated by Muslim thinkers who explicitly distance themselves from the classical shariʿa conception of human rights, especially as far as women's rights are concerned. They are firmly committed to sweeping reform – understood in this context as a major change in the rules. This includes the abandonment of numerous injunctions of the shariʿa and their replacement by Western norms. Most of the representatives of this group are human rights activists, including Necla Kelek,[62] Wafa Sultan,[63] Hirsi Ali,[64] Abdel-Hakim Ourghi and others. Their approach is often based on their personal experiences in Muslim societies or in migration milieus in Western countries. They often consider the behavior of some conservative groups as being representative of the general Muslim conception of gender roles. When it comes to debates on classical theory and the interpretation of sources such as the Quran and sunna, a generalizing process is used. Wafa Sultan argues in this regard:

> Islam is a sealed flask. Its stopper allows no ventilation [...]. The human mind is programmed to feel inferiority or mastery in accordance with

---

62   Necla Kelek is a famous German activist. In her publications, she presents both the negative experience of women in Turkey and the misbehavior of Muslim men towards women in migration milieus in Western societies. See her *Himmelsreise: Mein Streit mit den Wächtern des Islam* (Cologne: Kiepenheuer & Witsch, 2010), 128–60.

63   In her book *A God Who Hates*, Sultan narrates her story about living within conservative Muslim society. See Wafa Sultan, *A God Who Hates: The Courageous Woman Who Inflamed the Muslim World Speaks out against the Evils of Islam* (New York: St. Martin's Press, 2009), 155–77.

64   Ayaan Hirsi Ali, *Heretic: Why Islam Needs a Reformation Now* (New York: Harper Collins Publishers, 2015). In this book, she narrates about her life as a teenager in Nairobi, while at the same time asking questions about the tenets of the Muslim religion, such as why the prayer should be held five times a day (153ff.).

the status of each party [...]. Muhammad, to impose his authority, sowed unease in the hearts of his followers by linking obedience to God with obedience to himself. Then he added a third party to this "holy duality" in the form of the ruler, through whom he could control the rest of his folk.[65]

Necla Kelek makes her "Dispute with the Guardians of Islam" (*Mein Streit mit den Wächtern des Islam*) the main theme of her 2010 monograph entitled *Himmelsfahrt* ("Heavenly Journey"), in which she presents her own negative experience growing up in a conservative family. One chapter is dedicated to the "Role of Women in the Islamic Community".[66] There she explains the core concept of gender roles as follows: "The fact that traditional Muslims see and evaluate the relationship between the sexes quite differently is due to their religiously dominated view of the world and humanity."[67] This basic assumption is used to explain all negative positions regarding the role of women in Muslim communities. The special thing about this assumption is that the author presents herself in the first place as an affected woman, describing her own suffering under the power of her family. In the second step, she tells about her successful emancipation, thus the victim image becomes a pattern for emancipation. Kelek also sees the emancipation of Muslim women as the first step for the emancipation of Muslim men, using the pronoun "we" not only for Muslim women, but for both men and women. She ends the book by calling on Muslims to wage more individualism: "Muslims of all countries, confess the I, you have nothing to forsake but the shariʿa." With this statement, Kelek brings her discussion to its climax by pointing to the shariʿa, and not the Muslim man, as the cause of all evils.

The criticism and most of the arguments presented by Kelek, Sultan and others touch upon the problematic state of gender roles and relations in Muslim communities. The arguments and stories presented paint a truly dark image of this situation. However, the question should be asked as to whether this dark image is unjustly generalized and if there are any positive examples in Muslim culture. Furthermore, it is striking that the argumentation regarding shariʿa is based exclusively on practical experiences, so that the negative behavior of Muslim men towards women is seen as being representative of Islamic doctrine. The references relied on by the proponents of this paradigm are mostly limited to some general and short literature, so that in their works we often

---

65   Sultan, *A God Who Hates*, 155–59.
66   Kelek, *Himmelsfahrt*, 128–45.
67   Ibid., 128.

encounter a lack of understanding of Islamic law. It is true that the current understanding and implementation of Islamic law in many regions and by different groups is oppressive and one-dimensional, nevertheless, Islamic legal scholarship also offers different positions on gender roles, most specifically with regard to that of women.[68]

The three positions presented here – defensive, reconciliatory and rejectionist approaches – are often contrasted with each other. But despite their differences, one can also speak of methodological similarities: Both the rejecting and defensive paradigms are often selective when it comes to their presentation of the shariʿa and they lack a more comprehensive approach to the issues at stake. What speaks in favor of the harmonizing outlook is the fact that, on the one hand, its followers agree with criticisms of the current state of human rights in Muslim societies and accept the lead of Western concepts regarding human rights, while on the other hand, they strive to catch up by way of new interpretations of the Muslim tradition.

Research on the above three Muslim groups in relation to human rights has been strongly focused on their positions about women's roles, gender equality and the interpretation of religious sources regarding these subjects. On the one hand, there are numerous studies that deal with the interpretation of these topics in Islamic sources – especially in the Quran and the sunna of the Prophet Muhammad as well as in the classical legal texts. Different perspectives are presented that attempt to open up these sources in light of modern human rights and textual analysis methods. On the other hand, there are studies that deal with the representation of the situation of women in various regions of the Islamic world. These studies often deal decisively with women who suffer under archaic, patriarchal structures and take a critical position on this. Another direction counters any criticism of Islam defensively by paying tribute to the pre-modern positions on gender roles and positioning itself against any change in the status quo. In addition to the critics and defenders of the pre-modern positions, another group can be found that strives for a compromise between the two positions. This last perspective can be called the reconciliation approach. Therein, an attempt is made to defuse the passages of the pre-modern sources that are seen as problematic from today's perspective and to integrate modern conceptions of human rights into the discourse. This is intended to create a moderate position in order to enable a middle way between classical and modern positions.

---

68 As a case in point, Carolyn Baugh presents the different positions regarding minor marriages in Muslim legal literature. Cf. Baugh, *Minor Marriage*.

The two main positions on the interpretation of pre-modern Islamic conceptions of gender can be contrasted as follows: On the one side are conservative groups, who represent a rather defensive position. On the other side are the representatives of the emancipatory approach. They are highlighted as critical thinkers because they reject the pre-modern Islamic gender conception altogether and try to replace it with another conception. These two groups are irreconcilably opposed to each other because they deal with the same issues from opposing perspectives and with opposing arguments. The methodological approach on both sides is selective, as they each focus only on certain elements and events from the pre-modern Islamic context in order to confirm selected positions. Thus, issues such as honor killing and domestic violence are often attributed exclusively to religion by the representatives of the critical position, without considering other cultural or social motives. The representatives of the defensive position, on the other hand, try to justify such offences through religious arguments. The corresponding facts are partly generalized in order to be able to make an overall assessment of the situation of "women in Islam." The defensive actors often react to this with selectivity as well, by referring to certain moments in Islamic history or to certain passages in the source texts in order to derive generalized statements about the positive situation of women in Islam. Therefore, they see no reason for any changes or reform. Because both approaches present the topic selectively, a clear view regarding the classical conceptions is of great importance for the analysis of the topic.

7 Shariʿa and Human Rights in Muslim States

The human rights debate in the Islamic world is marked by contrasting, even contradictory, positions, which often leads to controversy and arguments. Conservative Muslims argue that the norms of modern human rights are contained within the main scriptures of Islam, therefore denying the need to change or adapt Islamic doctrine. Progressive liberal Muslims, on the other hand, feel they must free themselves from "outdated" Islamic norms and that international human rights should be fully ratified and implemented. A third group emphasizes the necessity of not only reforming Islam but also altering certain human rights to create a declaration that considers Muslim norms and is truly "universal." The development of the so-called Cairo Declaration of Human Rights in Islam, issued in 1990, brings another topic of debate to the fore. The declaration suggests that shariʿa norms should constitute a decisive factor in the contemporary treatment of human rights,[69] and it also declares several human rights to be illegitimate. Moreover, it allows some states to limit or even inhibit the application of certain human rights articles.

Historically speaking, the discussion about human rights in Muslim states appears to have reached its peak at the turn of the last century. Even in states such as Saudi Arabia, where human rights have always been limited, vivid engagement with the subject has begun. The rhetoric and attitude of many Muslim state agencies is based on two positions, or rather behavioral strategies: On the one hand, they acknowledge human rights in international panels and committees, hoping to thereby ensure their recognition as full members of the international community. Yet on the other hand, they continue to limit the implementation of international human rights to foreign actors, excluding their own legislation and society. In this regard, the 1990 Cairo Declaration of Human Rights in Islam aimed at replacing, or weakening, international human rights with a particularistic declaration – arguably without success. Contrary to the discussions that took place in the twentieth century, which were often considered to be elitist and limited to universities or political fora, contemporary human rights debates in Muslim states enjoy broad popularity. As the Arab Spring of 2011 made clear, human rights are no longer treated as the desideratum of the elite, but as a public desire.[70] It is noteworthy that contemporary human rights debates in the Islamic world differ among regions. While some states adopt a rather progressive attitude toward human rights, the matter seems to remain in its infancy elsewhere. Governments' official approaches toward human rights are typically reflected in state legislation and legal systems.[71] The legal reforms that have taken place in Muslim countries like Tunisia and Morocco have led to considerable changes in local legal conceptions. Among other things, these states have incorporated European legal concepts into their civil and criminal legal systems. This means that in these countries, debates about human rights have been narrowed down to specific juridical areas, primarily related to family law.[72] In other states which have thus far failed to undertake reforms, all juridical areas remain relevant in public debates on human rights. Women's rights and family rights play particularly important roles in these cases. The shari'a is frequently included in ongoing

---

69 Abdullah al-Ahsan, "Law, Religion and Human Dignity in the Muslim World Today: An Examination of OIC's Cairo Declaration of Human Rights," *Journal of Law and Religion* 24, no. 2 (2008), https://doi.org/10.1017/S0748081400001715.
70 Khalfaoui, "Das islamische Erbrecht," 75–82.
71 Otto, *Sharia Incorporated*.
72 Ibid.

discussions, either constituting the object of reform or a means of blocking certain articles contained in international human rights conventions.

The international Convention on the Elimination of all Forms of Discrimination Against Women (CEDAW) serves as a useful case study. A close look at the implementation of CEDAW allows for inferences about the legal status of women, particularly with regards to inheritance and marriage laws. Following the announcement of the international agreement in 1979, CEDAW was ratified by most Muslim states. Notwithstanding their ratification, Muslim state actors expressed reservations which were oftentimes based on religious arguments. For instance, many states pointed out that the shariʿa was not mutable and that each reform therefore posed a threat to Muslim identity. Until today, many governments have refused to implement certain articles of CEDAW, often with reference to their national sovereignty. The limited implementation of CEDAW is visibly reflected in the marriage laws of Muslim states, which are strongly influenced by classical shariʿa norms.

8   Conclusion

Despite the considerable efforts toward reconciliation, the relationship between Islamic doctrine and human rights law is still a challenging matter, both in the Islamic world and in Western states. In "the West," human rights are frequently put forth as a reason why shariʿa, or Islamic law, must be rejected or at least reformed. In contrast, shariʿa is treated as the main reason for the partial or absolute rejection of human rights in some parts of the Islamic world.[73] Since the discourse on Islam and human rights is primarily concerned with the interpretation of the shariʿa, it is important to reiterate that classical shariʿa norms, and their literal interpretation and practice in many Muslim states, fall below the standards of modern human rights.

The constant re-interpretation of Islamic doctrine confirms that shariʿa consists of multiple norms, which have been re-developed by Muslim scholars across time and space. According to this position, the legal provisions found in Islam were not delivered as a ready-made legal code, but emerged over time and in response to constantly changing situations and challenges. The constant alteration of Islamic law should strengthen the position of those calling for the

---

73 Jack Donnelly criticizes Islamic conceptions of human rights. Jack Donnelly, in his "Human Rights and Human Dignity: An Analytic Critique of Non-Western Conceptions of Human Rights," *The American Political Science Review* 76, no. 2 (June 1982), https://doi.org/10.2307/1961111.

reform of the shariʻa today. The historical flexibility of shariʻa norms facilitates the "modernization" of traditional Islamic verdicts regarding women, slaves, non-Muslims and children.

Besides external influences, which stem from, for instance, human rights organizations and activists, the present debate about the possible reconciliation of human rights and Islam is shaped considerably by rising internal pressure from within Muslim states. At the same time, Muslim scholars are forced to respond to questions raised by Muslim communities in Western states, primarily by young Muslims who seek equal rights.

In general, the situation outside the Muslim world provides a different picture. Here, Muslim groups and intellectuals engage in continuing discussion about Islam and human rights, especially in Western democratic states. Their debate is notably facilitated by the freedom of speech and religion. In addition, it appears that foreign legal discourse and interreligious dialogue may have an inspiring impact on Muslims in Western countries. However, as the example of Wilfried Murad Hofmann indicates, some Muslim intellectuals continue to maintain a rather defensive position, pleading for the development of a particular "Muslim position," while other groups emphasize the rejection of all forms of shariʻa law and call for adopting exclusively modern Western concepts of freedom.

A look at the human rights debate in Muslim states reveals that most arguments opposing the reform of the shariʻa and the implementation of human rights are politically motivated, lacking any reference to Islamic doctrine. In fact, deliberations concerning the application of human rights in Muslim states are strongly influenced by the interests of powerful elites.[74] In contrast, Muslim discussions about legal reforms in Europe and the West are primarily driven by Muslim scholars, who often do not live in Europe. Rather than emphasizing and fostering interreligious and intercultural similarities, they frequently attempt to develop particularistic rights for Muslims. The contributions made by Yusuf al-Qaradawi, for instance, but also by other religious authorities, have contributed to the development of so called "Muslim minorities laws." This notion risks putting Muslims in isolation and thus works against their attempted integration.[75]

---

74   Khalfaoui, "Public Theology," 89–101.
75   Mouez Khalfaoui, "Maqāṣid al-Sharīʻah as a Legitimization for the Muslim Minorities Law," in *The Objectives of Islamic Law: The Promises and Challenges of the Maqāṣid al-Sharīʻa*, ed. Idris Nassery et al. (Lanham: Lexington Books, 2018).

Bibliography

Al-Ahsan, Abdullah. "Law, Religion and Human Dignity in the Muslim World Today: An Examination of OIC's Cairo Declaration of Human Rights." *Journal of Law and Religion* 24, no. 2 (2008): 569–97, https://doi.org/10.1017/S0748081400001715.

Ali, Ayaan Hirsi. *Heretic: Why Islam Needs a Reformation Now.* New York: Harper Collins Publishers, 2015.

Ali, Kecia. "Marriage in Classical Islamic Jurisprudence: A Survey of Doctrines." In *The Islamic Marriage Contract: Case Studies in Islamic Family Law*, edited by Asifa Quraishi and Frank E. Vogel, 11–45. Cambridge, MA: Harvard Law School-Harvard University Press, 2008.

Ali, Shaheen Sardar. *Modern Challenges to Islamic Law.* Cambridge: Cambridge University Press, 2016.

An-Naʿim, Abdullahi Ahmed. "Islamic Law, International Relations, and Human Rights: Challenge and Response." *Cornell International Law Journal* 20, no. 2 (1987): 317–35.

An-Naʿim, Abdullahi Ahmed. *Toward an Islamic Reformation: Civil Liberties, Human Rights, and International Law.* New York: Syracuse University Press, 1990.

Baugh, Carolyn. *Minor Marriage in Early Islamic Law.* Leiden: Brill, 2017.

Benedek, Wolfgang, ed. *Understanding Human Rights: Manual on Human Rights Education.* Vienna: NWV, 2012.

Bielefeldt, Heiner. "Muslim Voices in the Human Rights Debate." *Human Rights Quarterly* 17, no. 4 (November 1995): 587–617.

Bielefeldt, Heiner. "Political Secularism and European Islam: A Challenge to Muslims and Non-Muslims." In *Muslims in Europe: From the Margin to the Centre*, edited by Jamal Malik, 147–60. Münster: LIT, 2004.

Cahen, Claude. "Ḏhimma." In *Encyclopaedia of Islam*, vol. II, 2nd ed., edited by P. Bearman, Th. Bianquis, C.E. Bosworth, E. van Donzel and W.P. Heinrichs, 227–31. Leiden: Brill, 1965.

Domingo, Rafael. *God and the Secular Legal System.* New York: Cambridge University Press, 2016.

Donnelly, Jack. "Human Rights and Human Dignity: An Analytic Critique of Non-Western Conceptions of Human Rights." *The American Political Science Review* 76, no. 2 (June 1982): 303–16, https://doi.org/10.2307/1961111.

Duderija, Adis. "Neo-Traditional Salafi Qur'an-Sunna Hermeneutics and Its Interpretational Implications." *Religion Compass* 5, no. 7 (July 2011): 314–25, https://doi.org/10.1111/j.1749-8171.2011.00285.x.

El-Maghraoui, Abdelaali. *Geld im Islamischen Recht: Die Grundzüge einer Geldtheorie nach der Rechtslogik ausgewählter Klassisch-Muslimischer Gelehrter.* Baden-Baden: Nomos, 2019.

Habermas, Jürgen. "Religion in the Public Sphere." *European Journal of Philosophy* 14, no. 1 (2006): 1–25, https://doi.org/10.1111/j.1468-0378.2006.00241.x.

Hamzah, Dawood Adesola. "Impact of International Law on the Application of Islamic Law in Saudi Arabia." PhD diss. SOAS, University of London, 2015.

Hofmann, Murad Wilfried. "Der Islam und die Menschenrechte." *Qantara*. Accessed November 29, 2019, https://de.qantara.de/inhalt/murad-wilfried-hofmann-der-islam-und-die-menschenrechte.

Al-Jaziri, Abdul Rahman. *Al-Fiqh 'ala al-Madhahib al-Arba'a*, vol. 4. Beirut: Dar al-Kutub al-'Ilmiyya, 2002.

Kelek, Necla. *Himmelsreise: Mein Streit mit den Wächtern des Islam*. Cologne: Kiepenheuer & Witsch, 2010.

Khalfaoui, Mouez. "Das islamische Erbrecht in Tunesien." *Electronic Journal of Islamic and Middle Eastern Law* 1 (2013): 75–83.

Khalfaoui, Mouez. "Das islamische Recht und das staatliche Recht aus muslimischer Perspektive." In *Handbuch Christentum und Islam in Deutschland: Grundlagen, Erfahrungen und Perspektiven des Zusammenlebens*, edited by Mathias Rohe, Havva Engin, Mouhanad Khorchide, Ömer Özsoy and Hansjörg Schmid, 304–40. Freiburg: Herder, 2014.

Khalfaoui, Mouez. "God's Law and Civil Law: Religious Norms in the Public Sphere." In *International Handbook of Practical Theology: A Transcultural and Transreligious Approach*, edited by Birgit Weyel, Annemie Dillen, Wilhelm Gräb, Emmanuel Lartey and Cas Wepener. Berlin: de Gruyter, forthcoming.

Khalfaoui, Mouez. "Maqāṣid al-Sharīʿah as a Legitimization for the Muslim Minorities Law." In *The Objectives of Islamic Law: The Promises and Challenges of the Maqāṣid al-Sharīʿa*, edited by Idris Nassery, Rumee Ahmed and Muna Tatari, 271–84. Lanham: Lexington Books, 2018.

Khalfaoui, Mouez. "Public Theology and Democracy: A Muslim Perspective." In *Religion and Democracy: Studies in Public Theology*, edited by Torsten Meireis and Rolf Schieder, 89–101. Baden-Baden: Nomos, 2017.

Khalfaoui, Mouez. "The Shift of Paradigms from Obligation to Right in Muslim Culture: Work Ethics as a Case Study." *Journal of Islamic Ethics*, forthcoming.

Khan, Muhammad Zafrullah. *Islam and Human Rights*. Islamabad: Islam International Publications Ltd., 1967.

Lewis, Bernard. *Race and Slavery in the Middle East: An Historical Enquiry*. New York: Oxford University Press, 1990.

Malik, Jamal. "Introduction." In *Muslims in Europe: From the Margin to the Centre*, edited by Jamal Malik, 1–18. Münster: LIT, 2004.

Mayer, Ann Elizabeth. "Islamic Rights or Human Rights: An Iranian Dilemma." *Iranian Studies* 29, no. 3/4 (1996): 269–96.

Mayer, Ann Elizabeth. "Universal Versus Islamic Human Rights: A Clash of Cultures or a Clash with a Construct?." *Michigan Journal of International Law* 15, no. 2 (1994): 307–429.

Nasrallah, Tony. "Charles Malik und die Universalität der Menschenrechte." In *Kultur, Identität und Menschenrechte: Transkulturelle Perspektiven*, edited by Sarhan Dhouib, 315–32. Göttingen: Velbrück, 2012.

Otto, Jan Michiel, ed. *Sharia Incorporated: A Comparative Overview of the Legal Systems of Twelve Muslim Countries in Past and Present.* Leiden: Leiden University Press, 2010.

Rohe, Mathias. *Das islamische Recht: Geschichte und Gegenwart.* Munich: C.H. Beck, 2009.

Rohe, Mathias. *Der Islam in Deutschland: Eine Bestandsaufnahme.* Munich: C.H. Beck, 2018.

Said, Abdul Aziz. "Precept and Practice of Human Rights in Islam." *Universal Human Rights* 1, no. 1 (January-March 1979): 63–79, https://doi.org/10.2307/761831.

Shah, Niaz A. "Women's Human Rights in the Koran: An Interpretive Approach." *Human Rights Quarterly* 28, no. 4 (November 2006): 868–903.

Sultan, Wafa. *A God Who Hates: The Courageous Woman Who Inflamed the Muslim World Speaks out against the Evils of Islam.* New York: St. Martin's Press, 2009.

Tahir, Atique. "A True Vision of Human Rights in Islam." *Al-Adwa* 28, no. 40 (2013): 7–22.

Waltz, Susan. "Universal Human Rights: The Contribution of Muslim States." *Human Rights Quarterly* 26, no. 4 (November 2004): 799–844, https://doi.org/10.1353/hrq.2004.0059.

CHAPTER 8

Islamic Law

The Struggle against Time

Reik Kirchhof

1   Introduction

"Everything was better in the good old days" is a familiar expression from everyday life which reflects the widespread belief in social or moral decline. Cognitive psychology explains this perception through reference to the tendency of our memory to rehearse and dwell on good things of the past more often than we do with bad events. This positivity bias applies for both autobiographical and collective memory and is believed to be driven by some sort of emotion regulation encompassing all cultures.[1] Recent research has suggested that this phenomenon is notably pronounced within contemporary Muslim legal thinking, which is often characterized "by an emulation of past perfection, and a dissatisfaction with an imperfect present," a feature that also translates into modern Muslim social formations.[2] This article attempts to address this phenomenon and investigates its possible reasons by applying a new concept of law and normative orders which I first introduced in *Grundlegung einer Soziologie der Scharia*.[3] Theoretical assumptions are essential prerequisites for understanding our social environment, thus the way we understand and explain our social world depends on the logical structures we set up towards our environment, as the history of ideas shows.

The study is framework-driven and thus does not exclude other possible reasons for the question under consideration. And as our theoretical model

---

[1] Margaret W. Matlin, "Pollyanna Principle," in *Cognitive Illusions: Intriguing Phenomena in Thinking, Judgment and Memory*, ed. Rüdiger F. Pohl (New York: Routledge, 2017). James Fentress and Chris Wickham, *Social Memory: New Perspectives in the Past* (Oxford: Blackwell, 1992).

[2] "Uses of the Past: Understanding Shariʿa – Custom, Gender, State and Violence," US-PPIP Project, accessed September 29, 2021, www.usppip.com/about/.

[3] Reik Kirchhof, *Grundlegung einer Soziologie der Scharia* (Wiesbaden: Springer VS, 2019). I am grateful to Jamal Malik, my Doktorvater, who encouraged me in my pursuit to raise greater attention to the theoretical assumptions of the study of Islamic law and to challenge its conventional thought patterns.

describes all normative traditions, Islamic or not, the choice of our object of investigation does not imply that other traditions are exempt from the same phenomenon, which is particularly true with regard to contemporary studies that link the rising conservatism and so-called right-wing or populist movements in "the West" to the cognitive positivity bias of collective memory.[4]

This chapter argues that a reason for the tendency in modern Muslim thought toward emulating the past lies in the classical logic of norm-generation in Islam, which is incapable of coping with an increasingly globalized social reality characterized by the perception of events in an unprecedentedly high frequency and volume. Like most non-Islamic concepts of normativity, the logic of Islamic normativity also assumes that norms are externally grounded. Decision-making thus requires a bridging between normative reality and its alleged foundations, which are commonly believed to lay somewhere in the past. The challenge of bridging the gap between past and present increases with the passing of time, which in Islam, in contrast to many Western concepts, is aggravated by the tenet of the predestination of norms. There is only one exception in the history of Islam in which this logic was not applied to the process of norm-making: the lifetime of the Prophet, which is of significance for the question under consideration.

In the first part of this article, the reader is introduced to a general concept of normative order and law that is methodologically distinct from the logical framework as it is mainly applied by the scholarship for the study of Islam. Scholars of Islamic law, including scholars of *usul al-fiqh*, almost universally take a legal positivist perspective towards the research object. They conceptualize law in the same way as most actors of the research object do, like jurists and lay-people.[5] Accordingly, law is understood as a rule-based system of social control, the rules of which are applied to practiced actions of its subjects by a judiciary, backed up by a threat of sanction. The rules are believed to be held in doctrinal repositories which are called legal sources and are manifest in civil or divine legislation and other precedents. The sources are a minimal abstract in comparison to any potential constellations of present social practice, which is logically unavoidable as every source predates its stream. For that reason, in almost every single act of application, it becomes necessary to argue about the meaning of those sources in order to bridge the gap between past and present,

---

4 Joris Lammers and Matt Baldwin, "Past-focused Temporal Communication Overcomes Conservatives' Resistance to Liberal Political Ideas," *Journal of Personality and Social Psychology* 114, no. 4 (2018), https://doi.org/10.1037/pspi0000121.

5 As also noted by A. Kevin Reinhart, "Law," in *Key Themes for the Study of Islam*, ed. Jamal J. Elias (Oxford: OneWorld, 2010), 220.

which is commonly described as interpretation or exegesis. This concept has proven more or less successful in practice, provided that all actors involved in this process agree that the source is the point of departure for all argumentation, regardless of whether the agreement is reached voluntarily or by threat of force, something that jurists usually describe with the enigmatic term "validity of law." However, this concept fails every time actors disagree on the validity of the source, or more vividly illustrated, every time the robber becomes the ruler. As this concept cannot transcend its assertion of validity,[6] its capacity to make predictions about normative structures is very limited. It rather serves to describe and, particularly, to legitimize the work of jurists, but it was not developed in order to understand or explain normative structures beyond normative assertions. In contrast, the theoretical framework of this study turns the tables and takes a non-normative approach towards normativity, beyond the realm of jurisprudence and its normative assumptions. It has no normative inclinations whatsoever, neither towards any tenets of Islam, any rights or wrongs, nor towards its theoretical propositions. The logical framework of this study identifies norms solely in facts of social practice and hence ignores any normative labels, because the statement, for example, not to drink alcohol does not say much about actual social practice and hence about a social norm, its genesis, evolution or involution. This concept aims at enlightening the far side of normativity, that is the non-normative side of normative orders. As this concept positions itself beyond the native traditions of Western and Islamic jurisprudence alike, it allows for a new perspective on Islamic normativity.

Based on this framework, the second part of this article assesses the classical Islamic concept of Islamic normativity from a diachronic perspective, taking historical events into consideration. It has had to resort to this method because scientifically acquired data about past social practices of Muslims are not at hand and are unlikely to ever be retrieved in a quality that could satisfy any general sociological analysis about the normative structures of past Muslim societies.[7] However, we suppose, in line with many other

---

[6] Any dispute on this matter is unthinkable for all jurists; cf. André-Jean Arnaud, "Droit et societé: Un Carrefour interdisciplinaire," *Revue interdisciplinaire d'études juridiques* 21, no. 2 (1988), 8–9. To this effect, Max Weber identified "the belief in legality" as "the most common form of legitimacy" of orders, idem, *Economy and Society: An Outline of Interpretive Sociology*, ed. Guenther Roth and Claus Wittich (Berkeley: University of California Press, 1978), 37.

[7] Mathias Rohe, *Das islamische Recht: Geschichte und Gegenwart* (Munich: C.H. Beck, 2009), 79; for selective studies, see for example Christian Müller, *Gerichtspraxis im Stadtstaat Córdoba: Zum Recht der Gesellschaft in einer mālikitisch-islamischen Rechtstradition des 5./ 11. Jahrhunderts* (Leiden: Brill, 1999); Gabriela Linda Guellil, *Damaszener Akten des 8./14. Jahrhunderts nach aṭ-Ṭarsūsīs Kitāb al-Iʻlām* (Bamberg: Klaus Schwarz, 1985).

scholars,[8] that the logical framework of Islamic normativity was well informed by societal developments and normative practice and thus evolved accordingly. As the study extrapolates data of social practice from the normative concept of shariʻa, this approach is hypothetical in nature.

Based on the results of this investigation, the third part of this article extends its assessment to modern developments and manifestations of Islam, offering explanations which demonstrate that a different conceptual proposition allows for distinct insights into modern Islamic social practices.

2 The Nature of Social Normativity and Law

This study assumes that social norms and orders exist. When we say "exist," we are not alluding to any variants of realism, which claim in different shades that elements of our universe have additional properties that one may call true or real. We simply start in a pragmatic way, with the common sense view of how things appear to be, and in this line, we identify social norms in the orderliness of consistent social behavioral patterns and structures of social practice.[9] We further consider ideas and concepts about our universe to be normative orders too, as long as they are perceivable by a third party and thus observable as social patterns.[10] Hence, we do not dispute, for example, the existence of God, because this idea is in excellent agreement with the observations of many actors and thus forms a normative order, whereas for his reality or properties, we recommend consulting the philosophers, whose hypotheses about God, again, we perceive as normative orders.

In contrast to jurists and the majority of scholars of Islamic law and normativity, who equate social norms with normative statements and assertions, we identify social norms in the congruence of normative statements and action, that is in the empirical realization of 'ought' in social practice.[11] The genesis

---

8   For a survey on this matter, see Patricia Crone, *Roman, Provincial and Islamic Law: The Origins of the Islamic Patronate* (Cambridge: Cambridge University Press, 1987), 1–17.

9   Which are commonly labelled as, for example, custom, law, moral, etiquette, language, fashion, eating- and drinking habit, whose demarcations, however, are hard to identify in spite of all scholarly efforts; cf. Jack P. Gibbs, "Norms: The Problem of Definition and Classification," *The American Journal of Sociology* 70, no. 5 (1965).

10 They are the non-normative flipside of what normatively inclined actors today commonly call ideologies in contrast to the original meaning of the term as "science of ideas." Cf. Brian W. Head, *Ideology and Social Science: Destutt de Tracy and French Liberalism* (Dordrecht: Martinus Nijhoff Publishers, 1985), 31.

11 Talcott Parsons viewed "mutual expectations" or the "complementarity of expectations" as the prerequisite of social order; cf. Talcott Parsons and Edward A. Shils,

of Islamic norms starts with the individual differentiation of meaning from the contingency of the universe in order to answer fundamental questions about existence and the self within this universe: Is the entropy of the universe increasing? Is it created by God? Considering that all actors have equal starting conditions, that is an infinite number of possibilities for action, and that thus with regard to potential interaction, all actors know that all actors know that everybody could act differently – something that Talcott Parsons called the state of "double contingency" – the question arises as to how norms find congruency and how they integrate, if not by fortunate coincidence.[12] A popular answer, which dominates sociological research today, is that this is achieved through learning. Actors learn from existing social normative patterns, from a "cultural inheritance" of a "shared symbolic system"[13] about the norms that actors can expect from others in order to make successful communication and action possible. While this logic is in agreement with a great number of our observations, it cannot explain the emergence of new norms, like the norm of Islam, the norm of the Big Bang, or any norms of art and invention.[14] With regard to the genesis of norms, it becomes clear that this argument is based on a logical fallacy, as it supports a claim with a premise that itself presupposes the claim. Therefore, we assume that congruency of individual norms and thus the genesis and evolution of a social pattern is based on decisions. This applies as much to the individual differentiation of norms and meaning from contingency as it does to the occurrence of mutual expectations, and thus to social norms.

As time passes and the present slips into another present, a nascent social norm instantly comes under attack by subsequent events and environmental change, that is due to time. The passing of time implies that expectations

---

"Categories of the Orientation and Organization of Action," in *Toward a General Theory of Action: Theoretical Foundations for the Social Sciences*, ed. Talcott Parsons and Edward A. Shils (New York: Harper & Row, 1962), 106; Talcott Parsons, "The Theory of Symbolism in Relation to Action," in *Working Papers in the Theory of Action*, ed. Talcott Parsons et al. (New York: Free Press, 1953), 35–36.

12 For the development of the concept of integration in sociology, see Rüdiger Peuckert and Albert Scherr, "Integration," in *Grundbegriffe der Soziologie*, ed. Bernhard Schäfers (Opladen: Leske und Budrich, 2003).

13 Parsons and Shils, "Categories of the Orientation," 106; Peter L. Berger and Thomas Luckmann, *The Social Construction of Reality: A Treatise in the Sociology of Knowledge* (London: Penguin Books, 1967).

14 This has been pointed out by Johan Galtung, "Expectations and Interaction Processes," *Inquiry: An Interdisciplinary Journal of Philosophy* 2, no. 1–4 (1959): 225–26, https://doi.org/10.1080/00201745908601296; as well as by Niklas Luhmann, *Rechtssoziologie*, vol. 1 (Opladen: Westdeutscher Verlag, 1987), 33.

about norms are constantly disappointed, which requires actors to constantly make decisions about their colliding expectations in order to overcome their disappointments.[15] Actors may affirm their disappointed norms, accepting the risk of repeatedly colliding expectations on a particular matter, or they may adjust their normative expectations in order to integrate their opposing individual norms into each other. They may decide jointly about disputed social norms, refer such decision to a third party or make a joint decision to defer the decision to the afterlife, but whatever the case, they have to make decisions in order to uphold any practiced social pattern against time. It is granted that actors may also opt to cease further social interaction altogether by living in social seclusion. We call these procedures, in which decisions on social norms are made, institutions; and in institutions, disappointments are expressed and normative expectations are integrated to constitute and maintain social normative orders.[16]

To decide about colliding norms, by oneself or together with others, means to argue about their justification, which is expressed by preexisting or newly created norms. As actors keep track of one another's expectations and their inferential use of norms, norms which have the highest score in referring to successful social understanding are the most compatible to this practice.[17] The function of those patterns evolving from social interaction lies in the stabilization of ongoing social relationships of interaction in order to avoid

---

15   The way actors deal with their disappointments is the access for investigating the evolution of normative structures, which was prominently pointed out by Niklas Luhmann, ibid., 41–42.

16   Such a notion of process is conveyed by, e.g., Lynne G. Zucker, "The Role of Institutionalization in Cultural Persistence," *American Sociological Review* 42, no. 5 (October 1977), https://doi.org/10.2307/2094862; Ronald L. Jepperson, "Institutions, Institutional Effects, and Institutionalism," in *The New Institutionalism in Organizational Analysis*, ed. Walter W. Powell and Paul J. DiMaggio (Chicago: University of Chicago Press, 1991); Niklas Luhmann, "Institutionalisierung – Funktion und Mechanismus im sozialen System der Gesellschaft," in *Zur Theorie der Institution*, ed. Helmut Schelsky (Düsseldorf: Bertelsmann Universitätsverlag, 1982). In contrast, the "institutional legal positivism" assumes a notion of substance. Its prototype of an institution is the lawmaker or the parliament that draws on a corpus of existing positive rules; cf. Neil MacCormick and Ota Weinberger, *An Institutional Theory of Law: New Approaches to Legal Positivism* (Dordrecht: D. Reidel, 1986). However, its proponents must always anticipate the institution that is actually the result of its institutionalization. This implies that power-conferring laws (that is Hart's secondary rules) are assigned validity without basis, which is the reason why institutional legal positivism is unable to answer the question of how institutionalization evolves or changes if its grounds follow its existence.

17   Robert B. Brandom, *Making It Explicit: Reasoning, Representing, and Discursive Commitment* (Cambridge, MA: Harvard University Press, 1994), 67–140, 496–97.

the uncertainty of not knowing how other actors will react to one's behavior, thus reducing the social complexity of interaction.[18] However, this function is achieved not because actors align with the meaning of past patterns of normativity, but rather because actors take part in the process of ongoing mutual engagement of decision-making, which operates like an unceasing normativity generator: Disappointed expectations into the use of norms are processed in institutionalized procedures of decision-making, the results of which serve as new normative expectations for further interaction. Hence, norms are practice-immanent and have no external ground, which is the pivotal difference from traditional concepts of law. Normative orderliness does not evolve because actors follow norms, but it exists because actors permanently create norms ad hoc through social practice.[19] This conceptual shift implies that our decisions are not determined by the past and that in consequence, as Heinz von Foerster put it, "only those questions that are in principle undecidable, we can decide,"[20] because otherwise every decision would have already been decided. Even though all arguments advanced in the decision-making process might originate in past individual experiences, decisions are incalculable, and thus contingent. This logical framework renders normativity in terms of use and social practice, rather than in terms of representation or its relation of reference to the world. It can explain the alteration of norms and the genesis of new norms, taking into account time, that is the individual perception of the environmental change of meaning.

Our observations suggest further that a kind of normative order exists which is distinct from other normative orders. It operates "expectations of a particular kind,"[21] which are characterized by particularly high investments into social interaction and are thus prone to especially deep disappointments,[22] which, if not contained by specific processes of decision-making, will cause

---

18 Thomas Raiser, *Grundlagen der Rechtssoziologie* (Tübingen: Mohr Siebeck, 2013), 162–63.
19 Robert B. Brandom, "Pragmatische Themen in Hegels Idealismus: Unterhandlung und Verwaltung der Struktur und des Gehalts in Hegels Erklärung begrifflicher Normen," *Deutsche Zeitschrift für Philosophie* 47, no. 3 (1999): 356, https://doi.org/10.1524/dzph.1999.47.3.355.
20 Heinz von Foerster, "Ethics and Second-order Cybernetics," *Cybernetics and Human Knowing* 1, no. 1 (1992): 14.
21 Max Weber, *Wirtschaft und Gesellschaft: Grundriss der Sozialökonomie*, vol. III, *Abteilung* (Tübingen: J.C.B. Mohr, 1922), 17: "auch (oder: nur) durch Erwartungen spezifischer äußerer Folgen, also: durch Interessenlage; aber: durch Erwartungen von besonderer Art." The end of this sentence has been omitted in the English translation.
22 This concept aligns with Eugen Ehrlich's concept of differentiating legal from non-legal orders by different "overtones of feelings" (*Gefühlstöne*): a transgression of law leads to a feeling of revolt (*Empörung*), whereas a violation of morals corresponds with the feeling

the normativity generator to grind to a halt, thus resulting in the disintegration of normative order. We call those expectations legal expectations. Their chief characteristic is that they must be processed by non-competing decisions. We identify the congruence of those norms as "legal norms" and their institutional process as "legal order" or "law." In contrast, if a will of integration prevails, then non-legal orders, often labelled as morals, ethics, etiquettes, language, etc., are not necessarily affected by multiple and thus competing decisions on colliding expectations regarding the same matter. Hence, law is an important condition for societal integration and reflects structures of society by processes of integration and disintegration of normative orders.

3   The Formation of Islamic Normativity

According to Islamic tradition, the genesis and evolution of Islamic normativity was not at the beginning a problematic undertaking. It started with an event in 610 on Mount Hira, in which both God's and Muhammad's initially colliding expectations on the matter of prophethood were finally attuned, and as a result created the first social norm of Islam: *Muhammad rasul Allah*. The subsequent interaction between God and the Prophet, on the basis of this understanding, revealed God's expectations towards mankind regarding their behavior and the universe of meaning until the death of the Prophet. Whoever confessed to Islam and listened to Muhammad's ongoing proclamations adopted, by faith, God's expectations as their own. As far as those norms were practiced, Islamic normativity evolved. Profession of the new faith did not mean that existing social practice and procedures of decision-making were overwritten. Actors were still tracking each other's norms and their inferential use, which hardly differed from past normativity.[23] In contrast to the past, however, every norm which now became justified with reference to Islam was considered as more convincing in the process of decision-making than norms without that reference, of course especially among Muslims, which is why Islamic norms could therefore soon book the highest score in referring to successful understanding.

As time passed, the perception of ongoing events and environmental change inevitably produced collisions of God's expectations in the day-to-day practice of their integration, which required actors to deal with their disappointments by making decisions. However, actors did not need to decide on God's and thus

---

of indignation (*Entrüstung*), etc. Cf. *Fundamental Principles of the Sociology of Law* (New Brunswick, NJ: Transaction Publishers, 2002), 165–66.

23   Crone, *Roman, Provincial and Islamic Law*.

on their own expectations, but they only had to decide to listen to the Prophet in order to overcome their disappointments. As the revelation was an ongoing process over time, the Prophet continuously proclaimed decisions to all arising conflicts until his death, which were adopted by believers for their discursive practice. Although all arising questions were still principally undecidable, this was not of concern for those worldly actors. The indeterminacy of normativity was concealed by the belief that the knowledge of God is omniscient and infinite and thus determines the universe of meaning for all times. And since God was attending via his worldly agent the early evolution of Islamic normative practice, the past and the present appeared in this period as a unified entity to actors, an idea that alludes to the later philosophical concept that "God is time (*dahr*)."[24] This situation was a sanctuary from the eternal puzzling problem that decisions were regularly justified with references to past causalities while this concept consistently contradicted empirical observations, which suggested that normativity was a contingent empirical phenomenon, meaning that something could actually exist without reason. The idea of God solved this riddle, it was the ultimate answer to the question of reason and causality, one that could successfully conceal empirical observations, which in contrast suggested that meaning has no relation of reference to the world; an idea that many actors up to the present day consider unbearable, regardless of their ideological or religious affiliation, including lawyers.

Applying our logical framework to Islamic tradition, the structure of normativity during the lifetime of the Prophet featured all prerequisites to process law: All arising conflicts about colliding norms were decided in an institutionalized process that responded with non-competing decisions, and was hence able to satisfy the worldly demand for law. On this basis, we hypothesize that the event of Islamic revelation likely fell into a social environment which was defined by social disintegration, a state in which actors, demanding law, were seeking to integrate expectations with particularly high investments into social practice, but failed to institutionalize appropriate processes of decision-making, a state that scholarly findings underpin.[25] This aim was achieved by abandoning past normativity and interaction, that now became shunned as *jahiliyya*, or the times of ignorance, and by the recognition of a new process of normativity. Yet this safe shelter did not last long.

---

24   Gerhard Böwering, "Ibn al-'Arabī's Concept of Time," in *Gott ist schön und Er liebt die Schönheit*, ed. Alma Giese and Johann Christoph Bürgel (Bern: Peter Lang, 1994), 72.

25   An overview is given in the reference-work by F.E. Peters, ed., *The Arabs and Arabia on the Eve of Islam* (Oxon: Routledge, 2017).

With the death of the Prophet, the institution that processed Islamic law was lost and the difference between past and present was starting to grow with every new perceptible event that slipped into the present. Actors were still individually or jointly addressing God in order to overcome their disappointments, but God no longer answered with decisions. It was a shock: from now on actors had to decide by themselves. All that was left was the revelation of God and memories of arguments of the past inferential process of Islamic normativity which was therefore held precious. For obvious reasons, Muslims opted for a concept, that is today commonly known as legal source, assuming that all decisions to all normative conflicts are held in a reservoir of precedents, which not only comprised the transmitted and known words of God and reports about the Prophet's life, but also non-Islamic *sunan*[26] and customs, since norms of the latter still earned a high score in terms of inferential successful use. As time marched onwards and social practice became overwhelmingly complex, Muslims referred decision-making processes to particularly keen and well-versed actors, as had been the habit in the past, who began to discuss this troubling matter in a more academic atmosphere. So-called study circles emerged in vast numbers across the entire and still growing empire.[27] Therein members focused on the interpretation and understanding of the divine scripture, and thus on the task of making oneself understood. Those scholars were tracking both the inferentiality of the normative practice of their environment and of their internal discursive scholarly practice and were thus eventually able to reduce the gap between past and present by institutionalizing an Islamic normativity-generator.[28]

The problem was that out of academic curiosity, scholars were also observing other study circles, which served the demands of other actors for decisions. This made them realize that Islamic normativity differed among different study circles, which not only stood in glaring conflict with the idea that one God had predestined one normative order for one Muslim community, but even worse, suggested once again that even divine normativity was an

---

26   Wael B. Hallaq, *Sharīʿa: Theory, Practice, Transformations* (New York: Cambridge University Press, 2009), 41, 43.

27   Bernard Weiss speaks of a "Plethora" of different legal schools, "The Madhhab in Islamic Legal Theory," in *The Islamic School of Law: Evolution, Devolution, and Progress*, ed. Peri Bearman et al. (Cambridge, MA: Islamic Legal Studies Program, Harvard Law School, 2005), 2.

28   Behnam Sadeghi investigates in detail the genesis and evolution of such a decision-making process through the example of women and group prayer in the Hanafi tradition, *The Logic of Law Making in Islam: Women and Prayer in the Legal Tradition* (New York: Cambridge University Press, 2013).

empirical fact. As scholars were responsive to this issue and willing to reconcile and integrate their differences, a fusion of study circles set in, which after a period of two hundred years, came to a halt with the manifestation of four Sunni *madhahib*.[29] Although all the remaining *madhahib* based their decisions on the same sources, widely using the same norms for their processes of understanding, they differed in the results of their understanding and hence dissociated from each other along the lines of differences in social practice.[30] Still, each *madhahib* met the requirements for processing legal expectations as long as all actors, who interacted with each other, addressed continuously only one of those *madhahib*. This was feasible because the operative realm of each *madhhab* was mostly limited to a geographically defined area.[31] However, in cases where those different legal orders encountered each other on the translocal level, the integration of God's expectations became impossible and law could not be maintained, regardless of the actor's common faith or willingness toward integration.[32] For obvious reasons, this state of affairs was unsatisfying for religious scholars, who on a regular basis crossed the discursive borders of the different *madhahib*, because it contradicted God's will to establish a single order for just one community. Moreover, this situation once more corroborated the unpleasant empirical observation that normative reality developed independent of normative claims and statements. The traditional scholarly conceptualization of Islamic normativity reflects this predicament and illustrates the attempt to reconcile empirical observations with the idea that normativity is conferred by a relation to the world that has been antecedently specified by God: Overall, the decision-making process was characterized by a reluctance toward decision-making, by the deflection of responsibility for decisions and by the attempt to contain the number of contingent norms so as to reduce the number of conflicting expectations.

---

29 Which Hallaq describes as "a cardinal evolution" that brought "Islamic law to full maturity," *Sharī'a*, 60.

30 "Without differences in *ijtihād* and disagreement over matters of interpretation, and some distinctive contributions to juristic thought, separate *madhhabs* could not have come into existence." Mohammad Hashim Kamali, *Shari'ah Law: An Introduction* (Oxford: OneWorld, 2008), 10. For an example of this practice on the matter of alcohol consumption, see Najam Haider, "Contesting Intoxication: Early Juristic Debates over the Lawfulness of Alcoholic Beverages," *Islamic Law and Society* 20, no. 1–2 (2013).

31 Knut S. Vikør, *Between God and the Sultan: A History of Islamic Law* (New York: Oxford University Press, 2005), 103–4.; Rohe, *Das Islamische Recht*, 29–30.

32 As for the so-called four chief judgeships, which evolved since Mamluk times in major cities, and its possible ramifications for legal order, see Kirchhof, *Grundlegung*, 336–37.

Where unavoidable, individual decisions of scholars, the *fuqahaʾ*, were disguised with the term *ijtihad*, meaning the "exertion of mental energy for the sake of arriving, through reasoning, at a considered opinion."[33] In the same line, a joint decision was termed *ijmaʿ*, meaning consensus or unanimity, insinuating complementarity of individual norms by coincidence. This approach is understandable since, after all, to decide about God's expectations was surely a delicate and thus controversial undertaking, especially insofar as decisions were based on human reason governed by empirical observations of inferential practice of meaning, commonly referred to by scholars as free will. Since observations proved that all decisions, including those based on free will, had consequences for the present of the future, it became obvious that decisions representing free will were genuine creations of man and thus interfered in God's creation, which of course also applied for the creators of those decisions. Influenced by Greek philosophy, the Muʿtazila addressed these intricate issues and conveyed the idea that human reason is a prerequisite for accessing the meaning of the revelation, accepting man's responsibility for decisions based on free will. Although a philosophical school, it had many followers among the early *fuqahaʾ* who were known as *ahl al-raʾy*. This school's approach toward decision-making was the norm until its opponents, namely the traditionalists or *ahl al-hadith*, who rejected any reasoning that was not based on textual evidence, gained ground towards the end of the eighth century. For a short while in the early ninth century, the Abbasid caliph al-Maʾmun (r. 813–833) interfered in the field of discursive practice on the side of the Muʿtazilites by persecuting the traditionalists, an event that became known as the *mihna*. Nevertheless, the norm of free will could no longer assert successful understanding within the inferential scholarly discourse about Islamic normativity, thus eventually limiting the scope of possible future decisions.[34]

Regardless of whether man was granted the prerogative to make decisions, it was indeed inevitable that he would do so, since time continued to influence

---

33   Hallaq, *Sharīʿa*, 49–50. Sami A. Aldeeb Abu-Sahlieh defines it as "the action of straining the forces of one's spirit to their extreme limits to penetrate the intimate meaning of the Shariʿa (Quran and Sunna) in order to deduce a speculative rule (qaʿi-dah dhanniyyah)." See his *Introduction to Islamic Law: Foundation, Sources and Principles*, trans. Felix J. Phiri (St-Sulpice: Centre of Arab and Islamic Law, 2012), 152, whereas Rohe bluntly describes it as "independent decision-making." Rohe, *Das Islamische Recht*, 36.

34   Hallaq sees an approximation of both positions at the end of the fight, which he calls the "great synthesis" (*Sharīʿa*, 56). This epistemic issue was an old one, which Plato already described in his Allegory of the Cave and was discussed across religions. A summary with reference to Christianity is given by Ebrahim Moosa, "Allegory of the Rule (*Ḥukm*): Law as Simulacrum in Islam?," *History of Religions* 38, no. 1 (1998), https://doi.org/10.1086/463517.

present normativity, as it always had, which is why *fuqaha'* tried to deflect responsibility for their individual decisions. They chose to align with the most successful understanding within the discourse, which fortunately always originated in past decisions made by third parties. They could thus maintain the illusion that at no point, since the death of the Prophet, were decisions about God's norms made in the present. Decisions were not made, or let alone created, but were simply found in past normativity, which is the essence of the concept of legal source and is in line with the Platonic idea of representation. Scholars, whose decisions became the most successful norms, but who could not yet refer to past decisions, were obviously in the spotlight of such references. Those opinion leaders,[35] who for obvious reasons were mostly deceased at the time of referencing, were called *mujtahid*s. The earliest of those scholars set the normative agenda of a given *madhhab*, which is why they became highly revered by past scholars and why *madhahib* eventually bore their names.[36]

This development had different effects. Dissident opinions and new norms were increasingly marginalized within the game of reasoning with the result that *ijtihad*, meaning the individual determination of new norms which are yet contingent in social practice, became less practiced, which is why the number of *mujtahid*s necessarily decreased over time. This phenomenon eventually raised the question among contemporaries as to whether any *mujtahid*s still existed at all, consequently resulting in the concern over whether all questions about God's normativity had already been answered, a topos which towards the end of the eleventh century became known among scholars as "the *closing* of the *gates* of *ijtihad*."[37] This state of discourse is commonly described with the term *taqlid*, meaning "imitation" or "blind following"[38] of successfully practiced norms or the "mandatory adoption of dogmas."[39]

---

35   Who hold deontic authority, whereas scholars mainly insinuate a kind of epistemic authority when explaining the role of *mujtahidun*, highlighting their skills and knowledge. Cf., e.g., Hallaq, *Sharī'a*, 66–67.

36   For this reason, Norman Calder argues that *madhhab*s emerged later than commonly believed. See his *Studies in Early Muslim Jurisprudence* (Oxford: Clarendon Press, 1993). An overview on this topic is given by Knut S. Vikør, "The Truth about Cats and Dogs: The Historicity of Early Islamic Law," *Historisk Tidsskrift* 82, no. 1 (2003).

37   In contrast, scholars often explain this phenomenon with the complex order of succession and the high qualification required to be fit. Wael B. Hallaq, "Was the Gate of Ijtihad Closed?," *International Journal of Middle East Studies* 16, no. 1 (March 1984): 32, https://doi.org/10.1017/S0020743800027598.

38   Kamali, *Shari'ah Law*, 36, 327.

39   Rohe, *Das Islamische Recht*, 37.

Another approach was the containment of norms at the level of sources. This development started early on, when all *sunan* except the sunna of the Prophet were blacklisted, a decision which is often attributed to Imam al-Shafi'i (d. 820), who rose to prominence in the ninth century and who, after his death, became the eponym of the Shafi'i *madhhab*. However, scholars had to experience that this was not sufficient, because unfortunately the decision led to a dramatic increase in the number of prophetic *ahadith*, and thus to new norms, since this new concept required the substitution of past inferentially practiced norms.[40] For this reason, scholars had to delimit their numbers again with further norms, above all the evaluation of authenticity and the chain of transmission (*isnad*), with the help of which many so-called false reports could be uncovered and eventually contained, an undertaking which continues to the present day.[41] On the other hand, the containment of contingency by the recursive iteration of past successful norms had the welcoming effect that the different *madhahib* were eventually able to speak with one voice and could thus serve their communities' demand for law, yet it also made those institutions less reactive to unexpected events.

Despite all efforts, scholars still had to experience that every established understanding about past normativity was contingent in every finite present and therefore appeared relative to God's will. Against this background, a highly sophisticated process of understanding developed, which was characterized by a constructivist approach towards understanding and interpretation. Yet this inevitably came with normative relativism, known as *kull-u mujtahid musib*, ("every *mujtahid* is right"), which drew the ire of many scholars, Ibn Taymiyya (d.1328) being probably one of the most popular among them.[42] The European history of the idea of interpretation underwent a similar development. Friedrich Schleiermacher (d. 1834), following Platonic ideas of representation, was convinced that intersubjective understanding of texts is achievable if the appropriate tools of interpretation are at hand. Friedrich Ast (d. 1841), in contrast, recognized that present normativity pervades every single process of interpretation, which is why he explained intersubjective understanding as a hermeneutical circle in which present and past normativity, which are interrelated, approach each other. Wilhelm Dilthey (d. 1911) went further, describing interpretation as a creative act which has only limited relations to the past,

---

40 Hallaq, *Shari'a*, 45–46.
41 The question of authenticity has ever since been contested. A survey of the debate is given by Harald Motzki, "Dating Muslim Traditions: A Survey," *Arabica* 52, no. 2 (April 2005).
42 Mohamad M. Yunis Ali, *Medieval Islamic Pragmatics: Sunni Legal Theorists' Models of Textual Communication* (Richmond: Curzon Press, 2000), 89–90.

until Hans-Georg Gadamer cut ties with historicism altogether, arguing that the situation of interpretation is an act of constructing norms, one that happens in every finite present. However, the constructivist disillusion with the concept of intersubjectivity was not final. In order to save scientific reasoning from the abyss of insignificance, Jürgen Habermas proposed the feature of an external auditor, whose function is to critically ascertain how far constructivist decisions present a true view of the issue at stake. He described this interlocution with the concept of an "ideal speech situation" that is only realized in a "radical democracy,"[43] linking normativity of social practice and communication to nation state politics.[44] In the same line, *usul al-fiqh* established an ideal discourse as well: If all intricate rules of the discourse are observed, all results are by definition objectively true while at the same time relative to God's will.

The existence of different *madhahib* with different ideal discourses, however, prevented Islamic normativities from reaching a single truth. Therefore, scholars agreed on the concept of an ontological pluralism of a God-given universe of meaning.[45] The final integration of God's expectations was deferred to the afterlife, where God himself, as an external auditor, would establish intersubjectivity and eventually close the gap between past and present. Yet this recognition of an intrinsic *ikhtilaf* in this world implied that the institutionalization of Islamic law beyond each *madhhab* was impossible in this world.[46]

4   Islamic Normativities in Modern Times

Scholars of Islam widely agree on the assumption that the advent of modernity heralded the "demise of shariʿa" and traditional Islamic normativity, which is why they seek to relate this phenomenon to specific aspects of modernity.

---

43   Jürgen Habermas, "Reflections on the Linguistic Foundation of Sociology: The Christian Gauss Lectures (Princeton University, February-March 1971)," in *On the Pragmatics of Social Interaction: Preliminary Studies in the Theory of Communicative Action*, trans. Barbara Fultner (Cambridge, MA: MIT Press, 2001), 1–103; Idem, *Between Facts and Norms: Contributions to a Discourse Theory of Law and Democracy*, trans. William Rehg (Cambridge, MA: MIT Press, 1996), 371–72.

44   Therefore, scholars identify this concept as "democratic positivism." Peter Niesen and Oliver Eberl, "Demokratischer Positivismus: Habermas und Maus," in *Neue Theorien des Rechts*, ed. Sonja Buckel, et al. (Stuttgart: Lucius & Lucius, 2020).

45   Which Ahmed Fekry Ibrahim describes as "ontological multiplicity of truth," in his *Pragmatism in Islamic Law: A Social and Intellectual History* (New York: Syracuse University Press, 2015), 49.

46   Whereas many scholars celebrate the "ijtihadic pluralism" of the shariʿa as its "defining feature par excellence," in contrast to Western law. Cf., e.g., Hallaq, *Sharīʿa*, 368–69.

Scholars commonly list the colonialist ventures of European imperialism and an ushering in of an "internalization of the concept of nationalism" as the most important reasons for this development, rendering the "persisting crisis" of Islamic normativity and its social formations as a continual struggle against Western hegemony.[47] Taking a relation between the demise of the shariʿa and the arrival of modernity as a premise, this study adopts a different perspective, challenging the orthodox hierarchy of causes. By focusing on the subtleties of social normative structure and the importance of time for its genesis and evolution, as described in the previous paragraphs, this study offers a different explanation for the demise of traditional Islamic normativity and its various developments in modern times.

Modern times are characterized by the perception of events at an unprecedentedly high frequency. Time, understood as the perception of events,[48] is accelerating, driving past and present further apart with increasing speed, which stresses traditional normativity-generators. Running on the Platonic concept of representation, these generators are beginning to arrive at their limits, something that also applies to normative orders of the so-called Western world.[49] New ways of communication, like the modern printing press, the telephone and later the internet, along with new means of transportation, allow norms to reach every corner of the social world. Social interaction thus becomes a global matter. As soon as a norm is perceived, the actors are required to decide about its inferential practice, which creates additional norms that spread throughout the world and require further decisions, and on and on. For this reason, the volume of norms increases exponentially. As successful social interaction requires keeping track of the inferential use of all norms among all potential interacting partners, all norms need to be taken into account in the process of decision-making.[50] Social norms, the inferential use of which might be insignificant in one corner of the world at a specific moment, might be a

---

47   Cf., for example, Hallaq, "Can the Shariʿa be Restored?," in *Islamic Law and the Challenges of Modernity*, ed. Yvonne Yazbeck Haddad and Barbara Freyer Stowasser (Walnut Creek, CA: AltaMira Press, 2004), 22; or Ebrahim Moosa, "Colonialism and Islamic Law," in *Islam and Modernity: Key Issues and Debates*, ed. Muhammad Khalid Masud et al. (Edinburgh: Edinburgh University Press, 2009), 166–67.
48   Ernst Pöppel, "Time Perception," in *Handbook of Sensory Physiology: Perception*, vol. 8, ed. Richard Held et al. (Berlin: Springer, 1978), 714, https://doi.org/10.1007/978-3-642-46354-9.
49   Karl-Heinz Ladeur, ed., *Public Governance in the Age of Globalization* (Oxon and New York: Routledge, 2004).
50   Which is why heuristics and biases must be applied to reduce the complexity of decision making. Daniel Kahneman, Paul Slovic and Amos Tversky, eds., *Judgment Under Uncertainty: Heuristics and Biases* (Cambridge: Cambridge University Press, 1982).

successful social norm in another corner; though this might change with any further event.

Since the advent of modernity, Islamic normativity became increasingly challenged by a flood of new norms of Islamic and non-Islamic origin. The number of Islamic norms increased, since more and more Muslims, who had traditionally processed their legal and non-legal expectations within a geographically determined ideal discourse, became aware that more and more decisions were actually competing with other decisions from different Islamic normative orders. Additionally, non-Islamic norms significantly increased in number among Muslim actors. For various reasons, Muslims were intensifying social interaction with non-Islamic actors and their respective universes of meaning, while at the same time Western actors likewise increasingly interacted with Muslims. Limiting the objectives of this development to the colonialist enterprise and to an external imposition of norms and ideas is empirically implausible, as this ignores the "multi-directionality of exchange." It is well established that actors voluntarily joined each other's universes of meaning for different reasons, such as for gaining knowledge, satisfying curiosity, increasing personal wealth or career chances, or simply for pleasure.[51]

The growing complexity of social interaction led to more and more norm-collisions, which required decisions in order to maintain social interaction. As usual, Muslims referred those norms to the ulama, who were traditionally supposed to produce decisions. However, the ideal Islamic discourses, which over centuries had been maintaining Islamic normativity for geographically designated Muslim communities, became overwhelmed by the flood of new norms and arguments and by the new entanglements of social interaction. The well attuned discourses, that were based on an intricate recursion to past normativity, lost track of the inferential use of Islamic norms, which were now practiced across *madhhab* borders. This had momentous consequences as soon as expectations with particularly high investments into social practice, that is legal expectation, required non-competing decisions.

Allegedly non-competing decisions, which were supposed to serve Muslims' legal demands, failed in practice, because interacting partners now increasingly asserted opposing legal decisions. While this had for centuries been common knowledge among *fuqaha'*, who had concealed the problem with the concept of an ontological pluralism of a God-given universe of meaning, this idea was not expedient for the social practice of Muslims, who wanted to make

---

51 Nebahat Avcioğlu and Finbarr Barry Flood, "Introduction: Globalizing Cultures: Art and Mobility in the Eighteenth Century," *Ars Orientalis* 39 (2010): 8.

a living and were thus in need of legal order. This had two mutually interrelated effects. On the one hand, Muslims became aware that the assumption of one God having predestined one normative order for one Muslim community was an illusion, which is why Muslims became increasingly disenchanted with traditional ulama. On the other hand, Muslims had to seek alternative institutions which corresponded to their new field of social interaction. They resorted to institutions that had for ages existed alongside *madhhab* procedures, like tribes, clans and families, or turned to newly developing nation states, which to some extent covered the new fields of trans-local interaction and also processed Islamic norms. The more Muslims addressed alternative processes of decision-making, the more the traditional institutions lost their practical significance, which is why *madhhab* procedures eventually collapsed. Altogether, this was a slow process which had already begun under Muslim rule in the Ottoman Empire.[52] The contradictions of the traditional concept of Islamic normativity were now lying in plain sight. However, the new normative constellations were not satisfying for all actors, particularly those who strived for a uniform Islamic normativity that they believed was divinely ordained, because neither clan or family structures, nor the new nation state structures were reflecting the new scope of social interaction as a whole. The situation was now comparable with the time of the formative period of Islam, prior to the emergence of the four Sunni *madhahib*, but with one crucial difference. This time, the experience of the existence of a vast number of institutions, which all claimed to process God's norms, was not only limited to scholars of the early study circles, but was now of concern for all Muslims.

This situation set the scene for all further developments of Islam in modern times up to the present in terms of conceptual propositions, which have been advanced by scholars, social movements and constellations in which Muslims are involved. Whereas lay Muslims are trying to find ways to institutionalize their legal demands in order to make a living, ideally in accordance with God's will, scholars are engaged in investigating the causes of the disarray of Islamic normativity or in advancing concepts to catch up on social practice (e.g., *talfiq*). In whichever case, as during the formative period of Islam, all conceptualizations of Islamic normativity have been highly informed by social practice.

As traditional Islamic normativity was overtaken by social practice and the ideal discourse drowned by a great number of new norms, scholars recognized that the matter of decision-making is crucial to preventing Muslims from turning to alternative institutions. Therefore, many scholars called for a renewal of

---

52 Vikør, *Between God and the Sultan*, 207–8, 231.

ijtihad, which in turn, however, compromised the practice of *taqlid*, that is the ideal discourse. This had far reaching implications, because *taqlid* consisted of a whole scholarly practice on the matter of understanding. Scholars tracked all frequently recurring arguments, in terms of their practical success, in order to make themselves understood in the discourse of understanding the divine message. The latter is commonly described as the methodological principles of *fiqh*, or as *usul al-fiqh*, consisting of an abundance of principles such as *naskh*, *ijma'*, *qiyas*, *istihsan*, *istislah*, *maslaha* and *maqasid*. Hence, all past successful social interaction inevitably became subject to revision.

As a result, the discourse that had processed Islamic normativity for centuries was set to zero. The world was as contingent as it was in the early days of Islam, which is why not surprisingly old epistemological controversies like the dispute between the Mu'tazila and Ash'ariyya, or the Maturidiyya, were reopened. As nothing was left to base an argument on, it is obvious why the Quran and sunna once more became the starting point of reference. Still maintaining that all answers to all questions are to be found in God's words and its inferential practice by the Prophet, scholars could not give up on the concept of legal source. The logical framework of this study, in contrast, understands the concept of legal source as simply a means to obscure the circular argument that would arise if the decision-maker had to admit that he himself is creating a norm that he is supposed to apply.[53] This unsettling insight evolved around the middle of the twentieth century in the discipline of legal theory, after empirical studies observed that so-called methodological principles of interpretation were not actually causative for the determination of norms or laws from a source.[54] Therefore, concepts shifted to a more constructivist approach, reversing the process of norm determination, positing the genesis of a norm not at the start, but at the end of a discursive process in which source and social circumstance are negotiated, as Friedrich Müller proposed in 1971.[55] Whereas this concept became widely accepted as "post-positivist legal thought" in legal

---

53   Niklas Luhmann, *Das Recht der Gesellschaft* (Frankfurt am Main: Suhrkamp, 1995), 306.
54   Josef Esser, *Vorverständnis und Methodenwahl in der Rechtsfindung: Rationalitätsgarantien der richterlichen Entscheidungspraxis* (Frankfurt am Main: Athenäum, 1972); Michel Rosenfeld, "Deconstruction and Legal Interpretation: Conflict, Indeterminacy and the Temptations of the New Legal Formalism," *Cardozo Law Review* 11 (1990); Werner Krawietz and Martin Morlok, eds., "Vom Scheitern und der Wiederbelebung juristischer Methodik im Rechtsalltag – ein Bruch zwischen Theorie und Praxis?," special issue *Juristische Methodenlehre, Zeitschrift für Rechtstheorie* 32, no. 2–3 (2001); Peter Stegmaier, *Wissen, was Recht ist: Richterliche Rechtspraxis aus wissenssoziologisch-ethnografischer Sicht* (Wiesbaden: vs Verlag, 2009).
55   Friedrich Müller, *Juristische Methodik* (Berlin: Duncker & Humblot, 3rd ed., 1989), 27.

theory,[56] only a few scholars of the study of Islam, such as Sherman Jackson, address this fundamental concern, arguing that the methods of *usul al-fiqh* do not generate or determine Islamic law, but rather validate desired law.[57]

However, for scholars, who for reasons of faith could not give up the idea of a legal source, the problem remained that the sources were still not easier to comprehend than in the early days, which is why they resorted to familiar and still practiced norms of *usul al-fiqh* for the purpose of interpretation. But since all those norms and principles were now contingent, due to the revived *ijtihad*, scholars were empowered to mix and match meanings of traditional norms or to transform past norms in order to justify present desired norms. Ever since, this has been the dominant "research question" of a normatively inclined scholarship, which is driven by the mission to "modernize" Islamic law.[58] Everything was now possible and everything now had a good prospect of gaining acceptance in social practice. The Sudanese scholar Mahmoud Taha, for example, reversed the established way of applying *naskh* by abrogating Medinan *sura*s with Meccan *sura*s in order to ground his and others' normative statements, for instance, with regard to the matter of the equality of men and women.[59]

While *ijtihad* had the potential to catch up on new social circumstances, its revival was not the remedy that many of its supporters had been hoping for. The re-opening of the game of reasoning produced a vast number of new Islamic norms. As a result, it became impossible for scholars to keep track of the normative attitudes towards one another within scholarly discursive practice, which, not by coincidence, corresponded with the wider social practice of Muslims that was torn apart in the global field of interaction. Since almost every norm could now be justified with a reference to Islam, it became impossible for Muslims to distinguish between appropriate and inappropriate behavior. Muslims lost track of a uniform Islamic orderliness in practice and hence of the very meaning of Islam itself. This startling observation eventually underlies the scholarly proposition that there is not one single Islam but

---

56 Nikolaus Forgó and Alexander Somek, "Nachpositivistisches Rechtsdenken," in *Neue Theorien des Rechts*, ed. Buckel et al.

57 Sherman A. Jackson, "Fiction and Formalism: Toward a Functional Analysis of *Uṣūl al-Fiqh*," in *Studies in Islamic Legal Theory*, ed. Bernard Weiss (Leiden: Brill, 2002); Sadeghi, *The Logic of Law Making*, 8–39.

58 See, e.g., Ann Elizabeth Mayer, *Islam and Human Rights: Tradition and Politics*, 4th ed. (Boulder, CO: Westview Press, 2007), or Mashood A. Baderin, *International Human Rights and Islamic Law* (New York: Oxford University Press, 2003).

59 Abdullahi Ahmed An-Naʿim, *Toward an Islamic Reformation: Civil Liberties, Human Rights, and International Law* (New York: Syracuse University Press, 1996), 60–61.

many,[60] thus glorifying the plurality of Islam in contrast to Western normative orders.[61] The vast plurality of Islamic practice in the global field of interaction was, however, not of concern for those Muslims who either processed their legal expectations with or without reverence to Islam within the new nation states, or interacted with fellow Muslims without being affected by the plurality of decisions on matters of Islam. However, Muslims who aimed at processing their expectations with reference to Islam with non-competing decisions within or beyond the nation state, were lost. They lost trust in interacting with fellow Muslims within as well as beyond nation states, regardless of their willingness toward integration, something that eventually amplified disintegration among Muslims.

Against this background, it becomes understandable why the call for Muslim unity developed into a powerful argument within the discourse.[62] Against all observations, scholars could still not admit that any Islamic order had its origin in social practice, as this would run counter to the assumption of its divine origin. Instead, they now hold social actors accountable for their conceptual flaws: The call for Muslim unity aimed at adjusting social practice to theory. The scope of this approach was extensive and could encompass all sorts of differences among the *umma*, including the *madhahib*-differences or even the Sunni-Shi'a divide, as was posited, for example, by Hassan al-Banna.[63] For this reason, the new *da'wa* movement, that developed in the early twentieth century and which is often linked with the names of al-Banna and the Muslim Brotherhood, addressed first and foremost Muslims and not unbelievers.[64] The idea aimed at imposing conformity across the plurality of Islamic orderliness by means of religious instructions, quite similar to the conventional wisdom in today's social sciences, which assumes that the evolution of normative orders is based on learning. Granted, the conformity of conscience of all Muslims, in other words, the congruence of all expectations into the preordained Islamic universe of meaning, would indeed amount to the realization

---

60 John L. Esposito, *Islam: The Straight Path* (New York: Oxford University Press, 1998), 223. An overview is given by Shahab Ahmed, *What Is Islam?: The Importance of Being Islamic* (Princeton: Princeton University Press, 2016), 129–52.
61 Hallaq, *Sharī'a*, 454.
62 Often linked with the names of Jamal al-Din al-Afghani and Muhammad 'Abduh. John L. Esposito, *Islam and Politics* (New York: Syracuse University Press, 1998), 48–49.
63 Evoking the old Islamic concept of "Islamic egalitarianism." Louise Marlow, *Hierarchy and Egalitarianism in Islamic Thought* (Cambridge: Cambridge University Press, 1997).
64 Jamal Malik, "Ideology, Practice, and Law in the Da'wa of the Muslim Brothers and Jama'at-e Islami," in *Culture of Dawa: Preaching in the Modern World*, ed. Jamal Malik and Itzchak Weismann (Salt Lake City: University of Utah Press, 2020), 62–63.

of God's normative expectations in this world: The world would be God. Yet such a concept of Islamic universalism would require, to begin with, a distinction between Islamic and non-Islamic norms and meanings, and would thus depend upon a uniform process of decision-making with global reach.

Muslims approached these problems with different strategies, all of which essentially aimed by various means at containing the number of practiced Islamic norms. Since the advent of modernity, considering the Printing Revolution as a threat, the ulama tried to inhibit the new ways of communication to protect their ideal discourse. Although the technology of modern printing has been known in Europe since the fifteenth century, it took four hundred years until it eventually became established in the Islamic world.[65] Everything that was considered as causative for the increase of norms, which was indeed a notable cause for the demise of traditional Islamic normativity, now became the subject of repudiation with the objective of delimiting the number of norms. In this light, the rejection of alleged Western norms becomes understandable. But the problem is that even norms which are considered as meaningless, like norms expressed by non-Muslims, have empirical meaning once they are perceived as norms and consequently need to be processed by decisions. This is why any rejection of a norm becomes futile the very moment this norm is differentiated from contingency, until the norm eventually falls into oblivion someday. On his quest to conceptualize Islam, this observation made Shahab Ahmed conclude that "all acts and statements of meaning-making for the Self by Muslims and non-Muslims that are carried out in terms of Islam should properly be understood as Islamic."[66]

Given the vast plurality of Islamic decision-making processes, the identification of Western norms was inconceivable, which was the reason why an all-inclusive rejection of the West, which in some cases extended to the notion of destruction, developed into a successful inferential practice in some Muslim normative orders. This also re-established the concept of *jahiliyya* in the discourse, but different from how it was used in earlier tradition by applying the term to "modern barbarity,"[67] rightly linking the troubling issue to the main characteristic of modernity, that is global communication. In this regard, in 2004 Tariq Ramadan offered a different but very simple solution, declaring

---

65 Francis Robinson, "Technology and Religious Change: Islam and the Impact of Print," *Modern Asian Studies* 27, no. 1 (1993): 232–33, https://doi.org/10.1017/S0026749X00016127.
66 Ahmed, *What is Islam?*, 544.
67 Malik, "Ideology, Practice, and Law," 65.

Islam to be a "Western religion," considering Western norms to be Islamic norms.[68]

Since norms and meanings are typically transported by individuals or by texts produced by individuals, the strategy of repudiation also turned-on actors or their works which were regarded as Western or non-Islamic. The objective was to limit the reach of social interaction in order to process the remaining norms in smaller, more manageable units which could respond with non-competing decisions. To some extent, the ban of communication and contact with Western individuals or their works became a successful practice. This attitude, although in a more sophisticated manner, also affected the scholarly discourse on the matter of Islam, which since modernity has inevitably evolved into a global academic discourse with both Muslim and non-Muslim participants. Particularly with reference to the paradigm of Orientalism – according to Edward Said, "a style of thought based upon an ontological and epistemological distinction made between 'the Orient' and 'the occident' "[69] – Muslims became engaged in isolating their scholarly practices from Western interference, especially from alleged non-Orientals, with the argument of "epistemological xenophobia."[70] Due to a poor methodological foundation of the discipline,[71] which in an environment of post-structuralist hegemony embraced the idea of cultural and epistemic relativism, the meaning of Orientalism developed into a successful social norm within academia, stalling the understanding of Islam in the modern world. The popular argument of "many Islams" may be regarded as a similar methodological flaw. While it is a truism, at least for a sociologist, that an abundance of existing normative orders all refer to Islam in their reasoning, from head-shopping to gay-marriage, the argument has the unfortunate potential to undermine the tracking of the object of investigation among scholars. After all, every argument can be successfully dismissed by claiming that a different Islam is the actual premise of the debate, driving an intersubjective understanding of Islamic normativity further apart. However,

---

68 Tariq Ramadan, *Western Muslims and the Future of Islam* (New York: Oxford University Press, 2004), 147; idem, *To Be a European Muslim: A Study of Islamic Sources in the European Context* (Leicester: The Islamic Foundation, 1999), 173, 178, 252.

69 Edward W. Said, *Orientalism* (London: Penguin Classics, 2003 [1978]), 2.

70 An example of this practice is the acrid dispute between Hallaq and Powers. Cf. Hallaq, "The Quest for Origins or Doctrine?: Islamic Legal Studies as Colonialist Discourse," UCLA *Journal of Islamic and Near Eastern Law* 2, no. 1 (2002–03); David S. Powers, "Wael B. Hallaq on the Origins of Islamic Law: A Review Essay," *Islamic Law and Society* 17, no. 1 (2010).

71 Abbas Poya and Maurus Reinkowski, eds., *Das Unbehagen in der Islamwissenschaft: Ein klassisches Fach im Scheinwerferlicht der Politik und der Medien* (Bielefeld: Transcript, 2008).

methodological deliberations do not greatly affect the normative practice of Muslims.

Since the number of Islamic norms was likewise increasing, the strategy of repudiation was also applied to those Muslims whose social practice was considered as either non-Islamic or Western. In order to limit the scope of social practice, actors were accused of *kufr* and *ilhad*, which despite all warnings of traditional scholars, developed into a successful social practice in modern times.[72] On the grounds of apostasy, Mahmoud Muhammad Taha was executed in an attempt to limit the number of participants involved in the discourse, and surely also to set a warning example. Practicing *ijtihad* was presumably as dangerous as it had been in the formative period of Islam.[73] The threat of negative sanctions or the promise of positive sanctions have all along been very successful arguments in any game of reasoning.[74]

Another method of dealing with the unmanageable number of new norms was the denial of the present. Since Muslims experienced that unwanted or allegedly meaningless norms do not easily or quickly fall into oblivion, and given the fact that time could not be rolled back to a point prior to the genesis of such new meanings, many Muslims, particularly those who aimed at processing their expectations with reference to Islam with non-competing decisions within or beyond the nation state, tried to live the present as if it was the past, avoiding exposing themselves to an environment which was pervaded by the new universe of meaning. In this context, it becomes understandable why an increasing number of Muslims dress, eat, pray and recite the Quran the way they believe the Prophet and his companions did these things. This exhibition of a traditional habitus of Islamic practice also had an additional advantage. Since the relation that gives content to an expression, as we have established, is not one of reference between an expression and the world, but one of inference between an expression and other expressions, an expressed norm asserted by an actor who adheres to the traditional habitus could earn a higher deontic score in the books of his counterparts than a norm that was

---

72   Camilla Adang et al., "Introduction," in *Accusations of Unbelief in Islam: A Diachronic Perspective on Takfīr*, ed. Camilla Adang et al. (Leiden: Brill, 2016), 3–4.

73   Fauzi M. Najjar, "Islamic Fundamentalism and the Intellectuals: The Case of Naṣr Ḥāmid Abū Zayd," *British Journal of Middle Eastern Studies* 27, no. 2 (2000), https://doi.org/10.1080/13530190020000529.

74   Which is why Habermas assumed that the ideal speech situation relies upon the anticipation of freedom from any non-rational coercive influences and domination. See his "Discourse Ethics: Notes on a Program of Philosophical Justification," in *Moral Consciousness and Communicative Action*, trans. Christian Lenhardt and Shierry Weber Nicholson (Cambridge, MA: MIT Press, 1990), 43–115.

asserted by an actor wearing a tie. At the same time, such expression could further serve as a defense against the most successful social norms in any Islamic game of reasoning, that is accusations of *kufr* and *ilhad*.

The struggle against the increasing fragmentation of Islamic normative orders also addressed the question of the institutional organization of Islamic normativity. Since the advance of modernity, scholars have increasingly discussed how the nation state figures into the equation of the shari'a. The increasing integration of Muslims' legal expectations into nation states, whose constitutions refer to the shari'a or established *madhahib* as one of several sources of jurisprudence,[75] amplified the disintegration of an alleged global Muslim *umma*, contravening the premise that one God had preordained one Islamic normative order for one Muslim community. For the same reason, the claim of establishing an Islamic state next to other Islamic states is a contradiction in terms. The idea of a coexistence of various Islamic states is only tenable by either dropping the idea of a global *umma* or by abandoning the idea that God's expectations are legal expectations.

In this context, the yearning for the founding period of Islam during the lifetime of the Prophet is often expressed through an emulation of past perfection. This is understandable because this was the only period in the history of Islam in which normativity according to God's expectations was processed with non-competing decisions, and in which Islamic law and Muslim society, the *umma*, coincided. The yearning for those heydays of Islam is the expression of an unfulfilled utopia, one that became apparent with the advent of modernity, but which goes back to the formative period of the shari'a. The dissatisfaction with the imperfect present may also explain why social formations often oppose or boycott nation states and their institutions. In light of this conflict, those ideas and social formations that strive for a uniform Islamic order with global reach appear very reasonable. A notable example is the idea of a global caliphate and the emergence of the Islamic State in Iraq and the Levant (ISIL), which has institutionalized an Islamic normative order with global aspirations beyond the Westphalian order of nation-states. Given that in the global field of Muslim interaction, Islamic orderliness became increasingly indistinguishable, it might bear some significance that ISIL's flag incorporates the historically first norm of Islam, the only common denominator of Islam that is left today – *La ilaha ila Allah, Muhammad rasul Allah*.

---

75 Jan Michiel Otto, ed., *Sharia Incorporated: A Comparative Overview of the Legal Systems of Twelve Muslim Countries in Past and Present* (Leiden: Leiden University Press, 2010).

5   Conclusion

The present article has shown that theoretical assumptions are essential prerequisites for navigating our understanding of data we gain from observing our environment. A logical framework, which is distinct from the mainstream positivist perspective on Islamic normativity, allows for distinct insights into Islam, which this article has only touched upon. This essay aims at encouraging the disciplines of the study of Islam to scrutinize their foundational research and to upgrade to more contemporary conceptual propositions in order to keep pace with modern Islamic social practices, which, largely unnoticed by observers, continuously develop their own concepts of understanding. A sociological approach towards Islam can furthermore bypass the obstructive epistemic Islam-West dichotomy and integrate a great many of the intractable positions that have become entrenched in the study of Islam since its globalization.

Bibliography

Abu-Sahlieh, Sami A. Aldeeb. *Introduction to Islamic Law: Foundation, Sources and Principles*. Translated by Felix J. Phiri. St-Sulpice: Centre of Arab and Islamic Law, 2012.

Adang, Camilla, Hassan Ansari, Maribel Fierro and Sabine Schmidtke. "Introduction." In *Accusations of Unbelief in Islam: A Diachronic Perspective on Takfīr*, edited by Camilla Adang, Hassan Ansari, Maribel Fierro and Sabine Schmidtke, 1–24. Leiden: Brill, 2016.

Ahmed, Shahab. *What Is Islam?: The Importance of Being Islamic*. Princeton: Princeton University Press, 2016.

Ali, Mohamad M. Yunis. *Medieval Islamic Pragmatics: Sunni Legal Theorists' Models of Textual Communication*. Richmond: Curzon Press, 2000.

An-Naʿim, Abdullahi Ahmed. *Toward an Islamic Reformation: Civil Liberties, Human Rights, and International Law*. New York: Syracuse University Press, 1996.

Arnaud, André-Jean. "Droit et societé: Un Carrefour interdisciplinaire." *Revue interdisciplinaire d'études juridiques* 21, no. 2 (1988): 7–32.

Avcioğlu, Nebahat and Finbarr Barry Flood. "Introduction: Globalizing Cultures: Art and Mobility in the Eighteenth Century." *Ars Orientalis* 39 (2010): 7–38.

Baderin, Mashood A. *International Human Rights and Islamic Law*. New York: Oxford University Press, 2003.

Berger, Peter L. and Thomas Luckmann. *The Social Construction of Reality: A Treatise in the Sociology of Knowledge*. London: Penguin Books, 1967.

Böwering, Gerhard. "Ibn al-'Arabī's Concept of Time." In *Gott ist schön und Er liebt die Schönheit*, edited by Alma Giese and Johann Christoph Bürgel, 71–91. Bern: Peter Lang, 1994.

Brandom, Robert B. *Making It Explicit: Reasoning, Representing, and Discursive Commitment*. Cambridge, MA: Harvard University Press, 1994.

Brandom, Robert B. "Pragmatische Themen in Hegels Idealismus: Unterhandlung und Verwaltung der Struktur und des Gehalts in Hegels Erklärung begrifflicher Normen." *Deutsche Zeitschrift für Philosophie* 47, no. 3 (1999): 355–81, https://doi.org/10.1524/dzph.1999.47.3.355.

Calder, Norman. *Studies in Early Muslim Jurisprudence*. Oxford: Clarendon, 1993.

Crone, Patricia. *Roman, Provincial and Islamic Law: The Origins of the Islamic Patronate*. Cambridge: Cambridge University Press, 1987.

Ehrlich, Eugen. *Fundamental Principles of the Sociology of Law*. New Brunswick, NJ: Transaction Publishers, 2002.

Esposito, John L. *Islam and Politics*. New York: Syracuse University Press, 1998.

Esposito, John L. *Islam: The Straight Path*. New York: Oxford University Press, 1998.

Esser, Josef. *Vorverständnis und Methodenwahl in der Rechtsfindung: Rationalitätsgarantien der richterlichen Entscheidungspraxis*. Frankfurt am Main: Athenäum, 1972.

Fentress, James and Chris Wickham. *Social Memory: New Perspectives in the Past*. Oxford: Blackwell, 1992.

Foerster, Heinz von. "Ethics and Second-order Cybernetics." *Cybernetics and Human Knowing* 1, no. 1 (1992): 9–19.

Forgó, Nikolaus and Alexander Somek. "Nachpositivistisches Rechtsdenken." In *Neue Theorien des Rechts*, edited by Sonja Buckel, Ralph Christensen and Andreas Fischer-Lescano, 123–38. Stuttgart: Lucius & Lucius, 2020.

Galtung, Johan. "Expectations and Interaction Processes." *Inquiry: An Interdisciplinary Journal of Philosophy* 2, no. 1–4 (1959): 213–34, https://doi.org/10.1080/00201745908601296.

Gibbs, Jack P. "Norms: The Problem of Definition and Classification." *The American Journal of Sociology* 70, no. 5 (1965): 586–94.

Guellil, Gabriela Linda. *Damaszener Akten des 8./14. Jahrhunderts nach aṭ-Ṭarsūsī's Kitāb al-I'lām*. Bamberg: Klaus Schwarz, 1985.

Habermas, Jürgen. *Between Facts and Norms: Contributions to a Discourse Theory of Law and Democracy*. Translated by William Rehg. Cambridge, MA: MIT Press, 1996.

Habermas, Jürgen. Moral Consciousness and Communicative Action. Translated by Christian Lenhardt and Shierry Weber Nicholson. Cambridge, MA: MIT Press, 1990.

Habermas, Jürgen. *On the Pragmatics of Social Interaction: Preliminary Studies in the Theory of Communicative Action*. Translated by Barbara Fultner. Cambridge, MA: MIT Press, 2001.

Haider, Najam. "Contesting Intoxication: Early Juristic Debates over the Lawfulness of Alcoholic Beverages." *Islamic Law and Society* 20, no. 1–2 (2013): 48–89.

Hallaq, Wael B. "Can the Shariʿa be Restored?." In *Islamic Law and the Challenges of Modernity*, edited by Yvonne Yazbeck Haddad and Barbara Freyer Stowasser, 21–53. Walnut Creek, CA: AltaMira Press, 2004.

Hallaq, Wael B. *Sharīʿa: Theory, Practice, Transformations.* New York: Cambridge University Press, 2009.

Hallaq, Wael B. "The Quest for Origins or Doctrine?: Islamic Legal Studies as Colonialist Discourse." UCLA *Journal of Islamic and Near Eastern Law* 2, no. 1 (2002–03): 1–32.

Hallaq, Wael B. "Was the Gate of Ijtihad Closed?." *International Journal of Middle East Studies* 16, no. 1 (March 1984): 3–41, https://doi.org/10.1017/S0020743800027598.

Head, Brian W. *Ideology and Social Science: Destutt de Tracy and French Liberalism.* Dordrecht: Martinus Nijhoff Publishers, 1985.

Ibrahim, Ahmed Fekry. *Pragmatism in Islamic Law: A Social and Intellectual History.* New York: Syracuse University Press, 2015.

Jackson, Sherman A. "Fiction and Formalism: Toward a Functional Analysis of *Uṣūl al-Fiqh*." In *Studies in Islamic Legal Theory*, edited by Bernard Weiss, 177–201. Leiden: Brill, 2002.

Jepperson, Ronald L. "Institutions, Institutional Effects, and Institutionalism." In *The New Institutionalism in Organizational Analysis*, edited by Walter W. Powell and Paul J. DiMaggio, 143–63. Chicago: University of Chicago Press, 1991.

Kahneman, Daniel, Paul Slovic and Amos Tversky, eds. *Judgment Under Uncertainty: Heuristics and Biases.* Cambridge: Cambridge University Press, 1982.

Kamali, Mohammad Hashim. *Shariʿah Law: An Introduction.* Oxford: OneWorld, 2008.

Kirchhof, Reik. *Grundlegung einer Soziologie der Scharia.* Wiesbaden: Springer VS, 2019.

Krawietz, Werner and Martin Morlok, eds. "Vom Scheitern und der Wiederbelebung juristischer Methodik im Rechtsalltag – ein Bruch zwischen Theorie und Praxis?." Special issue *Juristische Methodenlehre, Zeitschrift für Rechtstheorie* 32, no. 2–3 (2001): 135–371.

Ladeur, Karl-Heinz, ed. *Public Governance in the Age of Globalization.* Oxon and New York: Routledge, 2004.

Lammers, Joris and Matt Baldwin. "Past-focused Temporal Communication Overcomes Conservatives' Resistance to Liberal Political Ideas." *Journal of Personality and Social Psychology* 114, no. 4 (2018): 599–619, https://doi.org/10.1037/pspi0000121.

Luhmann, Niklas. *Das Recht der Gesellschaft.* Frankfurt am Main: Suhrkamp, 1995.

Luhmann, Niklas. "Institutionalisierung – Funktion und Mechanismus im sozialen System der Gesellschaft." In *Zur Theorie der Institution*, edited by Helmut Schelsky, 27–41. Düsseldorf: Bertelsmann Universitätsverlag, 1982.

Luhmann, Niklas. *Rechtssoziologie*, vol. 1. Opladen: Westdeutscher Verlag, 1987.

MacCormick, Neil and Ota Weinberger. *An Institutional Theory of Law: New Approaches to Legal Positivism*. Dordrecht: D. Reidel, 1986.

Malik, Jamal. "Ideology, Practice, and Law in the Daʿwa of the Muslim Brothers and Jamaʿat-e Islami." In *Culture of Dawa: Preaching in the Modern World*, edited by Jamal Malik and Itzchak Weismann, 61–78. Salt Lake City: University of Utah Press, 2020.

Marlow, Louise. *Hierarchy and Egalitarianism in Islamic Thought*. Cambridge: Cambridge University Press, 1997.

Matlin, Margaret W. "Pollyanna Principle." In *Cognitive Illusions: Intriguing Phenomena in Thinking, Judgment and Memory*, edited by Rüdiger F. Pohl, 315–35. New York: Routledge, 2017.

Mayer, Ann Elizabeth. *Islam and Human Rights: Tradition and Politics*, 4th ed. Boulder, CO: Westview Press, 2007.

Moosa, Ebrahim. "Allegory of the Rule (*Ḥukm*): Law as Simulacrum in Islam?." *History of Religions* 38, no. 1 (1998): 1–24, https://doi.org/10.1086/463517.

Moosa, Ebrahim. "Colonialism and Islamic Law." In *Islam and Modernity: Key Issues and Debates*, edited by Muhammad Khalid Masud, Armando Salvatore and Martin van Bruinessen, 158–81. Edinburgh: Edinburgh University Press, 2009.

Motzki, Harald. "Dating Muslim Traditions: A Survey." *Arabica* 52, no. 2 (2005): 204–53.

Müller, Christian. *Gerichtspraxis im Stadtstaat Córdoba: Zum Recht der Gesellschaft in einer mālikitisch-islamischen Rechtstradition des 5./11. Jahrhunderts*. Leiden: Brill, 1999.

Müller, Friedrich. *Juristische Methodik*. Berlin: Duncker & Humblot, 3rd ed., 1989.

Najjar, Fauzi M. "Islamic Fundamentalism and the Intellectuals: The Case of Naṣr Ḥāmid Abū Zayd." *British Journal of Middle Eastern Studies* 27, no. 2 (2000): 177–200, https://doi.org/10.1080/13530190020000529.

Niesen, Peter, and Oliver Eberl. "Demokratischer Positivismus: Habermas und Maus." In *Neue Theorien des Rechts*, edited by Sonja Buckel, Ralph Christensen, and Andreas Fischer-Lescano, 13–28. Stuttgart: Lucius & Lucius, 2020.

Otto, Jan Michiel, ed. *Sharia Incorporated: A Comparative Overview of the Legal Systems of Twelve Muslim Countries in Past and Present*. Leiden: Leiden University Press, 2010.

Parsons, Talcott. "The Theory of Symbolism in Relation to Action." In *Working Papers in the Theory of Action*, edited by Talcott Parsons, Robert Freed Bales and Edward Shils, 31–62. New York: Free Press, 1953.

Parsons, Talcott and Edward A. Shils. "Categories of the Orientation and Organization of Action." In *Toward a General Theory of Action: Theoretical Foundations for the Social Sciences*, edited by Talcott Parsons and Edward A. Shils, 53–109. New York: Harper & Row, 1962.

Peters, F.E., ed. *The Arabs and Arabia on the Eve of Islam*. Oxon: Routledge, 2017.

Peuckert, Rüdiger and Albert Scherr. "Integration." In *Grundbegriffe der Soziologie*, edited by Bernhard Schäfers, 152–55. Opladen: Leske und Budrich, 2003.

Pöppel, Ernst. "Time Perception." In *Handbook of Sensory Physiology: Perception*, vol. 8, edited by Richard Held, Herschel W. Leibowitz and Hans-Lukas Teuber, 713–29. Berlin: Springer, 1978, https://doi.org/10.1007/978-3-642-46354-9.

Powers, David S. "Wael B. Hallaq on the Origins of Islamic Law: A Review Essay." *Islamic Law and Society* 17, no. 1 (2010): 126–57.

Poya, Abbas and Maurus Reinkowski, eds. *Das Unbehagen in der Islamwissenschaft: Ein klassisches Fach im Scheinwerferlicht der Politik und der Medien*. Bielefeld: Transcript, 2008.

Raiser, Thomas. *Grundlagen der Rechtssoziologie*. Tübingen: Mohr Siebeck, 2013.

Ramadan, Tariq. *To Be a European Muslim: A Study of Islamic Sources in the European Context*. Leicester: The Islamic Foundation, 1999.

Ramadan, Tariq. *Western Muslims and the Future of Islam*. New York: Oxford University Press, 2004.

Reinhart, A. Kevin. "Law." In *Key Themes for the Study of Islam*, edited by Jamal J. Elias, 220–44. Oxford: OneWorld, 2010.

Robinson, Francis. "Technology and Religious Change: Islam and the Impact of Print." *Modern Asian Studies* 27, no. 1 (1993): 229–51, https://doi.org/10.1017/S0026749X00016127.

Rohe, Mathias. *Das islamische Recht: Geschichte und Gegenwart*. Munich: C.H. Beck, 2009.

Rosenfeld, Michel. "Deconstruction and Legal Interpretation: Conflict, Indeterminacy and the Temptations of the New Legal Formalism." *Cardozo Law Review* 11 (1990): 1211–67.

Sadeghi, Behnam. *The Logic of Law Making in Islam: Women and Prayer in the Legal Tradition*. New York: Cambridge University Press, 2013.

Said, Edward W. *Orientalism*. London: Penguin Classics, 2003 [1978].

Stegmaier, Peter. *Wissen, was Recht ist: Richterliche Rechtspraxis aus wissenssoziologisch-ethnografischer Sicht*. Wiesbaden: VS Verlag, 2009.

US-PPIP Project. "Uses of the Past: Understanding Shariʿa – Custom, Gender, State and Violence." Accessed September 29, 2021, www.usppip.com/about/.

Vikør, Knut S. *Between God and the Sultan: A History of Islamic Law*. New York: Oxford University Press, 2005.

Vikør, Knut S. "The Truth about Cats and Dogs: The Historicity of Early Islamic Law." *Historisk Tidsskrift* 82, no. 1 (2003): 1–17.

Weber, Max. *Economy and Society: An Outline of Interpretive Sociology*, edited by Guenther Roth and Claus Wittich. Berkeley: University of California Press, 1978.

Weber, Max. *Wirtschaft und Gesellschaft: Grundriss der Sozialökonomie*, vol. III, Abteilung. Tübingen: J.C.B. Mohr, 1922.

Weiss, Bernard. "The Madhhab in Islamic Legal Theory." In *The Islamic School of Law: Evolution, Devolution, and Progress*, edited by Peri Bearman, Rudolf Peters and Frank E. Vogel, 1–9. Cambridge, MA: Islamic Legal Studies Program, Harvard Law School, 2005.

Zucker, Lynne G. "The Role of Institutionalization in Cultural Persistence." *American Sociological Review* 42, no. 5 (October 1977): 726–43, https://doi.org/10.2307/2094862.

CHAPTER 9

Negotiating Everyday Lived Islam
A Case Study of Pakistani Diaspora in Canada

Syed FurrukhZad

In his seminal study *Islam in South Asia*, Jamal Malik contends that studies on Islam and Muslims should be carried out in the light of articulations of specific social and cultural realities, as textual normativity alone does not contribute significantly toward the understanding of a phenomenon.[1] The same applies to the study of religion in general, so that the context and content of mundane ordinary life must not be overlooked by primarily focusing on theological reflections, prescribed normativity and institutionalized religion. David Hall also claims that a religious historian "knows next-to-nothing about religion as practiced" in the everyday lives of lay people in terms of meaning, ritualization and narrative.[2] Everyday experiences of believers allow for a wider interpretation of religions, as lived and situated within specific contexts. This argument is anchored in the concept of "lived religion" (*la religion vécue*), derived from the French sociology of religion, which provides an ethnographic framework for comprehending everyday practices, attitudes and experiences of religious agents. Meredith McGuire explains it as the actual experiences of people, as distinct from the prescribed religion of institutionally defined beliefs and practices.[3] Lived religion is based more on such everyday embodied practices rather than on orthodox theology, which are necessarily neither logical nor consistent among believers and practitioners. Religious people enact religion in specific local contexts to maintain what it means to be religious. Everyday religion is thus based upon what counts as religious on an individual level rather than on a social level. In this context, Orsi argues that theologies are not made in a single venue only, but instead in the streets as well as the churches, at shrines or

---

1 Jamal Malik, *Islam in South Asia: A Short History* (Leiden: Brill, 2008), 401. This book's revised, enlarged and updated second edition was published in 2020.
2 David D. Hall, ed., *Lived Religion in America: Toward a History of Practice* (Princeton: Princeton University Press, 1997), vii.
3 Meredith B. McGuire, *Lived Religion: Faith and Practice in Everyday Life* (New York: Oxford University Press, 2008), 12.

in people's living rooms.⁴ According to this view, social agents as narrators and interpreters of their own spiritual experiences and religious practices are more valuable than theological texts, rituals, and institutions, because their experiences and interpretations hold lived meaning and serve as sources of text analyses. Everyday social and cultural context is imperative because it embodies the poly-focality of individual identities, since construction of the self with reference to scriptures is not germane.⁵ This sort of interest in the study of religion also derives from the variety of ways in which religious practitioners relate to religious doctrines, authoritative texts and normative practices within their life trajectories. Therefore, the everyday lived religion approach is flexible, inventive and holistic, as it seeks to provide practical insights into the reconfiguration of religious selves in terms of dilemmas faced by diaspora communities during their relocation process of space-making.

The study of lived religion in everyday contexts is also significant because less visible religious expressions are not only constitutive of social action in private spaces, but also in regulating interaction with formal structures in the public space. In the last decades, there has been an increasing interest among scholars in focusing on the "invisible religion" to comprehend social "systems" through laying bare individual practices.⁶ In this respect, de Certeau's study of everyday life is pragmatic in the sense that he does not ground his analysis on popular culture or regimes of power, but rather focuses on the synoptic view of the processes and ways that individuals take to navigate through everyday life, unconsciously and repeatedly. This is the process by which one poaches on the strategic territory of the others, employing existing culturally internalized rules tactically to live life with pragmatic deliberation.⁷ Employing the metaphor of walking through a city, he argues that a city is generated by various institutions, mapping it through grand strategies, while the walker walks through

---

4   Robert Orsi, "Everyday Miracles: The Study of Lived Religion," in *Lived Religion in America*, ed. Hall.
5   Jamal Malik, "Introduction," in *Religious Pluralism in South Asia and Europe*, ed. Jamal Malik and Helmut Reifeld (New Delhi: Oxford University Press, 2004).
6   See, for example, Thomas Luckmann, *The Invisible Religion: The Problem of Religion in Modern Society* (New York: Macmillan, 1967); Stephen Hunt, *Religion and Everyday Life: The New Sociology* (Oxon and New York: Routledge, 2005); Nancy Tatom Ammerman, *Sacred Stories, Spiritual Tribes: Finding Religion in Everyday Life* (New York: Oxford University Press, 2014); idem, *Everyday Religion: Observing Modern Religious Lives* (New York: Oxford University Press, 2007); Marion Bowman and Ülo Valk, eds., *Vernacular Religion in Everyday Life: Expressions of Belief* (Oxon and New York: Routledge, 2012); McGuire, *Lived Religion*.
7   Michel de Certeau, *The Practice of Everyday Life*, trans. Steven F. Rendall (Berkeley: University of California Press, 1984), xix.

this layout by means of his own tactical skills, which are distinct and different from the strategic planning of the institutions. One is influenced by the grand strategies which are not of his own creation, but in turn, he influences these processes through his tactical ingenuity. These "arts of doing," as de Certeau puts it, are invented and enacted by ordinary individuals in their mundane everyday existence through "creative resistance" to repressive formulations of life.[8] These strategies are all-pervasive socio-cultural mechanisms deployed for ordinary people, while tactics are the ways used by practitioners to reclaim their autonomy from the grand design. Thus, human life and culture cannot simply be comprehended by grand strategic designs, but are made sensible by understanding the tactical ways that ordinary people employ to live life. Lefebvre conceptualized this phenomenon of reproduction of social relations as *spatialization*: the process of the (re)production of space. To him, space is a social product or a construction with its own norms, values and meaning-making processes that affect spatial practices and perceptions.[9] He argues that every society, or for that matter every mode of social construction, produces a certain space, its own space, with different modes of production and construction, moving from natural or absolute space to more complex spaces. All spaces are socially produced and made productive in social practices of everyday life at the intersection of power and marginality.[10] Ordinary individuals select, interpret and employ multiple cultural resources in their everyday lives in flexible, pragmatic and inventive ways, which "rarely resemble[s] the tidy, consistent, and theologically correct packages official religions promote."[11] However, these inventive and creative tactical outcomes of engagements and negotiations are embedded in dominant power structures and relations of everyday life.

As a sociological concept, religiosity refers to various aspects of religious behavior, experience, devotion and belief system whereby people anchor religion in their everyday lives. Religiosity is an individual trait that expresses the degree of agreement with the values, norms and corresponding consequences of behavior specified by one's religion.[12] It is also formed by the religious attitudes, behavior and experiences of individuals through the centrality

---

8   Ibid.
9   Henri Lefebvre, *The Production of Space*, trans. Donald Nicholson-Smith (Oxford: Blackwell, 1991), 26.
10 Ibid.
11 McGuire, *Lived Religion*, 17.
12 Robert Kecskes and Christof Wolf, "Christliche Religiosität: Konzepte, Indikatoren, Messinstrumente," *Kölner Zeitschrift für Soziologie und Sozialpsychologie* 45, no. 2 (1993).

of existing religious constructs within a personality, as well as by theological understanding and influence. According to George Kelly, everyday life is shaped by such social constructions of reality, which is subjective and is dependent on the past experiences or socialization of an individual.[13] Moreover, as religiosity embodies the centrality of the religious construct of reality for a religious person, the more centrally it is woven into the personal ensemble of hierarchically arranged constructs, the more it determines and regulates his conduct.[14] An individual in whom these internalized religious constructs are displayed through frequent and fervent religious observances, expressions, values, attitudes and symbols is seen as "religious." In a way, this expressed religiosity is a value trait of individual personality which motivates him to "live" (by) his selected religious creed and doctrines. This is regulated by a functionally autonomous motivational system and can be measured empirically. Allport and Ross identify two dimensions of religiosity: extrinsic and intrinsic. Extrinsic religiosity is self-serving, whereby religious individuals seek utilitarian ends, whereas intrinsic religiosity serves as the master motive for life in religion, as individuals internalize their faith: "The extrinsically motivated person uses his religion, whereas the intrinsically motivated person lives his religion."[15] According to Glock and Stark, religiosity is a multi-dimensional "commitment" that expresses itself phenomenologically in several forms: experiential, ritualistic, ideological, intellectual and consequential.[16] Yoshio Fukuyama identifies four other dimensions of religiosity, namely the cognitive, cultic, creedal and devotional dimensions:[17]

> The cognitive dimension is concerned with what individuals know about religion, i.e., religious knowledge. The cultic dimension makes reference to the individual's religious practices, i.e., ritualistic behavior. The creedal dimension is concerned with a personal religious belief, and the

---

13 George A. Kelly, *The Psychology of Personal Constructs*, vol. 1 (New York: Norton, 1955), 50.
14 Stefan Huber, "Religion Monitor 2008: Structuring Principles, Operational Constructs, Interpretive Strategies," in *What the World Believes: Analysis and Commentary on the Religion Monitor 2008,* ed. Bertelsmann Stiftung (Gütersloh: Verlag Bertelsmann Stiftung, 2009).
15 Gordon W. Allport and J. Michael Ross, "Personal Religious Orientation and Prejudice," *Journal of Personality and Social Psychology* 5, no. 4 (1967), https://doi.org/10.1037/h0021212.
16 Charles Y. Glock and Rodney Stark, *Religion and Society in Tension* (Chicago: Rand McNally, 1965), 20.
17 Yoshio Fukuyama, "The Major Dimensions of Church Membership," *Review of Religious Research* 2, no. 4 (Spring 1961), https://doi.org/10.2307/3510955.

devotional dimension refers to a person's religious feelings and experiences, i.e., the experiential dimension.[18]

These various dimensions of religiosity have been widely studied across such academic disciplines as theology, pedagogy, psychology, politics and sociology. This study addresses three expressions of religiosity – creedal, ritual and devotional – in a diaspora context in Canada. It is pertinent to mention that there is a substantial amount of quantitative scholarship on Muslim religiosity from various perspectives, seeking to identify what it entails and how it can possibly be measured.[19] These various studies have sought to assess Muslims' religiosity in different contexts quantitatively. Furthermore, in the West, the religious identity of Muslims remains exaggeratedly politicized, to which Jeldtoft opines that "by focusing on institutionalized forms of Islam, we run the risk of reifying Muslims as being all-about Islam."[20] However, there are multiple global and local Muslim and non-Muslim traditions that influence the lived religious experiences of the communities.

The Pakistani-Canadian Muslim community can be identified as a social collectivity that exhibits collective national and/or cultural identity through a shared sense of internal cohesion, with sustained ties to the homeland through the globalization of economy and communication. As such, a diaspora community is not just a representation, subjectivity and consciousness, rather it is a whole shared network of local associations and transnational linkages beyond national borders.[21] With the formation of new frames of reference and networks of association, diaspora communities evolve in a social space

---

18   Jerry D. Cardwell, *The Social Context of Religiosity* (Washington, DC: University Press of America, 1980), 6.

19   See, for example, Alex Wilde and Stephan Joseph, "Religiosity and Personality in a Moslem Context," *Personality and Individual Differences* 23, no. 5 (November 1997): 899–900, https://doi.org/10.1016/S0191-8869(97)00098-6; Abdullah Sahin and Leslie Francis, "Assessing Attitude Toward Islam among Muslim Adolescents: The Psychometric Properties of the Sahin-Francis Scale," *Muslim Education Quarterly* 19, no. 4 (2002); Yasemin El-Menouar, "The Five Dimensions of Muslim Religiosity: Results of an Empirical Study," *Methods, Data, Analyses* 8, no. 1 (2014), https://doi.org/10.12758/mda.2014.003; Yunusa Olufadi, "Muslim Daily Religiosity Assessment Scale (MUDRAS): A New Instrument for Muslim Religiosity Research and Practice," *Psychology of Religion and Spirituality* 9, no. 2 (2017), http://dx.doi.org/10.1037/rel0000074.

20   Nadia Jeldtoft, "Lived Islam: Religious Identity with 'Non-organized' Muslim Minorities," *Ethnic and Racial Studies* 34, no. 7 (2011), https://doi.org/10.1080/01419870.2010.528441.

21   Fiona B. Adamson and Madeleine Demetriou, "Remapping the Boundaries of 'State' and 'National Identity': Incorporating Diasporas into IR Theorizing," *European Journal of International Relations* 13, no. 4 (2007).

where traditional borders lose significance, and identities and loyalties oscillate between different centers. These are neither fixed nor exclusive, but fluid, inclusive and multi-layered, with some intrinsic identities becoming more salient depending upon the contexts. With regard to the Canadian multicultural migration context, these are shaped and influenced by multiple factors and interests, contextualized by instances of social mobilization and transformation. However, re-negotiations of Islamic normativity, practice and doctrines remain more or less geographically and culturally independent of others among the first-generation diaspora, but change in the second and third generations. This study examines dimensions of Pakistani Muslim diaspora religiosity in order to explain what tactical mechanisms of negotiation they adopt to (re)live Islam in Canada's multicultural society.

The present chapter draws on five chronicles from ethnographic fieldwork conducted by the author in 2019 among members of the Pakistani diaspora living in Canada. All of the interlocutors were immigrants, who arrived in Canada within the last two decades and lived in the city of Calgary in Alberta province. Their average age was 36.4, with more females than males, and all held a high school diploma or higher (university education). The chronicles draw from semi-structured interviews of first-generation Muslims of Pakistani origin. These were conducted in Punjabi, Urdu and English, with translations, editions and additions made by the author. The researcher participated in private meetings and social gatherings, conducting thirteen open-ended interviews with five men and eight women who were selected through snowball sampling. To avoid the obvious biases that this method usually carries in relation to representativeness of age, occupation, sex, education, marital and economic status, etc., it was ensured that these interlocutors were identified and recruited from different places and networks. Despite all of the precautions taken in the selection of the five interlocutors, it is recognized that there will always remain a certain degree of bias in this snowball sampling method.[22] Moreover, the focus was placed on analyzing diverse expressions of religiosity in different settings and with varied challenges: from home to work, and from food to dress code. Some of these challenges have become major controversies at various forums and levels of state and society, yet this study does not delve into

---

22   It is also recognized that ethnographic research design, data, sampling and analysis can also be affected by a researcher's perceived identity(ies). My identity as a Pakistani Muslim immigrant male would have surely impacted the premises and outcomes of the study. Nevertheless, this does not exclude me from undertaking such a study, and in fact, it offers the opportunity for a more nuanced approach to locating and situating the everyday lived expressions of Pakistani culture.

those questions. It instead details and analyzes how ordinary individuals, in the course of their mundane daily existence, negotiate and relocate their individualized religiosity in private and public spheres, taking into account that the globalization of movement and communication has opened new vistas of interaction and possibilities for dialogue between cultures.[23] Furthermore, it needs to be stressed that the various dimensions and expressions of religiosity are not a unidimensional aspect of Muslim lives. The following chronicles illustrate the interlocutors' enactments of Islamic religiosity through practicing and making sense of their faith. The interviewees also reflected on everyday negotiations of practicing their Islamic faith within domestic and public spaces. This study interprets these challenges and struggles of settlement, negotiation and assimilation in order to document lived religiosity, beyond the politicized and mediatized meta-narratives that they are often subject to for common analysis.

1 First Chronicle: Domestic Religion

I moved to Canada seven years ago, in 2012, from a small village in Punjab and have been living in a two-room basement with my wife and three children. I had completed my university degree in pharmacy before moving here. It took me three years to get a relevant job in a lab [...]. These years have been beset with tough economic times as I had worked as a taxi driver, worked in a convenient store at night and as security. After years of saving and hard work, we have now bought our home in Canada. My previous landlords were a Sikh storeowner from India, a Catholic Filipino technician and an Iranian office assistant. We shared our living space with people of different faiths and cultures. It was not bad [...]. But now we have finally got our home. I am thankful to Allah Almighty that now I can finally transform my home with artefacts that can remind us of our great religious faith and tradition. My children will grow up living in Canada knowing that we are Muslims and how our religion is important to us [...]. It sums up our whole life and this is what should be reflected when someone enters our home, to know how important it is to my life. My parents will visit us next summer and they can see that we are living according to our religion. Nothing is lost during this transition [...]. My children and I practice our religion in Canada fully as it is a free country,

---

23   Jamal Malik, "Islamic-Christian Dialogue," *Journal of Oriental Studies* 15 (2005).

with freedom to live my life according to my cultural norms and religious dictates.

MAQSOOD, [24] 41 years old, taxi driver/lab worker

Maqsood told this story on a cold September night in 2019 at a housewarming party in his new home. With his not-so-fluent English, he explained how humble and thankful he felt for all that he had worked for and achieved since migrating to Canada. His three children, two of whom were attending high school, spoke English fluently with Canadian accents and were observant Muslims. The interior of his home was a living reminder of a middle-class home back in Pakistan, with fine arrangements and decorations, although its exterior design and architecture was that of a typical North American home, with a large lawn, a garage and a two-room basement, which he intends to sublet to make extra money. Once inside the home, one is welcomed by an enormous calligraphic inscription of *ayat al-kursi* (a Quranic verse, 2:255), which is customarily hung in Muslim homes to safeguard them from evil and any ill-omens. After that, proceeding through the living room, kitchen, hallways and bedrooms, one similarly finds further normative Quranic inscriptions of various sizes adorning the walls throughout the house. There is also a painting, depicting a village scene from the Punjab with a woman wearing a *chaddar* (long scarf for covering the head and upper body) and cooking outside in the open air with her four children sitting beside her. Also depicted is an old man sitting on a traditional bed, smoking a *hookah* (traditional tobacco pipe) with livestock grazing nearby. The entire image relates to the family's cultural roots, from which religious meanings are usually deciphered, and it conveys to the younger generation the image of a joint family home, with clearly defined roles for elders and women. Maqsood remains standing in front of the painting for a moment and reminds us of how life was back home. Suddenly, we hear the *adhan* (Muslim call to prayer) coming from a clock which is set for the prayer timings in Pakistan. Everyone remains reverentially silent and after the *adhan*, Maqsood explained that this has been a major problem living in rented property, as landlords would often be disturbed by the sound. But now he is free to hear it and can offer prayers at the specified times. He also has two other significant images displayed in his home, one of the Ka'ba (in the Holy Mosque in Mecca) and another of Al-Masjid al-Nabawi (the Prophet's mosque in Medina), which are reminiscent of the sacred in the Islamic tradition. Additionally, there is a calendar featuring scenic pictures of various places in

---

24 The names of the respondents have been changed to ensure their anonymity.

Canada, most of which he has visited, as he tells the guests. In his children' room, there are Canadian flags and a portrait of a Canadian ice hockey team with a cup. Although there is no strict gender segregation for the guests, the women are sitting with small children in the living room with a kitchen adjacent to it, while the men are on the first floor, watching TV news from back home. The time for prayer transforms the place into a prayer hall, with everyone, including the children, joining the congregation. He invites his son to recite from the Quran, which he has completed the study of online with an imam from Pakistan. Maqsood has more than two sets of books comprising the Quran with Urdu translation and commentary. There are CDs with Islamic lectures as well as Urdu and Punjabi songs that he loves to listen to, although the family sometimes uses YouTube and other sites to deepen their knowledge of Islam. Various other artifacts, like a traditional South Asian dinner set, utensils, rugs, bedsheets, etc., are constant reminders of the cultural setting, which is, however, mixed with local items purchased in Canada. And finally, there is the typical smell of South Asian cuisine with traditional spices, prepared according to *halal* dietary requirements in accordance with Islamic normativity. He is pleased that he resides in a neighborhood where *halal* meat and a range of traditional Pakistani food items are readily accessible.

Maqsood's chronicle along with the researcher's participatory observation at this event attest to how religion and culture are tactically domesticized for personal consumption when far from home. For immigrants, home is the place where devotion to the sacred finds expression in its entirety through various signs, symbols and observances. Serving as a cultural buffer zone, it is the space where they can reclaim religion and reconstruct their religious experience to avoid socio-psychological disintegration. The home is transformed from a mere physical structure into a religious and cultural space, which serves as the initial phase of identity formation. This transformation is achieved through various signs, symbols, rituals, practices and values, all incorporated into the performance of domestic religion within this space.[25] These various visual and material artifacts, their placement, sense of time and place in juxtaposition with local tastes and necessities, fill the home. These items are incorporated into the home to communicate values, norms and the tradition that was left behind. Thus, the home remains the locus of personal faith, which is displayed through concrete rituals and symbolic expressions. Domestic decoration is usually replete with religious themes, with various

---

25   Shampa Mazumdar and Sanjoy Mazumdar, "The Articulation of Religion in Domestic Space: Rituals in the Immigrant Muslim Home," *Journal of Ritual Studies* 18, no. 2 (2004).

paintings, pictures, sculpted art, carved doorframes and sacred texts either expressing or invoking devotion to the sacred. The entrance demarcates a border between two worlds, of past and present, of sacred and profane, informing those who enter of an identity, enmeshed with culture and religion. The sacred art, through its various manifestations, reminds insiders of their affiliations as well as of the holy bond that they are related to. In a way, the home is the locus of expressions and communications that help to create a religious environment, which is of course conducive to the practice of religion.

Moreover, these artifacts cultivate the self-realization of the diaspora. With these reminders of religion, culture and identity, the home becomes an actualized expression of the religious/Islamic self. Such physical and symbolic expressions of religiosity are not ordained by sacred texts or by orthodox religious accounts, yet they explain how a physical place is transformed into a religious space for the display of religiosity in the everyday lives of believers. Berger and Luckmann have called this process "physical objectifications" of the religion that migrants leave behind and which they seek to reinvent and reconstruct in new spaces.[26] These artifacts of religious devotion kept within domestic spaces also point to family concerns, including protection of the home's inhabitants, the welfare of the family/household, the prosperity of business and profession, and finally, the protection from demonic forces and the evil eye. Thus, these religious practices work through re-imagination and re-configuration that fit into the transmuted worlds through which individuals redefine, reconstruct and renegotiate their lives. This renegotiation of religious practices and even beliefs seems especially plausible in light of the enormous cultural variations among Muslims, who adjust these religious prescriptions in varied ways in migration contexts.

2 Second Chronicle: Ritual Practice

> I moved to Canada after getting married to my cousin in an arranged marriage. I have got a Master's degree in English Literature. Immigration was a unique and unexpected experience as I never thought of living abroad, away from my family and my country. Our marriage has been stable, but one major concern that I have been feeling since I moved

---

26 Peter L. Berger and Thomas Luckmann, *The Social Construction of Reality: A Treatise in the Sociology of Knowledge* (Garden City, NY: Doubleday, 1966), 92.

here is how to keep my faith alive and transmit it to my two kids. What I like about Canada is the religious freedom as well as the opportunities to practice my faith. There has never been a problem, but still we live as a minority. We have family relations with a lot of Muslim families from Pakistan and India. We arrange our religious functions and perform rituals with special care [...]. This was not the case in Pakistan, where we would do this as a routine, now I have to be particular and be ready for these events. My kids get weekend lessons on Islam and participate in local Muslim clubs that organize functions and activities for children [...]. I can tell that when we moved in this home, we did a lot of religious rituals with my friends and family. Like, we thoroughly cleaned the home again although it was handed over neat and clean. We shampooed carpets because these had not been replaced by the landlord. We washed kitchen appliances like the refrigerator, the oven and the stove as non-permitted items might have been used here. After this we arranged a family event, in which close families were invited. We lit *agarbatti*,[27] so that the house gets purified. Everybody recited the Holy Quran and a special female Islamic reciter was also invited. This is called *Quran khanni*, something we used to have in our home back in Pakistan twice a year. A male member gave the *adhan* in the house [...]. Our kids participated fervently, and afterwards we had a sumptuous Pakistani dinner. This was really satisfying for us to live for some time in a home and perform our religion.

NIGHAT, 29 years old, housewife

These details show how domestic religion is formed and performed here. Nighat is attempting to practice her religiosity in a minority situation within an unfamiliar and circumscribed religious setting through the performance of rituals. Moving into a house with these cultural-religious rituals, an attempt is made to bring blessings for the space and the people residing in it. It is expected that this will bring good luck and further prosperity for the family, yet in this diaspora situation, more important than the blessing is the attempt to purify the house from any *haram* (religiously non-permitted) elements. It expresses her attempts as a housewife to navigate through the profane and to pragmatically carve out a sacred space for herself and her family. Mahmood argues that such materialities endow "the self" with distinction,

---

27   This is a small wooden stick covered in a substance that produces a pleasant smell when burned. It is commonly used for religious ceremonies and other occasions in Asia.

when repeatedly performed either in public or private.[28] Rituals are symbolic actions which take on significant roles in the formation of both individual and communal identities. They symbolize socially structured human agency that finds its expression in historically informed perceptions of subjectivity. They also reflect processual dimensions of everyday lived religious navigations and negotiations, which are realized by being performed. These are not neutral moments of religious life, but rather those of seeking accommodation, settlement and stability. Performance of such rituals among migrants demonstrates "mechanisms of individual and social bricolage concerning religious issues."[29] Religion in its lived form is more varied and richer than is commonly imagined in textually-based analysis.[30] However, lived religion in the diaspora situation struggles to reduce the complexities of migration through accommodation, as McGuire concluded from her research, in which she discovered that only a tiny minority struggles to work for tight consistency and uniformity among their beliefs, values and practices.[31] To that end, Muslims individually and collectively reconfigure religious beliefs and faith practices in a flexible manner, as opposed to strictly conforming to tight religious normativities. This is not only understandable, but it is also more pragmatic and rational. Nighat's performance of such religiosity cultivates a distinct religious culture for her entire family, though especially for her growing children. This cultic experience is marked by a renegotiation and recreation of religion with its own regulatory boundaries because it is through these processes that our subjectivities and identities are expressed. Furthermore, as a trans-spatial and trans-temporal feature of lived religion embedded in our cultural subjectivities, such domestic rituals are the core of social-psychological processes, serving as a solid means of communicating our relationship with past and present. This is of even further importance because these rituals also transmit religious sensibilities and practices to subsequent generations, something that Nighat was precisely striving to achieve. Moreover, by performing these sacred rituals, she, like Maqsood, invents her domestic religiosity and carves out an individualized

---

28 Saba Mahmood, *Politics of Piety: The Islamic Revival and the Feminist Subject* (Princeton: Princeton University Press, 2005), 147.
29 Chantal Saint-Blancat, "Islam in Diaspora: Between Reterritorialization and Extraterritoriality," trans. Karen George, *International Journal of Urban and Regional Research* 26, no. 1 (March 2002), https://doi.org/10.1111/1468-2427.00368.
30 Jennifer A. Selby, Amélie Barras and Lori G. Beaman, *Beyond Accommodation: Everyday Narratives of Muslim Canadians* (Vancouver: University of British Columbia Press, 2018), 124.
31 McGuire, *Lived Religion*, 16.

and privatized religious space within the environs of a foreign home. As a display of intrinsic and extrinsic religiosity, Nighat seeks her master motive for life through religion, where her other needs of improved social status and economic prosperity are brought into harmony with her religious beliefs and doctrines of devotion, holiness and piety.

3   Third Chronicle: Dietary Practices

While leaving alone for Canada a year ago for my studies, one of the major concerns of my family was *halal* food. Although I do not come from a family where religion was so strictly followed, we would celebrate religious festivities and rudimentarily observe religion, but after moving here this emerged as a major issue. My family wanted me to live according to the culture and religion that I was brought up with. Perhaps, it was more sensitive as I am a female [...]. Among other things, my family ensured that *halal* food is available where I was moving, and they also discussed about abstaining from alcohol and the illicit. Personally, I was also not ready and open to taking food that was not religiously sanctioned. I was aware that there were Muslim communities living in Calgary, yet I was not sure about the easy availability of *halal* food. When I arrived, my first query during the first two days was about *halal* restaurants and grocery shops. My classmates and others took me to these shops and informed that there are many in the city. I took a sigh of relief, and bought more than enough quantity of *halal* items, especially meat. To my surprise, I later found out that even 'non-Muslim' grocery stores and supermarkets had shelves, indicating *halal* items [...]. At university food events, such culinary differences are acknowledged and are cared for by the community. I have many friends who are vegetarians, especially from India, and to them this is not an issue. I would say that even I am not a good practicing Muslim, still I care about the *halal* food. I abstain from alcohol, pork and its products, like sausages, salami, ham and bacon, and these are absolutely absent from my diet table. Interestingly, on *halal* shelves, these local specialties are prepared with halal meat, and many a times I tried these and have developed a taste for that [...]. I share my apartment with a Sikh girl from India who is a vegetarian. As she does not eat meat, I would rarely prepare it at the apartment, only when she is not there, or after informing her first. For this, I would use different utensils, as she is very particular about it. But we prepare other food items together, as it is

> the same like when we cook back home [...]. I like to taste many of the local cuisines, with the only restriction of *halal*.
> AYESHA, 24 years old, university student

Food consumption and preparation is another significant practice which corresponds to beliefs and values of human groups, especially of religious ones. It is through these embodied practices that humans express their identity and group solidarity.[32] Such culinary practices, which include specific food ingredients, preparation procedures and consumption protocols, establish walls of virtue and difference with those who eat different things and in different ways.[33] Mary Douglas argues that human food habits are highly organized and classified as an identity-marker whereby not only what we eat is important, but also what we do not eat.[34] This question surfaces as the major motivational force for religious observance for Ayesha. This explains how her religious subjectivity emerges in the diaspora setting, where she seems to be in dialogue with her faith in a specific and significant manner. Even for secular and cultural Muslims, this is an implicit expression of their identity and quiescent religiosity. Although there are specific Islamic norms dealing with food consumption, influenced by local traditions of culinary cultures in Muslim societies across the globe, by adhering to these specific food practices in a diaspora context, Muslims engage in a dialogue with their religious beliefs and sensitivities. Depending upon the context, such religiously sanctioned practices are not rigid, but are (re)negotiated in a multitude of ways. Ayesha's chronicle details how she reworks these practices while sharing them with her Sikh flatmate and the majority non-Muslim community she lives in. Even food preparation codes are being re-worked in her new setting, oscillating between cultural norms and local constraints. This regulatory behavior of food consumption becomes a significant aspect of her intrinsic religiosity and identity maintenance, which she chooses to live by. This should be seen as an attempt to engage in dialogue with the environment to seek inter-culturalism beyond religious essentialism, for it is not different religious traditions that encounter each other, but rather

---

[32] Elsa Mescoli, "Islamic Food Practices in a Migration Context: Ethnography among Moroccan Women in Milan (Italy)," in *Everyday Life Practices of Muslims in Europe*, ed. Erkan Toğuşlu (Leuven: Leuven University Press, 2015).
[33] Rachel Brown, "'Tell Me What You Eat and I'll Tell You What You Are': The Literal Consumption of Identity for North African Muslims in Paris (France)," in *Everyday Life Practices*, ed. Toğuşlu.
[34] Mary Douglas, "Deciphering a Meal," *Daedalus* 101, no. 1 (Winter 1972).

ordinary people anchored in differing religious systems that meet and seek ways of mutual existence.[35]

Although Islamic injunctions like the prohibition of alcohol, pork and non-ritually slaughtered meat regulate dietary practices of the believers, it would be wrong to say that all Muslims follow the religious injunctions for *halal* (licit) and *haram* (illicit) food both within and outside their societies. Due to differences in expressing their religiosity, Muslims instead continuously negotiate and rework their interpretations of *halal*. Elsa Mescoli suggests that while for some Muslims in migration contexts *halal* meat means lawful animals that are ritually slaughtered; for others it is only the flesh of lawful animals, not necessarily only those that are ritually slaughtered; and for others still, it means only non-pork meat.[36] Similar observations can be made regarding the consumption of alcohol, since while Islamic scholars assert a strict prohibition, this is less uniformly adhered to. Some practicing Muslims abstain from non-*dhabiha* (meat which is not slaughtered according to traditional Islamic requirements) and from food items that contain gelatin and other non-conforming substances, such as monosodium glutamate. However, as Ayesha details in her chronicle, she chooses to abstain from non-permitted food items, yet she seeks to expand her culinary taste buds, trying local cuisine that is sanctioned for consumption by her religiosity. This can be read in view of de Certeau's thesis on how ordinary people in their everyday lives restructure socio-cultural mechanisms with their own individual tactics to reclaim their autonomy from the grand designs. Thus, Ayesha employs inventive resources to produce her own private religious space from the unfamiliar outside, a personal space which resembles "the tidy, consistent, and theologically correct packages official religions promote."[37]

4 Fourth Chronicle: Reconfiguring Dress

We immigrated to Canada through my husband's brother within the family stream program. Coming from a humble background in Lahore (Pakistan), we both were college lecturers and wanted to upgrade our education and economic condition. After the completion of a teaching diploma at a community college, I was able to get a part-time job in a public school. I have lived here for the last six years and feel myself fully

---

35 Malik, "Introduction," in *Religious Pluralism*.
36 Mescoli, "Islamic Food Practices."
37 McGuire, *Lived Religion*, 17.

integrated into the society on account of my English fluency and also because I have developed a strong and vast network of friends, colleagues and relatives [...]. My husband and I are very social and like to interact with new people and travel to new places. Our economic condition is now very stable, and my son is about to finish high school and is going to join the university to study engineering [...]. Before moving to Canada, I already knew a lot about life in Calgary, especially its weather. We did not face any major issue, as our family and other relatives managed to take care of everything. It was a smooth transition. The one major issue that I faced was dress, with reference to my conservative cultural and religious background. I used to wear *burqa* with my face covered while in Pakistan, but when I landed here, I was wearing *abbaya* and a scarf. My relatives here would use the same *abbaya* and headscarf [...]. This was uncomfortable for me, but I discussed it with my husband, who asked me for this change. When I started community college, I felt a little more uncomfortable with this over-dressing, as my younger classmates would wear jeans and other western attire. After the completion of my studies, when I started applying for jobs and went for interviews, I felt more uneasy. I again talked with my husband and other female relatives, who counseled me to try jeans. This was a major dilemma for me, as since my adolescence I had always worn *burqa*. My dress has been a sort of impediment for me in my professional ambitions, although there was never a word said to me over this issue directly, nor did I face any physical or verbal abuse due to my dress. I made a bold personal decision, and kept the headscarf, but started wearing trousers with long shirts. This worked and I felt more accepted and comfortable in the society. It has now been four years and I feel satisfied with my new attire and looks, as I want not only to live here for a short time, but want to assimilate into Canadian society. I know about Muslim women veil/scarf/dress as an issue of political debate on TV screens and newspaper headlines, but for me in Canada, it is working well, and I perform my religion with equal ease and comfort. So, no regrets.

  RIFFAT, age 33 years, schoolteacher

This chronicle is a common ordeal for Muslim immigrant women in Canada, although in many cases the women choose differently, instead opting for more conservative dress, especially headscarves, *abbaya* (robe-like dress or cloak) or, in rare cases, *burqa*s (garment covering the body and the face, with a window across the eyes). As Riffat narrates her migration challenge, unlike other interlocutors, she seeks a common space for settlement and assimilation. She does not denounce her faith by forgoing her traditional veil, rather she reworks it in order to assimilate and be accepted in her new society by adopting a new dress code. Dress, like many other markers of belonging, is a potent symbol of cultural and religious identification. In diaspora contexts, it becomes an expression of the cultural visibility of new immigrants. According to Eicher, dress functions as a kind of coded sensory system of non-verbal communication that aids human interaction across time and space.[38] Emphasizing its social communicative meanings, she links it with processes of inclusion and exclusion, as a coded sign that a person belongs to a certain cultural group. The strategic positioning of power in and through dress functions as a powerful political language of aesthetics, morality, religiosity and culture.[39] Riffat's chronicle demonstrates how the positioning of dress between the individual self and the social world can render it capable of simultaneous insights into debates that seek negotiation, dialogue and accommodation. Caught between the tradition-sanctioned dress that she wears and its limited utility with reference to social mobility in her new cultural space, she along with her family chooses to reconfigure this aspect of their religiosity. This is not, however, an unsettling experience for all of them, rather it is one of negotiating space in a new society. Such dialogue, as Malik suggests, offers opportunities and strategies for constructing a more inclusive, pluralistic, communicative and peaceful societal order, breaking conservative structures and schemas.[40]

Moreover, types of clothing that Muslims traditionally wear in their communities are anchored in the cultural mores of South Asian societies and rarely carry specific religious meanings. Despite this, they are inadvertently connected to Islamic faith as an expression of religious piety. In South Asian cultures, they are worn by all religious groups, including religious and culturally conservative milieus alike. There has been a considerable increase in the use of such conservative attire as the *kebaya, batik, shalwar-kameez, sari, thobe, abbaya, dasiqui* and *boubou* among religiously conservative Muslim diaspora groups, especially in second and third generation Muslims, as an assertion of cultural/group identity. Beards, headscarves and *burqas* have

---

[38] Joanne B. Eicher, "Introduction: Dress as Expression of Ethnic Identity," in *Dress and Ethnicity: Change across Space and Time*, ed. Joanne B. Eicher (Oxford: Berg Publishers, 1995), 1–5, http://dx.doi.org/10.2752/9781847881342.

[39] Jean Allman, "Fashioning Africa: Power and the Politics of Dress," in *Fashioning Africa: Power and the Politics of Dress,* ed. Jean Allman (Bloomington: Indiana University Press, 2004), 2.

[40] Malik, "Introduction," in *Religious Pluralism*.

become significant identity markers of Islamic-ness or Muslim-ness. Such a dress code survives the migration experience as an embodiment of diaspora memory and as an expression of distant spatial roots within communities. Riffat sees her clothing as carrying cultural and religious significance and meaning, yet in the process of relocation, settlement and assimilation, she honestly negotiates its replacement with apparel that can fit into the new environment. In some cases, the result is the opposite: When individuals or groups seek to stress their religious, cultural or political message and turn towards conservative religious values during crises of identity and settlement, they start using more conservative dress codes like the face-veil or headscarf. For Riffat and her immediate family, the desire to be more at ease and comfortable as well as to engage with the new social environment leads them to their choices, but without any ensuing conflict in terms of a religious or cultural break or violation. Nevertheless, in the West, it is Muslim female attire that has attracted undue criticism from a broad spectrum of groups like secular feminists, ultra-nationalists and others who interpret it as slavish and a sign of the oppressive patriarchy that such critics assign to Muslim cultures.[41] Within Muslim communities across the globe, multiple local codes are operative, even when these are not legally or religiously mandated. A near consensus among Muslim communities and religious scholars on obligatory modest dress for both genders is that any clothing which is not revealing is acceptable, including Western-style clothing. More religiously conservative Muslim women, especially of a Salafi background, might wear an *abayya*, that is a gown with an accompanying headscarf or a complete veil. Muslim women like Riffat largely follow hybridized dress codes when living in Western societies; depending upon social status, mobility, acceptance and assimilation; as an expression of their religious piety, personal privacy and cultural identity. Yet this always requires the re-configuration of learned Islamic normativity and embedded religiosity in new social spaces, which can be interpreted as a part of their accommodation and assimilation tactics, as in the case of Riffat.

---

41 See, for example, Lila Abu-Lughod, *Do Muslim Women Need Saving?* (Cambridge, MA: Harvard University Press, 2013); Leila Ahmed, *A Quiet Revolution: The Veil's Resurgence, from the Middle East to America* (New Haven: Yale University Press, 2011); Haideh Moghissi, *Feminism and Islamic Fundamentalism: The Limits of Postmodern Analysis* (London: Zed Books, 1999).

5   Fifth Chronicle: Workplace Prayers

I came to Canada as a refugee, escaping political persecution back in Pakistan. It has now been almost twenty years, and I am now a Canadian citizen, living with my wife and four kids. Coming here was an abrupt decision, and I was unable to see my family and my daughter for four years. It was a time of hardship as I had no work and skills and I had to send money to my family so that they could survive. Anyway, the time is over, and I studied here, got a mechanical diploma and have a relatively modest job. Three of my kids are also working, one of them is married. When I reflect back on coming to Canada, I have mixed feelings. There [Pakistan] my life was threatened, and here I am cut off from my extended family, friends and society. Some five years back, I decided to return, but my kids did not approve of it and I do not wish to live separated from them again. I come from a religiously conservative family and I work hard to keep myself and my family as good observant and practicing Muslims. As a practicing Muslim, I have to offer my prayer five times a day on time, and also to fast during the month of Ramadan. I do not like mixing with females due to my religious convictions. That is why I had to make many compromises about practicing my faith. I work in a high-rise building in downtown as a machine operator. Normally, I have to work eight hours, but sometimes it is longer, which is okay with me as far as work is concerned. But the issue is at prayer time, when I am at work, it is not easy to leave and offer prayer which does not take more than ten minutes. My colleagues support me, but often I am stuck and cannot say the prayer in time. Initially, my supervisor and colleagues were really upset, as time-out for prayer, the place to offer prayer and the noisy conditions of the penthouse made this messy, but it is now kind of managed somehow. The main problem is the winter season when I have to offer four out of five prayers during work. Ramadan was initially a big issue, my colleagues would jeer at me, offer me drinks and food, but this does not happen anymore now. They have learnt and we manage. I could not work well during the last days of Ramadan, which affected my job and I was about to get fired. Similarly, working with females, especially as senior management, would put me in awkward situations as I would look down, not to their eyes or face directly, and they would find it offensive and rude. I had to explain it, especially because my English was not very good. I have a beard and I always cover my head with a small white cap. I was not used to wearing shirts and trousers, and even today I am not comfortable. Initially, when I tried to come to work in *shalwar-kameez*,[42] it was terrifying for many, even for security. Back then, there were not many Muslims here, so it was a strange sight for all. At work, I wear the approved worker dress now, but I keep my white cap on my head, even while I wear a protective helmet. I think I have changed a lot and have learnt to live here and they also accept me and treat me specially, recognizing my faith obligations. I am thankful to Allah for all this.

MUSTAFA, 54 years old, technician

Mustafa's chronicle is a typical instance of conflict, engagement, negotiation and accommodation that immigrants encounter when relocating and settling in new cultures. The increasing visibility of Muslim religious practices in the West, especially the ritual of prayer (*salat*), has generated heated debates as to how to deal with the challenges of cultural and religious diversity.[43] Being the major religious prescription in Islam for all believers, it consists of five daily prayers, which are to be offered at specific times and are preceded by ritual ablutions of the hands, mouth, nose, face, ears and feet.[44] These daily prayers can overlap with normal working hours, especially the noon prayer (*zuhr*), the afternoon prayer (*'asr*) and the early evening prayer (*maghrib*). These prayer times are synchronized with the movement of the sun (according to the lunar calendar), and not with specific clock times. They are thus constantly shifting, which of course creates complexity and problems for (re)scheduling in majority non-Muslim societies.[45] Moreover, as Mustafa recounts, taking regular breaks at work can be challenging for the employers as well as for the organization and other staff, depending upon the nature of the work. Therefore, praying strictly on time, especially in secular/neutral settings, can only be possible to the extent that the context allows it. Secondly, employers are hard-pressed to provide space that meets the specific requirements of ritual prayer (facing the Ka'ba and a clean quiet place). These issues are further compounded due to the variations of practice among Muslims over the exact time and duration of

---

42 This is a long, loose-fitting shirt worn in South Asia by both men and women, and which comes in different stitching styles and designs.
43 Nadia Fadil, "Performing the Salat [Islamic Prayers] at Work: Secular and Pious Muslims Negotiating the Contours of the Public in Belgium," *Ethnicities* 13, no. 6 (2013).
44 David Waines, "Islam," in *Religions in the Modern World: Traditions and Transformations*, ed. Linda Woodhead et al. (London and New York: Routledge, 2002).
45 Heiko Henkel, " 'Between Belief and Unbelief Lies the Performance of Salāt': Meaning and Efficacy of a Muslim Ritual," *Journal of the Royal Anthropological Institute* 11, no. 3 (2005), https://doi.org/10.1111/j.1467-9655.2005.00247.x.

the prayers, as well as over the permissibility of skipping or combining prayers or praying later.[46] As such, apart from the observance of these prayers, there are no hard and fast rules among Muslims, a situation that has the potential to lead to frustrating situations. Many Muslim employees attend just the *jumma* (Friday noon prayer), which is only offered in congregation. Although the performance of this practice has not created a larger public outcry, it continues to surface as a thorny issue with employers. Mustafa explains how troublesome it was in the beginning to manage it in a predominantly secular setting, yet through his persistent engagement and through the accommodation shown on the part of office management and staff, he finally worked it out. At times, demands for breaks during work hours in order to perform obligatory religious acts result in tensions with employers, and sometimes employees leave jobs that are not willing to accommodate their requests. Usually, Canadian employers make allowances due to legal requirements that stress policies like equal opportunity, non-discrimination, cultural pluralism and reasonable accommodation.[47] However, this involves more a two-way process of tactical negotiation, as it also includes employers' interests in maintaining the loyalty and goodwill of the workforce by accommodating such demands, especially where this does not impinge upon work performance and the overall business environment. With an increasing Muslim labor force in Canada, over time, employers have tackled this issue with provisions like allowing short breaks, introducing schedule changes to accommodate the observation of religious festivities or showing sensitivity towards dietary restrictions, religious dress, symbols and practices in the work place, based on the neutrality principle of a "bona fide occupational requirement or as reasonable or justifiable."[48] Yet usually these negotiated practices are not formally included in organizational rules and are thus sorted out on a case-by-case basis with due care for the law. Some public institutions employ a large number of Muslim personnel in their work force, such as the public transport service, and there such practices are refused on similar grounds of neutrality, because it is feared that other religious communities would demand similar allowances, leading to a disruption of public services. Nevertheless, neutrality is upheld by the law, which prohibits discrimination on the basis of religious beliefs and ensures that employees do not have to choose between their employment and their beliefs, and are also

---

46　Fadil, "Performing the Salat."
47　See, for example, Gérald A. Beaudoin and Ed Ratushny, eds., *The Canadian Charter of Rights and Freedoms* (Toronto: Carswell, 1989).
48　Alberta Human Rights Act, Revised *Statutes of Alberta* 2000, Chapter A-25.5, current as of June 11, 2018, accessed December 11, 2018, www.qp.alberta.ca/documents/Acts/A25P5.pdf.

not denied services because of their religious beliefs.⁴⁹ Prayer, fasting, religious holidays, pilgrimage as well as dietary and clothing requirements are all major aspects of religious life for Muslims, and these are thus given legal cover in the Canadian Charter of Rights and Freedoms. Human rights legislation also prohibits discriminatory practices by private actors and individuals on the basis of religion in the areas of employment, accommodation and the provision of goods, services and facilities.⁵⁰ Consequently, employers are prohibited from discriminating against employees on the basis of religion. Moreover, they are obliged to accommodate the religious observances of their employees, where doing so would not cause undue hardship for the employer. The purpose of accommodation is based on the recognition that rules and procedures apply equally to everyone, even if they do not affect everyone in an equal manner. Therefore, regular rituals like *salat* often produce challenges to accommodation when these are performed in a different cultural context. However, practicing Muslims like Mustafa chart out the means for performing these through negotiating various tactics.

6   Conclusion

This chapter, by way of interviews and participant observation, sheds light on everyday Islam as lived and practiced among members of the Pakistani diaspora in Canada. The chronicles presented here offer insights into the space-making experience of our interlocutors during the settlement phase of their relocation. In examining these vignettes, I have focused on rituals, practices and creative engagements and negotiations, facets which are central to the anthropological study of lived Islam. In their response to the challenges of migration, these varied expressions of religiosity are reflective of inventiveness, plurality and flexibility, rather than of rigid orthodoxy. According to Malik, this religious-cum-cultural space is gradually developing in response to a multi-dimensional, discovery-oriented dialogue between different social agents in the diaspora context.⁵¹ Individual Muslims employ various tactics

---

49   Fadil, "Performing the Salat."
50   Canadian Charter of Rights and Freedoms, section 15, Part I of the Constitution Act, Schedule B to the Canada Act 1982 (UK), c. 11., accessed December 11, 2018, https://www.canada.ca/content/dam/pch/documents/services/download-order-charter-bill/canadian-charter-rights-freedoms-eng.pdf.
51   Jamal Malik, "Integration of Muslim Migrants and the Politics of Dialogue: The Case of Modern Germany," *Journal of Muslim Minority Affairs* 33, no. 4 (2013), https://doi.org/10.1080/13602004.2013.866350.

to live according to a multiplicity of Islamic injunctions, and thereby create individual religious selves along with private and public religious spaces in Canada. As Malik argues, some sort of inter-cultural hermeneutics that interprets these contextualized engagements is imperative in order to comprehend these evolving negotiations.[52] These dimensions of Muslim life in diaspora contexts are partially explored by recent anthropological studies of Islam that focus on such context-based everyday encounters between various cultural entities. The underlying assumption is that Islam is not simply a religion of submission derived from an invariable set of scriptural codes, rather it is a dynamic lived experience in the everyday lives of its followers, one that allows room for transformation and invention. Michael Gilsenan argues along the same lines when he states that it is crucial to study the lived practices of Muslims, since it is the experience that constructs the self. Accordingly, Islam should be situated within the framework of everyday life and the contexts in which Muslim communities grow.[53] Deeb and Harb also point out that everyday Islam yields the tactics employed by Muslims to draw on ideas that they understand to be rooted in tradition in order to figure out everything from handshaking to prayer, from dress to which cafés to frequent and what social invitations to accept.[54]

Religiosity is something one chooses to perform from a multiplicity of available religious injunctions and interpretations. Talal Asad and Saba Mahmood refer to this religiosity as a symbolic marker of faith which reflects a temporal and spatial state of mind, rather than a constituting activity.[55] This religiously-based Muslim/Islamic identity is not a new invention, but in order for it to be determined, it is crucial to take into account the context, as the construction of a Muslim "self" cannot be comprehended with reference to sacred scriptures alone.[56] The chronicles on which this study is based establish that diaspora religiosity creates compelling challenges to settlement in the public and private negotiations of religious space-making. Religion of the diaspora is located in individual, private and domestic realms, but it operates in an invasive way in the public sphere as well. Ayesha and Riffat confront material opportunities

---

52 Jamal Malik, "Introduction," in *Muslims in Europe: From Margin to Center*, ed. Jamal Malik (Münster: LIT, 2004), 4.
53 Michael Gilsenan, *Recognizing Islam: Religion and Society in the Modern Middle East* (London and New York: I.B. Tauris, 2000), 19.
54 Lara Deeb and Mona Harb, *Leisurely Islam: Negotiating Geography and Morality in Shi'ite South Beirut* (Princeton: Princeton University Press, 2013).
55 Talal Asad, *Genealogies of Religion: Discipline and Reasons of Power in Christianity and Islam* (Baltimore: John Hopkins University Press, 1993); Mahmood, *Politics of Piety*.
56 Malik, "Introduction," in *Muslims in Europe*.

to make flexible compromises through negotiation tactics pertaining to food and dress in a minority situation. Nighat's chronicle illustrates how rituals are the expression of free choice and articulates the spirit of relocation and settlement in distant lands. Maqsood's chronicle also demonstrates that embodied practices of religiosity are significant, in the sense that these retain and transmit faith through regular rituals within the domestic space and are woven into everyday Muslim diaspora life in Canada. They conform to the rationality that is central to the diaspora life, wherein contested challenges of space-making are resolved through individual deliberation and public negotiation. These negotiations are internal dialogues within the community about how to act and react in specific situations, navigating the pros and cons of their actions, interacting with and attending to the power dynamics around them.[57] They allow social agents to carve out arrangements in pragmatic and practical ways with respect to internal and external challenges, which are not fixed but are instead contingent on numerous factors. This also points to the fact that power relations are always an indispensable aspect of these engagements and negotiations, being constitutive of and ingrained in everyday life. Stuart Hall argues that such negotiations allow for alternative spaces, while (re)producing the privileged structures of power.[58] Mustafa prays at work and maintains his personal religious code of interaction in a secular space through dialogue, rather than through forceful demands. He continuously finds ways to adhere to these religious practices, which have at times conflicted with his job requirements, while still engaging in his professional activities. These "tactics," which de Certeau also points to, are invisible. They consist of seizing opportunities within the prevalent power structures, charting out one's "own rules" by way of adjusting and adapting to the meta-strategies of the dominant structures.[59]

Thus, these individual religiosities reformulate the parameters of power structures, submerged under the rhetoric of "reasonable accommodation" in Canada.[60] As the above five chronicles reflect, these multiple expressions of religiosity are constantly being (re)invented, (re)produced and (re)formed by migrants amid constructions of religious space through implicit and explicit negotiations with society at large. They explain how diaspora Muslims reproduce their religious selves as potent expressions of their identities that provide practical coherence to otherwise incoherent religiosity. Smith contends that

---

57 Selby, Barras and Beaman, *Beyond Accommodation*.
58 Stuart Hall, "Cultural Studies: Two Paradigms," *Media, Culture and Society* 2, no. 1 (January 1980).
59 De Certeau, *The Practice of Everyday Life*, 37.
60 Selby, Barras and Beaman, *Beyond Accommodation*, 156.

migration itself can be a "theologizing experience,"[61] which is commonly taken for granted with regard to the social lives of Muslim migrants. During this relocation phase, religion offers psychological comfort by invoking meaning for their social existence in an uprooted condition, and thus relieving the stress of the transition to an unfamiliar place and culture. During phases of relocation and settlement, religious communities continuously enact their religiosity and anchor their lives in their chosen religious ideals. Moreover, these chronicles illustrate diaspora negotiations of displacement through (re)invented religiosity in the mundane moments of day-to-day existence. Malik stresses the need for engagements as "dialogues of life" that concentrate on everyday living in order to develop mechanisms of negotiation to improve host-migrant community relations:

> Fundamentally, dialogue itself is a benefit in intercultural communication and decisive for understanding the others and even oneself. For, in the dynamic process of construction and reconstruction of the other—through projection and introjections—one's self-perception changes at the same time, resulting in the constant modification of one's own perception as well as that of the others. Imagined ideas about subjects like essentialism, purity, homogeneity, and national cultures are therefore subject to permanent change. Consequently, on and above all, between both sides, a whole series of societal transitions can be perceived that can have quite a positive effect as they offer social space for the most varied—including religious—identity and discourse levels.[62]

These aspects of religious life are not made evident by studying only sacred scriptures and canonical texts. The main argument of this study is that the religious dynamics of a diaspora cannot simply be studied by means of theological texts or the contestations of regimes of power alone. It is rather through developing an understanding of the informal tactics of negotiation and processes of space-making within mundane life that a comprehensive understanding of these dynamics can be achieved. Drawing upon the scholarship of Jamal Malik, this chapter recounts the imperative of dialogue and negotiation, beyond religious essentialism and towards inter-culturalism, as this offers pragmatic opportunities for constructing a more inclusive, pluralistic, communicative and peaceful social order, breaking down divisive power

---

61   Timothy L. Smith, "Religion and Ethnicity in America," *American Historical Review* 83, no. 5 (December 1978), https://doi.org/10.1086/ahr/83.5.1155.
62   Malik, "Islamic-Christian Dialogue."

structures and cognitive schemas. He notes that this is gradually developing as a multi-directional, discovery-oriented dialogue between multiple groups for comprehending varied sociopolitical constructions.[63] This dialogue does not simply address the needs of those in power, but it also hearkens to the voices of the disenfranchised and the hitherto unheard.

Bibliography

Abu-Lughod, Lila. *Do Muslim Women Need Saving?*. Cambridge, MA: Harvard University Press, 2013.

Adamson, Fiona B. and Madeleine Demetriou. "Remapping the Boundaries of 'State' and 'National Identity': Incorporating Diasporas into IR Theorizing." *European Journal of International Relations* 13, no. 4 (2007): 489–526.

Ahmed, Leila. *A Quiet Revolution: The Veil's Resurgence, from the Middle East to America.* New Haven: Yale University Press, 2011.

Allman, Jean. "Fashioning Africa: Power and the Politics of Dress." In *Fashioning Africa: Power and the Politics of Dress*, edited by Jean Allman, 1–10. Bloomington: Indiana University Press, 2004.

Allport, Gordon W. and J. Michael Ross. "Personal Religious Orientation and Prejudice." *Journal of Personality and Social Psychology* 5, no. 4, (1967): 432–43, https://doi.org/10.1037/h0021212.

Ammerman, Nancy Tatom. *Everyday Religion: Observing Modern Religious Lives.* New York: Oxford University Press, 2007.

Ammerman, Nancy Tatom. *Sacred Stories, Spiritual Tribes: Finding Religion in Everyday Life.* New York: Oxford University Press, 2014.

Asad, Talal. *Genealogies of Religion: Discipline and Reasons of Power in Christianity and Islam.* Baltimore: John Hopkins University Press, 1993.

Beaudoin, Gérald A. and Ed Ratushny, eds. *The Canadian Charter of Rights and Freedoms.* Toronto: Carswell, 1989.

Berger, Peter L. and Thomas Luckmann. *The Social Construction of Reality: A Treatise in the Sociology of Knowledge.* Garden City, NY: Doubleday, 1966.

Bowman, Marion and Ülo Valk, eds. *Vernacular Religion in Everyday Life: Expressions of Belief.* Oxon and New York: Routledge, 2012.

Brown, Rachel. "'Tell Me What You Eat and I'll Tell You What You Are': The Literal Consumption of Identity for North African Muslims in Paris (France)." In *Everyday*

---

63 Malik, "Integration of Muslim Migrants," 495–96.

Life Practices of Muslims in Europe, edited by Erkan Toğuşlu, 41–56. Leuven: Leuven University Press, 2015.

Cardwell, Jerry D. *The Social Context of Religiosity.* Washington, DC: University Press of America, 1980.

De Certeau, Michael. *The Practice of Everyday Life.* Translated by Steven F. Rendall. Berkeley: University of California Press, 1984.

Deeb, Lara and Mona Harb. *Leisurely Islam: Negotiating Geography and Morality in Shi'ite South Beirut.* Princeton: Princeton University Press, 2013.

Douglas, Mary. "Deciphering a Meal." *Daedalus* 101, no. 1 (Winter 1972): 61–81.

Eicher, Joanne B. "Introduction: Dress as Expression of Ethnic Identity." In *Dress and Ethnicity: Change across Space and Time,* edited by Joanne B. Eicher, 1–6. Oxford: Berg Publishers, 1995, http://dx.doi.org/10.2752/9781847881342.

El-Menouar, Yasemin. "The Five Dimensions of Muslim Religiosity: Results of an Empirical Study." *Methods, Data, Analyses* 8, no. 1 (2014): 53–78, https://doi.org/10.12758/mda.2014.003.

Fadil, Nadia. "Performing the Salat [Islamic Prayers] at Work: Secular and Pious Muslims Negotiating the Contours of the Public in Belgium." *Ethnicities* 13, no. 6 (2013): 729–50.

Fukuyama, Yoshio. "The Major Dimensions of Church Membership." *Review of Religious Research* 2, no. 4 (Spring 1961): 154–61, https://doi.org/10.2307/3510955.

Gilsenan, Michael. *Recognizing Islam: Religion and Society in the Modern Middle East.* London and New York: I.B. Tauris, 2000.

Glock, Charles Y. and Rodney Stark. *Religion and Society in Tension.* Chicago: Rand McNally, 1965.

Hall, David D., ed. *Lived Religion in America: Toward a History of Practice.* Princeton: Princeton University Press, 1997.

Hall, Stuart. "Cultural Studies: Two Paradigms." *Media, Culture and Society* 2, no. 1 (January 1980): 57–72.

Henkel, Heiko. "'Between Belief and Unbelief Lies the Performance of Salāt': Meaning and Efficacy of a Muslim Ritual." *Journal of the Royal Anthropological Institute* 11, no. 3 (2005): 487–507, https://doi.org/10.1111/j.1467-9655.2005.00247.x.

Huber, Stefan. "Religion Monitor 2008: Structuring Principles, Operational Constructs, Interpretive Strategies." In *What the World Believes: Analysis and Commentary on the Religion Monitor 2008,* edited by Bertelsmann Stiftung, 17–51. Gütersloh: Verlag Bertelsmann Stiftung, 2009.

Hunt, Stephen. *Religion and Everyday Life: The New Sociology.* Oxon and New York: Routledge, 2005.

Jeldtoft, Nadia. "Lived Islam: Religious Identity with 'Non-organized' Muslim Minorities." *Ethnic and Racial Studies* 34, no. 7 (2011): 1134–51, https://doi.org/10.1080/01419870.2010.528441.

Kecskes, Robert and Christof Wolf. "Christliche Religiosität: Konzepte, Indikatoren, Messinstrumente." *Kölner Zeitschrift für Soziologie und Sozialpsychologie* 45, no. 2 (1993): 270–87.

Kelly, George A. *The Psychology of Personal Constructs*. New York: Norton, 1955.

Lefebvre, Henri. *The Production of Space*. Translated by Donald Nicholson-Smith. Oxford: Blackwell, 1991.

Luckmann, Thomas. *The Invisible Religion: The Problem of Religion in Modern Society*. New York: Macmillan, 1967.

Mahmood, Saba. *Politics of Piety: The Islamic Revival and the Feminist Subject*. Princeton: Princeton University Press, 2005.

Malik, Jamal. "Integration of Muslim Migrants and the Politics of Dialogue: The Case of Modern Germany." *Journal of Muslim Minority Affairs* 33, no. 4 (2013): 495–506, https://doi.org/10.1080/13602004.2013.866350.

Malik, Jamal. "Introduction." In *Muslims in Europe: From Margin to Center*, edited by Jamal Malik, 1–20. Münster: LIT, 2004.

Malik, Jamal. "Introduction." In *Religious Pluralism in South Asia and Europe*, edited by Jamal Malik and Helmut Reifeld, 1–20. New Delhi: Oxford University Press, 2004.

Malik, Jamal. "Islamic-Christian Dialogue." *Journal of Oriental Studies* 15 (2005): 129–37.

Malik, Jamal. *Islam in South Asia: A Short History*. Leiden: Brill, 2008 [revised, enlarged and updated second edition in 2020].

Mazumdar, Shampa and Sanjoy Mazumdar. "The Articulation of Religion in Domestic Space: Rituals in the Immigrant Muslim Home." *Journal of Ritual Studies* 18, no. 2 (2004): 74–85.

McGuire, Meredith B. *Lived Religion: Faith and Practice in Everyday Life*. New York: Oxford University Press, 2008.

Mescoli, Elsa. "Islamic Food Practices in a Migration Context: Ethnography among Moroccan Women in Milan (Italy)." In *Everyday Life Practices of Muslims in Europe*, edited by Erkan Toğuşlu, 19–39. Leuven: Leuven University Press, 2015.

Moghissi, Haideh. *Feminism and Islamic Fundamentalism: The Limits of Postmodern Analysis*. London: Zed Books, 1999.

Olufadi, Yunusa. "Muslim Daily Religiosity Assessment Scale (MUDRAS): A New Instrument for Muslim Religiosity Research and Practice." *Psychology of Religion and Spirituality* 9, no. 2 (2017): 165–79, http://dx.doi.org/10.1037/rel0000074.

Orsi, Robert. "Everyday Miracles: The Study of Lived Religion." In *Lived Religion in America: Toward a History of Practice*, edited by David D. Hall, 3–21. Princeton: Princeton University Press, 1997.

Sahin, Abdullah and Leslie Francis. "Assessing Attitude Toward Islam among Muslim Adolescents: The Psychometric Properties of the Sahin-Francis Scale." *Muslim Education Quarterly* 19, no. 4 (2002): 35–47.

Saint-Blancat, Chantal. "Islam in Diaspora: Between Reterritorialization and Extraterritoriality." Translated by Karen George, *International Journal of Urban and Regional Research* 26, no. 1 (March 2002): 138–51, https://doi.org/10.1111/1468-2427.00368.

Selby, Jennifer A., Amélie Barras and Lori G. Beaman. *Beyond Accommodation: Everyday Narratives of Muslim Canadians*. Vancouver: University of British Columbia Press, 2018.

Smith, Timothy L. "Religion and Ethnicity in America." *American Historical Review* 83, no. 5 (December 1978): 1158–85, https://doi.org/10.1086/ahr/83.5.1155.

Waines, David. "Islam." In *Religions in the Modern World: Traditions and Transformations*, edited by Linda Woodhead, Paul Fletcher, Hiroko Kawanami and David Smith, 210–34. London and New York: Routledge, 2002.

Wilde, Alex and Stephan Joseph. "Religiosity and Personality in a Moslem Context." *Personality and Individual Differences* 23, no. 5 (November 1997): 899–900, https://doi.org/10.1016/S0191-8869(97)00098-6.

PART 4

Islamic Mysticism and Globalization

CHAPTER 10

Prophetic Descent in the Early Modern *Tariqa Muhammadiyya Khalisa*

Soraya Khodamoradi

1   Introduction: Eighteenth-Century Muhammad

In eighteenth-century Europe, besides the already established medieval and early modern polemical image of Muhammad as a false prophet and impostor,[1] several authors began to portray him as a zealous religious reformer, a lawgiver to his people and a great conqueror and statesman.[2] The French historian Henri de Boulainvilliers (d. 1722), for example, presented the Prophet in his *La Vie de Mahomed* as a messenger who was sent to emancipate the Orient from the arbitrary rule of the Persians and Romans. According to him, the Prophet established a direct relationship between God and faithful human beings and rejected irrational and undesirable aspects of Christianity, such as the veneration of icons and relics, the despotic power of avaricious and superstitious priests, monks and clergy who had made religion subservient to their passions.[3] Some decades later, Claude-Emmanuel Pastoret (d. 1840), a French author and politician who was elected member of the Académie des inscriptions et belles-lettres because of his book *Zoroastre, Confucius et Mahomet, Comparés Comme Sectaires, Législateurs et Moralistes*, discussed the Prophet of Islam as one of the world's greatest legislators and the model that eighteenth-century Europeans would be wise to follow. For him, Muhammad was a

---

1   Medieval Latin texts on Islam and the Prophet mainly depict Muhammad in the various guises of a false prophet, anti-saint, a precursor to the Antichrist or the final manifestation of the Antichrist himself, a pagan god and a heretic. See Michelina Di Cesare, "The Prophet in the Book: Images of Muhammad in Western Medieval Book Culture," in *Constructing the Image of Muhammad in Europe*, ed. Avinoam Shalem (Berlin: de Gruyter, 2013), 10–11, https://doi.org/10.1515/9783110300864.9.
2   John Tolan, "Impostor or Lawgiver?: Muhammad through European Eyes in the 17th and 18th Centuries," in *The Image of the Prophet Between Ideal and Ideology: A Scholarly Investigation*, ed. Christiane Gruber and Avinoam Shalem (Berlin: de Gruyter, 2014), 261–62, https://doi.org/10.1515/9783110312546.261.
3   Henri de Boulainvilliers, *The Life of Mahomet*, trans. anon. (London: W. Hinchliffe, 1731), 179, 206–7, and 222.

religious reformer who was more interested in adapting received religious and cultural ideas and practices into the framework of his own mission than in dropping them completely.[4] Even Napoleon Bonaparte (d. 1821) propounded a triumphantly victorious image of the Prophet, turning him into something of a role model and understanding himself as a new world conqueror and legislator walking in Muhammad's footsteps.[5]

Emphasizing the socio-political aspect of Muhammad's life was not only a European, outsider approach. Similarly, in the milieu of Islamic thought of the eighteenth century, many outstanding Muslim Sufis and scholars focused on his historical aspect and worldly occupations, enthusiastically stressed his social and political role and conduct, and presented him as a religious and social reformist leader, a process Jamal Malik called the "subtle humanization of the Prophet."[6] Muhammad ibn ʿAbd al-Wahhab (d. 1792), the founder of the well-known Wahhabi movement, for instance, asserted in his biography of the Prophet entitled *Mukhtasar Sirat al-Rasul* ("Concise Biography of the Prophet") that Muhammad's success was primarily due to his utilizing warfare and his building a community of believers. In elaborating Muhammad's characteristics, he mainly highlighted the Prophet's military abilities and bravery in battle and focused on his Medinan phase of life, which most embodies his political and social life and manifests the military and legal aspects of his mission. There, Ibn ʿAbd al-Wahhab distanced himself from the Prophet's heavenly and spiritual image, which had been the concern of Muslim minds for centuries due to, among other factors, the domination of mysticism and ecstasy-oriented Sufism. Unlike many other types of the *sira* (biography of Muhammad) genre, *Mukhtasar* passed over many episodes in the life of the Prophet which elevated his status beyond that of an ordinary human. The book explicitly included episodes demonstrating Muhammad as a fallible human being, an image that contrasted with the dominant understanding of the infallible and pure Prophet who had been considered sheer light for centuries.[7]

---

4   Claude-Emmanuel Joseph Pierre de Pastoret, *Zoroastre, Confucius et Mahomet: Comparés Comme Sectaires, Législateurs et Moralistes* (Paris: Buisson, 1787), 267 and 320.
5   In his exile on the British island of Saint Helena, where he wrote his memoirs, including the description of his Egyptian campaign, Napoleon developed his portrait of Muhammad as a model statesman, lawmaker and conqueror. See Tolan, "Impostor or Lawgiver?," 269.
6   Jamal Malik, *Islam in South Asia: Revised, Enlarged and Updated Second Edition* (Leiden: Brill, 2020), 269.
7   Martin Riexinger, "Rendering Muḥammad Human Again: The Prophetology of Muḥammad b. ʿAbd al-Wahhāb (1703–1792)," *Numen* 60, no. 1 (2013): 103–5, and 116; Muhammad ibn ʿAbd al-Wahhab, *Mukhtasar Sirat al-Rasul* (Cairo: Maktabat al-Sunna al-Muhammadiyya, 1956), 77–82, 104–5, 140–48.

In India, which this chapter is mainly concerned with, Ibn 'Abd al-Wahhab's contemporary Shah Wali Allah of Delhi (d. 1762), who was an erudite reformist scholar and Naqshbandi Sufi, also depicted the Prophet as a successful reformer. Muhammad, in his viewpoint, brought his people, who had deviated from the true religion of Isma'il (Abraham's first son), to their proper original state by rectifying the already prevailing principles and traditions.[8] According to Wali Allah's narrative, the children of Isma'il in Arabia had inherited the codes of their forefather and had followed that divine law until the time of 'Amr bin Luhayy, a legendary Arab noble and trader[9] who had allegedly interpolated such things as idol worship into the religion of Isma'il, thus leading the Arabs astray. Wali Allah believes that although the people of the *jahiliyya* (period of "ignorance," referring to Arabian paganism before Islam) at the time of the Prophet retained some elements of the religion of Isma'il, such as belief in the mission of the prophets, requital and piety, their religiosity was falsified and its sound elements were mixed with corrupt ones.[10] Struggling to straighten their deviation from the true religion, Muhammad forbade the corrupt customs and commanded the sound ones.[11] Wali Allah argues that while Muhammad banned certain pre-Islamic Arabian practices, mainstays of the shari'a, such as regulations concerning marriage, divorce, prayer, fasting and pilgrimage, are modified versions of pre-Islamic Arabian custom (*'urf*). According to Wali Allah, Arabs followed the shari'a not only because of their belief in the Prophet, but also due to the proximity of the shari'a to their custom.[12] Therefore, Muhammad was indeed a reformer who partly relied on local customary law that he asserted was a corrupted form of Abraham's initial shari'a.

In Delhi, another renowned eighteenth-century Naqshbandi known for his absolute commitment to and imitation of the sunna, Mirza Mazhar Jan-i Janan (d. 1781),[13] continued the school of Ahmad Sirhindi (d. 1624), the significant

---

8   Shah Wali Allah, *The Conclusive Argument from God: Shāh Walī Allāh of Delhi's Ḥujjat Allāh al-Bāligha*, trans. Marcia K. Hermansen (Leiden: Brill, 1996), 361–62.
9   For the legend of 'Amr bin Luhayy in early Muslim accounts, see Reynold A. Nicholson, *A Literary History of the Arabs* (London: T. Fisher Unwin, 1907), 63–64; Abd al-Malik ibn Hisham, *Das Leben Mohammed's nach Mohammed ibn Ishak*, trans. Gustav Weil (Stuttgart: J.B. Metzler, 1864), 51; and Hisham ibn Muhammad al-Kalbi, *Kitab al-Asnam (Tankis al-Asnam): Tarikh-i Parastish-i Arab pish az Zuhur-i Islam*, trans. Muhammadriza Jalali Na'ini (Tehran: Sukhan, 2006), 9–13 and 53–58.
10 Wali Allah, *The Conclusive Argument*, 361–62.
11 Ibid.
12 M. Reza Pirbhai, *Reconsidering Islam in a South Asian Context* (Leiden: Brill, 2009), 140.
13 For Mazhar's approach, see SherAli Tareen, "The Perils and Possibilities of Inter-Religious Translation: Mirza Mazhar Jan-i Janan on the Hindus," *Sagar: A South Asia Research Journal*

Muslim reviver and precursor of the Indian *Tariqa Muhammadiyya*,[14] who maintained that a believer should realize not only the spiritual, but also the political and social aspects of the Prophet's legacy in this world.[15] Sirhindi's numerous letters and treatises claimed that, in the second millennium of Islam, he could help reverse the growing separation of the Prophet from his community.[16] According to him, the person of the Prophet was central to the definition of Islam, for it was Muhammad who demarcated the borderline between Islam and infidelity.[17] The way such Muslim scholars and Sufis of the early modern era reinterpreted the beginnings of Islamic history explores their expectation of the function of the Prophet as a reviver. It reflects the emphasis they laid on the character of Muhammad as a human religious and social reformer who had come to rectify and reform creeds and moral codes. Thus, according to Jamal Malik, "While prophetic sunna was considered a model for social and political reform, Muhammad came to be humanised."[18]

In general, during the socio-political instability of eighteenth-century India,[19] with the Mughal Empire disintegrating into smaller entities and facing the internal uprisings of the Marathas, Jats and Sikhs, as well as the external invasions of the Afghans and Persians,[20] the leaders of Sufi orders and reformist

---

22 (2014); and Muhammad Umar, "Mirza Mazhar Jan-i Janan: A Religious Reformer of the Eighteenth Century," *Studies in Islam* 6 (1969).

14　The Muhammadan Way is a broad theory that constructs the doctrinal foundation of not only several Sufi currents, but also anti-Sufis who refer to it from a different perspective. For a general survey of the notion of Muhammadan mysticism, see Mark Sedgwick, *Saints and Sons: The Making and Remaking of the Rashīdi Aḥmadi Sufi Order, 1799–2000* (Leiden: Brill, 2005), 27–49; Fazlur Rahman, *Islam* (Chicago: University of Chicago Press, 1979), 193–212; and Zachary Valentine Wright, *On the Path of the Prophet: Shaykh Ahmad Tijani and the Tariqa Muhammadiyya* (Atlanta: The African American Islamic Institute, 2005), 1–12 and 39–44.

15　Muhammad 'Abdul Haq Ansari, *Sufism and Shari'ah: A Study of Shaykh Ahmad Sirhindi's Effort to Reform Sufism* (London: The Islamic Foundation, 1986), 63.

16　John F. Richards, *The Mughal Empire* (Cambridge: Cambridge University Press, 1995), 99.

17　Ansari, *Sufism and Shari'ah*, 63.

18　Malik, *Islam in South Asia*, 18.

19　Jamal Malik clarifies the socio-political setting of post-Aurangzeb India and explains how the traditional social structure was confronting serious political and economic challenges. Pointing to new social formations in this period, he argues that, despite the disintegration of the Mughal Empire, the society was highly dynamic in various dimensions. See Malik, *Islam in South Asia*, 295–306.

20　On the political and social instability in eighteenth-century India that was, however, simultaneous with regional prosperity and development, see Malik, *Islam in South Asia*, 255–79. The desperate social and political instability in this era, especially in Delhi, has been described in detail in Rahman, *Islam*, 193–212; and John Obert Voll, *Islam: Continuity and Change in the Modern World* (Syracuse, NY: Syracuse University Press, 1994), 56–68.

Muslim scholars tried to motivate the desperate Muslim community by giving them a strong impetus to return to the time of the Prophet. This movement enthusiastically longed for the early age of Islam, when the Prophet had created a community with glory and power that was described as "the best of all nations" (*khayr al-umma*). This once glorious nation, however, now seemed unable to counteract the invasions by local rival groups and later by European powers. The ideal of Indian Muslims of the eighteenth century was the time when Muhammad led Muslims from victory to victory, hence they endeavored to return back to him and his age in the hopes that their community might be delivered from crisis.[21]

2 Mir Dard's Prophetology

Against this background of eighteenth-century India and in concordance with the social and religious challenges of his time, Khwaja Mir Dard (d. 1785) of Delhi,[22] a significant Sufi-scholar and theoretician of the *Tariqa Muhammadiyya Khalisa* ("Pure Muhammadan Path"), propagated his path. He declared that the only way of salvation for the people of Delhi, who were being subjected to unceasing attacks, famines and political instability, was a return to the Prophet in terms of both mystical return to and union with Muhammad's essence as well as reforming the character of individual Muslims according to his model of "descent."[23] Dard calls his path the "Comprehensive Way" (*Tariqa Jami'a*) and "the way of balance" (*i'tidal*), in order to show its most fundamental feature of encompassing both interior and exterior aspects of the believers' personality and reforming both their worldly and otherworldly life.[24] However,

---

21 Annemarie Schimmel, *And Muhammad is His Messenger: The Veneration of the Prophet in Islamic Piety* (Chapel Hill, NC: University of North Carolina Press, 1985), 225.
22 More information regarding the life and works of Dard and his father can be found in: Annemarie Schimmel, *Pain and Grace: A Study of Two Mystical Writers of Eighteenth-Century Muslim India* (Leiden: Brill, 1976), 31–102; Homayra Ziad, "Quest of the Nightingale: The Religious Thought of Khvājah Mīr Dard (1720–1785)" (PhD diss., Yale University, 2008), 28–106; Muhammad Seddiq Shibli, "Khwaja Mir Dard Dihlawi," in *Otharhwi Sadi 'Isawi Me Barr-i Saghir Me Islami ke Fikr ke Rahnoma*, ed. Muhammad Khalid Mas'ud (Islamabad: Idara-i Tahqiqat-i Islami, 2008), 275–301; and Zahir Ahmad Seddiqi, *Khwaja Mir Dard* (New Delhi: Taraqqi Urdu Bureau, 1983), 7–29.
23 Khwaja Mir Dard [hereafter: Dard], *'Ilm al-Kitab* (Delhi: Matba'a-i Ansari, 1890), 88–89 and 110–11.
24 Ibid., 164; Soraya Khodamoradi, "*Ṭarīqah Muḥammadiyyah* as *Ṭarīqah Jāmi'ah*: Khwājah Mīr Dard's Experience Beyond *Jamāl* and *Jalāl*," *Islamic Studies* 51, no. 4 (2012): 369.

his Pure Muhammadan Path is basically an exterior-oriented doctrine, as he accentuates the character of the Prophet as a perfect man who returned from his spiritual union with God back to the material world to guide humankind.[25] In Dard's thought, the Prophet, who in the minds of Muslim thinkers had been exalted into the deepest layers of the interior for centuries, needed to take the journey of descent from that exaltation to the lower world of witnessing, creatures and humankind, through the process of affirmation (*ithbat*) and subsistence (*baqa'*).[26]

Dard's prophetology thus displays a shift of focus in the perception and function of Muhammad compared to his dominant image in medieval and early Sufism.[27] This shift from the interior to the exterior, from annihilation in God to subsistence with Him, from identity and union with God to otherness and differentiation from Him, from ascent to descent, and finally from the otherworldly to this-worldly prophetic character can be well clarified through studying several key concepts that Dard propounded in his works. These include (a) "vicegerency of God" (*khalifat Allah*), (b) "patience and gratitude" (*sabr wa shukr*), (c) "clear and hidden announcement" (*balagh-i mubin wa balagh-i khafi*) and (d) the "pure Muhammadness" (*Muhammadiyya khalisa*). These notions are among the principles Dard uses to conceptualize the Prophetic descent from the heavens to the earth, and from a mystical entity and light to a social reformer and worldly human being who acquired even his spiritual status by virtue of his attachment with the material world.

---

25 Dard, *'Ilm al-Kitab*, 115–16.
26 Ibid., 313–14. *Ithbat* refers to the second half of the Muslim profession of faith (*shahada*), namely "but God," while the first half, or "there is no god," refers to *nafy* or negation. Hence, the affirmation points to divine immanence and the negation to divine transcendence. The concept of *baqa'* – which is usually used *vis-à-vis fana'* ("annihilation") – here shows that the ecstatic identification of the human self with God is merely a transient state and it is the "subsistence" with God which is a more advanced experience, permitting the simultaneous experience of God and the world, a state equivalent to prophetic consciousness.
27 For the dominant medieval image of the Prophet as light, a performer of miracles, ascendant to the heavens, the bridge between the Divinity and the created world, and a Logos chosen by God from the very moment of creation, all of which formed the mindset of the medieval Muslim folk, see Riexinger, "Rendering Muḥammad Human Again," 114–15; Gerhard Böwering, ed., *The Mystical Vision of Existence in Classical Islam: The Qur'ānic Hermeneutics of the Ṣūfī Sahl At-Tustarī (d. 283/896)* (Berlin: de Gruyter, 1980), 149–64, https://doi.org/10.1515/9783110837056.

2.1 Khalifat Allah

The vicegerency of God is a well-known Sufi concept modelled on the Prophet Muhammad himself.[28] As the Chishti Sufi Rukn al-Din Kashani (d. after 1337), a disciple of the Indian Chishti master Burhan al-Din Gharib (d. 1337), writes: "[R]eal vicegerency belonged to Lord Adam. As God said, 'I am placing a vicegerent on the earth'.[29] Then it came to Lord David [...]. Then it came to revered Prophet: 'I am the vicegerent of God'."[30] In Sufism in general, the vicegerent of God is also connected with the idea of the Perfect Man (*al-insan al-kamil*), who is defined as a spiritually transcendent personality united with God, so that his hearing and speaking and acts are considered as the very hearing and speaking and acts of God.[31] The Perfect Man is "comprehensive" (*jamiʿ*) of both the interior and the exterior.[32] In Ibn ʿArabi's (d. 1240) point of view, the divine vicegerent "becomes manifest within the cosmos displaying the names of God and his properties" in the same way that the sun becomes manifest in the moon, and the illuminated moon, wherein the sun sees itself, is then called the "full moon."[33] The image of *khalifat Allah* is thus connected with mystical union.

In explaining the concept of *khalifat Allah*, Dard highlights a specific aspect of God's vicegerent which had been undervalued due to the domination of ecstasy-oriented Sufism in India. That aspect is the vicegerent's awareness of the things belonging to the "lower" or material world and its partial details (*juzʾiyyat*). Dard believes that without such awareness, God's vicegerent would be unable to achieve mystical perfection. Yet this cognition is only possible through attachment of the soul to the body, since acquiring the knowledge of things requires a relationship with and attachment to them. Thus, the attachment of the human soul to the lower world is an inevitable process by means of which the human soul achieves the capability of knowing things

---

28 A.C.S. Peacock, *Islam, Literature and Society in Mongol Anatolia* (Cambridge: Cambridge University Press, 2019), 99, https://doi.org/10.1017/9781108582124.

29 Q 2:30.

30 Rukn al-Din Kashani, *Shamaʾil al-Atqiya*, ed. Sayyid ʿAtaʾ Husayn (Hyderabad: Matbuʿat Ashraf Press, 1928–29), 32–33, trans. in Carl W. Ernst, *Refractions of Islam in India: Situating Sufism and Yoga* (New Delhi: SAGE Publications/Yoda Press, 2016), 71.

31 William C. Chittick, "The Perfect Man as the Prototype of the Self in the Sufism of Jāmī," *Studia Islamica* 49 (1979), https://doi.org/10.2307/1595320.

32 Toshihiko Izutsu, *Sufism and Taoism: A Comparative Study of Key Philosophical Concepts* (Berkeley: University of California Press, 2016), 234–35.

33 Muhyi al-Din Ibn ʿArabi, *Al-Futuhat al-Makkiyya*, ed. Osman Yahya, vol. 11 (Cairo: Al-Hayʾa al-Misriyya al-ʿAmma li al-Kitab, 1972), 556; trans. in William C. Chittick, *The Sufi Path of Knowledge: Ibn al-ʿArabi's Metaphysics of Imagination* (Albany, NY: SUNY Press, 1989), 383.

and realities in the realm of the exterior and emanation, aside from its awareness of things and realities in the spiritual arena of the interior. This comprehensiveness encompasses both realms of matter and command (*khalq* and *amr*) in Quranic terms, which refer to the created universe as well as what is beyond that, containing the divine force that rules upon the material world.[34] Encompassing both the realms of *khalq* and *amr* is what Dard calls "the status of Muhammadan comprehensiveness"' (*jam'-i Muhammadi*), which is a cornerstone of his *Tariqa Muhammadiyya Khalisa*, also called *Tariqa Muhammadiyya Jami'a* ("Comprehensive Muhammadan Path").[35]

Although Dard considers such comprehensiveness an essential feature of *khalifat Allah*, in his discussions of the concept, he usually emphasizes the exterior realm of the material world. He asserts that the exterior is so important that if we were not attached to it and if we had not appeared in the seen world, we would not be able to be aware of the secrets of the unseen world. For him, becoming aware of the detachment of the rational soul (*tajarrud-i nafs-i natiqa*) is only possible when it is associated with the material and when material implements are achieved. Connected to this attachment is the "acquired knowledge" (*'ilm-i husuli*) or the "knowledge of details" (*'ilm-i tafsili*), which is highly significant as a necessary part of intuitional knowledge and human mystical perfection, since for Dard, the ascent of humankind is based on his knowledge, and acquiring knowledge depends on his possession of material implements belonging to the external world. This means that it is impossible to reach the eternal beatitude without noticing the world of emanation and attachment to the body.[36] In this way, in response to the damage caused by ecstasy-oriented Sufism in India, which had led to contempt for and devaluing of this-worldly life, Dard's interpretation of the prophetic attribute of God's vicegerency shifts the focus from the vicegerent's interior aspect, related to the spiritual ascent, to the exterior aspect, that is the need for the body and the external world for his perfection.

2.2 Sabr *and* Shukr

The subject of "patience and gratitude" has attracted the attention of various Muslim intellectuals, both before and after Dard. For instance, Ibn Qayyim

---

34 Q 7:54. For details about *khalq* and *amr*, see Abu al-Fazl Rashid al-Din Maybodi, *Kashf al-Asrar wa 'Udat al-Abrar*, vol. v, ed. 'Ali Asghar Hikmat (Tehran: Amir Kabir, 2003), 165; and Muhammad A'la ibn 'Ali al-Tahanawi, *Kashshāf Iṣṭilāḥāt al-Funūn*, ed. Aloys Sprenger et al. (Calcutta: Asiatic Society of Bengal, 1862), 1054.

35 Dard, *'Ilm al-Kitab*, 297; idem, *Chahar Risala* (Bhopal: Matba'a-i Shah Jahani, 1892), 30.

36 Idem, *'Ilm al-Kitab*, 298; and *Chahar Risala*, 31.

al-Jawziyya (d. 1350), the noteworthy medieval Hanbali jurist-theologian and the foremost student of the controversial and influential Sunni reformer Ibn Taymiyya (d.1328), dedicated a book to this topic entitled *'Uddat al-Sabirin wa Dhakhirat al-Shakirin* ("Supply of the Patient and Repertoire of the Thankful"), wherein he conceived of faith as a whole of which one half is patience and the other half is gratitude.[37] In Sufism, patience and gratitude are two mystical stages among various foundational stages through which the initiate must pass. Sufis believe that there are a myriad ways to God, and the disciple has to proceed through certain stages of spiritual development.[38] Many Sufi authors and Muslim thinkers, such as Abu Talib al-Makki (d. 998), al-Qushayri (d. 986), al-Ghazali (d. 1111) and Shahab al-Din Yahya Suhrawardi (d. 1191), dedicated chapters of their works to these stages,[39] and some of them, like 'Abd Allah Ansari (d. 1088), composed entire books devoted to this subject.[40] Different Sufi writers have enumerated these spiritual degrees on the path of mystical perfection in varying lists and sequences thereof, including penitence (*tawba*), patience (*sabr*), gratitude (*shukr*), hope (*raja*), fear (*khawf*), poverty (*faqr*), asceticism (*zuhd*), unity (*tawhid*), dependence upon God (*tawakkul*) and love (*mahabba*).[41]

In Sufi literature, it is often mentioned that whatever is manifested as misfortune/hated and fortune/favored is, in fact, the act of the divine Beloved, and one should be satisfied and show gratitude when confronting it. For several

---

[37] Ibn Qayyim al-Jawziyya, *'Uddat al-Sabirin wa Dhakhirat al-Shakirin* (Damascus and Beirut: Dar ibn Kathir, 1989), 10.

[38] Among the maxims Sufis refer to in this regard is "the ways towards God are as many as the believers [or as many as the created things]." See Margaret Smith, *Rābi'a the Mystic and Her Fellow-Saints in Islām* (Cambridge and New York: Cambridge University Press: 1984), 50. For a comparative study of the mystical stages, see Saeed Zarrabi-Zadeh, "Practical Mysticism: Its Definition, Parts and Characteristics," *Studies in Spirituality* 19 (2009), https://doi.org/10.2143/SIS.19.0.2043669.

[39] Shahab al-Din Yahya ibn Habash Suhrawardi, *Sih Risalih az Shaykh-i Ishraq: Al-Alwah al-'Amadiyya, Kalimat al-Tasawwuf, al-Lamhat*, ed. Najafquli Habibi (Tehran: Anjuman-i Shahanshahi-yi Falsafa-yi Iran, 1977), 122–27; Khwaja 'Abd Allah Ansari, *Majmu'i-yi Rasa'ili Farsi*, ed. Muhammad Sarwar Mawlayi (Tehran: Tus, 1994), 16; Abu Hamid al-Ghazali, *Kimiya-yi Sa'adat*, vol. 2 (Tehran: Intisharat 'Ilmi Farhangi, 1987), 317,307,480,606; 'Abd al-Karim ibn Hawazin al-Qushayri, *Tarjama-yi Risala-yi Qushayriyya*, ed. Badi' al-Zaman Furuzanfar (Tehran: Intisharat-i 'Ilmi Farhangi, 1998), 135–466.

[40] *Manazil al-Sa'irin* or "Stations of the Wayfarers" (Persian version: *Sad Maydan*) is one of the pillars of practical Sufism which details the spiritual stages leading to annihilation in and union with God. See A.G. Ravân Farhâdi, *'Abdullāh Anṣārī of Herât (1006–1089 C.E.): An Early Ṣūfī Master* (Richmond, Surrey: Curzon Press, 1996), 73–77.

[41] Abu Talib al-Makki, *Qut al-Qulub fi Mu'amalat al-Mahbub*, ed. Sa'id Nasib Makarim, vol. 1 (Beirut: Dar Sadir, 1995), 361.

early Sufis, insofar as satisfaction (*rida'*) and gratitude are natural responses to circumstances pleasing to the soul, they are not the consequence of any real moral struggle or effort, and therefore are not particularly distinctive virtues. Instead, true virtue is found in experiencing satisfaction in the face of the bitter blows of fate and in response to those circumstances of loss that produce distress, anxiety, suffering and pain.[42] The stories and words of many Sufis support and encourage the behavior of gratitude in response to misfortune – as a status of spiritual and moral virtue.[43] A famous tale in this regard, repeated in the books of early Sufis, is narrated in *Hadiqat al-Haqiqa* ("The Garden of Truth") of the Sufi-poet Sana'i (d. ca. 1130):

> An Iraqian Sufi visited a sheikh from Khurasan and asked him about real Sufism as taught in his country. He replied that, when God sent them something they would eat it and be grateful, if not, they would endure patience and take the wish out of the heart. Whereupon the Iraqian Sufi replied: "That kind of Sufism is what our dogs do in Iraq–when they find a bone they eat it, otherwise they are patient and leave it." Being asked by his companion how he, then, would define Sufism, he answered: "When we have anything we prefer others to ourselves [i.e., give it away], if not, we occupy ourselves with thanks and pray for forgiveness."[44]

Dard views the mystical perspective reflected in such Sufi stories as the result of the cessation of the senses and detachment from the physical world, due to which the Sufi saints express words indicating their unawareness of reality under the domination of mystical intoxication. Conceiving of *sabr* and *shukr* as prophetic attributes, he reconsiders these concepts and uses them as containers for explaining the importance of the exterior. He argues that considering the difference between fortune and misfortune as simply illusory, as Sufis experience in the status of intoxication, is inconsistent with several examples from the Quran and hadith about the patience the prophets displayed while experiencing misfortune in their lives. In his viewpoint, if cessation of the senses

---

42 Atif Khalil, "Contentment, Satisfaction and Good-Pleasure: *Rida* in Early Sufi Moral Psychology," *Studies in Religion/Sciences Religieuses* 43, no. 3 (2014): 375, https://doi.org/10.1177/0008429814538227.
43 For the famous story of Rabi'a (d. 801) in this regard, see al-Makki, *Qut al-Qulub*, vol. 2, 80.
44 Abu al-Majd Majdud Sana'i Ghaznawi, *Hadiqat al-Haqiqa wa Shari'at al-Tariqa*, ed. Muhammad Taqi Mudarris Razawi (Tehran: Tehran University Press, 1950); trans. in Annemarie Schimmel, *Mystical Dimensions of Islam* (Chapel Hill, NC: University of North Carolina Press, 1975), 125.

and lack of emotion toward and reaction against this-worldly matters was the true way, the prophets would be neither grateful nor patient. Finding the idea of equating fortune and misfortune, based on viewing good as identical with evil, as harmful for society, Dard tried to warn Muslims that the equating of fortune and misfortune belongs only to the arena of spiritual intoxication and is related to the inner world. For him, the rules and the conditions of the realm of the interior are different from those of the exterior, and it is necessary in the external and worldly life to differentiate between fortune and misfortune. Dard also asserts that considering misfortune and fortune as identical is meaningless and goes against both reason and tradition. Even if one supposes that they are really identical, it is not relevant and important, because that is also the status which every stone or any other inanimate object enjoys.[45]

In this manner, Dard invites Muslims to accept the reality of fortune and misfortune as distinct experiences and to take the position of patience while confronting misfortune, and of gratitude while confronting fortune. Nevertheless, based on the principle of comprehensiveness, he does not deny the value of equating good with evil and fortune with misfortune as a stage in the process of mystical wayfaring. However respectable such a level of identification may be, Dard's final mystical dwelling place is the stable stage of awareness after intoxication (*sahw-i b'ad az sukr*), which is the prophetic status of the highest perfection in which one differentiates every degree from other degrees. Here, if something happens to the perfected Sufi that he is supposed to be patient towards, he shows patience, and if something happens to him that he is supposed to be grateful for, he is so. Dard's ideal, consistent with his comprehensive mysticism, is when the capacity for witnessing divine unity is achieved, while at the same time man differentiates between things and realities and returns back to the multiplicity of the material world after the experience of unity.[46]

2.3 Balagh-i Mubin *and* Balagh-i Khafi

Clear announcement or *balagh-i mubin* has been considered as one of the tasks and attributes of prophets by many Muslim interpreters of the Quran. This concept means that prophets are obliged to express the message of God clearly and without any ambiguity or obscurity. If people do not accept and act according to the clear messages of the prophets, then the prophets would not be responsible for such people's ignorance.[47] As mentioned in the Quranic

---

45 Dard, *Chahar Risala*, 5 and 16.
46 Idem, *'Ilm al-Kitab*, 313–14.
47 See "Tafsir al-Mizan [of Tabataba'yi]," Quran Anhar, accessed March 26, 2020, quran.anhar.ir/tafsirfull-13749.htm.

verse "yet is aught for the Messengers, but to deliver the manifest Message?,"[48] Dard also conceives of clear announcement as a prophetic act and attribute and he defines his own mission as being along the lines of those of the prophets, while differentiating it from the teachings of the Sufi *shaykh*s, which he considers hidden. In his viewpoint, "hidden announcement" (*balagh-i khafi*) means to speak with people of matters that are internal, incomprehensible, unachievable and unclear, contrary to clear announcement, which is to speak with them about matters which are external, understandable, achievable and lucid. Following the declarations of the prophets that "it is only for us to deliver the Manifest Message,"[49] Dard asserts that the function of a Muhammadan (follower of Dard's path) is to affirm those affairs that are, contrary to internal affairs (*amr-i mubtin*), clear and external (*zahir va rowshan*) for every ordinary man. According to him, clear announcement addresses both common Muslims and elites and makes both aware of the righteousness of their exterior matters in order to help them achieve salvation. His effort to shift from the well-established language of Sufism to that of the Quran and hadith in order to make Sufism comprehensible for the majority of Muslims is also based on a change in orientation from the interior to the exterior.[50]

Additionally, Dard declares that through clear announcement, God's messengers speak of the injunctions of the shari'a, its orders and prohibitions which clearly define right and wrong, Islam and blasphemy, the right of God and the right of His servants, and the benefits and interests (*maslahat*) of this world and the other. All these topics, which are expressed and taught under the title of clear announcement, affirm the external degrees, viz., those that occur during the process of mystical descent. This process consists of turning towards this world during the mystical journey of self-perfection and experiencing God's process of creation and reaffirming the degrees and differences (*ithbat-i maratib*).[51] Therefore, although the message of the Muhammadans contains the interior, it is explained and announced in the form of the exterior and affirmation.[52] Due to their method of clear announcement, the Muhammadans abstain from ecstatic utterances, and their speech respects the external rites (*adab*) of the shari'a, though while also containing the interior truth as well. Hence, the exterior should be stressed because, on the one hand, it supplies for the needs of those who have the potential for spiritual development and are in

---

48   Q 16:35 (Arberry translation).
49   Q 36:17 (Arberry translation).
50   Dard, *'Ilm al-Kitab*, 3 and 6.
51   Ibid., 355–56.
52   For "affirmation" or *ithbat*, see footnote 26 above.

search of truth and deeper arenas of reality, and on the other, it is a secure way of life for the masses, protecting them from moral deficiencies caused by the unclear way of the interior.[53] This is a prophetic method of announcing God's message among the people and addressing the different strata of society.

Thus, the Prophet's task of addressing the people with a clear message, his attribute of God's vicegerency and his behavior of patience and gratitude all reflect the focus in Dard's Sufism on the aspects of the exterior, awareness, subsistence and descent. They also exhibit how Dard's teachings represent a change with regard to how Muhammad's character and function is perceived. All these attributes and behaviors are also applied to Dard's followers, pure Muhammadis, who in his viewpoint join their identities with that of the Prophet and are annihilated in him in the mystical stage of "pure Muhammadness."[54]

2.4 Prophetic Descent and "Pure Muhammadness"

Notwithstanding his strong emphasis on the exterior, Dard does not undervalue the interior realm. Such underestimation would not be consistent with his Comprehensive Way, whose slogan is indeed a balance in both internal and external arenas.[55] The interior aspect of the Prophet in Dard's doctrine is manifested in a significant mystical principle and stage that is central to the Pure Muhammadan Path, namely "annihilation in the Prophet" (*fana' fi al-Rasul*). Dard asserts that although the general knowledge of the Muhammadan Path is primarily based on the Quran and hadith, the followers of this Path are in every moment in a direct relationship with Muhammad, gain knowledge directly from him and follow his pure essence, which is the ontological cause of all existents. He considers Muhammadis as those who are one step further than all other Muslims due to their immediate connection with the Prophet through union with the Muhammadan reality (*haqiqa Muhammadiyya*). According to Dard, this perfection can be achieved through his father and Sufi master Muhammad Nasir 'Andalib (d. 1758), whom he describes as having reached the final of all perfections (*khatam-i kamalat*) and a master experiencing the most complete annihilation in the reality of Muhammad or *Muhammadiyya Khalisa*. This experience is the highest stage in Dard's practical mysticism,[56] incorporating all levels of mystical ascent (towards God) and descent (from God). In this spiritual fulfillment, the wayfarer's attention to both God and creation is

---

53 Dard, *'Ilm al-Kitab*, 61, 283–84.
54 Soraya Khodamoradi, *Sufi Reform in Eighteenth Century India: Khwaja Mir Dard of Delhi (1721–1785)* (Berlin: EB-Verlag, 2019), 232.
55 Ibid.
56 Dard, *'Ilm al-Kitab*, 83–85 and 113.

balanced and he achieves the quality of real certitude (*haqq al-yaqin*). Here, both exterior and interior stages are passed through and man is entrusted with the responsibility of guiding others,[57] similar to the Prophet Muhammad, who had access to both the stages of annihilation in Allah and subsistence with Him due to the divine will.[58]

Annihilation in the Prophet as presented in Dard's doctrine refers to a state traversing sainthood, reaching prophethood and becoming stable in the most particular state of "pure Muhammadness." It is the stage of both annihilation in and subsistence with Muhammad, which not only contains all his interior states, including intoxication into and identification with God, but it also involves awareness, sobriety, subsistence, guidance, prophetic mission, differentiation between good and evil, and propounding the regulations of the shariʿa based on the conditions of the exterior realm. Emphasizing these latter Prophetic aspects, Dard considers them as principles which the Muslim society of his time was in growing and urgent need of. Thus for him, it was imperative that they understand and apply these principles in their individual lives and in society.[59]

3   Sacralizing vs. Humanizing the Prophet before Mir Dard

The image of Muhammad as the "prophet of ascent and the interior," which alongside his being the "prophet of descent and the exterior" forms the highest mystical experience in Dard's *Tariqa Muhammadiyya Khalisa,* had already been constructed in earlier Muslim thought, specifically during the medieval era in the context of prevailing notions such as Muhammadan pre-existence, "Muhammadan light" (*nur-i Muhammadi*) and "Muhammadan reality" (*haqiqa Muhammadiyya*). The concept of Muhammad's pre-existence, which was widely developed by Sufis, is indeed rooted in the early Islamic tradition. In a hadith transmitted in the canonical compilation of al-Tirmidhi (d. 892), in reply to the question of when prophethood was decreed for him; Muhammad says that it was "When Adam was between the spirit and the body."[60] This hadith, which was widely circulated, suggests that Muhammad's prophetic mission

---

57   Ibid., 88.
58   Ibid., 115–16.
59   Ibid., 207.
60   Muhammad ibn ʿIsa al-Tirmidhi, *Sunan al-Tirmidhi,* ed. Muhammad Nasir al-Din al-Albani (Riyadh: Maktabat al-Maʿarif, n.d.), 821, Hadith no. 3609.

was predetermined before the appearance of any of the other prophets, in fact during the time that Adam's creation was still in process.

In the imagination of some Muslims and specifically Sufis, it came to be believed that the light of Muhammad was the primordial substance from which all other elements of creation, including the prophets, were brought forth. This idea originated in early biographies of the Prophet, such as Ibn Ishaq's *sira*, which describes how before Muhammad was conceived, his father's forehead was shining with light.[61] In addition to biographies, the image of Muhammad as light is also reflected in certain hadith. For instance, a tradition that goes back to Jabir ibn 'Abd Allah and that was frequently referenced and interpreted by pre-modern Sufis in legitimating the theory of Muhammadan primogeniture reads: "The first thing that God created was my light."[62] Sufis commonly interpretated this hadith to mean that Muhammad was created out of God's light and therefore his creation preceded that of Adam and the world itself. In the Sufi context, Sahl al-Tustari (d. 896) was among the earliest to bring forth the notion of the pre-eternal *nur-i Muhammadi*.[63] Later on, the well-known Sufi al-Hallaj (d. 922) wrote that the Prophet was the cause and goal of creation, supporting this assertion by quoting a *qudsi* ("sacred") hadith that says: "If you [Muhammad] had not been, I would not have created the heavens."[64] This theme came to be addressed in other Sufi texts like the works of 'Ayn al-Qudat Hamadani (d. 1131), especially his *Tamhidat*, as well as the writings of Najm al-Din Kubra (d. 1221) and Najm al-Din Razi (d. 1256). In Ibn 'Arabi's school, the term *al-insan al-kamil* was used as a mystical stage identified with the spirit of Muhammad, or the eternal Muhammadan reality.[65] Hence, the notion of

---

61 Alfred Guillaume, *The Life of Muhammad: A Translation of Ishāq's Sīrat Rasūl Allāh* (New York: Oxford University Press, 1955), 68–69.

62 On this hadith, see 'Ayn al-Qudat Hamadani, *Tamhīdāt*, trans. Christiane Tortel [as *Les tentations métaphysiques*] (Paris: Les Deux Océans, 1992), 130, 169, 229, 238, 266; and Uri Rubin, "Pre-existence and Light: Aspects of the Concept of Nūr Muḥammad," *Israel Oriental Studies* 5 (1975): 98–104.

63 Claude Addas, "At the Distance of Two Bows' Length or Even Closer: The Figure of the Prophet in the Work of 'Abd al-Karīm al-Jīlī (Part 1)," *Journal of the Muhyiddin Ibn 'Arabi Society* 45 (2009): 72; Böwering, *The Mystical Vision of Existence*, 149–51. See also Abu Muhammad Sahl ibn 'Abd Allah al-Tustari, *Tafsir al-Qur'an al-'Azim*, ed. M. Basil 'Uyun al-Suwd (Beirut: Dar al-Kutub al-'Ilmiyya, 2002), 68–69.

64 Schimmel, *Mystical Dimensions of Islam*, 215. This hadith is mentioned in Muhammad ibn 'Ali al-Shawkani, *Al-Fawa'id al-Majmu'a fi al-Ahadith al-Mawdu'a*, vol. 1, ed. Muhammad 'Abd al-Rahman 'Awad (Beirut: Dar al-Kitab al-'Arabi, 1986), 346. *Qudsi* hadith are the Prophet's sayings the content of which is from God, but the words are from Muhammad. Although these hadiths are revealed directly from God to Muhammad, they do not form part of the Quran and are rather considered as Prophetic tradition.

65 Ibn 'Arabi, *Al-Futuhat al-Makkiyya*, vol. 1, 134–35 and 144–45.

Muhammadan light that played a significant role in constructing the image of a heavenly Prophet in Muslim minds can be traced back to the ninth century, with further development in Sufi literature especially after the twelfth century.

Elevating Muhammad to a divine level and proliferating a kind of devotion to and even worshipping of the Prophet in medieval Muslim culture developed partly through popular poetry that used to be recited in Sufi lodges (*khanaqah*) during rituals or on the occasion of Muhammad's birthday. For centuries before Dard's time, the idea of the pre-existence of the light of Muhammad and its origination at the beginning of creation and its migration through the loins of the Prophet's ancestors had become an integral element of the paradigmatic *mawlid* narrative.[66] Such poetry, besides other attributes of the Prophet, extolled his physical beauty and moral virtues (*shama'il* and *fada'il*), recalling and elaborating on qualities like *'isma* ("infallibility") and Muhammadan light.[67]

Similar to the experience of a *heavenly* Prophet, the image of a *human* Prophet and attention to his worldly figure and functions has been an aspect of Muslim thought since the beginning of Islam, although in several discourses, such as in medieval Sufism, where it was marginalized and lost its color under the shade of the more prevalent image of a heavenly Prophet. In fact, focusing on the human side of Muhammad before the eighteenth century raised voices in opposition to the mystical concepts and forms of piety that had gradually become dominant elements of Muslim devotion to the Prophet. Long before the *Tariqa Muhammadiyya Khalisa* brought forth the theoretical basis for calling attention to the human side of Muhammad and the descending and exterior aspects of his prophethood, one can see outstanding cases of questioning and criticizing approaches and rituals that elevate the Prophet to a superhuman status. One of the most vigorous among these voices here was al-Ghazali, whose works were energetically restudied and taught by Sufi reformers of the modern era. Interpreting the hadith "I am the first of the prophets to be created, and the last of them to be sent," he argued that the word "created" means that God determined the existence of Muhammad rather than bringing him into existence. Thus, before his mother gave birth to him, the Prophet was not created and did not exist. Al-Ghazali likens the priority of Muhammad to the map of a house that pre-exists its construction in the mind of the builder.

---

66   Marion Holmes Katz, *The Birth of the Prophet Muhammad: Devotional Piety in Sunni Islam* (Abingdon and New York: Routledge, 2007), 15.

67   Riexinger, "Rendering Muḥammad Human Again," 104; Tilman Nagel, *Allahs Liebling: Ursprung und Erscheinungsformen des Mohammedglaubens* (Munich: Oldenbourg, 2008), 153–80, 351–52; and Rubin, "Pre-existence and Light," 62–119.

Although the finished house is the last stage of its physical construction, this finished house is first pre-figured in the imagination of the architect.[68]

Another figure who also criticized the idea of the Prophet's pre-existence and primordial light is Ibn Taymiyya. He declared that, like all other prophets and human beings, Muhammad was born from his parents and his spirit was breathed into him by God. Ibn Taymiyya also challenged the idea of the infallibility of the Prophet, for example through asserting the historicity of the story of the cranes. This account refers to the event of the migration of Muhammad's followers to Ethiopia due to their persecution by the Quraysh, when Muhammad's followers in Mecca gathered to pray in public and Muhammad recited *sura* 53 of the Quran. After mentioning the three goddesses in verses 19–20 ("Have you considered al-Lat and al-'Uzza and al-Manat, the third, the other?"), Satan puts, according to the story, the following words into the Prophet's mouth: "they are the high flying [or exalted] cranes whose intercession is to be asked for." On this occasion, thinking that Muhammad had now accepted the pagan goddesses, the pagans of Mecca prostrated themselves. Here, Ibn Taymiyya affirms that the Prophet, as any human individual, is liable to making mistakes.[69] Later on in the eighteenth century, Ibn 'Abd al-Wahhab also followed Ibn Taymiyya and affirmed the historicity of the story.[70]

4 Positive Approach to the World and Mir Dard's Prophetology

The propensity of eighteenth-century Sufis to focus on the Prophet as a human, to underscore his social and political character, and to emphasize his descent and subsistence, had its roots in an increasing tendency among well-known Muslim Sufis and scholars towards a general worldly approach to various dimensions of life. On the one hand, Sufis and scholars of this time emphasized the mystical stages related to the world of creatures, matter and the body, such as distinction and sobriety. On the other hand, they stressed the benefits of moral and social felicity in this world.[71] They also propounded

---

68 Katz, *The Birth of the Prophet Muhammad*, 14. See Abu Hamid al-Ghazali, *Nafkhu al-Ruh wa al-Taswiya*, ed. Ahmad Hijazi al-Saqa (Cairo: Maktabat al-Madina al-Munawwara, 1979).

69 Taqi al-Din Ahmad ibn Taymiyya, *Minhaj al-Sunna al-Nabawiyya fi Naqd Kalam al-Shi'a wa al-Qadariyya*, vol. 1, ed. Muhammad Rashad Salim (Riyadh: Jami'at al-Imam Muhammad ibn Sa'ud, 1986), 471.

70 Rexinger, "Rendering Muḥammad Human Again," 105 and 111–14. See Ibn 'Abd al-Wahhab, *Mukhtasar Sirat al-Rasul*, 63.

71 Rahman, *Islam*, 209.

worldly-oriented interpretations of religious beliefs, as can be observed in Wali Allah's discussing the requital for man's practices in this world as well as results of human actions on earth in the afterlife.[72]

Against such a background, Dard calls Muslims' attention to the more visible level of reality. His mysticism is a portrait of his endeavor to bring Muslims back from the interior (*batin*) realm of life – related to mystical experiences, particularly the experience of union with God, and the mystical states of intoxication and ecstasy – to its exterior (*zahir*) sphere related to normal worldly and social life. His strong emphasis on awareness (*agahi*), wakefulness (*bidari*), alertness (*hushyari*), sobriety (*sahw*), subsistence (*baqa'*), descent (*nuzul*), morality (*adab/akhlaq*), regulations of the shari'a and the exterior aspect of the Quran and hadith[73] indicates a shift of emphasis in the *Tariqa Muhammadiyya Khalisa* from the interior domain of life to its exterior sphere, which in his view had been underestimated by the extreme attention Sufis paid to mystical ecstasy.[74]

Dard considers experiencing a good worldly life (*husn-i ma'ash*) as important as achieving a good otherworldly life (*husn-i ma'ad*). In this regard, he emphasizes the endeavor of humans to rectify their bodies (*islah-i ajsad*) and to reform their hearts (*islah-i qulub*),[75] which indicates his change of approach to the world from negative to positive. This alteration was, among other things, a reaction to the view of intoxication-oriented Sufism, which considered the world as image, illusion, non-existent and therefore worthless.[76] The widespread outlook on the world as illusion and devaluating it as insignificant among Indian Muslims under the influence of the ideology of *hama ust* ("everything is He") had led to moral deficiencies such as indifference, ease and lack of responsibility in South Asian Muslim society.[77] Cessation in the realm of the interior, according to Dard, leads to moral deficiencies due to transcending evil and good in the state of mystical union and intoxication, and subsequently ignoring free will and responsibility for one's deeds.[78]

Although, due to his adherence to the mystical principle of union, Dard is not reluctant to consider this world as a mere image, he takes this image

---

72 Wali Allah, *The Conclusive Argument*, 96, 115–16.
73 Khodamoradi, *Sufi Reform in Eighteenth Century India*, 173–87.
74 Dard, *'Ilm al-Kitab*, 98, 120, 151–52, 183, 313–14 and 355–56.
75 Ibid., 74.
76 Arthur John Arberry, *Sufism: An Account of the Mystics of Islam* (London: Allen & Unwin, 1950), 5.
77 Soraya Khodamoradi, "Sufi Reform and the Mystical Ideology of Divine Unity," *Peshawar Islamicus* 3, no. 2 (July-December 2012).
78 Dard, *'Ilm al-Kitab*, 74.

seriously, maintains recognition and authenticity for it, and warns others against ignoring this world simply because of its being an image.[79] Thus, he opposes using and expanding the conditions of mystical union (which transcends any duality and diversity, including that of good and evil) to the world of multiplicity and declares that as long as humans live in this world of distinction, they are in need of morality as a significant requisite for worldly life.[80] In this connection, Dard discusses the problem of the contradiction between human free will and the divine name of the Advocator (*Wakil*) and asserts that to exercise reasonable management and to care about external matters does not go against reliance upon God and accepting His absolute advocacy. Human policy (*tadbir*) is a part of divine destiny and an element of human perfection, and true Sufis deal with all affairs of life according to the intellect and reason.[81]

Dard also sees the "science of ethics" (*'ilm-i akhlaq*) from a worldly perspective. He suggests applying the methodology and rules of the science of medicine to ethics, calling this the "medicine of ethics" (*tib-i akhlaq*) or "interior medicine" (*tib-i batini*). He intends to propound a method of clear examination and treatment of problems of the soul in the same way the problems of the body are examined. In this technique, moral deficiencies are considered illnesses that can be remedied by prophets and saints, who play the role of physicians and professionals in treating such spiritual illnesses.[82] He also exhibits his worldly approach through the advocacy of happiness rather than sorrow, emphasizing cheerfulness and criticizing sourness as an anti-moral feature.[83] Dard's strong positive approach toward the world through his accentuation of such concepts as a "good worldly life" and the "rectification of bodies," his emphasis on the active role of humans in this life, especially based on the value of human policy and the observation of external causes, and his concentration on ethics in terms of medicine, is indeed aligned with his emphasis on the descent aspect of Muhammad's prophethood.[84]

---

79   Ibid. In some of his works, Dard shows a tendency toward seclusion and distance from the world. See, for example, idem, *Chahar Risala*, 20–21, 33 and 37. In *Diwan-i Dard* (Lahore: Majlis-i Taraqqi-i Adab, 1962) he looks at the world as a dream or a tale; see also Schimmel, *Pain and Grace*, 101.
80   Dard, *'Ilm al-Kitab*, 75; and idem, *Chahar Risala*, 43.
81   Idem, *'Ilm al-Kitab*, 215, 220. However, Dard occasionally prefers love over intellect in his poetry, for instance in Dard, *Diwan-i Farsi* (Delhi: Matba'a-i Ansari, 1891), 8.
82   Idem, *'Ilm al-Kitab*, 233–36.
83   Ibid., 224 and 309–10; Idem, *Diwan-i Farsi*, 6.
84   After the eighteenth century, one can observe the academic efforts in producing history-based literature on the life of the Prophet. In a recent paper, Jamal Malik propounds a critical summary of such development in German scholarship. See Jamal Malik, "A

5   Conclusion

Over the course of the eighteenth century, while European authors such as Boulainvilliers and Pastoret portrayed Muhammad as a religious legislator and statesman, outstanding Muslim reformers such as Shah Wali Allah and Muhammad ibn ʿAbd al-Wahhab were stressing the Prophet's social and political role and presenting him as a reformist social leader. Some of these scholars and activist Sufis distanced themselves critically from the Prophet's heavenly spiritual image that had been the concern of Muslim minds and the focus of their spiritual sentiments during the preceding centuries due to, among other factors, the domination of mysticism and ecstasy-oriented Sufism. Against this background, Dard called Muslims' attention to the more visible level of reality and emphasized Sufi notions pointing to the world of creation and mystical stages related to the initiate's returning back to the material world during his or her spiritual advancement, such as the exterior, awareness, wakefulness, alertness, sobriety, subsistence and descent. He focused on the worldly and external aspect of Muhammad rather than his mystical dimension that had been extensively predominant in medieval Islam. In Dard's doctrine, the Prophet, who had been exalted into the deepest layers of the interior for centuries, takes the journey of descent from that exaltation to the lower world of witnessing, creatures and humankind, through the process of affirmation and subsistence, which are mystical stages pointing to the presence of a saint in the material sphere and in worldly social life.

Dard's interpretation of the Sufi subjects of the "vicegerent of God," "clear and hidden announcement" and "patience and gratitude" forms the theoretical foundation for a shift of focus on the figure and function of the Prophet compared to Muhammad's dominant image in medieval and early Sufism. This shift represents the descent of the Prophet from the heavens to the earth, and from a mystical perfect man, a spiritual entity and light to a worldly human being living among and guiding the people; a Prophet who even acquired his spiritual status by way of his attachment to the material world. Dard evinces such a change in orientation by depicting a journey of the Prophet from the interior to the exterior, from annihilation in God to subsistence with Him, from identity and union with God to otherness and differentiation from Him, and from ascent to descent. For Dard, the *khalifat Allah*, whose most complete example is Muhammad, not only acquires the ability to know things and

Survey and Assessment of German Approaches to *Sīrah*," *Islamic Studies* 58, no. 3 (July-September 2019).

realities in the realm of the exterior by means of attachment to the body and matter, but he also achieves his spiritual detachment through his association with material implements. The ascent of the *khalifat Allah* is based on "acquiring knowledge," which itself depends on the possession of material apparatuses belonging to the external world. After accomplishing the highest process of ascent, the *khalifat Allah* descends from union with God and turns his face once again to the world in order to guide others.

Dard believes that, since the Prophet's final dwelling place is the external world of witnessing, he shows gratefulness when experiencing fortune and patience when confronting misfortune, a behavior that is in line with the conditions of worldly life, contrary to satisfaction with misfortune, which is a behavior related to the arena of mystical intoxication. Dard's ideal man, consistent with his comprehensive mysticism, is a person who has achieved the ability of witnessing divine unity, while at the same time differentiating between things and realities of the material world. The inhabitants of this stage are the descended prophets who speak clearly with people about matters which are external, achievable and lucid, as opposed to the hidden and incomprehensible messages of Sufi *shaykh*s. A significant component of these external and clear issues is the shari'a and its orders and prohibitions, which reform both the worldly and otherworldly lives of the believers.

The prophetic attribute of the vicegerency of God, his displaying patience and gratitude, and his task of addressing people with a clear message all reflect Dard's accentuation of the aspects of the exterior, awareness, subsistence and descent in his Sufism. His thought thus represents a significant change in how Muhammad's function and character were perceived. All of these attributes and behaviors are also applied to Dard's followers, namely the pure Muhammadis, who in his viewpoint join their identities with that of the Prophet and are annihilated in him. Notwithstanding his considerable stress on subsistence and the exterior, Dard does not, however, undervalue the interior. He in fact affirms that his followers are in every moment in a direct relationship with Muhammad, gaining knowledge from and following his pure essence.

Bibliography

Addas, Claude. "At the Distance of Two Bows' Length or Even Closer: The Figure of the Prophet in the Work of 'Abd al-Karīm al-Jīlī (part 1)." *Journal of the Muhyiddin Ibn 'Arabi Society* 45 (2009): 65–88.

Ansari, Khwaja 'Abd Allah. *Majmu'i-yi Rasa'il-i Farsi*, edited by Muhammad Sarwar Mawlayi. Tehran: Tus, 1994.

Ansari, Muhammad 'Abdul Haq. *Sufism and Shari'ah: A Study of Shaykh Ahmad Sirhindi's Effort to Reform Sufism*. London: The Islamic Foundation, 1986.

Arberry, Arthur John. *Sufism: An Account of the Mystics of Islam*. London: Allen & Unwin, 1950.

Böwering, Gerhard, ed. *The Mystical Vision of Existence in Classical Islam: The Qur'ānic Hermeneutics of the Ṣūfī Sahl At-Tustarī (d. 283/896)*. Berlin: de Gruyter, 1980, https://doi.org/10.1515/9783110837056.

Chittick, William C. "The Perfect Man as the Prototype of the Self in the Sufism of Jāmī." *Studia Islamica* 49 (1979): 135–57, https://doi.org/10.2307/1595320.

Chittick, William C. *The Sufi Path of Knowledge: Ibn al-'Arabi's Metaphysics of Imagination*. Albany, NY: SUNY Press, 1989.

Dard, Khwaja Mir. *Chahar Risala*. Bhopal: Matba'a-i Shah Jahani, 1892.

Dard, Khwaja Mir. *Diwan-i Dard*. Lahore: Majlis-i Taraqqi-i Adab, 1962.

Dard, Khwaja Mir. *Diwan-i Farsi*. Delhi: Matba'a-i Ansari, 1891.

Dard, Khwaja Mir. *'Ilm al-Kitab*. Delhi: Matba'a-i Ansari, 1890.

De Boulainvilliers, Henri. *The Life of Mahomet*. Translated by anon. London: W. Hinchliffe, 1731.

De Pastoret, Claude-Emmanuel Joseph Pierre. *Zoroastre, Confucius et Mahomet: Comparés comme Sectaires, Législateurs et Moralistes*. Paris: Buisson, 1787.

Di Cesare, Michelina. "The Prophet in the Book: Images of Muhammad in Western Medieval Book Culture." In *Constructing the Image of Muhammad in Europe*, edited by Avinoam Shalem, 9–32. Berlin: de Gruyter, 2013, https://doi.org/10.1515/9783110300864.9.

Ernst, Carl W. *Refractions of Islam in India: Situating Sufism and Yoga*. New Delhi: SAGE Publications/Yoda Press, 2016.

Farhâdi, A.G. Ravân. *'Abdullāh Anṣārī of Herāt (1006–1089 C.E.): An Early Ṣūfī Master*. Richmond, Surrey: Curzon Press, 1996.

Al-Ghazali, Abu Hamid. *Kimiya-yi Sa'adat*, 2 vols. Tehran: Intisharat 'Ilmi Farhangi, 1987.

Al-Ghazali, Abu Hamid. *Nafkhu al-Ruh wa al-Taswiya*, edited by Ahmad Hijazi al-Saqa. Cairo: Maktabat al-Madina al-Munawwara, 1979.

Guillaume, Alfred. *The Life of Muhammad: A Translation of Isḥāq's Sīrat Rasūl Allāh*. New York: Oxford University Press, 1955.

Hamadani, 'Ayn al-Qudat. *Tamhīdāt*. Translated by Christiane Tortel [as *Les tentations métaphysiques*]. Paris: Les Deux Océans, 1992.

Ibn 'Abd al-Wahhab, Muhammad. *Mukhtasar Sirat al-Rasul*. Cairo: Maktabat al-Sunna al-Muhammadiyya, 1956.

Ibn 'Arabi, Muhyi al-Din. *Al-Futuhat al-Makkiyya*, vols. I and II, edited by Osman Yahya. Cairo: Al-Hay'a al-Misriyya al-'Amma li al-Kitab, 1972.

Ibn Hisham, Abd al-Malik. *Das Leben Mohammed's nach Mohammed Ibn Ishak*. Translated by Gustav Weil. Stuttgart: J.B. Metzler, 1864.

Ibn Taymiyya, Taqi al-Din Ahmad. *Minhaj al-Sunna al-Nabawiyya fi Naqd Kalam al-Shi'a wa al-Qadariyya,* vol. 1, edited by Muhammad Rashad Salim. Riyadh: Jami'at al-Imam Muhammad ibn Sa'ud, 1986.

Izutsu, Toshihiko. *Sufism and Taoism: A Comparative Study of Key Philosophical Concepts.* Berkeley: University of California Press, 2016.

Al-Jawziyya, Ibn Qayyim. *'Uddat al-Sabirin wa Dhakhirat al-Shakirin.* Damascus and Beirut: Dar ibn Kathir, 1989.

Al-Kalbi, Hisham ibn Muhammad. *Kitab al-Asnam (Tankis al-Asnam): Tarikh-i Parastish-i Arab pish az Zuhur-i Islam.* Translated by Muhammadriza Jalali Na'ini. Tehran: Sukhan, 2006.

Kashani, Rukn al-Din. *Shama'il al-Atqiya',* edited by Sayyid 'Ata' Husayn. Hyderabad: Matbu'at Ashraf Press, 1928–29.

Katz, Marion Holmes. *The Birth of the Prophet Muhammad: Devotional Piety in Sunni Islam.* Abingdon and New York: Routledge, 2007.

Khalil, Atif. "Contentment, Satisfaction and Good-Pleasure: *Rida* in Early Sufi Moral Psychology." *Studies in Religion/Sciences Religieuses* 43, no. 3 (2014): 371–89, https://doi.org/10.1177/0008429814538227.

Khodamoradi, Soraya. "Sufi Reform and the Mystical Ideology of Divine Unity." *Peshawar Islamicus* 3, no. 2 (July-December 2012): 1–20.

Khodamoradi, Soraya. *Sufi Reform in Eighteenth Century India: Khwaja Mir Dard of Delhi (1721–1785).* Berlin: EB-Verlag, 2019.

Khodamoradi, Soraya. "*Ṭarīqah Muḥammadiyyah* as *Ṭarīqah Jāmi'ah*: Khwājah Mīr Dard's Experience Beyond *Jamāl* and *Jalāl*." *Islamic Studies* 51, no. 4 (2012): 367–402.

Malik, Jamal. "A Survey and Assessment of German Approaches to *Sīrah*." *Islamic Studies* 58, no. 3 (July- September 2019): 335–58.

Malik, Jamal. *Islam in South Asia: Revised, Enlarged and Updated Second Edition.* Leiden: Brill, 2020.

Maybodi, Abu al-Fazl Rashid al-Din. *Kashf al-Asrar wa 'Udat al-Abrar,* vol. v, edited by 'Ali Asghar Hikmat. Tehran: Amir Kabir, 2003.

Al-Makki, Abu Talib. *Qut al-Qulub fi Mu'amalat al-Mahbub,* 2 vols, edited by Sa'id Nasib Makarim. Beirut: Dar Sadir, 1995.

Nagel, Tilman. *Allahs Liebling: Ursprung und Erscheinungsformen des Mohammedglaubens.* Munich: Oldenbourg, 2008.

Nicholson, Reynold A. *A Literary History of the Arabs.* London: T. Fisher Unwin, 1907.

Peacock, A.C.S. *Islam, Literature and Society in Mongol Anatolia.* Cambridge University Press, 2019, https://doi.org/10.1017/9781108582124.

Pirbhai, M. Reza. *Reconsidering Islam in a South Asian Context.* Leiden: Brill, 2009.

Quran Anhar. "Tafsir al-Mizan [of Tabataba'yi]." Accessed March 26, 2020, https://quran.anhar.ir/tafsirfull-13749.htm.

Al-Qushayri, ʿAbd al-Karim ibn Hawazin. *Tarjama-yi Risala-yi Qushayriyya*, edited by Badiʿ al-Zaman Furuzanfar. Tehran: Intisharat-i ʿIlmi Farhangi, 1998.

Rahman, Fazlur. *Islam*. Chicago: University of Chicago Press, 1979.

Rexinger, Martin. "Rendering Muḥammad Human Again: The Prophetology of Muḥammad b. ʿAbd al-Wahhāb (1703–1792)." *Numen* 60, no. 1 (2013): 103–18.

Richards, John F. *The Mughal Empire*. Cambridge: Cambridge University Press, 1995.

Rubin, Uri. "Pre-Existence and Light: Aspects of the Concept of Nūr Muḥammad." *Israel Oriental Studies* 5 (1975): 62–119.

Sanaʾi Ghaznawi, Abu al-Majd Majdud. *Hadiqat al-Haqiqa wa Shariʿat al-ariqa*, edited by Muhammad Taqi Mudarris Razawi. Tehran: Tehran University Press, 1950.

Schimmel, Annemarie. *And Muhammad is His Messenger: The Veneration of the Prophet in Islamic Piety*. Chapel Hill, NC: University of North Carolina Press, 1985.

Schimmel, Annemarie. *Mystical Dimensions of Islam*. Chapel Hill, NC: University of North Carolina Press, 1975.

Schimmel, Annemarie. *Pain and Grace: A Study of Two Mystical Writers of Eighteenth-Century Muslim India*. Leiden: Brill, 1976.

Seddiqi, Zahir Ahmad. *Khwaja Mir Dard*. New Delhi: Taraqqi Urdu Bureau, 1983.

Sedgwick, Mark. *Saints and Sons: The Making and Remaking of the Rashīdi Aḥmadi Sufi Order, 1799–2000*. Leiden: Brill, 2005.

Al-Shawkani, Muhammad ibn ʿAli. *Al-Fawaʾid al-Majmuʿa fi al-Ahadith al-Mawduʿa*, vol. 1, edited by Muhammad ʿAbd al-Rahman ʿAwad. Beirut: Dar al-Kitab al-ʿArabi, 1986.

Shibli, Muhammad Seddiq. "Khwaja Mir Dard Dihlawi." In *Otharhwi Sadi ʿIsawi Me Barr-i Saghir Me Islami ke Fikr ke Rahnoma*, edited by Muhammad Khalid Masʿud, 275–301. Islamabad: Idara-i Tahqiqat-i Islami, 2008.

Smith, Margaret. *Rābiʿa the Mystic and Her Fellow-Saints in Islām*. Cambridge and New York: Cambridge University Press: 1984.

Suhrawardi, Shahab al-Din Yahya ibn Habash. *Sih Risalih az Shaykh-i Ishraq: Al-Alwah al-ʿAmadiyya, Kalimat al-Tasawwuf, al-Lamhat*, edited by Najafquli Habibi. Tehran: Anjuman-i Shahanshahi-yi Falsafa-yi Iran, 1997.

Al-Tahanawi, Muhammad Aʿla ibn ʿAli. *Kashshāf Iṣṭilāḥāt al-Funūn*, edited by Aloys Sprenger et al. Calcutta: Asiatic Society of Bengal, 1862.

Tareen, SherAli. "The Perils and Possibilities of Inter-Religious Translation: Mirza Mazhar Jan-i Janan on the Hindus." *Sagar: A South Asia Research Journal* 22 (2014): 42–51.

Al-Tirmidhi, Muhammad ibn ʿIsa. *Sunan al-Tirmidhi*, edited by Muhammad Nasir al-Din al-Albani. Riyadh: Maktabat al-Maʿarif, n.d.

Tolan, John. "Impostor or Lawgiver?: Muhammad through European Eyes in the 17th and 18th Centuries." In *The Image of the Prophet Between Ideal and Ideology: A Scholarly Investigation*, edited by Christiane Gruber and Avinoam Shalem, 261–72. Berlin: de Gruyter, 2014, https://doi.org/10.1515/9783110312546.261.

Al-Tustari, Abu Muhammad Sahl ibn 'Abd Allah. *Tafsir al-Qur'an al-'Azim,* edited by M. Basil 'Uyun al-Suwd. Beirut: Dar al-Kutub al-'Ilmiyya, 2002.

Umar, Muhammad. "Mirza Mazhar Jan-i Janan: A Religious Reformer of the Eighteenth Century." *Studies in Islam* 6 (1969): 118–54.

Voll, John Obert. *Islam: Continuity and Change in the Modern World.* Syracuse, NY: Syracuse University Press, 1994.

Wali Allah, Shah. *The Conclusive Argument from God: Shāh Walī Allāh of Delhi's Ḥujjat Allāh al-Bāligha.* Translated by Marcia K. Hermansen. Leiden: Brill, 1996.

Wright, Zachary Valentine. *On the Path of the Prophet: Shaykh Ahmad Tijani and the Tariqa Muhammadiyya.* Atlanta: The African American Islamic Institute, 2005.

Zarrabi-Zadeh, Saeed. "Practical Mysticism: Its Definition, Parts and Characteristics." *Studies in Spirituality* 19 (2009): 1–13, https://doi.org/10.2143/SIS.19.0.2043669.

Ziad, Homayra. "Quest of the Nightingale: The Religious Thought of Khvājah Mīr Dard (1720–1785)." PhD diss., Yale University, 2008.

CHAPTER 11

Dynamics of Mystical Islam in the American Space
Ahmed Abdur Rashid's "Applied Sufism"

Michael E. Asbury and Saeed Zarrabi-Zadeh

1 Introduction

Before the major mystical trend in Islam, mainly referred to as Sufism, began to have a visible presence in the West during the late eighteenth century, it had undergone a lengthy process of evolution in the Muslim world.[1] Its "formative period" (ca. 650–950) began with ascetic movements that emerged after the death of the Prophet Muhammad, with personalities such as al-Hasan al-Basri (d. 728) choosing the way of self-denial and abstinence from worldly pleasures for both spiritual and political reasons.[2] These ascetic movements and some other spiritually-oriented currents are often seen as having gradually developed, around the turn of the ninth century, into mystical currents which added the language of love, intimacy and even unity with the divine to the earlier ascetic vocabulary. Subsequent to the critical reaction of parts of the Muslim community to this rhetoric, exemplified in the execution of al-Hallaj in 922, the history of Islamic mysticism entered a second phase, that of

---

1   A few studies have tried to present a global narrative of Sufism in terms of successive waves. Using the (European) categories of early medieval, medieval, early modern and modern, Nile Green (*Sufism: A Global History* [Chichester: Wiley-Blackwell, 2012]) divides the history of Sufism into four periods of "origins, foundations and rivalries" (850–1100), "an Islam of saints and brothers" (1100–1400), "empires, frontiers and renewals" (1400–1800), and "from colonization to globalization" (1800–2000). Also, Julian Baldick in his *Mystical Islam: An Introduction to Sufism* (London: I.B. Tauris, 1989) introduces four phases of "Sufi beginnings" (before 922), "from construction to systematization" (922–1240), "elders and empires" (1240–1700), and "into the modern world." The set of phases mentioned in this chapter is a revised version of the seven-fold schematic chronology suggested by Jamal Malik in his introduction to *Sufism in the West*, ed. Jamal Malik and John Hinnells (London and New York: Routledge, 2006), 2–11. Malik's sixth and seventh phases (1900 onwards) are not included here.

2   For a thoughtful, critical history of al-Hasan al-Basri, who is claimed by medieval sources to be both the founder of asceticism (*zuhd*) and a forefather of Sufism, see Suleiman Ali Mourad, *Early Islam between Myth and History: Al-Ḥasan Al-Baṣrī (d. 110H/728CE) and the Formation on His Legacy in Classical Islamic Scholarship* (Leiden: Brill, 2006).

"systematization and apologism" (ca. 950–1100).³ Sufi figures tried to organize the chaotic mass of teachings and techniques of earlier generations of mystics into an orderly system of theory and practice that was congruous with Islamic principles. These endeavors reached their apex in the works of the Sufi-jurist-philosopher al-Ghazali (d. 1111), whose religious authority was crucial in keeping and further establishing Sufism within (Sunni) Islam.

Such establishment paved the way for the next phase of Sufi history, that is its "organizational and intellectual development" (ca. 1100–1300). In this period, mystical groups and communities developed into several Sufi orders (*tariqas*), each with its own lineage (*silsila*), internal hierarchy and distinctive techniques.⁴ This phase also witnessed remarkable intellectual evolution, as attested to by the theoretical mysticism of the likes of Ibn ʿArabi (d. 1240) and the production of masterpieces of Sufi literature by such mystics as Rumi (d. 1273). These developments preceded the fourth phase of the "institutionalization of Sufi orders" (ca. 1300–1700), in the time when three powerful empires in the western (Ottoman), central (Safavid) and eastern (Mughal) territories of Islam were established. While Sufis and elites had both mutually beneficial and antagonistic relationships from quite early on, Sufism came to be increasingly utilized by rulers for the purposes of empire-building, expansion and the cultural integration of ruled peoples.⁵ Sufi orders were integrated into professional groups such as guilds and were increasingly engaged with the ruling elites. The institution of Sufism was further developed through the reformulation of membership, the elaboration of bureaucracy and hierarchy and the creation of new codes of conduct. The centuries that followed could be considered the fifth phase of "Sufi reform" (ca. 1700–1900), when the political decentralization and collapse of Muslim empires was accompanied by a sense of social, religious and moral decline among many Muslims.⁶ While the followers of Muhammad ibn ʿAbd al-Wahhab (d. 1792) rejected Sufism *in toto* as unlawful innovation, appended to the original pristine Islam, Sufi reformers initiated a program of self-critique and sought to revise medieval Sufi tradition according

---

3   In his informative study of early Sufism, Ahmet T. Karamustafa points out that this systematization was mainly the outcome of Sufis' self-conscious efforts at tradition-building rather than a defensive strategy against their detractors. See *Sufism: The Formative Period* (Edinburgh: Edinburgh University Press, 2007), 175.
4   On the rise of *tariqas* in this phase in both Sunni and Shiʿi contexts, see Alexander Knysh, *Islamic Mysticism: A Short History* (Leiden: Brill, 2000), 172–244.
5   On the role of Sufism in the early stage of these three empires, see Green, *Sufism*, 132–47.
6   Regarding the controversy surrounding Sufi reform and "neo-Sufism," see the conclusion section below.

to the needs of their time.⁷ Once Western (and Russian) powers began colonizing Muslim territories, these Sufi reformists and their extended networks played a significant role in mobilizing the masses for anti-colonial resistance.

Focusing now on the trajectory of Sufism in the "Occident," in spite of limited encounters with Sufism in the Middle Ages, specifically through travelers,⁸ the first serious interactions of Westerners with Sufism occurred during the colonial period. While activist Sufi orders and fighting dervishes were seen as major enemies and a significant threat to colonial rule, the acquaintance of colonial administrators and Orientalist scholars with Islamicate languages resulted in the "discovery" of an attractive Sufi tradition found in a body of classical literature, especially in poetic form, advocating such notions as love, religious pluralism and latitudinarianism.⁹ This understanding became the basis for the construction of the concept of "Sufi-ism" and the commencement of the first stage of Sufi presence in the West, which may be termed "early literary Sufism" (ca. 1770–1900).¹⁰ Sufi texts written in Islamic languages such as Arabic, Persian and Turkish were rendered into European languages, particularly by Westerners fascinated with the "mystical East."¹¹ Among them, the Romanticists of the first two-thirds of the nineteenth century, especially in German-speaking lands, played a significant role in the translation movement, as can be seen in the works of Joseph von Hammer-Purgstall (d. 1856) and Friedrich Rückert (d. 1866).¹²

---

7   On eighteenth-century reform, see Ahmad S. Dallal, *Islam without Europe: Traditions of Reform in Eighteenth-Century Islamic Thought* (Chapel Hill: The University of North Carolina Press, 2018).

8   Among the first texts written by a Western European on Sufi ideas and practices, see *Tractatus de moribus, condicionibus et nequicia Turcorum* [Treatise on the Customs, Habits and Perversity of the Turks] (Rome: n.p, 1480) penned by Georgius de Hungaria (d. 1502) and *Trattato de costumi et vita de Turchi* [Treatise on the Customs and Life of the Turks] (Florence: n.p, 1548) by Giovan Antonio Menavino (d. ca. 1550). Both authors lived for some years in the Ottoman territories.

9   Carl W. Ernst, *Sufism: An Introduction to the Mystical Tradition of Islam* (Boston and London: Shambhala Publications, 2011), 8–18.

10 The approximate date of 1770 corresponds roughly to the start of the Romantic era and the first rendering of the poetry of Hafiz into English by Sir William Jones (d. 1794). The point that Sufism entered the West in the late eighteenth century, first as literature and later through individuals and institutions, does not entail that the "image" of Sufis and dervishes had not been present in Europe prior to that time.

11 On the perception of the East as "mystical" by Orientalists and Romanticists, see Richard King, *Orientalism and Religion: Postcolonial Theory, India and 'The Mystic East'* (London and New York: Routledge, 1999), 24–34.

12 Among other Sufi texts, Hammer-Purgstall translated the *Gulshan-i Raz* of Mahmud Shabistari (d. 1340) under the title *Rosenflor des Geheimnisses* (Pesth and Leipzig: Hartleben, 1838). Like Rückert, he also translated poems by Rumi.

Subsequent to this inceptive step, the second stage in the history of Sufism in the West, or "universalist Sufism" (ca. 1900–1960), began around the turn of the twentieth century. Several spiritual teachers inspired by Sufi discourse and practice, as a part of the mystical traditions of the East, appeared in this period, such as the Swedish painter Ivan Aguéli (d. 1917), the Greco-Armenian master G.I. Gurdjieff (d. 1949) and the French intellectual René Guénon (d. 1951).[13] These figures, along with a small number of Sufi teachers who migrated to the West, notable among them Inayat Khan (d. 1927), set out upon inserting Sufism into Western esotericism in the form of a *philosophia perennis*, that is a perennial and universal wisdom shared by all religions. This transpired during the time of the psychologization of mysticism by scholars such as William James (d. 1910), who were de-theologizing the mystical and casting off its local religious and metaphysical entanglements.[14] In the second half of the twentieth century, when the harsh critique against the principles of "modernity" and its universal meta-narrative resulted in the emergence of the post-modern or high modern[15] era, Sufism was one of the available options to be used in the rapidly expanding counter-culture and the nascent "New-Age" movements. This marks the third stage of "syncretic Sufism" (ca. 1960–1975), a period when Sufism extended its sphere from within the limited circles of a few elites into the public sphere and became a part of popular syncretic forms of spirituality. Such development was intensified via the publication of well-received works on Sufism, such as those written by the self-publicist Idries Shah (d. 1996).

Yet the last quarter of the twentieth century saw a renewed accentuation in the West of Sufism's connection to Islamic normativity, partly in reaction to the eclectic attitude of the New Age and the underemphasis on Islam among universalist Sufis.[16] This stage can be labeled as "re-orthodoxized Sufism" (since ca. 1975).[17] On the one hand, Western spiritual seekers increasingly came into

---

13 A discussion of these spiritual teachers and their contributions to Sufism in the Occident can be found in Mark Sedgwick, *Western Sufism: From the Abbasids to the New Age* (New York: Oxford University Press, 2017), part III, 135–85.

14 The four marks of mystical experience suggested in James' classic *The Varieties of Religious Experience: A Study in Human Nature* (New York: Longmans, Green and Co., 1902), 379, namely ineffability, noetic quality, transiency and passivity, are for the most part universal and free from specific ecclesiastical traditions.

15 Anthony Giddens, *Modernity and Self-Identity: Self and Society in the Late Modern Age* (Stanford: Stanford University Press, 1991).

16 In this regard, see, for example, the section entitled "Situating the Transplants" in Hermansen's chapter in this volume.

17 Though the term "orthodoxy" is utilized out of convenience here, one should be careful in making use of it in reference to Islam and in singular form. See Wilfred Cantwell Smith, *Modern Islām in India: A Social Analysis* (London: Victor Gollancz Ltd., 1946), 305, which

contact with traditional Sufi orders based in the Muslim world, even establishing branches of those *tariqa*s in their homelands, as can be observed in the cases of the Scottish Sufi Ian Dallas (b. 1930), also known as Abdalqadir as-Sufi, and the American convert Nuh Ha Mim Keller (b. 1954).[18] On the other hand, the large-scale migration from Muslim majority areas into the West starting in the second half of the twentieth century facilitated the activities of various branches of more "orthodox" Islamic Sufi orders, including the Naqshbandiyya and Shadhiliyya, in the western setting.[19] As a result of this four-fold trajectory of Sufism in the West, the current Western scene includes all forms of (neo-)Romantic, universalist, syncretic and re-orthodoxized Sufism simultaneously, though with different degrees of popularity and with various internal modifications.[20]

The current chapter explores the dynamics of mystical Islam in a hitherto unstudied Sufi lineage that extended its presence into the West in the above-mentioned fourth stage. This line traces its particular spiritual practices back to the nineteenth-century *shaykh* Sayyid ʿAbd al-Bari Shah (1859–1900), who is said to have established standardized curricula for training in five traditions: a non-Mujaddidi branch of the Naqshbandiyya[21] as well as the

---

suggest "orthopraxy" instead of "orthodoxy," and SherAli Tareen, "Normativity, Heresy, and the Politics of Authenticity in South Asian Islam," *The Muslim World* 99, no. 3 (June 2009): 526, https://doi.org/10.1111/j.1478-1913.2009.01284.x, which sees "normativity" as a justifiable alternative.

18   For a concise overview of Abdalqadir's Darqawiyya-Habibiyya and the "ultra-orthodoxy" of Keller, see Marcia Hermansen, "Global Sufism: 'Theirs and Ours,'" in *Sufis in Western Society: Global Networking and Locality*, ed. Ron Geaves, Markus Dressler and Gritt Klinkhammer (Abingdon and New York: Routledge, 2009), 34–37.

19   For more detail on these four stages, see Jamal Malik and Saeed Zarrabi-Zadeh, "Introduction," in *Sufism East and West: Mystical Islam and Cross-Cultural Exchange in the Modern World*, ed. Jamal Malik and Saeed Zarrabi-Zadeh (Leiden: Brill, 2019), 8–17. An elaborate study of Sufi presence in the West can be found in *Sufism in Western Contexts*, ed. Marcia Hermansen and Saeed Zarrabi-Zadeh (Leiden: Brill, forthcoming).

20   In addition, several variants of hybrid Sufism, blurring the borders between these forms of Sufism, have also grown in the garden of Western Sufism. The perennialist-Guénonian interpretation of the Naqshbandiyya Haqqaniyya by the French Philippe De Vos is a case in point. See his *Sheikh Nâzim: la Preuve de la Générosité* (Avignon: Les éditions du Relié, 1997); and Thierry Zarcone, "Rereadings and Transformations of Sufism in the West," *Diogenes* 47, no. 187 (September 1999): 115, https://doi.org/10.1177/039219219904718711.

21   The "non-Mujaddidi Naqshbandiyya" here refers to a lineage that is said to have passed via non-physical (*uwaysi*) connection from the fourteenth-century Bukharan Baha' al-Din Naqshband (d. 1389) to the nineteenth-century Indian *shaykh* Sayyid ʿAbd al-Bari Shah. His Shadhili and Qadiri lines are also both exclusively *uwaysi*, while the Mujaddidi and Chishti lines were passed through physically embodied *shaykhs* alongside *uwaysi* connections to significant foundational figures. Azad Rasool, *Turning Toward*

Naqshbandiyya-Mujaddidiyya, Chishtiyya, Shadhiliyya and Qadiriyya.²² Its expansion into the West while maintaining its connection to Islamic normativity was primarily accomplished by the Indian *shaykh* Azad Rasool (1921–2006). In our exploration, we focus on Rasool's US-based *khalifa*, Ahmed Abdur Rashid (b. 1942), in order to show the internal dynamics of the lineage after the Indian *shaykh* was succeeded by an American one and the environment shifted from South Asia to the United States. This cultural translation is studied by means of juxtaposing a carefully selected sampling of Abdur Rashid's teachings in three areas, namely cosmo-psychology, mystical practices and the role of the Sufi guide and community, with those of his immediate forebears. As we will see below, while maintaining considerable continuity with his own teacher, his approach to implementing adaptations in the lineage can serve as an example of "tradition-based" dynamics and as evidence for the insufficiency of the dichotomous categories of change *vis-à-vis* continuity in studying modern mystical Islam.

2 Ahmed Abdur Rashid, the World Community and Legacy International

Noticing the large number of Westerners coming to India in search of spirituality, the Indian Sufi *shaykh* Azad Rasool established the Institute of Search for Truth (IST) in Delhi in 1975 as a way of introducing them to Sufi practices.²³ One such seeker from the United States was Ahmed Abdur Rashid, *né* J.E. Rash (b. 1942), who arrived later the next year and began his training under Rasool. Early on in his biography, one can detect spirituality and positive engagement in the world as the twin pillars of his life work and teachings: By the late 1960s, and prior to meeting Rasool, Abdur Rashid had been active in the civil rights movement as well as in protesting the Vietnam War, but he had also, since his teens, explored a number of spiritual paths of Eastern origin that had begun to arrive in the West, including Buddhism, Taoism and Yoga. He had come to be a Yoga teacher and in 1970, he founded, along with a group of his students,

---

the Heart: Awakening to the Sufi Way, Forty Questions and Answers with Shaykh al-Tariqat Hazrat Azad Rasool (Louisville, KY: Fons Vitae, 2002), 119.

22   Ibid., 113–23; idem, *The Search for Truth: The Life & Teaching Methods of the Indian Sufi Shaykh Hazrat Maulvi Muhammad Saʿid Khan (r)* (Louisville, KY: Fons Vitae, 2010), 50–52, 60.

23   Ibid., 75.

the Prema Dharmasala *ashram*, or what is now a *khanqah* called the World Community in the rural woodlands of southern Virginia. It was intended to be a utopian ideal, an alternative, back-to-the-land, self-sufficient shared community that would allow them to engage continuously in spiritual practices and where they would grow their own organic foods, practice homeopathy and run a Montessori school for the children born there, as well as engage in service in the world.

Over time, Abdur Rashid began to feel something missing in Yoga, perhaps it was in part due to his ever-present emphasis on serving humanity and building "a better world," rather than escaping it for self-realization. Thus in 1977, he decided to return to India, where he had traveled as a Yogi, to continue his spiritual search, which then led him to Rasool, under whom he immediately began his tutelage. After a few transitional years from a universalist practice of Yoga to Islamic Sufism, the majority of the residents of the World Community gradually embraced Sufism and Islam and by 1984, Rasool gave *ijaza* ("authorization") to Abdur Rashid to train students of his own and appointed him as his *khalifa* ("deputy"). Like Rasool, who affirmed "the inseparability of the Sufi rose from its Islamic rosebush"[24] while also accepting non-Muslim students, and unlike earlier universalist varieties of Sufism in the West, Abdur Rashid upholds the need for Sufism to retain its Islamic foundation. Much in line with his forebears, his approach to Islam can be characterized as seeking its inner meaning and what he sees as its essential principles, along with emphasizing contextual adaptivity and intra/interfaith pluralism, but also living "on the margins of the mainstream," aloof of the individualism and materialism of Western society as well as the exoteric-dogmatism and empty ritualism he sees being practiced among some Muslims.[25] Now, nearly 50 years after the founding of the community, his students number altogether less than 100 people, mostly residents at the World Community. Many of them were founding members or were born and raised there, but there are also others who have joined over the years. Additionally, Abdur Rashid has individual disciples scattered in different areas of the globe, often in Muslim-majority countries.[26]

Abdur Rashid also founded Legacy International, a secular non-profit NGO that seeks to promote peace and well-being through engaged citizenship. Originally established as the Institute for Practical Idealism in 1979, Legacy grew out of a summer camp for students of the community's Montessori school, the World Community Education Center (WCEC), which was founded

---

24 Idem, *Turning Toward the Heart*, 3.
25 Examples can be found throughout Abdur Rashid's *Applied Sufism*.
26 Ahmed Abdur Rashid, interview by Michael E. Asbury, Bedford, VA, January 3–4, 2017.

on the hope of creating "compassionate and visionary leaders for a global society faced with many challenges."[27] The camp would evolve into the Global Youth Village (GYV), an international leadership program that has welcomed participants from more than 120 different countries since its first year in 1979. GYV uses various activities to promote respect, service and global perspectives, including their intercultural dialogue and conflict prevention curriculum called *LivingSidebySide*. Abdur Rashid explained that it furthermore seeks to affirm the overarching Legacy principles of universal values, which he feels transcend limitations like culture, religion, race and gender.[28]

Over the decades since, Legacy has widened its mission and added a number of additional programs, expanding their leadership training to include not only youths, but also citizen exchanges involving early to mid-career professionals, government employees from around the world and socially responsible business entrepreneurs. Participants across Legacy's diverse array of programs are encouraged to identify their own "core values" and find ways to practically put them into action in the form of service to their communities, and thus to the world. Legacy also provides access to resources and mentorship after training events to assist participants in, for instance, developing civil society initiatives in their home regions.[29] Members of the World Community view the activities of the WCEC and Legacy as a practical application of their Sufism. Thus, the twin pillars of Abdur Rashid's life work, spirituality and engagement in the world, are inextricably intertwined, converging in what he calls "Applied Sufism."[30]

3   Abdur Rashid's "Applied Sufism"

Abdur Rashid holds that "Sufism is a means to a personal experience of the presence of Allah."[31] For him, such an experience has a multi-faceted transformative effect on the individual, which he describes in a number of ways, expounding upon different aspects of the relationship between the seeker and

---

27   Brochure for the WCEC.
28   Ahmed Abdur Rashid, Email, August 2, 2019.
29   The WCEC and Legacy are covered in detail in Michael E. Asbury, "Seeing with the Heart: The Mysticism of an Islamic Sufi Lineage from India in the West" (PhD diss., University of Erfurt, 2020).
30   Like much in Abdur Rashid's thought, one might find yet another level of meaning in the term "Applied Sufism" aside from what is explained below, as referring to its applicability to different temporal, geographic and cultural contexts, such as the contemporary West.
31   Ahmed Abdur Rashid, *Why?* (Bedford, VA: The Circle Group, 2011), 13.

God. Yet he repeatedly emphasizes the need to manifest the transformation that the encounter with the divine is held to produce *in the world* through refined conduct and morality – oftentimes referring to the necessity of maintaining a balance between inner (*batin*) and outer (*zahir*). He exhorts to reflecting the names and attributes of God, like the Compassionate and the Merciful, in the way one lives, which for him and his students often takes the form of service to humanity and the world, including the environment.[32] His teacher, Azad Rasool, similarly saw the purpose of Sufism as being "to transform the seeker into a highly humane and moral person" through spiritual training.[33] Yet Rasool's greatest emphasis seems to have been on encouraging students in the diligent performance of the practices, allowing the results to emerge on their own, while Abdur Rashid, with no lesser emphasis on the practices, distinctively highlights the application of their results.

Abdur Rashid's orientation toward application can be observed by comparing his approach to disseminating Sufism and manifesting the results thereof to that of his immediate forebears. Rasool, and before him Muhammad Saʿid Khan (1907–1976) and Hamid Hasan ʿAlawi (1871/72–1959), sought to propagate their particular lineage as a realization of a promise that God is said to have made to ʿAbd al-Bari Shah that his teachings would spread "from East to West, and from land to sea."[34] Their efforts involved annual touring circuits in which they visited disciples around South Asia, something Rasool expanded locally and internationally to include the US, UK and Australia.[35] Such an approach has been carried even further by Hamid Hasan (b. 1961), Rasool's son and only other living successor, who currently heads IST and the School of Sufi Teaching (SOST) and who has maintained and extended such regular travel even further, to areas like Germany, Poland, Russia, Brazil, Malaysia and Singapore. Abdur Rashid, however, continues the mission of his predecessors in a somewhat different direction. While he travels frequently as the president of Legacy International, he rarely does so in his capacity as a Sufi *shaykh*. Most of his students live and work at the World Community, often at the WCEC or Legacy, and can see him in person on a daily basis.[36] The comparatively small and centrally located nature of Abdur Rashid's student base demonstrates how

---

32 See, for example, Idem, *Dhaahir and Baatin* (Bedford, VA: The Circle Group, 2010).
33 Rasool, *The Search for Truth*, 43.
34 Idem, *Turning Toward the Heart*, 123.
35 Idem, *The Search for Truth*, 30–31, 83–84; "Hazrat Hamid Hasan Alawi (r.a)," School of Sufi Teaching, accessed November 2, 2019, www.sufischool.org/orders/hazrat-hamid-hasan-alawi-r-a.html.
36 Abdur Rashid, interview, January 3–4, 2017.

his focus is not so much on spreading a particular set of Sufi practices, but more on encouraging the students he already has to manifest the outcome of such practices in the world. He sees the work of Legacy and the WCEC as the tangible results of their Sufi practice, results that emanate beyond the Muslim and Sufi community. Thus he provides spiritual training for his small core of students, seeking to transform their characters as they in turn work to bring out the "universal values," which Abdur Rashid equates with the names and attributes of God (see below), in persons of all faiths or of no faith at all. He and his students strive to do this, inter alia, through Legacy's portfolio of civic education, peace education and leadership development programs, with the aim of "catalyzing transformative leaders" for bringing about what they see as a better world.[37]

In examining Abdur Rashid's Applied Sufism, we concentrate here on his mystical teachings in comparison with those of his immediate predecessors, especially Rasool. In doing so, our discussion is arranged around five key terms which Rasool used prominently in elaborating his mainly practice-oriented Sufism[38] and to which Abdur Rashid also refers in his more application-oriented teachings. These terms are *nisbat* ("relationship"), *lata'if* ("subtleties," or "subtle centers of consciousness"), *muraqaba* ("meditation"), *dhikr* ("remembrance [of God]"), and *tawajjuh* ("spiritual attention/transmission"). They receive considerable treatment in both of Rasool's English language books, having separate sections devoted to them, and each term also has its own page on SOST's current website.[39] For our discussion, these terms are addressed under three major categories, namely (a) mystical cosmo-psychology (*nisbat, lata'if*); (b) practices performed by the student (*muraqaba, dhikr*); and (c) the role of the *shaykh* and the community (*tawajjuh, nisbat*).[40]

---

37   Idem, interview by Michael E. Asbury, Bedford, VA, June 26, 2018.
38   In *The Search for Truth* (49–50), Rasool lists these terms in a succinct summary of this lineage's approach to "spiritual training," which he says "is given through spiritual attention/transmission [*tawajjuh*], spiritual affinity [*nisbat*] and the awakening of the subtle centers of consciousness [*lata'if*]. [...] For this training, remembrance of God [*dhikr*], [...] meditation [*muraqaba*], awareness of the heart, and spiritual friendship with the shaykh are obligatory." He also mentions a sixth key term associated with the *lata'if*, that is *indiraj al-nihayat fi al-bidayat* ("inclusion of the end in the beginning"), which was not referred to as often by Abdur Rashid in the sources consulted and was thus excluded from the list of terms for comparison here.
39   Rasool, *Turning Toward the Heart*, 86–91, 94–101 and 104–8; idem, *The Search for Truth*, 52–59; and SufiSchool.org.
40   As explained below, Abdur Rashid uses at least three meanings for *nisbat*, out of which the first and third senses are related to cosmo-psychology and the second to the Sufi guide and community.

3.1 Cosmo-psychology

In Sufi tradition, especially after the substantial developments in theoretical mysticism during the thirteenth century, cosmology and psychology meet each other and are merged into a single sphere that could be called "cosmo-psychology." Therein, various layers of the soul correspond with different levels of the cosmos, the microcosm (psyche) thus reflecting the macrocosm (universe). Sufis have developed complex expositions of the structure of the cosmos to chart the inner journey toward, in and from God—whom they consider as the origin of the entire world and also accessible at the core of one's inner being. They utilize notions such as "the arc of ascent" (*qaws al-suʿud*) for spiritual movement towards God and from multiplicity to unity, which aims at reversing, or returning back along, "the arc of descent" (*qaws al-nuzul*), that is the manifestation of creatures and the emergence of multiplicity out of divine unity. These two arcs together constitute a circle connecting man/creation and God.[41] For those Sufis emphasizing mystical sobriety (*sahw*) over intoxication (*sukr*) and subsistence (*baqaʾ*) over annihilation (*fanaʾ*), man returns, or descends again, to the created world after having ascended to the divine and been absorbed in His unity.[42]

Rasool only briefly touches upon such cosmo-psychology, the *lataʾif* being the only aspect that he expounds upon in any significant detail, likely because of their central role in the practices. In expressing his emphasis on practice, he affirms that spiritual travelers "undertake a concrete program of training. They do not speculate on cosmic principles [...]. They work." He exhorts such seekers after ultimate Truth to "throw away their books and meditate."[43] Abdur Rashid, however, in his massive output of recorded and transcribed lectures and pamphlets, expounds at length on a vast range of topics, including the various levels of Sufi cosmo-psychology that one ascends through in approaching God, while simultaneously emphasizing man's descent from the divine. One of the major concepts both men utilize in discussing this spiritual ascent and

---

41 On these two arcs in Ibn ʿArabi's speculative mysticism, see William C. Chittick, *The Self-Disclosure of God: Principles of Ibn al-ʿArabī's Cosmology* (Albany, NY: SUNY Press, 1998), 233–36.

42 This feature is characteristic of the four-fold Mujaddidi path culminating in a return to creation transformed. See Arthur F. Buehler, *Revealed Grace: The Juristic Sufism of Ahmad Sirhindi (1564–1624)* (Louisville, KY: Fons Vitae, 2011), 36–38. On the twin notions of *fanaʾ* and *baqaʾ* and their role in the mystical schools advocating *sukr* and *sahw* in early Sufi Sūfism, see Andrew Wilcox, "The Dual Mystical Concepts of Fanāʾ and Baqāʾ in Early Sūfism," *British Journal of Middle Eastern Studies* 38, no. 1 (April 2011), https://doi.org/10.1080/13530191003794681.

43 Rasool, *Turning Toward the Heart*, 84.

descent is that of *nisbat*. Following Rasool, Abdur Rashid uses the concept in two major ways: (a) as the affinity that can develop between God and man, and (b) the affinity among people, such as with a particular *tariqa*, but especially the "cordial relationship" one ought to have with their *shaykh* as a means for attaining the first type of affinity, though he more often uses the related word *munasaba* for this second sense. He does not seem to employ Rasool's third use of *nisbat* as a comprehensive placeholder for a wide range of mystical concepts and practices,[44] likely because Abdur Rashid discusses an immense array of concepts individually and in detail in his *dars* (lectures).[45] He does, however, give it a third meaning of his own, as "one's relatedness to everything, one's affinity, one's awareness of everything."[46] This theme returns time and again in his lectures and is directly relevant to his hallmark of Applied Sufism, wherein the idea of the unity and interconnectedness of all of existence, Abdur Rashid's third meaning of *nisbat*, comes to the service of his call for social responsibility and engagement, service to all of creation. His first and third meanings of *nisbat* are addressed in this section, while the second meaning will be discussed in the section "*Shaykh* and Community" below.

One recurring theme in Abdur Rashid's cosmo-psychological teachings relating to the concept of *nisbat* – as the affinity between God and man and the interrelatedness of all things – is the divine names and attributes, a central topic used extensively by Ibn 'Arabi and his followers in connecting Sufi cosmology and psychology. This Andalusian mystic, also known as "the Greatest Shaykh" (*al-Shaykh al-Akbar*) for his pivotal role in the evolution of Sufi thought from the thirteenth century onwards is often referred to by Abdur Rashid, who considers him among the major influences on his own thought.[47] According to Ibn 'Arabi, the assumption of the divine attributes is the very goal of mystical perfection and the medium of the affinity of man and God. Moreover, the same names and attributes, being various manifestations of Allah yet all united in God's presence, are the ideal forms and the virtual being of all creatures and the origin of their interconnectedness.[48] Emphasis on the issue of the names and attributes represents one major difference between Abdur Rashid and his teacher, as Rasool cautioned him against concentrating too much on them, because the goal is to go beyond the names and attributes to their source,

---

44 Idem, *The Search for Truth*, 43, 53–54.
45 Abdur Rashid's lectures are discussed in the section "*Shaykh* and Community" below.
46 Abdur Rashid, interview, January 3–4, 2017.
47 Ibid.
48 William C. Chittick, *The Sufi Path of Knowledge: Ibn-al-'Arabi's Metaphysics of Imagination* (Albany, NY: SUNY Press, 1989), especially parts on theology (31–76) and ontology (77–143).

i.e., the very essence (*dhat*) of God.⁴⁹ This difference is far from arbitrary and Abdur Rashid's focus on the names and attributes can be connected to the two main pillars of his teachings, achieving a profound awareness of God (ascent) and living it in one's life (descent). On the first, he sees the names and attributes as means through which the seeker can relate to God, and on the latter, they are means by which the seeker can manifest that relationship with God in their dealings in the world.⁵⁰

Pertaining to the ascent, after noting how Rasool would say to him "Don't keep stressing the Divine Names," Abdur Rashid explains that he questioned why, since for him these are ways in which "people can relate to Allah." He describes how Rasool, in contrast, maintained that the students should relate to God through the practices, yet Abdur Rashid felt that he needed "to do both," to teach the practices and to help students relate to God conceptually by discussing the names and attributes,⁵¹ which are easier to conceive of than the abstract notion of a divine essence and unity beyond all attributes. This is of course also tied to his own use of lectures alongside the practices, relating to God both conceptually through the former and intuitionally through the latter. He sees this two-pronged approach as necessary since not everyone is at the same level of spiritual development, nor are all equally diligent in the practices.⁵² He also explains that while the divine essence should govern one's inner life, the names and attributes should govern one's outer life,⁵³ thus leading us to consider the descent and activity in the world.

Referring to a hadith in which God says of His servant whom He loves: "I am his hearing through which he hears, his sight through which he sees, his hand through which he grasps, and his foot through which he walks,"⁵⁴ Abdur Rashid explains that the Sufi must strive to reflect the names and attributes of God in their own daily life, and since the Sufi is to be "well integrated into the community, into the society," such a reflection of these divine characteristics

---

49   In one lecture, Abdur Rashid explains how the ultimate objective is to travel "in the essence, not in the attributes," and that "This is why Hazrat [Rasool] was so strong with me about being careful about teaching too much about the attributes." Ahmed Abdur Rashid, "Muraqabah in the Naqshbandi-Mujaddidi Order: The Spiritual Road Map of Contemplation/Niyyat," lecture, June 20, 2013, 4–5.
50   Idem, interview, June 26, 2018.
51   Ibid.
52   Idem, "Proof of the Divine: Seeing the Unseen through the Unseen Accelerating the Circles of the Laṭā'if," lecture, September 19, 2012, 9.
53   Idem, "Practices of Muraqabah: History and References, Rābita of the Shaykh," lecture, September 20, 2012, 12.
54   *Sahih Bukhari*, vol. 8, book 76, no. 509.

also benefits those around them.⁵⁵ He does not limit this to only Muslims, saying that the "(d)ivine attributes are legacies from God to every being of His creation, regardless of race, ethnicity, nationality or religion. [...] The challenge for all humans is the pursuit of the Divine attributes—learning to note, realize, embrace and activate them in our daily lives."⁵⁶ Not only does this highlight his pluralism and orientation toward application, but his referring to the divine attributes as "legacies" is especially significant as it invokes the name of the non-profit organization he founded, Legacy International. He in fact uses the term "universal values" as nearly interchangeable with the divine names and attributes, with Legacy and all of its programs being built around the concept of universal values.

Abdur Rashid's delving into theoretical mysticism leads to another important aspect of his Sufism, that is his engagement with "new science." While before him Saʿid Khan spoke of the potential for a complementary relationship between science and spirituality⁵⁷ and Rasool made appeals to the scientific method to encourage potential students to empirically test the practices out for themselves,⁵⁸ Abdur Rashid goes a significant step further by actually engaging with the findings of scientific disciplines to find parallels to the inner insights of Sufism, or what he sees as approaching the same Truth from different angles. On the issue of *batin* and *zahir*, for example, he maintains: "This understanding of both the outer and inner reality is similar to our understanding of the atomic or sub-atomic world that exists beyond the normal sensory perceptions."⁵⁹ He also compares the great Sufis of the past to physicists like Einstein, Planck and Heisenberg, since both groups "were dealing with non-sensory experiences of reality, and non-duality" and just as physicists have used "metaphoric" terms to describe seemingly paradoxical realities, so the Sufis have made use of "poetic language" in expressing apparently self-contradictory ideas. Harking back to his understanding of *nisbat*, Abdur Rashid asserts: "Quantum science deals with the interconnectedness of all things; so does *Tasawwuf* and so does Islam."⁶⁰

Another concept related to this lineage's cosmo-psychology is the "subtle centers of consciousness" or *lata'if*, that in Sufi tradition have been associated

---

55   Ahmed Abdur Rashid, *What?* (Bedford, VA: The Circle Group, 2011), 21.
56   J.E. Rash, *Islam and Democracy: A Foundation for Ending Extremism and Preventing Conflict* (Bedford, VA: Legacy International, 2006), 40.
57   Rasool, *The Search for Truth*, 117–19, 125–29.
58   Ibid., 152–55.
59   Ahmed Abdur Rashid, *Who?* (Bedford, VA: The Circle Group, 2012), 5.
60   Ibid., 9.

with different levels of the cosmos, various prophets and colors, as well as locations within the body to which the practitioner directs their attention, especially during meditation. Abdur Rashid describes these centers in several ways, such as vehicles for the spiritual ascent and receptors for divine grace (*baraka*) and guidance, but most often as subtle organs for the perception of both inner and outer realities. Like Rasool and Sa'id Khan before him, he connects these with a transformational process in which the *lata'if* are sequentially awakened or activated, one in which a kind of inner potential is accessed that has concrete ethical implications in how one lives and contributes to the betterment of the world. Pertaining to the role of the *lata'if* in perception, however, Abdur Rashid makes a distinctive contribution. During the mystical practices (see below), the practitioner directs their attention to one or more of the *lata'if*, which serve as supra-sensory organs for the inner spiritual journey, and it is this meaning that seemed primary for Rasool and Sa'id Khan.[61] Yet Abdur Rashid places a great deal of emphasis on their role in perceiving the outer world alongside the inner, saying "You see through, you hear through, and you understand through the refined *lataa'if*."[62] This takes place through balancing one's perception of the exterior world via the outer physical senses – which he associates with the four elements of earth, air, fire and water – with our perceiving the interior world through the inner senses, "through the organs of perception of the *lataa'if*: *qalb* ["heart"], *ruuh* ["spirit"], *sirr* ["secret"], *khafee* ["hidden"], *akhfaa* ["most hidden"] and *nafs* ["self"]."[63] Thus we see an identical set of subtle centers as taught by Rasool and nearly every other Mujaddidi *shaykh* for which data is available.[64] Of all these centers, Abdur Rashid explains that the heart is the only organ existing simultaneously in both the outer and the inner, and it is there, where these two worlds meet in the microcosm of man, that the "expressions of Allah are reflected, like in a mirror, in the heart of a human."[65] The *lata'if* function as "lenses" that must be properly aligned

---

61 Rasool, *Turning Toward the Heart*, 86–91; idem, *The Search for Truth*, 54–56, 129–37.
62 Ahmed Abdur Rashid, *Prophet Musa: The Journey from the Mountain* (Bedford, VA: The Circle Group, 2013), 31.
63 Idem, <u>Dhaahir and Baatin</u>, 5.
64 The ten *lata'if* structure consists of the five of the *'alam-i amr* ("world of divine command," or the spiritual world), viz., *qalb*, *ruh*, *sirr*, *khafi* and *akhfa*; along with the five of the *'alam-i khalq* ("world of creation"), namely the *nafs* and the four elements of earth, water, fire and wind. For an overview of this fairly standard Mujaddidi *lata'if* model, along with an historical overview of its development in Sufi thought and its relation to broader cosmology, see Arthur F. Buehler, *Sufi Heirs of the Prophet: The Indian Naqshbandiyya and the Rise of the Mediating Sufi Shaykh* (Columbia, SC: University of South Carolina Press, 1998), 105–20.
65 Abdur Rashid, <u>Dhaahir and Baatin</u>, 15.

and through which the practitioner must "learn how to perceive,"[66] and it is only when the physical senses are aligned with them that one can truly see.[67] Such emphasis on the outer perceptive aspect of the *lata'if* falls in line with Abdur Rashid's Applied Sufism: "Through the eyes of the heart, through love, we respond differently to the world than we respond when we are acting only through the intellect, through reason, or through our normal emotional reactions."[68] The subtle centers thus have the capacity "to create the most humane human beings."[69]

3.2 *Mystical Practices*

Rasool trained disciples in the curricula that are said to have been fully standardized by 'Abd al-Bari Shah in the late nineteenth century. Each is comprised of a series of intentions for *muraqaba*, which are intended to lead the student through various levels of mystical cosmo-psychology back to the divine source, augmented by a daily *wazifa*. The latter consists of forms of *dhikr* like *nafy wa ithbat* ("negation and affirmation," or repeating *la ilaha illa Allah*, "There is no god but God") and *dhikr ism-i dhat* ("remembering the name of the divine essence," that is repeating *Allah*), along with the recitation of *al-Fatiha* (the opening chapter of the Quran), supplications for blessings upon the Prophet (*durud sharif*) and honoring the saints of the *silsila* (*khatm sharif*).[70] Abdur Rashid teaches exactly the same curricula, with the various recitations and the procedure for performing *muraqaba* and the intentions that initiate the practice being identical to that taught by Rasool.[71] Abdur Rashid also describes *muraqaba* in similar ways as his teacher, as time to turn away from the world and sit waiting for blessings, allowing thoughts of "everything other than God" to subside while directing one's attention to the divine essence by way of the *lata'if*.[72] Moreover, both Rasool and Abdur Rashid warn not to become overly preoccupied with any visions that may take place and both quote Sirhindi's statement that these only serve "to please the seeker's heart. The final

---

66 Idem, *Applied Sufism: Classical Teachings for the Contemporary Seeker* (Livermore, CA: WingSpan Press, 2006), 64.
67 Ibid., 128.
68 Ibid., 63.
69 Idem, "Proof of the Divine," 13.
70 Rasool, *The Search for Truth*, 63–67.
71 Abdur Rashid, interview, January 3–4, 2017.
72 Rasool, *Turning Toward the Heart*, 98–102; idem, *The Search for Truth*, 58–59; Abdur Rashid, "Practices of Muraqabah," 1.

destination lies ahead."⁷³ Abdur Rashid, again echoing his teacher, says that the aim is not to focus one's thoughts but to awaken one's heart. Yet, unlike Rasool, who considered *muraqaba* as entirely post-rational, he does accord the intellect a role to play at the very outside of the practice, in making the intention that begins this journey beyond the mind. He has also described these intentions as a "spiritual roadmap," drawn up by the saints of the past who derived them from their own experiences traversing the path so that others may journey to the same experience for themselves.⁷⁴

Abdur Rashid also follows Rasool in urging students toward daily consistency in the performance of the practices, but in contrast to his teacher's comparatively practice-oriented teachings and in line with his own application-oriented focus on manifesting the results of such practices, he also encourages them to move "beyond the practices as practices," so they are not simply something that one does, rather they become a part of one's way of being, of who one is.⁷⁵ While Rasool made use of broader meanings for the words *muraqaba* and *dhikr*, namely "vigilance" and "remembrance," even considering any conduct not in violation of the shari'a as an act of remembrance,⁷⁶ Abdur Rashid does so much more frequently, using his words to inspire his students to achieve such states in parallel with their performance of the practices. So, for example, he emphasizes how *muraqaba* not only refers to the practice of sitting in meditation, but it is also a state that one can reach and maintain in daily life wherein one is "actively paying attention to the Divine Presence."⁷⁷ Likewise, time and again he states that *dhikr* is not just repeating *la ilaha illa Allah* or *Allah, Allah, Allah* but, drawing from Quran 2:115, it is realizing and feeling the divine presence. According to him, *dhikr* "in its most comprehensive form [...] is a process of making everything a reminder of the Divine Presence," that is everything that one sees, hears, thinks, does or that happens to one.⁷⁸ He even notes that "when you say, 'This is beautiful', you have just said the name of Allah, *al-Jamal*."⁷⁹

---

73 Abdur Rashid differentiates here between practicing horseback riding and actually riding a horse. See Abdur Rashid, "Practices of Muraqabah," 1–3, 5, 10; Rasool, *Turning Toward the Heart*, 36.
74 Abdur Rashid, "Muraqabah in the Naqshbandi-Mujaddidi Order."
75 Idem, "Tafakkur/Contemplation: The Bridge to the Eternal," lecture, February 28, 2018.
76 Rasool, *Turning Toward the Heart*, 100 and 108; idem, *The Search for Truth*, 56.
77 Abdur Rashid, *Applied Sufism*, 64.
78 Idem, *Transformation: The Challenge to Remember* (Bedford, VA: The Circle Group, 2017), 23.
79 Idem, *Who?*, 28.

Such broader meanings relate to how Abdur Rashid makes substantial use of lectures in training his students, seeking to bring about their transformation not only through assigned practices involving the *lata'if*, but also through the intellect. In contrast to Rasool and Sa'id Khan, who emphasized how in the modern era the heart has been neglected in favor of the mind and reason,[80] Abdur Rashid, without any lesser emphasis on the heart, also highlights the mind and its ability to affect the heart. Here, he incorporates additional means that are supplemental to Rasool's teachings, exhorting his students to the daily practices of accounting for oneself (*muhasabat al-nafs* or *muhasaba*) as well as conscious reflection (*fikr*). Abdur Rashid sees *muhasaba* as a major tool for building character[81] and modeling one's life after the Prophet,[82] and he considers it a crucial part of the spiritual journey that consists of actively seeking to discover one's own "strengths and weaknesses," cultivating and nurturing the former while rectifying the latter. He laments how, especially in contemporary times, people are reluctant to engage in such self-criticism, to the point that it has even become an anathema.[83] Moreover, reflecting his characteristic emphasis on societal engagement, in addition to taking account of oneself as an individual, Abdur Rashid points out that "*Muḥaasabah* also has a collective implication,"[84] meaning that one should also examine and rectify the state of society.

Abdur Rashid also frequently encourages setting aside the time to contemplate or reflect (*fikr* or *tafakkur*) daily on the signs of the divine presence in the outer world and within oneself,[85] which like *muhasaba* was not among the main practices taught by Rasool and his teachers. While the debate among Sufis over whether the intuitional practice of *dhikr* or the intellectual practice of *fikr* is superior has resulted in a general consensus on the primacy of the former,[86] Abdur Rashid describes an interdependent and mutually supportive relationship, seeing *fikr* as a personal responsibility that compliments *dhikr*.[87]

---

80   Rasool, *The Search for Truth*, 117–29, 152–55.
81   Abdur Rashid, *Applied Sufism*, 207–11.
82   Idem, *Seeing by the Light of the Moon: The Prophet Muhammad* (Bedford, VA: The Circle Group, 2013), 21.
83   Idem, *Transformation*, 32.
84   Idem, *Seeing by the Light of the Moon*, 21; for further discussion of *muhasaba* by Abdur Rashid, including a description of the actual practice, see his *Applied Sufism*, 272–76.
85   In this regard, he often draws upon Quran 41:53, which states, "We will show them Our signs in the horizons and within themselves until it becomes clear to them that it is the truth" (trans. Saheeh International).
86   Louis Gardet, s.v. "Fikr," in *Encyclopaedia of Islam*, 2nd ed., ed. P. Bearman et al. (Leiden: Brill, 1960–2007), http://dx.doi.org/10.1163/1573-3912_islam_SIM_2366.
87   Ahmed Abdur Rashid, "Consciousness: Tafakkur and Tadhakkur," lecture, August 18, 2018.

Concerning the former, we again see Abdur Rashid's emphasis on application, as he states "The desire for beauty and peace in the world, that's great contemplation,"[88] and he says that *fikr* is not simply seeing the beautiful, but it is also looking at "the ugly, upsetting, painful, frightening, disturbing, [since] you can learn a lesson from it, how to avoid it, how to fix it."[89] Moreover, the notion that the heart can be affected by the intellect relates not only to Abdur Rashid's reliance on lectures (*dars*) as one means of spiritual training, but also, in a secular context, to the educational activities of the WCEC as well as of Legacy in seeking to empower and inspire emerging leaders, affecting their hearts through their intellects by way of their peace education, civic education and professional development programs.

Yet another example of an additional practice which cannot be found in Rasool's teachings is the weekly collective vocalized *dhikr* (*hadra*). This is a marked shift from Rasool's preference for silent over vocal recitation. Abdur Rashid describes how the silent practices which he, like Rasool, primarily teaches (namely *muraqaba* and the *wazifa*) are particularly beneficial in refining intuitional perception and furthermore that "the mind can run continuously" whether inhaling, exhaling or holding one's breath, but that they are nevertheless more difficult to master than vocalized *dhikr*. Abdur Rashid feels that his students respond well to the loud *dhikr*, and he also reports that Rasool's stated grounds for avoiding it was so as not to create controversy with the neighbors.[90] This might indeed be a problem if one has "reformist-leaning" neighbors in a Muslim-majority area of bustling Delhi, but would be less of an issue at a *khanqah* tucked away in the forested hinterlands of Virginia.

3.3 Shaykh *and Community*

Speaking of the collective aspect of spiritual training, the *shaykh* and a group of fellow seekers play crucial roles in the teachings of this lineage and Abdur Rashid has retained the importance of the spiritual guide along with instilling a strong sense of community, in some ways even more so than was fostered by his teacher. Rasool emphasized the need for a relationship of spiritual affinity (*nisbat*), or a bond (*rabita*), with the *shaykh*. He considered this necessary for facilitating the student's progress on the path through *tawajjuh*, the non-physical transmission of *baraka* from teacher to student.[91] While upholding

---

88 Idem, "Tafakkur/Contemplation: Visualizing Who You Want to Become," lecture, March 3, 2018.
89 Idem, "Tafakkur/Contemplation: Paying Attention is Healing," lecture, March 8, 2018.
90 Idem, *Transformation*, 7; idem, interview, January 3–4, 2017.
91 Rasool, *Turning Toward the Heart*, 74–83, 94–98; idem, *The Search for Truth*, 52–54.

the significance of such means of spiritual training, Abdur Rashid additionally emphasizes keeping in the physical company of the *shaykh* (*suhbat*). He highlights the need for a spiritual affinity with the teacher, often using the term *munasaba*, and describes sending the transmissions of the order to students in other parts of the world, when they are not able to travel to sit with him in person. Yet he warns that such transmission should not be used as an excuse for not making the effort to be in the physical company of the *shaykh*.[92] He maintains that although *tawajjuh* serves as a crucial link for the student to the lineage leading back to the Prophet and ultimately to God, the *shaykh*'s range of functions, such as assessing the student's progress on the path, assigning practices and providing spiritual guidance, are best facilitated by close contact between him and his students. Therefore, he believes that *nisbat* and *tawajjuh* ought to be supported and sustained with *suhbat*, that is keeping in the physical company of the *shaykh* – whether that be performing the practices or simply spending time together, talking and attending the *shaykh*'s lectures. Otherwise, he says, one becomes one's own *shaykh* and loses the benefit of having a "mirror" or "litmus test" to gauge one's spiritual progress, noting also that "a book is not a mirror."[93] Of further note, characteristic of his application-orientation, Abdur Rashid extends *tawajjuh* to also mean the student directing his or her own spiritual attention toward not only their *lata'if* and God, but also other people or situations.[94]

While the importance of *suhbat* was also noted by Sa'id Khan as well as by Rasool,[95] the greater stress on non-physical aspects in the latter's writings compared with the more apparent emphasis on physical company for Abdur Rashid may be directly tied to institutional differences in their respective approaches to spreading their Sufi lineage. Whereas some students of Hamid Hasan 'Alawi, Sa'id Khan and Rasool might have only seen their *shaykh* in person once per year during their tours, most of Abdur Rashid's students reside at the World Community and can thus see him on a daily basis. Students living in other areas of the US or abroad come to visit the *shaykh* there, instead of vice versa, supplemented with email and telephone contact as well as attending his lectures remotely via telephonic or online conferencing platforms.[96]

---

92 Abdur Rashid, interview, January 3–4, 2017.
93 Ibid.
94 Idem, *Transformation*, 14.
95 Rasool, *The Search for Truth*, 85; Ahmed Abdur Rashid and Azad Rasool, *A Guide to Modern Sufi Teaching: Questions and Answers for the Sincere Seekers* (Bedford, VA: The Circle Group, 2015), 10, 12.
96 Abdur Rashid, interview, January 3–4, 2017.

Regarding travelling as a *shaykh*, Rasool made an analogy that in the past, people went to the well to get water whereas now, pipes bring water to the people.[97] Accordingly, Abdur Rashid sees his own more stationary approach as a return to an earlier way of doing things, one in which it is incumbent upon the student to go to the well.[98]

With regard to community, Rasool, in between his visits, encouraged weekly group meetings among his students, in their various locations within India and abroad, for the purpose of performing the practices together.[99] Abdur Rashid similarly highlights the importance of community, but to an even greater degree, as the majority of his students live together, perform the practices daily as a group and work side-by-side at the WCEC or Legacy. Accordingly, he extends the meaning of *suhbat* to include "being in the company of the *shaykh* and fellow seekers, for spiritual purposes,"[100] and he has sometimes gone even further, in tune with his pluralism, using it in reference to keeping company with "good Muslims, good Christians, good Jews, good Hindus, good whatever. Good people."[101]

A final difference between Rasool and Abdur Rashid regarding the role of the *shaykh*, one that has been present throughout this chapter, is the latter's extensive use of lectures (*dars*). Abdur Rashid acknowledges this difference, saying: "My Shaykh didn't give lots of *dars* like I do, but taught vis-à-vis only the practices."[102] Nevertheless, Abdur Rashid explained that he was indeed "given very specific permission [from Rasool] to write and to give *dars*" and that although Rasool emphasized practices over reading and speculation, he even directed his own disciples who were eager for reading material towards Abdur Rashid's writings.[103] Each week, he normally gives three lectures as *suhbat*, around an hour each, in addition to a Friday *khutba*. These are broadcast online and recorded for students to return to at their leisure. The topics vary widely and build upon the teachings of Rasool, while also including Abdur Rashid's own spiritual insights as well as his research into a wide range of Islamic thought, primarily Sufi but also including other sources such as early Isma'ili thinkers, as well as modern science. He makes quite clear, however,

---

97 Rasool, *Turning Toward the Heart*, 46.
98 Abdur Rashid, interview, January 3–4, 2017.
99 Rasool, *Turning Toward the Heart*, 46–49.
100 Abdur Rashid, *Transformation*, 30.
101 Idem, "The Purpose of Activating the Laṭā'if is to Return to its Origin," lecture, July 13, 2013, 9.
102 Idem, *What?*, 22.
103 Idem, interview, January 3–4, 2017.

that attending the lectures is no replacement for performing one's assigned practices, and that these are actually crucial for students in order to fully benefit from the *dars*.[104] He in fact sees the *dars* as a practice in and of itself, both for his audience as well as for himself personally, and he advises listeners to seek to not only understand his words, but also to attune themselves to receive the "the message behind the words" or "the inner message," along with the transmission of *baraka* that accompanies it.[105] For him, the *dars* is a form of *dhikr* and it is not simply articulating about God, but being in the presence of the Truth.[106]

So we have seen that for Abdur Rashid, spiritual training is given through transmission (*tawajjuh*) from and spiritual affinity (*nisbat*) with the *shaykh* supported by keeping in his company and that of fellow seekers (*suhbat*), including attending the shaykh's lectures (*dars*), while also performing practices that are intuitional (*muraqaba* and *dhikr*) and intellectual (*muhasaba* and *tafakkur*) in nature. Such training is held to result in the awakening of the *lata'if* and an affinity (*nisbat*) with God which manifests as engaged and profoundly refined ethical conduct in the world.

4 Conclusion: Change in Continuity

Juxtaposition of the American *shaykh* with his immediate Indian forebears reveals much continuity, but also several instances of divergence or shifts in emphasis from the conventions of the lineage. With regard to mystical cosmopsychology, while Rasool cautioned against concentrating too much on the divine names and attributes in his lectures, the topic is a prominent theme in Abdur Rashid's elaboration of the relationship (*nisbat* in its first and third meanings) between God and man. Specifically, he emphasizes the "descent" of man from God, after ascending towards him through the divine names and attributes, in the service of his call for positive engagement in the world: while the divine essence governs the inner life, the names and attributes should regulate the outer life. By considering the divine names and attributes as "universal values," he makes Sufi teachings beneficial for a broader audience. Likewise, his endeavor to find analogies between Sufism and modern science has the potential to make mystical Islam more acceptable for a modern mind. Concerning man's subtle centers of consciousness (*lata'if*), which make spiritual ascent

---

104 Idem, interview, June 26, 2018.
105 Idem, *Dooste Haghighi: The True Friend* (Bedford, VA: The Circle Group, 2012), 17.
106 Idem, interview, June 26, 2018.

possible, Abdur Rashid goes beyond his teacher's focus on their function as supra-sensory organs for the inner journey by highlighting their role in also perceiving the external world and thus facilitating societal engagement.

Abdur Rashid's mystical practices exhibit substantial continuity, but also cases of difference from those of his immediate predecessors. He continues to teach the same five curricula of practices attributed to 'Abd al-Bari Shah unchanged from how he received them from Rasool. These consist of complex series of intentions for meditation (*muraqaba*) alongside different forms of the remembrance of God (*dhikr*) and other recitations. Through his lectures, he stresses that these terms denote more than the mystical techniques to which they refer, that is as parts of one's manner of being and states that can be attained and realized in everyday life. He also incorporates additional techniques beyond and supplemental to the practices he was taught by Rasool, including the sessions of vocalized *dhikr* called *hadra*, inward accounting (*muhasaba*) and conscious reflection (*fikr*). Again, Abdur Rashid goes beyond conventional understandings of Sufi practices and gives *muhasaba* a collective function in examining the deficiencies of society and improving its condition. Similarly, conscious reflection is introduced not only as contemplating the signs of the divine, but also as a desire for peace and well-being in the world and using the intellect to achieve such aims. Concerning the role of the *shaykh* and the relation between him and his students (*nisbat* in its second meaning), in addition to the *shaykh*'s function in orienting his spiritual attention towards disciples (*tawajjuh*), Abdur Rashid places more emphasis than his predecessors on direct, physically embodied mentorship of the Sufi guide and the students' need to personally accompany him. For those not actually residing at the World Community, their visits for such companionship (*suhbat*) are augmented by continuous contact between student and guide by means of recent advances in communication technologies.

The differences observed between Abdur Rashid and his nineteenth- and twentieth-century Indian forebears can be clustered into two categories. The first is those distinctions resulting from his extending the meaning and/ or function of mystical elements already present in the teachings of Rasool and others of the lineage. With regard to Rasool's above-mentioned five key terms, we saw how Abdur Rashid gives a seemingly novel meaning to *nisbat*, as the interconnectedness of all things; expands the function of the *lata'if* to perceiving the external world as well as the inner; highlights broader senses of *muraqaba* and *dhikr* as continuous awareness of God and making everything in life a reminder of the divine presence; and extends *tawajjuh* to include the student directing his or her own spiritual attention toward other people and circumstances as well as toward the *lata'if* and toward God. The latter two senses are actually closer to the original meaning of *tawajjuh* among the early Naqshbandis, as nearly synonymous with *muraqaba*.[107] In addition to Rasool's five central terms, Abdur Rashid further broadens the scope of the practice of *suhbat*. While primarily using it to mean keeping the company of the *shaykh*, he also extends it to refer to fellow Sufi practitioners, and on some occasions, he has even used it with reference to good people in general, regardless of faith. Moreover, the earlier attention Rasool and Saʿid Khan paid towards modern science evolved into Abdur Rashid's engagement with the findings of scientific disciplines and his endeavor to draw analogies and find common ground with Sufism, as approaching the same Truth from different angles.

The second category of distinctions between Abdur Rashid and his predecessors includes those resulting from his restoration, mainly in revised form, of some Sufi elements that are not prominent in Rasool's writings, but that can be found in medieval Sufi tradition. An example of such re-introduction is his emphasis on theoretical mysticism and one of its major themes, the divine names and attributes, which can be regarded as Abdur Rashid's return to earlier Sufi traditions, including the early Naqshbandiyya. In the case of the latter, many of the first *shaykh*s of this order were among the major interpreters of Ibn ʿArabi, the founder of *al-tasawwuf al-nazari* ("theoretical Sufism"), Naqshbandi figures such as Muhammad Parsa (d. 1420), Yaʿqub Charkhi (d. 1447) and ʿAbd al-Rahman Jami (d. 1492) were crucial in disseminating the Ibn ʿArabi school.[108] Even the founder-figure of the Naqshbandiyya Mujaddidiyya, Ahmad Sirhindi, whose critique of certain aspects of Ibn ʿArabi's thought resulted in the waning of interest in the Andalusian *shaykh* among later Naqshbandis, was himself well acquainted with Ibn ʿArabi's teachings, including those concerning the divine names and attributes, and showed respect and reverence towards him.[109]

Another instance of Abdur Rashid's restoration of Sufi elements, which like the previous example shows his emphasis on a two-pronged intuitional and intellectual approach to spiritual training, is his regular and extensive use of lectures (*dars*). This addition can also be seen as a return to the Sufi tradition of teaching and lecturing popular among various Sufi orders. This tradition can

---

107 Necdet Tosun, "Murāqabah and Tawajjuh," trans. Muhammed F. Bayraktar, accessed November 16, 2020, http://maktabah.org/blog/?p=2447.
108 Hamid Algar, "Reflections of Ibn ʿArabi in Early Naqshbandî Tradition," *Journal of the Muhyiddin Ibn ʿArabi Society* 10 (1991).
109 Alberto Ventura, "A Letter of Šayḫ Aḥmad Sirhindī in Defense of the *Waḥdat al-Wuǧūd*," *Oriente Moderno* 92, no. 2 (2012). For more literature on the relationship between Sirhindi and Ibn ʿArabi, see footnote 1 of Ventura's article.

be observed, for instance, in South Asia in the *malfuzat* literary genre, which emerged out of the written records of audiences and question-and-answer sessions of notable Sufis or scholars.¹¹⁰ Additionally, all three of the above-listed techniques which Abdur Rashid integrated into the regimen of practices – viz., vocalized *dhikr*, *muhasaba* and *fikr* – also have roots in earlier Sufi tradition. The former is an important ingredient of several Sufi orders, even being practiced by some Naqshbandis, past and present, for whom silent over vocal recitation is a hallmark.¹¹¹ Moreover, both *muhasaba* and *fikr* are practiced in other lineages, though in various ways, and Abdur Rashid himself refers to the medieval Sufi heritage and early Islamic tradition in substantiating his incorporation of these practices.¹¹²

But we may ask, is there any main underlying motivation behind Abdur Rashid's modifications to the conventions of this lineage? It seems that the most significant red thread connecting his amendments and additions is his concern with Applied Sufism—that is achieving a profound awareness of God, spiritually and intellectually, and manifesting that in daily life through ethical conduct and service. Such results-oriented Sufism with emphasis on social engagement,¹¹³ which aims at bringing the outer world and inner world into alignment, is yet not developed through integrating totally new or alien elements into the lineage, but mainly via unearthing earlier Sufi tradition and utilizing the potentialities of such mystical past for the present. The Naqshbandi tradition plays a central role here, as the very concept of Applied Sufism can be seen as a reformulation of the Naqshbandi pillar of Sufi activism in the new context of the West, while emphasizing contextual adaptivity and having a

---

110 On this genre, see Amina Steinfels, "His Master's Voice: The Genre of Malfūẓāt in South Asian Sufism," *History of Religions* 44, no. 1 (August 2004), https://doi.org/10.1086/426655.
111 Muhammad Parsa, for instance, accepted the practice of vocal *dhikr* for beginners in the Naqshbandi brotherhood. See the edition and translation of one of Parsa's treatises in Jürgen Paul, "Muhammad Parsa: Sendschreiben über das Gottesgedenken mit Vernehmlicher Stimme," in *Muslim Culture in Russia and Central Asia*, vol. 3, *Arabic, Persian and Turkic Manuscripts (15th–19th Centuries)*, ed. Anke von Kügelgen, Asirbek Muminov, and Michael Kemper (Berlin: Klaus Schwarz, 2000), 17–41.
112 Ahmed Abdur Rashid, "Tafakkur/Contemplation: A Positive Relationship with Science," lecture, March 24, 2018; idem, "Our Ability to Perceive Signs in this World with Faith in the Unseen," lecture, February 24, 2018.
113 Concerning social engagement and activism, Abdur Rashid asserts that he is not pushing any sort of political agenda, though outspoken on a number of issues that do have ramifications in the sphere of politics, namely his main goals of promoting peace and well-being for all of humanity. Abdur Rashid, interview, January 3–4, 2017.

more pluralistic scope.¹¹⁴ This attitude towards re-orientation can be better understood if it is compared with other reformulations of Sufism in the West. The revision of mystical Islam by figures such as Inayat Khan, Idries Shah and Frithjof Schuon (d. 1998), for example, included incorporating elements outside Sufi heritage and even Islamic tradition, be it through syncretism with other systems such as Western esotericism, ancient Eastern religions, occult sciences, Freemasonry and Native Americans customs, or through innovations of their own.¹¹⁵

The re-orientation of mystical Islam in the Applied Sufism of Abdur Rashid brings us to critically reconsider the notions of "continuity" and "change" in understanding and analyzing the history of Sufism. A notorious example of debates around these notions is the academic controversy starting in the 1990s about "neo-Sufism," a term first utilized by Fazlur Rahman in reference to the Sufi reformism of the eighteenth and nineteenth centuries.¹¹⁶ While the scholars supporting the idea of neo-Sufism, notable among them Reinhard Schulze, emphasized the emergence of "new" elements in Sufism during those centuries, their fiery critics, especially Bernd Radtke, claimed that many of the allegedly new things are nothing but "old" ideas and practices that can be found in earlier Sufi heritage.¹¹⁷ In this discourse, "change" mainly denotes innovative

---

114 Itzchak Weismann considers "orthodoxy" and "activism" as the two main distinctive features of this *tariqa*. See his *The Naqshbandiyya: Orthodoxy and Activism in a Worldwide Sufi Tradition* (Abingdon and New York: Routledge, 2007).

115 Olav Hammer considers Inayat Khan's Sufism to be a "quintessentially Western phenomenon," since, as Hammer claims, he did not represent the teachings and practices of the Chishtiyya despite being a member of that order ("Sufism for Westerners," in *Sufism in Europe and North America*, ed. David Westerlund [London and New York: RoutledgeCurzon, 2004], 134–36). Sedgwick also believes that Schuon's Sufi group was never more than formally subordinate to its Algerian leadership, and it became formally independent after Schuon's vision of the Virgin Mary ("Western Sufism and Traditionalism," accessed September 15, 2019, www.traditionalists.org/write/WSuf.htm). In her *Mystical Dimensions of Islam* (Chapel Hill: The University of North Carolina Press, 1975), 9, Annemarie Schimmel warns that "Idries Shah, *The Sufis*, as well as his other books, should be avoided by serious students."

116 Fazlur Rahman, *Islam* (Chicago and London: University of Chicago Press, 1979), 206.

117 See, for example, Reinhard Schulze, "Was ist die islamische Aufklärung?," *Die Welt des Islams* 36, no. 3 (January 1996), https://doi.org/10.1163/1570060962597391; and R.S. O'Fahey and Bernd Radtke, "Neo-Sufism Reconsidered," *Der Islam* 70, no. 1 (1993), https://doi.org/10.1515/islm.1993.70.1.52. For Jamal Malik's contribution to this debate, see, for instance, "Muslim Culture and Reform in 18th Century South Asia," *Journal of the Royal Asiatic Society* 13, no. 2 (2003): 227–43 and "Some Ideas on Pre-Colonial Modernity: The Case of Indian Muslim Pietists," *Exemplar: The Journal of South Asian Studies* 1, no. 1 (2012). A critical summary of the debate can be found in Alexander Knysh's *Sufism: A New History of Islamic Mysticism* (Princeton: Princeton University Press, 2017), 141–44.

additions disconnected from the past, while "continuity" signifies the flow of earlier elements in the new context. Yet the reformulation of mystical Islam by Abdur Rashid, who creates new mystical elements through re-connecting with earlier tradition, shows the insufficiency of the dichotomy of change versus continuity as an analytic tool for investigating the internal movement within Sufi orders and communities. Therefore, instead of this black-and-white division, one may utilize the category of "dynamics," a central theme of the current volume, in reference to Abdur Rashid's re-activation of the past for the sake of the present and the future.[118] Indeed, the concept of "dynamics," which refers to the motions within a system resulting from the internal interaction of its components or from their external interaction with the environment outside the system, can better reflect the spectrum of hybrid areas of Sufi activity which can be located between two sides of total innovation/newness and absolute continuity/oldness. This concept can be used not only for scrutinizing the *behavior* of groups and their members, as is the case in the fields of social dynamics and system dynamics, but, for the study of Sufism, it can also be extended to include all of the different aspects of mysticism, including theoretical, practical, institutional, aesthetic and even experiential dimensions.[119] For such a broad sense of dynamism, Abdur Rashid's change-in-continuity is an illuminating example.

Bibliography

Abdur Rashid, Ahmed. *Applied Sufism: Classical Teachings for the Contemporary Seeker*. Livermore, CA: WingSpan Press, 2006.

Abdur Rashid, Ahmed. "Consciousness: Tafakkur and Tadhakkur." Lecture, August 18, 2018.

Abdur Rashid, Ahmed. *Dhaahir and Baaṭin*. Bedford, VA: The Circle Group, 2010.

Abdur Rashid, Ahmed. *Dooste Haghighi: The True Friend*. Bedford, VA: The Circle Group, 2012.

---

118 For a similar concept which blurs the dichotomy of "integrationism" and "rejectionism" in studying the dynamics of mystical Islam, see Saeed Zarrabi-Zadeh, "Sufism in the Modern West: A Taxonomy of Typologies and the Category of 'Dynamic Integrejectionism'," in *Sufism East and West*, ed. Malik and Zarrabi-Zadeh, 180–208.

119 On multi-dimensional definitions of mysticism, see for example Peter Moore, s.v. "Mysticism [Further Consideration]," in *Encyclopedia of Religion*, 2nd ed., ed. Lindsay Jones (Detroit: Macmillan Reference USA, 2005), 6356; and Bernard McGinn, *The Presence of God: A History of Western Christian Mysticism*, vol. 1, *The Foundations of Mysticism* (New York: Crossroad, 1991), xvi.

Abdur Rashid, Ahmed. Interview by Michael E. Asbury. Bedford, VA, January 3–4, 2017.
Abdur Rashid, Ahmed. Interview by Michael E. Asbury. Bedford, VA, June 26, 2018.
Abdur Rashid, Ahmed. "Muraqabah in the Naqshbandi-Mujaddidi Order: The Spiritual Road Map of Contemplation/Niyyat." Lecture, June 20, 2013.
Abdur Rashid, Ahmed. "The Purpose of Activating the Laṭā'if is to Return to its Origin." Lecture, July 13, 2013.
Abdur Rashid, Ahmed. "Our Ability to Perceive Signs in this World with Faith in the Unseen." Lecture, February 24, 2018.
Abdur Rashid, Ahmed. "Practices of Muraqabah: History and References, Rābita of the Shaykh." Lecture, September 20, 2012.
Abdur Rashid, Ahmed. "Proof of the Divine: Seeing the Unseen through the Unseen, Accelerating the Circles of the Latā'if." Lecture, September 19, 2012.
Abdur Rashid, Ahmed. *Prophet Musa: The Journey from the Mountain*. Bedford, VA: The Circle Group, 2013.
Abdur Rashid, Ahmed. *Seeing by the Light of the Moon: The Prophet Muhammad*. Bedford, VA: The Circle Group, 2013.
Abdur Rashid, Ahmed. "Tafakkur/Contemplation: A Positive Relationship with Science." Lecture, March 24, 2018.
Abdur Rashid, Ahmed. "Tafakkur/Contemplation: Paying Attention is Healing." Lecture, March 8, 2018.
Abdur Rashid, Ahmed. "Tafakkur/Contemplation: The Bridge to the Eternal." Lecture, February 28, 2018.
Abdur Rashid, Ahmed. "Tafakkur/Contemplation: Visualizing Who You Want to Become." Lecture, March 3, 2018.
Abdur Rashid, Ahmed. *Transformation: The Challenge to Remember*. Bedford, VA: The Circle Group, 2017.
Abdur Rashid, Ahmed. *What?*. Bedford, VA: The Circle Group, 2011.
Abdur Rashid, Ahmed. *Who?*. Bedford, VA: The Circle Group, 2012.
Abdur Rashid, Ahmed. *Why?*. Bedford, VA: The Circle Group, 2011.
Abdur Rashid, Ahmed and Azad Rasool. *A Guide to Modern Sufi Teaching: Questions and Answers for the Sincere Seekers*. Bedford, VA: The Circle Group, 2015.
Algar, Hamid. "Reflections of Ibn 'Arabi in Early Naqshbandî Tradition." *Journal of the Muhyiddin Ibn 'Arabi Society* 10 (1991): 45–66.
Asbury, Michael E. "Seeing with the Heart: The Mysticism of an Islamic Sufi Lineage from India in the West." PhD diss., University of Erfurt, 2020.
Baldick, Julian. *Mystical Islam: An Introduction to Sufism*. London: I.B. Tauris, 1989.
Buehler, Arthur F. *Revealed Grace: The Juristic Sufism of Ahmad Sirhindi (1564–1624)*. Louisville, KY: Fons Vitae, 2011.
Buehler, Arthur F. *Sufi Heirs of the Prophet: The Indian Naqshbandiyya and the Rise of the Mediating Sufi Shaykh*. Columbia, SC: University of South Carolina Press, 1998.

Chittick, William C. *The Self-Disclosure of God: Principles of Ibn al-'Arabī's Cosmology*. Albany, NY: SUNY Press, 1998.

Chittick, William C. *The Sufi Path of Knowledge: Ibn-al-'Arabi's Metaphysics of Imagination*. Albany, NY: SUNY Press, 1989.

Dallal, Ahmad S. *Islam without Europe: Traditions of Reform in Eighteenth-Century Islamic Thought*. Chapel Hill: The University of North Carolina Press, 2018.

De Hungaria, Georgius. *Tractatus de moribus, condicionibus et nequicia Turcorum* [Treatise on the Customs, Habits and Perversity of the Turks]. Rome: n.p, 1480.

De Vos, Philippe A. *Sheikh Nâzim la Preuve de la Générosité*. Avignon: Les éditions du Relié, 1997.

Ernst, Carl W. *Sufism: An Introduction to the Mystical Tradition of Islam*. Boston and London: Shambhala Publications, 2011.

Gardet, Louis. s.v. "Fikr." In *Encyclopaedia of Islam*, 2nd ed., edited by P. Bearman, Th. Bianquis, C.E. Bosworth, E. van Donzel and W.P. Heinrichs. Leiden: Brill, 1960–2007, http://dx.doi.org/10.1163/1573-3912_islam_SIM_2366.

Giddens, Anthony. *Modernity and Self-Identity: Self and Society in the Late Modern Age*. Stanford: Stanford University Press, 1991.

Green, Nile. *Sufism: A Global History*. Chichester: Wiley-Blackwell, 2012.

Hammer, Olav. "Sufism for Westerners." In *Sufism in Europe and North America*, edited by David Westerlund, 127–43. London and New York: RoutledgeCurzon, 2004.

Hermansen, Marcia. "Global Sufism: 'Theirs and Ours'." In *Sufis in Western Society: Global Networking and Locality*, edited by Ron Geaves, Markus Dressler and Gritt Klinkhammer, 26–45. Abingdon and New York: Routledge, 2009.

Hermansen, Marcia and Saeed Zarrabi-Zadeh, eds. *Sufism in Western Contexts*. Leiden: Brill, forthcoming.

James, William. *The Varieties of Religious Experience: A Study in Human Nature*. New York: Longmans, Green and Co., 1902.

Karamustafa, Ahmet T. *Sufism: The Formative Period*. Edinburgh: Edinburgh University Press, 2007.

King, Richard. *Orientalism and Religion: Postcolonial Theory, India and 'The Mystic East'*. London and New York: Routledge, 1999.

Knysh, Alexander. *Islamic Mysticism: A Short History*. Leiden: Brill, 2000.

Knysh, Alexander. *Sufism: A New History of Islamic Mysticism*. Princeton: Princeton University Press, 2017.

Malik, Jamal. "Introduction." In *Sufism in the West*, edited by Jamal Malik and John Hinnells, 1–27. London and New York: Routledge, 2006.

Malik, Jamal. "Muslim Culture and Reform in 18th Century South Asia." *Journal of the Royal Asiatic Society* 13, no. 2 (2003): 227–43.

Malik, Jamal. "Some Ideas on Pre-Colonial Modernity: The Case of Indian Muslim Pietists." *Exemplar: The Journal of South Asian Studies* 1, no. 1 (2012): 56–64.

Malik, Jamal and Saeed Zarrabi-Zadeh. "Introduction." In *Sufism East and West: Mystical Islam and Cross-Cultural Exchange in the Modern World*, edited by Jamal Malik and Saeed Zarrabi-Zadeh, 1–29. Leiden: Brill, 2019.

McGinn, Bernard. *The Presence of God: A History of Western Christian Mysticism*, vol. 1, *The Foundations of Mysticism*. New York: Crossroad, 1991.

Menavino, Giovan Antonio. *Trattato de costumi et vita de Turchi* [Treatise on the Customs and Life of the Turks]. Florence: n.p, 1548.

Moore, Peter. s.v. "Mysticism [Further Consideration]." In *Encyclopedia of Religion*, 2nd ed., edited by Lindsay Jones, 6355–59. Detroit: Macmillan Reference USA, 2005.

Mourad, Suleiman Ali. *Early Islam between Myth and History: Al-Ḥasan Al-Baṣrī (d. 110H/728CE) and the Formation on His Legacy in Classical Islamic Scholarship*. Leiden: Brill, 2006.

O'Fahey, R.S. and Bernd Radtke. "Neo-Sufism Reconsidered." *Der Islam* 70, no. 1 (1993): 52–87, https://doi.org/10.1515/islm.1993.70.1.52.

Paul, Jürgen. "Muhammad Parsa: Sendschriben über das Gottesgedenken mit Vernehmlicher Stimme." In *Muslim Culture in Russia and Central Asia*, vol. 3, *Arabic, Persian and Turkic Manuscripts (15th–19th Centuries)*, edited by Anke von Kügelgen, Asirbek Muminov, and Michael Kemper, 5–41. Berlin: Klaus Schwarz, 2000.

Rahman, Fazlur. *Islam*. Chicago and London: University of Chicago Press, 1979.

Rash, J.E. *Islam and Democracy: A Foundation for Ending Extremism and Preventing Conflict*. Bedford, VA: Legacy International, 2006.

Rasool, Azad. *The Search for Truth: The Life & Teaching Methods of the Indian Sufi Shaykh Hazrat Maulvi Muhammad Saʿid Khan (r)*. Louisville, KY: Fons Vitae, 2010.

Rasool, Azad. *Turning Toward the Heart: Awakening to the Sufi Way, Forty Questions and Answers with Shaykh al-Tariqat Hazrat Azad Rasool*. Louisville, KY: Fons Vitae, 2002.

Schimmel, Annemarie. *Mystical Dimensions of Islam*. Chapel Hill: The University of North Carolina Press, 1975.

Schulze, Reinhard. "Was ist die islamische Aufklärung?." *Die Welt des Islams* 36, no. 3 (January 1996): 276–325, https://doi.org/10.1163/1570060962597391.

Sedgwick, Mark. "Western Sufism and Traditionalism." Accessed September 15, 2019, www.traditionalists.org/write/WSuf.htm.

Sedgwick, Mark. *Western Sufism: From the Abbasids to the New Age*. New York: Oxford University Press, 2017.

Shabistari, Mahmud. *Rosenflor des Geheimnisses*. Translated by Joseph von Hammer-Purgstall. Pesth and Leipzig: Hartleben, 1838.

Smith, Wilfred Cantwell. *Modern Islām in India: A Social Analysis*. London: Victor Gollancz Ltd., 1946.

Steinfels, Amina. "His Master's Voice: The Genre of Malfūẓāt in South Asian Sufism." In *History of Religions* 44, no. 1 (August 2004): 56–69, https://doi.org/10.1086/426655.

SufiSchool.org. "Hazrat Hamid Hasan Alawi (r.a)." Accessed November 2, 2019, www.sufischool.org/orders/hazrat-hamid-hasan-alawi-r-a.html.

Tareen, SherAli. "Normativity, Heresy, and the Politics of Authenticity in South Asian Islam." *The Muslim World* 99, no. 3 (June 2009): 521–52, https://doi.org/10.1111/j.1478-1913.2009.01284.x.

Tosun, Necdet. "Murāqabah and Tawajjuh." Translated by Muhammed F. Bayraktar. Accessed November 16, 2020, http://maktabah.org/blog/?p=2447.

Ventura, Alberto. "A Letter of Šayḫ Aḥmad Sirhindī in Defense of the *Waḥdat al-Wuǧūd*." *Oriente Moderno* 92, no. 2 (2012): 509–17.

Weismann, Itzchak. *The Naqshbandiyya: Orthodoxy and Activism in a Worldwide Sufi Tradition*. Abingdon and New York: Routledge, 2007.

Wilcox, Andrew. "The Dual Mystical Concepts of *Fanāʾ* and *Baqāʾ* in Early Sūfism." *British Journal of Middle Eastern Studies* 38, no. 1 (April 2011): 95–118, https://doi.org/10.1080/13530191003794681.

Zarcone, Thierry. "Rereadings and Transformations of Sufism in the West." *Diogenes* 47, no. 187 (September 1999): 110–21, https://doi.org/10.1177/039219219904718711.

Zarrabi-Zadeh, Saeed. "Sufism in the Modern West: A Taxonomy of Typologies and the Category of 'Dynamic Integrejectionism'." In *Sufism East and West: Mystical Islam and Cross-Cultural Exchange in the Modern World*, edited by Jamal Malik and Saeed Zarrabi-Zadeh, 180–208. Leiden: Brill, 2019.

CHAPTER 12

"Transplanted" Sufism
Complications of a Category

Marcia Hermansen

One of the continuing interests of Prof. Jamal Malik has been the interactions of East and West and the fact that these categories are highly complex—marked and transgressed over long historical interactions and reciprocal[1]—if not isomorphic, exchanges over the longue durée. South Asian Sufism and Western expressions of Sufism, both academic and popular, have also been interrogated in his thorough and probing studies and edited volumes.[2] In this brief chapter, composed for his Festschrift, I would like to revisit and elaborate a category or ideal type of Western Sufism that I initially proposed in the 1997 article "In the Garden of American Sufism: Hybrids and Perennials," which was one of the first academic treatments of multiple Sufi movements in America.[3] The garden metaphor of the title was carried through in the body of the piece in which I only very briefly alluded to a further category beyond the hybrids and perennials, that of the transplants. "Transplants," or what might also be called "transplanted Sufism," was the term I used to refer to "Sufi movements conducted among small circles of immigrants with less adaptation to the American context."[4] I later revisited the category in a chapter seeking to identify some distinctive features of Sufi movements in the United States:

---

1 Jamal Malik, ed., *Perspectives of Mutual Encounters in South Asian History 1760–1860* (Leiden: Brill, 2000). This volume and the conference on which it was based specifically invoked the term "reciprocity" in terms of cross-cultural encounter between Europeans and South Asians during the crucial period from 1760 to 1860.
2 Jamal Malik and John Hinnells, eds., *Sufism in the West* (New York: Routledge, 2006); Jamal Malik and Saeed Zarrabi-Zadeh, eds., *Sufism East and West: Mystical Islam and Cross-Cultural Exchange in the Modern World* (Leiden: Brill, 2019).
3 Marcia Hermansen, "In the Garden of American Sufi Movements: Hybrids and Perennials," in *New Trends and Developments in the World of Islam*, ed. Peter B. Clarke (London: Luzac Oriental Press, 1997). I note that Gisela Webb's chapter "Tradition and Innovation in Contemporary American Islamic Spirituality: The Bawa Muhaiyadeen Fellowship," in *Muslim Communities in North America*, ed. Yvonne Yazbeck Haddad and Jane Idleman Smith (Albany, NY: SUNY Press, 1994), appeared even earlier.
4 Hermansen, "In the Garden."

What's American about American Sufi Movements? On initial consideration, this question seems most likely to be posed from a European comparativist perspective. After all, someone from the Muslim world, say Egypt or South Asia, would likely think of the West as an undifferentiated whole. At the same time Sufi movements that are essentially "transplants" of orders active in Muslim countries that retain the same clientele and language among immigrants in the United States or Europe—might not be thought of as significantly "Western" at all. However, other Sufi movements that have made substantial adjustments to a new context and attract larger numbers of Europeans or North Americans would more likely be seen as generically "Western."[5]

I wrote this while being based in Chicago and interacting quite intensively with South Asian Muslims in personal and academic encounters. I was therefore familiar with a variety of small groups who in some cases gathered with local Sufi teachers or the representatives of Sufi leaders from abroad to perform rituals such as *milad*s (celebrating the birthday of the Prophet Muhammad) or *dhikr* (Sufi recollection of God) sessions. I had also been in contact with similar groups in the San Francisco Bay area and Washington, DC and had participated in some of their gatherings.

Subsequent scholarship on diverse Sufi movements in the "global West"[6] has at times adopted and at other times critiqued or proposed alternatives to the categories of perennial, hybrid and transplant. In particular, the idea of transplantation relates to lively theoretical discussions regarding how to conceptualize such movements in the light of migration, networking and globalization theory. Questions of how to theorize such movements of people, practices and ideas across and within changing "scapes"[7] and contexts has resulted in a proliferation of metaphors, keywords and framings that seek to capture salient elements of these emerging phenomena – crossing and dwelling, travelling and settling, diasporic, transnational, translocal, glocal, multi-sited, etc. In terms of how consideration of this category engages the current

---

5 Marcia Hermansen, "What's American about American Sufi Movements?," in *Sufism in Europe and North America*, ed. David Westerlund (New York: Routledge, 2004), 36–37.
6 The geographical and intellectual framing of the "Global West" reflects both the role played by the interactions between people from diverse religions and cultures in the development of Western ideals and institutions in the modern era, as well as the globalization of these very ideals and institutions. This expression is utilized by Kambiz GhaneaBassiri and Frank Peter in their series *Islam of the Global West* from Bloomsbury Press.
7 Arjun Appadurai, *Modernity at Large: Cultural Dimensions of Globalization* (Minneapolis: University of Minnesota Press, 1996).

volume's theme, "Dynamics of Islam in the Modern World," the movement of Muslims to the West is a relatively recent phenomenon and one that provides fresh and challenging contexts of cultural encounter.

Among contemporary manifestations of Sufism in the global West, one can easily recognize the universal or New Age forms, the perennialists or Traditionalists who view Sufism as one articulation of higher eternal wisdom, and the hybridized Sufi orders that attract Western converts to Islam as well as a new generation of legacy Muslims.[8] Sufi transplants, on the other hand, have garnered less attention and one purpose of this chapter is to consider the reasons for this.

While in previous studies of Sufi movements in the West, I defined the category of "transplants" as primarily consisting of smaller groups of co-ethnics who follow a Sufi teacher and/or Sufi order in much the same way as they might have done in their original cultural settings, I hardly ventured into elaborating and critiquing the category through specific examples. On reflection, some of the issues raised by the "transplant" category are: the scope and applicability of theories of locality – are these groups trans-national, multi-national, multi-sited, etc.? Where to position groups such as Deobandis, Barelwis or the Turkish Nur movements, who display some elements of Sufism but are not identified with any single *tariqa* or who have dispensed with traditional institutional structures? Do transplant Sufi groups inevitably hybridize over time, and if not, why not? In what ways does the size of a group matter?

Imagine a "transplant" in the field of botany – which factors will enable it to survive and flourish – and over time, will the new local weather and soil conditions cause modifications in the very nature of the entity? These are some of the challenges that we face when deciding whether a Sufi movement in the West is a transplant or a hybrid. Perhaps we might conclude that the adaptations of hybrid Sufi orders are more rapid, deliberate and strategic. We may further look at the membership of a Sufi group and determine how ethnically homogenous it is, concluding that ethnic uniformity is a salient feature of transplants.[9] We might further assess its practices in terms of the group's adaptability in gesture, costume, language usage and gendered behaviors.

---

8 The term "legacy Muslim" has been suggested as an alternative to "born Muslim," "native Muslim," etc.
9 As elaborated by Nile Green in *Sufism: A Global History* (Chichester: Wiley-Blackwell, 2012), 221.

1   Situating the Transplants

Locating transplant groups benefits from the nuanced discussion that has occurred in the field of migration studies as to the purview of the terms diaspora versus transnational. In a summary assessment, sociologist Thomas Feist observes that:

> The use of diaspora as a descriptive and analytical category has a strong tradition. Examples [...] include Safran's and Cohen's taxonomies of diaspora and Sheffer's effort to systematically analyse diaspora politic.[10] Making frequent references to family trees, roots, replanting and ancestral soil, such taxonomies often use agrarian or gardening tropes – a trend Cohen[11] has noted in diaspora studies overall. Sometimes these definitions border on essentialist notions of organic social development. By contrast, conceptualisations of transnationalism are more rooted in geographic and sociological images such as "space" and "field," which are often either used heuristically, or associated with claims towards applying key notions of social theory.[12]

It is important to note Feist's caution regarding the employment of agricultural, horticultural or "gardening" terms, as these may inject essentialist notions about the messy process of adaptation. In fact, scholars of Western Sufism have engaged in a prolific interrogation of appropriate categories to differentiate diverse aspects of Sufi movements, struggling with the implicit normativization embedded in terms such as "New Age," "universalist" or even "non-Islamic" Sufis,[13] while also resisting the inflexibility of compartmentalization itself. Scholars of religion have likewise argued against rigid categorization in favor of aquatic metaphors that allow for more fluidity in conceptualizing

---

10   Gabriel Sheffer, *Diaspora Politics: At Home Abroad* (New York: Cambridge University Press, 2003).
11   Robin Cohen, *Global Diasporas: An Introduction* (London: UCL Press, 1997), 177–78.
12   Thomas Faist, "Diaspora and Transnationalism: What Kind of Dance Partners?," in *Diaspora and Transnationalism: Concepts, Theories and Methods*, ed. Rainer Bauböck and Thomas Faist (Amsterdam: Amsterdam University Press, 2010), 16–17. The last citation references Sanjeev Khagram and Peggy Levitt, eds., *The Transnational Studies Reader: Intersections and Innovations* (New York: Routledge, 2008).
13   This refers to the schema proposed by Alan Godlas on the webpage "Sufism, the West, and Modernity," accessed February 16, 2020, http://islam.uga.edu/sufismwest.html, on Islamic, quasi-Islamic and non-Islamic Sufi organizations or orders.

transient, ephemeral and complex interactions.[14] Mobility, fluidity and rupture versus identifying permanent patterns and universal "deep" categories marked a transition in the academic study of religion during the 1960s and 70s.[15] These sorts of shifts are reflected in scholarly efforts to heuristically make sense of the varieties of Sufi movements in the West. Religious studies scholar Thomas Tweed argued that more fluid metaphors avoid "essentializing religious traditions as static, isolated, and immutable substances."[16]

This imperative in categorization was cited by William Dickson in support of his claim that non-Islamic orders can be traditional while Islamic orders can be universal, thereby asserting the inadequacy of these terms.

> Ostensibly "New Age," "universal," or "non-Islamic" Sufis are in many ways deeply "traditional" and grounded in a broader sense of Islam, while those who practice a form of Sufism more in line with mainstream Islamic orthodoxy retain universalistic perspectives and can hold to a generally pluralistic understanding of the legitimate forms that Sufism can take.[17]

Since transplants are "Islamic" Sufis, I suppose the crucial point here is what makes a movement a "Sufi" movement. If certain practices, attitudes toward charismatic authority and a sense of lineage qualify, then Dickson has made his point. I would, however, issue a caveat in the case of transplant Sufis. While they may embrace a certain universalism in the sense that all is a manifestation of one divine presence or emanation, in my experience, one would need to be a Muslim to be considered a member of such groups, although outsiders on occasion might visit a meeting or be welcome to attend a more public ritual. They would be guests in this context, however, rather than members of the group.

In differentiating forms of Sufism that have emerged in the West, some researchers have favored historical periodization of waves or phases, beginning with Gisela Webb, who suggested three phases: the first wave marking the beginning of the twentieth century, the second wave rising in the 1960s and

---

14   William Rory Dickson, *Living Sufism in North America: Between Tradition and Transformation*. (Albany, NY: SUNY Press, 2015), 213; drawing on Thomas A. Tweed, *Crossing and Dwelling: A Theory of Religion* (Cambridge, MA: Harvard University Press, 2006).

15   David Chidester, "Mobility," in *Religion: Material Dynamics* (Oakland: University of California Press, 2018), 152–65.

16   Tweed, *Crossing and Dwelling*, 60.

17   Dickson, *Living Sufism*, 213.

70s, and the third wave occurring after the mid-1990s.[18] More recently, Jamal Malik and Saeed Zarrabi-Zadeh stretched this framework further back into the past by adding and amending to produce the four phases of (a) early literary Sufism (ca. 1700–1900); (b) universalistic Sufism (ca. 1900–1960); (c) New Age Sufism (ca. 1960–1975); and (d) re-orthodoxized Sufism (ca. 1975-).[19] In a related initiative, I attempted to push the historical phases of American (or even global) Sufism even further forward by designating two more recent trends as "Authenticity Sufism" (ca. 1995–2010) and "Affective Sufism" (ca. 2010 onwards).[20]

Mark Sedgwick traces Western Sufism in the first half of the twentieth century to three streams: Inayat Khan's Sufi Movement, Frithjof Schuon's Traditionalist Alawiyya, and the Gurdjieff movement,[21] none of which was transplanted Sufism, according to our definition. It was only in the 1960s, when the West experienced extensive migration from traditionally Muslim societies, that more Islamic forms took hold. In a later chapter of his book, Sedgwick discusses how even the earlier, more perennialist streams, or at least two of the three (excluding Gurdjieff), moved more towards Islamic identities in the latter part of the century.[22] While transplanted Sufis are not part of his analysis, we may imagine that their presence would be subsumed under Islamic forms that emerged due to increased migration.

Another way of categorizing Sufism in the West in the postcolonial period was proposed by Nile Green, who develops the categories "community Sufis," "entrepreneurial Sufis" and "fusion Sufis."[23] "Community Sufis" is the closest to our transplant distinction and Green characterizes this mode as:

> [...] the importation of Sufi groups as part of the larger establishment of immigrant communities. In such cases, the styles of Sufism varied in

---

18 Gisela Webb, "Third-Wave Sufism in America and the Bawa Muhaiyaddeen Fellowship," in *Sufism in the West*, ed. Malik and Hinnells.

19 Jamal Malik and Saeed Zarrabi-Zadeh, "Introduction," in *Sufism East and West*, ed. Malik and Zarrabi-Zadeh, 17.

20 Marcia Hermansen, "American Sufis and American Islam: From Private Spirituality to the Public Sphere," in *Islamic Movements and Islam in the Multicultural World: Islamic Movements and Formation of Islamic Ideologies in the Information Age*, ed. Denis Brilyov (Kazan: Kazan Federal University Publishing House, 2014), 193ff.

21 Mark Sedgwick, *Western Sufism: From the Abbasids to the New Age* (New York: Oxford University Press, 2017), 189.

22 Mark Sedgwick, "The Islamisation of Western Sufism after the New Age," in *Global Sufism: Boundaries, Narratives, and Practices*, ed. Francesco Piraino and Mark Sedgwick (London: Hurst, 2019).

23 Green, *Sufism: A Global History*, 221.

accordance with the regional, class and educational backgrounds of the migrant community in question and adapted as the religious preferences of those migrants themselves changed as a result of their experiences in their new homes.[24]

Green notes that while the context within which Sufi migrants find themselves in Europe or the United States might be new to them, the experience of Sufis migrating as part of broader movements of population was much older.

Søren Christian Lassen, focusing on the Burhaniyya in Europe, also offers a tripartite schema of Sufi groups in the West in which he characterizes certain orders as "diaspora phenomena" that mainly attract immigrants from Asian or African countries who were Muslim by birth. "As the disciples move to the West, so does the Sufi environment."[25] This is clearly another way of describing transplant Sufis. Lassen's other types are Sufi groups that seek to attract converts to Islam, and finally, those that he labels "new age Sufis," for whom Islamic affiliation is not a prerequisite. Interestingly, Lassen traces the presence of the Burhaniyya Order in Germany back to a group of New Age converts in the 1970s who Islamicized and formed an attachment to Sudan.[26] Among the new generation of born in Germany Burhaniyya Sufis are those of both European and Sudanese backgrounds. Thus this movement, at least in Northern Europe, does not neatly fit into either the "diaspora" or the "New Age" category according to Lassen's analysis, but it would perhaps accord with Green's "fusion Sufis" that feature membership largely raised in the West, either of Muslim background or converts to Islam.

Thus, Sufi transplants, for the most part, do not fit so easily into the historical "wave" theory of the coming of Sufism to the West. This is because they are most likely local and ephemeral, such that the vagaries of migration patterns continue to bring transplants along with them. For example, in the north of Chicago, a district favored by many new immigrants, there exists a mosque that serves primarily Nigerian immigrants, and in which there is a strong current of Sufism within the community itself. The dominant *tariqa* practiced in the Nigerian community in Chicago, especially in the Nigerian Islamic Association Center is the Tijaniyya. The Sufi lodges (*zawiya*s), in the sense of Chicago-based Sufi practice, were established by Sheikh Mohammad Rabiu Adebayo

---

24 Ibid.
25 Søren Christian Lassen, "Growing up as a Sufi: Generational Change in the Burhaniyya Sufi Order," in *Sufis in Western Society: Global Networking and Locality*, ed. Ron Geaves, Markus Dressler and Gritt Klinkhammer (New York: Routledge, 2009), 148.
26 Ibid., 153–54.

from Nigeria in 1991. A Sufi litany recitation (*wazifa*) has been practiced in the mosque daily since then, between sunset and evening prayers, except on Fridays, when the *wurdi* (*wird*; devotional liturgy) is performed between afternoon and sunset prayers. Celebration of the *milad* has also become an annual event in the community, particularly at the NIA on the north side of Chicago. Shakiru Nasiru, the NIA Imam, is also the leader of this Order's activities in the city. Tijani *shaykh*s come to the Chicago area for visits, usually staying for about a month.[27] While established in the 1990s, transplanted Nigerian Sufism in Chicago is replenished by continuing and increasing immigration as well as persisting connections to a homeland.

Italian sociologist and researcher on European Sufism, Francesco Piraino, along with his co-author, Spanish anthropologist Antonio de Diego González, in a recent article employ "transplants" as one among other categories to sort Sufi movements in Latin Europe. After noting the "never-ending dialogue between global and local, exogenous and endogenous, orthodox and heterodox," they present Latin European Sufism as a complex phenomenon drawing from diverse sources and therefore manifesting in several broad categories. The first of these that they discuss is in fact (a) "transplanted Sufism," which they describe as "formed by Sufi orders whose members are the first and second generation of migrants, strongly influenced by ethnic and cultural identities and bonds."[28] Piraino and de Diego González then present Sufism according to further categories of (b) "European esotericism," especially as derived from the works of René Guénon and Frithjof Schuon, (c) "New Age culture" or the "cultic milieu" and (d) "scholarly Sufism," which has often moved beyond an academic context to influence contemporary Sufism; in order to categorize the diverse manifestations among Sufi groups.[29] Further elaborating on the "transplant" category, in the same article, they offer several examples of such groups.

> Marcia Hermansen uses the term "transplant" to identify Sufi orders in Western countries that reproduce the doctrines, rituals and organisational structures of the country of origin. Examples of transplanted Sufi orders in Latin Europe are the Muridiyya (Senegal), the Tijaniyya (Western Africa), and the Chishtiyya (Bangladesh), which are increasingly widespread among the immigrant population. These orders, mainly

---

27 Details provided by Imam Misbah Rifai, private email communication, January 4, 2020.
28 Hermansen, "What's American about American Sufi Movements?," 36–37.
29 Francesco Piraino and Antonio de Diego González, "Sufism in Latin Europe (France, Spain, Italy)," in *Sufism in Western Contexts*, ed. Marcia Hermansen and Saeed Zarrabi-Zadeh (Leiden: Brill, forthcoming).

constituted of first- and second-generation migrants, are particularly difficult to study, since they are less visible in the public sphere and generally not interested in proselytism. Transplanted Sufi orders are quite homogenous from the ethnic point of view,[30] although they may occasionally attract Sufi-inclined converts, and they seem rather impermeable to specifically European religious influences, such as Western esotericism, anti-modernism, and New Age culture. Furthermore, their composition and presence is strongly related to the migration process.[31]

At the same time, Piraino and de Diego González comment on the instability of the identification of certain groups with this transplant category as they increasingly adapt to local contexts, noting that, "Similar to the other Sufi orders and currents analysed above, these religious movements are not static. In fact, recently some branches of these Orders [Murids and Tijanis] in Latin Europe have overcome the 'status of transplanted' and opened towards the surrounding societies."[32] One example they offer is the Fayda Tijaniyya Order, which is attracting new disciples both among white European converts and lifelong Muslims of diverse ethnic backgrounds. In contributing to "the production of Islamic knowledge, as has also been described by the term 'Afropolitanism'"[33] it may be transitioning from 'transplanted' status."[34]

Focusing on Latin Europe, Piraino and de Diego González furnish several examples of transplanted groups, primarily from Africa, such as the Murids and Tijanis from Senegal, as well as groups from other African countries, including Nigeria. Aside from the African Sufi orders, he notes that Bangladeshi Chishti Sufis have a presence that has not yet been studied. In describing the Senegalese Muridiyya, they elaborate that:

> [T]he Murīdiyya functions as a welfare state, a network, and a cultural mediator between migrants and the surrounding "new" society. In fact, the *zāwiya* or *dāira*, which in Wolof and Arabic means "circle," is the

---

30 Gina Gertrud Smith, "Religious Retreats and Transcultural Challenges: Recreating Senegalese Tijani Islam in Metropolitan France," *Journal of Muslims in Europe* 3, no. 1 (2014), https://doi.org/10.1163/22117954-12341277.
31 Piraino and González, "Sufism in Latin Europe."
32 Ibid.
33 Zachary Wright, "Afropolitan Sufism: The Contemporary Tijaniyya in Global Contexts," in *Global Sufism*, ed. Piraino and Sedgwick.
34 Piraino and González, "Sufism in Latin Europe."

main space of socialisation for its members.³⁵ The Murīdiyya also provides its followers with esoteric materials (talismans, medicines, etc.) and informal religious education. These functions are also exercised by other transplanted Sufi orders, each of whom gathers migrants from a single ethnic group.³⁶

The above paragraph enumerates certain key elements that Piraino and de Diego González associate with transplant Sufis: a welfare function, socialization, esoteric mediation/healing, religious education and ethnic uniformity. In German-speaking Europe, one finds similar developments among orders such as the Sudanese Burhaniyya,³⁷ while in Denmark, a series of studies by Mikkel Rytter focus on small-scale activities of the Pakistan-based Saifiyya branch of the Naqshbandiyya Mujaddidiyya.³⁸

2   Encounters with Sufi Transplants

This reflection on the "transplant" category might be an occasion to speak of two experiences I had with groups that I considered as examples of the category of transplanted Sufism. It was in Toronto, Ontario in the early 1970s that I encountered a group that met around then Professor of Islamic Studies at the University of Toronto, Dr. Mirza Qadeer Baig (d. 1988).³⁹ Baig was not only an academic who had written his thesis on the dispute between Ahmad Sirhindi (d. 1624) and Ibn 'Arabi (d. 1240), but he was also the *khalifa* (representative) of a little known branch of the Chishti Order, the Guderi Shahis. In fact, Baig was originally from Ajmer, the main site of Chishti pilgrimage in India.

---

35   Sophie Bava, "Reconversions et nouveaux mondes commerciaux des mourides à Marseille," *Hommes & Migrations* 1224 (March-April 2000), https://doi.org/10.3406/homig.2000.3479.
36   Piraino and González, "Sufism in Latin Europe."
37   Lassen, "Growing up as a Sufi."
38   Mikkel Rytter, "The Hair of the Prophet: Relics and the Affective Presence of the Absent Beloved among Sufis in Denmark," *Contemporary Islam* 13, no. 1 (April 2019), https://doi.org/10.1007/s11562-017-0400-z; idem, "Back to the Future: Religious Mobility among Danish Pakistani Sufi Muslims," *Journal of Ethnic and Migration Studies* 44, no. 16 (2018), https://doi.org/10.1080/1369183X.2017.1389031.
39   This group received scholarly attention in an article by Regula Qureshi, "Lineage, Shrine, Qawwali, and Study Circle: Spiritual Kinship in Transnational Sufism," *Religious Studies and Theology* 22, no. 1 (2003): 62–84, https://doi.org/10.1558/rsth.v22i1.63.

I was a student in his undergraduate course on Sufism and he invited me and one other Canadian student to attend weekly private Sufi gatherings at his apartment on Bay Street near the university. It was a heady cultural experience. I had already gotten on a plane and travelled to India in search of gurus, which did not pan out as I had intended, but left me with a permanent fascination and a determination to learn Urdu, so the South Asian cultural component was not completely new to me. I had also already participated in two camps of the Sufi Order in the West conducted by Pir Vilayat Khan (d. 2004) in Woodstock, NY and Chamonix, France.

At Baig's apartment, a small group of South Asian Muslims would gather, males on one side of the living room and a few related female attendees on the other, no more than fifteen or twenty persons total. His wife and young children sat at one end of the rectangular living room during the sessions. Baig would offer some discourses in English and tell stories of his Pir, Nawab Sahib (Nawab Mohammad Khadim Hasan Shah, d. 1970), and then he would play cassette tapes, I believe, non-commercial ones, of Sufi *qawwali*s in Persian and Urdu. Afterwards, tea and sweets would be served, with gatherings often running until the early morning hours, say three or four am.

In a 2003 article, Regula Qureshi compared the Toronto "Chishti Study Circle in Canada" established by Baig in the 1960s with a different branch of the Order located in Karachi. Qureshi was interested in the adaptations and challenges of Chishti Sufism in new contexts, observing in particular the fact that after Baig's passing there was no shrine and no annual ʿ*urs* (death anniversary celebration, literally "wedding") established in his memory. The context of Toronto in the 1970s and 80s also tended to work against specifically South Asian cultural performances and even language usage. For example, there were difficulties in finding capable *qawwali* performers, as well as in communicating the Chishti tradition to interested Canadians with no South Asian linguistic ability or cultural background.[40] Qureshi's anthropological and ethnomusicological approach suggests that if transplant Sufi orders are to persist, many adaptations to new settings would need to take place. Changes in the material circumstances and technologies that impact religious experience, as well as the absence of social structures in which hereditary kinship lineages convey authority and cement affiliations, portend a declining presence over time. In this regard, Qureshi's observation about the impact of Professor Baig's institutional location at the University of Toronto, together with the fact that many of the recruitment/outreach activities of the group were centered around that

---

40 Ibid., 75.

platform, suggest that this group increasingly began to move away from being a "transplant" manifestation. In the time of Baig's successor, Syed Mumtaz 'Ali (d. 2009), Qureshi found there to be fewer disciples who were less "intellectually and socially eminent."[41] It also seems that a rapid increase in South Asian Muslim immigration and the growing influence of global Islamization led the immigrant leaders of the Chishti Study Circle to become more involved in activities such as contestations over mosque leadership in Toronto and the involvement of 'Ali, himself a lawyer, in promoting shari'a arbitration councils in the Canadian province of Ontario.[42] 'Ali's obituary, for example, cites his being the first Muslim lawyer in Canada and a past president of the Canadian Society of Muslims.[43]

In attempting to ascertain the more recent situation of this group, I had occasion to contact a Canadian of non-Muslim background who had been an early initiate and whose presence at some of the gatherings was likely contemporary to my own. His observations, that had taken place over a longer period, were rather different than mine in that he recalled the circle around Professor Baig as primarily consisting of white Canadian spiritual seekers, many of whom were connected to the University of Toronto. According to his view of the group, it had not been Baig's mission or purpose to establish a permanent Chishti branch in Toronto, such that after his passing away there was no formally designated succession. Clearly the process of "transplantation" in this case is complicated, and may suggest that while personal charisma can transcend cultural limitations and challenges for a time, a lack of traditional structures may result in a transplanted group not taking root in the new environment.

The second main encounter that impacted my sense of "transplanted" Sufism occurred some twenty years later in Chicago. This was with the Chishti-Nizami circle that gathered around a *shaykh* from Hyderabad, India, Muhammad Afzaluddin Nizami (d. 2006). Afzaluddin Nizami was a disciple of Khwaja Hasan Nizami (d. 1955), a literary figure and activist associated with the shrine of the revered medieval Chishti saint Nizamuddin Awliya'

---

41 Ibid., 76.
42 In 2004, Syed Mumtaz 'Ali declared that an "Islamic Institute of Civil Justice" would begin "arbitrating family matters on the basis of sharia law." This led to a very contentious and public debate in Canada that has been studied academically in numerous publications. 'Ali himself authored several statements and articles on the topic.
43 "Syed Mumtaz Ali, 1st Muslim lawyer in Canada, dies at 82," Canadian Broadcasting Corporation, accessed December 25, 2020, https://www.cbc.ca/news/canada/syed-mumtaz-ali-1st-muslim-lawyer-in-canada-dies-at-82-1.823391.

(d. 1325) in New Delhi. Yet Khwaja Hasan Nizami also spent quite a lot of time in the Deccan and the brother of Shaykh Afzaluddin, the prominent architect Fayyazuddin Nizami (d. 1977), was often his host in Hyderabad, as well as being his disciple and *khalifa*.[44] Interestingly, a picture of Fayyazuddin Nizami with the well known American Sufi teacher Samuel Lewis (d. 1971) is featured in the latter's book, *Sufi Vision and Initiation,* in a section documenting his 1956 trip to India.[45] Thus it seems that some degree of transnational Chishti networking and transfer was occurring even in that early period.

Shaykh Afzaluddin Nizami emigrated to Chicago, where several of his children had settled, in 1978, at which point he may have been about seventy years of age. He became recognized in the South Asian community there as a healer and resolver of difficulties, receiving requests from persons in all sorts of health, financial and family crises.[46] In addition, a small group of disciples gathered around him, some directly initiated as Chishtis and some already affiliated with other Sufi *tariqa*s. Monthly *dhikr* sessions were conducted at private homes that included a Chishti *dhikr* lasting some forty minutes followed by a communal meal. The group was not large, perhaps a maximum of fifteen persons and a few female relatives who also attended seated in a separate room or behind the men. Isolated disciples occasionally hosted the *shaykh* in Los Angeles or New Jersey, but no consistent groups emerged there.

An annual *'urs* (a celebration to commemorate the death of a Sufi master) in honor of Mu'inuddin Chishti (d. 1236) was conducted in a local banquet hall. This event would be attended by perhaps 100–150 persons and would feature *qawwali* music and on some occasions speeches. The *qawwali* would conform to the rituals associated with South Asian Chishti Sufism, such as money being presented through the *shaykh* or his representative. Moreover, attendees would occasionally achieve an ecstatic state (*wajd*), such that the particular line of poetry that had brought about this spiritual intoxication would be repeated to sustain it until their bliss subsided and they returned to a more

---

[44] Afzaluddin actually lists Fayyazuddin as an intermediary between himself and Khwaja Hasan Nizami in the Chishti lineage. Abu Yusuf Muhammad Afzaluddin Nizami Chishti, *Dawa'i Chishtiyya fi al-Tariq Silsila Nizamiyya* (Mardan: Kawthar Press, 1972), 14.

[45] Samuel L. Lewis, *Sufi Vision and Initiation: Meetings with Remarkable Beings* (San Francisco: Ruhaniat Press, 1986), 138.

[46] Marcia Hermansen, "Dimensions of Islamic Religious Healing in America," in *Religion and Healing in America,* ed. Linda L. Barnes and Susan S. Sered (New York: Oxford University Press, 2005).

stable condition.[47] Favorite *qawwalis* of Shaykh Afzaluddin, some penned by the Hyderabadi poet, Amjad (d. 1961), would be high on the request list.

The group remained constant until the passing of the *shaykh* in 2006. Despite attempts on the part of Nizami's son, Shaykh Mazharuddin Nizami, to develop a "Chishti youth" segment, most participants were South Asian males above fifty years of age. Often, they were experiencing some sort of immigration, financial or family instability and the group, as well as the attention of the *shaykh*, provided a source of hope and comfort. Specific instruction in *suluk* (spiritual path) or the recitation of regular litanies did not seem to be part of the practice,[48] which might not have conformed to Western expectations of Sufi training, but was probably consistent with Sufi practice in contemporary Hyderabad. Over the course of the 1990s, the speeches and the public presentations became increasingly "Islamic" and less explicitly mystical, although musical performance and ecstasy were still part of events. As time passed, many remaining members of the group around Baba Nizami (d. 2006) passed away, some in the US and some after returning to Hyderabad, and the group gradually ceased to function.

These few examples may suggest some features of transplanted Sufism while also indicating some further complicating factors to be considered when constructing and applying the category more broadly. In the case of Shaykh Nizami, the particular historical situation of Hyderabadi Muslims as transplanted Sufis is relevant, since their imaginary homeland is a lost one, ending with the "Police Action" of 1948, when the realm of the Nizam was forcibly integrated into broader India.[49] While family ties of members to Hyderabad remained, in most cases, the Sufi element was not multi-sited or translocal to any great extent. A further observation is that for South Asian Sufis in America, the road to India or Pakistan obviously passes through Mecca and Medina. This geographical fact, combined with the increasing Islamization of the 1980s and 90s, made ties to specific Sufi shrines, such as those of Mu'inuddin Chishti in Ajmer or Nizamuddin Awliya' in Delhi, less compelling and viable. Thus, in my observation, for Hyderabadis these sites were usually not on a pilgrimage itinerary, and probably had not even been highly visited when participants lived in South Asia. Further considering the case of Indian Chishtis specifically, the two major shrines in India are not under the control of any single charismatic

---

47 Regula Burckhardt Qureshi, *Sufi Music of India and Pakistan: Sound, Context, and Meaning in Qawwali* (Cambridge: Cambridge University Press, 1986).

48 On occasion, disciples were presented with the book of Chishti Nizami litanies compiled by Shaykh Afzaluddin Nizami. See Nizami Chishti, *Dawa'i Chishtiyya*, 14.

49 Karen Leonard, *Hyderabad and Hyderabadis* (New Delhi: Manohar, 2014).

leader, but rather over time, complex networks and hierarchies of representatives of the shrines developed and divided up patrons and their donations. This further militated against transplanted loyalty to a specific Indian Sufi shrine.

What sustained and maintained the Chicago Chishti group was the charismatic presence of a Sufi master, Baba Nizami, as well as a certain social support network among his affiliates. The *shaykh* was to a degree recognized in the broader Muslim community and within the hybrid Sufi networks that were beginning to emerge in the United States through such activities as the *milad*s hosted in Chicago by the Naqshbandiyya Foundation for Islamic Education.[50] This is also noteworthy in the sense that the *milad*[51] ceremony and recitation of the *Burda* poem[52] were Sufi-inflected aspects of Islamic ritual that attracted a broader, more loosely affiliated segment of the South Asian Muslim immigrant population. After the death of the *shaykh*, one Hyderabadi Muslim attending the Chishti *dhikr* group in Chicago, who was in fact a Qadiri affiliate, began asserting his leadership by incorporating a *Burda* recitation as part of the proceedings. While an isolated example, this could serve to illustrate forces acting to dilute specific *tariqa* identity over time.

One question to be asked is for how long a Sufi movement in the West will remain considered as a transplant? Another is the impact of the size of a Sufi movement and whether it makes any explicit efforts to either recruit new members or to transmit teachings and practices to the new generation. Thus, by definition, transplants may be ephemeral.

It should further be noted that the phenomenon of very small Sufi groups clustered around a single *shaykh* is not something that uniquely emerges in the West, but rather such groups are not uncommon in South Asian Islam. Not every Sufi *shaykh* is looking for disciples or promotion. Such small groups may result from an individual's refusal to initiate disciples without some explicit sign, for example, Baba Nizami would say that Nizamuddin Awliya' told him to make a certain person a disciple.

---

50 See Marcia Hermansen, "Global Sufism: 'Theirs and Ours,'" in *Sufis in Western Society*, ed. Geaves et al., 29–30 for a brief discussion of this group.

51 On American *milad*s and specifically Chicago ceremonies, see Marcia Hermansen, "Milad/Mawlid: Celebrating the Prophet Muhammad's Birthday," in *The Practice of Islam in America: An Introduction,* ed. Edward E. Curtis IV (New York: New York University Press, 2017), https://doi.org/10.2307/j.ctt1pwtb7t.10; Justine Howe, "Contemporary Mawlids in Chicago," in *Global Sufism*, ed. Piraino and Sedgwick.

52 *Qasida al-Burda* or "Ode of the Mantle" is a poem composed by Imam al-Busiri (d. 1294) in praise of the Prophet Muhammad.

3 Conclusion

When anthropologist Pnina Werbner considered transplant or multi-local Sufi practices in Britain, she alluded to a "local diasporic public sphere, almost entirely hidden from the gaze of outsiders."[53] The "hiddenness" of many transplanted groups, especially smaller ones, is one factor in the lack of their inclusion in studies of Sufism in the West. One American participant in the Burhaniyya Order's branch in New Jersey described transplant Sufi groups in the US as being "pockets of traditionalism,"[54] in the positive sense that they preserved both the religious and the cultural ethos of authentic Sufi Islam.

Ron Geaves, when writing about Chishti mosques or organized centers in Britain, used the phrase "dispersed influence" to describe broader Barelwi communities whose "shared focal point remains the 'recollection of a personal and corporate identity rooted in the place of origin'."[55] Geaves further identifies several Sufi groups in Britain that had been organized around ethnicity: the Shadhili Alawiyya (Yemen), the Bani Alawiya and the Tijanis.[56]

To persist over time, it seems a transplant Sufi group must hybridize. Sufi transplants, in fact, compete in the same space with hybrid groups whose broader membership and more aggressive claims regarding their *shaykhs*' charisma seem to attest to their spiritual efficacy, or at least the potential benefits of joining their network. The case of the "hybrid" Naqshbandi-Haqqanis in Britain and the US during the 1990s is such a case in point. The very diversity of their membership and their global reach, combined with a less-specifically ethnic style of Sufism, attracted some immigrant Muslims who might otherwise have stayed in the transplant Sufi sphere, or might have eschewed Sufi practice altogether. Green would call movements like the Naqshbandi-Haqqanis "entrepreneurial Sufism."[57] In addition, South Asian affiliates of transplanted groups may at the same time participate more loosely in Barelwi type practices,[58] such

---

53 Pnina Werbner, "Theorising Complex Diasporas: Purity and Hybridity in the South Asian Public Sphere in Britain," *Journal of Ethnic and Migration Studies* 30, no. 5 (2004): 898, https://doi.org/10.1080/1369183042000245606.
54 Telephone interview, Ibrahim Abd al-Aziz, February 1, 2020.
55 Ron Geaves, *The Sufis of Britain: An Exploration of Muslim Identity* (Cardiff: Cardiff Academic Press, 2000), 90, quoting Stephen Barton on Bengalis (1986).
56 Ibid., 101ff.
57 Green, *Sufism: A Global History*, 221–22.
58 Within South Asia, a large proportion of the Sunni Muslim population follows interpretations that encompass popular Sufi attitudes to shrine and saint veneration and allot a superhuman role and powers to the Prophet Muhammad, including his continued spiritual presence. See Usha Sanyal, *Devotional Islam and Politics in British India: Ahmad Riza Khan Barelwi and his Movement, 1870–1920*, 2nd ed. (New York and Delhi: Oxford

as *milad*s or rituals conducted by a different order or visiting *shaykh*. Therefore, among South Asian Muslim immigrants, *milad*s, beard hair viewings and *Burda* recitations all qualify as trans-*tariqa* Sufi inflected practices that might be held as free-standing events or incorporated into *tariqa*-organized performances. Each of these rituals, with perhaps the exception of certain Americanized *milad*s,[59] attracts primarily audiences from Muslim-majority areas, but at the same time, they may blur the boundaries of what is Sufi affiliation and identity, since none of these rituals is specific to a single *tariqa* or its followers. Therefore, South Asian Barelwism sometimes fits the category of transplanted Sufism, and sometimes tests its limits.

Certain insights from cultural geography may be applied to Sufi transplants. For example, the concept of "rootedness" is understood as a firm relationship between identity and territory. Yet even in diasporic settings, we may find a reemergence of territorialized notions of belonging in new "soil." The locations for transplanted Sufism may no longer be shrines or *zawiya*s – but certain mosques, homes, families[60] and even banquet halls and cemeteries, may acquire, even if transiently, Sufi coloring. For example, in the case of Chicago's Devon Avenue, the heart of the local South Asian diaspora community, sites such as the Bombay Banquet Hall hosted *qawwali*s or *dhikr* sessions for Sufis, while accommodating weddings or political events for other, increasingly diverse, groups.[61] Rosehill Cemetery on Peterson Avenue, near Devon Avenue, receives not only processions from a nearby Sufi-inflected "basement" mosque, the Hameediyya, on occasions such as *shab-e barat*,[62] but it is also where the grave of Baba Nizami is located, since the Muslim section of this graveyard is the primary burial ground for city-dwelling Muslims.

University Press, 1999). This usually does not include affiliation or practice within a Sufi Order, but it also does not preclude it.

[59] For example, those held at the University of Chicago and directed to both a broad Muslim and interfaith audience. See Hermansen, "Milad/Mawlid."

[60] Clemens Greiner and Patrick Sakdapolrak, "Translocality: Concepts, Applications and Emerging Research Perspectives," *Geography Compass* 7, no. 5 (May 2013), https://doi.org/10.1111/gec3.12048.

[61] One example of a Chishti performance is "August-2008 Chicago: An Evening of Sufi-Style Devotional Qawwali," accessed December 30, 2019, https://www.youtube.com/watch?v=1PxycSH6Vy0.

[62] The middle night of the Islamic month of *Sha'ban* on which South Asian Muslims believe destinies are determined for the coming year and when deceased ancestors are commemorated.

Transplant Sufis themselves embody an element of locality. They are often not global franchises, like Deobandis, Barelwis or Nurcus are. Furthermore, transplants usually have a single *tariqa* identity, they are neither post-*tariqa* nor multi-*tariqa*. They may meet in private homes or rented halls, establish their own centers, or meet in mosques usually dominated by the same, single, Sufi-friendly community. Transplanted Sufis may gather around an immigrant *shaykh* or a *shaykh*'s representative (*khalifa*) who is available locally or they may be served by visiting Sufi masters from abroad. They generally attract immigrants and therefore only expand through further immigration, despite some attempts to engage the new generation, otherwise they gradually fade away.

Bibliography

Appadurai, Arjun. *Modernity at Large: Cultural Dimensions of Globalization.* Minneapolis: University of Minnesota Press, 1996.

Bava, Sophie. "Reconversions et nouveaux mondes commerciaux des mourides à Marseille." *Hommes & Migrations* 1224 (March-April 2000): 46–55, https://doi.org/10.3406/homig.2000.3479.

Canadian Broadcasting Corporation. "Syed Mumtaz Ali, 1st Muslim lawyer in Canada, dies at 82." Accessed Dec. 25, 2020, https://www.cbc.ca/news/canada/syed-mumtaz-ali-1st-muslim-lawyer-in-canada-dies-at-82-1.823391.

Chidester, David. *Religion: Material Dynamics.* Oakland: University of California Press, 2018.

Cohen, Robin. *Global Diasporas: An Introduction.* London: UCL Press, 1997.

Dickson, William Rory. *Living Sufism in North America: Between Tradition and Transformation.* Albany, NY: SUNY Press, 2015.

Faist, Thomas. "Diaspora and Transnationalism: What Kind of Dance Partners?." In *Diaspora and Transnationalism: Concepts, Theories and Methods,* edited by Rainer Bauböck and Thomas Faist, 9–34. Amsterdam: Amsterdam University Press, 2010.

Geaves, Ron. *The Sufis of Britain: An Exploration of Muslim Identity.* Cardiff: Cardiff Academic Press, 2000.

Godlas, Alan. "Sufism, the West, and Modernity." Accessed February 16, 2020, http://islam.uga.edu/sufismwest.html.

Green, Nile. *Sufism: A Global History.* Chichester: Wiley-Blackwell, 2012.

Greiner, Clemens and Patrick Sakdapolrak. "Translocality: Concepts, Applications and Emerging Research Perspectives." *Geography Compass* 7, no. 5 (May 2013): 373–84, https://doi.org/10.1111/gec3.12048.

Hermansen, Marcia. "American Sufis and American Islam: From Private Spirituality to the Public Sphere." In *Islamic Movements and Islam in the Multicultural World: Islamic*

Movements and Formation of Islamic Ideologies in the Information Age, edited by Denis Brilyov, 189–208. Kazan: Kazan Federal University Publishing House, 2014.

Hermansen, Marcia. "Dimensions of Islamic Religious Healing in America." In *Religion and Healing in America,* edited by Linda L. Barnes and Susan S. Sered, 407–22. New York: Oxford University Press, 2005.

Hermansen, Marcia. "Global Sufism: 'Theirs and Ours'." In *Sufis in Western Society: Global Networking and Locality,* edited by Ron Geaves, Markus Dressler and Gritt Klinkhammer, 26–45. New York: Routledge, 2009.

Hermansen, Marcia. "In the Garden of American Sufi Movements: Hybrids and Perennials." In *New Trends and Developments in the World of Islam,* edited by Peter B. Clarke, 155–78. London: Luzac Oriental Press, 1997.

Hermansen, Marcia. "Milad/Mawlid: Celebrating the Prophet Muhammad's Birthday." In *The Practice of Islam in America: An Introduction,* edited by Edward E. Curtis IV, 123–38. New York: New York University Press, 2017, https://doi.org/10.2307/j.ctt1pwtb7t.10.

Hermansen, Marcia. "What's American about American Sufi Movements?." In *Sufism in Europe and North America,* edited by David Westerlund, 36–62. New York: Routledge, 2004.

Hermansen, Marcia and Saeed Zarrabi-Zadeh, eds. *Sufism in Western Contexts.* Leiden: Brill, forthcoming.

Howe, Justine. "Contemporary Mawlids in Chicago." In *Global Sufism: Boundaries, Narratives, and Practices,* edited by Francesco Piraino and Mark Sedgwick, 119–35. London: Hurst, 2019.

Khagram, Sanjeev and Peggy Levitt, eds. *The Transnational Studies Reader: Intersections and Innovations.* New York: Routledge, 2008.

Lassen, Søren Christian. "Growing up as a Sufi: Generational Change in the Burhaniyya Sufi Order." In *Sufis in Western Society: Global Networking and Locality,* edited by Ron Geaves, Markus Dressler and Gritt Klinkhammer, 148–61. New York: Routledge, 2009.

Leonard, Karen. *Hyderabad and Hyderabadis.* New Delhi: Manohar, 2014.

Lewis, Samuel L. *Sufi Vision and Initiation: Meetings with Remarkable Beings.* San Francisco: Ruhaniat Press, 1986.

Malik, Jamal, ed. *Perspectives of Mutual Encounters in South Asian History 1760–1860.* Leiden: Brill, 2000.

Malik, Jamal and John Hinnells, eds. *Sufism in the West.* New York: Routledge, 2006.

Malik, Jamal and Saeed Zarrabi-Zadeh. "Introduction." In *Sufism East and West: Mystical Islam and Cross-Cultural Exchange in the Modern World,* edited by Jamal Malik and Saeed Zarrabi-Zadeh. Leiden: Brill, 2019.

Malik, Jamal and Saeed Zarrabi-Zadeh, eds. *Sufism East and West: Mystical Islam and Cross-Cultural Exchange in the Modern World.* Leiden: Brill, 2019.

Nizami Chishti, Abu Yusuf Muhammad Afzaluddin. *Dawa'i Chishtiyya fi al-Tariq Silsila-i Nizamiyya*. Mardan: Kawthar Press, 1972.

Piraino, Francesco and Antonio de Diego González. "Sufism in Latin Europe (France, Spain, Italy)." In *Sufism in Western Contexts*, edited by Marcia Hermansen and Saeed Zarrabi-Zadeh. Leiden: Brill, forthcoming.

Qureshi, Regula Burckhardt. "Lineage, Shrine, Qawwali, and Study Circle: Spiritual Kinship in Transnational Sufism." *Religious Studies and Theology* 22, no. 1 (2003): 62–84, https://doi.org/10.1558/rsth.v22i1.63.

Qureshi, Regula Burckhardt. *Sufi Music of India and Pakistan: Sound, Context, and Meaning in Qawwali*. Cambridge: Cambridge University Press, 1986.

Rytter, Mikkel. "Back to the Future: Religious Mobility among Danish Pakistani Sufi Muslims." *Journal of Ethnic and Migration Studies* 44, no. 16 (2018): 2667–83, https://doi.org/10.1080/1369183X.2017.1389031.

Rytter, Mikkel. "The Hair of the Prophet: Relics and the Affective Presence of the Absent Beloved among Sufis in Denmark." *Contemporary Islam* 13, no. 1 (April 2019): 49–65, https://doi.org/10.1007/s11562-017-0400-z.

Sanyal, Usha. *Devotional Islam and Politics in British India: Ahmad Riza Khan Barelwi and his Movement, 1870–1920*, 2nd ed. New York and Delhi: Oxford University Press, 1999.

Sedgwick, Mark. "The Islamisation of Western Sufism after the New Age." In *Global Sufism: Boundaries, Narratives, and Practices*, edited by Francesco Piraino and Mark Sedgwick, 35–54. London: Hurst, 2019.

Sedgwick, Mark. *Western Sufism: From the Abbasids to the New Age*. New York: Oxford University Press, 2017.

Sheffer, Gabriel. *Diaspora Politics: At Home Abroad*. New York: Cambridge University Press, 2003.

Smith, Gina Gertrud. "Religious Retreats and Transcultural Challenges: Recreating Senegalese Tijani Islam in Metropolitan France." *Journal of Muslims in Europe* 3, no. 1 (2014): 26–48, https://doi.org/10.1163/22117954-12341277.

Tweed, Thomas A. *Crossing and Dwelling: A Theory of Religion*. Cambridge, MA: Harvard University Press, 2006.

Webb, Gisela. "Third-Wave Sufism in America and the Bawa Muhaiyaddeen Fellowship." In *Sufism in the West*, edited by Jamal Malik and John Hinnells, 86–102. London and New York: Routledge, 2006.

Webb, Gisela. "Tradition and Innovation in Contemporary American Islamic Spirituality: The Bawa Muhaiyadeen Fellowship." In *Muslim Communities in North America*, edited by Yvonne Yazbeck Haddad and Jane Idleman Smith, 75–108. Albany, NY: SUNY Press, 1994.

Werbner, Pnina. "Theorising Complex Diasporas: Purity and Hybridity in the South Asian Public Sphere in Britain." *Journal of Ethnic and Migration Studies* 30, no. 5 (2004): 895–911, https://doi.org/10.1080/1369183042000245606.

Wright, Zachary. "Afropolitan Sufism: The Contemporary Tijaniyya in Global Contexts." In *Global Sufism: Boundaries, Narratives, and Practices*, edited by Francesco Piraino and Mark Sedgwick, 55–74. London: Hurst, 2019.

PART 5

Islamic Pluralism and Dialogue

∴

CHAPTER 13

Discourses of Tolerance and Dialogue in Contemporary Islam

Itzchak Weismann

Tolerance is one of the major philosophical ideas associated with the European Enlightenment. Coming out of the "persecuting society" of the Reformation and Counter-Reformation, the eighteenth-century *philosophes* rejected the divine order of society, offering in its stead "secular" ideals such as freedom of thought and speech, man's responsibility to himself and to his fellow men, and tolerance for religious minorities, philosophical dissenters and sexual deviants.[1] These thinkers, who usually sought to reform religion by reason rather than to abolish it, were cognizant of the inherent tensions between such ideals and the requirements of public order and moral solidarity. Nevertheless, to them the great diversity of faiths, customs and morals amongst the peoples of humankind suggested that at least some measure of tolerance was indispensable for social harmony, the pursuit of knowledge, and just and peaceful politics.[2]

Dialogue became an established mode of interfaith and intercultural encounter in the twentieth century. Forcefully stated in the 1893 Parliament of World's Religions in Chicago, it was reinforced by the missionary intra-Christian ecumenical movement, which expanded to encompass other religions. The Vatican Council II of 1962–1965 ushered in a revolution in the field, declaring in its *Nostra aetate* that the Catholic Church "reflects at the outset what humans have in common and what tends to promote fellowship among them. All humans form but one community." A secretariat for non-Christian religions was set up to implement this new policy.[3] Since then, there has been a proliferation of interreligious and intercultural initiatives, among them the foundation of Religions for Peace in 1970, the declaration of a Global Ethic

---

[1] Peter Gay, *The Enlightenment: An Interpretation*, vol. 2, *The Science of Freedom* (New York: W.W. Norton, 1977), 398–401.
[2] Ole Peter Grell and Roy Porter, eds., *Toleration in Enlightenment Europe* (Cambridge: Cambridge University Press, 2000), 1–2.
[3] Leonard Swidler, "The History of Inter-Religious Dialogue," in *The Wiley-Blackwell Companion to Inter-Religious Dialogue*, ed. Catherine Cornille (Chichester: Wiley-Blackwell, 2013), 3–10.

at the centennial Chicago World Parliament of Religions in 1993, and King Abdallah ibn Saud's interfaith and intercultural dialogue initiative from 2007.

As against this, one cannot deny that in the Middle East, political tyranny and religious fanaticism are rampant. Despite predictions of change,[4] which peaked during the "Arab Spring," genuine democracy, pluralism and respect for human rights continue to evade the region. Government intolerance is rooted in ruling patrimonial elites' employment of secular ideologies and a docile Islam to maintain social acceptance for their authoritarian regimes.[5] Islamist intolerance springs from the struggle of religious opposition to forge an alternative political order and identity in the national and international arenas. Albeit at loggerheads, governments and Islamists often join hands in repressing freedom of opinion[6] and in persecuting people with different sexual inclinations. With growing authoritarianism in Iran and Turkey, the failure of the Arab Uprisings of 2011, and the atrocities of al-Qaeda and ISIS, this "tolerance deficit" seems only to increase.[7]

Still, from the very beginnings of the encounter with Western modernity, there have been attempts to form an Islamic concept of tolerance that will correspond with Enlightenment ideals and join in interfaith and intercultural dialogue.[8] Early initiatives came from among Muslim intellectuals and academics living in the West or in India.[9] As a German citizen of Pakistani origin, Jamal Malik was engaged in both arenas, from the comparative approach as well as from the perspective of Muslim migration to Europe.[10] They were later joined by men of religion from Muslim-majority countries. This chapter focuses on

---

4　Robert W. Hefner, ed., *Remaking Muslim Politics: Pluralism, Contestation, Democratization* (Princeton: Princeton University Press, 2005).

5　Charles Tripp, "Islam and the Secular Logic of the State in the Middle East," in *Islamic Fundamentalism*, ed. Abdel Salam Sidahmed and Anoushiravan Ehteshami (Boulder, CO: Westview Press, 1996), 54–55.

6　For a glaring example, see George N. Sfeir, "Basic Freedoms in a Fractured Legal Culture: Egypt and the Case of Nasr Hamid Abu Zayd," *Middle East Journal* 52, no. 3 (1998).

7　Ann Elizabeth Mayer, *Islam and Human Rights: Tradition and Politics*, 5th ed. (New York: Routledge, 2018).

8　Aaron Tyler, *Islam, the West, and Tolerance: Conceiving Coexistence* (New York: Palgrave Macmillan, 2008).

9　Itzchak Weismann, "Between *Daʿwa* and Dialogue: Religious Engagement in Muslim-minority Environments," *Islam and Christian–Muslim Relations* 30, no. 4 (2019), https://doi.org/10.1080/09596410.2019.1601909.

10　Jamal Malik and Helmut Reifeld, eds., *Religious Pluralism in South Asia and Europe* (New Delhi: Oxford University Press, 2004); Jamal Malik, "Integration of Muslim Migrants and the Politics of Dialogue: The Case of Modern Germany," *Journal of Muslim Minority Affairs* 33 (2013).

four major religious elements from the Middle East (each representing a different type of agency and drawing on a different part of the Muslim tradition) that have pursued this course since the onset of the Islamic resurgence of the 1970s. These are the Egyptian-born Islamist "global mufti" Shaykh Yusuf al-Qaradawi, the Sufi-oriented Turkish Gülen Movement, the Iranian exile philosopher Abdolkarim Soroush and the Saudi-Wahhabi sponsored national and international dialogue initiative. In each case, I analyze the discourse and action, discern the motivations and clarify the internal shortcomings and external detriments underlying the ultimate failure of these elements to challenge the prevailing mood of intolerance and conflict in the contemporary Middle East.

1 Tolerance and Dialogue in Islamic Scriptures and in History

Public views on Islam and its attitudes toward other religions and cultures are prone to stumble into one of two "ideological" pitfalls. Western critics tend to judge "Islam" with the measuring rod of the Enlightenment in order to demonstrate that it is, in its essence, an intolerant religion. In contrast, Muslim apologists are busy scrutinizing the canonical sources and the historical record in search of evidence to "prove" that Islam has always respected the Other and that today's manifestations of coercion and violence are but an aberration. Accepting the normative validity of tolerance and dialogue on one hand, and the need to examine the ways in which they are conceptualized and practiced among Muslims on their own terms on the other, we refer to them as a mixed legacy in a continuous process of multiple interpretations in response to external influences and internal developments.

Islam's attitude toward other communities was formed against the backdrop of the realities of Muslim rule over religiously heterogeneous populations along with its phenomenal success in propagating the faith among other peoples. As in most other premodern systems, it had no conception of mutual understanding or of interaction on an equal basis. There is thus no specific concept of either tolerance or dialogue in the Quran or the hadith, nor are such notions to be found in the classical books of law, theology or mysticism. The modern Arabic term for tolerance – *samaha* or *tasamuh*, the latter conveying a sense of reciprocity – or any other term from the linguistic root *s-m-h* is absent from the Muslims' holy book. The modern term for dialogue, or *hiwar*, appears several times in the Quran, but only in its basic meaning of conversation, between friends (Q 18:34, 37) or between a man and his wife (Q 58:1).

On the other hand, various verses in the Quran and reports from the hadith convey attitudes and values that seem compatible with the modern notion of tolerance. Among the most cited are Q 49:13, "O mankind, We have created you male and female, and appointed you races and tribes, that you may know one another. Surely the noblest among you in the sight of God is the most godfearing of you," and Q 2:256, which asserts that, "There is no compulsion in religion." Yet the former confirms the supremacy of the believers, while the latter could be construed as acknowledging that one cannot be forced into belief, as opposed to being a command to refrain from forcing the faith on others.[11] Some verses also come close to the practice of dialogue, most prominently Q 16:125, "Call to the way of your Lord with wisdom and good instruction, and argue with them in a way that is best." This too, however, points to the means of conveying the Truth, rather than to sorting this out between equal interlocutors.

Similar ambiguities characterize the classical concepts that have regulated Muslims' relations with other faiths, most notably struggle in the path of God (jihad), apostasy (*ridda*) and protection (*dhimma*).[12] For Islam's opponents, jihad is the epitome of the intolerant nature of this religion and proof for its innate violence and incompatibility with civilized norms. It is the main doctrine used to justify today's Islamist suicide terrorism and the barbarity of al-Qaeda and ISIS.[13] Numerous verses in the Quran enjoin fighting the enemies of Islam, ranging from the mere permission being given to those who emigrated to Medina to wage war against their Meccan oppressors (Q 2:216) to the absolute command in the "verse of the sword" to kill the polytheists wherever they are found (Q 9:5). The compendiums of Islamic law declared jihad a pious duty aimed at the expansion of the political sway of Islam (as distinct from forced conversion). Its rules permitted offensive war and the killing or enslaving of prisoners, but also stipulated that opening hostilities must be preceded by an invitation to join Islam (*daʿwa*) and that the lives of non-combatants should be spared. Still, jihad has retained a much wider semantic range, signifying any effort in the path of God. For Sufis, the "greater jihad" against one's self is superior to the "lesser jihad" of armed combat.[14]

The rules governing the treatment of apostates in Islam are harsher than those pertaining to infidels. The Quran warns on several occasions against people who abandoned Islam and reverted to their former faith. Often cited by

---

[11] Yohanan Friedmann, *Tolerance and Coercion in Islam: Interfaith Relations in the Muslim Tradition* (Cambridge: Cambridge University Press, 2003), 102–6.

[12] Donna E. Arzt, "The Role of Compulsion in Islamic Conversion: *Jihad, Dhimma* and *Ridda*," *Buffalo Human Rights Law Review* 8 (2002).

[13] See, e.g., Daniel Pipes, "What is Jihad?," Middle East Forum, accessed October 17, 2018, www.danielpipes.org/990/what-is-jihad.

[14] David Cook, *Understanding Jihad* (Berkeley: University of California Press, 2005).

Islamists today in this context is Q 5:44: "Those who judge not according to what God has sent down, they are the unbelievers." Following the death of the Prophet, the first Caliph, Abu Bakr, initiated the "wars of apostasy" (*hurub al-ridda*) against Arab tribes that had renounced their loyalty to Islam. The basic choice between repentance and death given to apostates by the classical jurists was no different from other civilizations of the time. It amounted to compulsion in religion, but it also reserved the possibility of indefinite postponement of the sentence or substituting it with imprisonment.[15]

On the other hand, treatment of non-Muslims in *dar al-Islam* ("abode of Islam") is more lenient than of apostates or infidels in *dar al-harb* ("abode of war"). In terms of faith, non-Muslims are generally considered as nothing but unbelievers (*kuffar*), while in terms of Islamic law, they are divided between, on one hand, the recipients of a divinely revealed scripture (*ahl al-kitab*), particularly Jews and Christians, and on the other, polytheists and heretics. According to the manuals of jurisprudence, Jews and Christians are allowed to retain their respective faiths and are entitled to protection (*dhimma*), so long as they accept Muslim rule and pay the poll tax. Yet polytheists, similar to apostates, are forced to choose between conversion and death. For practical reasons, protection was extended to other religious communities, notably Zoroastrians and Hindus, whereas the category of idolatry was confined to the Arabs of the Peninsula in the time of the conquests.[16]

Muslim history may seem like an endless series of wars, just like the history of any other political entity. Warfare filled a central role in Muhammad's career after he had constituted the Muslim community in Medina. There followed the great conquests by his successors, which Muslim historiography describes as *futuhat* ("openings [to the word of God]") rather than mere wars. But this was also a time of internal strife, resulting in the division of Islam between the Sunnis, Shi'a and the now almost defunct Khawarij. With the disintegration of the overextended Abbasid polity, jihad was taken up by frontier societies, often accompanied by mystics and preachers. Major setbacks included the Crusades in Palestine and the Mongol catastrophe, but nothing could prepare the Muslim world for the formidable modern colonial drive. The failure of jihadi resistance movements to repel European domination paved the way for a revision of the concept itself.[17]

---

15 Friedmann, *Tolerance and Coercion*, 121–33.
16 Anver M. Emon, *Religious Pluralism and Islamic Law: Dhimmīs and Others in the Empire of Law* (Oxford: Oxford University Press, 2014).
17 Michael Bonner, *Jihad in Islamic History: Doctrines and Practice* (Princeton: Princeton University Press, 2006).

The situation of non-Muslims under Muslim rule was generally more favorable than that of non-Christians in Europe. Actual persecution was rare, though the enforcement of restrictive regulations intensified after the Crusades and the Mongol invasions. Jews and Christians in Muslim countries could occupy high positions as administrators, financiers and physicians. They participated in Islamic civilization and contributed to its philosophy, science and literature, while retaining their internal communal identity and autonomy. In the sixteenth century, Jews expelled from Christian Spain were welcomed in the Ottoman Empire. Conversion to Islam was achieved through persuasion and economic enticement, rather than by force.[18]

Apostasy was also rare in Islamic history, and even rarer in the cases of regimes or countries. Charges of apostasy became a major issue when the Mongol rulers of Iran professed to adopt Islam, but continued to apply the *yasaq* law of Genghis Khan and the customs of the steppe. For the zealot Hanbali theologian Ahmad ibn Taymiyya, the ideological forefather of today's radical Islamic movements, they remained infidels, against whom it was obligatory to fight until they complied with the laws of God.[19]

Modernist Islamic reformers of the late nineteenth and early twentieth centuries usually acknowledged the value of tolerance. Especially when confronted by European interlocutors, thinkers such as Muhammad ʿAbduh assumed an apologetic stance in an effort to prove that, despite the appalling situation of the Muslims of their time, Islam itself was more tolerant toward learning and science than Christianity, and that if freed from ossified tradition, it would offer no impediment to wealth and progress.[20] The modernists tended to limit the legitimacy of jihad to defense, to substitute the protection of non-Muslim subjects with the patriotic idea of common citizenship in a shared fatherland, and to disregard the law of apostasy altogether.

The atrocities of World War I led the modernist Salafi leader Rashid Rida to approve of violence against imperialist Europe and denounce Muslim rulers who adopted Western secular laws in place of the shariʿa.[21] For the Muslim Brotherhood, the occupation of Arab lands by the colonial powers, alongside

---

18 Kate Zebiri, *Muslims and Christians Face to Face* (Oxford: OneWorld, 1997), 22–24; Mark R. Cohen, *Under Crescent & Cross: The Jews in the Middle Ages* (Princeton: Princeton University Press, 1994), 3–14.

19 Emmanuel Sivan, *Radical Islam: Medieval Theology and Modern Politics* (New Haven: Yale University Press, 1985), 97–99.

20 Mark Sedgwick, *Muhammad Abduh* (London: OneWorld, 2010), 83–93.

21 Emad Eldin Shahin, "Muḥammad Rashīd Riḍā's Perspectives on the West as Reflected in *al-Manār*," *The Muslim World* 79, no. 2 (April 1989), https://doi.org/10.1111/j.1478-1913.1989.tb02841.x.

their encouragement of Zionism, represented a revival of Christian crusading fanaticism, aimed at the "slow annihilation and profound and complete corruption of Islam."[22] In such circumstances, the task at hand was to demonstrate the continuing intolerance of Western Christianity, and of local Christian and Jewish minorities, as against the innate tolerance of Islam.[23] The basic Salafi-Wahhabi principle of *al-wala' wa al-bara'* – loyalty to believers, disavowal of unbelievers – was opposed to any tolerance toward non-Muslims, Shi'a and even non-Salafi Sunni Muslims.[24] It was only after independence, and with the onset of globalization, that an opening was made for ideas of tolerance and initiatives for interfaith and inter-civilizational dialogue.

2   Yusuf al-Qaradawi's Middle Way

Shaykh Yusuf al-Qaradawi (b. 1926) is arguably today's most prominent Sunni Muslim scholar. A graduate of al-Azhar University in Cairo, he joined the Muslim Brotherhood in the 1940s and has remained associated with it ever since. In 1961, he relocated to Qatar, making it the base for his growing worldwide activity. Qaradawi was elected president of the European Council for Fatwa and Research in 1997 and the International Union of Muslim Scholars in 2004, and has been involved in various global campaigns, some of them ecumenical, others controversial.[25]

Qaradawi's reputation rests on his prolific writing, with an output of more than a hundred books and *fatwa* collections, augmented by his popular TV program "Sharia and Life" on Al Jazeera and the internet website IslamOnline. Purporting to guide fellow believers toward full Muslim life, Qaradawi combines a modernist quest for reform and progress with insistence on the religious law. In the footsteps of Hasan al-Banna, he seeks to steer the "Islamic awakening" in the face of both external and internal threats. His "Islamic solution" lies in striking a middle way (*wasatiyya*) between the extremes of authenticity and innovation, excess and neglect, rigidity and extremism. More

---

22   Richard P. Mitchell, *The Society of the Muslim Brothers* (Oxford: Oxford University Press, 1969), 227–31.

23   See especially Muhammad al-Ghazali, *Al-Ta'assub wa al-Tasamuh bayn al-Masihiyya wa al-Islam: Dahd Shubuhat wa Radd Muftarayyat* (Cairo: Dar al-Kutub al-Haditha, 1965).

24   Uriya Shavit, "Can Muslims Befriend non-Muslims? Debating *al-Walā' wa-al-Barā'* (Loyalty and Disavowal) in Theory and Practice," *Islam and Christian-Muslim Relations* 25, no. 1 (2014), https://doi.org/10.1080/09596410.2013.851329.

25   Bettina Gräf and Jakob Skovgaard-Petersen, eds., *The Global Mufti: The Phenomenon of Yusuf al-Qaradawi* (New York: Columbia University Press, 2009).

recently, he has devoted much attention to Muslim life in the West and Islam's place in globalization.[26]

The earliest mentions of tolerance in Qaradawi's writings go back to the 1970s, and are related to the treatment of non-Muslims under Muslim rule. Adopting a modernist apologetic tone, he set out to prove through both shariʻa and history that relations with *ahl al-dhimma* "were based on strong foundations of tolerance, justice, kindness and compassion," and that their rights and freedoms were guaranteed while their obligations were minimal. Islam's "spirit of tolerance," he argued, far surpassed modern secular ideologies, which, as the Muslim Brothers' experience under Nasser showed, ruthlessly persecuted and eliminated adversaries as well as partisans.[27] Returning to the topic in the 1990s, Qaradawi sought to demonstrate that the Islamic solution was fully compatible with the Quranic principle of "no compulsion in religion." Now, however, he spoke of minority rights, was ready to abandon the juristic term *dhimma* in favor of citizenship, and defined Islam as the shared cultural heritage of Muslims and non-Muslims in the abode of Islam.[28] His adoption of such universal discourse reflected a shift from scriptural to contextual reasoning, and a growing attention to the condition of Muslims under Western rule. Qaradawi was a leading figure in the formation of a new field, the jurisprudence of minorities (*fiqh al-aqaliyyat*), which justifies Muslim presence in the West for the benefit of the *umma* and its *daʻwa*, facilitates the lives of Muslims in the diaspora and pursues the middle way of integration, between assimilation and segregation.[29]

Qaradawi's discourse of holy war locates it somewhere between the purely physical combat of the jihadists and the spiritual struggle of the Sufis. In this light, he criticizes al-Qaeda and its ilk for using indiscriminate violence against non-Muslims as well as against Muslims whom they declare infidels. In his jurisprudence of jihad, Qaradawi distinguishes between peaceful struggle against injustice and corruption within the Muslim community and armed combat against external enemies, which is a personal obligation in the case

---

26   Armando Salvatore, "Qaraḍāwī's *Maṣlaḥa*: From Ideologue of the Islamic Awakening to Sponsor of Transnational Public Islam," in *The Global Mufti*, ed. Gräf and Skovgaard-Petersen.

27   Yusuf al-Qaradawi, *Ghayr al-Muslimin fi al-Mujtamaʻ al-Islami*, 2nd ed. (Cairo: Maktabat Wahba, 1983 [1977]), 5, 31–54, 69–78.

28   Yusuf al-Qaradawi, *Al-Aqaliyyat al-Diniyya* [...] *wa al-Hall al-Islami* (Amman: Dar al-Furqan, 1996), esp. 5, 16, 76.

29   Alexandre Caeiro and Mahmoud al-Saify, "Qaraḍāwī in Europe, Europe in Qaraḍāwī?: The Global Mufti's European Politics," in *The Global Mufti*, ed. Gräf and Skovgaard-Petersen, 115–18.

of defensive war and a collective duty in the case of offensive war. The latter, he opines, has become obsolete today, since new means of communication facilitate *da'wa* without obstruction. As the Hudaybiyya truce treaty the Prophet concluded with the pagans of Mecca demonstrates, Islam always prefers peaceful means.[30] This, however, is not the case in Palestine, where occupation makes resistance to the "Zionist entity" a defensive war. In his *fatwa*s from the Second Intifada, Qaradawi approved of suicide attacks on Israeli civilians, since "Palestinians had no other weapons at their disposal to defend their homeland but their bodies." For him, such "sacrificial martyrdom operations" were lawful terrorism.[31] Condemned and banned from entering the United States and the United Kingdom, in late 2016, Qaradawi revoked his earlier ruling on the grounds that the Palestinians' new capabilities rendered martyrdom operations no longer necessary.[32]

On the issue of apostasy, Qaradawi seems to be the least tolerant. He describes the severe punishments prescribed in the scriptures and Islamic law on "the crime of *ridda*" as necessary for maintaining the integrity of "the believing society." He furthermore expresses his understanding as to the motives of radicals in using *takfir* ("excommunication") against iniquitous rulers. Yet here too, for both juristic and contextual considerations, Qaradawi opts for the middle way. Attributing widespread contemporary Muslim apostasy to the inroads of Christian missionaries, Communist ideology and atheist secularization, he affirms the obligation to fight apostasy, but warns against the excesses of the jihadi organizations, which generate violence and threaten to tear Muslim society, and the Islamic movement itself, apart.[33] *Takfir* should not be used lightly; it must take into consideration the juristic distinctions between major and minor disbelief and between public and discreet apostasy, as well as the obligation to give apostates the chance to repent.[34]

Dialogue appears in Qaradawi's 1991 landmark *Priorities of the Islamic Movement in the Next Stage*. In this programmatic work, he urges the Islamic

---

30   Yusuf al-Qaradawi, *Fiqh al-Jihad: Dirasa Muqarina li Ahkamihi wa Falsafatihi fi Daw' al-Qur'an wa al-Sunna* (Cairo: Maktabat Wahba, 2009), 1:88–120, 231ff., 330ff.

31   Yusuf al-Qaradawi, *Khitabuna al-Islami fi 'Asr al-'Awlama* (Cairo: Dar al-Shuruq, 2004), 158–62. "Qaradawi's View on Martyrdom Operations," IslamOnline Archive, accessed October 17, 2018, https://archive.islamonline.net/?p=6549.

32   "Qaradawi Retracts Suicide Bombing Fatwa- Says No More Need," The Global Muslim Brotherhood Daily Watch, accessed October 17, 2018, www.globalmbwatch.com/2016/12/05/qaradawi-retractssuicide-bombing-fatwa/.

33   Yusuf al-Qaradawi, *Zahirat al-Ghulu fi al-Takfir* (Cairo: Maktabat Wahba, 1990), 3–15.

34   Yusuf al-Qaradawi, *Jarimat al-Ridda* [...] *wa 'Uqubat al-Murtadd fi Daw' al-Qur'an wa al-Sunna* (Amman: Dar al-Furqan, 1996).

movement to open up and engage the Other, since globalization renders self-seclusion neither desirable nor possible. Particularly important externally are dialogue with the dominant West, Christian-Muslim dialogue in the face of secularism and atheism, intellectual dialogue with Orientalists and political dialogue based on common interests rather than false images. Internally, dialogue must be pursued with sympathetic rulers and even with perceptive secular Muslims.[35]

On the other hand, Qaradawi blames Christian missionaries, the "crusader spirit" of European imperialism and colonialism, Islamophobia and the military and ideological "invasions" of the US, as major obstacles to good relations. His suspicions, fed by a sense of humiliation, pop up in times of crisis. Such was his response to Pope Benedict XVI's controversial Regensburg lecture in 2006, in which he cited offensive remarks made against Islam by a Byzantine Emperor. For Qaradawi, this was part of a long-standing Catholic mistreatment, which included French and Italian colonialisms in North Africa as well as more recently, the so-called War on Terror. Arguing that Islam is humane, rational and promotes peace, he brought to his aid sympathetic Western scholars who maintained that the rapid spread of Islam was accomplished by its merits, not by the sword. Qaradawi added a thinly veiled warning that although no Muslim wishes war, if forced to fight, he will do so with strength, bravery and patience, accepting only victory or martyrdom.[36]

Qaradawi's concept of tolerance is shaped by its antonym *ta'assub*, which means blind loyalty to one's group, in conjunction with emancipation (*taharrur*) – opening toward the Other and accepting a plurality of opinions. Seeking to anchor this new notion of tolerance in the scriptures, Qaradawi extracts from the Quran and sunna four principles that support it: the affirmation of religious diversity, deferring the judgment of unbelievers and the judgment of sinners until the Day of Reckoning, and the obligations to treat humanity with justice and respect. Tolerance is conducive to dialogue, which relies on the practical principles of argument, critique, flexibility and mutual learning.[37] This guarantees the internal unity of the Islamic awakening, which like Islamic jurisprudence, must be based on a multiplicity of perspectives and

---

[35] Yusuf al-Qaradawi, *Awlawiyyat al-Haraka al-Islamiyya fi al-Marhala al-Qadima* (Beirut: Mu'asasit al-Risala, 1991), 167–88.

[36] Yusuf al-Qaradawi, *Al-Baba wa al-Islam: Radd 'ala al-Baba Benedict al-Sadis 'Ashar fi Kalimatihi fi Almania allati As'a biha ila al-Islam* (Cairo: Maktabat Wahba, 2007), 17–27, 95–156.

[37] Yusuf al-Qaradawi, *Al-Sahwa al-Islamiyya min al-Murahaqa ila al-Rushd* (Cairo: Dar al-Shuruq, 2002), 213–40.

judgments. For Qaradawi, not only is such a notion of tolerance compatible with religion as the all-inclusive and final truth; but it actually makes tolerance as such an Islamic invention and posits Muslims as the only ones to practice it.[38]

3 The Gülen Movement and Islamic Enlightenment

The Gülen Movement has become one of the most influential religio-civil organizations in Turkey and in the Muslim world at large. Its founder and leader, *hocaefendi* Fethullah Gülen (b. 1941), embodies in his persona the combined roles of the Sufi *shaykh*, the *'alim* (scholar), the modern intellectual and the social activist. Formed as a loosely knit educational network, the Gülen Movement developed close ties with state institutions and became deeply involved in national politics, the economy and the media.[39] Gülen himself, who since 1999 has lived in a self-imposed exile in the United States, first allied with Erdoğan's Justice and Development Party (AKP). However, the apprehensions of the authoritarian Turkish President about the cleric's increasing power created a rift that led to his accusation of being the mastermind behind the failed coup attempt of July 2016 and a large-scale wave of purges, arrests and firings among his followers and sympathizers.

The appeal of the Gülen Movement relied on the charisma of its leader, who combined the activist Naqshbandi Sufi tradition of eastern Anatolia with the modernist teachings of the Kurdish luminary Said Nursi. Using a direct and emotive style, his public discourse was embedded in the Quran and sunna, with reference to European Enlightenment thought. He thus employed ideas from the likes of Kant, Sartre or Kafka to reinforce his interpretation of Islamic precepts to meet contemporary needs. Under his guidance, the Gülen Movement centered on the practical idea of *hizmet* – rendering service to the community, to Islam and to humanity, which echoes the Protestant ethic of working in this world in preparation for the hereafter. Its network of schools, boardinghouses (known as "lighthouses") and media outlets promoted moral values while offering ways to be Muslim, modern and Turk all at the same time.[40]

---

38   Yusuf al-Qaradawi, *Al-Sahwa al-Islamiyya bayna al-Ikhtilaf al-Mashru' wa al-Tafarruq al-Madhmum* (Cairo: Dar al-Shuruq, 2001), 106–14.
39   M. Hakan Yavuz, *Toward an Islamic Enlightenment: The Gülen Movement* (New York: Oxford University Press, 2013), 25–46.
40   Lester R. Kurtz, "Gülen's Paradox: Combining Commitment and Tolerance," *The Muslim World* 95, no. 3 (July 2005), https://doi.org/10.1111/j.1478-1913.2005.00100.x.

Tolerance and dialogue are major concepts in Fethullah Gülen's thought.[41] The inspiration for these "two roses of the emerald hills" comes from Sufi-like sentiments of love, mercy and forgiveness.[42] For Gülen, tolerance is the most essential element of any moral system, and it must permeate all walks of society. By way of definition, he emphasizes that it "does not mean being influenced by others or joining them, it means accepting others as they are and knowing how to get along with them." On the individual level, this entails "clos[ing] our eyes to the faults of others, to have respect for different ideas, and to forgive everything that is forgivable." On the national level, it is "our safest refuge and our fortress" against the hardships caused by factionalism and disagreement over Turkey's recovery and revival. Tolerance, Gülen insists, was introduced to the world by the prophets, is often mentioned in the Quran and sunna, and was realized in an exemplary manner by Muhammad and his companions. It is also embedded in the universal values of human rights, dignity and care for the environment, and is the prerequisite for democracy and peace. Absent in these troubled days, in which hatred, evildoing and rancor reign supreme, it is urgently needed to bring about reconciliation within society and in interfaith and inter-civilizational relations.[43]

Dialogue is the practical side of tolerance. In Gülen's simple definition, it is "the coming together of two or more people to discuss certain issues, and thus the forming of a bond between these people."[44] Dialogue is rooted, according to Gülen, in the Quranic injunction and the Prophet's way of spreading the message of Islam, by exemplary conduct and morality rather than preaching. It demands treating others with respect, mercy and forbearance, even responding to detractors with mildness and gentle words. Dialogue is the prerequisite for justice and stability within society, and the means of cooperation between diverse faiths for addressing the shared problems of humanity.[45]

In Gülen's thought, this universal discourse of tolerance and dialogue has largely overshadowed the classical concepts of *jihad*, *dhimma* and *ridda*. Jihad is a partial exception, mainly due to the bad reputation it gives to Islam. Gülen seeks to rehabilitate it by separating the struggle in the path of God, which

---

41 This analysis is based on the semi-official selection of articles and sermons: Fethullah Gülen, *Toward a Global Civilization of Love & Tolerance* (Somerset, NJ: The Light, Inc., 2004).
42 Ibid., 4–9.
43 Ibid., 33–45.
44 Ibid., 50.
45 Ali Ünal and Alphonse Williams, eds., *Advocate of Dialogue: Fethullah Gülen* (Fairfax, VA.: The Fountain, 2000), 14–34.

is, "in one respect [...] the purpose of our creation and our most important duty," from terrorism, which is the antithesis of dialogue. Following Sufi tradition, he distinguishes between the greater and the lesser jihad, the latter denoting active fulfilment of Islam's commandments and duties, but in the Enlightenment spirit, it is also "based on removing obstacles [...] so that people can choose freely between belief and unbelief." Gülen notes that the Prophet's mission to communicate the faith to unbelievers demanded reconciliation, even with his enemies. In stark contrast to Qaradawi, he asserts that no individual or organization is authorized to declare war, and that no *fatwa* can justify the killing of innocent people and suicide bombing. Terrorism is in Gülen's view total evil, and associating Islam with it is sheer ignorance on the part of both unbelievers and the terrorists themselves. Bin Laden and his cohorts are nothing but monsters who have sullied the bright face of Islam. Yet the way to fight them is not by warfare, but through peaceful jihad: by good education and by solving the problems faced by Muslims, such as poverty, foreign rule, civil turmoil and drug addiction.[46]

In place of *dhimma*, the Gülen Movement has promoted active engagement and support of religious and ethnic minorities. Gülen's guiding approach toward Jews and Christians in Turkey and on the global stage is dialogue that capitalizes on shared belief in God and shuns divisive issues, including even Muhammad's prophethood.[47] In this vein, he met during the 1990s with representatives of the Christian and Jewish communities and invited them to his "tolerance dinners."[48] The Gülen Movement also supported the right of Kurds in Turkey to use their language and opened educational institutions and a private TV channel to disseminate Kurdish culture. They have similarly propagated the idea of Sunni-Alevi brotherhood and assisted in constructing places of worship (*cemevi*) that also serve as spaces for dialogue.[49]

I could likewise hardly find any reference to *ridda* in Gülen's writings, an issue that is of great importance to Arab Islamists, but rarely an issue in Turkey. In principle, he compares apostasy to state treason, and like Qaradawi, he justifies the harsh punishments meted out in Islamic Law for renouncing the faith,

---

46 Gülen, *Toward a Global Civilization*, 171–90.
47 Ibid., 71–76.
48 Zeki Saritoprak and Sidney Griffith, "Fethullah Gülen and the 'People of the Book': A Voice from Turkey for Interfaith Dialogue," *The Muslim World* 95, no. 3 (July 2005), https://doi.org/10.1111/j.1478-1913.2005.00097.x.
49 Mustafa Demir and Omer Sener, "Normalisation of Minorities in Turkey: The Role of the Gulen Movement (September 21, 2013)," SSRN, accessed April 27, 2020, www.ssrn.com/abstract=2329078.

including the death penalty, on the grounds that it "breaks one's covenant with God" and "overturns the whole balance of creation and its relationship with the Creator."[50]

Still, despite its lofty discourse and avowed commitment to tolerance and dialogue, the Gülen Movement's motives remain highly controversial. The failed coup of July 2016 left even academic researchers confused. Detractors inside Turkey claim that it is seeking to infiltrate the state and dominate civil society in order to establish an Islamic state, or they depict it as an American puppet and a collaborator with the Pope and the Zionists. Its opponents in the West regard it as a Trojan horse that dissimulates its true goals (*taqiyya*), which are to resurrect the Caliphate and spread Islam by violence and terror.[51] As against these, stands the explicit discourse of the movement, which seeks to offer a non-authoritarian Islamic alternative for Turkey and to challenge the "clash of civilizations" approach on the global scene.

4 Abdolkarim Soroush and Islamic Democracy

Dr. Abdolkarim Soroush (b. 1945) is a prominent intellectual in post-revolutionary Iran, and one of the most influential religious intellectuals worldwide. Educated at the University of Teheran, he pursued his studies in London in a PhD program in the History and Philosophy of Science. In the wake of the Islamic Revolution of 1978–1979, he was appointed by Imam Khomeini to the Cultural Revolution Council and was entrusted with Islamizing the universities. Four years later, Soroush resigned and moved to the Institute for Cultural Research and Studies, his academic base for the following years. Subjected to harsh critique and physical threats from the regime's vigilantes, he has spent much of the last two decades as a visiting scholar at various universities abroad.[52]

Soroush's credentials are based on his prolific writing, which includes numerous learned treatises and newspaper articles, especially in the 1990s dissident

---

50 Fethullah Gülen, "The Quran Says: There is No Compulsion in Religion (2:256) What Does This Mean?," accessed October 17, 2018, www.web.archive.org/web/20121009104449/ http://en.fgulen.com/questions-and-answers/589-the-quran-says-there-is-no-compulsion-in-religion-2256-what-does-this-mean.

51 Doğan Koç, *Strategic Defamation of Fethullah Gülen: English vs. Turkish* (Lanham, MD: University Press of America, 2012).

52 Behrooz Ghamari-Tabrizi, *Islam & Dissent in Postrevolutionary Iran: Abdolkarim Soroush, Religious Politics and Democratic Reform* (London: I.B. Tauris, 2008), 89–129, 189–222.

monthly *Kiyan*, along with his popular and widely circulated speeches and debates. Of a philosophical mind, his thought is founded on the combination of mysticism – the rationalist theosophy of Mulla Sadra as well as Persian Sufi poetry – and science. His point of departure is that our understanding of religion changes and evolves over time in accordance with methodology, worldview and the advancement of the human sciences. In his view, current Islamic ideologies reduce the complexity of religion to a fixed, easy-to-grasp system of thought and turn it into a political tool for mobilizing and directing public opinion and behavior. Soroush rejects both the innovative ideas underlying Khomeini's Islamic Revolution and the official dogmatism of the present clerical establishment. For him, democracy and good relations with the West will guarantee a free and adequate interpretation of Islam in modern times.[53]

Invited recently to take part in a project in which prominent Muslim, Christian and Jewish thinkers sought "to defend religious liberty and tolerance from within their own faith traditions," Soroush chose, like Gülen, to focus on the legacy of the Quran and on Sufism. From the holy book, he deduces that Islam recognizes the pluralistic nature of the human condition and enjoins dealing with non-Muslims with kindness and justice. From the Persian Sufi-poets Hafez and Rumi, he learns that one should tolerate enemies as well as friends (though not the enemies of tolerance), despite the human propensity to err and sin, and that God gave people religion and reason to recognize the truth and worship Him, not to use them as weapons against antagonists. The Sufi quest for self-perfection and love is contrasted with the contemporary fundamentalist "plague" – of either the religious or the secular type, which out of a false sense of superiority easily succumbs to intolerance and destructive violence, even considering them sacrosanct.[54]

Soroush too has little interest in the classical concepts regulating Islam's relations with non-Muslims. He admits that some verses in the Quran seem to enjoin Muslims to wage war against infidels, but then points to the wider semantic field of the term jihad and argues that most of these verses actually refer to its peaceful and defensive brand. Soroush similarly favors jurists who tried to soften the decree to kill apostates by stipulating qualifications on its application. He distinguishes between sincere seekers of the truth, who may

---

[53] Valla Vakili, "Abdolkarim Soroush and Critical Discourse in Iran," in *Makers of Contemporary Islam*, ed. John L. Esposito and John O. Voll (New York: Oxford University Press, 2001).

[54] Abdolkarim Soroush, "An Islamic Treatise on Tolerance," in *Abraham's Children: Liberty and Tolerance in an Age of Religious Conflict*, ed. Kelly James Clark (New Haven: Yale University Press, 2012).

be persuaded to leave the faith in periods of universal quandary and doubt, such as in secular modernity, and conspirators, who frequently enter and leave the faith in order to trivialize and mock it, as was the case with the hypocrites at the beginning of Islam. The latter, in concurrence with Qaradawi, had to be treated with punitive measures, but the former should be confronted through proper logical argumentation.[55]

In place of these Islamic notions, Soroush resorts to the universal vocabulary of democracy and human rights, freedom of thought and public accountability. His reflections on tolerance are set against the religio-political repression in post-revolutionary Iran in general, and his own plight as a dissident intellectual in particular. "Today in Iran," he laments, "tolerance is seen as a vice rather than a virtue [...] we endure an intolerant, *religious* state."[56] Yet, in defying the secular idea of the separation of religion and politics, Soroush advances the notion of democratic religious government, which is neither a narrow-minded jurisprudential government, a thinly veiled reference to Khomeini's concept of *vilayat-i faqih*, nor the relativist liberalism of Western governments. It is rather a just representative government, in which reason and revelation converge and human rights are respected. Soroush can thus agree with the liberals that, "the government has no right to impose religion on its citizens. Nor should it have the prerogative to dictate a particular interpretation of a religion to the adherents of that religion," but also to affirm that democracy requires tolerance of different points of view, not renouncing one's own religious beliefs.[57]

Drawing from the scientific method of deliberation, Soroush has actively promoted dialogue among Iran's university students. Pointing to the hazards of Huntington's theory of the "clash of civilizations" on one hand, and Jalal Al-e Ahmed's concept of Westoxication (*gharbzadegi*) on the other, he instead suggests pursuing "dialogue of cultures" and "dialogue of religions." These are to be based on the distinction between static and materialist "civilization," such as technology, wealth and military force, and dynamic and spiritual "culture," as reflected in the universal language of human rights. Dialogue among philosophers, historians, artists and clerics is, for Soroush, "perhaps the most important thing that's left for humanity to do." Intra-cultural dialogue, he declares, must begin in the world of Islam itself, by overcoming ignorance and forging a greater unity. Muslims should thus initiate dialogue with Christians and especially Jews, because "Judaism has many more affinities with Islam,"

---

55   Mahmoud Sadri and Ahmad Sadri, eds., *Reason, Freedom, and Democracy in Islam: Essential Writings of Abdolkarim Soroush* (New York: Oxford University Press, 2000), 215–16, n. 19.
56   Soroush, "An Islamic Treatise," 288.
57   Sadri, *Reason, Freedom and Democracy*, 138–40.

and many Western scholars, "make the point that Islam was a kind of reform of Judaism"! The purpose of interfaith dialogue, Soroush emphasizes, is not to change the religion of our partner, but to better understand ourselves by dwelling on our commonalities. Dialogue, finally, should be the rule among Iranians themselves, rather than the coercion and violence that prevail in the Islamic Republic.[58]

5 Saudi Arabia's National and International Dialogue

Saudi Arabia has until lately been one of the least tolerant countries in the world. Founded in the early twentieth century on a politico-religious alliance between the Saudi royal family and the ultra-orthodox Wahhabi ulama, it has long been notorious for beheading offenders in the public square and for its prohibition against women driving. The founder, Muhammad ibn ʿAbd al-Wahhab (1703–1792), excommunicated (*takfir*) Bedouin, Sufis, Shiʿa, rival clerics and other Muslims who differed from his purist concept of God's unity (*tawhid*). Under the Saudi banner, his followers embarked upon uncompromising jihad, until suppressed by the Ottoman viceroy of Egypt. The increasing subservience of the Wahhabi establishment to Saudi political authority during the twentieth century generated an inner-Wahhabi protest movement – the Islamic Awakening (*al-Sahwa al-Islamiyya*), which erupted in the 1990s and turned violent under the spell of al-Qaeda. Until the turn of the present century, all Wahhabi factions subscribed to the xenophobic concept of loyalty to the believers, disavowal of the unbelievers.

As Saudi Arabia's state religion, the Wahhabi mission was embodied in the Committee for Commanding Right and Forbidding Wrong, the notorious religious police entrusted with surveillance of public morality. Propagation of the strict Wahhabi brand of Islam outside Saudi Arabia was entrusted to the Salafi movement, with whom Wahhabism became increasingly identified. The Wahhabi *daʿwa* experienced a great boom in the 1960s with King Faisal's establishment of several transnational religious organizations as part of his struggle against secular Nasserism and the Baʿth: the Organization of the Islamic

---

[58] "Dialogue of Cultures instead of Dialogue of Civilizations – Interview with Dr. Abdulkarim Soroush by Hamideh Safamanesh," May 5, 2007, accessed October 17, 2018, www.drsoroush.com/English/Interviews/E-INT-Dialogue%20of%20Cultures%20instead%20of%20Dialogue%20of%20Civilizations.html.

Conference (OIC), the Islamic University in Medina (IUM) and, above all, the Muslim World League (MWL).[59]

The Saudi-Wahhabi approach toward the Other began to change in the wake of the terror attacks of 9/11 and subsequent terror incidents on Arabian soil from 2003–2006. Yet there were some precedents, as meetings of Wahhabi ulama with the Vatican and with the main Protestant churches took place as early as 1972–1974 and included a European tour under the Saudi Minister of Justice. In 1986, the MWL Secretary General participated in "the pilgrimage to Assisi" to show solidarity with other religions.[60] Under the mounting critique of Wahhabi promotion of religious extremism after 9/11, Crown Prince and later King Abdallah urged the ulama to take on the task of creating a more moderate religious discourse.[61] The new policy resulted in the 2003 formation of the King Abdulaziz Center for National Dialogue (KACND). Its stated aims include consolidating national unity within the framework of the Islamic faith; presenting a moderate image of Islam; tackling social, cultural and political problems through dialogue; and strengthening civil society to ensure equality, justice and freedom of expression within the framework of the shariʿa. To effect these goals, training programs were developed and implemented throughout the kingdom, reaching one million participants by 2013,[62] and a series of annual meetings were convened, bringing together Saudi intellectuals of all shades – Wahhabis and non-Wahhabis, Sunnis and Shiʿa, men and women (though segregated) – to discuss such issues as religious extremism, women, youth, education, employment and relation to the Other.[63]

Subsequently in 2012, the King Abdullah bin Abdulaziz International Center for Interfaith and Intercultural Dialogue (KAICIID) was founded in Vienna. Preparatory meetings were held in the preceding years between the Saudi king and such world leaders as Pope Benedict XVI, UN General Secretary Ban-Ki Moon and King Juan Carlos I of Spain. An international Islamic conference for dialogue held in Mecca gave his initiative religious sanction. The avowed

---

59 Reinhard Schulze, *Islamischer Internationalismus im 20. Jahrhundert: Untersuchungen zur Geschichte der islamischen Weltliga* (Leiden: Brill, 1990), part 2.
60 Ataullah Siddiqui, *Christian-Muslim Dialogue in the Twentieth Century* (Basingstoke: Palgrave Macmillan, 1997), 183.
61 Muhammad al-Atawneh, "Wahhabi Self-Examination Post-9/11: Rethinking the 'Other', 'Otherness' and Tolerance," *Middle Eastern Studies* 47, no. 2 (2011), https://doi.org/10.1080/00263206.2011.544098.
62 Interview with Dr. Amal Yahya Almoallimi, Head of the Female Branch KACND, Vienna, November 19, 2013.
63 Mark C. Thompson, *Saudi Arabia and the Path to Political Change: National Dialogue and Civil Society* (London: I.B. Tauris, 2014), 58–87.

mission of KAICIID is "acting as a hub, facilitating interreligious and intercultural dialogue and understanding, to enhance cooperation, respect for diversity, justice and peace." Its board of directors includes a Shiʿa, clergy of various Christian denominations, a Jewish Rabbi as well as Hindu and Buddhist representatives. Its current projects include establishing interreligious dialogue in conflict areas in the Middle East and Africa, worldwide campaigns against violence in the name of religion, as well as supporting refugee integration in Europe and peace initiatives in Myanmar.[64] Today, the organization emphasizes its independent non-governmental character and the equal standing of the member states in its decision-making bodies, although Saudi Arabia continues to be the principal funder and the king's adviser, Faisal bin Muaammar, its secretary-general.[65]

The relative dearth of the notion of tolerance in the new Saudi-Wahhabi discourse points to the practical defensive nature of the move from daʿwa to dialogue. In the corridors of the 2013 inaugural conference of KAICIID in Vienna, which I attended along with nearly a thousand other participants from all major religions, many questioned whether its stated intentions were genuine. The Wahhabi standing becomes apparent from MWL Secretary-General Abdullah al-Turki's review of King Abdallah's initiative. Setting himself against the "clash of civilizations" theory, Turki asserts that neither religion nor the Enlightenment are the cause of pain and conflict in the world; it is rather imperialist designs dressed in the garb of religion and culture. Islam, he avers apologetically, has no association with terrorism, and Muslims have been at the forefront of openness and cooperation with other civilizations. Saudi Arabia itself, according to Turki, chose dialogue as a strategic option upon its foundation, and King Abdallah has reinitiated it in these troubled times "as the best example that the Islamic nation can set to solidify understanding and coexistence with members of all religions and difference [sic] cultures as a rebuff to the call of others to excesses and fanaticism." The followers of the different religions are best suited, according to both the King and the high cleric, to accomplish the task in light of their shared humanistic values and views.[66]

Still, while the establishment ulama acquiesced to the royal policy, they had difficulties in comprehending and adjusting to the alien concepts it introduced into the religious discourse. Salih bin Humaid, Chairman of the Supreme

---

64   For the KAICIID website, see www.kaiciid.org, accessed October 17, 2018.
65   Interview with Peter Kaiser, Director of Communications, KAICIID headquarters, Vienna, November 2, 2017.
66   Abdullah b. A. al-Turki, "Interfaith Dialogue: From Makkah to New York," in *Interfaith Dialogue: Cross-Cultural Views,* ed. anon. (Riyadh: Ghainaa Publications, 2010).

Judicial Council and, like Turki, a member of the Saudi Committee of Senior Scholars, confounds the Islamic and universal perspectives on relations with the Other. From the purely Islamic angle, he defines dialogue as the means to inspect the different thoughts, opinions and beliefs among people to distinguish the good from the bad. Interfaith dialogue is in this respect tantamount to "inviting people to Islam or explaining the truth to them," that is, *daʿwa*. More appropriate for the universal angle, however, is the Quranic injunction to interact with others of all cultures and civilizations so that people can come to know each other. Finally, against the prevailing Western feelings of civilizational supremacy and cultural dominance, "dialogue becomes an invitation to consultation to reach useful objectives and to avoid divergence, exploitation and isolation." This angle confirms that the Islamic call is itself universal and that universal values are ensconced in the Quran. Therefore, for Bin Humaid, dialogue is the basis for Islam's relations with others in the exchange of benefits and cooperation in developing the world, but also in establishing the truth of Islam and realizing its justice in an increasingly small and interconnected world.[67]

6   Conclusion

Shaykh Yusuf al-Qaradawi, the Gülen Movement, Dr. Abdolkarim Soroush and Saudi Arabia are among the major professed protagonists of the emerging discourse of tolerance and the practice of dialogue in the contemporary Middle East. The teachings and conduct of each are grounded in the particular religious strand to which they belong and respond to the specific circumstances with which they have to cope. For the scholarly Qaradawi, the point of departure is the juristic heritage. Concerned about the conditions of Muslims in their own secularized countries and also as minorities in the West, he shifts from *dhimma* to citizenship, attenuates the scope of *ridda* and jihad, and promotes dialogue with other elements in society. The Sufi-oriented Gülen views tolerance as an essential element of the Islamic moral system, grounding it in the Prophet's exemplary model, but also in modern concepts. Reflecting the Turkish condition, he further emphasizes that dialogue is the prerequisite for human rights, justice and stability. With the Shiʿi philosopher Soroush, the universal vocabulary of human and civil rights is even more pronounced. In

---

67   Salih bin A. bin Humaid, "The Islamic View of Dialogue with the Other," in *Interfaith Dialogue*.

opposition to post-revolutionary Iran's *vilayat-i faqih*, he proposes a democratic religious government based on freedom of thought, public accountability and inter-cultural dialogue. The approach of the Saudi-Wahhabi establishment is utterly practical. Seeking to counter accusations of extremism in the aftermath of 9/11, it embraces dialogue in the framework of the shariʻa and promotes projects of reconciliation in conflict areas around the world.

In spite of the endorsement of tolerance and dialogue by our four protagonists, their discourse is frequently met with deep suspicion, defamation or outright persecution. These emanate from three different quarters. One is Western opponents, who deny the sincerity of such endeavors out of the belief that Islam's ultimate goal is to dominate the world. Another is Muslim autocrats, who are convinced that such efforts are nothing but plots to replace their governments with an Islamic state. The third quarter consists of radical Islamists, for whom the proponents of tolerance and dialogue are mere agents of the infidel West, bent on destroying Islam from within. This widespread distrust of the Other reflects the deep-seated cleavages that dominate relations between "Islam and the West," and between Muslim governments and Islamic civil societies. Still, part of the blame for the failure rests with the protagonists themselves and the contradictions that blur their messages. Qaradawi's erstwhile support of suicide bombings in Palestine and his repeated campaigns against the West, the Gülen Movement's alleged attempts to infiltrate the Turkish state apparatus, Soroush's involvement in the closing of Iranian universities during the Islamic Revolution, and Saudi Arabia's long-standing backing of Wahhabi xenophobia and discrimination all remind us that tolerance and dialogue can flourish only where democracy, pluralism and peace prevail.

Bibliography

Arzt, Donna E. "The Role of Compulsion in Islamic Conversion: *Jihad, Dhimma* and *Ridda*." *Buffalo Human Rights Law Review* 8 (2002): 15–44.

Al-Atawneh, Muhammad. "Wahhabi Self-Examination Post-9/11: Rethinking the 'Other', 'Otherness' and Tolerance." *Middle Eastern Studies* 47, no. 2 (2011): 255–71, https://doi.org/10.1080/00263206.2011.544098.

Bin Humaid, Salih A. "The Islamic View of Dialogue with the Other." In *Interfaith Dialogue: Cross-Cultural Views*, ed. anon., 24–47. Riyadh: Ghainaa Publications, 2010.

Bonner, Michael. *Jihad in Islamic History: Doctrines and Practice*. Princeton: Princeton University Press, 2006.

Caeiro, Alexandre and Mahmoud al-Saify. "Qaraḍāwī in Europe, Europe in Qaraḍāwī?: The Global Mufti's European Politics." In *The Global Mufti: The*

Phenomenon of Yusuf al-Qaradawi, edited by Bettina Gräf and Jakob Skovgaard-Petersen, 109–48. New York: Columbia University Press, 2009.

Cohen, Mark R. *Under Crescent & Cross: The Jews in the Middle Ages*. Princeton: Princeton University Press, 1994.

Cook, David. *Understanding Jihad*. Berkeley: University of California Press, 2005.

Demir, Mustafa and Omer Sener. "Normalisation of Minorities in Turkey: The Role of the Gulen Movement." SSRN. Accessed April 27, 2020, www.ssrn.com/abstract=2329078.

Emon, Anver M. *Religious Pluralism and Islamic Law: Dhimmīs and Others in the Empire of Law*. Oxford: Oxford University Press, 2014.

Friedmann, Yohanan. *Tolerance and Coercion in Islam: Interfaith Relations in the Muslim Tradition*. Cambridge: Cambridge University Press, 2003.

Gay, Peter. *The Enlightenment: An Interpretation*, vol. 2, *The Science of Freedom*. New York: W.W. Norton, 1977.

Ghamari-Tabrizi, Behrooz. *Islam & Dissent in Postrevolutionary Iran: Abdolkarim Soroush, Religious Politics and Democratic Reform*. London: I.B. Tauris, 2008.

Al-Ghazali, Muhammad. *Al-Ta'assub wa al-Tasamuh bayn al-Masihiyya wa al-Islam: Dahd Shubuhat wa Radd Muftarayyat*. Cairo: Dar al-Kutub al-Haditha, 1965.

Gräf, Bettina and Jakob Skovgaard-Petersen, eds. *The Global Mufti: The Phenomenon of Yusuf al-Qaradawi*. New York: Columbia University Press, 2009.

Grell, Ole Peter and Roy Porter, eds. *Toleration in Enlightenment Europe*. Cambridge: Cambridge University Press, 2000.

Gülen, Fethullah. "The Quran Says: There is No Compulsion in Religion (2:256) What Does This Mean?." Accessed October 17, 2018, www.web.archive.org/web/20121009104449/http://en.fgulen.com/questions-and-answers/589-the-quran-says-there-is-no-compulsion-in-religion-2256-what-does-this-mean.

Gülen, Fethullah. *Toward a Global Civilization of Love & Tolerance*. Somerset, NJ: The Light, Inc., 2004.

Hefner, Robert W. ed. *Remaking Muslim Politics: Pluralism, Contestation, Democratization*. Princeton: Princeton University Press, 2005.

Koç, Doğan. *Strategic Defamation of Fethullah Gülen: English vs. Turkish*. Lanham, MD: University Press of America, 2012.

Kurtz, Lester R. "Gülen's Paradox: Combining Commitment and Tolerance." *The Muslim World* 95, no. 3 (July 2005): 373–84, https://doi.org/10.1111/j.1478-1913.2005.00100.x.

Malik, Jamal. "Integration of Muslim Migrants and the Politics of Dialogue: The Case of Modern Germany." *Journal of Muslim Minority Affairs* 33 (2013): 495–506.

Malik, Jamal and Helmut Reifeld, eds. *Religious Pluralism in South Asia and Europe*. New Delhi: Oxford University Press, 2004.

Mayer, Ann Elizabeth. *Islam and Human Rights: Tradition and Politics*, 5th ed. New York: Routledge, 2018.

Mitchell, Richard P. *The Society of the Muslim Brothers*. Oxford: Oxford University Press, 1969.

Pipes, Daniel. "What is Jihad?." *Middle East Forum*. Accessed October 17, 2018, www.danielpipes.org/990/what-is-jihad.

Al-Qaradawi, Yusuf. *Al-Aqaliyyat al-Diniyya* [...] *wa al-Hall al-Islami*. Amman: Dar al-Furqan, 1996.

Al-Qaradawi, Yusuf. *Al-Baba wa al-Islam: Radd 'ala al-Baba Benedict al-Sadis 'Ashar fi Kalimatihi fi Almania allati As'a biha ila al-Islam*. Cairo: Maktabat Wahba, 2007.

Al-Qaradawi, Yusuf. *Al-Sahwa al-Islamiyya bayna al-Ikhtilaf al-Mashru' wa al-Tafarruq al-Madhmum*. Cairo: Dar al-Shuruq, 2001.

Al-Qaradawi, Yusuf. *Al-Sahwa al-Islamiyya min al-Murahaqa ila al-Rushd*. Cairo: Dar al-Shuruq, 2002.

Al-Qaradawi, Yusuf. *Awlawiyyat al-Haraka al-Islamiyya fi al-Marhala al-Qadima*. Beirut: Mu'asasit al-Risala, 1991.

Al-Qaradawi, Yusuf. *Fiqh al-Jihad: Dirasa Muqarina li-Ahkamihi wa-Falsafatihi fi Daw' al-Qur'an wa al-Sunna*. Cairo: Maktabat Wahba, 2009.

Al-Qaradawi, Yusuf. *Ghayr al-Muslimin fi al-Mujtama' al-Islami*, 2nd ed. Cairo: Maktabat Wahba, 1983 [1977].

Al-Qaradawi, Yusuf. *Jarimat al-Ridda* [...] *wa 'Uqubat al-Murtadd fi Daw' al-Qur'an wa al-Sunna*. Amman: Dar al-Furqan, 1996.

Al-Qaradawi, Yusuf. *Khitabuna al-Islami fi 'Asr al-'Awlama*. Cairo: Dar al-Shuruq, 2004.

Al-Qaradawi, Yusuf. *Zahirat al-Ghulu fi al-Takfir*. Cairo: Maktabat Wahba, 1990.

Sadri, Mahmoud and Ahmad Sadri, eds. *Reason, Freedom, and Democracy in Islam: Essential Writings of Abdolkarim Soroush*. New York: Oxford University Press, 2000.

Salvatore, Armando. "Qaraḍāwī's *Maṣlaḥa*: From Ideologue of the Islamic Awakening to Sponsor of Transnational Public Islam." In *The Global Mufti: The Phenomenon of Yusuf al-Qaradawi*, edited by Bettina Gräf and Jakob Skovgaard-Petersen, 239–50. New York: Columbia University Press, 2009.

Saritoprak, Zeki and Sidney Griffith. "Fethullah Gülen and the 'People of the Book': A Voice from Turkey for Interfaith Dialogue." *The Muslim World* 95, no. 3 (July 2005): 329–40, https://doi.org/10.1111/j.1478-1913.2005.00097.x.

Schulze, Reinhard. *Islamischer Internationalismus im 20. Jahrhundert: Untersuchungen zur Geschichte der islamischen Weltliga*. Leiden: Brill, 1990.

Sedgwick, Mark. *Muhammad Abduh*. London: OneWorld, 2010.

Sfeir, George N. "Basic Freedoms in a Fractured Legal Culture: Egypt and the Case of Nasr Hamid Abu Zayd." *Middle East Journal* 52, no. 3 (1998): 402–14.

Shahin, Emad Eldin. "Muḥammad Rashīd Riḍā's Perspectives on the West as Reflected in *al-Manār*." *The Muslim World* 79, no. 2 (April 1989): 113–32, https://doi.org/10.1111/j.1478-1913.1989.tb02841.x.

Shavit, Uriya. "Can Muslims Befriend non-Muslims? Debating *al-Walā' wa-al-Barā'* (Loyalty and Disavowal) in Theory and Practice." *Islam and Christian-Muslim Relations* 25, no. 1 (2014): 67–88, https://doi.org/10.1080/09596410.2013.851329.

Siddiqui, Ataullah. *Christian-Muslim Dialogue in the Twentieth Century*. Basingstoke: Palgrave Macmillan, 1997.

Sivan, Emmanuel. *Radical Islam: Medieval Theology and Modern Politics*. New Haven: Yale University Press, 1985.

Soroush, Abdolkarim. "An Islamic Treatise on Tolerance." In *Abraham's Children: Liberty and Tolerance in an Age of Religious Conflict*, edited by Kelly James Clark, 278–89. New Haven: Yale University Press, 2012.

Swidler, Leonard. "The History of Inter-Religious Dialogue." In *The Wiley-Blackwell Companion to Inter-Religious Dialogue*, edited by Catherine Cornille, 3–19. Chichester: Wiley-Blackwell, 2013.

Thompson, Mark C. *Saudi Arabia and the Path to Political Change: National Dialogue and Civil Society*. London: I.B. Tauris, 2014.

Tripp, Charles. "Islam and the Secular Logic of the State in the Middle East." In *Islamic Fundamentalism*, edited by Abdel Salam Sidahmed and Anoushiravan Ehteshami, 51–69. Boulder, CO: Westview Press, 1996.

Al-Turki, Abdullah b. A. "Interfaith Dialogue: From Makkah to New York." In *Interfaith Dialogue: Cross-Cultural Views,* ed. anon, 10–21. Riyadh: Ghainaa Publications, 2010.

Tyler, Aaron. *Islam, the West, and Tolerance: Conceiving Coexistence*. New York: Palgrave Macmillan, 2008.

Ünal, Ali and Alphonse Williams, eds. *Advocate of Dialogue: Fethullah Gülen*. Fairfax, VA.: The Fountain, 2000.

Vakili, Valla. "Abdolkarim Soroush and Critical Discourse in Iran." In *Makers of Contemporary Islam*, edited by John L. Esposito and John O. Voll, 150–76. New York: Oxford University Press, 2001.

Weismann, Itzchak. "Between *Daʿwa* and Dialogue: Religious Engagement in Muslim-minority Environments." *Islam and Christian–Muslim Relations* 30, no. 4 (2019): 505–22, https://doi.org/10.1080/09596410.2019.1601909.

Yavuz, M. Hakan. *Toward an Islamic Enlightenment: The Gülen Movement*. New York: Oxford University Press, 2013.

Zebiri, Kate. *Muslims and Christians Face to Face*. Oxford: OneWorld, 1997.

CHAPTER 14

Religious Pluralism and Religious Plurality in Pakistan

Hasnain Bokhari

1   Introduction

A Festschrift for Jamal Malik would remain incomplete without mentioning madrasas in Pakistan, a topic with which he began his scholarly journey in the 1980s[1] and to which he continued to return throughout his academic career. In a finale of sorts, he conceived an idea to engage with major religious schools of thought in Pakistan by hosting a dialogical exchange involving both female and male madrasa students from Pakistan at the University of Erfurt in 2015. Acknowledging and appreciating the different facets of the Dars-i Nizami, as formulated by the early eighteenth-century scholar Mulla Nizam al-Din (d. 1748) and on which most South Asian madrasas base their curricula, the two-year project titled "Religious Pluralism and Religious Plurality: Towards an Ethics of Peace" (hereafter: *Towards an Ethics of Peace* project) examined the topic of religious (in)tolerance in Pakistan from the perspective of social, cultural and religious studies.[2] From 2016 through 2017, madrasa students belonging to Barelwi, Deobandi, Shiʿa, Ahl-i Hadith and Jamaʿat-i Islami schools of thought were invited to Erfurt to discuss issues, such as justice, religious pluralism, traditions, diversity and human rights, while grounding the discussion primarily within Islamic cultures and traditions.[3] The present study is an attempt to discuss various aspects of that project, present some thoughts that were shared by the madrasa students, and also learn about the participating madrasas and their networks in Pakistan.

---

[1]   The subject of Pakistani madrasas is discussed in Malik's very first monograph. See Jamal Malik, *Islamisierung in Pakistan 1977–84: Untersuchungen zur Auflösung autochthoner Strukturen* (Wiesbaden: Franz Steiner, 1989).

[2]   For the project's rationale, outcomes and participating madrasas, see "Religious Pluralism & Religious Plurality: Towards an Ethics of Peace," University of Erfurt, accessed April 6, 2021, www.uni-erfurt.de/en/philosophische-fakultaet/seminare-professuren/religionswissen schaft/professuren/islamic-studies/research/religious-pluralism-religious-plurality-towards -an-ethics-of-peace.

[3]   The author was fortunate to be associated with the project as its principal coordinator.

Madrasas in Pakistan have received significant attention throughout the past two decades from media outlets, think tanks, non-governmental organisations (NGOs) and academia. This profound interest stems partly from the tragic incidents of 9/11.[4] This brought madrasas in Pakistan into global geopolitical debates, where they were minutely scrutinised for what was seen as their role in encouraging hate speech and violent extremism.[5] It has been argued that madrasa pedagogy fans intolerance and incites fanaticism, which are detrimental to pluralism and multicultural coexistence.[6] It has also been alleged that madrasas introduce students to extremely traditional and conservative socio-political worldviews, which is seen as an imminent threat to local and global political orders.[7] In a Cold War context, evidence does indicate that several graduates of Pakistani madrasas went to fight in Afghanistan during its Soviet occupation.[8] These developments along with the changing global calculus has since increased interest about madrasas, but what resulted from this curiosity has at times been hurried approaches dealing with "what" questions in reviewing the role of madrasas and less emphasis on "why" in analysing its graduates' worldviews. Just a cursory mention of a madrasa graduate commonly evokes the assumption that the person is a male, yet madrasas offer education to both male and female students. In Pakistani madrasas, the boys' section is referred to as the *banin*, whereas the girls' section is called the *banat*. In 2019 alone, there were 962,872 female students enrolled in Deobandi madrasas, not to mention the other schools of thought.[9] Most scholarship seems to give less prominence to females at madrasas, often glossing over their existence and instead focussing on the males. This and the practice of using a generic yardstick in studying madrasas, as Francis Robinson and

---

4 Jamal Malik, "Introduction," in *Madrasas in South Asia: Teaching Terror?*, ed. Jamal Malik (Oxon: Routledge, 2007), 1; Muhammad Moj, *The Deoband Madrassah Movement: Countercultural Trends and Tendencies* (London: Anthem Press, 2015).
5 Farish A. Noor, Yoginder Sikand and Martin van Bruinessen, eds., *The Madrasa in Asia: Political Activism and Transnational Linkages* (Amsterdam: Amsterdam University Press, 2008).
6 Robert W. Hefner and Muhammad Qasim Zaman, eds., *Schooling Islam: The Culture and Politics of Modern Muslim Education* (Princeton: Princeton University Press, 2010).
7 Zahid Hussain, *Frontline Pakistan: The Path to Catastrophe and the Killing of Benazir Bhutto* (New Delhi: Penguin Books India, 2008).
8 Robert D. Crews and Amin Tarzi, eds., *The Taliban and the Crisis of Afghanistan* (Cambridge, MA: Harvard University Press, 2009).
9 Abdul Majid, "Wafâq Al-Madâris al-Arabia: Introduction and Contribution," WifaqulMadaris .org, accessed October 9, 2020, www.wifaqulmadaris.org/pages/introduction.php.

Usha Sanyal suggest,[10] tends to place madrasas in one homogenous category. There seems to be less emphasis on the genealogical disposition of madrasas or their epistemological and theological denominations. Within academic circles, there have been a number of inspiring and stimulating studies, such as by Barbara D. Metcalf, Francis Robinson, Muhammad Qasim Zaman, Tariq Rahman, Masooda Bano, William Dalrymple or Matthew J. Nelson.[11] In particular, Metcalf and Robinson's works from the pre-9/11 era are some of the leading sources for understanding historical currents of the last three centuries. There are also some fresh scholarly perspectives provided by Ebrahim Moosa or Brannon Ingram[12] focussing on madrasas in South Asia. However, when it comes to understanding contemporary madrasas in Pakistan, Jamal Malik's *Islamisierung in Pakistan 1977–84: Untersuchungen zur Auflösung autochthoner Strukturen*, along with its English version,[13] can be considered as a pioneering work that helps contextualise madrasas in Pakistan.

Over the past thirty years, Pakistan has gone through several structural, political, cultural, social and of course religious transformations.[14] In the aftermath of Zia ul-Haq's (the sixth President of Pakistan; d. 1988) policy of Islamisation, the state television started to give more prominence to the Arabic language by introducing a daily news bulletin in Arabic. Persian, which was the lingua franca of the Mughal Empire and is the language of Pakistan's

---

10 Francis Robinson, "Islamic Reform and Modernities in South Asia," *Modern Asian Studies* 42, no. 2–3 (March 2008): 259–81, https://doi.org/10.1017/S0026749X07002922; Usha Sanyal, *Ahmad Riza Khan Barelwi: In the Path of the Prophet* (Oxford: Oneworld, 2012).

11 Barbara D. Metcalf, ed., *Islam in South Asia in Practice* (Princeton: Princeton University Press, 2009); Francis Robinson, *Islam and Muslim History in South Asia* (New Delhi: Oxford University Press, 2000); Muhammad Qasim Zaman, *The Ulama in Contemporary Islam: Custodians of Change* (Princeton: Princeton University Press, 2010); Tariq Rahman, "Madrasas: The Potential for Violence in Pakistan?," in *Madrasas in South Asia: Teaching Terror?*, ed. Jamal Malik, 1st ed. (Oxon: Routledge, 2007); Masooda Bano, "Beyond Politics: The Reality of a Deobandi Madrasa in Pakistan," *Journal of Islamic Studies* 18, no. 1 (January 2007): 43–68, https://doi.org/10.1093/jis/etl043; William Dalrymple, *The Last Mughal: The Fall of Delhi, 1857* (London: Bloomsbury Publishing, 2009); Matthew J. Nelson, "Muslims, Markets, and the Meaning of a 'Good' Education in Pakistan," *Asian Survey* 46, no. 5 (October 2006): 699–720, https://doi.org/10.1525/as.2006.46.5.699.

12 Ebrahim Moosa, *What Is a Madrasa?* (Chapel Hill: The University of North Carolina Press, 2015); Brannon D. Ingram, "'Modern' Madrasa: Deoband and Colonial Secularity," *Historical Social Research / Historische Sozialforschung* 44, no. 3 (169) (2019): 206–25.

13 Jamal Malik, *Colonialization of Islam: Dissolution of Traditional Institutions in Pakistan* (New Delhi: Manohar; Lahore: Vanguard, 1996).

14 Masooda Bano, *The Rational Believer: Choices and Decisions in the Madrasas of Pakistan* (Ithaca and London: Cornell University Press, 2012).

national anthem, has heavily inspired Urdu's vocabulary and prose. However, Zia's policy of Islamisation also brought Arabic influence on Persian expressions used in Urdu. An example is how saying goodbye with the originally Persian *khuda hafiz* ("may God protect you") in Pakistan has been gradually replaced by *Allah hafiz*,[15] an expression that Arabs themselves do not use. At local schools and colleges, debate competitions and sports matches were often accompanied with *na't* (poetry extolling the Prophet) recitals or *hamd* (praise unto God) competitions.[16] After Zia's sudden death, Pakistan experimented with parliamentary democracy, but the seeds of extremism and violent sectarianism sowed during and after Zia's martial law kept cropping up in the form of various militant outfits.[17] General Musharraf (the tenth President of Pakistan; b. 1943) tried to appear different from his predecessors. He styled himself as a kind of latter-day Ataturk and proffered the idea of enlightened moderation.[18] Nevertheless, violent sectarian discourse and shrinking space for religious sects as well as minorities in Pakistan became more evident in daily life.[19] Among the most recent casualties have been Christian churches, Shi'a places of worship[20] and Sufi shrines, the latter of which have been mercilessly targeted by suicide bombers.[21] Religious seminaries, on the other hand, have grown by leaps and bounds. Their outreach and student intake has

15 Syed Hamad Ali, "In Pakistan, Saying Goodbye Can Be a Religious Statement," *The Guardian*, accessed October 9, 2020, www.theguardian.com/commentisfree/belief/2012/apr/17/pakistan-goodbye-allah-hafiz.
16 Shafiqua Haq, "Moral Education in Pakistan," *Journal of Moral Education* 9, no. 3 (May 1980): 156–65, https://doi.org/10.1080/0305724800090302.
17 Frédéric Grare, "The Evolution of Sectarian Conflicts in Pakistan and the Ever-Changing Face of Islamic Violence," *South Asia: Journal of South Asian Studies* 30, no. 1 (April 2007): 127–43, https://doi.org/10.1080/00856400701264068.
18 Afiya Zia, "Faith-Based Politics, Enlightened Moderation and the Pakistani Women's Movement," *Journal of International Women's Studies* 11, no. 1 (November 2009): 225–45.
19 Irm Haleem, "Ethnic and Sectarian Violence and the Propensity Towards Praetorianism in Pakistan," *Third World Quarterly* 24, no. 3 (June 2003): 463–77, https://doi.org/10.1080/0143659032000084410.
20 Ian Talbot, "Understanding Religious Violence in Contemporary Pakistan: Themes and Theories," in *Religion, Violence and Political Mobilisation in South Asia*, ed. Ravinder Kaur (New Delhi: SAGE Publications, 2005), 145–65.
21 Shamil Shams, "Pakistan Shrine Attack – No Place for 'Soft Islam' in a Hard Country," accessed October 9, 2020, www.dw.com/en/pakistan-shrine-attack-no-place-for-soft-islam-in-a-hard-country/a-37595893; Declan Walsh, "Pakistan Bomb Kills Several at Sufi Shrine," *The Guardian*, accessed October 9, 2020, www.theguardian.com/world/2010/oct/25/bomb-sufi-shrine-pakistan.

reached into the thousands and millions, respectively.[22] In 2002, following the start of the US and NATO missions in Afghanistan, General Musharraf came under international pressure to introduce reforms in religious seminaries.[23] However, the reform initiatives and international pressures have not hindered the growth of these seminaries.[24]

In 2015, three decades after his initial research on madrasas, Malik once again turned his focus toward madrasas in Pakistan. Yet this time he sought to engage with future leaders, that is, the students of religious seminaries, who have often been stereotyped and perceived as having a very narrow outlook by international policy institutions and sometimes also by recent scholarship.[25] Yet, little is actually known about how they approach current affairs. What kind of perceptions do they have about a religiously plural society in general and about academic developments in the rest of the world? Thus, the idea was to engage with the students of religious seminaries in a meaningful and academic dialogue by revisiting some classic Islamic texts with them and also by introducing them to Western scholarship. The project employed a unique dialogical approach and was the first of its kind ever attempted by any Western university, inviting both female and male students from five major religious schools of thought in Pakistan: Deobandi, Barelwi, Ahl-i Hadith, Jamaʿat-i Islami and Shiʿa madrasas. The project proposed three main workshops on the topics of historiography, social sciences and human rights to be held in Erfurt along with twelve follow-up workshops in Pakistan. The workshops were designed as such to encourage participants to advance their own solutions from within their respective traditions while also employing the scientific tools and epistemological insights provided during the workshops. These workshops also emphasised the cultural translation of knowledge. The project not only aimed to benefit selected students, but it also focussed on encouraging and providing attendees the skills necessary to host similar workshops at their home institutions for fellow madrasa students upon returning to Pakistan.

It is, however, interesting to note the undercurrents at play that led to the engagement with the ulama (religious scholars) of the major schools of

---

22 Mujeeb Ahmad, "Understanding the Barelwi Madaris of Pakistan: Case Study of the *Tanzim al-Madaris (Ahl-i-Sunnat) Pakistan*," *Journal of South Asian and Middle Eastern Studies* 40, no. 3 (April 2017): 15–34.
23 Bano, "Beyond Politics."
24 Sanaa Riaz, *New Islamic Schools: Tradition, Modernity, and Class in Urban Pakistan*, ed. Sanaa Riaz (New York: Palgrave Macmillan, 2014).
25 University of Erfurt, "Religiöse Vielfalt und Friedensethik," accessed October 9, 2020, www.uni-erfurt.de/forschung/forschen/forschungsprojekte/religioese-vielfalt-und-friedensethik.

thought. Similarly, equally interesting is the kind of motivation and reception the University of Erfurt showed towards such cooperation. In fact, in a meeting in March 2016 when the project was presented at the madrasa of Mufti Taqi Usmani, the Jamiʿa Dar al-ʿUlum in Karachi, the panel, comprising (among others) Rafi Usmani and Zubair Usmani, posed a pertinent and thought-provoking question. While appreciating the effort to build bridges between German academia and Pakistani madrasas, the panel wondered why the West in general and the University of Erfurt in particular had developed a soft spot for the madrasas in Pakistan? This legitimate question requires some elaboration.

By 2001, Huntington's thesis on the Clash of Civilisations was nine years old. Although its framework has been the subject of much criticism, its relevance and significance has continuously increased amidst developments across the globe like the Taliban's take-over of Kabul in 1996, wars in former Soviet republics and, of course, the US-led missions in Afghanistan and Iraq post-9/11.[26] Similarly, in Europe, particularly in Germany, the debate about the integration of Muslim migrants had also picked up momentum.[27] These events led Malik to host an interfaith dialogue event in 2002 at the University of Erfurt entitled "Islam in the West." It brought together academics from the West and from Muslim majority areas in an attempt to revisit master narratives and review the growing distrust on both ends.[28] The event familiarized participants with various developments and issues in contemporary Muslim history, such as the challenges faced by Muslims in Europe as well as the impact of the works of Rushdie and Huntington on both academia and global politics.

This exercise was not only useful for the visiting scholars, but also for those studying and working at the Chair of Muslim Cultural and Religious History (CMCRH) at that time. These include, for example, Albrecht Fuess (then an

---

26 Jeffrey Haynes, "Religion and International Relations After '9/11'," *Democratization* 12, no. 3 (June 2005): 398–413, https://doi.org/10.1080/13510340500126814; Armando Salvatore, "From Tension to Dialogue?: The Mediterranean between European Civilization and the Muslim World," in *Civilizational Dialogue and World Order: The Other Politics of Cultures, Religions, and Civilizations in International Relations*, ed. Michális S. Michael and Fabio Petito (New York: Palgrave Macmillan US, 2009), 217–37.
27 Ruud Koopmans, "Germany and Its Immigrants: An Ambivalent Relationship," *Journal of Ethnic and Migration Studies* 25, no. 4 (1999): 627–47.
28 University of Erfurt, "Summer School: 'Muslims in the West'," accessed April 6, 2021, www.uni-erfurt.de/en/philosophische-fakultaet/seminare-professuren/religionswissenschaft/professuren/islamic-studies/workshops/conferences/summer-school-muslims-in-the-west. The author happened to be present at that event, then as an undergraduate fellow from Pakistan. See "25 Köpfe: Hasnain Bokhari ist geblieben," Hochschulkommunikation Universität Erfurt, accessed October 9, 2020, https://25jahre.uni-erfurt.de/25jahre.uni-erfurt.de/25-koepfe-hasnain-bokhari/index.html.

assistant professor and later a professor at Philipps University in Marburg), Jan-Peter Hartung (then a doctoral fellow and later an associate professor at Georg-August University in Göttingen) and Mouez Khalfaoui (then a graduate fellow and later a professor at Tübingen University). This 2002 interfaith dialogue was to be repeated for the next fifteen years in the form of summer schools, with its sponsors, the University of Erfurt and the German Academic Exchange Service (DAAD), realising the need for such a discursive and dialogical space and continuing to extend their cooperation. On the other hand, global events such as the US-led mission in Iraq beginning in 2003, the Madrid train bombing (2004), the London bombing of 7/7, the Danish cartoon controversy (2005) or the Charlie Hebdo shootings in Paris (2015) not only continuously fuelled mutual distrust, but it also and alternatively provided the opportunity for engagement in meaningful dialogue. Deeply enriched with philosophical and theoretical concepts from social sciences and the humanities, the summer school's proactive approach to dialogue opened doors for mutual learning, perceptive growth and respecting differing views and opinions. In a way, this summer school served as a laboratory wherein several themes were debated and contested, such as the significance of stereotypes and the problematization thereof, the making of master narratives, identity, the differences between tolerance and pluralism, and the appreciation of diversity.

Two topics in particular that Malik kept returning to were madrasas and Islam in South Asia. It remained his wish to digitise manuscripts available at various shrines in Pakistan. He also hosted an international conference in Erfurt on madrasas in South Asia in 2005/2006 where its attendees sought to question misperceptions on the curricular trends surrounding madrasas in South Asia.[29] Another important precursor to the 2016–2017 *Towards an Ethics of Peace* project was the DAAD's higher education dialogue initiative with universities in the Islamic world (*Hochschuldialog mit der islamischen Welt*).[30] In the aftermath of the multiple civil uprisings across the Arab world in 2011, the CMCRH was engaged with Pakistani universities in studying the role of social media.[31] The three-year project, entitled "Changing Role of Social Media in

---

29 Jamal Malik, *Madrasas in South Asia: Teaching Terror?*, 1st ed. (Oxon: Routledge, 2007).
30 "Social Media in muslimischen Ländern: Studierende aus Erfurt und Peshawar arbeiten zusammen," University of Erfurt, Press Release (June 19, 2012), accessed October 9, 2020, www2.uni-erfurt.de/cms-alt/pressemitteilungen-archiv/www.uni-erfurt.de/uni/einrichtungen/presse/pressemitteilungen/2012/102-12/index.html.
31 "Changing Role of Social Media in Muslim Countries," University of Erfurt, accessed April 6, 2021, www.uni-erfurt.de/en/philosophische-fakultaet/seminare-professuren/religionswissenschaft/professuren/islamic-studies/research/changing-role-of-social-media-in-muslim-countries.

Muslim Countries," was followed by a multipronged endeavour consisting of dialogue activities, field work, joint curriculum development and collaboration with civil society institutions. Malik's frequent visits to Pakistan not only served to renew interest in engaging in academic research with institutions in Pakistan, but these visits also brought participants from Germany in closer contact with issues like shrinking pluralist discourse and diminishing religious tolerance in Pakistan. During the period from 2000 to 2015, the building blocks were laid, in terms of institutional support and intellectual growth, that would eventually lead to the making of *Towards an Ethics of Peace*.[32]

I would like to return here to the March 2016 meeting at the Jamia Dar al-ʿUlum in Karachi in which Rafi Usmani's panel waited anxiously, yet patiently, for the University of Erfurt to explain its motivation behind the project. The response to their query touched on most of the topics outlined above, but more importantly, it was asserted that for a meaningful dialogue to take place, it was crucial that the dialogue partners take equal responsibility for and ownership of the project. Similarly, in pursuing such a project, it was imperative to also evaluate the knowledge acquired by the participants. Furthermore, the organisers wished to use evaluation criteria that could reflect the CMCRH's experiences from two decades of hosting dialogue events and other academic projects. This was achieved by consulting the earlier enumerated academic concepts which emerged from the summer school debates. Out of a multiplicity of potential notions, a handful were shortlisted to aid in designing key performance indicators for the evaluations. Those ideas finally selected were gender, plurality, harmony, stereotypes, diversity, identity and pluralism.

To initiate contact with the different madrasas, the project pursued a two-step approach by first meeting the senior ulama in Pakistan at their administrative centres, known as *wafaq al-madaris* (see table 14.1). In a second step, the representatives of all five madrasa boards (*wafaq*s) were invited to Erfurt to discuss the project's contents in detail.

All of the five major religious schools of thought in Pakistan – Deobandi, Barelwi, Ahl-i Hadith, Shiʿa and Jamaʿat-i Islami – have their own administrative and examination bodies. Every madrasa is supposed to be registered with its respective *wafaq* to conduct centralised annual exams. It was important to

---

32   Among the projects managed by the CMCRH during this period are "Dialogue(s) with Islam(s) in European and South-Asian Perspectives" and "Mobilisation of Religion in Europe." See "Mobilisierung von Religion in Europa," University of Erfurt, accessed April 6, 2021, www.uni-erfurt.de/philosophische-fakultaet/seminare-professuren/religionswissenschaft/professuren/philosophische-fakultaet/seminare-professuren/religionswissenschaft/professuren/islamwissenschaft/forschung/mobilisierung-von-religion-in-europa.

TABLE 14.1 List of madrasa boards (*wafaqs*) in Pakistan

No.	Name	Denomination	Sect	Headquarters
1	Wafaq al-Madaris al-ʿArabiyya	Deobandi	Sunni/Hanafi	Multan
2	Tanzim al-Madaris Ahl-i Sunnat	Barelwi	Sunni/Hanafi	Lahore
3	Wafaq al-Madaris al-Salafiyya	Ahl-i Hadith	Sunni/Hanafi	Faisalabad
4	Rabita al-Madaris	Jamaʿat-i Islami	Sunni/Hanafi	Lahore
5	Wafaq al-Madaris al-Shiʿa	Shiʿa	Shiʿa / Jaʿfariyya	Lahore

visit these five *wafaq*s and personally present this project, as madrasas students do not generally take part in student exchange with foreign universities. Therefore, the project team reached out to all five madrasa boards, holding discussions with Mufti Munibur Rehman and Abdul Mustafa Hazarvi (Tanzim al-Madaris Ahl-i Sunnat), Hanif Jalandhari (Wafaq al-Madaris al-ʿArabiyya), Yaseen Zafar (Wafaq al-Madaris al-Salafiyya), Syed Riaz Hussain Najfi (Wafaq al-Madaris Shiʿa) as well as Ataur Rehman and Abdul Malik (Rabita al-Madaris). The receptions were thoroughly welcoming.

In a second step, the leading representatives of all five *wafaq*s (see figure 14.1) were hosted by the University of Erfurt to review the modules of all the workshops, meet with professors of Religious Studies at the university and also to meet the rest of the project team, consisting of graduate and doctoral fellows. Using this as an opportunity, a podium discussion entitled "Talking Euro Islam" was also organised to give the University of Erfurt a chance for open interaction.[33] This discussion came at an important juncture, as European countries were struggling to come to terms with the refugee crisis. It seemed thoughtful of Mufti Munibur Rehman to argue that Muslims living in Europe and in Germany ought to treat it as *dar al-aman* ("house of safety"), and it is their duty

---

[33] "Podium Discussion: Talking Euro Islam," University of Erfurt, accessed October 9, 2020, www.uni-erfurt.de/en/philosophische-fakultaet/seminare-professuren/religionswissen schaft/professuren/islamwissenschaft/research/religious-pluralism-religious-plurality -towards-an-ethics-of-peace/agenda-setting-workshop.

FIGURE 14.1 Representatives of all five *wafaq*s at Hafez-Goethe monument in Weimar (from right to left: Jamal Malik, Mohammad Akram, Hanif Jalandhari, Munibur Rehman, Yaseen Zafar, Ataur Rehman, Syed Muhammad Naqvi and Hasnain Bokhari)
COPYRIGHT: HASNAIN BOKHARI

to follow the country's rules and laws. In fact, he even went on to write an opinion piece in a Pakistani newspaper with details of his visit to the University of Erfurt and of the cooperation with the Pakistani madrasas.[34] Mufti Munibur Rehman's article served as an acknowledgement of the project's objectives and as encouragement to participate, not only for the Barelwi madrasas, but for the madrasas of other schools of thought as well.

2   Questions of Historiography – Preparing the First Workshop

All five madrasa boards follow variations of the Dars-i Nizami curriculum. The project's aim was to invite 'Alamiyya (Master) or Takhassus (M.Phil) students for the workshops in Germany (for a complete list of madrasa degrees/certificates, see table 14.2). The choice of these students was important so as

---

34   Mufti Munibur Rahman, "Few Days in Germany," *Daily Dunya*, accessed October 9, 2020, https://e.dunya.com.pk/colum.php?date=2016-05-14&edition=KCH&id=73744_88264699.

to maintain compatibility with participating students from the University of Erfurt. The project strongly advocated for the participation of female madrasa students during the workshops in both Germany and Pakistan. As discussed earlier, female voices within Pakistan's religious discourse are rarely heard. The project team specifically visited female madrasas within Lahore, Karachi, Sheikhupura, Multan and Faisalabad to encourage the institutional heads to give their female students due representation. Malik's vast body of scholarly work on South Asia, extended cooperation within South Asian academic networks and the involvement of Muslim female staff within the project team encouraged the madrasas to allow both male and female students to take part in the workshops. Participating madrasas even took self-initiatives to organise English language courses for the shortlisted students.

The world inside a madrasa, including its etiquette and administrative system, has some notable differences from the university system. To begin with, madrasas do not use the Gregorian calendar. They rely instead on the Islamic Hijri calendar, which starts with the month of Muharram and ends with Dhu al-Hijja. The admission process begins in the third month (Rabi' al-'Awwal) whereas the exam period commences at the end of the seventh month (Rajab). The madrasas remain closed during the fasting month of Ramadan followed by the festive holiday of 'Eid al-Fitr at the beginning of the next month. Over the course of two years, the project had to accommodate both calendrical systems.

TABLE 14.2 Madrasa degrees/certificates in Pakistan

No.	Madrasa Degree/Certificate	Years of study	Equivalence
1	Shahada al-Ibtida'iyya	5	Primary education
2	Shahada al-Mutawassita	3	Secondary education
3	Shahada al-Thaniyya al-'Amma	2	–
4	Shahada al-Thaniyya al-Khassa	2	Higher Secondary/College
5	Shahada al-'Aliyya	2	Bachelor/Undergraduate
6	Shahada al-'Alamiyya	2	Master/Graduate
7	Shahada al-Takhassus fi al-Fiqh al-Islamiyya	2	M.Phil

The experience of visiting madrasas in Pakistan brought the project organisers in contact with male and female students from extremely diverse backgrounds. A common pattern observed while interacting with these madrasa students is that they were fond of studying Islamic history. Most of their frames of reference about worldly problems were informed by or drawn from events from the history of the early centuries of Islam. Similarly, there were a number of students who did not find any appeal in noncurricular reading. For those who did find time for such reading, like Urdu fiction, their choices were also inspired by religious undertones, such as the novels depicting Islamic history by Naseem Hijazi (d. 1996) or those written by a younger generation of novelists like Nemrah Ahmed's *Jannat ke Pattay* ("Leaves of Heaven") or Umaira Ahmed's *Pir-e Kamil* ("Perfected Elder"). Only a few students preferred reading Urdu classics, such as those by Patras Bokhari, Ghulam Abbas, Mumtaz Mufti or Bano Qudsia.

These observations along with the madrasa students' keen interest in history provided a suitable point of departure for the first workshop (Questions of Historiography) in Erfurt. The art of documenting history, both oral and written, as Malik and Rosenthal[35] remind us, is a complex and multi-layered process. It represents the approaches available to historians of a particular period along with the literary expression(s) involved in reproducing the historical accounts of that period. In due process, narratives tend to reflect a power discourse, and there remains a fear of those voices that either remained quiet or were silenced. In this regard, the workshop emphasized the gender disparity in the historiographical process, namely that in comparison to male authors, there seem to be very few female voices/authors. The project also invited the entire Department of Religious Studies at the University of Erfurt, thus providing madrasa students an opportunity to interact with scholars of Greek and Roman religions, Judaism, Orthodox Christianity and Protestantism. These alternative and equally important perspectives on the concepts and experiences of religious traditions other than Islamic ones had neither ever been taught nor were known to the madrasa students.

The initial sprouts of self-reflection were witnessed within the first two days of the workshop. Most of the Pakistani participants introduced themselves as students of the Dars-i Nizami curriculum studying in a *dini* ("religious") madrasa. The discussions that followed resulted in some pertinent questions, such as when did madrasas become *dini*? And what does Nizami mean

---

35 Jamal Malik, *Islam in South Asia: Revised, Enlarged and Updated Second Edition* (Leiden: Brill, 2020); Franz Rosenthal, *A History of Muslim Historiography* (Leiden: Brill, 1968).

in the very name of the curriculum? On the latter question, students did not have any difficulty in linking it to Mulla Nizam al-Din, but on the former, one could sense multiple expressions of surprise and curiosity. It was also, in fact, interesting for the participants from the University of Erfurt to encounter the transformation of madrasas to *religious* madrasas. This navigation through the history of madrasas in South Asia posed several questions for the participants to review and reanalyse regarding Muslim presence in India, particularly in the eighteenth century and under British rule in later years.

Understanding Farangi Mahall in the evolution of madrasas in South Asia is an important precursor to understanding how madrasas were perceived, what was taught and how the different schools of thought that currently exist in Pakistan developed. Farangi Mahall (lit. "palace of the Franks [Europeans]") received its name after a wealthy French visitor was allowed to stay at this palace in Lucknow by the Mughal ruler Aurangzeb (d. 1707).[36] It was also during this period that Nizam al-Din developed the Dars-i Nizami Curriculum, which advocated the teaching of rational sciences (*maʿqulat*) alongside the study of religion (*manqulat*), including hadith studies, Quran exegesis (*tafsir*) and Islamic jurisprudence (*fiqh*).[37] While the curriculum contained only one work on hadith (*Mishkat al-Masabih*), the *maʿqulat* included a diverse range of themes, such as philosophy (*hikma*), logic (*mantiq*), dialectical theology (*kalam*), rhetoric and astronomy. Some scholars have claimed that even music was an essential part of the Nizami curriculum.[38] The madrasa of the eighteenth century in India served as a springboard for young ulama, who would go on to serve in administrative positions in the Mughal government.

Navigating through the history of madrasas helped the madrasa students in several ways as they first retranslated traditional belief contents and/or symbols into their original historical contexts and later subjected them to critique to draw fresh interpretations suitable to the current situation. Similarly, students were also encouraged to address the questions of Islamic cultural articulations, including oral and textual traditions, and to review the process of historicising shariʿa. Both madrasa students and those from Erfurt interpreted and dealt with the concept of "ethics of peace." In doing so, they worked together in reviewing texts by the Iranian philosopher and historian Ibn

---

36 Zaman, *The Ulama in Contemporary Islam*.
37 Malik, *Madrasas in South Asia*.
38 Muhammad Farooq, "Political Change and Madrasa Curriculum: A Historical Analysis of Dars-i-Nizami," *Journal of Research (Faculty of Languages & Islamic Studies)* 12 (2007): 59–81; Syed Ejaz Hussain, "Islamic Philosophy of Education and the Indian Madrasahs," *Studies in Humanities and Social Sciences, Shimla* VII, no. 2 (2000): 109–18.

Miskawayh (d. 1030)[39] or by the Indian historian and diplomat K.A. Nizami (d. 1997)[40] to see if and what lessons could be drawn for promoting the values of peace and coexistence.

The two-week exercise was attended by 57% female and 43% male madrasa students, which led to some interesting results with equally varying views. Madrasa students seemed genuinely willing to embrace new knowledge, yet their perceptions seemed contradictory. They acknowledged the need for diversity, tolerance and flexibility, yet they appeared reluctant to experience these on the basis of religious boundaries. They expressed their belief in gender equality, yet they felt that the most important job for women is to look after the family. It was surprising to notice that even some female madrasas students seemed comfortable with such self-restriction and gender roles. On the other hand, the students from Erfurt inclined towards critical examination of religious issues. Appreciating religious pluralism, they showed curiosity, openness and acceptance as well as gave importance to jointly celebrating interfaith festivities (such as Christmas and 'Eid al-Fitr). Madrasa students, on the other hand, remarked that interfaith festivities help in creating harmony,[41] yet they also pointed out that these should not be jointly celebrated.

This first workshop enjoyed an impressive reception by governmental representatives from both Germany and Pakistan. In Erfurt, Head of the State Chancellery Benjamin-Immanuel Hoff welcomed the madrasa delegates on behalf of the Thuringian state government, whereas in Berlin, the Pakistani Ambassador to Germany Jauhar Saleem received the delegation while also highlighting the important role of educational exchange between Germany and Pakistan.

---

39   Ahmad ibn Muhammad ibn Miskawayh, *The Refinement of Character: A Translation from the Arabic of Ahmad ibn-Muhammad Miskawayh's Tahdhib al-Akhlaq*, trans. Constantine Zurayk (Beirut: American University of Beirut, 1968).

40   Khaliq Ahmad Nizami, *On History and Historians of Medieval India* (New Delhi: Munshiram Manoharlal, 1983).

41   Some of these views are also depicted in the two video documentaries produced during the project, one filmed in Erfurt and Berlin and the other in Lahore. In both documentaries, the madrasa students as well as their administrators highlight how these workshops and dialogical methods opened a new door of learning, as well as memorisation, for them. See "Religious Pluralism & Religious Plurality: Towards an Ethics of Peace," Religious Pluralism, accessed April 6, 2021, youtu.be/jvn8dwSGSnc and "Religious Pluralism & Religious Plurality: Towards an Ethics of Peace," accessed April 6, 2021, youtu.be/WAI6yG5fglc.

3 Historiography and the Cultural Translation of Knowledge

Sustainability and continuity were among the key aspects of the *Towards an Ethics of Peace* project. To reach a larger number of madrasa students in Pakistan, every madrasa student that took part in the Erfurt workshop was tasked to host a workshop of their own based on the same pattern back at her/ his madrasa. This was aimed at encouraging the madrasa students to not only improve their interpersonal, organisational and leadership skills, but this exercise in cultural translation was also intended to benefit their peers by sharing the experiences they gained in Erfurt, discussing social similarities and dissimilarities as well as learning new methodologies and didactics – not necessarily as a benchmark, but perhaps as an additional approach. They were encouraged to invite students from other seminaries, even from different schools of thought, to these workshops. The first follow-up workshops were hosted in three historic madrasas, namely Jamiʿa Khair al-Madaris (Multan), Jamiʿa Salfia (Faisalabad) and Jamiʿa Naeemia (Lahore).

The workshop in Multan was inaugurated by Hanif Jalandhari, the principal of Jamiʿa Khair al-Madaris who also holds the important position of secretary general in Wafaq al-Madaris al-ʿArabiyya (Deobandi). The madrasa was originally set up in the Indian city of Jalandhar in 1931 by Jalandhari's father, Khair Mohammad Jalandhari (d. 1970), but after India's partition, he migrated to Pakistan and founded Jamiʿa Khair al-Madaris in Multan in 1947. In the 1950s, he was also the driving force behind bringing all Deobandi madrasas under one administrative body, eventually establishing the Wafaq al-Madaris al-ʿArabiyya in Multan on October 19, 1959.[42] Since then, Multan has remained the centre of the administrative structure for Deobandi madrasas. Instead of only engaging with madrasa teachers, the lecturers even came from NGOs and Multan's Bahauddin Zakariya University (BZU). It seemed quite progressive for a Deobandi madrasa to invite lecturers who could engage madrasa students in discussions on the role of commentaries/glosses and to highlight their significance for understanding canonical texts. For instance, BZU's Professor for Islamic Studies, Saeed-ur-Rahman, focused on early religious historiography and the importance of literature produced in later centuries. His emphasis on understanding history through the tradition of commentaries reminds one of a character from the short story "The Dream of a Madrasa,"[43] a madrasa

---

42 Abdul Majid, "Wafāq al-Madāris al-Arabia: Introduction and Contribution."
43 "The Dream of a Madrasa: A Short Story from Pakistan" is a piece of what we might call "academic fiction" by Jamal Malik and Bushra Iqbal. It depicts a story of a madrasa student named Salik who is in awe of his teacher Maulana Rizwi, who in several conversations

student named Salik, who encounters various underdiscussed and forgotten facets of the institution of the madrasa through the guidance of his teacher. The second follow-up workshop took place in Faisalabad at Jami'a Salfia, which also serves as an administrative centre for the Ahl-i Hadith school of thought. Unlike the Multan workshop, Jami'a Salfia followed a co-education pattern by inviting both male and female students. Madrasas in Pakistan, as pointed out earlier, normally segregate genders. But here they were in an Ahl-i Hadith madrasa, where the apparent hesitation, visible reluctance and understandable nervousness on the part of both genders dominated the session for the first couple of hours. For the third follow-up workshop in Lahore, Jami'a Naeemia (Barelwi) also brought together madrasa students from different schools of thought in a co-education format. Their workshop included female instructors as well as historical accounts of other religions, such as Christianity and Sikhism. For Pakistani madrasas to host co-education classes in their seminaries, discuss religious historiography of not just Islam, but also of other religions and to invite female lecturers from not only madrasas, but also from NGOs and universities, is quite progressive and might be seen as an adaptive endeavour to remain relevant.

4 Liturgy, Rituals and Symbolism – Empirical Approaches to Religion

After the first workshop on historiography in Erfurt, news of the project spread out to other madrasas who expressed their interest in also taking part. One such case was one of the largest Deobandi madrasas in Karachi, Jami'a Binoria Al-Aalmia. During a visit to Germany, the representatives of Jami'a Binoria also visited the CMCRH in Erfurt in July 2019 and expressed their desire to join the project. Jami'a Binoria was then headed by Mufti Naeem (d. 2020), who was an influential figure in Pakistan's Deobandi circles and an active member of the executive committee of the Deobandis' administrative board. Similarly, two Barelwi madrasas in Karachi, namely the Aleemiyah Institute of Islamic Studies and Islamic University International, came on board as well. The project also echoed well in Punjab province, with Dar al-'Ulum Muhammadia Ghousia expressing their interest in taking part. This Dar al-'Ulum is a historic Barelwi madrasa in Bhera Sharif and was established in 1925 by Ghazi Hafiz Pir

---

walks him through the evolution of the institution of the madrasa, including the importance of rational studies during the time of the Ottoman and Mughal empires. See Jamal Malik and Bushra Iqbal, "The Dream of a Madrasa: A Short Story from Pakistan," Fikrun wa Fann, accessed October 9, 2020, www.goethe.de/ges/phi/prj/ffs/the/a101/en13019366.htm.

Muhammad Shah.[44] The madrasa is headed by Muhammad Amin Ul Hasnat Shah, who also served as the Minister of State for Religious Affairs and Interfaith Harmony during the Nawaz Sharif government (2013–2018).[45] Partners continued to increase as the Shiʿa madrasa in Islamabad, Jamiʿa al-Kauthar also joined. These partners added religious and sectarian diversity to the workshops. In fact, this diverse range of madrasas put the second workshop (Social Sciences & Religion) in Germany to good test as it focused on how and why societal dynamics inform religious behaviour and vice versa, seeking to understand what roles ritual and liturgy, organization and dissemination can play.

In addition to historiography, the project sought to discuss different theoretical and empirical discourses on the entanglement of society at large and the religious field within the social sciences sphere. The madrasa students were introduced to theories and methods in the social sciences and their utility for studying religion. Apart from dealing with the history of the sociology of religion, the workshop introduced the participants to classical texts by Max Weber (d. 1920) and Emile Durkheim (d. 1917), but also Shah Waliullah (d. 1762) and Ibn Khaldun (d. 1406). Studying these texts aimed at appreciating how a holistic view could better inform understandings of the problems faced today. For madrasa students, some important questions arose: How can a lived religion be measured? How do methods and techniques from the social sciences help us negotiate with lived experience? To answer these, students were introduced to the basics of social science research and the steps involved in conducting field research, such as interviews and participatory observation. Students were taken on a field trip to Berlin where they were divided into smaller groups to visit different places of worship, including a mosque, church, Buddhist temple and Sikh gurdwara. This exercise put methods of the social sciences into practice and introduced participants to how people belonging to different religions in the German capital practice their faiths. The fieldwork conducted served as a workable blueprint for religious pluralism for madrasa students. Their questions for the representatives of these different religions in Berlin ranged from the concept of God to gender roles as well as the core values and prohibitions of these faiths.

The majority of the madrasa students had not previously studied social science research and their enthusiasm while conducting and presenting the fieldwork indicated their curiosity about the subject. Regarding the role of

---

44 "Introduction," Dar-ul-Uloom Muhammadia Ghousia, accessed October 9, 2020, https://sites.google.com/site/dmglhr.

45 "Personal Profile: Pir Muhammad Amin Ul Hasnat Shah," National Assembly of Pakistan, accessed October 9, 2020, na.gov.pk/en/profile.php?uid=734.

rituals and religious festivities, more than half of the participants expressed that celebrating such events together can create harmony among different religious groups. Most of the participants admitted that they invite people of other faiths to their own religious events. Similarly, more than 50% of participants also said that they participate in events when people of other faiths invite them. Pertaining to religious pluralism, participants seemed curious to find answers through sources other than their own religion. Nevertheless, over 80% of the madrasa students did believe that their own religion/sect had the most authentic doctrine for understanding religious issues. Their responses showed that their religion provides them a complete set of beliefs which they are expected to live according to. About one-third of the participants believed that the foremost responsibility of women is to take care of family matters in order to ensure stability in society. These observations were surprising, as almost 55–60% of students within these workshops were female. Their institutional heads were also working women. For instance, one of the participating institutions is Jamiʿa Naeemia Sirajia in Lahore, which is headed by Ms. Nabeera Indleeb. She single-handedly runs her madrasa in Lahore. Moreover, she also carried a legislative portfolio as a member of Punjab's provincial assembly.

5   Society and Religion in Cultural Translation

The *Towards an Ethics of Peace* project also provided a unique opportunity for madrasas to cooperate with one another. Before the 1970s, the sectarian differences among religious sects in Pakistan were limited to publications or communicated via loudspeakers during Friday sermons. However, when these disagreements took a violent turn in the 1980s, Pakistan's pluralist fabric and sectarian differences started to impact societal, cultural, interpersonal and of course, political norms. With the *Towards an Ethics of Peace* project, the workshops in Erfurt invited scholars from different sects who could indirectly encourage participating institutions to also invite students as well as guest speakers from other sects for workshops in Pakistan. From the follow-up workshops in Pakistan, it appears that the participating madrasas found that approach necessary for their image-building. All the madrasas invited participants as well as speakers from multiple schools of thought to their madrasas. The four follow-up workshops for Social Sciences and Religion took place at Dar al-ʿUlum Muhammadia Ghousia (Bhera), Jamiʿa Binoria (Karachi), Aleemiyah Institute of Islamic Studies (Karachi) and Jamiʿa Naeemia (Lahore). These institutions invited lecturers from not only their own madrasas, but also from different universities and other madrasas. Jami'a Binoria in Karachi, for instance, engaged with Allama Mohsin Naqvi (Shi'i) and the Bishop Nazeer Alam from the United Church of Pakistan to discuss inter-sectarian dialogue and human morality as a shared religious heritage. Such progressive attempts could also be witnessed at the Aleemiyah Institute of Islamic Studies in Karachi, where students focused on Sufi discourses by presenting the history and evolution of Sufi devotional music (*qawwali*). They performed the Sufi song "*Dama Dam Mast Qalandar*," which was originally written by Amir Khusraw in homage to the Sufi saint of Sindh, Lal Shahbaz Qalandar (1177–1274). Although madrasas are usually seen as synonymous with rigidity, the echoes of students' brief rendition of *qawwali* could be heard throughout the entire Aleemiyah Institute. The students of the Dar al-'Ulum Muhammadia Ghousia also tried to include creative and interactive exercises by planning two field visits to the Sher Shah Suri Mosque and an *imam bargah* (a devotional place used by Twelver Shi'a Muslims) in Bhera. During their field visit to the *imam bargah*, students had several questions about the rituals among Shi'a Muslims, particularly about *'ashura* (a holiday commemorating the martyrdom of the third Shi'a Imam), *ta'ziya* ("mourning"), the *'alam* ("holy flag") and *tabut* (coffin-carrying ritual). Dar al-'Ulum Muhammadia Ghousia in Bhera was the only madrasa whose lecturers discussed the system of madrasa education and its compatibility with modern education. The interactions of students belonging to different sects highlighted an important fact: knowing or interacting with the sectarian or religious other is restricted in Pakistan.

6   Human Rights and Ethics of Peace

Active engagement of the participating madrasas in organising workshops in Pakistan with the freedom to choose the literature and guest speakers had multiple impacts. It increased their sense of ownership and having a substantial voice in the overall project. Due to their active participation, Jami'a Naeemia in Lahore and Jami'a Binoria in Karachi became two important centres for the *Towards an Ethics of Peace* project, hosting the largest numbers of follow-up workshops in Pakistan. Such an active contribution in the project by these madrasas was also reflected in the improvement of workshop quality whereas the incentive to receive recognition also created a sense of competition. For the third and final workshop (Human Rights and the Contribution of Religions) in Erfurt in July 2017, two additional madrasas; namely Dar al-'Ulum Naeemia in Karachi – a Barelwi madrasa headed by Mufti Munibur Rehman – and Dar al-'Ulum Haqqania in Akora Khattak – a Deobandi madrasa which was then headed by Maulana Sami ul-Haq (d. 2018); joined as cooperating partners. The workshop focused on the impact and influence of world religions on values of social justice, human rights and peace ethics. It employed different theoretical perspectives to study the entanglement of cultural, historical, political, ethnic as well as religious factors that contribute to the recognition and implementation of universal human rights. Group assignments conducted during the workshop looked at religions as a set of systems that help (re)shape people's lives. Religious pluralism, as the workshop discussions argued, is the situation in which, or the idea that, people of different faiths or ways of life can co-exist in society and exercise their human rights. In this respect, pluralism needs to be clearly distinguished from the concept of tolerance, which serves as the first step towards reaching a religiously pluralistic society. Yet it only indicates acceptance of and tolerance towards the other without interacting with the other. For pluralism, interactions and mutual exchange are among the prerequisites. However, it seemed difficult, as some of the madrasa students vocally expressed, for an individual to acknowledge other points of view, to learn from the other and/or to distance oneself from previous standpoints.

The workshop presented interesting scenarios for the young madrasa students. One instance in this context was the lecture by Mufti Mohammad Abdullah, which focused on human rights, religion and gender. He was asked about women's right to veil as well as their freedom to pursue an occupation. Mufti Abdullah's response left the participants, including veiled female madrasa students, stumped for a while. He argued that there is no compulsion to wear the veil (*niqab*) according to the Hanafi school. It would be a separate debate whether out of respect for cultural norms women choose to veil themselves. Cultural norms do not exist in a static, unchanging state, but are instead dynamic and continuously evolving, developing, changing and even disappearing.

7 Human Rights in Cultural Translation

By October 2017, the *Towards an Ethics of Peace* project was well into its concluding phase. Based on the enthusiasm and motivation shown by the participating madrasas, it was decided to hold four follow-up workshops in Pakistan. Jami'a Binoria offered to host two of these for both Barelwi and Deobandi students. Jami'a Binoria is situated on twelve acres of land in Karachi and is attended by Pakistanis as well as foreigners. Despite being unwell, the principal of Jami'a Binoria, Mufti Muhammad Naeem (d. 2020), personally gave the project team a tour of various departments as well as the shelter home he established. In Lahore, the principal of Jamiʿa Naeemia, Raghib Naeemi, showed similar enthusiasm towards this collaboration. His madrasa in Lahore has been known for its moderate views and was at the forefront of establishing Wafaq al-Madaris Ahl-i Sunnat, as the first-ever meeting of Barelwi ulama took place in 1960 in Jamiʿa Naeemia to discuss the madrasa curriculum.[46] Naeemi's father, Sarfaraz Ahmed Naeemi (d. 2009), was among Pakistan's first clerics to publicly denounce militancy in the name of religion[47] and the third workshop took place in the seminar hall built in honour of his memory.

The fourth workshop was held in Jamiʿa al-Kauthar's Al Mustafa Auditorium, named after Mustafa Gokal. Jamiʿa al-Kauthar is a Shiʿa madrasa situated in the heart of Pakistan's federal capital. It brought together madrasa students from four different schools of thought, namely from Dar al-ʿUlum Haqqania (Deobandi), Dar al-ʿUlum Muhammadia Ghousia (Barelwi), Jamiʿa Salfia (Ahl-i Hadith) and Jamiʿa al-Kauthar (Shiʿa). The madrasa was founded in 1992 by the Al-Khoei Foundation. Its organisers gave participating students and the project team a guided tour of the campus as well as its 2,500-person capacity mosque, where the bulbs and crystals within its chandelier reflected symbolism associated with Shiʿa Islam. Madrasa students expressed their contentment with being provided a unique opportunity to engage in debates and discuss various aspects of religion through interactive sessions and group work, which they had never experienced in their respective madrasas before. This is a pertinent observation as the madrasa education system predominantly relies on learning by rote. Moreover, very rarely would the students from Pakistan's dominating and contesting sectarian backgrounds, such as Deobandi, Barelwi and Ahl-i Hadith, converge under one roof (particularly in a Shiʿa madrasa) to participate in joint academic activities. More than 90% of participating students of the Jamiʿa al-Kauthar workshop said that they had never been to a Shiʿa madrasa, let alone the heavily guarded Jamiʿa al-Kauthar in Islamabad.

8   Concluding Remarks

In the past few years, several NGOs, diplomatic missions and successive governments in Pakistan have voiced their opinions about reforms in the curricula

---

46 "Brief Introduction," Tanzim al-Madaris Ahl-i Sunnat, accessed October 10, 2020, https://tanzeemulmadaris.com/Contents/Downloads/Taruf-Tanzeem-ul-madaris.pdf.

47 Unfortunately, these views cost Sarfaraz Naeemi his life when a suicide bomber killed him. See "State Funeral for Late Sarfaraz Naeemi," Dawn, accessed October 11, 2020, www.beta.dawn.com/news/879900/state-funeral-for-late-sarfaraz-naeemi.

taught in madrasas. Madrasas themselves have become cautious about their identity, the interest groups they interact with and their underlying agendas as well as the sources of funding that are offered to them. In a highly conservative society and within the guarded environment of the madrasa, it is exceptionally rare to send off young students, particularly females, to participate in academic programmes abroad. The principals of the participating institutions (see table 14.3) deserve much recognition for this since, despite some reluctance even from within their own madrasas, they showed no objection to allowing their female students to participate in the workshops, either in Germany or in Pakistan. They were accommodating enough to introduce the provision of a joint guardian (a madrasa teacher) who travelled along with them for every workshop in Erfurt. The guardian's presence worked as a positive assurance for the madrasas, their administration and particularly for the parents of participating female students. The madrasas' principals believed in the project's academic value and showed personal interest in supporting the returning madrasa students as they organised follow-up workshops in their madrasas. They allocated their seminar rooms, libraries and auditoriums as well as their administrative staff to conduct these workshops. To his credit, Malik's work on madrasas will remain a substantial contribution in bringing the subject into mainstream scholarship.

The *Towards an Ethics of Peace* project was among the first attempts at encouraging madrasa students to make use of dialogical didactics and critical thinking rather than rote learning. Several madrasas introduced co-education formats for their workshops without any insistence or intervention from the project organisers. The principals of participating madrasas were invited to the project's review meeting in December 2017 at the University of Erfurt. They acknowledged that perhaps while focusing more on debate, the madrasa as an institution has not been able to encourage a dialogue culture. The representative of Jami'a Binoria (Karachi), Farhan Naeem stated in his remarks that the project was able to draw students' attention towards both curricular and non-curricular reading. Similarly, the representative of Jami'a Nizamia Rizvia (Sheikhupura), Ghulam Murtaza Hazarvi believed that the project had a unique impact on his institution as it was benefitting from returning students' feedback on his institution's administrative and didactic culture. Jami'a Salfia's principal and the secretary general of Wafaq al-Madaris al-Salafiyya, Yasin Zafar opined that the project provided a space for introspection, as he felt that madrasa students sometimes do not have a good command of South Asian history. For Jami'a Naeemia (Lahore)'s representative, Raghib Naeemi, the project gave him a chance to look beyond theological discourse and explore scientific methods in the study of religion. The way madrasas have appreciated the

TABLE 14.3 List of participating madrasas in *Towards an Ethics of Peace* project

No.	Madrasa	Gender	Denomination	City
1	Dar al-ʿUlum Naeemia	Male	Barelwi	Karachi
2	Jamiʿa Naeemia	Male	Barelwi	Lahore
3	Jamiʿa Nizamia Rizvia	Male	Barelwi	Lahore
4	Jamiʿa Naeemia Sirajia	Female	Barelwi	Lahore
5	Jamiʿa Nizamia Rizvia	Female	Barelwi	Sheikhupura
6	Dar al-ʿUlum Ghousia	Male	Barelwi	Behra
7	Aleemiyah Institute of Islamic Studies	Male	Barelwi	Karachi
8	Islamic University International	Female	Barelwi	Karachi
9	Jamiʿa Salfia	Male	Ahl-i Hadith	Faisalabad
10	Jamiʿa Binoria	Male/Female	Deobandi	Karachi
11	Dar al-ʿUlum Haqqania	Male	Deobandi	Akora Khattak
12	Khair al-Madaris	Male	Deobandi	Multan
13	Jamiʿa al-Kauthar	Male	Shiʿa	Islamabad

efforts of the University of Erfurt for international collaboration shows that they needed to establish trust with an international collaborating partner – which is exactly what they did in *Towards an Ethics of Peace* project.

Bibliography

Ahmad, Mujeeb. "Understanding the Barelwi Madaris of Pakistan: Case Study of the Tanzim al-Madaris (Ahl-i-Sunnat) Pakistan." *Journal of South Asian and Middle Eastern Studies* 40, no. 3 (April 2017): 15–34.

Ali, Syed Hamad. "In Pakistan, Saying Goodbye Can Be a Religious Statement." *The Guardian*. Accessed October 9, 2020, www.theguardian.com/commentisfree/belief/2012/apr/17/pakistan-goodbye-allah-hafiz.

Bano, Masooda. "Beyond Politics: The Reality of a Deobandi Madrasa in Pakistan." *Journal of Islamic Studies* 18, no. 1 (January 2007): 43–68, https://doi.org/10.1093/jis/etl043.

Bano, Masooda. *The Rational Believer: Choices and Decisions in the Madrasas of Pakistan*. Ithaca and London: Cornell University Press, 2012.

Crews, Robert D. and Amin Tarzi, eds. *The Taliban and the Crisis of Afghanistan*. Cambridge, MA: Harvard University Press, 2009.

Dalrymple, William. *The Last Mughal: The Fall of Delhi, 1857*. London: Bloomsbury Publishing, 2009.

Dar-ul-Uloom Muhammadia Ghousia. "Introduction." Accessed October 9, 2020, https://sites.google.com/site/dmglhr.

Dawn. "Madressah Registration, Reform Can Mitigate Most Negative Consequences." Accessed October 10, 2020, www.dawn.com/news/1386370.

Dawn. "State Funeral for Late Sarfaraz Naeemi." Accessed October 11, 2020, www.beta.dawn.com/news/879900/state-funeral-for-late-sarfaraz-naeemi.

Farooq, Muhammad. "Political Change and Madrasa Curriculum: A Historical Analysis of *Dars-i-Nizami*." *Journal of Research (Faculty of Languages & Islamic Studies)* 12 (2007): 59–81.

Grare, Frédéric. "The Evolution of Sectarian Conflicts in Pakistan and the Ever-Changing Face of Islamic Violence." *South Asia: Journal of South Asian Studies* 30, no. 1 (April 2007): 127–43, https://doi.org/10.1080/00856400701264068.

Haleem, Irm. "Ethnic and Sectarian Violence and the Propensity Towards Praetorianism in Pakistan." *Third World Quarterly* 24, no. 3 (June 2003): 463–77, https://doi.org/10.1080/0143659032000084410.

Haq, Shafiqua. "Moral Education in Pakistan." *Journal of Moral Education* 9, no. 3 (May 1980): 156–65, https://doi.org/10.1080/0305724800090302.

Haynes, Jeffrey. "Religion and International Relations After '9/11'." *Democratization* 12, no. 3 (June 2005): 398–413, https://doi.org/10.1080/13510340500126814.

Hefner, Robert W. and Muhammad Qasim Zaman, eds. *Schooling Islam: The Culture and Politics of Modern Muslim Education*. Princeton: Princeton University Press, 2010.

Hochschulkommunikation Universität Erfurt. "25 Köpfe: Hasnain Bokhari ist geblieben." Accessed October 9, 2020, https://25jahre.uni-erfurt.de/25jahre.uni-erfurt.de/25-koepfe-hasnain-bokhari/index.html.

Hussain, Syed Ejaz. "Islamic Philosophy of Education and the Indian Madrasahs." *Studies in Humanities and Social Sciences, Shimla* VII, no. 2 (2000): 109–18.

Hussain, Zahid. *Frontline Pakistan: The Path to Catastrophe and the Killing of Benazir Bhutto*. New Delhi: Penguin Books India, 2008.

Ingram, Brannon D. "'Modern' Madrasa: Deoband and Colonial Secularity." *Historical Social Research / Historische Sozialforschung* 44, no. 3 (169) (2019): 206–25.

Koopmans, Ruud. "Germany and Its Immigrants: An Ambivalent Relationship." *Journal of Ethnic and Migration Studies* 25, no. 4 (1999): 627–47.

Majid, Abdul. "Wafâq Al-Madâris al-Arabia: Introduction and Contribution." WifaqulMadaris.org. Accessed October 9, 2020, www.wifaqulmadaris.org/pages/introduction.php.

Malik, Jamal. *Colonialization of Islam: Dissolution of Traditional Institutions in Pakistan.* New Delhi: Manohar; Lahore: Vanguard, 1996.

Malik, Jamal. "Introduction." In *Madrasas in South Asia: Teaching Terror?*, edited by Jamal Malik, 1–22. Oxon: Routledge, 2007.

Malik, Jamal. *Islam in South Asia: Revised, Enlarged and Updated Second Edition.* Leiden: Brill, 2020.

Malik, Jamal. *Islamisierung in Pakistan, 1977–1984: Untersuchungen zur Auflösung autochthoner Strukturen.* Wiesbaden: Franz Steiner, 1989.

Malik, Jamal. *Madrasas in South Asia: Teaching Terror?.* 1st ed. Oxon: Routledge, 2007.

Malik, Jamal and Bushra Iqbal. "The Dream of a Madrasa: A Short Story from Pakistan." Fikrun wa Fann. Accessed October 9, 2020, www.goethe.de/ges/phi/prj/ffs/the/a101/en13019366.htm.

Metcalf, Barbara D., ed. *Islam in South Asia in Practice.* Princeton: Princeton University Press, 2009.

Miskawayh, Ahmad ibn Muhammad ibn. *The Refinement of Character: A Translation from the Arabic of Ahmad ibn-Muhammad Miskawayh's Tahdhib al-Akhlaq.* Translated by Constantine Zurayk. Beirut: American University of Beirut, 1968.

Moj, Muhammad. *The Deoband Madrassah Movement: Countercultural Trends and Tendencies.* London: Anthem Press, 2015.

Moosa, Ebrahim. *What Is a Madrasa?.* Chapel Hill: The University of North Carolina Press, 2015.

National Assembly of Pakistan. "Personal Profile: Pir Muhammad Amin Ul Hasnat Shah." Accessed October 9, 2020, na.gov.pk/en/profile.php?uid=734.

Nelson, Matthew J. "Muslims, Markets, and the Meaning of a 'Good' Education in Pakistan." *Asian Survey* 46, no. 5 (October 2006): 699–720, https://doi.org/10.1525/as.2006.46.5.699.

Nizami, Khaliq Ahmad. *On History and Historians of Medieval India.* New Delhi: Munshiram Monoharlal, 1983.

Noor, Farish A., Yoginder Sikand and Martin van Bruinessen, eds. *The Madrasa in Asia: Political Activism and Transnational Linkages.* Amsterdam: Amsterdam University Press, 2008.

Rahman, Ataur. "Râbitah Al-Madâris: Constitution and Curriculum." Accessed October 9, 2020, www.rabtatulmadaris.com.pk/ur/doc/DASTOR_RABITA.pdf.

Rahman, Mufti Munibur. "Few Days in Germany." *Daily Dunya.* Accessed October 9, 2020, https://e.dunya.com.pk/colum.php?date=2016-05-14&edition=KCH&id=73744_88264699.

Rahman, Tariq. "Madrasas: The Potential for Violence in Pakistan?." In *Madrasas in South Asia: Teaching Terror?*, edited by Jamal Malik, 61–84. Oxon: Routledge, 2007.

Riaz, Sanaa. *New Islamic Schools: Tradition, Modernity, and Class in Urban Pakistan.* Edited by Sanaa Riaz. New York: Palgrave Macmillan, 2014.

Robinson, Francis. *Islam and Muslim History in South Asia.* New Delhi: Oxford University Press, 2000.

Robinson, Francis. "Islamic Reform and Modernities in South Asia." *Modern Asian Studies* 42, no. 2–3 (March 2008): 259–81, https://doi.org/10.1017/S0026749X07002922.

Rosenthal, Franz. *A History of Muslim Historiography.* Leiden: Brill, 1968.

Salvatore, Armando. "From Tension to Dialogue?: The Mediterranean between European Civilization and the Muslim World." In *Civilizational Dialogue and World Order: The Other Politics of Cultures, Religions, and Civilizations in International Relations*, edited by Michális S. Michael and Fabio Petito, 217–37. New York: Palgrave Macmillan US, 2009.

Sanyal, Usha. *Ahmad Riza Khan Barelwi: In the Path of the Prophet.* Oxford: Oneworld, 2012.

Shams, Shamil. "Pakistan Shrine Attack – No Place for 'Soft Islam' in a Hard Country." Accessed October 9, 2020, www.dw.com/en/pakistan-shrine-attack-no-place-for-soft-islam-in-a-hard-country/a-37595893.

Talbot, Ian. "Understanding Religious Violence in Contemporary Pakistan: Themes and Theories." In *Religion, Violence and Political Mobilisation in South Asia*, edited by Ravinder Kaur, 145–65. New Delhi: SAGE Publications, 2005.

Tanzim al-Madaris Ahl-i Sunnat. "Brief Introduction." Accessed October 10, 2020, https://tanzeemulmadaris.com/Contents/Downloads/Taruf-Tanzeem-ul-madaris.pdf.

University of Erfurt. "Changing Role of Social Media in Muslim Countries." Accessed April 6, 2021, www.uni-erfurt.de/en/philosophische-fakultaet/seminare-professuren/religionswissenschaft/professuren/islamic-studies/research/changing-role-of-social-media-in-muslim-countries.

University of Erfurt. "Mobilisierung von Religion in Europa." Accessed April 6, 2021, www.uni-erfurt.de/philosophische-fakultaet/seminare-professuren/religionswissenschaft/professuren/philosophische-fakultaet/seminare-professuren/religionswissenschaft/professuren/islamwissenschaft/forschung/mobilisierung-von-religion-in-europa.

University of Erfurt. "Podium Discussion: Talking Euro Islam." Universität Erfurt. Accessed October 9, 2020, www.uni-erfurt.de/en/philosophische-fakultaet/seminare-professuren/religionswissenschaft/professuren/islamwissenschaft/research/religious-pluralism-religious-plurality-towards-an-ethics-of-peace/agenda-setting-workshop.

University of Erfurt. "Religiöse Vielfalt und Friedensethik." Accessed October 9, 2020, www.uni-erfurt.de/forschung/forschen/forschungsprojekte/religioese-vielfalt-und-friedensethik.

University of Erfurt. "Religious Pluralism & Religious Plurality: Towards an Ethics of Peace." Accessed April 6, 2021, www.uni-erfurt.de/en/philosophische-fakultaet/seminare-professuren/religionswissenschaft/professuren/islamic-studies/research/religious-pluralism-religious-plurality-towards-an-ethics-of-peace.

University of Erfurt. "Social Media in muslimischen Ländern: Studierende aus Erfurt und Peshawar arbeiten zusammen." Press Release, June 19, 2012, www2.uni-erfurt.de/cms-alt/pressemitteilungen-archiv/www.uni-erfurt.de/uni/einrichtungen/presse/pressemitteilungen/2012/102-12/index.html.

University of Erfurt. "Summer School: 'Muslims in the West'." Accessed April 6, 2021, www.uni-erfurt.de/en/philosophische-fakultaet/seminare-professuren/religionswissenschaft/professuren/islamic-studies/workshops/conferences/summer-school-muslims-in-the-west.

Walsh, Declan. "Pakistan Bomb Kills Several at Sufi Shrine." *The Guardian*. Accessed October 9, 2020, www.theguardian.com/world/2010/oct/25/bomb-sufi-shrine-pakistan.

Zaman, Muhammad Qasim. *The Ulama in Contemporary Islam: Custodians of Change*. Princeton: Princeton University Press, 2010.

Zia, Afiya. "Faith-Based Politics, Enlightened Moderation and the Pakistani Women's Movement." *Journal of International Women's Studies* 11, no. 1 (November 2009): 225–45.

Afterword

Dynamics of Islam in Context

Pnina Werbner

It is rare to encounter in the work of a single writer truly visionary understanding along with immense, in-depth and wide-ranging scholarship. The essays in this book attest to the inspiring influence of that unique combination. Jamal Malik's vision is above all one of religion as heterogenous, dialogical, responsive to change, to encounters with other faiths and evolving contexts. Rather than closed, homogeneous, monolithic and essentially static, Islam is understood by Malik *in context*, as interacting with politics, economics and changing times. It may be syncretic or hybrid, diffuse or sharply adversarial, moving from violent confrontation to absorption. Whatever the case, its variability is only a starting point for analysis. Whether the encounter is between East and West, modernity and tradition, diaspora and home, or between different strands within the same religious milieu, to understand such encounters requires empirical research as well as in-depth understanding.

Malik's *Colonialization of Islam,* first published in 1996, is an example of the theoretical and comparative inspiration that can be derived from detailed empirical research, in this case of the rise and expansion of Deobandi and Barelwi madrasas in Pakistan.[1] The book laid the grounds for all subsequent historical and sociological research on madrasas in South Asia, including the dilemmas they face finding jobs for a surplus of graduates, and their increasing centrality for some classes in Pakistani society. Over the years, these themes have emerged as central not only in Religious Studies but also in the geopolitics of Pakistan and South Asia more generally. Ultimately, the book heralded Malik's exciting project on religious plurality in Pakistan.[2] As Hasnain Bokhari tells us in this volume, Malik's early work on madrasas turned into a lifetime scholarly journey. His project "Religious Pluralism and Religious Plurality: Towards an Ethics of Peace" aimed to examine the topic of religious (in)tolerance in Pakistan from the perspective of social, cultural and religious studies. It brought together clerics and students from several key religious schools in Pakistan

---

1 Jamal Malik, *Colonialization of Islam: Dissolution of Traditional Institutions in Pakistan* (New Delhi: Manohar, 1996).
2 Before starting this project, Malik edited, with Helmut Reifeld, the volume *Religious Pluralism in South Asia and Europe* (New Delhi: Oxford University Press, 2004).

with students and other scholars in Erfurt for discussion and debate. The students deliberated over issues such as justice, religious pluralism, tolerance and intolerance, diversity and human rights, as these are grounded in Islamic cultures and traditions. What is particularly exciting about the project is the way it refuted common assumptions about the madrasas. As Bokhari reminds us, as a background to the project it was widely alleged that

> madrasa pedagogy fans intolerance and incites fanaticism, which are detrimental to pluralism and multicultural coexistence. It has also been alleged that madrasas introduce students to extremely traditional and conservative socio-political worldviews, which is seen as an imminent threat to local and global political orders.

This is in a context in which "violent sectarian discourse and shrinking space for religious sects as well as minorities in Pakistan became more evident in daily life." Against the stream, Malik's project has sought to engage with madrasa students, employing a "unique dialogical approach." It invited both female and male students from five major religious schools of thought in Pakistan: Deobandi, Barelwi, Ahl-i Hadith, Jamaʿat-i Islami and Shiʿa madrasas to participate in a series of workshops on a variety of topics chosen by participants (gender, plurality, harmony, stereotypes, diversity, identity and pluralism) and encouraged them to host similar workshops in Pakistan. Without going into detail (see Chapter 14 above) the workshops turned out to be an astonishing success, with animated discussions across the various themes actively debated by both male and female students, and mutual hosting and visiting between madrasas in Pakistan, as well as interaction with German academics and students. More broadly, Itzchak Weizmann (Chapter 13) shows how key figures in the Middle East have espoused "dialogue" and a discourse of tolerance, human rights and citizenship. Yet these are often met with suspicion and even outright rejection.[3]

When I met Jamal in Manchester, midway through the project, he was enormously excited about it. And indeed, the project was groundbreaking – challenging stereotypes and confounding expectations. Religion (in this case

---

[3] In Chapter 4, Tariq Rahman discusses the "peaceful interpretations of jihad" by some contemporary modernist Muslims who believe that the accepted norms of international behavior are harmonious with Islam. Also in Chapter 5, Jan-Peter Hartung presents a case study of the visions which emphasized the co-existence of all religious communities in an undivided India after British colonial rule.

Islam), it seems, was in motion; open to new ideas, encouraging debate, hospitality and mutual dialogue.

Of course, tolerance and communication are only one half of the story. As I write this afterword, the Taliban have taken over the government in Afghanistan. Outwardly, they seem to have changed, for example promising to allow women to work and study. But the reality being played out on the ground is still opaque. Policewomen are being assassinated. Anyone who worked for the American or NATO forces has either fled or is in hiding. Women and men are prohibited from studying together. Journalists are being persecuted. Girls are not welcome as high school students. Protests have been prohibited, as have music and performing arts. Let us recall that Taliban leaders are religious mullahs who emerged from Pakistani Deobandi madrasas, which follow a strict interpretation of the Quran and Hadith. They may be willing to compromise temporarily with wider cosmopolitan values in order to be granted humanitarian aid, but there is no evidence that they have abandoned their doctrinaire religious stance on issues of gender, freedom of speech or democracy.

Several issues are evident in the Taliban takeover. First, it highlights the imbrication of religious movements in politics and economics. There is no pure religion, in and of itself. The intersectionality of religion and politics, including the political ideology of nationalism, makes it impossible to think of religion on its own. To the extent that the Taliban are patriotic, placing the interests of the nation high on the agenda, so too the possibilities for religious compromise increase. As Afghanis themselves try to figure out whether the Taliban have "changed," no one is disputing that there are many strands of Islam that are tolerant, open-minded on gender rights, peace-loving and hospitable. The question is – when and how is doctrinaire extremism converted into a more open kind of Islam? Here the dynamics of Islam in the modern world, invoked by the title to this volume, are tested. The essays in this book address these dynamics from different perspectives as summarised in a masterly introduction by Ali Altaf Mian.

One of the striking achievements of Malik's work is his capacity to take in the fine details not simply of global trends but of the local in all its infinitesimal intricacy and ambiguity. In an essay on the Urdu literary critique of Islamic popular religion in South Asia and the cult of shrines, Malik takes up the work of the progressive writer Ahmad Nadim Qasimi.[4] In a short story,

---

4 Jamal Malik, "The Literary Critique of Islamic Popular Religion in the Guise of Traditional Mysticism, or the Abused Woman," in *Embodying Charisma: Modernity, Locality and the Performance of Emotion in Sufi Cults*, ed. Pnina Werbner and Helene Basu (London: Routledge, 1998).

Qasimi criticises the practices at saints' shrines, but, Malik argues, his reformist ideas and arguments are "still bound up with norms and symbols rooted in a long tradition."[5] Ironically, he shows, the narrative structure deployed by Qasimi follows a pattern similar to an underlying mystical Sufi discourse. This indicates, Malik argues, that modernist reformist values are influenced by a common symbolic framework.

What is impressive in the essay is the deep and extensive familiarity Malik displays with scholarly Islamic works from the Middle East as well as South Asia, written by historians as well as anthropologists; he draws on Urdu literature, ethnography and critical reformist works, while also recognising the impact of British colonial criticisms of the cult of shrines. In particular, he highlights the development of a new brand of Urdu urban literature – *social realism*. Its young writers, he tells us, drew on a mixture of "tradition" and "modernity."[6] These young writers formed the Progressive Writers' Association (PWA). Ahmad Nadim Qasimi, himself the son of a *pir*, was an early representative of the PWA.

Having provided the background to this movement, Malik then moves to a detailed analysis of a single story. It is here that he displays his interpretive and hermeneutical skills. The tragic story is of a beautiful young girl captured by the shrine, her visionary capacity destroyed, ultimately leading to her death. The mystical dimensions of her spiritual ascent underline the corruption and cruelty of the shrine authorities, particularly in their relations with women, and the gender bias this implies about Sufi shrines.

Malik's contextualising insights and interpretive perspicacity are also evident in another of his early essays, this time on a Barelwi politician, Shah Ahmed Nurani, President of the JUP.[7] Malik shows how Nurani's charismatic leadership is constructed, among other things, from his spiritual role as saviour or saint. His miraculous powers, his farsightedness or *ma'rifa* (gnosis), his saintly descent and his alleged beauty, all imbue his secular modern leadership with a "numinous" charisma.

Unlike the new scripturalists of the nineteenth century, the Deobandis, Ahl-i Hadiths and later Jama'at-i Islamis, who appealed to an emerging new Islamic intelligentsia, the Barelwis continued to rely on the teachings and sayings of holy men, and indeed, their messages were not meant, it seems, for the colonial

---

5   Ibid., 187.
6   Ibid., 190.
7   Jamal Malik, "The Luminous Nurani: Charisma and Political Mobilisation among the Barelwis in Pakistan," *Social Analysis* 28, *Special Issue: Person, Myth and Society in South Asian Islam* (1990).

public. For the Barelwis, the Prophet was still "present or existent." They supported the creation of Pakistan, and after Partition, helped with the integration of refugees fleeing from India. Without going into the details of Nurani's birth and religious-cum-political career as outlined by Malik, the key point he makes is that Nurani was among the few popular leaders "who was able to combine political and religious leadership with charisma, by using traditional modes of social discourse and thereby taking advantage of the symbolic dynamics of his society."[8] Nurani, we are told, was particularly famous for his "luminous speeches." Propagating the millennium, they promised equality and justice for all. By 1978, Nurani had been elevated to the position of holy man, a *pir*, whose speeches and recitations propagated a mood of experiential unity. Politically, the Barelwi under Nurani demanded ritual recognition for their prayers and processions, and representation in major religious forums. Nurani claimed to be "full of light" (of the Prophet), and linked his movement, the Barelwis, to the four main *tariqa*s in South Asia and the four holy centres of Islam.

By 1984, Nurani was regarded as the "perfect leader" and "saviour." Malik shows how the symbolic language of dreams elevated him to almost-prophetic status. So too were his representations in calligraphy. Both dreams and calligraphy used a language of religious symbolism "beyond grammatical speech."[9] In the end, however, Nurani was unsuccessful in realising his political ambitions. Nonetheless, he was for a time a unifying figure, Malik tells us, transcending divisions and uniting followers.

This case study illustrates in subtle detail the dynamic interaction between Islamic mysticism and politics. To understand the rise of a single figure, Malik shows, requires a full grasp of the social, historical and sociological context along with a fine understanding of religious symbolism and language. Without these, the figure of a man like Shah Ahmad Nurani remains an enigma, which only in-depth analysis can fully explain.

As a social historian, for Malik, modernity in South Asia is inextricably linked to British colonialism, with the rise of civil society, political parties, secularism and identity politics, all impacted by the colonial encounter,[10] while he has also considered the roots of pre-colonial, native modernities developing in India during the eighteenth century (see also Chapter 10 above).[11] In

---

8   Ibid., 42.
9   Ibid., 47–48.
10   Jamal Malik, *Islam in South Asia: Revised, Enlarged and Updated Second Edition* (Leiden: Brill, 2020), 22. See also idem, *Perspectives of Mutual Encounters in South Asian History 1760–1860* (Leiden: Brill, 2000).
11   Jamal Malik, "Muslim Culture and Reform in 18th Century South Asia," *Journal of the Royal Asiatic Society* 13, no. 2 (2003); idem, "Some Ideas on Pre-Colonial Modernity: The Case

the present volume, the focus on modernity has yet extended to also include the Middle Eastern encounter with "Europe" and key historical figures that influenced the way Islam came to be interpreted in the Arab world following this encounter (Chapters 1 and 2). The same era also led to innovative medical developments (Chapter 3).

Beyond modernity, as a social historian, Malik's enduring interest is in the *encounter*, not only between religions but more broadly, between cultures, political groups, institutional arrangements and ways of life. Much of his work pursues different kinds of encounters, but equally importantly, he wants to probe the way in which confrontations in dogma can be transcended by the everyday. As he points out, "[a]s long as we consider the fuzzy and non-ideological potential of everyday lived religious reality as something viable for the process of cultural integration, we may be on the safe side." According to him, lived Islam offers "a broad panoply of internal arrangements, beyond dogmas and debates about normativity."[12] Above all, it offers a way of living beyond essentialism and beyond simplistic dichotomies. This is equally true in the field of law: Islamic jurisprudence had a long history before the encounter with colonialism, but it too was challenged radically by this encounter. In the present volume, Mouez Khalfaoui (Chapter 7) asks: are Islam and human rights compatible? They are, he says, if they are reconceptualised to fit into current international rights discourse. Similar arguments are made by Reik Kirchhoff and Syed FurrukhZad in their contributions (Chapters 8 and 9).

Over the years, Malik has repeatedly considered one particular encounter: that of Muslim migrants and the Muslim diaspora with Europe or the West more generally.[13] Malik[14] is mainly concerned with the extent to which an Islamic European identity has emerged, and how this has been impacted by developments in the post-9/11 era. To what extent has a sphere of intercultural communication emerged, both among different Muslim groups and between

---

of Indian Muslim Pietists," *Exemplar: The Journal of South Asian Studies* 1, no. 1 (2012). In Chapter 1 above, Reinhard Schulze also emphasizes the "indigenous" mechanisms for dividing consciousness and social life in the Muslim world and that the notion of the secularization of the social order has not only happened in the Euro-American sphere.

12 Malik, *Islam in South Asia*, 26.
13 See, for instance, Jamal Malik, *Muslims in Europe: From the Margin to the Centre* (Münster: LIT, 2004); idem, "Muslims in the West – A Muslim 'Diaspora'?," in *Religion and Secular State: Role and Meaning of Religion in a Secular Society from Jewish, Christian, and Muslim Perspectives*, ed. Stefan Schreiner (Zurich and Sarajevo: European Abrahamic Forum, 2008).
14 Jamal Malik and John Hinnells, eds., *Sufism in the West* (London and New York: Routledge, 2006).

them and the majority? To what extent have Muslim minorities achieved recognition? Writing more specifically about Sufism among migrants in the West, he is mainly concerned with the most recent phase of Sufism, in which diasporic Sufi orders may be regarded "as part of the Muslim global diaspora, providing for yet new identities and solidarity systems and making meaningful the diasporic situation for a variety of new social formations by expanding its semantics."[15] Several chapters in the present volume consider the diasporic encounter (Chapters 6, 9, 11 and 12).

One of the most fascinating Islamic religious encounters relates to the early historical expansion of Sufism into the West, and then back again, analysed in a volume dedicated to Annemarie Schimmel, Malik's teacher. In *Sufism East and West*,[16] the contributors attempt to explore "the fluidity between East and West, the oscillating processes in that *space of resonance* which create the very elusiveness which defies such categorizations." The editors explain that

> Resonance is more than consonance and mere echo, it can help distinguish the self from the other, it is elusive and transformative for all sides involved. Yet, it is more than mere dissonance, too, for it allows for contact and encounter without nostrification or assimilation. It is bidirectional with an experience towards the productive efficacy of the actors in their involvement.[17]

In the present volume, tracing the historical development of Sufism since its foundation with the spread of Islam, and moving on to analyse the phases of Sufism in the West since the nineteenth century, Michael Asbury and Saeed Zarrabi-Zadeh (Chapter 11) examine the final phase of this western expansion through an in-depth analysis of the so-called "applied" Sufism of Abdur Rashid, who continued the tradition of his master in India in the USA. In particular, the authors point out

> [...] the insufficiency of the dichotomy of change versus continuity as an analytic tool for investigating the internal movement within Sufi orders and communities. Therefore, instead of this black-and-white division, one may utilize the category of 'dynamics', a central theme of the current

---

15 Jamal Malik, "Introduction," in *Sufism in the West*, ed. Malik and Hinnells, 10–11.
16 Jamal Malik and Saeed Zarrabi-Zadeh, eds., *Sufism East and West: Mystical Islam and Cross-Cultural Exchange in the Modern World. In Memory of Professor Annemarie Schimmel (1922–2003)* (Leiden: Brill, 2019).
17 Ibid., 2.

volume, in reference to Abdur Rashid's re-activation of the past for the sake of the present and the future. Indeed, the concept of 'dynamics', which refers to the motions within a system resulting from the internal interaction of its components or from their external interaction with the environment outside the system, can better reflect the spectrum of hybrid areas of Sufi activity which can be located between two sides of total innovation/newness and absolute continuity/oldness.

The term "dynamics" is thus intended to deny simple dichotomies in favour of a focus on the interplay of ideas, practices and traditions in the encounter with the modern world in all its complexity. We have seen the way such dialectical interplays are shown by Malik to be manifested in the figure of a Barelwi JUP leader in Pakistan, and in new realist Urdu short stories about Sufi shrines. The existence of such dynamics also raises questions about the future trajectory of the Taliban in Afghanistan. All the essays in this volume probe the dynamics of different approaches and strands of Islam over the *longue durée*.

To conclude, I am honoured and privileged to have been asked to write an afterword to this splendid volume of essays written as a tribute to Jamal Malik's rich and varied *oeuvre*. Over the years, our paths have crossed countries and continents as we attended shared conferences and workshops or lived for a while in the North of England. A particularly memorable event was my attendance at a conference convened by Jamal in mid-winter in 2001 when my flight was delayed and I arrived in Frankfurt too late for the last train to Erfurt. I will never forget driving a rented car on an almost-empty autobahn, snowflakes falling, in the early days when there were still no satnavs. Luckily, I noticed a sign to Erfurt and arrived in a deserted town centre at midnight. I was escorted by two policemen to the conference hotel. Whenever I have wanted to understand a particularly thorny question to do with South Asian Islam or Islamic observance, I have turned to Jamal. He has never failed me.

Bibliography

Malik, Jamal. *Colonialization of Islam: Dissolution of Traditional Institutions in Pakistan.* New Delhi: Manohar; Lahore: Vanguard, 1996.

Malik, Jamal. "Introduction." In *Sufism in the West*, edited by Jamal Malik and John Hinnells, 1–27. London and New York: Routledge, 2006.

Malik, Jamal. *Islam in South Asia: Revised, Enlarged and Updated Second Edition.* Leiden: Brill, 2020.

Malik, Jamal. "Muslim Culture and Reform in 18th Century South Asia." *Journal of the Royal Asiatic Society* 13, no. 2 (2003): 227–43.

Malik, Jamal. *Muslims in Europe: From the Margin to the Centre*. Münster: LIT, 2004.

Malik, Jamal. "Muslims in the West – A Muslim 'Diaspora'?." In *Religion and Secular State: Role and Meaning of Religion in a Secular Society from Jewish, Christian, and Muslim Perspectives,* edited by Stefan Schreiner, 147–52. Zurich and Sarajevo: European Abrahamic Forum, 2008.

Malik, Jamal. *Perspectives of Mutual Encounters in South Asian History 1760–1860*. Leiden: Brill, 2000.

Malik, Jamal. "Some Ideas on Pre-Colonial Modernity: The Case of Indian Muslim Pietists." *Exemplar: The Journal of South Asian Studies* 1, no. 1 (2012): 56–64.

Malik, Jamal. "The Literary Critique of Islamic Popular Religion in the Guise of Traditional Mysticism, or the Abused Woman." In *Embodying Charisma: Modernity, Locality and the Performance of Emotion in Sufi Cults*, edited by Pnina Werbner and Helene Basu, 187–208. London: Routledge, 1998.

Malik, Jamal. "The Luminous Nurani: Charisma and Political Mobilisation among the Barelwis in Pakistan." *Social Analysis* 28, *Special Issue: Person, Myth and Society in South Asian Islam* (1990): 38–50.

Malik, Jamal and Helmut Reifeld, eds. *Religious Pluralism in South Asia and Europe*. New Delhi: Oxford University Press, 2004.

Malik, Jamal and John Hinnells, eds. *Sufism in the West*. London and New York: Routledge, 2006.

Malik, Jamal and Saeed Zarrabi-Zadeh, eds. *Sufism East and West: Mystical Islam and Cross-Cultural Exchange in the Modern World. In Memory of Professor Annemarie Schimmel (1922–2003)*. Leiden: Brill, 2019.

Honoring Jamal Malik

Tabula Gratulatoria

Ishrat Abbasi
Yasser Abdelrehim
Bekim Agai
Imtiaz Ahmad
Moinuddin Ahmad
Hilal Ahmed
Anwar Alam
Arshad Alam
Muzaffar Alam
Shahid Alam
Seema Alavi
Ahmed S. Al-Mesri
Katajun Amirpur
Tanvir Anjum
Humayun Ansari
Sarah Ansari
Ali Asani
Ednan Aslan
Shahrul Azman
Helene Basu
Mark Chalîl Bodenstein
Monika Boehm-Tettelbach
Michael Borgolte
Syed Mehboob Bukhari
Christoph Bultmann
Ursula Seibold-Bultmann
Ikram Chaghatai
Rachida Chih
Stephan Conermann
Vasudha Dalmia
Günther Distelrath
David Doss
Markus Dressler
Michael Dusche
Amir Dziri
Dale F. Eickelman
Andus Emge
Carl W. Ernst
Ute Falasch
Michael Fisher
Katharina Fleckenstein
Patrick Franke
Ulrike Freitag
Jürgen Wasim Frembgen
Albrecht Fuess
Marc Gaborieau
Malte Gaier
Werner Gephart
Christine Gieraths
Andreas Gotzmann
Heike Grimm
Kai Hafez
Hans Harder
Zoya Hasan
Sarah Holz
Beate Huppertz
Yousra Ibrahim
Hartmut Ihne
Navid Kermani
Muhammad Afzal Khan
Muhammad Yasir Ali Khan
Hans G. Kippenberg
Verena Klemm
Gritt Klinkhammer
Benedikt Kranemann
Klaus Kreiser
Dieter Langewiesche
Kiran Latif
Bruce B. Lawrence
Vasilios Makrides
Iftikhar Malik
Bindu Menon Mannil
Silvia Martens
Muhammad Khalid Masud

Zahra Saffia Réka Uta Máté
Barbara Metcalf
Sana Migati
Gail Minault
Hussain Muhammad
Faiza Muhammad-din
Volker Nenzel
Johannes Pahlitzsch
Margrit Pernau
Alix Philippon
Anja Pistor-Hatam
Claudia Preckel
Ali Usman Qasmi
Maryam Rahmani
Zakir Hossain Raju
Abdul Rauf
Dietrich Reetz
Misbahur Rehman
Francis Robinson
Ekkehard Rudolph
Jörg Rüpke
Jörn Rüsen
Ehsan Safaeimoghadam
Neda Saghaee
Armando Salvatore
Usha Sanyal
Christine Schirrmacher

Hansjörg Schmid
Gudrun Schubert
Isabella Schwaderer
Tilman Seidensticker
Muhammad Shafique
Udo Steinbach
Guido Steinberg
Wolfgang Struck
Georges Tamer
Abdulkader Tayob
Levent Tezcan
Alexander Thumfart
Christian W. Troll
Muhammad Usman
Katharina Waldner
Mohammad Waseem
Stefan Weber
Paul Weller
Heinz Werner Wessler
Nina Wiedl
Rotraud Wielandt
Stefan Wild
Michael Winkels
Monika Wohlrab-Sahr
Philipp Zehmisch
Miraj ul Islam Zia
Wolfgang-Peter Zingel

Jamal Malik's Publication List

Monographs

2020   *Islam in South Asia: Revised, Enlarged and Updated Second Edition.* Handbook of Oriental Studies, section 2 South Asia, vol. 37. Leiden: Brill.

2008   *Islam in South Asia: A Short History.* Leiden: Brill; Indian edition, Hyderabad: Orient BlackSwan, 2012.

1997   *Islamische Gelehrtenkultur in Nordindien: Entwicklungsgeschichte und Tendenzen am Beispiel von Lucknow.* Leiden: Brill.

1996   *Colonialization of Islam: Dissolution of Traditional Institutions in Pakistan.* New Delhi: Manohar Publications; Lahore: Vanguard; 2nd ed., 1998 (reprint); Dhaka: The University Press Ltd., 1999 (reprint).

1989   *Islamisierung in Pakistan 1977–1984: Untersuchungen zur Auflösung autochthoner Strukturen.* Wiesbaden: Franz Steiner.

Edited Volumes

2020   *Culture of Daʿwa: Islamic Preaching in the Modern World.* Salt Lake City: University of Utah Press (co-author and co-editor with Itzchak Weismann).

2019   *Sufism East and West: Mystical Islam and Cross-Cultural Exchange in the Modern World. In Memory of Professor Annemarie Schimmel (1922–2003).* Leiden: Brill (co-author and co-editor with Saeed Zarrabi-Zadeh).

2016   *Religionen in Bewegung: Interreligiöse Beziehungen im Wandel der Zeit.* Münster: Aschendorff (co-author and co-editor with Michael Gabel and Justyna Okolowicz).

2015   *Sufi-Sufi Diaspora: Fenomena Sufisme di Negara-Negara Barat.* Jakarta: Mizan Publika (co-author and co-editor with John Hinnells).

2010   *Mobilisierung von Religion in Europa.* Frankfurt am Main: Peter Lang.

2009 *Religionsproduktivität in Europa: Markierungen im religiösen Feld.* Münster: Aschendorff (co-author and co-editor with Jürgen Manemann).
2008 *Madrasas in South Asia: Teaching Terror?.* London and New York: Routledge; paperback, 2009.
2007 *Religion und Medien: Vom Kultbild zum Internetritual.* Münster: Aschendorff (co-editor and co-author with Jörg Rüpke and Theresa Wobbe).
2006 *Mahnungen und Warnungen: Die Lehre der Religionen über das rechte Leben. Vorlesungen des Interdisziplinären Forums Religion der Universität Erfurt.* Münster: Aschendorff (co-editor with Christoph Bultmann and Claus-Peter März).
2006 *Sufism in the West.* London and New York: Routledge (co-author and co-editor with John Hinnells).
2004 *Religious Pluralism in South Asia and Europe.* New Delhi: Oxford University Press (co-author and co-editor with Helmut Reifeld).
2004 *Muslims in Europe: From the Margin to the Centre.* Münster: LIT.
2001 *Pluralismus in der europäischen Religionsgeschichte: Religionswissenschaftliche Antrittsvorlesungen.* Marburg: Diagonal (co-author and co-editor with Andreas Gotzmann, Vasilios N. Makrides and Jörg Rüpke).
2000 *Perspectives of Mutual Encounters in South Asian History 1760 – 1860.* Leiden: Brill.
1993 *A Map of Shahjahanabad from about 1850.* Bonn: Geographisches Institut der Universität Bonn.
1989 *Pakistan: Destabilisierung durch Kontinuität, eine Dokumentation des Südasienbüro.* Wuppertal: Südasienbüro.

Book Chapters

2022 "Analytic Essay: Sufism in Western Regional Settings." In *Sufism in Western Contexts*, edited by Marcia Hermansen and Saeed Zarrabi-Zadeh. Leiden: Brill (forthcoming).
2022 "Muslim*innen und religiöse Bildung in Südasien mit Schwerpunkt Indien." In *Handbuch Islamische Religionspädagogik*, edited by Ednan Aslan, Teil 2. V&R unipress (forthcoming).

2022	"Der Islam in Südasien II." In *Religionen der Menschheit*, vol. II, *Vom Beginn des 20. Jahrhunderts bis heute*, edited by Peter Antes. Stuttgart-Vaihingen: Kohlhammer (forthcoming).
2022	"Der Islam in Südasien I." In *Religionen der Menschheit*, vol. I, *Von der Entstehung bis zum Ende des 19. Jahrhunderts*, edited by Georges Tamer. Stuttgart-Vaihingen: Kohlhammer (forthcoming).
2021	"The Prophet, Law and Constitution in Pakistani Society." In *The Presence of the Prophet in Early Modern and Contemporary Islam*, vol. II, *Heirs of the Prophet: Authority and Power*, edited by Rachida Chih, David Jordan and Stefan Reichmuth, 293–322. Leiden: Brill.
2020	"Introduction." In *Culture of Daʿwa: Islamic Preaching in the Modern World*, edited by Itzchak Weismann and Jamal Malik, 1–12. Salt Lake City: The Utah University Press (co-authored with Itzchak Weismann).
2020	"Ideology, Practice and Law in the Daʿwa of the Muslim Brothers and Jamaʿat-e Islami." In *Culture of Daʿwa: Islamic Preaching in the Modern World*, edited by Itzchak Weismann and Jamal Malik, 61–78. Salt Lake City: The Utah University Press.
2019	"Introduction." In *Sufism East and West: Mystical Islam and Cross-Cultural Exchange in the Modern World. In Memory of Professor Annemarie Schimmel (1922–2003)*, edited by Jamal Malik and Saeed Zarrabi-Zadeh, 1–29. Leiden: Brill (co-authored with Saeed Zarrabi-Zadeh).
2019	"Sufi Amnesia in Sayyid Ahmad Khan's *Tahdhib al-Akhlaq*." In *Sufism East and West: Mystical Islam and Cross-Cultural Exchange in the Modern World. In Memory of Professor Annemarie Schimmel (1922–2003)*, edited by Jamal Malik and Saeed Zarrabi-Zadeh, 76–103. Leiden: Brill.
2019	"Toward Historicizing an Indian Nationalist Salafī: The Case of Abū l-Kalām Āzād." In *Muslim Minorities in Modern Times*, edited by Yohanan Friedmann, 69–90. Jerusalem: The Israel Academy of Sciences and Humanities.
2018	"Sayyid Abu al-Aʿla al-Mawdudi, al-Jihad fi al-Islam (1930)." In *Geschichte des politischen Denkens. Das 20. Jahrhundert*, edited by Manfred Brocker, 217–32. Frankfurt am Main: Suhrkamp.
2018	"Literarische Salons im Indien des 18. Jahrhunderts: Ein Beitrag zur Moderne im Islam?." In *Islam in der Moderne, Moderne im Islam: Eine Festschrift für Reinhard Schulze zum 65. Geburtstag*, edited by Monica Corrado, Johannes Stephan, Florian Zemmin, 301–27. Leiden: Brill.

2018   "The Sociopolitical Entanglements of Sufism." In *The Wiley Blackwell History of Islam,* edited by Armando Salvatore, Roberto Tottoli and Babak Rahimi, 587–606. Oxford: John Wiley & Sons Ltd.

2016   "Orientalismus in Mitteldeutschland: Der Fall des Grafen von Gleichen." In *Religionen in Bewegung: Interreligiöse Beziehungen im Wandel der Zeit,* edited by Michael Gabel, Jamal Malik and Justyna Okolowicz, 197–211, Münster: Aschendorff.

2016   "Andaman Islands in Muslim Cultural Memory and Fadl-e Haqq Khairabadi." In *Manifestations of History: Time, Space and Community in the Andaman Islands,* edited by Frank Heidemann and Philipp Zehmisch, 18–36. Delhi: Primus Books.

2015   "Integration of Muslim Migrants and the Politics of Dialogue: The Case of Modern Germany." In *The Issue of Religious Harmony in Europe, South Asia and the Middle East,* edited by Naveed Ahmad Tahir, 38–54. Karachi: Area Study Centre for Europe-University of Karachi.

2015   "Islamic Law and Mediation." In *Rechtskulturen im Übergang /Legal Cultures in Transition: Von Südafrika bis Spanien, von Nachkriegsdeutschland bis zum Aufbruch der arabischen Welt,* edited by Werner Gephart, Raja Sakrani and Jenny Hellmann, 201–30. Frankfurt am Main: Vittorio Klostermann (co-authored with Misbahur Rehman).

2015   "Pendahuluan." In *Sufi-Sufi Diaspora: Fenomena Sufisme di Negara-Negara Barata,* edited by Jamal Malik and John Hinnells, 13–57. Jakarta: Mizan Publika.

2015   "Constructions of the Past in and about India: From Jahiliyya to the Cradle of Civilization. Pre-colonial Perceptions of India." In *Globalized Antiquity: Uses and Perceptions of the Past in South Asia, Mesoamerica, and Europe,* edited by Ute Schüren, Daniel Marc Segesser and Thomas Späth, 51–72. Berlin: Reimer.

2014   "Modernity, Diversity, and the Public Sphere: Religious Identities in 18th–20th Century India. Some Ideas on Pre-Colonial Modernity: The Case of Indian Muslim Pietists." In *Open Pages in South Asian Studies,* edited by Alexander Stolyarov (convenor) and Joe Pellegrino, 111–31. Woodland Hills, CA: South Asian Studies Association.

2013 "Gewalt und Verfolgung im Islam: Versuch einer historischen Perspektive auf den Koran." In *Wege und Hindernisse religiöser Toleranz: Zur friedensschaffenden Kraft der Religionen,* edited by Maria Eder, Elmar Kuhn and Helmut Reinalter, 31–47. Weimar: VDG.

2013 "Wirkungsgeschichte und Konsequenzen – Aus der Sicht des Islams: Semantische Erweiterungen und politische Deutungen." In *Wege und Hindernisse religiöser Toleranz: Zur friedensschaffenden Kraft der Religionen,* edited by Maria Eder, Elmar Kuhn and Helmut Reinalter, 61–74. Weimar: VDG.

2012 "Some Critical Remarks on Madrasa Reforms as Proposed by the Government of Afghanistan (2007)." In *Conference Proceedings of the International Conference of the Department of Political Science, University of Peshawar: The Dynamics of Change in Conflict Societies: Pakhtun Region in Perspective,* 112–19. Peshawar: al-Qalam Publishers.

2012 "Foreword." In *Perceptions of Islam and Muslims in Europe,* edited by Moonis Ahmar, III–V. Karachi: Area Study Centre for Europe – University of Karachi.

2011 "Historische, philosophische und theologische Voraussetzungen des interreligiösen Dialogs aus islamischer Sicht." In *Interreligiosität und Interkulturalität: Herausforderungen für Bildung, Seelsorge und Soziale Arbeit im christlich-muslimischen Kontext,* edited by Josef Freise and Mouhanad Khorchide, 80–97. Münster: Waxmann.

2010 "Muslime in Westeuropa – eine muslimische Diaspora?." In *Islam und Muslime in (Südost) Europa im Kontext von Transformation und EU-Erweiterung,* edited by Christian Voß and Jordanka Telbizova-Sack, 33–51. Munich and Berlin: Otto Sagner.

2010 "Einleitung." In *Mobilisierung von Religion in Europa,* edited by Jamal Malik, 1–10. Frankfurt am Main: Peter Lang.

2010 "Muslim Culture and Reform in 18th Century South Asia." In *Islam in South Asia: Critical Concepts in Islamic Studies,* vol. I, *South Asian Islam in Historical and Cultural Context*, edited by David Taylor, 398–418. London: Routledge, [reprint of article from *Journal of the Royal Asiatic Society* 13, no. 2 (July 2007): 227–43].

2010 "Was lehren die Madrasen?." In *Indien und Pakistan: Atommächte im Spannungsfeld regionaler und globaler Veränderungen. Beiträge zur Außen- und Sicherheitspolitik Südasiens,* edited by Rüdiger von Dehn and Sebastian Buciak, 316–28. Berlin: Dr. Köster.

2010 "Religion as a Catalyst for Conflict: The Case of Islam." In *Superpower Rivalry and Conflict: The Long Shadow of the Cold War on the Twenty-First Century,* edited by Chandra Chari, 176–88. London: Routledge.

2009 "Rolle islamischer Nichtregierungsorganisationen (NGOs) und dem Wahhabismus auf dem Balkan." In *Jahresbericht 2008/2009, Fritz Thyssen Stiftung für Wissenschaftsförderung,* 223–25.

2009 "Islam und Entwicklung." In *Religion und globale Entwicklung: Der Einfluss der Religionen auf die soziale, politische und wirtschaftliche Entwicklung,* edited by Jürgen Wilhelm and Hartmut Ihne, 40–50. Berlin: Berlin University Press.

2008 "Interreligiöser Dialog: Ein Integrationswerkzeug?." In *Interreligiöser Dialog auf dem Prüfstand: Kriterien und Standards für die interkulturelle und interreligiöse Kommunikation,* edited by Gritt Klinkhammer and Ayla Satilmis, 141–63. Münster: LIT.

2008 "Muslims in the West – A Muslim 'Diaspora'?." In *Religion and Secular State: Role and Meaning of Religion in a Secular Society from Jewish, Christian, and Muslim Perspectives,* edited by Stefan Schreiner, 147–52. Zurich and Sarajevo: European Abrahamic Forum [as "Muslimani na zapadu – musilmanska "dijaspora?." In *Religija I Sekularna Drzava,* Sarajevo, 221–28].

2008 "Religion und Staat im Islam." In *Wissen im Alter hat Zukunft – Kreativität im Alter,* edited by Das Europäische Zentrum für universitäre Studien der Senioren, 46–53. Bad Meinberg: Staats.

2008 "Der Islam in Deutschland im Prozess der Neuformierung." In *Religion und Bildung: Orte, Medien und Experten religiöser Bildung,* edited by Bertelsmann Stiftung, 98–104. Gütersloh: Bertelsmann (co-author with Michael Kiefer).

2008 "Introduction," and "In Lieu of a Conclusion." In *Madrasas in South Asia: Teaching Terror?,* edited by Jamal Malik, 1–22 and 165–67. London and New York: Routledge.

2007 "From the Margin to the Centre: Muslims in Europe." In *Terrorism Democracy: The West & The Muslim World,* edited by Abdul Rashid Moten and Noraini M. Noor, 277–90. Singapore: Thomson Learning.

2007 "Introduction." In *Punjab Main Khanqahi Kalchar*, edited by Ghafir Shahzad, 9–18. Lahore: Fiction House.

2007 "Das islamische System der sozialen Sicherung: Theorie und Praxis." In *60 Jahre Pakistan: Aufbruch, Errungenschaften und Herausforderungen*, edited by Saeed Chaudhry, Hermann Kreutzmann, Paul Lehrieder and Norbert Pintsch, 89–99. Bonn, Berlin and Lahore: Ferozsons.

2007 "Religion in den Medien – Medien der Religion: Diaspora, Medien und Muslime." In *Religion und Medien: Vom Kultbild zum Internetritual*, edited by Jamal Malik, Jörg Rüpke and Theresa Wobbe, 43–57. Münster: Aschendorff.

2006 "Die EU in ihrem Verhältnis zu Religionsgemeinschaften und ihrem religiösen Erbe: Inwieweit ist Europa ein christliches Projekt?." In *Politik und Religion in der Europäischen Union: Zwischen nationalen Traditionen und Europäisierung*, edited by Hartmut Behr and Mathias Hildebrandt, 95–100. Wiesbaden: GWV.

2006 "The Social Situation of Muslims in India." In *Fikrun wa Fann*. Goethe-Institut, www.goethe.de/ges/phi/prj/ffs/the/iss/en1734638.htm (accessed February 5, 2011).

2006 "Der islamische Fundamentalimus – einige Bemerkungen." In *Gemeinsame Bibel – Gemeinsame Sendung: 25 Jahre Rheinischer Synodalbeschluss zur Erneuerung des Verhältnisses von Christen und Juden*, edited by Siegfried Kreuzer and Frank Ueberschaer, 127–29. Neukirchen: Neukirchener – Vandenhoeck & Ruprecht.

2006 "Perspectives of Mutual Encounters in South Asian History, 1750–1850." In *Rising India – Europe's Partner?: Foreign and Security Policy, Politics, Economics, Human Rights and Social Issues, Media, Civil Society and Intercultural Dimensions*, edited by Klaus Voll and Doreen Beierlein, 865–77. Berlin: Weißensee.

2006 "Encountering Muslims in Germany." In *'East is East and West is West?': Talks on Dialogue in Beirut*, edited by Leslie A. Tramontini, 137–50. Würzburg: Ergon.

2006 "The Right to be Different: Mutual Respect, Freedom of Religion, and their Respective Limits: Muslims in the Western Diaspora-Legal Implications and Everyday Experiences." In *Visions of a Just Society: Fears, Hopes, and Chances for Living Together in a Globalized World from Jewish, Christian, and Muslim Perspectives*, edited by Stefan Schreiner, 100–7. Sarajevo: Abrahamic Forum and Konrad-Adenauer-Stiftung.

2006 "Introduction." In *Sufism in the West,* edited by Jamal Malik and John Hinnells, 1–27. London and New York: Routledge.

2006 "Madrasah in South Asia." In *The Blackwell Companion to Contemporary Islamic Thought,* edited by Ibrahim M. Abu-Rabi', 105–22. Malden, Oxford; Victoria: Blackwell.

2005 "Der Neue Nahe Osten: Der Islam und Europa." In *Der 'neue' Nahe Osten?, edited by* Wolfgang Bergsdorf, Dietmar Herz, Hans Hoffmeister and Wolf Wagner, 55–69. Erfurt: Rhino.

2005 "Der Islam in Europa–Integration oder Ghettoisierung." In *Konferenzberichte: Islam, Staat und moderne Gesellschaft in der Türkei und in Europa,* edited by Konrad-Adenauer-Stiftung, 101–16. Ankara: Konrad-Adenauer-Stiftung.

2004 "Introduction." In *Religious Pluralism in South Asia and Europe,* edited by Jamal Malik and Helmut Reifeld, 1–20. New Delhi: Oxford University Press.

2004 "Gewalt und Gewaltlosigkeit im Islam." In *Religion – Christentum – Gewalt: Einblicke und Perspektiven,* edited by Wolfgang Ratzmann, 57–73. Leipzig: Evangelische Verlagsanstalt.

2004 "Der Islamische Fundamentalismus: Einige Bemerkungen." In *Religion und Politik: Zu Theorie und Praxis des theologisch-politischen Komplexes,* edited by Manfred Walther, 387–90. Baden-Baden: Nomos.

2004 "Introduction." In *Muslims in Europe: From the Margin to the Centre,* edited by Jamal Malik, 1–18. Münster: LIT.

2004 "Nationale und religiöse Fremd- und Selbstbilder: Muslime in Deutschland." In *Nation und Religion in Europa: Mehrkonfessionelle Gesellschaften im 19. und 20. Jahrhundert,* edited by Heinz-Gehard Haupt and Dieter Langewiesche, 281–302. Frankfurt am Main and New York: Campus.

2004 "Gewalt und Gewaltverzicht im Islam." In *Religion, Gewalt, Gewaltlosigkeit: Probleme – Positionen – Perspektiven,* edited by Christoph Bultmann, Benedikt Kranemann and Jörg Rüpke, 70–82. Münster: Aschendorff.

2004 "Politischer Islam: Eine Spielart muslimischer kultureller Artikulation." In *Wartburg Gespräche*, Katholischer Burschenschafter IV. Band 2000–2003, 171–75. Bonn: Selbstverlag des Vorbereitenden Komitees der Wartburg Gespräche, Druck JF Carthaus Bonn.

2003 Texts by Sayyid Ahmad Khan, Shibli Nuʿmani, M. Iqbal, A.H. Ali Nadwi and I.H. Qureshi, In *Historical Thinking in South Asia: A Handbook of Sources from Colonial Times to the Present*, edited by Michael Gottlob, 124–27, 134–39, 163–67, 242–46, 246–49. New Delhi: Oxford University Press.

2003 "Die gesellschaftliche Situation indischer Muslime." In *Indien heute: Brennpunkte seiner Innenpolitik*, edited by Subrata K. Mitra and Bernd Rill, 121–32. Munich: Hanns-Seidel-Stiftung.

2003 "Islamic Institutions and Infrastructure in Shâhjahânâbâd." In *Shâhjahânâbâd / Old Delhi: Tradition and Colonial Change*, edited by Eckart Ehlers and Thomas Krafft, 2nd ed., 71–92. New Delhi: Manohar.

2003 "Der Islamischer Fundamentalismus: Einige Bemerkungen." In *Ethik, Politik und Kulturen im Globalisierungsprozess: Eine interdisziplinäre Zusammenführung*, edited by Ralf Elm, 216–19. Bochum: Projekt.

2003 "Traditional Islamic Learning and Reform in Pakistan." In *Local Forms of Religious Organisation as Structural Modernisation: Effects on Religious Community Building and Globalisation*, edited by Karl-Fritz Daiber and Gerdien Jonker, 113–20. Marburg: Philipps Universität Marburg, http://archiv.ub.uni-marburg.de/uni/2003/0001/relorg.pdf.

2003 "Reform in Südasien: Das 18. Jahrhundert." In *Südasien in der 'Neuzeit': Geschichte und Gesellschaft, 1500–2000*, edited by Karin Preisendanz and Dietmar Rothermund, 72–89. Wien: Promedia.

2002 "Einleitung: Die Reform des Islam im 18. Jahrhundert." In *Die muslimische Sicht (13. bis 18. Jahrhundert), Geschichtsdenken der Kulturen: Eine kommentierte Dokumentation*, 8 vols., *Südasien – von den Anfängen bis zur Gegenwart (Band I bis III)*, edited by Stephan Conermann, Jörn Rüsen and Sebastian Manhart, vol. II, 295–313. E-book: Humanities online.

2002 Texts by Sayyid Ahmad Khan, Shibli Nuʿmani, M. Iqbal, A. Maududi, A.H. Ali Nadwi and I.H. Qureshi. *Historisches Denken im modernen Südasien (1786 bis heute), Geschichtsdenken der Kulturen: Eine kommentierte Dokumentation*, 8 Bände, *Südasien – von den Anfängen bis zur Gegenwart (Band. I bis III)*, edited by Michael Gottlob, Jörn Rüsen and Sebastian Manhart, vol. III, 195–200, 210–18, 253–60, 304–8, 385–95. E-book: Humanities online.

2002 "The *MULLĀ* and the State: Dynamics of Islamic Religious Scholars and their Institutions in Contemporary Pakistan." In *Islam in the Era of Globalization: Muslim Attitudes Towards Modernity and Identity,* edited by Johan Meuleman, 225–32. London and New York: RoutledgeCurzon.

2002 "Islam auf dem indischen Subkontinent." In *Indien – Wege zum besseren Verstehen: Fächerübergreifende Unterrichtsmaterialien,* edited by Clemens Jürgenmeyer et al., 121–24. Gotha and Stuttgart: Klett-Perthes (co-author with Jan-Peter Hartung).

2001 "Europäische Muslime oder muslimische Europäer?." In *Pluralismus in der europäischen Religionsgeschichte: Religionswissenschaftliche Antrittsvorlesungen,* edited by Andreas Gotzmann, Vasilios N. Makrides, Jamal Malik and Jörg Rüpke, 79–90. Marburg: Diagonal.

2001 "Islam in Deutschland." *Religion und Politik in Deutschland und Großbritannien, Prinz-Albert-Studien,* vol. 19, edited by Richard Bonney, Franz Bosbach and Thomas Brockmann, 155–63. Munich: K.G. Saur.

2001 "Canons, Charismas and Identities in Modern Islam." In *Charisma and Canon: Essays on the Religious History of the Indian Subcontinent. Festschrift for Professor Heinrich von Stietencron,* edited by Vasudha Dalmia, Angelika Malinar and Martin Christof-Fuechsle, 374–87. Delhi: Oxford University Press.

2001 "Europa als Herausforderung für den Islam – Islam als Herausforderung für Europa." In *Christenheit – Europa 2000: Die Zukunft Europas als Aufgabe und Herausforderung für Theologie und Kirchen,* edited by Walter Fürst and Martin Honecker, 123–35. Baden-Baden: Nomos.

2001 "Muslim Societies in British India." In *Explorations in the History of South Asia: Essays in Honour of Dietmar Rothermund,* edited by George Berkemer, Tilman Frasch, Hermann Kulke and Jürgen Lütt, 257–76. New Delhi: Manohar.

2001 "Historische Entwicklung des Islam in Asien." In *Islam in Asien,* edited by Klaus H. Schreiner, 18–29. Bad Honnef: Horlemann.

2000 "Die soziale Lage der Muslime in Indien." In *Indien 2000: Politik, Wirtschaft, Gesellschaft,* edited by Werner Draguhn, 131–47. Hamburg: Institut für Asienkunde.

2000 "Introduction." In *Perspectives of Mutual Encounters in South Asian History 1760 – 1860,* edited by Jamal Malik, 1–22. Leiden: Brill.

2000 "Encounter and Appropriation in the Context of Modern South Asian History." In *Perspectives of Mutual Encounters in South Asian History 1760 – 1860*, edited by Jamal Malik, 315–32. Leiden: Brill.

2000 "Bakkalaureus- und Magisterstudiengänge an der Universität Erfurt." In *Bachelor und Master in Wirtschafts-, Rechts- und Sozialwissenschaften, Dokumention und Materialien*, edited by Deutscher Akademischer Austauschdienst, 401–5. Bonn: DAAD.

1999 "Koloniale Dialoge und die Kritik am Orientalismus." In *Aneignung und Selbstbehauptung: Antworten auf die europäische Expansion*, edited by Dietmar Rothermund, 161–81. Munich: Oldenbourg.

1999 "Muslimische Identitäten zwischen Tradition und Moderne." In *Religion und Identität: Im Horizont des Pluralismus*, edited by Werner Gephart and Hans Waldenfels, 206–29. Frankfurt am Main: Suhrkamp.

1998 "Kolonialisten und Islamgelehrte im 18. und 19. Jahrhundert." In *Annäherung an das Fremde: XXVI. Deutscher Orientalistentag vom 25. bis 29.9.1995 in Leipzig, Vorträge*, edited by Holger Preißler and Heidi Stein, 34–43. Stuttgart: Franz Steiner.

1998 "Das islamische System der sozialen Sicherung: Theorie und Praxis." In *Betriebliche Personal- und Sozialpolitik*, edited by Alois Clermont and Wilhelm Schmeisser, 109–22. Munich: Vahlen.

1998 "Between National Integration and Islamism: Lucknow's Nadwat al-Ulama." In *Knowledge, Power & Politics: Educational Institutions in India*, edited by Mushirul Hasan, 221–38. New Delhi: Roli Books.

1998 "Briefe, autobiographische Aufzeichnungen und Gefängnisliteratur." In *Lesarten eines globalen Prozesses: Quellen und Interpretationen zur Geschichte der europäischen Expansion. Festschrift für Dietmar Rothermund zu seinem 65. Geburtstag*, edited by Andreas Eckert and Gesine Krüger, 52–66. Hamburg: LIT.

1998 "The Literary Critique of Islamic Popular Religion in the Guise of Traditional Mysticism, or the Abused Woman." In *Embodying Charisma: Modernity, Locality and the Performance of Emotion in Sufi Cults*, edited by Pnina Werbner and Helene Basu, 187–208. London: Routledge.

1998 "Fundamentalismus aus Sicht des Islam." In *Religion und Politik, Interne Studien 151*, edited by Stephan Eisel and Christian Koecke, 71–75. St. Augustin: Konrad-Adenauer-Stiftung.

1998 "Islam in Südasien." In *Der islamische Orient: Grundzüge seiner Geschichte,* edited by Albrecht Noth and Jürgen Paul, 505–46. Würzburg: Ergon.

1997 "Rushdie, Migration, Mysticism or the Double Vision." In *Encounters of Words and Texts: Intercultural Studies in Honor of Stefan Wild on the Occasion of His 60th Birthday, March 2, 1997, Presented by His Pupils in Bonn,* edited by Lutz Edzard and Christian Szyska, 125–30. Hildesheim: Georg Olms.

1997 "Dynamics among Traditional Religious Scholars and their Institutions in Contemporary Pakistan." In *Madrasa: La Transmission du Savoir dans le Monde Musulman,* edited by Nicole Grandin and Marc Gaborieau, 168–82. Paris: Éditions Arguments.

1997 "Gesellschaftliche Dynamik und muslimische Identitäten." In *Internationales Personalmanagement,* edited by Alois Clermont and Wilhelm Schmeisser, 35–48. Munich: Vahlen.

1997 "Die 'Erfindung' von Tradition: Islamgelehrte und Kolonialherren." In *Transformation der Europäischen Expansion vom 16. bis zum 20. Jahrhundert: Beiträge der vierten Jahrestagung des DFG-Schwerpunktprogramms, Forschungen zur kognitiven Interaktion europäischer mit außereuropäischen Gesellschaften,* edited by Andreas Eckert and Jürgen Müller, 75–85. Rehburg-Loccum: Evangelische Akademie Loccum.

1996 "Der Rat der Islamgelehrten zwischen nationaler Integration und Islamismus." In *Religion – Macht – Gewalt: Religiöser 'Fundamentalismus' und Hindu-Moslem-Konflikte in Südasien,* edited by Christian Weiß, Tom Weichert, Evelin Hust and Harald Fischer-Tiné, 152–71. Frankfurt am Main: IKO.

1993 "16th Century Mahdism: The Rawshanîya Movement among Pakhtun Tribes." In *Islam and Indian Regions,* vol. 1, *Texts,* edited by Anna Libera Dallapiccola and Stephani Zingel-Avé Lallemant, 31–59. Stuttgart: Franz Steiner.

1993 "Islamic Institutions and Infrastructure in Shâhjahânâbâd." In *Shâhjahânâbâd / Old Delhi: Tradition and Colonial Change,* edited by Eckart Ehlers and Thomas Krafft, 43–64. Stuttgart: Franz Steiner.

1992 "Traditionale islamische Institutionen und muslimischer Staat im Spannungsverhältnis: Stiftungen, Almosen und religiöse Schulen." In *Pakistan: Zweite Heidelberger Südasiengespräche,* edited by Dieter Conrad and Wolfgang-Peter Zingel, 77–82. Stuttgart: Franz Steiner.

1992	"Islam und Entwicklung." In *Nord-Süd-Dialog : Entwicklungsländerforschung an der Universität Bonn,* edited by M.G. Huber, 37–40. Bonn: Horlemann.
1991	"Change in Traditional Institutions: *Waqf* in Pakistan." In *Islam, Politics and Society in South Asia,* edited by André Wink, 81–116. Delhi: Manohar.
1991	"Zum Spannungsverhältnis zwischen islamischer Tradition und islamischem Staat in Pakistan." In *Die 'Re-orientalisierung' des Orients?: Zur Rolle der Tradition in Gesellschaftskonflikten der achtziger Jahre: Beiträge eines Kolloquiums vom 24. Oktober am Bereich Orientforschung des Instituts für Allgemeine Geschichte,* edited by Dietrich Reetz, 68–96. Berlin: Akademie.
1990	"Fallstudie zum System der sozialen Sicherung in den ländlichen Gebieten des Mardan Distrikts der Islamischen Republik Pakistan." In *Überlebenssicherung durch Kaufkraft-Transfers,* edited by Bernd Schubert and Geert Balzer, 131–44. Berlin: GTZ.
1990	"The Luminous Nurani: Charisma and Political Mobilisation among the Barelwis in Pakistan." In *Person, Myth and Society in South Asian Islam,* edited by Pnina Werbner, 38–50, Social Analysis 28, Adelaide.
1989	"Urdu Kurzgeschichten." In *Pakistan: Destabilisierung durch Kontinuität, eine Dokumentation des Südasienbüro,* edited by Jamal Malik, 86–91. Wuppertal: Südasienbüro.

Articles (Journals and Internet)

2022	"Islamic Revival and Millennial Movements in the 16th and 17th Centuries: The Case of Ahmad Sirhindi (1564–1624 CE)." *The Journal of South Asian Intellectual History* 4, no. 1 (forthcoming).
2019	"A Survey and Assessment of German Approaches to *Sīrah*." *Islamic Studies* 58, no. 3: 335–58.
2018	"*Fiqh al-Daʿwa*: The Emerging Standardization of Islamic Proselytism." *Die Welt des Islams* 58, no. 2: 206–43.
2016	"Madrase ka khawab." *Adabiyaat* 110 [Islamabad]: 126–52 (co-author with Bushra Iqbal).

2014	"From Salafism to Secularism: The Dialectic of Political Islam and Secular Nationalism in the Case of Azad's Thoughts." *Journal of South Asian and Middle Eastern Studies* 37, no. 4: 32–45.
2014	"Die Madrassa eines Traumes." *Südasien* 3–4: 10–18 (co-author with Bushra Iqbal).
2014	"The Dream of a Madrasa: A Short Story from Pakistan." Edited by Stefan Weidner. *Fikrun wa Fann* 101 [Goethe-Institute e. v.]: 5–13 (co-author with Bushra Iqbal).
2013	"Integration of Muslim Migrants and the Politics of Dialogue: The Case of Modern Germany." *Journal of Muslim Minority Affairs* 33, no. 4: 495–506, https://doi.org/10.1080/13602004.2013.866350.
2013	"Islamisches Recht und Schlichtung (Teil 2)." *Zeitschrift für Jugendkriminalrecht und Jugendhilfe* 24, no. 4: 371–77 (co-author with Misbahur Rehman).
2013	"Islamisches Recht und Schlichtung (Teil 1)." *Zeitschrift für Jugendkriminalrecht und Jugendhilfe* 24, no. 3: 269–79 (co-author with Misbahur Rehman).
2013	"Islam and the Sermon on the Mount." *Islam and Christian–Muslim Relations* 24, no. 1: 43–56, https://doi.org/10.1080/09596410.2013.746173.
2012	"Orientalism and Occidentalism: The Case of Earl of Gleichen." *Islamic Studies* 51, no. 2: 119–37.
2012	"Some Ideas on Pre-Colonial Modernity: The Case of Indian Muslim Pietists." *Exemplar: The Journal of South Asian Studies* 1, no. 1: 56–64.
2012	"Bergpredigt und Islam." *Theologische Zeitschrift* 68, no. 1: 57–79.
2010	"Welches akademisch gebildete Personal benötigen die muslimischen Gemeinden in Deutschland?," https://studylibde.com/doc/11653291/jamal-malik--welches-akademisch-gebildete.
2010	"De la tradición compartida al particularismo: los casos de India, Pakistán y Bangladesh." *Culturas* 6 [Sevilla]: 89–102, http://revistaculturas.org/wp-content/uploads/2013/02/De-la-tradici%C3%B3n-compartida-al-particularismo-los-casos-de-India-Pakist%C3%A1n-y-Bangladesh.pdf.
2009	"Crises and Cleavages in Pakistan." Friedrich-Naumann-Stiftung: Virtuelle Akademie, International Online-Conference, http://focus-pakistan.virtuelle-akademie.fnst.org/webcom/show_blog.php?wc_c=26322 (accessed April 15, 2010).
2009	"Maudūdī's *al-Jihād fī'l-Islām*: A Neglected Document." *Zeitschrift für Religionswissenschaft* 17, no. 1: 61–70, https://doi.org/10.1515/zfr.2009.17.1.61.

2009 "Madrasas in Pakistan: Breeding Ground for Terrorism?." *Orient*, no. 1: 22–28.

2008 "Abraham im Islam." *zur debatte. Themen der Katholischen Kirche in Bayern* 6: 17–19.

2007 "Fadl-e Haqq Khairabadi aur 1857." *Ta'rikh* 35 [Lahore], no. 2: 188–203.

2007 "Riwayati tasawwuf ke bhais main 'awami islam ka adabi muhakimah." *Ta'rikh* 33 [Lahore]: 138–68.

2007 "Islamkonferenz zwischen Religion und Politik." *Blickpunkt Bundestag* 1 [Berlin]: 33, http://www.bundestag.de/blickpunkt/101_Themen/0701/0701033.htm (accessed October 3, 2011).

2007 "Medien reduzieren Muslime auf ihre Religion." *Tages-Anzeiger* [Switzerland] (08.12.2007).

2006 "Religion in the Media; the Media of Religion: Migration, the Media, and Muslims." *Islamic Studies* 45, no. 3: 413–28.

2006 "Letters, Prison Sketches and Autobiographical Literature: The Case of Fadl-e-Haqq Khairabadi in the Andaman Penal Colony." *Indian Economic and Social History Review* 43, no. 1: 77–100.

2005 "Islamic-Christian Dialogue." *The Journal of Oriental Studies* 15 [Japan]: 129–37.

2005 "Ausbildung und Rolle der Imame in der Moschee." *Ausbildung von Imamen und Seelsorgern in Deutschland für die Herausforderungen von morgen. Tagung der Georges-Anawati-Stiftung am 27. September 2005 in St. Georgen in Frankfurt/Main*, 11–19.

2004 "Dialogues Between Christianity and Islam" [in Japanese]. *Oriental Academic Research* 43 [Japan], no. 1: 140–51.

2003 "Die 'fundamentalistische Falle'." *Die Politische Meinung* 48, no. 408: 41–44.

2003 "Muslim Culture and Reform in 18th Century South Asia." *Journal of the Royal Asiatic Society* 13, no. 2, 227–43, https://doi.org/10.1017/S1356186303003080.

2002 "Traditional Islamic Learning and Reform in Pakistan." *International Institute for the Study of Islam in the Modern World – ISIM Newsletter* 10 [Leiden]: 20–21.

2001 "Islam in Südasien: Historische Voraussetzungen aktueller Entwicklungen im politischen Islam." *Religion – Staat – Gesellschaft* 2 [Leipzig], no. 2: 173–203.

2001 "Islamischer Fundamentalismus oder politischer Islam." *Gewerkschaftliche Monatshefte* 11–12: 686–93.

2001 "Mit jeder neuen Bombe auf Kabul wächst der Hass." *Handelsblatt* (October 9): 10.

2000 "European Islam." *Mutualities: Britain and Islam*: 14 [The British Council, London].

1999 "Religionswissenschaft an der Universität Erfurt." *Historische Anthropologie* 7, no. 3: 488–89 (co-author with Andreas Gotzmann, Vasilios Makrides and Jörg Rüpke).

1998 "Muslimische Gesellschaften in Südasien." *Aktuelle Profile der islamischen Welt, Reihe Berichte & Studien der Hanns-Seidel-Stiftung* 76 [Munich], edited by Bernd Rill: 299–312.

1998 "Making Sense of Islamic Fundamentalism." *International Institute for the Study of Islam in the Modern World – ISIM Newsletter* 1 [Leiden]: 27.

1998 "Christen und Muslime sind Nachbarn: Fragen an Gesellschaft und Kirchen – oder wie kann das Islam-Bild entschleiert werden." *Evangelische Verantwortung* 4 [Bonn]: 10–12.

1998 "Ein Zentrum für Islam in Europa Studien, Bonn: Ein Positionspapier." *Forum Mittelmeerraum. Lernziel Konvivialität: Hoffnung durch Ernüchterung? Mittelmeerverbindungen in Wissenschaft und Bildung. Bericht vom MultiplikatorInnen-Workshop 12. / 13. Dez. 1997, Haus der Kulturen der Welt, Berlin*, edited by Deutsche UNESCO-Kommission in Zusammenarbeit mit dem Haus der Kulturen der Welt und Unterstützung der Heinrich-Böll-Stiftung e.v.: 28–30.

1998 "Islamic Mission and Call: The Case of the International Islamic University, Islamabad." *Islam and Christian-Muslim Relations* 9, no. 1: 31–45.

1997 "Muslimische Identitäten, autochthone Institutionen und kulturelle Hybridität: Einige Forschungsperspektiven." *Mitteilungen der Anthropologischen Gesellschaft in Wien* 127 [Vienna]: 67–78.

1997 "Dynamics among Traditional Religious Scholars and their Institutions in Contemporary South Asia." *The Muslim World, Special Issue on Islam in South Asia* 87 [Hartford], no. 3–4: 199–220, https://doi.org/10.1111/j.1478-1913.1997.tb03636.x.

1997 "Islam in Südasien." *Südasien* 7–8 [Dortmund]: xiii–xxvii.

1996 "Orientalisches Seminar, Regina Pacis-Weg 7, 53 113. Bonn, Germany. 7 IX 95: Comment on Pnina Werbner's: 'Allegories of Sacred Imperfection: Magic, Hermeneutics, and Passion in The Satanic Verses'." *Current Anthropology* 37 [Chicago], Supplement (February): 77–80.

1996	"Muslim Identities Suspended between Tradition and Modernity." *Comparative Studies of South Asia, Africa and the Middle East* 16 [Durham], no. 2: 1–9, https://doi.org/10.1215/1089201X-16-2-1.
1995	"The Literary Critique of Islamic Popular Religion in the Guise of Traditional Mysticism, or the Abused Woman." *Die Welt des Islams* 35, no. 1: 70–94, https://doi.org/10.1163/1570060952597941.
1995	"Traditional and Islamic Social Welfare Systems in North West Pakistan." *The Bulletin of the Henry Martyn Institute of Islamic Studies* 14 [Hyderabad, Deccan], no. 3–4: 64–83.
1994	"The Making of a Council: The Nadwat al-ʿUlamâ." *Zeitung der Deutschen Morgenländischen Gesellschaft* 144, no. 1: 60–91.
1994	"The Making of a Council: The Nadwat al-ʿUlama." *Islamic Culture, The Hyderabad Quarterly Review* LXVIII [Hyderabad, Deccan], no. 1: 11–40.
1992	"Islamische Gelehrsamkeit in Nordindien." *PERIPLUS 1992* [Münster]: 152–63.
1991	"Islamisierungspolitik und ihre Früchte." *Südasien* 5 [Wuppertal]: 48–51.
1990	"*Waqf* in Pakistan: Change in Traditional Institutions." *Die Welt des Islams* 30, no. 1–4: 63–97, https://doi.org/10.2307/1571046.
1990	"Moslems in Indien." *Südasien* 10 [Wuppertal], no. 2–3: 50–54, and no. 4–5: 52–56.
1990	" 'Sultan', Kurzgeschichte aus Pakistan." *Südasien* 2–3 [Wuppertal]: 60–65.
1990	" 'Todesklage', Kurzgeschichte aus Pakistan." *Südasien* 7–8 [Wuppertal]: 56–62.
1989	"Islamization in Pakistan 1977–1985: The Ulama and their Places of Learning." *Islamic Studies* 28 [Islamabad], no. 1: 5–27.
1989	"Legitimizing Islamization: The Case of the 'Council of Islamic Ideology' in Pakistan, 1962–1984." *Orient* 30 [Opladen], no. 2: 251–68.
1989	"Große Herausforderung für Benazir Bhutto: Unruhen erschüttern Karachi." *Südasien* 5–6 [Wuppertal]: 35–43 (co-author with Christine Gieraths).
1989	"Regierung steht unter Legitimationsdruck; ein Kommentar zum Interview mit Benazir Bhutto." *Südasien* 8–9 [Wuppertal]: 56–58.
1987	"Islamization of the Ulama and their Places of Learning in Pakistan 1977–1984." *ASIEN* 25 [Hamburg]: 41–63.

Encylopaedia Entries

2020 "Gentry in South Asia." In *The Encyclopaedia of Islam*, 3rd ed., edited by Kate Fleet, Gudrun Krämer, Denis Matringe, John Nawas and Everett Rowson, 37–40. Leiden: Brill.

2018 "Jīvan, Aḥmad." In *The Encyclopaedia of Islam*, 3rd ed., edited by Kate Fleet, Gudrun Krämer, Denis Matringe, John Nawas and Everett Rowson, 132–34. Leiden: Brill.

2016 "Colonialism," "Jamaʿat-e Islami," "Jamʿiyat ʿUlama-e Hind," "Jamʿiyat ʿUlama-e Islam," "Jamʿiyat ʿUlama-e Pakistan," and "Maududi, Abu l-Aʿla' (1903–1979)" [revised and updated versions]. In *Encyclopedia of Islam and the Muslim World*, 2nd ed., edited by Richard C. Martin, vol. I, 229–32, 575–77, 578, 578–80, 580–81, vol. II, 708–10. New York: Macmillan Reference USA.

2015 "Faḍl-i Ḥaqq Khayrābādī." In *The Encyclopaedia of Islam*, 3rd ed., edited by Kate Fleet, Gudrun Krämer, Denis Matringe, John Nawas and Everett Rowson, 104–6. Leiden: Brill.

2013 "Āzād Bilgrāmī, Ghulām ʿAlī." In *The Encyclopaedia of Islam*, 3rd ed., edited by Kate Fleet, Gudrun Krämer, Denis Matringe, John Nawas and Everett Rowson, 40–41. Leiden: Brill.

2011 "Amānallāh Pānīpatī." In *The Encyclopaedia of Islam*, 3rd ed., edited by Kate Fleet, Gudrun Krämer, Denis Matringe, John Nawas and Everett Rowson, 49–51. Leiden: Brill.

2009 "Aḥrār Movement." In *The Encyclopaedia of Islam*, 3rd ed., edited by Kate Fleet, Gudrun Krämer, Denis Matringe, John Nawas and Everett Rowson, 27–29. Leiden: Brill.

2005 "Islamisch-christlicher Dialog." In *Neues Handbuch theologischer Grundbegriffe*, vol. 2, edited by Peter Eicher, 235–42. Munich: Kösel.

2004 "Colonialism," "Jamaʿat-e Islami," "Jamʿiyat ʿUlama-e Hind," "Jamʿiyat ʿUlama-e Islam," "Jamʿiyat ʿUlama-e Pakistan," and "Maududi, Abu l-Aʿla' (1903–1979)." In *Encyclopedia of Islam and the Muslim World*, edited by Richard C. Martin, vol. I, 152–55, 371–73, 374, 374–75, 375, vol. II 443–44. New York: Macmillan Reference USA.

2002 "Minderheiten (Islam)." In *Die Religion in Geschichte und Gegenwart: Handwörterbuch für Theologie und Religionswissenschaft*, vol. 5, 4th ed., edited by Hans Dieter Betz, Don S. Browning, Bernd Janowski and Eberhard Jüngel, 1250. Tübingen: J.C.B. Mohr.

1998 "Akbar." In *Die Religion in Geschichte und Gegenwart : Handwörterbuch für Theologie und Religionswissenschaft*, vol. 1, 4th ed., edited by Hans Dieter Betz, Don S. Browning, Bernd Janowski and Eberhard Jüngel, 252–53.Tübingen : J.C.B. Mohr.

1995 "International Islamic University at Islamabad." In *The Oxford Encyclopedia of the Modern Islamic World*, vol. 11, edited by John L. Esposito, 209–11. New York and Oxford: Oxford University Press.

Book Reviews

2021 Christian W. Troll, Charles M. Ramsey and Mahboob Basharat Mughal. *The Gospel According to Sayyid Ahmad Khan (1817–1898): An Annotated Translation of Tabyīn al-Kalām (Part 3)*. Leiden: Brill, 2020. Review in *CIBEDO-Beiträge* 2: 92–94.

2018 Joppke, Christian and John Torpey. *Legal Integration of Islam: A Transatlantic Comparison*. Cambridge, MA: Harvard University Press, 2013. Review in *Islamic Studies* 57, no. 1–2: 159–62 (co-author with Dylan Lewis).

2010 Masud, Muhammad Khalid (ed.). *Travellers in Faith: Studies of the Tablīghī Jamāʿat as a Transnational Islamic Movement for Faith Renewal*. Leiden: Brill, 2000. Review in *Internationales Asienforum* 41, no. 3–4: 348–51.

2009 Mourad, Suleiman Ali. *Early Islam between Myth and History: Al-Ḥasan Al-Baṣrī (d. 110H/728CE) and the Formation of His Legacy in Classical Islamic Scholarship*. Leiden: Brill, 2006. Review in *Theologische Literaturzeitschrift* 134, no. 11: 1170–72 (co-author with Saeed Zarrabi Zadeh).

2009 Hüttermann, Jörg. *Islamische Mystik – Ein 'gemachtes Milieu' im Kontext von Modernität und Globalität*. Würzburg: Ergon, 2002. Review in *Die Welt des Islams* 49, no. 1: 130–33.

2008 Asani, Ali S. *Ecstasy and Enlightenment: The Ismaili Devotional Literature in South Asia*. London: Islamic Publications, 2002. Review in *Die Welt des Islams* 48, no. 2: 240–42.

2000 Markovits, Claude (ed.). *Histoire de l'Inde moderne 1480–1950*. Paris: Fayard, 1994. Review in *Der Islam* 77, no. 1: 192–94.

1999   Eaton, Richard M. *The Rise of Islam and the Bengal Frontier, 1204–1760*. Berkeley: University of California Press, 1993. Review in *Der Islam* 76, no. 1: 169–71.

1998   Conermann, Stephan. *Die Beschreibung Indiens in der 'Riḥla' des Ibn Baṭṭūṭa: Aspekte einer herrschaftssoziologischen Einordnung des Delhi-Sultanates unter Muḥammad Ibn Tughluq*. Berlin: Klaus Schwarz, 1993. Review in *Der Islam* 75, no. 1: 129–31.

1998   Russell, Ralph. *The Pursuit of Urdu Literature: A Select History*. London: Zed Books Ltd., 1992. Review in *Der Islam* 75, no. 1: 127–29.

1997   Schimmel, Annemarie. *Berge, Wüsten, Heiligtümer: Meine Reisen in Pakistan und Indien*. Munich: Beck, 1994. Review in *Die Welt des Islams* 37, no. 1: 127–29.

1997   Haghayeghi, Mehrdad. *Islam & Politics in Central Asia*. London: Macmillan Press, 1995. Review in *Das Historisch-Politische Buch* 45: 12–13.

1997   Basu, Helene. *Habshi Sklaven, Sidi-Fakire: Muslimische Heiligenverehrung im westlichen Indien*. Berlin: Das Arabische Buch, 1994. Review in *Die Welt des Islams* 37, no. 2: 226–29.

1997   Gonnella, Julia. *Islamische Heiligenverehrung im urbanen Kontext am Beispiel von Aleppo (Syrien)*. Berlin: Klaus Schwarz, 1995. Review in *Die Welt des Islams* 37, no. 2: 226–29.

1995   Gaborieau, Marc, Alexandre Popovic and Thierry Zarcone (eds.). *Naqshbandis: Historical Developments and Present Situation of a Muslim Mystical Order*. Istanbul: Institut Francais d'Études Anatoliennes, 1990. Review in *Die Welt des Islams* 35, no. 1: 145–47.

1995   Currie, P. M. *The Shrine and Cult of Muʿin al-dīn Chishti of Ajmer*. Delhi: Oxford University Press, 1989. Review in *Die Welt des Islams* 35, no. 1: 132–34.

1994   Ernst, Carl W. *Eternal Garden: Mysticism, History and Politics at a South Asian Sufi Centre*. Albany, NY: State University of New York Press, 1992. Review in *Der Islam* 71, no. 2: 348–52.

1993   Frembgen, Jürgen. *Alltagsverhalten in Pakistan*. Rieden: Mundo, 1990, 2nd ed. Review in *Die Welt des Islams* 33, no. 1: 155–56.

1992   Troll, Christian W. (ed.). *Muslim Shrines in India: Their Character, History and Significance*. Delhi: Oxford University Press, 1989. Review in *Die Welt des Islams* 32, no. 1: 161–64.

1992   Khalidi, Omar. *Hyderabad: After the Fall.* Wichita, KS: Hyderabad Historical Society, 1988. Review in *Die Welt des Islams* 32, no. 2: 275–78.

1991   Rothen-Dubs, Ursula (ed.). *Allahs indischer Garten: Ein Lesebuch der Urdu Literatur.* Frauenfeld: Verlag im Waldgut, 1989. Review in *Internationales Asienforum* 22, no. 1–2: 148–49.

Index

Abbasid dynasty 216, 351
'Abd al-Raziq, Mustafa 47
'Abduh, Muhammad 43–47, 52n63, 56, 127, 155, 156, 225n62, 352
Abdur Rashid, Ahmed 8–9, 297–318, 404–5
Abou-Nagie, Ibrahim 164
Abrahamic triad 128–33
"acting Muslim," as political performance 147
activism. *see* political activism
'ada 48–49
Adebayo, Mohammad Rabiu 329–30
Advice Center on Radicalization 166
adyan 130, 131, 132n41, 133
AfD (Alternative für Deutschland) 151
Al-Afghani, Jamal al-Din 43–47, 52n63, 56, 155–56, 225n62
Afropolitanism 331
Afsaruddin, Asma 94
Afzaluddin Nizami, Muhammad 334–36
Aguéli, Ivan 295
Ahl-i Hadith 10, 74, 76, 84, 371, 375, 378–79, 386, 391, 393, 399, 401
Ahmad, Mirza Ghulam 111
Ahmadiyya 111, 143, 144
Alam, Nazeer 389
'alam 31, 389
'Alawi, Hamid Hasan 300, 311
Al-Albani, Muhammad Nasir al-Din 157
Aleemiyah Institute of Islamic Studies 386, 388–89
'Ali, Chiragh 108
'Ali, Syed Mumtaz 334
Aligarh Muslim University 67
Allama Mohsin Naqvi 389
'almana 25
'almani 19, 24, 30
Amjad 336
amr 274
Al-Amriki, Abu Adam Jibril 102
'Andalib, Muhammad Nasir 279
Anjuman Astan-e Fazal 82–83
Anjuman Himayat al-Islam 68
An-Na'im, Abdullahi Ahmed 193–95
Ansari, 'Abd Allah 275
Ansari, Mukhtar Ahmad 122n3

anti-liberalism 23
Antun, Farah 51
Applied Sufism 8–9, 299–301, 303, 307, 316–17, 404
Arab Spring (2011) 199, 348
Arkoun, Muhammad 44, 55–57
Armaghan-i Hijaz (Iqbal) 126
Al-'Arwi, 'Abdallah 51
Asad, Talal 22, 29, 142, 154, 168, 258
asceticism 275, 292
Ast, Friedrich 218
Attia, Iman 147–48, 154–55
Aurangzeb 383
Avicenna 70
Ayurvedic Medicine 63, 66–69, 76–77. *see also* Unani Medicine
Azad (Abul Kalam Makki) 6, 121–37
Azhar, Maulana Mas'ud 95, 102, 107–8
Al-Azmeh, Aziz 51
'Azzam, 'Abdullah 98, 99

Bahauddin Zakariya University (BZU) 385
Bahrinipour, Amir 70
Baig, Mirza Qadeer 332–34
balagh-i khafi 272, 278
balagh-i mubin 272, 277–79
Barelwi Sunnis 76, 325, 338–40, 371, 375, 378, 399, 401–2, 405
  madrasas of 380, 386, 389–91, 398
Al-Basri, Al-Hasan 292
Bauer, Thomas 148
Bedouin 363
belonging *vs.* non-belonging 144–45
Benedict XVI (pope) 356, 364
Bennabi, Malek 51
Beydoun, Khaled A. 147
Bhatti, Vir Singh 121
Bin Baz, 'Abd al-'Aziz 98
Bin Humaid, Salih 365–66
Bin Laden, Osama 98, 99
Boulainvilliers, Henri de 267, 286
Britain and British colonialism 66, 124–25, 134, 136, 338, 383, 401, 402
British India 66, 67, 68, 69, 121–22, 133, 399n3. *see also* India

Brockhaus' Conversations-Lexikon 24
Buddhism 297, 365, 387
Burhaniyya 329, 332, 338

Cairo Declaration of Human Rights in Islam
 (1990) 192, 198–99
Canada
 Charter of Rights and Freedoms 257
 Chishtiyya 333–35
 deradicalization process in 165–66
 EXIT-program 166
 Pakistani Muslim experiences in 240–57
Canadian Society of Muslims 334
Canadian Terrorists by the Numbers (Wilner
 and Yar) 147
capitalism 28–29
Castoriadis, Cornelius 30
Catholicism 24, 41, 347, 356
causality 45
Chair of Muslim Cultural and Religious
 History (CMCRH, Erfurt) 376, 378
"Changing Role of Social Media in Muslim
 Countries" project 377–78
Charter of Rights and Freedoms
 (Canada) 257
children's rights 180–81. *see also*
 human rights
Chishti, Muʿinuddin 335
Chishtiyya 273, 297, 330–38
Christianity 6, 19, 24, 33, 100, 110, 134, 142,
 216n34, 267, 352, 353, 382, 386
clash of civilizations theory 362, 365,
 376
clothing and religious identity 250–53. *see
 also* religious identity
Colonialization of Islam (Malik) 114, 398
commanding right and forbidding
 wrong 115, 363
community Sufis 328–29
composite nationalism 126
Convention on the Elimination of all Forms
 of Discrimination against Women
 (CEDAW) 200
Cook, Michael 115
cosmo-psychology 302–7
countering radicalization to violence
 (CRV) 165–66
counterterrorism 146–47
cultural translation of knowledge 385–86

dahri 30, 31
Dallas, Ian 296
Dantschke, Claudia 162
dar al-aman 379–80
dar al-harb 351
dar al-Islam 351
Dar al-ʿUlum 67, 126–27
Dar al-ʿUlum Haqqania 389, 391
Dar al-ʿUlum Muhammadia Ghousia 386,
 388, 389, 391
Dar al-ʿUlum Naeemia 389, 391
Dard, Khwaja Mir 271–77, 279, 283–87
dars-i nizami 123–24, 380, 383
Dawson, Lorne 161
Daʿish 115
daʿwa 157, 225, 350, 354–55, 363, 365–66. *see
 also* street-*daʿwa*
De Certeau, Michel 237, 238, 250, 259
Declaration of Human Rights (1948)
 177, 180
deconfessionalization 21–22, 28n30
De Diego González, Antonio 330–32
defensive paradigm 189–93
democracy 149, 167, 179, 184–86, 189, 219,
 348, 358, 360–63
denominationalism 20–22
Deobandi Sunnis 76, 122, 127n20, 325
 madrasas of 371, 372, 375, 378, 385, 386,
 389–91, 398, 399
deradicalization process 165–66
dhikr 301, 307–10, 313–14, 324, 335, 337
dhimma 350, 351, 354, 358, 359, 366
Dickson, William Rory 327
dietary practices and religious identity 248–
 50. *see also* religious identity
Dihlawi, Shah Waliullah 127n20, 134n54,
 269, 284, 286, 387
Dilthey, Wilhelm 53, 218
din 4, 30–31, 33, 126, 128–35
Din aur Shariʿat (Khan) 110–11
discriminatory legislation 146–47, 180, 256–
 57. *see also* human rights
dividing epistemologies 4–5
Dost Mohammad. *see* Multani, Sabir
Douglas, Mary 249
"The Dream of a Madrasa" (Malik and
 Iqbal) 385–86
dress and religious identity 188, 228, 250–
 53. *see also* religious identity

dunya 4, 30, 31, 33
dunyawi 18n2, 19, 24, 30
Durkheim, Emile 21, 160, 387
dynamic processes 1, 77–82
dynamics, as term 405

emerging public sphere, as concept 40
empirical discourses on religion 386–88
Enayat, Hadi 23
Enlightenment 3, 44, 142, 347–49, 357–59, 365
essentialism 145–48, 153, 161, 168, 177, 249, 260, 403. *see also* othering
EXIT-program (Canada) 166
extremism 10, 144–45, 147, 151, 155, 159–60, 164–65, 364, 372, 374, 377

Fada'il-e Jihad (Mas'ud) 103–4
Fair, C. Christine 99, 102
Farahi, Hamiduddin 112
Fath al-Jawwad (Mas'ud) 105
Fayda Tijaniyya 329, 330, 331
Federal Association of Muslim Pathfinders in Germany (BMPPD) 149–50, 153, 167
Feist, Thomas 326
female madrasa students 371, 372, 375, 381–84, 386, 390, 392, 399. *see also* gender issues in Muslim modernity; madrasa culture
fikr 309–10, 314, 316
fitna 96, 106, 110, 112–13
food habits and religious identity 248–50
Foroutan, Naika 142, 153
Freedom of Religion or Belief report (UN) 161
Fuess, Albrecht 376–77
fuqaha' 216–17, 221

Gadamer, Hans-Georg 219
Galen 65
Gandhi, Mohan Das "Mahatma" 122
Geaves, Ron 338
Geissinger, Aysha 42
gender issues in Muslim modernity 42, 180–81, 196. *see also* female madrasa students; women's rights
German Academic Exchange Service (DAAD) 377
Germany
  history of Islam in 142–44
Muslim youth and Salafism 6–7, 141–42, 162–67
Ghamidi, Jawad Ahmad 94, 112–14
Gharaibeh, Mohammad 156
Al-Ghazali, Abu Hamid 49n47, 128n26, 156, 275, 282, 293
Glaser, Michaela 159, 162
Global Youth Village (GYV) 299
Graeco-Islamic medicine 63n3, 66, 77, 81, 84. *see also* Unani Medicine
gratitude 274–77, 279, 286–87
Great Western Transmutation (GWT) 2–3, 11
Greek Medicine. *see* Unani Medicine
Green, Nile 328–29
Griffel, Frank 155–56, 168
Guénon, René 295, 330
Gülen, Fethullah 357–61
Gülen Movement 9, 349, 357–60, 366–67
Gurdjieff, G.I. 295
Gurdjieff movement 328

Habermas, Jürgen 20, 219, 228n74
habit (*'ada*) 48–49
Haddad, Yvonne 42
Hadiqat al-Haqiqa (Sana'i) 276
Hafez 361
Al-Hallaj 281, 292
Hallaq, Wael B. 215n29, 216nn33–34
Hamadani, 'Ayn al-Qudat 281
Hamdard (pharmaceutical company) 67
Hammer-Purgstall, Joseph von 294
Hanbal, Ahmad b. 155–56, 275
haqiqa 64, 76
  haqiqa Muhammadiyya 279–80
Harakat al-Mujahidin 103
Hendrich, Geert 41
hermeneutical approaches to Quran 52–54
hikmat, as term 65. *see also* Unani Medicine
Himmelsfahrt (Kelek) 196
Himmelstrand, Ulf 30
Hinduism 6, 110, 134–36, 365
Hippocrates 65
Hirsi Ali, Ayaan 195
historical scholarship 43, 154–57
historiographies 38–43, 51–57, 380–86
Hodgson, Marshall 2–3, 11
Hoff, Benjamin-Immanuel 384
Hofmann, Murad Wilfried 188, 189–93, 201
Holyoake, George Jacob 25

homeopathy 63, 67, 69, 298. *see also* Unani Medicine
House of One 144
Hudaybiyya treaty 101, 355
human rights 177–79. *see also* children's rights; women's rights
    are indivisible 183–84
    Cairo Declaration on 198–99
    in cultural translation 390–91
    defensive paradigm on 189–93
    discriminatory legislation against 146–47, 180
    ethics of peace and 389–90
    Hofmann on 189–90
    Islamic democracy on 360–63
    modern concept of 180–83
    reconciliatory paradigm on 193–95
    rejectionist paradigm on 195–98
    shari'a and 185–86, 198–200
    Tahir on Muslim discourse on 178n7
    UDHR on 177, 180, 183–84, 193
Humoral Medicine. *see* Unani Medicine
Hünermann, Peter 41
Huntington, Samuel 183n31, 362, 376
Husayn, Taha 43n25, 47
Al-Husayni, Amin 143

Ibn 'Abd al-Wahhab, Muhammad 156, 268–69, 283, 286, 293, 363. *see also* Wahhabism
Ibn 'Arabi 31n36, 83, 273, 281, 293, 302n41, 303, 315, 332
Ibn Khaldun 46, 387
Ibn Miskawayh 383–84
Ibn al-Nihas, Abu Zakariyya 104
Ibn Rushd-Goethe Mosque 144, 150
Ibn Saud, King Abdallah 348, 364
Ibn Taymiyya 156, 218, 275, 283, 352
Idea of an Anthropology of Islam (Asad) 154
identity. *see* religious identity
identity debates 38–43. *see also* religious identity
Iftikhar, Asif 112
ijtihad 190, 215n30, 216–17, 223, 224, 228
India
    under British rule 66, 67, 68, 69, 121–22, 133, 399n3
    Islamic revival in 4
    Unani Medicine in 64–68

Indian National Congress (INC) 122, 122n3
Indleeb, Nabeera 388
al-insan al-kamil 273, 281
Institute for Practical Idealism 298
Institute of Search for Truth (IST) 297
inter-religious initiatives 347–48, 364–65, 376
intersectionality 149–51
intra-faith coherency 6
Iqbal, Muhammad 121, 125–27
islahi 44, 56–57
Islahi, Amin Ahsan 112
"Islam and Human Rights" (*Der Islam und die Menschenrechte*, Hofmann) 189
Islamic Awakening 363
Islamic democracy 360–63
Islamic law 205–12, 230
Islamic mysticism. *see* Sufism
Islamic normativity. *see also* social normativity and law
    formation of 212–19
    in modern times 219–29
    shari'a and 7
Islamic State of Iraq and Syria (ISIS) 187
Islamic State of Iraq and the Levant (ISIL) 229
Islamic University in Medina (IUM) 364
Islamic University International 386
Islam in South Asia (Malik) 4, 12, 236–37
"Islam in the West" event (2002) 376
Islamisation policy (Zia) 373, 374
Islamisierung in Pakistan 1977–84 (Malik) 373
Islamism, defined 28n30, 95–96, 154
ithbat 272

Jabir ibn 'Abd Allah 281
Jahangir 135
jahiliyya 213, 226–27, 269
Jaish-e-Mohammad 102–3
Jalal, Ayesha 94
Jalandhari, Hanif 379, 385
Jama'at-i Islami 121, 371, 375, 378, 399, 401
James, William 295
Jami'a al-Kauthar 387, 391
Jami'a Binoria Al-Aalmia 386, 388–90, 392
Jami'a Dar al-'Ulum 376, 378
Jami'a Khair al-Madaris 385
Jami'a Naeemia Sirajia 385, 386, 388, 391

Jami'a Nizamia Rizvia   392
Jami'a Salfia   385, 386, 391
Jam'iyyat al-'Ulama'-i Hind   126
Janan, Mirza Mazhar Jan-i   269
Al-Jawziyya, Ibn Qayyim   274–75
jihad   114–17
   Ayesha Jalal on Quranic interpretations of   94–95
   militant Quranic interpretations on   98–108
   modernist Quranic interpretations on   108–14, 350
   peaceful Quranic interpretations on   6, 97–98, 109–11
   tawhid and   157
   as term   93
Al-Jihad fi al-Islam (Mawdudi)   98
Juan Carlos I (king)   364
Judaism   27–28, 99–100, 351–53, 361–63, 365
Al-Jundi, Anwar   49–50
Jung, Dietrich   39, 40

kalam   48–49, 383
Karamustafa, Ahmet T.   293n3
Kashani, Rukn al-Din   273
Kashmir   101–3
Kelek, Necla   195, 196
Keller, Nuh Ha Mim   296
Kelly, George   239
Kepel, Gilles   158–59, 168
Al-Khair Free Tibbi Hospital   82–83
Khaksar Movement   11, 121
khalifat Allah   273–74, 286–87
khalq   274
Khan, Inayat   295, 317, 328
Khan, Muhammad Sa'id   300
Khan, Sayyid Ahmed   108–11
Khawarij sect   351
Khomeini, Ayatollah   360, 361, 362
King Abdulaziz Center for National Dialogue (KACND)   364
King Abdullah bin Abdulaziz International Center for Interfaith and Intercultural Dialogue (KAICIID)   364, 365
Klawe, Willy   145
Kleine, Christoph   23
Koehler, Daniel   160
Koselleck, Reinhard   40–41
Kubra, Najm al-Din   281

Kulturkampf   20, 22, 25n21, 26–27
Kurds   359

la dini   24n20
laïcité   26, 121
Lashkar-e-Tayyaba   98
Lassen, Søren Christian   329
lata'if   301–2, 305–7, 309, 311, 313–14
Lau, Sven   162
Lauzière, Henri   155, 168
La Vie de Mahomed (de Boulainvilliers)   267
Legacy International   298–300
Lessing, Gotthold Ephraim   142
Lewis, Samuel   335
LGBT*IQ Competence Centre   150
LGBTQ+   149
LivingSidebySide program   299
Luhayy, 'Amr bin   269
Luhmann, Niklas   19n5, 20, 210n15

Madani, Husayn Ahmad   122, 126–28
madhhab (pl. *madhahib*)   215–19, 221–22, 225
madrasa culture   10, 380–92
   of Barelwi Sunnis   380, 386, 389–91, 398, 399, 401–2, 405
   of Deobandi Sunnis   371, 372, 375, 378, 385, 386, 389–91, 398, 399
   in Pakistan   372–75
Madrasas in South Asia (ed. Malik)   11, 93
Mahall, Farangi   383
Mahmood, Saba   246, 258
Makki, Abul Kalam.   *see* Azad (Abul Kalam Makki)
Al-Makki, Abu Talib   275
Malik, Charles   177n2
Malik, Jamal
   about   10–12, 398–405
   Colonialization of Islam   114, 398
   on dialogues of life   260
   "The Dream of a Madrasa" (with Bushra Iqbal)   385–86
   Islam in South Asia   4, 12, 236–37
   Islamisierung in Pakistan 1977–84   373
   on madrasas in Pakistan   371, 373, 375, 392
   Madrasas in South Asia (ed.)   11, 93
   on post-Aurangzeb India   270n19
   "Religious Pluralism and Religious Plurality" project   371, 398
   on Sufism in East and West   323

marriage 163, 181–82, 186–89, 192, 194, 197n68, 200, 245, 269
Al-Mashriqi ('Inayatullah Khan) 121
Massignon, Louis 155
Mas'ala-yi Khilafat va Jazira-yi 'Arab (Azad) 127
Mas'ud Azhar, Mawlana 95, 102–8
Mawdudi, Syed Abul A'la 98, 112, 121, 125–28, 131, 133
Al-Mawrid 112
McGuire, Meredith 236, 247
Mein Streit mit den Wächtern des Islam (Kelek) 196
Merton, Robert 160
Mescoli, Elsa 250
Metcalf, Barbara 122, 373
militancy and Islam 98–108, 116–17
Mirza, Hakim Arshad 69–70
modernist, defined 96
modernity 5, 38–43
Moon, Ban-Ki 364
Muaammar, Faisal bin 365
Al-Mubarak, 'Abd Allah bin 103
Mughal Empire 66, 135, 270, 293, 373, 383
Muhammadan Way 270
mujtahid 217–18
Müller, Friedrich 223
Multani, Sabir
  about 5, 64, 68–70
  on dynamic processes 77–82
  Simple Organ Theory of 69, 70–77, 81–84
Muqaddima (Ibn Khaldun) 46
muraqaba 307–8, 310, 313–15
Muridiyya 330–32
Musharraf, Pervez 374–75
Muslim Brotherhood 149, 225, 352–53
Muslim League (ML) 121
Muslim modernity 38–43
Muslim World League (MWL) 364
Muslim Youth in Germany (MJD; organization) 149, 153, 167
Muslim youth in Germany and Salafism 6–7, 141–42, 162–67
Muttahida Qawmiyyat awr Islam (Madani) 122
mystical practices 64, 307–10
mystical union 284–85

Nadwat al-'Ulama' 67
Naeem, Farhan 392
Naeem, Mufti Muhammad 386, 390–91
Naeemi, Raghib 391, 392
Naeemi, Sarfaraz Ahmed 391
Napoleon Bonaparte 268
Naqshbandiyya 269, 296–97, 315–16, 332, 338, 357
Naqshbandiyya Foundation for Islamic Education 337
Naqshbandiyya-Mujaddidiyya 297, 332
naskh 96
National Socialist Underground (NSU) 144
Nedza, Justyna 156, 157
Nehru, Jawaharlal 122
Neo-Muslima 152
neo-Sufism 293n6, 317
Neumann, Peter 165
Nigerian Islamic Association Center 329
Nizam al-Din, Mulla 371, 383
Nizami, Baba 336, 337, 339
Nizami, Fayyazuddin 335
Nizami, K.A. 384
Nizami, Khwaja Hasan 334–35
Nizami, Mazharuddin 336
Nordau, Max 28
Nurani, Shah Ahmed 401, 402

objectification, defined 115
Organization of the Islamic Conference (OIC) 363–64
Orientalism 23, 108, 227, 294, 356
othering 141, 144–50, 159
Ottoman empire 40, 142, 222, 293, 352
Özsoy, Ömer 53–54

Pakistan. *see also* madrasa culture
  religious pluralism in 371–80
  Unani Medicine in 64–68
Pakistani-Canadian Muslim community 240–57
Palestine-Israel conflict 101–2
Parliament of World's Religions 347
Parsons, Talcot 18, 27, 209
Pastoret, Immanuel 267, 286
peace 6, 76, 94, 97–99, 101, 106–11, 115, 135, 310, 314, 347, 356, 358–59, 365, 371, 383–85, 389–93, 399n3

INDEX

PEGIDA (Patriotic Europeans Against the Islamization of the Occident) 151
Piraino, Francesco 330, 331
political activism 6–7, 48–51
Political Islam (ed. Volpi) 95
pop Islam movement 149
positivity bias 205–6
postcolonial theory 148
post-secularism 20–22
Prema Dharmasala 298
"Prevent-Strategy" (U.K.) 147
Priorities of the Islamic Movement in the Next Stage (Qaradawi) 355–56
prisoners and religious worship 142–43
Progressive Writers' Association (PWA) 401
Prophet Muhammad 8, 267–87
Prussian empire 142. *see also* Germany
"pure Muhammadness" 8–9, 272, 279–80

Qadiriyya 297, 337
Al-Qaradawi, Yusuf 9–10, 201, 349, 353–57, 359, 362, 366–67
Qasimi, Ahmad Nadim 400–401
Qawwali 333, 335–36, 339, 389
queer Muslim community 149, 150–51
Quranic hermeneutics 48–49, 53–54, 93–117, 349–51
Quraysh 99, 283
Qureshi, Regula 333–34
Qutb, Sayyid 47, 49–50, 158

radical Islamism 6
  defined 93, 95
radicalization 158–62
Radtke, Bernd 317
Rahman, Fazlur 43n25, 52, 97, 317
Rash, J.E. *see* Abdur Rashid, Ahmed
Rashid Rida, Muhammad 47, 111, 127, 155, 352
Rasool, Azad 297–98, 300–15
Razi, Najm al-Din 281
reconciliatory paradigm 193–95
Rehman, Mufti Munibur 379–80, 389
rejectionist paradigm 195–98
Religions for Peace 347
religiosity 151–53, 238–42, 245–60
religious identity 5. *see also* identity debates
  dietary practice and 248–50
  dress and 250–53

ritual practice and 245–48
workplace experiences and 254–57
"Religious Pluralism and Religious Plurality" project 371, 398
religious pluralism in Pakistan 371–80
ridda 191, 350–51, 355, 358–60, 366
right-wing extremism 144, 151
ritual practice 245–48. *see also* religious identity
Rosati, Massimo 20
Roy, Olivier 158–59, 168
Rückert, Friedrich 294
Rumi 293, 294n12, 361
Rustin, Michael 30
Rytter, Mikkel 332

sabr 274–77
saddle time, as concept 40–41, 57
Saeed-ur-Rahman 385
Safavid empire 293
Said, Edward 23, 227
Sa'id, Hafiz Muhammad 95, 98–102, 106
Salafi and Salafism
  German Muslim youth and 6–7, 141–42, 162–67
  as movement 157–62
  as term and concept 154–56, 167
Salafiyya Bookstore 155
Saleem, Jauhar 384
Sallam, Abu 'Ubayd al-Qasim ibn 96
Sami ul-Haq, Maulana 390
Sana'i 276
Sattelzeit. see saddle time
Saudi Arabia 98, 157, 182, 187n39, 199, 363–67
Savarkar, "Vir" Vinayak Damodar 121
Sa'id, Hafiz Mohammad 95, 98–99
Schimmel, Annemarie 12, 317n115, 404
Schleiermacher, Friedrich 218
Schluchter, Wolfgang 28–29
Scholem, Gershom 27–28
School of Sufi Teaching (SOST) 300
Schulze, Reinhard 4–5, 317
Schuon, Frithjof 317, 328, 330
secular historiographies 51–57
secularism, as term 18, 22, 25
secularity
  as concept 18–20
  Islam and 4–5, 19–34

secularization, as term   18, 34
seculum   31
Sedgwick, Mark   317n115, 328
Shadhiliyya   296, 297, 338
al-Shafi'i, Abu 'Abd Allah ibn Idris   96, 218
Shah, Ghazi Hafiz Pir Muhammad   386–87
Shah, Idries   295, 317
Shah, Muhammad Amin Ul Hasnat   387
Shah, 'Abd al-Bari   296, 300, 307
Shahin, Rafiq   84
"Sharia and Life" (TV program)   353
Sharif, Nawaz   99
shari'a   50, 58, 74, 76, 105, 178–79, 192–97,
　　208, 216n33, 219–20, 229, 269, 278,
　　280, 284, 287, 308, 334, 352, 354, 364,
　　367, 383
　　defined   186–88
　　human rights and   180–82, 184–86,
　　　198–202
　　Islamic normativity and   7
　　Unani Medicine and   64
Shari'ati, 'Ali   49–50
Al-Sharkawi, Mahmud   49–50
shaykh   278, 287, 296–97, 301, 303, 306, 310–
　　15, 330, 334, 335–40, 357
Shi'a
　　in Germany   144
　　history of   50, 363
　　madrasas of   371, 374, 375, 378–79,
　　　387, 391
　　rituals of   389
shukr   274–77
Siddha medicine   63. *see also* Unani
　　Medicine
Sikhism   121, 164, 386, 387
Simple Organ Theory (Multani)   69, 70–
　　77, 81–84
Singh, Tara   121
Sirhindi, Ahmad   269–70, 307, 315, 332
slavery   180
social normativity and law   208–12. *see also*
　　Islamic normativity
Soroush, Abdolkarim   349, 360–63, 366–67
space of resonance   404
Spengler, Oswald   49
Speziale, Fabrizio   84
strategic essentialism   148. *see also*
　　essentialism

street-*da'wa*   141, 163–64
Striving in the Path of God (Afsaruddin)   94
Sufism   8–9, 307–10. *see also* Sufi transplants
　　Applied Sufism   8–9, 299–301, 303, 307,
　　　316–17, 404
　　development of   292–97
　　medicine and   66, 69, 84
　　on patience and gratitude   274–77
　　prophetology and   272
　　Soroush on   361
　　transplanted Sufism, as
　　　category   9, 323–25
　　Wahhabism and   363
Sufism East and West (ed. Malik and
　　Zarrabi-Zadeh)   404
Sufi transplants   326–40. *see also*
　　transplanted Sufism, as category
Sufi Vision and Initiation (Lewis)   335
Suhrawardi, Shahab al-Din Yahya   275
Sultan, Wafa   195–96
sunnat Allah   45
Sura al-Muhammad   108
Surat al-Hajj   112
Surat al-Ma'ida   99
Surat al-Tawba   95, 100–101
surveillance   149

ta'assub   356
tadniya   34
tafsir   127
Tafsir al-Manar (Rida)   127
Tafsir-e Surat-e Yusuf (Sa'id)   102
taghut   105–6
Taha, Mahmoud Mohammed   193–94, 224
takfir   100, 107, 158, 355, 363
Taoism   297
Tariqa Muhammadiyya Khalisa (Dard)   270,
　　271–72, 280, 282
tariqa   64, 74, 76, 293, 296, 303, 325, 329, 335,
　　337, 339–40, 402
Tarjuman al-Qur'an (Azad)   121, 124, 128–29,
　　131, 136, 137
Taylor, Charles   24, 30, 34
tibb.   see Unani Medicine
tibbiyya colleges   67, 68
Tibi, Bassam   146
Tijaniyya   329–31, 338
Al-Tirmidhi   280

tolerance and dialogue
    as concept   347–49
    Gülen movement on   357–60
    in Islamic scriptures and history   9–10, 349–57
    in Saudi Arabia   363–66
    Soroush on   360–63
Toward an Islamic Reformation (An-Na'im)   193
"Towards an Ethics of Peace" project   377, 378, 385, 388–92
Toynbee, Arnold   49
transplanted Sufism, as category   9, 323–25.
    see also Sufi transplants
travel bans on Muslim-majority countries by U.S.   147
Troeltsch, Ernst   34
The True Jihad (Khan)   110
Trump, Donald   147
Al-Tustari, Sahl   281
Two-Nation-Theory   121

'Uddat al-Sabirin wa Dhakhirat al-Shakirin (Ibn Taymiyya)   275
Unani, Ayurvedic and Homeopathic Practitioners Act (1965)   67
Unani Medicine   5
    doctrine of   65–68
    on dynamic processes   77–82
    history of   64–65
    Simple Organ Theory   69, 70–77, 81–84
United States
    Applied Sufism in   8–9, 299–301, 303, 307, 316–17
    discriminatory legislation in   146–47
Universal Declaration of Human Rights (UDHR; 1948)   177, 180, 183–84, 193
Usmani, Rafi   376, 378
Usmani, Zubair   376
usul al-fiqh   206, 219, 223, 224

vahdat-i din   129, 132, 135–36
Vatican Council II   347
Verlockender Fundamentalismus (Heitmeyer et al.)   151–52

vilayat-i faqih   362, 367
Violence Prevention Network   166
violent extremism   144, 151, 164, 166
Vogel, Pierre   162, 164
Von Foerster, Heinz   211

Wafaq al-Madaris Ahl-i Sunnat   391
Wafaq al-Madaris al-'Arabiyya   385
Wahhabism   156, 363–66. *see also* Ibn 'Abd al-Wahhab, Muhammad
Wahiduddin Khan, Maulana   94, 108–10
wasatiyya   353–54
Webb, Gisela   327–28
Weber, Max   25, 28–29, 207n6, 387
Western Islamic Studies, as discipline   48
Westoxication   362
WHO Medical Atlas   68
Wiedl, Nina   157
Wiktorowicz, Quintan   157–58
Wohlrab-Sahr, Monika   23
women's rights   42, 180–81, 196, 199–200, 363. *see also* female madrasa students; gender issues in Muslim modernity; human rights
workplace and religious identity   254–57.
    see also religious identity
World Community Education Center (WCEC)   298–99, 300, 311
World War II   143

Yasmeen, Samina   99–100
Ya'qub, Mawlavi Muhammad   123
Yemen   338
Yoga   297, 298
youth and Salafism   6–7, 141–42, 162–67
Yunani Tibb.   *see* Unani Medicine

Zafar, Yasin   392
zawiya   329, 331, 339
Zemmin, Florian   27
Zia ul-Haq   373, 374
Zionism   27–28, 353
Zoroastre, Confucius et Mahomet (Pastoret)   267